ROUTLEDGE LIBRARY EDITIONS: SOUTH AFRICA

Volume 21

A HISTORY OF SOUTH AFRICA TO 1870

A HISTORY OF SOUTH AFRICA TO 1870

Edited by
MONICA WILSON and
LEONARD THOMPSON

LONDON AND NEW YORK

First published by Croom Helm Ltd in 1982.

This edition first published in 2023
by Routledge
4 Park Square, Milton Park, Abingdon, Oxon OX14 4RN

and by Routledge
605 Third Avenue, New York, NY 10158

Routledge is an imprint of the Taylor & Francis Group, an informa business

© 1982 Monica Wilson and Leonard Thompson

All rights reserved. No part of this book may be reprinted or reproduced or utilised in any form or by any electronic, mechanical, or other means, now known or hereafter invented, including photocopying and recording, or in any information storage or retrieval system, without permission in writing from the publishers.

Trademark notice: Product or corporate names may be trademarks or registered trademarks, and are used only for identification and explanation without intent to infringe.

British Library Cataloguing in Publication Data
A catalogue record for this book is available from the British Library

ISBN: 978-1-032-30347-5 (Set)
ISBN: 978-1-032-31627-7 (Volume 21) (hbk)
ISBN: 978-1-032-31637-6 (Volume 21) (pbk)
ISBN: 978-1-003-31065-5 (Volume 21) (ebk)

DOI: 10.4324/9781003310655

Publisher's Note
The publisher has gone to great lengths to ensure the quality of this reprint but points out that some imperfections in the original copies may be apparent.

Disclaimer
The publisher has made every effort to trace copyright holders and would welcome correspondence from those they have been unable to trace.

This is a reissue of a previously published book. The language is reflective of the time in which this book was published. In reissuing this book, no offence is intended by the Publishers to any reader.

A HISTORY OF
SOUTH AFRICA
TO 1870

EDITED BY MONICA WILSON
AND LEONARD THOMPSON

CROOM HELM
London and Canberra

© Monica Wilson and Leonard Thompson

Croom Helm Ltd., Provident House, Burrell Row, Beckenham,
Kent, BR3 1AT, England

British Library Cataloguing in Publication Data
A History of South Africa to 1870
  1. South Africa—History
  I. Wilson, Monica   II. Thompson, Leonard
  968   DT766

ISBN 0-7099-2778-9

Printed and bound in South Africa

CONTENTS

LIST OF ABBREVIATIONS	7
PREFACE TO THE 1982 EDITION	9
THE PLATES	19
PREFACE TO THE 1969 EDITION	31

I. THE ARCHAEOLOGICAL BACKGROUND. By R. R. INSKEEP
(This chapter has been omitted from this edition)

II. THE HUNTERS AND HERDERS. By MONICA WILSON
   1. Characteristics and Distribution — 41
   2. Economy and Social Structure of the Hunters — 47
   3. Economy and Social Structure of the Herders — 55
   4. Relationships between Groups — 63

III. THE NGUNI PEOPLE. By MONICA WILSON
   1. Demarcation and Distribution — 75
   2. Relations with Other Groups — 95
   3. Economy — 107
   4. The Structure of Nguni Society — 116

IV. THE SOTHO, VENDA, AND TSONGA. By MONICA WILSON
   1. The Sotho
      (a) Distribution in Space and Time — 131
      (b) Economy — 142
      (c) Social Structure — 153
      (d) Relations with Other Groups — 163
   2. The Venda — 167
   3. The Tsonga — 176
   4. Conclusion — 179

V. WHITE SETTLERS AND THE ORIGIN OF A NEW SOCIETY, 1652–1778. By M. F. KATZEN
   1. The Foundation of the Cape Station — 187
   2. Agriculture and Immigration — 192
   3. Pastoral Farming — 208
   4. VOC Government at the Cape — 213
   5. The White Colonial Community — 228

CONTENTS

VI. CO-OPERATION AND CONFLICT: THE EASTERN CAPE FRONTIER. By MONICA WILSON
1. The Beginnings of Interaction — 233
2. Intermediaries — 246
3. Fragmentation and Pressure on Land — 250
4. The Pagan Reaction — 256
5. Civilization by Mingling — 260
6. Conflicting Attitudes — 268

VII. THE CONSOLIDATION OF A NEW SOCIETY: THE CAPE COLONY. By T. R. H. DAVENPORT — 272
1. The Diversification of Culture — 273
2. The Diversification of the Economy — 287
3. The Extension of Freedom under Law — 297
4. The Move towards Responsible Government — 311

VIII. CO-OPERATION AND CONFLICT: THE ZULU KINGDOM AND NATAL. By LEONARD THOMPSON — 334
1. The Zulu Kingdom — 336
2. The Voortrekker Republic — 364
3. The British Colony — 373

IX. CO-OPERATION AND CONFLICT: THE HIGH VELD. By LEONARD THOMPSON
1. The *Difaqane* and its Aftermath, 1822–36 — 391
2. The Great Trek, 1836–54 — 405
3. Afrikaner Republics and African States, 1854–70 — 424

INDEX — 447

LIST OF ABBREVIATIONS

AJPA	Americal Journal of Physical Anthropology
AS	African Studies
AYB	Archives Year Book for South African History
Bas. Rec.	G. M. Theal, Basutoland Records
Bel. Hist. Dok.	G. M. Theal, Belangrijke Historische Dokumenten verzameld in die Kaap en Elders
Boëseken (1)	Anna Boëseken, 'Die Nederlandse Kommissarisse en die 18de Eeuse Samelewing aan die Kaap', in AYB, 1944
Boëseken (2)	Anna Boëseken, Nederlandsche Kommissarissen aan die Kaap, 1657–1700
BGSA	Bulletin of the Geological Society of America
Br. Parl. Pap.	British Parliamentary Papers
BS	Bantu Studies
CA	Current Anthropology
Campbell, 1813	J. Campbell, Travels in South Africa
Campbell, 1820	J. Campbell, Travels in South Africa . . . being a Narrative of a Second Journey
CGH	Cape of Good Hope
CHBE	Cambridge History of the British Empire
CMM	Cape Monthly Magazine
JAH	Journal of African History
JRAI	Journal of the Royal Anthropological Institute
Misc. S. Rhod.	Miscellaneous Publications of the National Museum of Southern Rhodesia
Occ. S. Rhod.	Occasional Papers of the National Museum of Southern Rhodesia
PA	Palaeontologica Africana
RCC	G. M. Theal, Records of the Cape Colony
SAAB	South African Archaeological Bulletin
SAAR	South African Archival Records
SAJS	South African Journal of Science
S.A. Mus.	Annals of the South African Museum
SwJA	Southwestern Journal of Anthropology
TGSSA	Transactions of the Geological Society of South Africa
TRSSA	Transactions of the Royal Society of South Africa
VFPA	Viking Fund Publications in Anthropology
VRJ	Journal of Jan van Riebeeck
VRS	Van Riebeeck Society
1st PAC	L. S. B. Leakey, Proceedings of the First Pan-African Congress on Prehistory
3rd PAC	J. D. Clark, Third Pan-African Congress on Prehistory
4th PAC	Actes du IVe Congrès panafricain de préhistoire et de l'étude du Quaternaire: Annales du Musée Royal de L'Afrique Centrale, série in-8^c, n. 40
1883 Report	Report and Proceedings of the Government Commission on Native Laws and Customs, 1883

PREFACE TO THE 1982 EDITION

THE first volume of *The Oxford History of South Africa* is the only comprehensive, scholarly survey of South African history from the beginning through 1870. Consequently, when the Delegates of the Oxford University Press, for reasons related to the economics of the publishing industry in the United Kingdom, decided not to produce further reprints of many of their established books, including this one, we were delighted that David Philip agreed to reproduce the greater part of it in Cape Town.

In this illustrated paperback edition, we have omitted the extensive bibliography that was part of the Oxford edition. We have done so because there is ample documentation in the footnotes throughout the volume. Readers who wish to consult a bibliography that includes more recent works are referred to C. F. J. Muller et al., *South African History and Historians: A Bibliography*, which was published in 1979.[1]

We have also omitted the first chapter of the Oxford edition—R. R. Inskeep's contribution on 'The Archaeological Background'. Archaeologists have been excavating sites in South Africa at an astonishing rate in the last decade; consequently that chapter is largely out of date. Inskeep himself has incorporated many of the findings in a vivid account of early human activity in the region, *The Peopling of Southern Africa*, which was published by David Philip in 1978.[2] In place of that chapter we have included in this edition illustrations chosen according to their significance for the history of the period before 1870.

In the following pages we discuss some recent trends in the historiography of South Africa before the beginning of large-scale mining operations in Kimberley in 1870.[3] For the aeons before the foundation of the Dutch settlement at the Cape of Good Hope in 1652, we draw attention to the deepening of the time scale produced by the archaeologists.

There is still argument about when man emerged and what his distinguishing characteristics were,[4] but the earliest stone tools in

[1] Pretoria, 1979.
[2] Cape Town, 1978.
[3] For a recent summary of the history of Southern Africa to 1870 see Philip Curtin et al., *African History* (Boston, 1978), Chs. 9 and 10.
[4] J. Z. Young, E. M. Jope, K. P. Oakley (organizers), *The Emergence of Man*, Philosophical Transactions of the Royal Society, London, B (292) 1–216 (1918); J. Desmond Clark, 'Africa in Prehistory: Peripheral or Paramount?' (Huxley Memorial Lecture, 1974), *Man* (new ser.) 10, 175–98.

South Africa probably date back to between one and two million years ago. There followed a long, long procession of hunting and gathering peoples who made stone tools until, two thousand years ago, communities of shepherds established themselves on the coast east of the Cape peninsula. By the fourth century A.D., people who worked iron and cultivated the soil and kept cattle as well as small stock were in the Transvaal and moving into Swaziland and Natal. By the seventh century such people were on the coast of the Transkei and the Ciskei.

Between Early and Late Iron Ages dominant lineages moved gradually into South Africa both north and south of the Drakensberg. From the tenth century onwards there is continuity in pottery styles at Phalaborwa in the northern Lowveld and it is likely that their descendants—Sotho-speakers—have been in occupation through to the present day. South-east of the Drakensberg, people who built on ridges, and are probably the principal ancestors of the modern Nguni-speakers, spread in what is now Natal in the eleventh century, probably absorbing earlier occupants of river valleys who, too, were iron-workers and farmers.[5] The westward movement of both Early and Late Iron Age peoples was limited by summer rainfall. They did not settle west of a line between the present Port Elizabeth and Somerset East, since there the combination of cattle-keeping and cultivation of the grains, legumes, and cucurbits grown further north in Africa was not possible. Ecology continued to be a major influence on settlement and the growth of kingdoms, as fruitful studies by Tim Maggs, Colin Webb, and Jeff Guy have shown. Archaeological work is now proceeding so fast that dates are tentative: they may well go back earlier than is suggested here before this book is published. What the reader must understand is that South Africa is finding her past, an exciting tale, and much remains to be discovered.

A second contribution to early historiography comes from historians proper who have criticized anthropologists for a 'static view' of African societies. Indeed, African societies were changing before anthropologists began to examine them (as most anthropologists were aware). Change can be documented from the seventeenth century onward as well as being traced through centuries by archaeologists, but anthropologists are right to insist on differences in the *pace*

---

[5] Five key papers out of many are: R. J. Mason, 'Early Iron Age Settlements at Broederstroom', *SAJS*, 77 (Sept. 1981); R. J. Mason, J. M. Houmoller, and R. Steel, 'Archaeological Survey of the Magalies Valley', *SAJS*, 77 (July 1981); T. Maggs, 'Iron Age Patterns and Sotho History on the Southern Highveld', *World Archaeology*, 7 iii (1976), and 'The Iron Age Sequence South of the Vaal and Pongola Rivers: Some Historical Implications', *JAH*, 21, i (1980); N. J. van der Merwe and T. K. Scully, 'The Phalaborwa Story', *World Archaeology*, 2, iv (1971).

of change. In most isolated societies radical change in techniques and social structure, as opposed to change in office holders and dynasties, is exceedingly slow compared with such change in the modern world.

An important factor in change was the growth of trade. Here a great deal of evidence has been assembled by archaeologists and historians showing the extent of trade between the Moçambique coast and inland metal mines from the thirteenth century onward; the eighteenth- and nineteenth-century trade into Zululand; the nineteenth-century trade from both the eastern Cape and Durban to the Transkei, and also from the eastern Cape to the 'interior', as far as Botswana. Evidence of extensive trade from the Zimbabwe plateau to the east coast goes much further back and the growth of large settlements associated with this trade is now demonstrated.[6] This supports the view expressed on pages 179–81 that the large settlements of the Tswana were connected with their trade in metal and furs. In *The House of Phalo*, a historian, J. B. Peires, uses archival material together with field work, to show the spread of a dominant lineage, the Tshawe, and the development of a Xhosa chiefdom between 1750 and 1850. The question of whether two (or more) independent chiefdoms existed at any particular date turns upon criteria of independence: the seniority and moral authority of the Gcaleka chief was clearly acknowledged but he could not enforce judgment in a dispute between his juniors, Ngqika and Ndlambe, when Ngqika received Colonial support.[7]

A third major contribution to the understanding of early South Africans comes from R. B. Lee and others[8] who have made meticulous studies of the subsistence of hunting peoples and who show them, even in a desert environment, to be communities with relative leisure, not obliged to spend all day and every day in search of food. The extent of rock painting, of dancing, and elaborate mythology described by Bleek and others thus becomes more intelligible.

Studies in the use of language and symbolism by anthropologists have been particularly useful. Mafeje's analysis of 'The Role of the Bard in Contemporary African Society'[9] has implications for the traditional societies also, showing how the bard was not only the praiser but also the critic of the chief. This had been noted earlier by A. C. Jordan[10] but its implications were not grasped by us when we

[6] D. N. Beach, *The Shona of Zimbabwe, 900–1850* (London, 1980), pp. 39–47, 95–6.
[7] J. B. Peires, *The House of Phalo* (Johannesburg, 1981).
[8] R. B. Lee and I. deVore (eds.), *Man the Hunter* (Wenner Gren, 1968); essays by R. B. Lee and James Woodburn.
[9] A. Mafeje, 'The Role of the Bard in a Contemporary African Community', *Journal of African Languages*, 6, viii (1967, actually published 1969).
[10] A. C. Jordan, *Towards an African Literature* (Berkeley and Los Angeles, 1973).

wrote on chieftainship. Jordan drew attention to bards' criticisms of the harsh policies of the Zulu chief Dingane and the Thembu chief Ngangelizwe, who died respectively in 1840 and 1884. The *mbongi* almost filled the role of the licensed fool in Shakespeare's tragedies, or of a modern political cartoonist. D. Mzolo also adds to our understanding of the use of clan praises.[11]

Much of the substantial body of material published on religion centres on the interaction of traditional ideas and Christianity in contemporary economic conditions (Pauw, Setiloane, Whisson and West, and Hammond-Tooke).[12] However, two books are outstanding for the light they throw on symbolism, which has ancient roots: Axel-Ivar Berglund, *Zulu Thought-Patterns and Symbolism*, and Harriet Ngubane, *Body and Mind in Zulu Medicine*.[13] These provide a level of analysis far deeper than anything previously available on thought-patterns in Southern Africa. Harriet Ngubane also shows that the phrase used in the traditional ritual of chieftainship celebrated in December, on which Gluckman based his theory of *Rituals of Rebellion*,[14] was, in fact, a mistranslation by Bryant. She interprets the ritual as a purification, not a symbolic rebellion (Ngubane, pp. 152–3), and purification is, indeed, the explicit intention of somewhat similar annual rituals further north. Zulu thought-patterns fit closely with those of other Africans who speak Bantu languages. The fact that the great *incwala* ritual was not an occasion for the expression of rebellion, as Gluckman supposed, is relevant to the study of the Zulu polity.

Considerable attention has been paid by anthropologists to further analysis of kinship systems including detailed discussion of marriage in a money economy with widespread migrant labour. Most of the discussion relates to the post-1870 period, but one essay considers evidence on Xhosa marriage from 1635 onward, showing that traditional forms have continued though new legal forms exist alongside them; and Philip Mayer is concerned with 'The Origin and Decline of Two Rural Resistance Ideologies', which have roots stretching back before 1850.[15]

[11] D. Mzolo, 'Zulu Clan Praises', in J. Argyle and E. Preston-Whyte (eds.), *Social System and Tradition in Southern Africa* (Cape Town, 1978).

[12] B. A. Pauw, *Christianity and Xhosa Tradition* (Cape Town, 1975); G. M. Setiloane, *The Image of God among the Sotho–Tswana* (Rotterdam, 1976); M. G. Whisson and Martin West, *Religion and Social Change in Southern Africa* (Cape Town, 1975); W. D. Hammond-Tooke, *Boundaries and Belief* (Johannesburg, 1981).

[13] A.-I. Berglund, *Zulu Thought-Patterns and Symbolism* (Uppsala, London and Cape Town, 1975); Harriet Ngubane, *Body and Mind in Zulu Medicine* (London, 1977).

[14] Max Gluckman, *Rituals of Rebellion in South East Africa* (Manchester, 1952).

[15] Monica Wilson, 'Xhosa Marriage in Historical Perspective', in E. J. Krige and J. L. Comaroff (eds.), *Essays on Marriage in Southern Africa* (Cape Town, 1981). Philip Mayer (ed.), *Black Villagers in an Industrial Society* (Cape Town, 1980).

Recent research in the Dutch and Cape archives has resulted in a considerable deepening of our knowledge of the Dutch colonial period. While May Katzen's chapter in this volume is a reliable introduction to the subject, people who wish to probe it more deeply should supplement this chapter with *The Shaping of South African Society, 1652–1820*, edited by Richard Elphick and Hermann Giliomee, which incorporates much of the best new research.[16] It includes careful accounts of the different population groups in the Dutch colony, of the Dutch administrative institutions, and of the frontier interactions with Khoisan and Bantu-speaking farming peoples. It closes with a review of the structure of European domination in the colony throughout the period.

Elphick has made a meticulous study of the Dutch East India Company records in the Cape, the Hague, and Amsterdam, and provides a summary of his findings about the Khoikhoi people and their changing relationships with Dutch settlers.[17] He demonstrates the decline in Khoikhoi population and cattle-holdings even before the smallpox epidemic of 1713 and traces the movement of men to work for the Dutch. Shula Marks has shown the extent of 'Khoisan Resistance to the Dutch in the Seventeenth and Eighteenth Centuries'.[18] Robert Ross narrates the history of one remarkable mixed group, descendants of Khoikhoi, San, and white, in *Adam Kok's Griquas* and inquires into the development of stratification in South Africa.[19]

Although Calvinism undoubtedly became a powerful influence in Afrikaner nationalism in the late nineteenth century,[20] *The Shaping of South African Society* convincingly refutes the notion that it was Calvinism or, alternatively, frontier conditions that were responsible for the creation of a racial ideology and racial practices in South Africa. Rather, the editors attribute the origins of Afrikaner racism to the prejudices and practices of the Dutch East India Company. They show that 'It was ... the Company's distinctions among legal status groups, which initially structured Cape society,'[21] and that racial differentiation was intensified by the nature of the colonial economy.

Recent work has also deepened our understanding of the rise of the Zulu kingdom and its repercussions—that major transformation of African societies that reached a crescendo shortly before the Voor-

---

[16] Cape Town and London, 1979.
[17] Richard Elphick, *Kraal and Castle: Khoikhoi and the Founding of White South Africa* (New Haven and London, 1977).
[18] Shula Marks, 'Khoisan Resistance to the Dutch in the Seventeenth and Eighteenth Centuries', *JAH*, 13, i (1972), 55–80.
[19] Robert Ross, *Adam Kok's Griquas* (Cambridge, 1976).
[20] W. A. de Klerk, *The Puritans in Africa* (London, 1975); T. Dunbar Moodie, *The Rise of Afrikanerdom* (Berkeley and Los Angeles, 1975).
[21] *The Shaping of South African Society*, p. 364.

trekkers penetrated into the eastern part of South Africa. The main thrust of this new work shows that the crisis in Nguni society had been developing throughout the eighteenth century. Focusing on social and economic processes, it constitutes a corrective to the earlier concentration on the personality and role of Shaka. Jeff Guy makes a major contribution by analyzing the ecological factors in Zulu history.[22] He shows that kwaZulu is an area of closely juxtaposed variations of climate, altitude, and vegetation, which necessitated the seasonal transhumance of cattle; and that by the late eighteenth century cattle-grazing over a long period had caused environmental deterioration and thereby reduced the carrying capacity of the land. As noted on page 253, the adoption of maize as a food crop may have accelerated the growth of population at the cost of contributing to the degeneration of the soil, hence the population growth which was almost certainly a major factor behind the *mfecane* can be related to changes in the material environment. Soon, we may expect more mature syntheses of the entire *mfecane* process. Colin Webb and J. B. Wright are editing *The James Stuart Archive of Recorded Oral Evidence Relating to the History of the Zulu and Neighbouring Peoples*, which comprises transcriptions of interviews which Stuart, an excellent Zulu linguist, made with numerous people in the late nineteenth and early twentieth centuries.[23]

The history of white expansion into the lands previously occupied by Bantu-speaking farming societies has received a great deal of fresh attention. Peter Sanders and Leonard Thompson have both written biographies of Moshweshwe, the founder of the kingdom of Lesotho, whose life straddled the entire epoch from isolated autonomy to white hegemony.[24] *The Frontier in History: North America and Southern Africa Compared*, edited by Howard Lamar and Leonard Thompson, places this crucial aspect of South African history in a comparative perspective, treating the frontier processes in North America and Southern Africa as contemporaneous expressions of the same global phenomenon.[25] Though both cases were generated by the same forces and had much in common, their differences were profound; and these differences help us to see features of the South

---

[22] Jeff Guy, 'Ecological Factors in the Rise of Shaka and the Zulu Kingdom', in Shula Marks and Anthony Atmore (eds.), *Economy and Society in Pre-Industrial South Africa* (London, 1980), pp. 102–19. See also the first part of Jeff Guy, *The Destruction of the Zulu Kingdom: The Civil War in Zululand 1879–1884* (London and Johannesburg, 1979).

[23] Six volumes of the *The James Stuart Archive* are projected. Volumes 1, 2, and 3 were published in Pietermaritzburg and Durban in 1976, 1979, and 1982, respectively. They are superbly edited.

[24] Peter Sanders, *Moshoeshoe: Chief of the Sotho* (London and Cape Town, 1975); Leonard Thompson, *Survival in Two Worlds: Moshoeshoe of Lesotho, 1786–1870* (Oxford, 1975).

[25] New Haven and London, 1981.

African situation which, without the comparative perspective, might go unnoticed. First, by the end of the nineteenth century, when the frontiers had closed and whites had established hegemony, the survivors of the indigenous peoples of the United States amounted to fewer than one half of one per cent of the total population, whereas the Bantu-speaking peoples were still a large majority of the population of Southern Africa. Second, white settlers in North America rarely used Indian labour, whereas from an early stage the white Southern African economies depended on the labour services of indigenous people as well as imported slaves. Third, before 1870 Southern Africa was very loosely linked to external markets, whereas from the very beginning the white settlements in North America had significant roles in the burgeoning capitalist world economy. Besides integrative chapters by the editors, *The Frontier in History* contains parallel essays by North American and South African specialists, including Hermann Giliomee, Christopher Saunders, Robert Ross, and Richard Elphick.

In a most ambitious study, George Fredrickson has compared the entire history of race relations in the two regions.[26] He contends that, although both the south-western Cape and the southern colonies in North America were based on racial slavery, white Americans were more ruthless than white South Africans in dispossessing the indigenous peoples and were also less tolerant of racial mixing. In Fredrickson's analysis, the situation was only reversed after the industrialization process began in South Africa towards the end of the nineteenth century.

Shula Marks and Anthony Atmore have edited a series of essays derived from their graduate seminar in the University of London, with the title *Economy and Society in Pre-Industrial South Africa*.[27] In their Introduction, they use the Marxist categories of social formation, mode of production, and forces and relations of production, and they say, with specific reference to the *Oxford History*, that they regard their work as 'an attempt to get beyond the liberal "problematic"'.[28] These essays are a series of case studies that add significantly to our knowledge of several key aspects of that history; in particular, of the changes in African societies in the first three quarters of the nineteenth century. In a revised version of an essay that was first circulated in 1971, Martin Legassick shows that I. D. MacCrone's thesis

---

[26] George M. Fredrickson, *White Supremacy: A Comparative Study in American and South African History* (New York, 1981).
[27] London, 1980.
[28] *Economy and Society*, p. 1. They use their Marxist categories somewhat awkwardly; as in fn. 9, p. 38, which is a dense 400-word discussion of the attributes of the concepts social formation and mode of production.

that white South African racism was predominantly a product of the frontier experiences of the trekboers in the eighteenth century is no longer tenable. 'The pattern of racial relationships established in the eighteenth century Cape', writes Legassick, 'must be seen in the light of the formation of the colonist as a whole, the form of his inheritance from Europe, and the exigencies of the situation he had to face.'[29] Philip Bonner characterizes the African farming societies, in terms of the debate among Marxists about pre-capitalist modes of production. The editors summarize his hypothesis as 'the articulation of two separate modes of production, that of the lineage ... and that of the tributary state'.[30] He shows the part played by captives 'who remained perpetual minors' in Swazi economy, and the extent to which children were traded as 'apprentices' to Boer farmers in the Transvaal.[31] Roger Wagner shows how white hunters and their men in the Zoutpansberg also seized children to serve as 'apprentices' on white farms.[32] Both Swaziland and the Zoutpansberg adjoined areas in which slaving was rampant, and there never has been any doubt that the Nguni raided for slaves once they were established north of the Limpopo (see p. 121). Patrick Harries has shown that there was more sale of Tsonga by Nguni than we indicated, even south of the Limpopo,[33] but though Inhambane was for long a port for the slave trade (as we noted), and Lourenço Marques also, Port Natal (Durban) was not. William Beinart shows how the Mpondo people responded successively to the *mfecane* and the intrusion of white people, first by concentrating for defence in larger village settlements under increased chiefly control, and then by producing an agricultural surplus for the market with a decline of chiefly control over production. Colin Bundy demonstrates that Africans in the Herschel district of the Cape Colony responded to market opportunities during the middle of the nineteenth century by producing a surplus of crops for sale, but that at a later stage they were reduced to sub-subsistence farming, dependent on wages from migrant labour.[34] In an essay reminiscent of Eric Williams's critique

[29] *Economy and Society*, p. 68. In revising this essay for publication in this book, Legassick has gone to great lengths to respond to the criticisms of Harrison M. Wright in *The Burden of the Present: Liberal–Radical Controversy over Southern African History* (Cape Town and London), 1977.
[30] *Economy and Society*, p. 11. The wording is that of Marks and Atmore summarizing Bonner.
[31] *Economy and Society*, pp. 96–7.
[32] Roger Wagner, 'Zoutpansberg: The Dynamics of a Hunting Frontier, 1848–67' in *Economy and Society*, pp. 332–3.
[33] Patrick Harries, 'Slavery, Social Incorporation and Surplus Extraction; The Nature of Free and Unfree Labour in South East Africa', *JAH*, 22 (1981), 309–30.
[34] See also Colin Bundy, *The Rise and Fall of the South African Peasantry* (Berkeley and Los Angeles, 1979). For a more mature treatment of the subject, see Frederick Cooper, 'Peasants, Capitalists, and Historians: A Review Article', in *Journal of Southern African Studies*, 7, ii (April 1981), 284–314.

of the British emancipation movement in *Capitalism and Slavery*,[35] Susan Newton-King highlights the material interests behind the Cape colonial ordinances of 1828 that removed the restrictions on the movements of Khoikhoi ('Hottentots') and permitted Bantu-speaking Africans to obtain work inside the colony. 'Ordinance 50, like Ordinance 49,' she says, 'represented an attempt to increase the labour supply available to the colonists.'[36] In similar vein, Stanley Trapido examines the material bases of nineteenth-century Cape 'liberalism', while in another essay he discusses the origins of class differentiation among Afrikaners in the Transvaal.

Most recent Afrikaans historiography has continued to deal with traditional themes. Representative of the best of such scholarship, with its thorough control of the South African archival sources, is C. F. J. Muller's magisterial study of the origins of the Great Trek.[37] Archival research has also led to some fresh interpretations. J. A. Heese's exhaustive study of the Slagters Nek Rebellion has shed a great deal of light on the cleavages in early nineteenth-century trekboer society and on the relations between various trekboer factions and the British colonial administrators.[38] He shows that the majority of the substantial Boer frontiersmen sided with the government in suppressing the 1815 rebellion and that it was they who later provided the leaders and participants in the Great Trek, while the Bezuidenhouts and their accomplices were not the heroic figures they have been represented to be by a generation of Afrikaner historians and publicists. Similarly, B. J. Liebenberg's biography of Andries Pretorius subjects that major Voortrekker leader to a searching reappraisal, with the result that Pretorius's reputation, too, is somewhat tarnished.[39] Recently, F. A. van Jaarsveld, the most prolific and influential Afrikaner historian of his generation, has exposed the fallacies in the Afrikaner traditions concerning 16 December, the 'Day of the Covenant'.[40] Younger scholars, notably André du Toit and Hermann Giliomee, are systematically reviewing the intellectual and cultural history of the Afrikaner people.[41] What is still conspicuously absent from the historiography is a major input from black

[35] Eric Williams, *Capitalism and Slavery* (2nd ed., London, 1964).
[36] *Economy and Society*, p. 197.
[37] C. F. J. Muller, *Die Oorsprong van die Groot Trek* (Cape Town and Johannesburg, 1974).
[38] J. A. Heese, *Slagtersnek en sy Mense* (Cape Town and Johannesburg, 1973).
[39] B. J. Liebenberg, *Andries Pretorius in Natal* (Pretoria and Cape Town, 1977).
[40] F. A. van Jaarsveld, 'An Historical Mirror of Blood River', in A. König and H. Keane (eds.), *The Meaning of History* (Pretoria, 1980), pp. 8–59. Other recent works by Van Jaarsveld include *Geskiedkundige Verkenninge* (Pretoria, 1974).
[41] Hermann Giliomee and André du Toit are working on a three-volume history of *Afrikaner Political Thought*. The first volume will soon be published by David Philip, Cape Town and the University of California Press.

South Africans[42]—a sad reflection of the present structure of South African society.

MONICA WILSON
LEONARD THOMPSON
May 1982

[42] But see W. M. Tsotsi, *From Chattel to Wage Slavery: A New Approach to South African History* (Maseru, 1981).

PUBLISHER'S NOTE

As explained by the Editors on page 9, chapter I and the Bibliography of *The Oxford History of South Africa*, vol. i, have been omitted from this paperback edition, and many more illustrations have been added. Although some preliminary and Index pages have been renumbered or rearranged, the text of *OHSA*, vol. i, has not otherwise been altered.

An asterisk (*) in the margin indicates that a reference in the text applies to *OHSA*, not to this book; where further comment would be helpful, it is added at the foot of the page concerned.

ACKNOWLEDGEMENTS

Acknowledgement is made to the following copyright holders for the illustrations reproduced (illustration numbers in parentheses): William Fehr Collection, Cape Town (1, 6, 7, 8, 9, 10, 11, 12, 13, 14); Africana Museum, Johannesburg (15, 16, 17, 18, 19, 20, 21, 22, 23, 24, 25); Mr. Lorenzo Cloete (2); Albany Museum, Grahamstown (3); Akademische Druck- und Verlagsanstalt, Graz (4); A. A. Balkema, Cape Town (5).

Acknowledgement is due also to the William Fehr Collection for permission to reproduce the cover illustration, 'Meeting of Governor Janssens with Kaffir Chief Gaika at the Kat River, 1803' (Maj. Johann Christoph Ludwig Alberti, 1810).

1 'Namaqua Hottentot on loose horned Riding Ox and his Bushman' (Thomas Baines, 1865)

2 'Xhosa riding an Ox, Tyhume' (Thomas Baines, c. 1850)
3 'Mr Hume's Waggons with Ivory and Skins from the Interior of Africa on Grahamstown Market' (Thomas Baines, 1850)

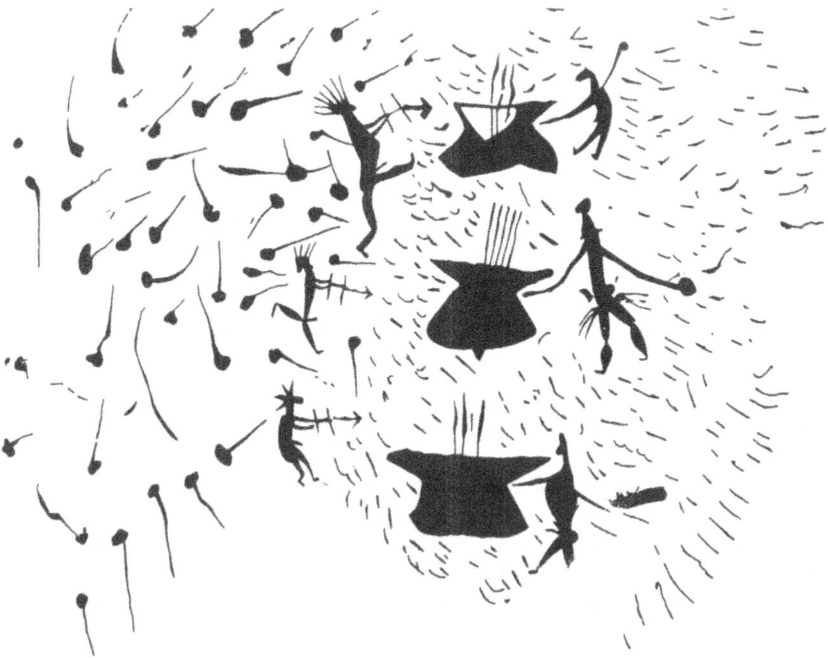

4 Battle between San and Bantu-speakers
5 Battle between two groups of Bantu-speakers (Lichtenstein, Rouxville, O.F.S.)

6 'Bush-men Hottentots armed for an Expedition' (Samuel Daniell, 1831)
7 'Booshuana Women manufacturing Earthen Ware' (Samuel Daniell, 1831)

8 'The Town of Leetakoo' (Samuel Daniell, 1831)
9 'A Boosh-wannah Hut' (Samuel Daniell, 1801)

10 'Kaffir Chief Macoma' (Charles Davidson Bell, *c.* 1849)
11 'Genadendal' (George French Angas, 1849)

12 'Gudu's Kraal at the Tugela. Women making Beer' (George French Angas, 1849)
13 'Matabele Kraal' (Sir William Cornwallis Harris, c. 1836)

14 'State of Cradock's Pass in 1840' (Charles Cornwallis Michell, 1840)
15 'Phillipolis' (*sic*) (James Backhouse, *c.* 1844)

16 'Houses and Yard of Sinosee, in Kurreechane' (John Campbell, c. 1822)
17 'A Boor's House' (Samuel Daniell, 1805)

18 The Village of Tulbagh (William J. Burchell, *c.* 1824)
19 'A View in the Town of Litakun' (William J. Burchell, *c.* 1824)

20 'Hottentot Levy' (Charles Davidson Bell)
21 'The Namaqua Kraal' (James Chapman, after a drawing by Charles Davidson Bell, c. 1868)

22 'Sandili, Häuptling der Gaika (Ama-Ngqika)' (Gustav Fritsch, c. 1868)

23 'Hintza' (Charles Cornwallis Michell, c. 1837)

24 'A Korah Girl' (Samuel Daniell, c. 1820)

25 'A Hottentot' (Samuel Daniell, c. 1804)

PREFACE TO THE 1969 EDITION

THIS work derives from our belief that the central theme of South African history is interaction between peoples of diverse origins, languages, technologies, ideologies, and social systems, meeting on South African soil.

It is peculiarly difficult to write the history of a society which has become as rigidly stratified as South African society. Recent histories of South Africa illustrate the difficulties.[1] Nearly every one of them embodies the point of view of only one community. The group focus is seen in the structures of the works as well as in the interpretations they give to events. They are primarily concerned with the achievements of white people in South Africa, and their relations with one another. The experiences of the other inhabitants of South Africa are not dealt with at any length: they are treated mainly as peoples who constituted 'Native', or 'Coloured', or 'Indian' problems for the whites. Where these works differ from each other is in their assessment of the policies which whites have adopted in grappling with such problems. The histories in the English language tend to be sympathetic to the policies of the British government, of missionaries, and of 'liberals', and critical of the policies of local white governments; and the Afrikaans *Geskiedenis* the reverse.

The reasons for these limitations are evident. Group focus is the product of the social milieu in a plural society, where communication between the different communities is restricted and the individual historian is conditioned by the assumptions and prejudices of his own community, whether it is a community of religion, or class, or language, or race, or some combination of two or more of these factors. Hence the religious histories of Reformation and Counter-Reformation Europe, the aristocratic histories of eighteenth-century Europe, and the nationalistic histories of nineteenth-century Europe; and hence, too, the racial focus in some histories of the southern States of the United States, as well as those of South Africa. Focus on one physical type is not, of

[1] Eric A. Walker, *A History of South Africa*. It was re-issued with additions in 1935, published in a second edition in 1940, re-printed with minor corrections in 1947, published in a third edition under the title *A History of Southern Africa* in 1957, and further corrected in 1959 and 1962.
CHBE, vol. viii, *South Africa, Rhodesia, and the Protectorates*, ed. A. P. Newton and E. A. Benians, Cambridge, 1936; and E. A. Walker, Cambridge, 1963.
Geskiedenis van Suid-Afrika, ed. A. J. H. van der Walt, J. A. Wiid, and A. L. Geyer, Cape Town/Bloemfontein/Johannesburg, 2 vols., 1951; and D. W. Krüger, 1 vol., 1965.

course, confined to societies where the barrier is a barrier of colour. As Jan Vansina has shown, the traditional historiography in Rwanda was essentially the historiography of an African minority (the Tutsi) which formerly dominated the majority of the people (the Hutu), who were also dark-skinned but physically different from themselves.[1]

In a rigidly stratified society historical writing (or historical tradition, orally transmitted) is not merely a *reflection* of social inequality; it is also a powerful instrument for the *maintenance* of inequality. This is certainly the case in South Africa, where much historical writing promotes the perpetuation of language and race barriers, and some of it does so intentionally.[2]

This account cannot be free from the limitations set on the authors by their environment. We have profited from the work of our predecessors, and disagreed with them when the evidence led us to do so, but we, too, are the products of our time and place. We live, or have lived, in a caste society, and we are all white. This last unbalance occurs because in South Africa today few Africans, or Asians, or Coloured people have the opportunity for unfettered research and writing; and those who have the training and opportunity are for the most part occupied with other commitments. A deliberate attempt is made to look at the roots of South African society and to take due account of all its peoples: how far it succeeds must be for readers of the various groups to judge.

A further limitation in most contemporary historical writings on South Africa is that they have a marked disciplinary focus, construing history in narrow terms. The South Africa volume of the *Cambridge History of the British Empire* includes a social anthropologist's summary of the condition of the inhabitants of South Africa before they mingled with people from Europe; an account of the early contacts of the East African coast with the outside world; and chapters which analyse the effects of contact upon the African peoples. This was pioneering work when these chapters were first written, but our knowledge of African archaeology and anthropology has increased rapidly in recent years. In the second edition there is also a chapter on South African art, literature, and sport. Nevertheless, the effect is additive rather than integrative, for the bulk of the work is concerned with white people and with politics.

Whereas group focus is a product of social division and becomes less conspicuous as a society becomes more homogeneous, the disciplinary limitation exists in all modern societies. It arises from the partition of

---

[1] J. Vansina, *L'Évolution du Royaume Rwanda des Origines à 1900*.
[2] L. M. Thompson, 'Afrikaner Nationalist Historiography and the Policy of Apartheid', *JAH*, 3 (1962), 125–41; 'South Africa', Robin Winks (ed.), *The Historiography of the British Empire-Commonwealth*, pp. 212–36.

knowledge between the disciplines in modern universities. This is not the original tradition of the universities of Europe. In the medieval universities Theology was Queen, and knowledge was an integrated whole around the throne; but with the dethronement of theology, the rise of Cartesian philosophy, and the proliferation of data, knowledge became divided into different disciplines, each claiming an independent validity. In this process history became divorced from most of the social sciences and mainly political in content. The process has now been arrested in varying degrees. Everywhere Marx and his successors have gone a long way towards bringing economics back into history; and an historian is no longer suspect if he makes use of the modes of analysis of the anthropologist and the sociologist. Nevertheless, the structure of most modern universities, where different professors teach different courses, labelled history, economics, anthropology, and sociology, to different groups of students, continues to exert a narrowing influence; and it is this narrowness which is reflected in the three basic surveys of South African history.

A work which largely escapes these limitations is C. W. de Kiewiet's *A History of South Africa: Social and Economic*,[1] and it has had a deep influence on many who are sensitive to the need for a broad approach. De Kiewiet wrote twenty-five years ago that 'The true history of South African colonization describes the growth, not of a settlement of Europeans, but of a totally new and unique society of different races and colours and cultural attainments.'[2] But the focus of his book is on the growth of the modern sector of the South African economy; and, as its title indicates, it is scarcely concerned with the political aspect.

One difficulty inherent in co-operation between members of different disciplines is that they ask different questions and are not agreed as to what facts are relevant. The historian is likely to concentrate on *what happened*, and the succession of events, while the anthropologist is more interested in *what is* and *why it is*, and he seeks to answer 'why' partly through comparison with other societies. In making comparisons, he may disregard time and his account become static. The problem of providing meat for the specialist and at the same time being intelligible to the layman is also most acute when members of several disciplines collaborate. What has emerged in this book is the fruit of mutual criticism, but no attempt has been made to eliminate the differences in viewpoint between various chapters.

Five misleading assumptions have shaped writing about South African history, though they have seldom been made explicit. Most authors write as if South African history began with the discovery of the Cape

[1] Oxford, 1941.   [2] Ibid., p. 19.

by the Portuguese, and the significant time span for historians is, at the most, five hundred years; more commonly it is thought of as beginning with the arrival of the Dutch in 1652. The rich archaeological evidence has been largely ignored. This assumption of the brevity of significant time is an aspect of parochialism; it is one of the characteristics of a small-scale society that it conceives of all history as packed into a few generations.

Secondly, it has been assumed that the traditional societies of Africa were static; that there was no structural change, only a succession of office-holders. Even so eminent a scholar as Professor Trevor-Roper, broadcasting in 1963, expressed the view that there is no African history, only the history of Europeans in Africa. He went on:

I do not deny that men existed even in dark countries and dark centuries, nor that they had political life and culture, interesting to sociologists and anthropologists; but history, I believe is essentially a form of movement. . . . The positive content of history, to all these writers . . . [of the eighteenth century] consisted not in the meaningless fermentation of passive or barbarous societies but in the movement of society, the process, conscious or unconscious, by which certain societies, at certain times, had risen out of barbarism once common to all and, by their efforts and example, by the interchange and diffusion of arts and sciences, gradually drawn or driven other societies along with them to 'the full light and freedom of the eighteenth century'.[1]

At what point 'barbarism' ceases, and 'movement' begins, is not defined.

In fact, archaeological evidence demonstrates a succession of economies in pre-colonial southern Africa; anthropologists have described a variety of cultures; and through the use of oral tradition and written record we are beginning to piece together the gradual transformation from one to another. One social revolution—the growth of kingdoms where previously there had existed only small chiefdoms—is discussed in some detail in this volume. It is true that the *pace* of change in very small societies is often extremely slow—the Xhosa between 1686 and 1857 are an example—but it is only the ignorant who suppose that radical change in social structure does not occur among preliterate peoples. Myth and tradition in Africa still continually refer to the revolutions which took place when men first learnt to make fire; when iron weapons supplanted those of stone and bone; when domesticated animals were introduced; when the institution of chieftainship was first established and law and order were extended beyond one tiny village or hunting band.

A third assumption—perhaps the most misleading of all—is that

[1] H. Trevor-Roper, 'The Rise of Christian Europe', *The Listener*, 28 November 1963, p. 871.

PREFACE TO THE 1969 EDITION

physical type, language, and economy are *necessarily* correlated. Generations of South Africans have grown up believing that 'Bushmen', a distinct dwarf physical type, were all hunters, and all spoke one or another form of a 'Bushman language'; that 'Hottentots' were distinct physically, that they were all pastoralists, and that they all spoke the 'Hottentot language'; that those who spoke a Bantu language were again physically distinct and that they all combined cultivation with herding; and that whites remained quite distinct in physical type, language, and manner of life from all the preceding groups. But it has long been known, and recent research has further demonstrated, that the cleavages in physical type, language, and economy do *not* fit at all exactly. It has been shown, for example, that a negroid people, the Dama, speak Nama, a so-called 'Hottentot' language;[1] that various hunting groups speak languages close to Nama and far from 'Bushman';[2] that the physical anthropologists can define no one 'Hottentot' physical type, and argue as to how to differentiate 'Hottentot' from 'Bushman';[3] that some of those who speak Bantu languages are part caucasian in physical type; that many caucasians, speaking a Germanic language, have lived as nomadic herdsmen in a manner vastly different from the peasants and townsmen of Europe from whom they sprang; and that persons who, to all appearance, are bush-boskop or negroid may have as their home language Afrikaans or, more rarely, English.

Because correlations are so far from exact, different terms are used in this book for physical type, language, and economy. We speak of bush-boskop, negroid, and caucasian when referring to physical type; of San, Khoikhoi, Bantu, and Germanic languages; and when discussing mode of subsistence, of hunters, herders, cultivators, peasants (who have begun trading with the outside world), farmers, and townsmen.

If precise terminology is used, the fourth assumption, that each of the four physical types formed a 'pure race' which, at least in the seventeenth and eighteenth centuries, had the exclusive occupation of a specific area and remained isolated from the others, can be shown to be absurd. It is equally untrue to suggest that cultural groups were quite separate. The journals of shipwrecked travellers—Portuguese, Dutch, and English—from the sixteenth century onwards show that no consistent distinction was made between 'Bushmen' and 'Hottentots' in physique; that hunters and herders were interspersed around the Cape; and that both groups were living in close association with dark-skinned cultivators who were also cattle-owners along the south-eastern coast.

---

[1] H. Vedder, 'The Berg Damara', in *The Native Tribes of South West Africa*, p. 41.
[2] E. Westphal, 'The Linguistic Prehistory of Southern Africa', *Africa*, 33 (1963), 2.
[3] P. Tobias, 'Physical Anthropology and Somatic Origins of the Hottentots', *AS*, 14 (1955), 1-14.

The evidence from skeletal remains, blood groups, and language alike demonstrates an ancient intermingling of physical types and language groups. Statements about *exclusive* occupation by different 'races' of defined areas, and of a distaste for mingling, reflect the present preoccupation with race and the present social structure, rather than any historical reality. The myth that white settlers occupied an 'empty land' likewise reflects present values of the ruling group and not demographic fact. This will be shown in succeeding chapters.

The fifth assumption implicit in most academic studies in South Africa is that it is improper for the historian to be concerned with social structure and improper for the anthropologist to study all races. Historians have been *mainly* concerned with the political and economic development of whites; anthropologists *mainly* with the more isolated 'tribal' communities of blacks. For an historian to study demographic change, or the relation between changing forms of the family and political institutions, or for an anthropologist to study the caste system in a South African city, or the organization of a church, or a secret society, among whites, is aberrant.

The spelling of names of people and places in South African history has been chaotic, largely because historians have rarely troubled to learn any African language and have mixed singular, plural, and locative forms with happy abandon; but also because orthographies have differed from one dialect and language to another, and have changed in time. In this history the rules set out by the International African Institute thirty years ago are followed.[1] The stem only of a Bantu or Khoikhoi word is used without prefix or suffix, and we refer to the *Sotho, Zulu, Tswana,* and *Khoikhoi,* rather than *Basotho, Amazulu, Betshwana,* and *Khoikhoin*; *Xhosa country* rather than *emaXhoseni*. The form used is that of the current orthography in the language of the people concerned, except in direct quotation. Thus we have the Ndebele form *Mzilikazi* rather than the Sotho form *Moselekatse*, except when quoting Moffat and other Sotho speakers. There is a further difficulty in that two orthographies for southern Sotho exist; we use the international form current in the Republic. Two exceptions are made to the dropping of prefixes: Lesotho is used for the kingdom of Moshweshwe and his successors, known for a hundred years as Basutoland, and Botswana for what has been called Bechuanaland, for Lesotho and Botswana are the names now used by the people themselves in international affairs. Further departures from the rule of no prefixes may indeed follow in English usage as the claims of African languages are pressed, and more English speakers learn to manipulate Bantu nouns.

[1] 'Orthography of Africa's Tribal Names', *Africa*, 6 (1933), 479.

PREFACE TO THE 1969 EDITION 37

South Africans are commonly classified by race and we refer to the three main groups in the country by the terms they themselves prefer: 'whites' meaning those classified as descendants of settlers from Europe and a handful from America; 'Coloured' meaning those of mixed descent (mulatto), and 'African' meaning dark-skinned part-negro people. But 'African' is not a very precise term, for already South Africans of all complexions are beginning to talk of 'white Africans' as well as 'black Africans', and the word 'Afrikaner'[1] means specifically a white South African whose home language is Afrikaans. Tension over the exclusive use of 'African' and 'Afrikaner' is, indeed, a reflection of the struggle for power and the claim to rights based on prior occupation. 'Native' is almost a term of abuse, but white and black and Coloured alike claim to be native to the country. The most egregious term of all, 'foreign Native', is used in official documents to describe black Africans who have come from outside the Republic: its parallel is 'African South African' used of themselves by some blacks born within the Republic. 'Bantu' is now the official term for black Africans, but it is disliked by those to whom it is applied, and therefore avoided here, except in its original usage meaning a category of languages. We use 'Asian' for descendants of all settlers from Asia, rather than 'Indian' and 'Chinese'. But the official terms appear in direct quotations.

After this Preface, there is a survey of the archaeological data, * emphasizing the links between South Africa[2] and the rest of the continent, and between the more remote and the more recent past in South Africa. This is followed by three chapters which describe the hunting, herding, and cultivating peoples who lived in South Africa for many centuries before the advent of people from Europe, and who were the ancestors of the vast majority of the present inhabitants. Chapter V describes the foundation at the Cape of Good Hope of a colonial society, with a dominant community of white officials and settlers, and subordinate communities of people absorbed from the indigenous hunters and herders, and of slaves imported from tropical Africa, Malagasy, and south-east Asia; and the expansion of that society until the 1770s. Chapter VI reviews the relations between the peoples of the Cape Colony and the Nguni cultivators on its eastern frontier, from their first meetings until about 1870. The next chapter describes the growth of the plural society in the Cape Colony from the 1770s to 1870.

[1] This meaning of *Afrikaner* has become considerably narrowed in recent years because of the tendency of the Nationalist Party to equate membership of the party with the word *Afrikaner*.
[2] In this book we mean by South Africa the area south of the lower reaches of the Limpopo and Orange rivers and east and south of the Kalahari desert—more precisely, the present Republic of South Africa, Lesotho, Swaziland, and a part of Botswana.
* Omitted from this 1982 edition; see new Preface, p. 9.

The last two chapters of this volume describe the rise of the Zulu kingdom, its repercussions on the High Veld (including the rise of the Ndebele and southern Sotho kingdoms), the intrusion into both areas of Afrikaner Voortrekkers from the Cape Colony, and the foundation of the British colony of Natal and the Afrikaner Republics in the Orange Free State and the Transvaal. The volume terminates in 1870, which marks the beginning of the diamond-mining industry and of the entry of South Africa into the world economy.

* We start the second volume with a brief analysis of economic conditions in the 1860s. This is followed by an account of the economic growth which has taken place. The next three chapters examine the development of the three basic social complexes of modern South Africa: the communities of African and Coloured peasants in the rural areas reserved by law for their exclusive occupation; the plural communities engaged in commercial farming in the rural areas reserved by law for exclusive *ownership* by white people; and the plural communities in the industrial and commercial towns. The next five chapters consider the impact of the forces which have dominated the political scene in modern South Africa: British imperialism, which was dominant from the 1870s until the beginning of the twentieth century; the attempt which was then made to establish a compromise between Boer and Briton; the rise and triumph of Afrikaner nationalism; and the challenge which is being presented to Afrikaner nationalism by African nationalism. Finally there is a review of the relations between South Africa and the world beyond its borders. The work terminates in the year 1966.

The reader's attention is drawn to the maps which have been specially
* prepared for both volumes. They contain a great deal of necessary information which is not repeated in the text. The illustrations, too, illuminate some key aspects of South African history.

We are keenly aware that this work has shortcomings. Apart from our own limitations and those of our collaborators, there are inescapable weaknesses in any survey of South African history that is published at the present time. There is still a dearth of monographs on many vital aspects of South African history. For example, in recent decades archaeological work has not advanced as rapidly in South Africa as it has in some other parts of the continent, including the contiguous Rhodesia. Far too little systematic excavation has been done on the crucial site at Mapungubwe; and on Iron Age sites in the Orange Free State, Natal, and the Transkei. Then again there are insufficient studies of the experiences of specific African communities since they came into contact with white people and, more particularly, of the relations between the white, African, and Coloured peoples on white-owned farms, in country towns, and on the main industrial complex of the

Witwatersrand. Analysis of these relationships by African and Coloured historians, economists, and anthropologists, as well as their account of past wars and alliances, are long overdue.

Nevertheless, we hope that this survey may advance that understanding of the South African past which is essential to an appreciation of the South African promise and problems in the late twentieth century; and if we and our collaborators have succeeded thus far, we shall not be disappointed.

MONICA WILSON   LEONARD THOMPSON

ACKNOWLEDGEMENTS

WE gratefully acknowledge support received from the African Studies Center and the Research Committee of the University of California, Los Angeles, which reduced Leonard Thompson's teaching commitments in the academic year 1966–7 and provided funds for research assistance. Leonard Thompson is also grateful for the Fulbright-Hays Fellowship which made it possible for him to visit South Africa for research and for editorial consultations in 1965–6. Monica Wilson thanks the University of Cape Town for research leave and a contribution towards research assistance.

Acknowledgements to individuals will be found at the beginnings of the appropriate chapters.

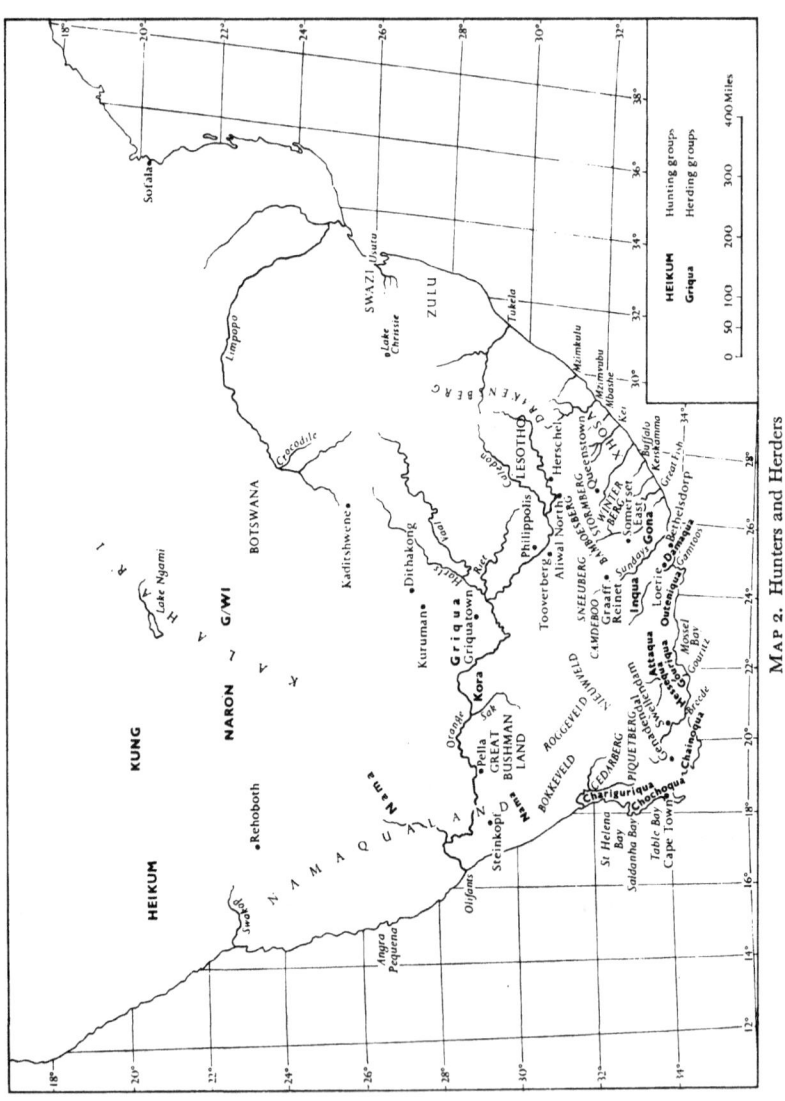

MAP 2. Hunters and Herders
(Placing of groups after Maingard, Vedder, Schapera)

II

THE HUNTERS AND HERDERS

1. *Characteristics and Distribution*

THE first people at the Cape about whom we have the reports of eye-witnesses were yellow-skinned hunters and herders. These are called in the literature 'Bushmen' and 'Hottentots', or simply 'Hottentots', because in the early accounts no systematic distinction was made between pastoralists with large herds of cattle and sheep and small groups of hunters and collectors who lacked stock. Distinctions can be made on the basis both of economy and of language and, as already noted (see p. ix), these vary independently. The Portuguese, ∗ when they first rounded the Cape in 1487, and on succeeding voyages, found yellow-skinned herders at Saldanha Bay, Table Bay, and Mossel Bay[1] who spoke a language characterized by clicks. They called themselves 'Khoikhoin'—'men of men'. They and their language are commonly referred to as 'Hottentot', but here they are called 'Khoikhoi', since 'Hottentot' is a nickname which has become a term of ridicule and abuse in South Africa.[2] The root *Khoikhoi* is used without the suffix *-n* for reasons already explained (see p. x). It was these Khoikhoi herdsmen who interacted closely with the Dutch from the first settlement of the Cape in 1652, and who were of great importance to them as suppliers of meat.

The Portuguese and Dutch found them spread parallel to the coast (but some way inland if the coast was barren) from the Swakop river on the Atlantic shore to the Buffalo on the Indian Ocean shore[3] (see map 2). They were nomadic, moving in search of grazing for stock,

---

[1] Da Gama, 'Diario da Viagem de Vasco da Gama', *Documents on the Portuguese in Mozambique and Central Africa*, 1494-1840, i. 3-11; G. M. Theal, *Records of South-Eastern Africa*, i. 4; E. Axelson, *South East Africa*, 1488-1530, pp. 12-36. The people encountered at St. Helena Bay in 1487 were hunters.

[2] T. Hahn, *Tsuni-//Goam, The Supreme Being of the Khoi-khoi*; O. Dapper, 'Kaffraria, or Land of the Kafirs', 1668, in I. Schapera (trans. and ed.), *The Early Cape Hottentots*, VRS, 1933, p. 71 and n. 81; L. F. Maingard, 'The Origin of the Word "Hottentot"', *BS*, 9 (1935); G. S. Nienaber, 'The Origin of the Name "Hottentot"', *AS*, 22 (1963), 65-89; H. Vedder, 'The Nama', in *The Native Tribes of South West Africa*, p. 112.

[3] P. Kolb (Kolbe, Kolben), *A Particular Account of the Several Nations of the Hottentots*, i. 60-80. For an assessment of Kolb's reliability see I. Schapera (ed.), *The Early Cape Hottentots*, pp. 162-7; L. F. Maingard, 'Lost Tribes of the Cape', *SAJS*, 28 (1931), 487-584; H. Vedder, *South West Africa in Early Times*, pp. 3-42.

∗ This page number refers to *OHSA*, vol. i; see p. 36 above.

and utilizing the lush pasture of the Cape in spring, when the country further north and east, which has summer rains, was dry. There is no evidence of their occupying the interior tableland south of the Orange, though Vedder[1] speaks of an ancient occupation by Khoikhoi as far as Lake Ngami, and the Khoikhoi language is still spoken by *hunters* living in the dry inland parts of the Kalahari.[2] According to van Riebeeck it was also spoken in 1652 by small groups of Strandlopers —hunters and collectors on the shore—whom he found in occupation of the Cape Peninsula.[3]

In the mountains of the western Cape, and throughout the mountain areas of southern Africa, there were other yellow-skinned hunters who spoke languages also characterized by clicks but distinct from Khoikhoi. They were called Bushmen by the whites, Twa by the Xhosa, Roa by the Sotho, and San (Saan) by the Khoikhoi.[4] San hunters occupied the Drakenstein and Cedarberg ranges, the Outeniqua, Camdeboo, Sneeuberg, Winterberg, Stormberg, and Drakensberg; they stretched along the Orange river and on to the plateau north of it; they occupied the valleys of the Vaal, Kei, Tsomo, Mzimvubu, and Tukela,[5] and were seen on the sea-shore.[6] The land they retained longest was stony or arid country, and mountain sour veld, frequented by eland, but unsuitable for permanent grazing for cattle.[7] They still occupy dry parts of Botswana, South West Africa, and Angola. They moved with the game, but, like the Khoikhoi herders, they had their regular beats.

Discussion on hunters and herders has been bedevilled because scholars have attempted to fit scientific classifications to popular usage and combine various criteria. Khoikhoi, Bantu-speakers, and white settlers alike classified people in terms of economy and skin colour. *All* the yellow-skinned hunters were San to Khoikhoi herders, Twa, or Roa, or Sarwa to Bantu-speakers, and 'Bushmen' to whites; yellow-skinned herders were Lawu or 'Hottentots'. The hunters were *assumed* by whites all to speak the same sort of language because they all clicked, and they were generally supposed to speak differently from the herders. Dorothea Bleek, a linguist working in 1921–2, recognized that 'the

---

[1] Vedder, 'Nama', pp. 114–15.   [2] Westphal, 237–64.
[3] D. Moodie, *The Record*, i. 16.
[4] E. Casalis, *Les Bassoutos*, p. 16; I. Schapera, *The Khoisan Peoples of South Africa*, p. 31.
[5] Moodie, i. 400–4.
[6] Almost all the early travellers reported meeting hunters. For the main sources on them see p. 44 note. Theal, *Records*, viii. 307. The hunters seen on the shore in 1647 near the Fish River mouth spoke a click language which might have been either Khoikhoi or San.
[7] Sour veld occurs in areas of high rainfall. The constituent grasses become unpalatable at an early stage in growth. It provides excellent grazing in spring and early summer, but is seldom much value for more than four or five months in the year. Sweet veld is palatable not only during the growing season but throughout the winter. D. Meredith (ed.), *The Grasses and Pastures of South Africa*, pp. 602–3.

CHARACTERISTICS AND DISTRIBUTION 43

Naron language was closely related to Nama' (a Khoikhoi language), but because the Naron were hunters not herders she classified the language as 'Bushman';[1] and Dr. Silberbauer, using economy, physical type, and language as criteria, classified G/wi as 'Bushman', though he noted that the language showed 'very close relationship to the Hottentot languages'.[2] Professor Westphal, using purely linguistic criteria, classified Naron and G/wi as 'Hottentot' (Khoikhoi).[3] The contradictions therefore arose because some scholars combined economic and physical criteria with linguistic criteria. Theophilus Hahn was aware of this: he wrote in 1881, 'the poor Namaquas are also called by the others Bushmen, especially when they are servants or lead a Bushman's life and have no cattle and sheep'.[4] In fact, the manner of life does not vary systematically with language, and this has long been recognized, because certain groups of negro hunters called Dama ('Berg Damara' or 'Bergdama')[5] were known to speak Nama (a Khoikhoi language), but they were treated as an 'exception'.

The picture is a more complex one than when it was supposed that language, economy, and physical type were inextricably linked. There were small groups of hunters scattered throughout the country. Some living on the sea-shore were particularly adapted to fishing; others were adapted to the desert; some spoke a San language, i.e. a language peculiar to hunters; others Khoikhoi. Adaptation to the desert was not correlated with one type of language rather than another, and there is no reason to suppose that fishing was either. There were also groups of herders, most of whom spoke Khoikhoi, but some (who do not concern us here since they live in South West Africa) spoke a Bantu language, Herero.[6] It is agreed that there were several San languages—recent research suggests four unrelated languages—and some authorities postulate several Khoikhoi ('Hottentot') languages, others only one.[7] Moffat remarked in 1842 that 'I have had in my presence genuine Hottentots, Corranas, and Namaquas, who had met from their respective and distant tribes for the first time, and they conversed with scarcely any difficulty', and he went on to comment on 'The variety of languages spoken by the Bushmen, even when nothing but a range of hills, or a river intervenes between the tribes, and none of these dialects is

[1] D. Bleek, *The Naron*, pp. 2–3, 66; *Comparative Vocabularies of Bushman Languages*.
[2] G. B. Silberbauer, *Bushman Survey* (Report to the Government of Bechuanaland), p. 13.
[3] Westphal, 244. I am indebted to Professor Westphal for helpful discussions of linguistic problems.
[4] Hahn, *Tsuni-//Goam*, p. 101; F. Galton, *Narrative of an Explorer in Tropical Africa*, p. 42.
[5] H. Vedder, 'The Berg Damara', in *The Native Tribes of South West Africa*, p. 41.
[6] H. Vedder, 'The Herero', in ibid., pp. 155–208.
[7] D. F. Bleek, 'The Distribution of Bushman Languages in South Africa', in *Festschrift Meinhof*, pp. 55–64; *Naron*, p. 2; G. W. Stow, *The Native Races of South Africa*, p. 42; Vedder, *South West Africa*, pp. 10–12, 78; Westphal, 244, 248–52.

understood by the Hottentots'.[1] This may be interpreted as meaning that all the yellow-skinned herders could understand one another, whereas the hunting peoples could not (see p. 103).

Our sources of evidence on hunters and herders are travellers' reports, beginning with the journals of Portuguese voyagers,[2] and, more important, the diary of van Riebeeck, the first Commander at the Cape,[3] and a collection of official papers relating to dealings between the Dutch and the aboriginal inhabitants.[4] The eyewitness accounts of the seventeenth and eighteenth centuries can be read in the light of investigations by a nineteenth-century linguist, W. H. I. Bleek, his daughter Dorothea Bleek, and his sister-in-law Lucy Lloyd; G. W. Stow, a geologist who began recording rock art, and visited San groups in Queenstown district in the second half of the nineteenth century; and more recent anthropological studies of hunters in Botswana and South West Africa.[5] There is no evidence to suggest that the !Kung, G/wi, and other hunting peoples recently described are descendants of the hunters who occupied the southern mountains; moreover, their manner of life is very closely adapted to the desert in which they live,[6] whereas the hunters of the Cape mountains and Drakensberg lived in well-watered country which abounded in game; nevertheless these anthropological studies are illuminating because the manner of life of all the surviving southern hunters shows marked resemblance in economy and social structure, and is comparable to what we know of earlier hunters within South Africa. There may, however, be diversity in ritual and belief, as there is in language, and these seem to vary independently. Although the !Kung speak a language somewhat resembling that spoken by the San of the Cape mountains, they have gods

[1] R. Moffat, *Missionary Labours*, pp. 6, 10.
[2] *Documents on the Portuguese*; Theal, *Records*. [3] *VRJ*.
[4] Moodie; of the travellers see particularly: A. Sparrman, *A Voyage to the Cape of Good Hope*, 1772-6; J. Barrow, *Travels into the Interior of Southern Africa*; J. Campbell, *Travels in South Africa* (1813), *First Journey*, 1815 (hereafter Campbell, 1813), 3rd edn., pp. 235-8; H. Lichtenstein, *Travels in Southern Africa*, 1812, VRS, 1928, ii. 281, 288 ff.; G. Thompson, *Travels and Adventures in Southern Africa*, pp. 73-74, 135; W. J. Burchell, *Travels in the Interior of South Africa*, ii. 244; J. Backhouse, *A Narrative of a Visit to the Mauritius and South Africa*, pp. 423, 426; A. Smith, *The Diary of Dr. Andrew Smith*, VRS, 1939-40, i. 191-3; ii. 281 ff.; W. C. Harris, *The Wild Sports of Southern Africa*, pp. 242-5, 255, 261 ff.; A. G. Bain, *Journals of Andrew Geddes Bain*, VRS, 1949, p. 23; T. Arbousset, *Voyage d'Exploration au nord-est de la colonie du Cap de Bonne Espérance*. See also: L. Fourie, 'The Bushmen of South West Africa' in *The Native Tribes of South West Africa*, pp. 79-105; S. S. Dornan, *Pygmies and Bushmen of the Kalahari*; E. F. Potgieter, *The Disappearing Bushmen of Lake Chrissie*; V. Ellenberger, *La Fin Tragique des Bushmen*; M. W. How, *The Mountain Bushmen of Basutoland*.
[5] E. M. Thomas, *The Harmless People*; Silberbauer, *Survey*; L. Marshall, four papers in *Africa*, referred to below; P. V. Tobias, eleven papers on physical anthropology, some referred to below.
[6] P. V. Tobias, 'Bushman Hunter-Gatherers: a Study in Human Ecology', in *Ecological Studies*; Thomas, pp. 12-14; Silberbauer, *Survey*, pp. 18-32.

CHARACTERISTICS AND DISTRIBUTION

other than the heavenly bodies which the San of the Cape worshipped,[1] and they and the Heikum and Dama hunters (who speak Khoikhoi) guard a sacred fire which is barely mentioned in accounts of the San of the Cape.[2] We do not even know whether differences in art—as between painters and engravers—coincided exactly with differences in language, as Stow supposed. He was assured that the painters could not understand the engravers of the Riet river;[3] but did *all* the painters speak the same language?

There are no anthropological studies of Khoikhoi herders, for no group of herders in the south has retained its ancient way of life to the degree to which some hunters, retreating into the desert, have retained theirs. We have, however, a valuable study of Nama religion by Theophilus Hahn, the son of a missionary, who grew up speaking Nama, and studies by professional anthropologists, which show how the descendants of Khoikhoi herdsmen lived as they settled and became peasants.[4] The standard work on the Khoikhoi and San is the very careful compilation published by Professor I. Schapera in 1930 entitled *The Khoisan Peoples of South Africa*, and he edited the important seventeenth-century journals of Dapper, Ten Rhyne, and Grevenbroek in a volume entitled *The Early Cape Hottentots*, and added illuminating notes. All later students are heavily indebted to his meticulous scholarship, though naturally a generation of further research necessitates modification of some of his conclusions. There is also a useful report made to the League of Nations in 1928, with chapters by various authorities which have already been quoted, and an important paper on physical anthropology by Professor Tobias.[5] Professor J. S. Marais's *Cape Coloured People* has also been drawn upon, though it refers rather to developments discussed in the second volume under 'The Growth of Peasant Communities'.

One oral tradition collected from Khoikhoi herders refers to their ancestors travelling with their faces towards the setting sun until they reached the 'great water', and then travelling southward down the Atlantic coast;[6] another tradition refers to the movement eastward to

---

[1] L. Marshall, '!Kung Bushman Religious Beliefs', *Africa*, 32 (1962), 221-2; Bleek, *Naron*, pp. 26-27; Schapera, *Khoisan*, pp. 172-7.
[2] Ibid., p. 97; Hendrik Jacob Wikar, *Journal*, 1779, VRS, 1935, p. 111.
[3] Stow, p. 42.
[4] A. W. Hoernlé, 'The Social Organization of the Nama Hottentots of Southwest Africa,' *American Anthropologist*, 27 (1925), 1-24; 'The Expression of the Social Value of Water among the Naman of South-West Africa', *SAJS*, 20 (1923), 514-26; and other articles cited below. E. Fischer, *Die Rehobother Bastards* (Jena, 1913), reprint Graz, 1961; W. P. Carstens, *The Social Structure of a Cape Coloured Reserve*.
[5] P. V. Tobias, 'Physical Anthropology and Somatic Origins of the Hottentots,' *AS*, 14 (1955), 1-22.
[6] Stow, pp. 267-8; Vedder, 'Nama', pp. 112-18.

the Zuurveld, after the arrival of the Dutch.[1] There is an obscure reference in the early tradition to the Khoikhoi having arrived in Africa in 'un grand panier',[2] but whence and when they came we do not yet know; nor do we know whether these traditions refer to the whole Khoikhoi-speaking population or, as is more likely, to a small group of immigrants absorbed by them. It is the eastern origin that is emphasized. Hahn reported:

> Every Nama from whom I inquired told me that this Heitsi-eibib [see p. 62] is their great grandfather, and a great powerful rich chief. He lived originally in the East and had plenty of cattle and sheep. Therefore they make the doors of their huts towards the East, where the sun and moon rise. This custom is so peculiar to them that those who possess waggons always put these vehicles alongside their houses, with the front towards sunrise. All the graves are directed towards the East, and the face of the deceased is also turned in that direction.[3]

Such alignment of the dead to face the direction whence they came—wheresoever it may be—is widespread also in Bantu Africa.

No hunters' traditions have been recorded which throw light on their early movements: they set little store by history (see p. 53). But the wealth of archaeological evidence in southern Africa is now being tapped, and links of San and Khoikhoi with certain stone cultures and rock art have been demonstrated (see pp. 21, 27–30, 105–6). The use of ivory and bone awls by herders was observed in the eighteenth century, and the use of stone knives is reported in the nineteenth century,[4] while the manufacture and use of bone and stone tools by hunters has been observed up until 1964.[5]

Whether San hunters were the only painters in the eighteenth century is uncertain. Later evidence indicates that some Sotho who lived and intermarried with them began painting;[6] moreover, Campbell illustrates paintings in the chief's hut in Kaditshwene in 1820 (see p. 139);[7] but the great development of painting was in areas such as Bamboesberg, Stormberg, and Queenstown district, known once to have been exclusively occupied by San.[8]

[1] Moodie, v, 12.   [2] Casalis, p. 8 n.
[3] Hahn, *Tsuni-//Goam*, p. 65.
[4] Kolb, i. 232; W. Ten Rhyne, 'A Short Account of the Cape of Good Hope', 1685, in *The Early Cape Hottentots*, p. 149.
[5] Stow, pp. 66–73, 140 (quoting actual observations); Bleek, *Naron*, pp. 13, 18; Thomas, pp. 9, 45; H. R. MacCalman and B. J. Grobbelaar, 'Preliminary Report on Two Stone-Working Ovatjimba Groups in the Northern Kaokoveld of South West Africa', *Cimbebasia*, Windhoek, 13 (1965).
[6] How, pp. 31–42; F. G. Gawston, 'A Consideration of the Bushmen's Paintings at Quthing', *SAJS*, 28 (1931), 470–1.
[7] J. Campbell, *Travels in South Africa*, 1820, Second Journey, 1822, i. 269 and Plate.
[8] Stow, pp. 198–204.

San and Khoikhoi speakers were both yellow-skinned and physically much alike; they differed from the darker negroid people, whether Bantu-speakers or Dama hunters. The early accounts do not distinguish 'Bushmen' and 'Hottentots' on physical grounds, though it is likely that the herders generally were taller than the hunters, as the Nama were taller than the San of the Cape mountains,[1] and hunters who become pastoralists have children taller than themselves.[2] The leading authority on physical types in South Africa concludes that not all the people who practised a 'Hottentot culture' were physically alike and no one 'Hottentot' physical type can be distinguished.[3] He does suggest, however, that shortness of stature was a physical asset to a hunter, as well as being admired by the women, and therefore cultural selection favoured shortness.[4]

There has been much speculation about the northward links of the yellow-skinned hunters and herders but little substantial evidence. Links between Khoikhoi and San languages and two click languages spoken in Tanzania—Hadza and Sandawe—have been postulated, but this is still a matter of debate. Are clicks indeed any criterion of linguistic affinity? Professor Westphal argues that they are not.

Since some (though not all) of the hunters in Botswana, South West Africa, and Angola speak Khoikhoi,[5] it is likely that certain groups in an ancient Khoikhoi hunting population received domestic animals from other immigrants, rather than that Khoikhoi-speakers themselves travelled from East Africa with stock, as was formerly supposed. There is a marked similarity in the techniques and material culture of all the hunters and herders, and some similarity in their religious ideas, which argues long interaction; but there are also cleavages, as between painters and non-painters; and the herders also have links in technology, ritual, and language with cattle-keeping agriculturalists, as will be shown (see pp. 104-5). Ritual links of the hunters with the agriculturalists exist, but are different and more tenuous (see p. 106).

2. *Economy and Social Structure of the Hunters*

The hunters and collectors described by the early travellers and settlers inhabited the mountains and the sea-shore. They had no domestic animals except the dog and lived off game, of which there were enormous herds in southern Africa; wild roots and berries, commonly

---

[1] Dapper, pp. 31, 37.
[2] P. V. Tobias, 'On the Increasing Stature of the Bushmen', *Anthropos*, 57 (1962), 801-10.
[3] Tobias, 'Physical Anthropology and Somatic Origins of the Hottentots', 12.
[4] Tobias, 'Bushmen Hunter-Gatherers'; L. Marshall, 'Marriage among !Kung Bushmen', *Africa*, 29 (1959), 349.
[5] Westphal, 243, 248, Maps.

called veldkos; caterpillars, termites, and locusts; wild honey; and fish. One of the early references to the hunters in the Cape mountains describes them as living by shooting dassie (*hyrax capensis*) 'with bow and arrow which they use with remarkable skill', and their dogs were trained 'to drag these animals out of their holes'. They brought a Dutch expedition a gift of dried fish and honey.[1] Recent studies in the Kalahari show that, even in the desert, vegetable foods play a major part in the diet of hunters,[2] and this is likely to have been the case when they occupied better-watered country. A digging stick, tipped with bone and weighted with a bored stone, and a skin cloak which also served as a bag, were the women's equipment among the mountain people, and these are still used in the desert, though the stick is not always tipped and weighted; in the desert ostrich eggshells, used for storing water, are a housekeeper's essential utensils.

Honey was so important that wild hives were marked as private property and a thief who stole from one might be killed by the owner.[3] Stow describes how wooden pegs were driven into cracks in a cliff face to enable a man to scale it and reach a nest.[4] The hunters of the mountains fished in the rivers with harpoons made of bone, and trapped eels, when opportunity offered, and the Strandlopers lived off shellfish and other fish caught on lines,[5] and in the fishgarths which are still visible along the Cape coast. All the hunters used bows and poisoned arrows. The effective range was small—twenty-five yards among the G/wi[6]— and hunters crept up on herds, sometimes disguising themselves in buck-skins or ostrich feathers.[7] Then they followed the wounded animal until the poison took effect; they were highly skilled in tracing a spoor. They dug traps for large game, and built stone or brushwood fences, or posts or cairns, the height of a hunter, and surmounted by feathers, to form converging lanes through which game was driven.[8] This suggests co-operation between a considerable number of men. Francis Galton, travelling in 1851 in the Kalahari,

> passed a magnificent set of pitfalls, which the Bushmen who live about these hills had made; the whole breadth of the valley was staked and bushed across. At intervals the fence was broken, and where broken deep pitfalls were made. The strength and size of timber that was used gave me a great idea of Bushman industry, for every tree had to be burned down and carried away from the hills, and yet the scale of the undertaking would have excited

[1] Dapper, p. 33; Moodie, i. 224.
[2] Silberbauer, *Survey*, p. 47; L. Marshall, '!Kung Bushman Bands', *Africa*, 30 (1960), 335.
[3] Ibid., 336.   [4] Stow, pp. 86–88, 356.
[5] Ibid., pp. 72, 92–93, 210; Barrow, i. 300; Moodie, i. 25–26; P. B. Borcherds, *An Autobiographical Memoir*, p. 112.
[6] Silberbauer, *Survey*, p. 47.   [7] Stow, Plate opposite p. 82.
[8] Ibid., pp. 84, 90–92.

astonishment in far more civilized nations. When a herd of animals was seen among the hills the Bushman drove them through this valley up to the fence; this was too high for them to jump so that they were obliged to make for the gaps, and there tumbled into the pitfalls.[1]

Baines painted just such a scene, with feathered posts marking the lanes. When meat from such a battue was plentiful, it was dried in strips and preserved for future use. The hunters also burnt the grass during winter to attract game to the fresh pasture and to make them more visible, and to encourage the growth of spring bulbs.[2] This firing of the grass was a common cause of friction with the herders,[3] who likewise burnt for fresh pasture, but who needed to preserve some areas of long grass to maintain their cattle. The hunters were fair-weather men, because their bows were not serviceable in the rain—the gut string snapped—,[4] and they always lay up in their caves during rain in the mountains[5] and, where they had the choice, selected drier rather than wetter country.

The hunt supplied not only food but clothing, which was made of skins, and the furs and feathers which were, and still are, traded to other peoples for iron and tobacco. Even the every-day utensils of ostrich-eggshell and tortoise carapace were hunters' trophies.

The hunters lived and still live in bands, each independent of the next, and their characteristic is isolation. The size of bands of !Kung hunters in the Kalahari averages twenty-five;[6] most G/wi bands (also in the Kalahari) have forty to sixty members, and Dr. Silberbauer estimates the optimum size at fifty to seventy.[7] Such scrappy evidence as we have of bands living in the Sneeuberg, Tarka, and Stormsberg in the eighteenth and early nineteenth centuries indicates that they might sometimes number more. Collins found in the Tarka in 1809 'two Bosjesman chiefs' who 'had about 200 of their people at this and a neighbouring farm', and he mentions a Nieuwveld band 'of nearly twenty families',[8] but he met another band of twenty persons and three 'consisting all together of about 70 persons'.[9] Stow speaks of 'large tribes' having existed on the Orange river and in the Bamboesberg and Queenstown area. A certain Lynx is said to have had about five hundred people under him in the Bamboesberg in 1797, and Madura had 'three hundred men under his jurisdiction' in 1849, but there is no eyewitness evidence of this. Nor is it certain that the villages with the remains of 'one hundred huts' had indeed been occupied by hunters as Stow supposed,[10] for huts such as he described were built by

---

[1] Galton, p. 106.   [2] Bleek, *Naron*, p. 17; Schapera, *Khoisan*, p. 140.
[3] Vedder, 'Berg Damara', p. 43.   [4] Campbell, 1813, p. 147.   [5] Stow, p. 42.
[6] Marshall, '!Kung Bands', 328, 345–6.   [7] Silberbauer, *Survey*, pp. 40, 62.
[8] Moodie, v. 6, 23.   [9] Ibid. v. 3, 5.   [10] Stow, pp. 32, 42, 171, 202.

Sotho (see p. 140), and the 'abandoned village of 1,133 huts' seen between Aliwal North and Herschel in 1823 was thought to have consisted of refugees who had gathered for protection against Boer commandos.[1] What Stow does demonstrate is that in the Queenstown district in the nineteenth century every band used a cave as its headquarters, and in each of these there was a painting which was sacred and from which a band took its name. One painting was of a python, another of springbok, another of eland, and so forth. The desert bands, on which we have evidence, have no headquarters, but each has a name,[2] which continues through time,[3] and each moves within a defined area. All the hunting groups have, and had, territories over which their prior rights are recognized.[4] Vedder even suggests that cairns of stone were sometimes piled near paths to mark boundaries.[5] Among the G/wi hunting rights over defined territories are exclusive. Among the !Kung prior rights are recognized over water and veldkos, but not over game, which may be shot in one territory and followed into another.[6] Mrs. Marshall's statement fits very closely with that of Kolb, who reported in 1707 that 'Hottentots of every kraal and nation have the liberty of hunting throughout all the Hottentot countries'.[7]

However, neither isolation nor the recognition of territory precluded movement over a hundred miles or perhaps much further. San living in the Drakensberg painted boats which could only have been seen near the coast, a hundred miles away, and mounds of shells from shellfish have been found on middens fifty miles inland. Hunting expeditions typically lure men far afield, and in the traditional histories of Africa it is most often the hunter who explores and settles in a new territory. The San were surely no exception. Interaction with only a small number of people is not to be confused with confinement to a limited area.

Among the !Kung, marriage between neighbouring bands is approved, and movement of families of parents and children from one band to another occurs, but only within the area recognizing some common unity. This includes thirty-six or thirty-seven bands and a thousand persons.[8] The diversity in language among the hunters, even neighbouring bands sometimes not understanding one another if Moffat was correct (see p. 43), is surely a reflection of long isolation.

Control over rights in water and vegetable foods is vested in a custodian among the !Kung. The office is hereditary, passing from father to son (or failing a son to a daughter and through her to her son), but

---

[1] D. Ellenberger and J. C. Macgregor, *History of the Basuto*, p. 10.
[2] Stow, pp. 32–33, 200–3.   [3] Marshall, '!Kung Bands', 330.
[4] Silberbauer, *Survey*, p. 29; Schapera, *Khoisan*, p. 77.
[5] Vedder, 'Nama', p. 132.   [6] Marshall, '!Kung Bands', 331–4.
[7] Kolb, i. 259.   [8] Marshall, '!Kung Bands', 327.

SOCIAL STRUCTURE OF THE HUNTERS

there is no chief with power to adjudicate in disputes and enforce judgements.[1] The custodian's precedence is recognized by his taking the head of the line when the band moves, and making the first fire in a new camp, from which others take brands, but he does not necessarily organize hunting parties or trading trips, and when theft or adultery occurs the wronged person will kill the one who has injured him, or they fight until both are killed. The whole band, however, is concerned to reconcile quarrelling members, for the loss of a hunter means a serious loss in food and, if weapons are used, the smallest scratch may mean death, since the poison with which arrows are smeared is deadly. Mrs. Marshall describes very vividly how men and women gather quickly, seeking to compose any quarrel that arises.[2] A fight once begun is feared almost like atomic warfare. Taking fire from the custodian is a recognition of his leadership among the !Kung, as among so many peoples in Africa. He himself starts the first fire at each camp with firesticks,[3] and even where hunters are clients of herders there is no fiction of inability to ignite a fire as among the pygmies.

No matter how wide the territory they occupy, or how much individual families may have to scatter during drought to find food, when a band moves as a group the members camp and build their shelters close together—so close that sisters in different households can hand things to each other. Mrs. Marshall illustrates how the !Kung 'settle for the night like migrating birds in the bushes',[4] and in the eighteenth century travellers to the Orange found clusters of shelters huddled together.[5] Jan Wessels, who lived north of the Orange 'at the time the country was filled with Bushmen', described to Stow how 'on visiting any of their caves, it was possible, although all the inhabitants were absent... to tell the exact number of men, women, and children who lived in it, as each of them made a small round hollow hole, like a nest, into which they individually coiled themselves, each man, woman, and child having his or her own allotted form ...'.[6] One of the jibes of the Sotho against the San was that all slept together without regard for decency, but eyewitness evidence shows that the !Kung camp in a regular order, each married couple establishing their shelter, or a symbol of it, beside their fire, and people sitting in their set order, men to the right of the fire facing the entrance to the shelter, women to the left. Boys from about the age of puberty sleep by their own fire with other boys of the band, and girls of the same age with some single woman, unless they

---

[1] Ibid., 348–53; Silberbauer, *Survey*, pp. 71–72.
[2] L. Marshall, 'Marriage among !Kung Bushmen', *Africa*, 29 (1959), 360–2.
[3] Marshall, '!Kung Bands', 352; Vedder, 'Berg Damara', pp. 68–70.
[4] Marshall, '!Kung Bands', Plate 2, 342.   [5] Barrow, i. 275, 284.
[6] Stow, p. 44.

themselves are already married.[1] Each person may indeed hollow out a sleeping place to escape the biting night wind.[2] The shelters and fires are huddled together in the wide expanse of the desert, and it might be that a stranger, coming on a deserted camp, would suppose that the whole band slept promiscuously. He would be mistaken, but relationships in an isolated band are necessarily intimate. This is reflected in each member recognizing the spoor of the others: a child recognizes its mother's footprints as it does her face, and a young man is pictured as falling in love with the footprints of an unknown girl.[3]

Among the !Kung each woman cooked the veldkos she had collected for her own husband and young children, but the meat of any animal shot was distributed, the man whose arrow had first struck the animal allocating portions, according to set rule, to individuals in the band, for no one eats alone 'like a lion'.[4]

The family of parents and children held together until a son married, when he went to live with his wife's band, and to hunt for his parents-in-law. Only after the birth of several children was he free to rejoin his own band, but he did not always do so, and no large descent groups, such as are common among the herders and cultivators, developed. Bands broke up and recombined and a grown man had some choice as to which he joined.[5] Among the !Kung and G/wi[6] (on whom we have evidence) a girl commonly married at seven or eight—well before puberty—and a boy at fourteen or fifteen. He then began his suitor-service, and his bride went to gather veldkos with the older women, and cooked in the evening for her husband at their own fire, and they slept in their own shelter. We do not know whether such very early marriage was general among the southern hunters—among the !Kung, as elsewhere, it was connected with the scarcity of brides—[7] but the pattern of marriage by service, whereby the groom comes to hunt for parents-in-law, was certainly widespread.

At her first menstruation a girl, even though already married, was secluded and observed various taboos, and a great dance miming the courtship of the eland bull was performed in her honour.[8] Circumcision was not a general practice among the hunters[9] (though the Sotho

---

[1] Marshall, '!Kung Bands', 342; Thomas, p. 41.
[2] Tobias, 'Bushman Hunter-Gatherers', p. 79; Thomas, pp. 40, 56.
[3] P. J. Schoeman, *Hunters of the Desert Land*, p. 6 *et passim*.
[4] Marshall, .'!Kung Bands', 334–6; L. Marshall, 'Sharing, Talking, and Giving: Relief of Social Tensions among !Kung Bushmen' *Africa*, 31, 1961, 236–41.
[5] Thomas, p. 11.
[6] Marshall, 'Marriage among !Kung', 335–65: G. B. Siberbauer. 'Marriage and the Girl's Puberty Ceremony of the G/wi Bushmen', *Africa*, 33, 1963, 12–23; Bleek, *Naron*, p. 33.
[7] M. Wilson, *Good Company*, p. 87.
[8] Marshall, 'Marriage among !Kung', 89; Bleek, *Naron*, pp. 23–6; Schapera, *Khoisan*, pp. 118–22.
[9] Ibid., pp. 122–6.

claim to have learnt it from the San), but a ritual which marked the attainment of adult status was celebrated for groups of boys. The elements emphasized by various writers are the testing of a boy's ability as a hunter; treatment with medicines to give him skill in hunting; and the performance of certain dances. The boy's rite preceded marriage, and among the !Kung it was a condition of marriage, for he must have proved himself as a hunter before he could marry, and bring to his bride's parents a large animal he, himself, had killed.[1] But among the G/wi Dr. Silberbauer met many married men who had never been initiated. The evidence on initiation among the hunters is confused, and it is not possible to demonstrate whether or not there are consistent differences between those hunters who speak a Khoikhoi language and those who do not, or whether there have been changes through the last century.

Though girls married so young they did not rear many children. According to Dorothea Bleek most Naron mothers did not rear more than three, and Mrs. Marshall's evidence confirms this.[2] It was recognized that a mother could not feed and travel with children who were less than three to five years apart, therefore if a baby was born too soon it was disposed of by the midwife—'thrown away' in the Naron phrase. Wide spacing of children was a condition of their survival. The difference of about seven years in the marriage-age of men and women permitted polygyny, which, in turn, accounted for the scarcity of brides. Among the !Kung polygyny was generally approved by men, though not favoured by the women.[3]

Property that could be inherited did not exist—except for certain rights over the water and veldkos in a given area—and kinship bonds in time, which are so closely tied to the inheritance of wealth, were not treated as important. Nor was there a veneration of the ancestors comparable to that general among the Bantu-speaking peoples.[4] Mrs. Marshall reports of the !Kung: 'The concept of having special relations with their own ancestors or of worshipping ancestors is lacking.'[5] The implications of this are profound. 'The !Kung are a present-orientated people who make no great effort to hold the past in memory or teach their history to their children.' 'The history and origin of settlement, and of individual bands is lost in the past.'[6]

The gods spoken of by the San of the Cape were Kaggen (Cagn, Qhang, 'Kaang) who made all things, and the mantis which was his embodiment. To J. M. Orpen's query: 'Where is !Kaang?' a hunter

---
[1] Marshall, 'Marriage among !Kung', 351.
[2] Bleek, *Naron*, p. 331; Marshall, '!Kung Bands', 327-8.
[3] Marshall, 'Marriage among !Kung', 347.   [4] Stow, p. 133.
[5] Marshall, '!Kung Beliefs', 241.   [6] Marshall, '!Kung Bands', 330.

replied: 'We don't know, but the elands do. Have you not hunted and heard his cry, when the elands suddenly started and ran to his call? Where he is the elands are in droves like cattle.'[1] It is as though Pan and the mantis held the poetic imagination in the south of Africa as on the Mediterranean shore. The hunters danced at the new moon and full moon, and prayed for good hunting, and Dorothea Bleek was told: 'We sing to the sun and stars, as well as to the moon.'[2] But these ideas were not held by all the hunters, and from the scanty material it is not possible to formulate any general beliefs which have continued through time. Nor do we know what were the symbolic associations of amputating a finger-joint, a practice which was widespread among the hunters.

For all that their food supply was precarious and search for food occupied most of their time, San hunters were prolific artists. They painted or engraved on stone and ostrich eggs; they made thousands of ostrich eggshell beads to adorn themselves; they told myths; and above all, they danced. The myths and paintings were connected and so, perhaps, were the dances, for they painted dances as well as animals and hunting scenes, and Stow describes how an old San couple were deeply moved by reproductions of paintings of a dance which he showed them, and began singing the appropriate songs.[3]

Every writer on the hunters, whatever the period, speaks of their dancing. Men and women, daily engaged in the strenuous search for food, nevertheless found strength at night to dance. Barrow noted a small, circular, dance floor as characteristic of San encampments south of the Orange in 1797;[4] Silberbauer in 1965 describes how a G/wi child in the Kalahari learns to dance before it can walk,[5] and Thomas noted a boy, seeing wildebeeste, 'unconsciously making a gesture representing the head and horns'.[6] In the dances the hunters regularly mimed animals: the courtship of the eland bull; the kudu; a gemsbok hunt; a hyena feeding off a carcass and keeping jackals at bay; vultures at the carcass of a zebra; ostriches.[7] It seems as if the acute observation of animals, necessary to a hunter, had to find some expression in artistic form, whether it be painting, or dancing, or myth. The Naron say 'in olden times the trees were people, and the animals were people . . .',[8] and the world view of all the hunters depicted a time when animals spoke like men, and there was friendship between them.[9]

[1] Stow, pp. 132-4.
[2] D. Bleek, 'Bushman Folklore', *Africa*, 2 (1929), 306; Schapera, *Khoisan*, pp. 172-7.
[3] Stow, pp. 103-5, 120-4.   [4] Barrow, i. 284.
[5] Silberbauer, *Survey*, p. 77.
[6] Thomas, p. 59.
[7] Bleek, *Naron*, p. 23; Fourie, pp. 96-98; Schapera, p. 119.
[8] Bleek, *Naron*, p. 26.
[9] Stow quoting Palgrave, pp. 130-2.

3. Economy and Social Structure of the Herders

The Khoikhoi herders had large flocks of fat-tailed sheep and herds of cattle, and milk was their staple food, men drinking cows' milk only, women and children that of ewes.[1] The Nama alone, who were trading with 'the goat people'—the Sotho-speaking Thlaping (see pp. 135, 149)—, had goats.[2] The cattle were the long-horned type, ancestral to the modern Afrikander strain,[3] and they were numerous in proportion to men. Van Riebeeck speaks of a camp of 'Saldanha men' with fifteen huts and a population of about two-hundred-and-fifty, men, women, and children, with fifteen or sixteen hundred cattle, and sheep besides[4]—six head of cattle per person. Another horde had eleven to twelve hundred cattle and six hundred sheep.[5] 'Cattle were in number like the grass in the field.'[6] The women milked, as they typically do among a people who are primarily pastoral and depend little, if at all, on agriculture, and life was geared to the need for pasture. Each group or horde (as defined below) was nomadic, moving on a regular beat which Herry, the interpreter to van Riebeeck, could predict.[7]

The herders did not ordinarily kill stock just for meat, but only in the celebration of rituals, and they depended for food not only on their herds but on hunting, fishing, and collecting veldkos and honey.[8] When meat was plentiful they dried it to make biltong, and honey was used to brew mead.[9] Like the hunters, the herders were knapsack carriers. The San painted them so, and early travellers described both men and women carrying loads on the back.[10] This is what forest people do, further north,[11] and perhaps it is characteristic of hunters and collectors, whereas among cultivators, living in open country like the Nguni and Sotho, the women carry loads on their heads.

Clothing was of skin—most often sheep-skin, but also ox-hide, and pelts of dassie, seal, jackal, wild-cat, and, for great men, otter or badger.[12] They wove rush mats to sleep on, and a man lined the hollow he dug out for himself to sleep in with one of these.[13] Men, as well as women, used sunshades of ostrich feathers tied to a stick,[14] and they all wore copper ornaments—the Nama had quantities of them[15]—and ivory bracelets, and glass beads which already, in 1668, came from trade with the Portuguese. Wikar's evidence, added to by Vedder, suggests that this trade was through the Ambo (Ovambo) northward to Angola,

[1] Moodie, i. 18; Kolb, i. 173; Dapper, p. 37.　　[2] Dapper, p. 37.
[3] H. H. Curson and R. W. Thornton, 'A Contribution to the Study of African Native Cattle', *Onderstepoort Journal of Veterinary Science and Animal Industry* (1936), 672; R. Singer and H. Lehmann, 'The Haemoglobins of Africander Cattle', in A. E. Mourant and F. E. Zeuner, *Man and Cattle*, pp. 119–25.　　[4] Moodie, i. 18.　　[5] Ibid. i. 50.　　[6] Ibid. i. 148.
[7] Ibid. i. 18, 24, 26, 28.　　[8] Wikar, pp. 87, 115, 121, 137; Kolb, i. 255.
[9] Vedder, 'Nama', p. 129.　　[10] Ten Rhyne, p. 119; Bleek, *Naron*, p. 8.
[11] Direct observation.　　[12] Ten Rhyne, p. 117; Dapper, p. 49.
[13] Moodie, i. 147.　　[14] Dapper, p. 39.　　[15] Dapper, p. 51

rather than through the Sotho to the east coast (see pp. 148–51). The beads were of Italian manufacture.[1] The Dutch bartered coral beads for cattle and these were highly prized. Knives were not in much demand, but copper wire was wanted and, above all, sheet copper.[2] Copper was mined in Nama country, but according to Wikar it was the Dama who were the smelters, and Nama power in relation to Dama increased as Nama acquired metal weapons.[3] Pots were made, different in shape from those of the Bantu-speakers.[4]

The Khoikhoi herders gelded animals and rode their oxen, fastening a bridle to a stick passed through the cartilage of the animal's nose. They were seen riding near Mossel Bay by the Portuguese in 1497; and there are numerous sketches of both men and women riding. When a camp was moved the mats and poles for the huts and household utensils were piled on the backs of pack-oxen, but there was no yoking of oxen for draught. Both oxen and bulls were used in war, as a shield for the fighting men, and Kolb describes vividly how a stranger might be charged by a fighting bull.[5] Le Vaillant painted an ox with horns pointing forward, as the type of fighting ox. The cattle were trained to answer a whistle, and one wretched party of shipwrecked Portuguese lost the cattle they had bought when the former owners whistled them home at night.[6] One man had even trained an ox for hunting.[7]

All this argues a long and close association between men and cattle, though the importance of sheep in ritual, as well as for clothing, supports the view that the Khoikhoi may have been shepherds before they were cattle-men (see p. 30). The contrast with the Nguni, who never use sheep in sacrifice to the shades, and whose language and poetry expressed their concentration on cattle alone, is marked.[8]

The areas that were occupied by Khoikhoi herdsmen in 1652 are not now good cattle country,[9] and it may well be asked why cattle-men lived there. Several possible reasons come to mind. The country was probably better grassed than it is now, for the ecological balance in dry parts of South Africa is precarious, and areas known once to have been good grazing veld have been destroyed by over-grazing;[10] furthermore,

---

[1] Dapper, p. 67; Wikar, pp. 79, 149; Vedder, *South West Africa*, pp. 28–29.
[2] Moodie, i. 30; Dapper, p. 53.
[3] Wikar, p. 79; Vedder, 'Nama', p. 126; *South West Africa*, p. 35.
[4] Kolb, i. 236; Hahn, *Tsuni-//Goam*, p. 21; J. F. Schofield, 'A Hottentot Pot from Pella District', *SAJS*, 33 (1937), 940–2.
[5] Kolb, i. 176–8; J. G. Grevenbroek, 'An Account of the Hottentots', 1695, in *The Early Cape Hottentots*, p. 189.   [6] Theal, *Records*, vi. 301.
[7] Sparrman, i. 253.   [8] M. Hunter, *Reaction to Conquest*, pp. 68–71, 371.
[9] A. M. Talbot and W. J. Talbot, *Atlas of the Union of South Africa*, Maps, pp. 16, 109.
[10] J. P. H. Acocks, *Veld Types of South Africa*, Memoir 28 in *Botanical Survey of South Africa*. I am indebted to Miss Jean Radloff, a farmer near Kimberley, for an illuminating discussion on this point.

SOCIAL STRUCTURE OF THE HERDERS 57

nomads could occupy country which settled farmers could not, for they moved when the grazing was no longer good; already in 1785 the Swedish botanist, Andrew Sparrmann, noted that pastures suffered more from Dutch farmers who were settled than from Khoikhoi who moved continually (see p. 253). But there may be another reason deep in Khoikhoi history. The Nama country from which the Khoikhoi dispersed is still suited to fat-tailed sheep. It is less arid than the desert called 'Great Bushmanland' immediately eastward, and the well-watered country beyond that was perhaps already occupied by Sotho before the Khoikhoi got cattle. They circled round the desert and the Sotho, and were moving towards better grasslands which some Khoikhoi had reached on the Keiskamma and Buffalo by 1686 (see p. 102). A Gona told Colonel Collins in 1809:[1]

They had resided at first much nearer the Peninsula, and were yet united under their last great chief, Quama, when the Europeans advanced from the Cape to the interior. Unable to prevent their encroachments, and unwilling to acknowledge their superiority, they removed towards the east; observing, that the country improved as they advanced, they continued their route to the territories of Tzeeo [Tshiwo]. This chief was as much dissatisfied at their approach as they had been at that of the christians, and unfortunately for them, he has as much the power as the inclination to show his displeasure.

After a considerable loss, both of their people and their cattle, they returned to the neighbourhood of the Great Fish River. Some settled on the fine plains on both banks of that stream. But the others apprehending that the wrath of Tzeeo might pursue them even that far, resolved to seek a less insecure though a more distant retreat.

With that view they proceeded to the north, where the Bosjesmen treated them as unkindly as the Caffres. Driven from the south, the east, and the north, the wanderers bent their last hope on the west. They followed the sun until stopped by the ocean, on whose borders their posterity are known by the name of Namaquas.

Tshiwo was a Xhosa chief who ruled in the first half of the eighteenth century, and some Khoikhoi had reached the Buffalo by the reign of his grandfather, Togu (see pp. 88, 102), but apart from the final sentence, which echoes much earlier Nama tradition, this account may indeed be close to what happened.

A group of 'Gonjemans Hottentots' also moved from the Cape to Algoa Bay, after losing their land to the Dutch settlers (see pp. 65, 103).

Taking all the evidence, the most probable hypothesis is that the Khoikhoi acquired cattle after they had sheep; that some of them had cattle well before 1488; but that cattle-men had not lived for many

[1] Moodie, v. 12.

generations before that in the western Cape, though shepherds doubtless did so. Riding was common in the Sahara and East Africa, and 'Ethiopians' who rode oxen and used them in war were reported near Sofala in the tenth century.[1] The absence of these techniques as an *ancient* tradition among the Nguni and Sotho peoples (see pp. 108, 143) suggests that some Khoikhoi ancestors may indeed have learnt from these men of Sofala, and remained isolated from Nguni and Sotho, thereafter, until the eighteenth century. If, as the evidence suggests (see pp. 143–6), the Sotho were the early smelters in South Africa, the riders (as distinct from Khoikhoi-speaking hunters) probably followed, rather than preceded, them.

Each Khoikhoi camp or village was made up of a circle of huts, sometimes surrounded by a fence of brushwood, within which the cattle were enclosed at night. They were trained to lie within the circle whether there was a fence or not.[2] Huts were made of a framework of poles (or whalebone on the barren Atlantic coast), covered with reed mats, and lined with skins in the winter. They commonly numbered thirty to fifty. Kolb describes the camps as having 'never ... less than twenty huts' and being small with 'a hundred souls'; Dapper describes the 'Saldanhars' living in fifteen or sixteen camps with four hundred to four hundred and fifty huts all told.[3]

The camp was occupied by men of one clan—descendants of a common ancestor in the male line—together with their wives and children, and dependent servants or clients. A number of such clans, together with their adherents, made up a horde,[4] an independent political unit which, though it had a kinship base, was never exclusively a kinship group. Membership of a clan depended on birth, but non-kinsmen were included in a camp or horde. Palgrave writing in 1876[5] gave the size of twelve hordes which ranged from six hundred to two thousand five hundred members; but there was a report in 1659 of a chief 'lying in Saldanha Bay with more than 16,000 of his Saldanhars'.[6] The clans within a horde often moved separately, though Winifred Hoernlé

[1] K. G. Lindblom, *The Use of Oxen as Pack and Riding Animals in Africa, passim*; J. Vansina, R. Mauny, and L. V. Thomas, *The Historian in Tropical Africa*, p. 100.
[2] Galton, pp. 19, 67.
[3] Ten Rhyne, p. 119; Kolb, i, Plate; Schapera, *Khoisan*, p. 228; Kolb, i. 216; Dapper, p. 23; I. Schapera, *Government and Politics in Tribal Societies*, p. 204, puts the average number in a camp at two hundred to three hundred people.
[4] *Horde* is used here to mean 'A tribe or troop of nomads dwelling in tents or wagons and migrating from place to place for pasturage' (*Shorter Oxford English Dictionary*). The word *tribe* is avoided, since it is widely used both for political units and linguistic groups, and it is difficult to confine it to any precise meaning.
[5] W. C. Palgrave, *Report of ... Mission to Damaraland and Great Namaqualand in 1876*, G. 50–77, p. 94.
[6] Moodie, i. 195.

speaks of 'representatives' of each clan remaining at a central camp, while the others moved in search of pasture.[1] Periodically a clan would split off to form an independent horde. In 1863 the Nama consisted of seven hordes; the dominant clans in five of these claimed descent from brothers, and the clans of the other two were later offshoots from one of the five.[2]

Seniority among a group of brothers and sisters was emphasized, and was expressed in the everyday kinship terms and usages. In a camp the relative status of each lineage, and of each man in a lineage, was reflected in the position of his hut in relation to that of his father or senior brother: seniors camped to the right, juniors to the left, in order of precedence, and unrelated dependents attached to rich cattle-owners camped as junior members of the household to which they were attached. The seniority of one clan within the horde was recognized; leadership was vested in it, and the position was hereditary, passing from father to son. Similarly, in each clan the senior lineage, and the senior son in the lineage, was the leader.

Children belonged to the clan of the father and marriage within a clan was prohibited, though marriage between cross-cousins—the children of brothers and sisters—was acceptable. The social identity of brothers was expressed in the practice of the levirate (so widespread in Africa and elsewhere), the custom whereby a man is expected to take the widow of a deceased brother to wife. A woman's sisters were likewise identified with her, and a younger sister might replace a wife who had died, or become a junior co-wife.[3]

A characteristic of the Khoikhoi kinship system was the formality and avoidance between brother and sister which precluded their even being alone together or speaking directly to one another.[4] Such avoidance between relatives-in-law is widespread, but between brother and sister it is peculiar in southern Africa to Khoikhoi and San-speakers—or some of the San.[5] This is one of the many details of custom and language which link Khoikhoi and San-speakers and differentiate them from Bantu-speakers.

Marriage could take place only after the initiation ritual of a girl, celebrated at her first menstruation, was complete, and after a youth had been initiated into the company of adult men, a rite commonly celebrated at 'about eighteen years', though the timing of it depended upon his father's ability to provide stock for a feast.[6] The groom supplied several sheep or an ox for the marriage feast, and the gall of the

[1] Hoernlé, 'Social Organization', 15.
[2] Ibid., pp. 4–14; Schapera, *Khoisan*, p. 225.
[3] Hoernlé, 'Social Organization', 23. [4] Ibid., 22.
[5] Marshall, 'Marriage among !Kung', 339; Vedder, 'Berg Damara', pp. 50, 55.
[6] Grevenbroek, p. 201; Kolb, i. 119.

slaughtered animal was poured over the feet of the bride. This was the essential wedding rite. A new hut was built for the bride near that of her mother, and her husband joined her there, serving his parents-in-law by hunting for them, until after the birth of a child. Only then was he free to take his bride home. When he did so, he presented his mother-in-law with two cows, and his mother welcomed her daughter-in-law by slaughtering a sheep. The importance of domestic animals in the marriage ritual, and the shorter period of suitor-service, marks the difference between the herders and hunters. The bride brought with her the poles and mats for her hut, and stock given her by her parents which remained her own property, distinct from that of her husband. She was the milker and controlled the milk in her husband's household, that from his stock as well as from the cows and ewes she brought with her.[1]

The milk ensured a better food supply than the hunters could find, and made it possible for more people to live together—the Khoikhoi horde was twenty to fifty times the size of a hunting band. Pack animals also made movement easier. Nevertheless the herders also thought that a mother could not rear two young children at the same time, therefore one of a pair of twins was commonly exposed,[2] and pregnancies were spaced.

The herders, like the hunters, feared lest a quarrel develop, for they also used poisoned arrows, and a scratch might be deadly. Kolb wrote in 1707: 'The Hottentots run to the suppression of strife that has seized a family as we do to putting out of a fire that has seized a house; and allow themselves no rest till every matter in difference is adjusted.'[3] This exactly fits with Mrs. Marshall's description of members of a !Kung band crowding round to mediate if a quarrel flared up.

Disputes were heard before all the men of a camp, assembled under the leadership of the senior kinsman of the clan. The chief of the horde, sitting with the heads of clans, tried disputes between members of different clans; he could and did sentence a man to death, himself striking the first blow, and others following. But he could not compel the kinsmen of a murdered man to accept compensation. They had not only the right but the *obligation* to take vengeance on the murderer.[4] A murderer or adulterer was not received by another Khoikhoi horde but might try to 'escape to the Buchies'—i.e. to hunters in the mountains.[5]

The institution of chieftainship thus emerges with the herders in South Africa, if we take arbitration in dispute and the enforcement of

---

[1] Schapera, *Khoisan*, p. 251.
[2] Kolb, i. 142–3; Ten Rhyne, p. 143; Grevenbroek, pp. 181–2.   [3] Kolb, i. 223.
[4] T. Hahn, evidence in *1883 Report on Native Laws and Customs*, G. 4, '83, ii. 249.
[5] Kolb, i. 295.

SOCIAL STRUCTURE OF THE HERDERS

a decision by a court of some sort as the mark of chieftainship. The custodian of a hunting band did not settle disputes; the senior kinsman of the senior lineage in a Nama horde did so; but his authority was limited. He could not interfere in disputes between members of the same clan, which were settled by the head of the clan without appeal to the chief of the horde; and he could not control a blood-feud between two of his clans.[1] The authority of a Khoikhoi chief was thus considerably less than that of any Nguni or Sotho chief—Charles Brownlee indeed maintained that the Gona had no chiefs at all.[2] Early writers speak of the respect with which Saldanha, Nama, and 'Ingua' chiefs were treated by their people,[3] and it is possible that they differed from the Gona in this regard, but even their power was very limited. Lichtenstein wrote of the Kora on the Orange in 1806:

> Their form of government is the same as with the other Hottentot tribes: the richest person in the kraal is the captain, or provost: he is the leader of the party, and the spokesman on all occasions, without deriving from this office any judicial right over the rest. His authority is exceedingly circumscribed, and no one considers himself as wholly bound to yield obedience to him; neither does he himself ever pretend to command them.[4]

Although each horde was independent, alliances between hordes for war occurred, and there was a trickle of trade between them. Hahn speaks of the 'large trade', 'chiefly in Buxu' (buchu), an aromatic herb.[5] Trade in dagga (hemp) between Khoikhoi of the western Cape and those on the Gamtoos or Keiskamma also occurred, and trade in metal between the Khoikhoi of the Longkloof and the Sotho—perhaps the Thlaping; as well as the indirect trade already referred to between the Nama and the Portuguese in beads.[6]

The Khoikhoi traditionally celebrated a series of rituals which Kolb, two centuries before van Gennep evolved his famous theory, recognized as *transition* rites,[7] and Theophilus Hahn (who knew more of Nama custom than any other writer) remarks that though Kolb's evidence was 'repeatedly doubted', this was 'without any good reason'.[8] Kolb describes rites at birth, puberty, marriage, and death which involved the sacrifice of a sheep, or an ox, or a cow; and the sprinkling of the person on whose behalf it was performed with an aromatic herb, *buchu*, and the gall of the slaughtered animal. The main participant also had to wear the fatty entrails of the animal killed. Winifred Hoernlé,

---

[1] Schapera, *Government and Politics*, p. 84.
[2] C. Brownlee, *Reminiscences of Kaffir Life and History*, p. 182.
[3] Moodie, i. 18, 436; Wikar, p. 27.
[4] Lichtenstein, ii. 319; Galton, p. 71.
[5] Hahn, *Tsuni-//Goam*, p. 23.
[6] Moodie, i. 437; Kolb, pp. 260-1.
[7] A. van Gennep, *Les Rites de passage*.
[8] Hahn, *Tsuni-//Goam*, p. 40.

writing in 1918,[1] again noted the stress on transition in the cycle of rituals. The form shows many similarities with Nguni and Sotho sacrifices; but there is no clear statement, as with them, that the offering is to the shades of the lineage, though Hahn speaks of 'an offering to the deceased or the Supreme Being', and of the amputation of a finger as an 'offering to //Guanab'.[2]

The Khoikhoi thought in terms of lineages—this is clear from their accounts of their history, and from the questions they asked whites. For example, an ensign visiting a Saldanha chief was asked 'whether the Dutch captain was also descended from a great family, and what were his ancestors, and those of the said ensign'.[3] They were concerned also about the graves of their ancestors: Hahn tells of a woman he knew praying at the grave of her father, for she said: 'We Khoikhoi always, if we are in trouble, go and pray at the graves of our grandparents and ancestors; it is an old custom of ours.'[4] But most of the rites on which we have evidence relate to founding heroes, not immediate ancestors. Cairns of stones associated with the hero Heitsi Eibib, who 'came from the east', are common in Namaqualand, and Tsuni-//Goam (Tsui-//Goab) was another founding hero, a 'powerful chief', 'the first Khoikhoib from whom all the Khoikhoi tribes took their origin'.[5] Their heroes were sky gods, who were identified with the Supreme Being,[6] and it was they who controlled the rain, in Khoikhoi thought. Rain was something holy—an attitude intelligible to all South Africans bred in drought—and the most important communal ritual was a sacrifice and prayer for rain, when the Pleiades appeared in spring. The Khoikhoi also danced at moonrise at the new moon and full moon,[7] and they respected the mantis as a sign of 'grace and prosperity'. If one alighted on a man they killed an ox as a thank-offering.[8]

The lesser importance of the shades among the Khoikhoi than among Bantu-speakers perhaps implied a lesser sense of unity and continuity through time. Certainly it implied less power for the chief, for (so far as the evidence goes) he did not pray on behalf of his people to his ancestors, and he was in no sense a 'divine king' on whose person the fertility of the country depended, as he was, in some degree, among all the Bantu-speakers of the south.

[1] A. W. Hoernlé, 'Certain Rites of Transition and the Conception of 'Nau among the Hottentots', *Harvard African Studies*, 2, 1918, 65–82.
[2] Hahn, *Tsuni-//Goam*, pp. 22, 87; Kolb, i. 308, links the amputation with widowhood.
[3] Moodie, i. 147.
[4] Hahn, *Tsuni-//Goam*, p. 113; Kolb, i. 137.
[5] Hahn, p. 61.
[6] Ibid., pp. 61–65.
[7] Ibid., pp. 40–44; A. W. Hoernlé, 'A Hottentot Rain Ceremony', *BS*, 1 (1922), 20–1; Schapera, *Khoisan*, pp. 366–89. Ten Rhyne, p. 139.
[8] Kolb, i. 99.

4. Relationships between Groups

In 1779 Wikar, a Swede, then travelling on the Orange river, made an observation which is one of the keys to South African history. He wrote: 'Every tribe that owns cattle also has a number of Bushmen under its protection',[1] and 'Bushmen' is used by him, as by other writers, to mean any group living solely by hunting and collecting. This relationship between hunters and herders is mentioned still earlier. Van der Stel on his journey to Namaqualand in 1685 reported: 'We found on inquiry and other information, that the Sonquas are like our poor in Europe, every tribe of Hottentots has some of them, and they are employed to give warning when they discover any strange tribe. They do not plunder any thing whatever from the kraals in whose service they are but from others.'[2] Kolb, writing of his visit to the Cape in 1707, says: 'Sonquas are mercenaries to other Hottentot nations, serving for food.'[3] He describes them as hunters and honey-gatherers, living in the mountains, among whom 'cattle great and small are very scarce'. They were 'not numerous'. A similar relationship continues to the present day in Botswana and South West Africa, where hunters attach themselves to cattle-owners and hunt or herd for them in return for food.[4] We call it *clientship*. It operates irrespective of race and language. So far back as our evidence goes, yellow-skinned Nama pastoralists had negro, Dama, clients who served them, in particular working metal for them;[5] the Tswana had clients when Moffat first came among them (see pp. 153, 155–6); white farmers have long had dependents whose relationship is closer to that of a client than that of an employee.[6] Ownership of stock gave the herders a much more secure food supply than the hunters had. After the whites arrived ownership of guns and horses was nearly as important, for a mounted man, armed with a musket, could kill much more game than could a man on foot with a bow. Thomas Baines shows something of the quality of the relationships in his nineteenth-century painting of 'Namaqua Hottentot on Riding ox with his Bushman'[7] (Plate I)—the possessive pronoun is revealing.

Some San bands remained wholly independent (so far as our evidence goes); others attached themselves intermittently to suppliers of food; others remained permanently dependent upon some patron. Those clients who remain hunters and only visit their patrons intermittently may retain much of their own culture, but those who settle do not. They learn the languages of their patrons and lose their own; their

---
[1] Wikar, p. 161.   [2] Moodie, i. 402, 403.   [3] Kolb, i. 76.
[4] Thomas, pp. 14–15, 18–21, 28, 165–7. (Observations 1951–5.)
[5] Vedder, 'Berg Damara', pp. 39–43.   [6] Thomas, pp. 172–4.
[7] Thomas Baines (1822–75), Fehr Collection, Rust en Vreugd, Cape Town.

crafts mostly disappear, and they become absorbed into the patron's culture.[1] Where land and game were plentiful the hunters remained independent—it was easy for them to vanish when they wished to do so (see p. 156); but where population grew more dense and game was shot out by men with firearms, the bow-and-arrow hunters could no longer subsist. They stole cattle and sheep and were themselves shot as thieves, or they became the permanent servants of herders and farmers. When the servant had no alternative means of subsistence, and no freedom of movement, clientship became slavery, or something akin to it.

Van Riebeeck describes how nervous the hunters were of meeting cattle-owners in 1652;[2] and Kolb how the 'Buchies' who stole cattle were hated by the 'Hottentots', who sent out parties in search of them[3] in 1707; and Wikar tells how much afraid hunters on the Orange river were of his 'large company of Hottentots' in 1779.[4] Tension therefore existed from early times, but it did not exclude communication. The hunters of van Riebeeck's day talked both with Saldanha and Nama herders, and the hunters on the Orange, 'though they spoke the Finch or Chinese language just like the Bushmen of the Sneeuwberg',[5] could communicate with the herders there.

The second type of relationship that existed between groups was that between traders and herders. Van Riebeeck was a buyer. He was the servant of a trading company, and his preoccupation, from the day he landed in South Africa until the day he left, was with the cattle trade, to provide food for his men and fresh supplies for scurvy-ridden ships. His diary records in minute detail how many cattle and sheep he was able to buy each day; what he paid for them; and how the limited number of animals were allocated to his men and to passing ships. It reflects his intense anxiety in the matter. When the Khoikhoi were reluctant to part with their stock he resisted the demands of his hungry men that he take their cattle by force, but pressed the advantages of doing so on his employers.[6] He was lavish in treating stock-owners to spirits, and he used every possible device to get them to part with cattle. The lives of his men, and his countrymen on the passing ships, as well as his own career, depended upon his success.

It has been shown that the Khoikhoi, like most pastoralists, were very careful of their breeding stock. They killed for rituals but not ordinarily for food, and though they were at first prepared to sell a limited number of cattle for copper, they were reluctant to part with many. Gradually,

---

[1] C. M. Turnbull, *The Forest People*, brilliantly analyses clientship between hunters and villagers in the Congo.
[2] Moodie, i. 20, 38, 59.   [3] Kolb, i. 89.   [4] Wikar, p. 161.
[5] Moodie, i. 404; Wikar, p. 161.   [6] Moodie, i. 23, 44, 50, 60.

however, the temptation of beads, tobacco, and brandy became too strong for them, and the hordes living close to the Cape lost most of their stock. It was these luxuries, rather than necessities, which made them part with cattle.[1] Ten Rhyne describes the Hessequa (who lived east of Swellendam) as still having large herds in 1685. The Commander sent a trading expedition to them annually; he got 447 horned cattle and 1,292 sheep the first time, and a hundred to two hundred cattle, as well as sheep, each succeeding year.[2]

A third type of relationship was that between settlers and herders. From the very beginning there was competition for pasture land: the settlers wanted exclusive occupation of the valley behind Table Bay and the Capemen argued that they had always been accustomed to pasture their cattle there. In 1659 the Capemen attempted to expel the Dutch,[3] and in 1660 van Riebeeck reported to the Chamber XVII in Holland:

the reasons advanced by them for . . . making war upon us last year, arising out of the complaints . . . that our people, living at a distance, and without our knowledge, had done them much injury, and also perhaps stolen and eaten up some of their sheep and calves etc. in which there is also some truth, and which it is very difficult to keep the common people from doing, when a little out of sight; so that they think they had cause for revenge, and especially, they said, upon people who had come to take and to occupy the land which had been their own in all ages, turning with the plough and cultivating permanently their best land, and keeping them off the ground upon which they had been accustomed to depasture their cattle, so that they must consequently now seek their subsistence by depasturing the land of other people, from which nothing could arise but disputes with their neighbours; insisting so strenuously upon the point of restoring to them their own land, that we were at length compelled to say they had entirely forfeited that right, through the war which they had waged against us, and that we were not inclined to restore it, as it now had become the property of the Company by the sword and the laws of war.[4]

From 1673 to 1677 there was war with the Gonnema of Saldanha Bay, again over land rights, and in 1707 Kolb noted that the Dutch occupied land that had belonged to 'Gunjeman' and 'Saldanhars'.[5] Thus the themes that dominated South African history for two centuries—the struggle for land and stock—emerged during the first decade of white settlement.

Employment of Khoikhoi by whites had begun even before the settlement, for the men of the wrecked ship *Haarlem* had used Khoikhoi

[1] Dapper, p. 73; Moodie, i. 301.   [2] Ten Rhyne, pp. 99, 135–7.
[3] Dapper, p. 13; Moodie, i. 58.   [4] Ibid. i. 206.
[5] We do not know the real names of most early Khoikhoi groups, therefore some form of the original spelling is used. Vedder, 'Nama', p. 113; Maingard, 'Lost Tribes'.

to gather firewood and cook for them.[1] They were not regarded as efficient workers, and van Riebeeck kept stressing the need for slaves or 'some industrious Chinese'; nevertheless, Khoikhoi were employed,[2] some even coming from the Swellendam area as migrant labourers, for Kolb reported that Hessequas entered the service of Europeans, and employed their wages to purchase cattle.[3]

At the time of the earliest contacts it was Khoikhoi who learnt Dutch or English rather than Europeans who learnt Khoikhoi, because the Europeans found Khoikhoi phonetics impossible.[4] They could not pronounce the clicks. Herry, leader of a small Strandloper group, had been taken in an English vessel to Batavia, and in 1652 he was referred to as 'the Ottentoo who speaks English' and who interpreted for van Riebeeck and his party in their first transactions with the people of the Cape.[5] Then in 1654 a man was kept on Dassen Island to 'try if he will learn Dutch . . . for he already understands it pretty well'—perhaps this was Claas Das, who replaced Herry during his absence.[6] The most fluent was Eva, a niece of Herry, who was brought up in van Riebeeck's household and baptized.[7] By 1668 'several' Khoikhoi from around the Fort were 'beginning to grasp the Dutch language'.[8] In 1663 the first Khoikhoi vocabulary was prepared ('in the Greek character') by G. F. Wreede, and this the Directors of the Company received, but they laid down the principle that 'The natives should learn our language, rather than we theirs'.[9] Later generations of settlers spoke Khoikhoi and San, learning as children from their nurses and playmates, but, except on the frontiers, it was Dutch, in the increasingly modified form of Afrikaans, which was spoken by the mixed population living on the farms and villages of the Cape.

Domestic employment and the learning of Dutch accompanied intermarriage and concubinage. Eva was married in 1664 to the explorer and chief surgeon, Pieter van Meerhoff, from the Commander's own house, and irregular unions between white men and Khoikhoi women were common.[10] The cleavage at that time was between Christian and non-Christian, rather than on the ground of colour, but marriage between white and Khoikhoi was rare.[11]

To further trade and maintain the security of the settlers the Governor of the Cape sought to exercise some authority over independent

---

[1] Moodie, i. 4, 31, 33.
[2] Ibid. i. 3; ii. 47, 49, 99 n., 154 n., 279.
[3] Kolb, i. 60, 167.
[4] Dapper, p. 71.
[5] Moodie, i. 9, 10, 14 n., 19, 21 n., 24.
[6] Ibid. i. 54 n., 70–71, 78.
[7] Ibid. i. 44, 82, 110, 115, 128–223.
[8] Dapper, pp. 45, 73.
[9] Moodie, i. 271 n., 273 notes.
[10] Ibid. i. 279–80, 400; Ten Rhyne, pp. 125–7; Fischer, genealogies; J. S. Marais, *The Cape Coloured People*, pp. 9–13.
[11] MacCrone, pp. 39–88.

RELATIONSHIPS BETWEEN GROUPS 67

Khoikhoi hordes. The chief of each horde recognized by the Company was presented with a copper-headed staff with the Company's mark, and in 1685 van der Stel speaks of 'the Cape Hottentots, Hessequas, Grigriquas and others who lived under the dominion of the Company'.[1] In 1685 he tried to mediate between 'Grigriqua' hordes,[2] and in 1689 the Council heard a complaint by a 'Hottentot captain' regarding the shooting of his son by members of another horde in a quarrel over a woman. A fine in stock was imposed, and the Council resolved to assist 'The Hottentot captains' in attacking him if he did not pay it.[3] Grevenbroek also describes the Governor mediating in a similar dispute between two hordes that war between them might be avoided.[4] Some sort of 'indirect rule' over neighbouring peoples had been established.

When groups interact influence is not in one direction only, and the settlers learnt much from the hunters and herders about the animals they shot for meat, and the grazing lands they used. Some of the whites adopted a life much closer to that of the Khoikhoi pastoralists than to that of seventeenth-century Europe whence their forebears came; they continued to live as pastoralists in the eastern and northern Cape until the early nineteenth century, and across the Orange for much longer. Their life differed from that of the Khoikhoi, however, in that they retained links with the outside world, on which they depended for firearms and gunpowder, and they held on to their literate and Christian tradition, though some frontiersmen grew up unable even to write their names.[5]

The Khoikhoi hordes which lost their land crumbled very quickly. In 1707 Kolb noted that the 'Gunjeman', whose land had been taken, 'dwell promiscuously with the Dutch', but among the 'Hessequas', who still lived independently on their own land, 'villages are larger, more in number and better peopled than those of any other Hottentot nation'.[6] The survival of a horde depended upon the use of a large territory within which it could circulate, pasturing stock and hunting. Once their land was gone the horde broke up into small groups of clients or farm servants, no longer independent, and slowly ceasing to speak their own language or follow traditional customs.

We do not know what the Khoikhoi population was when the settlers arrived, but a contributing reason for the disintegration of Khoikhoi culture was, perhaps, the smallness of the total population and its decrease through introduced diseases. Van Riebeeck's estimates of

[1] Moodie, i. 402, 406; Ten Rhyne, p. 135. [2] Moodie, i. 403; cf. i. 443, 445.
[3] Ibid. i. 445.   [4] Grevenbroek, p. 191.   [5] Borcherds, p. 55.
[6] Kolb, i. 60, 76.

particular groups range from '300 men capable of bearing arms' among the 'Gorinhaiquas' to '6 or 8,000 men' among the 'Saldanhars or Cochoquas'. The total population of the 'Cochoquas' is estimated at 16,000. One Nama group is estimated at 300 able-bodied men,[1] but Kolb, writing in 1707, said that the 'Great Nama' were 'able to take the field with 20,000 fighting men'. This, however, may have been north of the Orange. He lists sixteen Khoikhoi peoples,[2] and it is likely that the total Khoikhoi population south of the Orange was somewhere about 200,000 in 1652. This was the minimum figure given the Select Committee on Aborigines in 1837,[3] and is much closer to the reports of eye-witnesses than Theal's estimate of forty-five to fifty thousand. The smallpox epidemics of 1713, 1735, and 1767 so decimated the Khoikhoi that the very names of some hordes were forgotten,[4] and by 1805 the Cape census showed only 20,006 'Hottentots'. This included 'Bastards' and 'Bushmen', but excluded the people of Little Namaqualand and Bushmanland which were not yet part of the Cape Colony, nor did it include Nama north of the Orange. These estimates are, of course, not much more than informed guesses; quoted only to give a general indication of population size.

According to their own accounts, some remnants of groups which had occupied the Cape Peninsula retreated eastward and northward before the advance of the settlers, and they emerge in the eighteenth century as Gona (in the Eastern Cape), Kora (!Khora, Corans, or Koranna) on the Orange,[5] and Griqua (Xiri, ‡Kari-huriqua) moving northward along a line of springs towards the Orange river.[6]

The movement was a gradual one. The missionary John Campbell, when travelling some way south of the Orange in 1813, reported:

We came to a Hottentot kraal, where we would have halted for the night, but their fountain was dried up, so that they had no water for man or beast, and were to remove from it on the morrow. From their own account they had once a better place, but a boor having asked permission first to sow a little corn, then to erect a mill, they allowed it; after which he applied to government for a grant of the whole place, which they promised, not knowing that it was in possession of these Hottentots; of course they were driven from it. An old Hottentot told us that he remembered the time when the boors

---

[1] Moodie, i. 195, 208, 233, 234, 247.
[2] Kolb, i. 60–80; Maingard, 'Lost Tribes'; Vedder, 'Nama', pp. 113–14; Stow, pp. 246–7.
[3] Moodie, i. 61.   [4] Schapera, *Khoisan*, p. 45.
[5] Moodie, v. 12; Wikar, pp. 15, 143; L. F. Maingard, 'Studies in Korana History, Customs and Language', *BS*, 6, 1932, 103–62; Maingard, 'Lost Tribes'; Vedder, 'Nama'; J. A. Engelbrecht, *The Korana*, pp. 2–79; Stow, pp. 267–314. It is possible that some of the Kora had lived on the Orange before 1652 and never came south, but the evidence for this depends upon the statement of a single, ancient informant.
[6] In using *Griqua* we depart from our rules of orthography in order to be more readily understood. Stow, pp. 316–38.

RELATIONSHIPS BETWEEN GROUPS

were all within five days journey of Cape-Town, and the country was full of Hottentot kraals; but they have been gradually driven up the country to make room for the white people.[1]

The families pushed northward were often of mixed descent, and professing Christians.

The children of the Hottentot women, in whose veins Christian blood often flowed, were educated in Christianity: they learnt to sing psalms and to read; and were, even to receiving the sacrament of baptism, as good Christians as the pure offspring of the Europeans. At the death of one of these heads of families his servant would often assume his name; and not infrequently sought himself some little spot, to which he retired with all belonging to him, and gained a subsistence for himself and his family by the breeding of cattle. . . .

Many Hottentot families of this description had established themselves in the Lower Bokkeveld, when the increasing population of the colony occasioned new researches to be made after lands capable of cultivation; and the white children of the colonists did not hesitate to make use of the right of the strongest and to drive their half yellow relations out of the places where they had fixed their abodes. These Bastard Hottentots were then obliged to seek an asylum in more remote parts, till at length, driven from the Sack river, as they had been before from the Bokkeveld, nothing remained for them but to retreat to the Orange river.[2]

Professor Marais describes the bitter process as it continued into the nineteenth century.[3]

At the beginning of the nineteenth century some of the people who had moved up to the Orange lived 'after the manner of their forefathers',[4] in small nomadic hordes, and spoke only Khoikhoi. Campbell gives the names of fifteen Kora hordes living along the Orange river in 1813, with camps ranging from sixty to a hundred and fifty inhabitants.[5] Other groups were of mixed descent; they possessed firearms and horses; and some members spoke Dutch as their home language. In Sparrman's time (1775) the Khoikhoi were forbidden to possess horses,[6] but early in the history of the settlement they began to ride those of their employers, and they were trained to use firearms for hunting and serving on commando. It was the possession of horses and firearms that made certain groups so formidable on the Orange and which, together with the developing market in pelts and ivory, gave an impetus to hunting in Africa as in America. Lichtenstein describes them:

Colonel Gordon, at his journey to the Orange river, found a little colony established here of emigrant Bastard-Hottentots . . . they were clothed after

---

[1] Campbell, *1813*, p. 329.   [2] Lichtenstein, ii. 303-4.   [3] Marais, pp. 83-100.
[4] Lichtenstein, ii. 317.   [5] Campbell, *1813*, pp. 246-7, 276, 301-2.
[6] Sparrman, i. 253.

the European manner . . . they were converts to Christianity; they lived by breeding cattle, or by the chase; . . . they had good fire-arms in their possession; and . . . they obtained powder and ball, with other necessaries of civilized life, by a traffic in elephants' teeth with the inhabitants on the northern borders of the Colony.[1]

The other necessity was a wagon to transport the ivory and bring back ammunition, and this many families of mixed descent acquired.[2] Borcherds wrote of them: 'In dress, manners, and habits they resemble the farmers of the Frontier as also in their pursuits of cattle breeding and their addiction to hunting excursions.'[3] The two categories—those who spoke Khoikhoi and those who spoke Dutch—often combined in one horde, which might also have hunters ('Bojesmen') attached to it,[4] for men with fire-arms were food providers who inevitably attracted a following. In the early nineteenth century 'Kora' and 'Nama' were terms used primarily for those who spoke Khoikhoi, but Kok's 'Griqua' were of mixed descent and spoke Afrikaans. They had proudly called themselves 'Bastards' until, in 1813, Campbell 'represented to the principal persons the offensiveness of the word to an English or Dutch ear. . . . On consulting among themselves, they found the majority were descended from a person of the name of Griqua, and they resolved hereafter to be called Griquas.'[5] Indeed, they had links with the Chariguriqua (Grigriqua) who once lived between the Olifants river and St. Helena Bay.[6]

The refugees driven from the area adjoining the Cape Peninsula cannoned into other established groups: Gona into Xhosa and San (see p. 57); Kora and Griqua into San and later into Sotho living north of the Orange;[7] Nama from south of the Orange into their kinsmen living north of it, who, in turn, attacked the Herero;[8] and there were a number of lawless men who raided on their own account and attracted a following. Conspicuous among them was a Khoikhoi called Africaner, originally a farm servant in Tulbagh.[9]

The hunters were worse neighbours to both Khoikhoi and whites than other herders were because, as the population increased and wild game diminished, they stole domestic stock. White settlers, and their Khoikhoi and Coloured servants, and the independent Khoikhoi and Coloured hordes all made war on the hunters, driving them successively from one range after another: Drakenstein, Piquetberg, Roggeveld, Camdeboo,

---

[1] Lichtenstein, ii. 301-2. [2] Campbell, *1813*, pp. 245, 257-8, 284.
[3] Borcherds, p. 117. [4] Ibid. [5] Campbell, *1813*, pp. 252-3.
[6] Maingard, 'Lost Tribes'; Vedder, 'Nama', p. 114; Stow, pp. 243-4; Schapera, *Khoisan*, p. 46. [7] Stow, pp. 275-81, 316; Marais, p. 40.
[8] Vedder, 'Nama', p. 114; Galton, pp. 41-45.
[9] Campbell, *1813*, pp. 299, 305-6, 376-7.

Sneeuberg, Tarka, and even from 'Bushmanland' along the Orange river. Between 1715 and 1862 the hunters were hunted, almost as they themselves hunted animals, for many white farmers thought and spoke of them as if they were animals, and thousands were killed. They fought back furiously and tenaciously: there was no sign among the San of Camdeboo, Sneeuberg, and Tarka of that 'timidity' before other peoples which the !Kung manifest. Marais assembles the evidence of the bitter warfare.[1] What we do not know is what proportion of the total population of hunters the three to four thousand certainly killed represented.[2] Children were commonly taken home by members of commandos to be brought up and 'apprenticed' as farm servants—'tame Bushmen' the farmers called them—and indeed, the demand for servants was probably one of the reasons for commando expeditions against the hunters; Colonel Collins reported in 1809 'the prohibition to their carrying off women and children has greatly served to damp the ardour for commandos'.[3] Ten wagon-loads of children were taken from the Tooverberg, according to a survivor from the area.[4]

Extermination of the hunters lay on the consciences of some, and it was recognized as wasteful of potential labourers. Some farmers were successful in persuading hunters to become their servants—or at least their clients—in the way defined (see p. 63), and to care for their stock.[5] J. G. van Reenen and his father at Loerie and the Sak river, and Johannes van der Walt in the Tarka district and near the Orange–Caledon junction, were conspicuously successful.[6] Attempts were also made to stop San raids by turning the San into pastoralists on their own account. In the Roggeveld and Sneeuberg white farmers gave hunters sheep and goats—two thousand in one year in Graaff Reinet District.[7] This did indeed reduce raiding for a time, and Stockenström noted with satisfaction in 1820 that some San had taken to stockbreeding, but few bands of hunters—other than those attached to a mission station or a group of herders—seem to have been transformed into herders.[8] Some of the San grasped the importance of horses in hunting, and used the horses they stole to ride down eland,[9] but possession of horses did not transform them into stock-breeders, whereas Kora, Griqua, Xhosa, and Sotho, already familiar with the care of stock, began to breed horses as soon as they got them. The transformation

---

[1] Marais, pp. 15–29; L. Anthing (Civil Commissioner of Namaqualand), 1862, *Report*, A. 39, 1863.
[2] Moodie, v. 7–8; Marais, pp. 17, 18, 22, 28–29.   [3] Moodie, v. 23.
[4] Stow, p. 176. The grim story resembles that of the relations of Californian settlers with American Indian hunters and colleotors. T. Kroeber, *Ishi in Two Worlds*, pp. 40–100.
[5] Moodie, v. 3, 34.
[6] Moodie, iii. 64–65 n.; v. 3.   [7] Marais, pp. 20–22; Moodie, v. 3.
[8] Moffat, pp. 62–63; G. Thompson, p. 405.   [9] Moodie, v. 3.

of hunter to herder involves a radical shift in values, in particular the willingness to forgo immediate food in order to preserve breeding stock for future supply. Hunters were likely to eat all the stock they acquired. The determination of herders to preserve breeding stock and forgo immediate satisfactions in order to do so is a handicap in countries which are overstocked, and has been a matter of bitter criticism by whites against Bantu-speaking cattle-owners through Africa,[1] but the establishment of these values was clearly difficult, and an issue on which the revolution from hunting to pastoralism turned. It may be compared with the difficulty of an underdeveloped country in persuading its people to save and accumulate capital for development. Hunting and gathering continued for an immensity of time before pastoralism was invented, and it has continued since, showing how difficult is the change from one way of life to another. In Africa, as elsewhere, 'farming and the domestication of animals . . . crept in slowly'.[2]

The hunters could not acquire the skills and values of herders overnight, though they might attach themselves to a group of herders and hunt or pasture stock for them, but it is possible that some groups of herders *lost* their stock, and became hunters for a time, reverting to herding when they could. One small group of Strandlopers who occupied the Cape Peninsula in 1652 seem to have taken to herding immediately after they had stolen cattle from the whites.[3]

Those San who grew up on farms, either as captive children or as the descendants of clients, were absorbed into the mixed Coloured community. Culturally, they were no longer hunters, they no longer painted, and they mingled in race with negroid and Indonesian slaves, with whites, as well as with the descendants of herders who resembled them physically. It is not true to suggest that San could not adapt; many individuals did so (among them Andries Waterboer, who became chief of the Griqua);[4] but only in the desert, where they could retain their hunting grounds and their isolation, did their language and way of life survive. Nowhere has the painting and sculpture continued, in the great tradition, to this century, though some of the most lively paintings of Queenstown and the Drakensberg are of the mid nineteenth century (see pp. 105–6).

A careful study made by Professor Tobias gives the number of 'Bushmen' remaining within the Republic in 1957 at 20; those in Botswana at 31,000; and those in South West Africa at 20,311; he used as criteria language, and 'the common recognition of individuals and tribes as

---

[1] D. H. Houghton and E. M. Walton, *The Economy of a Native Reserve* (Keiskammahoek Rural Survey, vol. ii), pp. 164–73; J. Huxley, *Africa View*, pp. 81–83, 206–8.
[2] Grahame Clark and Stuart Piggott, *Prehistoric Societies*, p. 23.
[3] Moodie, i. 10, 12, 35, 43.   [4] Marais, p. 37.

Bushmen or Sarwa', but following Bleek and others he classified as 'Bushman' languages spoken by Sarwa which are close to Khoikhoi. Nor are all the 51,331 hunters: the figure includes those who are clients or servants of Bantu-speakers or whites, but who still speak their own click language.[1] The independent bands of hunters are becoming fewer, and their membership smaller, as farmers encroach on what were once hunters' springs, and more and more hunters settle on farms to be assured of food and water. The movement is accelerated by drought.[2] In local terminology, 'wild Bushmen' are becoming 'tame': as they have been doing over three centuries and more.

Those who talk about the process of change commonly make judgements of value, often without realizing that they are doing so. We have spoken of the 'loss' of traditional language and customs, and the 'disintegration' of bands or hordes. These are loaded terms. One may equally well speak of the 'adaptability' of the hunters and herders to new circumstances; of the readiness with which the Khoikhoi learnt a new language, accepted Christian teaching, and were educated in the ways of another society. Again the terms are loaded. Those who favour an anthropological zoo, or who think that cultural diversity is the supreme value, or have some mystical notion that culture is carried 'in the blood' and that those who abandon their traditional culture cannot acquire any other—speak of 'loss'. Those who value most highly Christian teaching, or technical development, or productivity, or scientific knowledge, or whatever else they term 'civilization', speak of 'education' and 'development'.

It is on the readiness of men to borrow inventions and accept new ideas and techniques that civilization has been built. Groups whose members fail to adapt to changing circumstances are, like dinosaurs, doomed to extinction, but those which do adapt may live transformed. Nomadism as a way of life is extinct in South Africa (save in remote desert places), but the descendants of nomads drive tractors and work in factories. The more efficient economy slowly drives out the less efficient, as hunters become clients of pastoralists; and subsistence farmers, in their turn, become migrant labourers in an industrial civilization, a position not unlike that of clients. The irony is that the descendants of settlers who taught the Khoikhoi and San and Bantu-speakers to desire trade goods and learn their language, and pressed them into their service as labourers, now demand that their descendants develop 'separately'.

[1] Tobias, 'Bushman Hunter-Gatherers', 68–69.
[2] Ibid. 83–84.

The ability to overcome fragmentation and create political units in which a large number of men may co-operate under the rule of law is one of the crucial achievements in the history of human society. As men gain more control over their physical environment, the size of the unit tends to increase. This process can be traced very clearly in South Africa, where, among the hunters, each band is independent and commonly numbered about thirty to fifty persons; but among the herders the horde acknowledging one chief might reach 2,500; and among the cattle-keepers and cultivators chiefdoms of 10,000 were common enough, and occasional kingdoms reached 200,000. These, in turn, were absorbed by still larger industrialized trading states with diverse populations. The connexion between the economy and the size of the political unit is not an absolute one, and there were, indeed, chiefdoms of cattle-keepers and cultivators smaller than the largest hordes of herders; nor does the density of population on the ground determine the size or form of political units,[1] but absence of technical skills, and isolation, preclude the growth of large states.

The tendency to fragment still bedevils men and we know very little of the conditions which enable a group to cohere. What are the conditions that restrain factionalism and make men accept the authority of a wider unit? Mastery of these is as important in the history of human society as the learning of new skills like domesticating animals, or harnessing them to plough, or making a wheel, or pumping water, or splitting the atom. We may compare the difficulty of a Nama chief in holding together several clans, and preventing raiding between them, with the difficulty of the United Nations Organization in preventing war between great states. The tendency to split is a problem that recurs repeatedly in South African history: it is traced in the following chapters among Xhosa, Sotho, Zulu, Voortrekkers, and settlers of the eastern Cape (pp. 119, 156, 325, 351, 357, 361, 366); sometimes it was controlled, and sometimes chiefdoms or colonizing parties fragmented. Perhaps the formation of a viable political unit is a creation comparable to the creation of a work of art, and the conditions of creation elude us.

We are left with other tantalizing questions: When and where did the ancestors of the Khoikhoi herders acquire the art of riding? How are the languages of the various hunting and herding peoples related one to another, and to other languages in Africa? Why did some of the hunters paint with such skill and vigour, and other peoples not paint at all? And what were the links through time between the painters of the south and those of Rhodesia and Zambia and Tanzania? Our knowledge of the history of the hunters and herders is still fragmentary.

[1] M. Fortes and E. E. Evans-Pritchard, *African Political Systems*.

III

THE NGUNI PEOPLE[1]

EVIDENCE on Nguni history comes from four main sources: contemporary documents, oral tradition, archaeological excavations, and linguistic studies. Documents date from 1486 when the Portuguese rounded the Cape, and there are some detailed accounts in the sixteenth and seventeenth centuries of the manner of life of Nguni-speaking people recorded by shipwrecked travellers. Their evidence can be interpreted in the light of our fuller knowledge of Nguni society from the eighteenth and nineteenth centuries.

1. *Demarcation and Distribution*

The Nguni are a people who can understand one another's speech,[2] though there are dialect differences among them as marked as between Kent and Cumberland. In the speech of the ordinary countryman there are no sharp lines of cleavage but a gradual merging from one dialect to the next, so that the common usage of a man living on the Fish river differs a little from that of a man living on the Mthatha (Umtata) and his, in turn, from that of a man on the Mzimvubu, and so northward across the Tukela (Tugela), and on to Kosi Bay.[3] Two of the more distant dialects were written down by missionaries in the nineteenth century—Xhosa as spoken on the Eastern Cape frontier (the valleys of the Fish, Keiskamma, and Buffalo) and Zulu as spoken north of the Tukela—and this has tended to stabilize two forms: Xhosa and Zulu.

[1] I am indebted to Mrs. T. Shifrin and Mr. C. C. Saunders, who worked as research assistants on this chapter; to Miss L. Levy of the School of African Studies, University of Cape Town, who with an eagle eye for detail has saved me from many mistakes in this and succeeding chapters; to Professor A. C. Jordan and my colleague Mr. S. M. Tindleni for generous help with Xhosa spelling; and to Mr. Leo Marquard, Mr. Archie Mafeje, and Professor L. M. Thompson for criticism.

[2] Some linguists term Nguni a 'language group', which 'indicates an aggregation of languages possessing common salient phonetic and grammatical features, and having a high degree of mutual understanding, so that members can, without serious difficulty, converse with one another' (C. M. Doke, *The Southern Bantu Languages*, p. 20). W. G. Bennie spoke of 'the Nguni language' and stressed its unity in A. M. Duggan Cronin, *The Bantu Tribes of South Africa*, iii (1), p. 13, as also does J. M. Nhlapo, *Nguni and Sotho*, pp. 18–21.

[3] D. D. T. Jabavu, personal communication. The late Professor Jabavu lectured on Bantu languages at Fort Hare for many years and was famous as an orator in Xhosa. He had travelled widely listening to dialect change.

An earlier distinction existed between those Nguni whose language reflected Sotho and Tsonga influence, who *tekela* in their speech using t in place of z, and those such as the Zulu proper who do not. The *tekela* Nguni live in the modern Swaziland and once occupied what is now Natal, between the great rivers Tukela and Mzimkhulu, while those Nguni who were not so influenced lived south of the Mzimkhulu, and in Zululand north of the Tukela.[1] During the wars of the early nineteenth century the population of Natal was so dispersed that local variations in speech were largely overlaid, and at Shaka's court Zulu was insisted upon,[2] but one *tekela* form, the Lala dialect, can still be traced in the speech of old women in some groups in Natal.[3]

Similarity in speech implies close interaction, and there is a marked tendency for differences in custom to coincide with differences in language, therefore the Nguni can be distinguished both in language and custom from the Tsonga to the north-east, the Sotho to the north and north-west, and the Khoikhoi and San to the south-west. Dialect differences *within* the Nguni group are also associated with differences in custom. But the connexion between language and custom is not inextricable, and there is no certainty that a change in vocabulary will be matched by a change in law. The Nguni area can be precisely defined only in terms of language.

In 1965 Nguni speakers numbered more than 7,000,000[4] and were found scattered all over southern Africa with outlying groups even beyond the Zambezi, but they spread, within historical times, from the area which lies between the Drakensberg mountains and the sea, from the Fish river to Swaziland. There has long been debate about their precise distribution in space and time, and it is therefore necessary to examine the earliest accounts of them in some detail.

[1] A. T. Bryant, *A Zulu–English Dictionary*, pp. 25–28; *Olden Times in Zululand and Natal*, pp. 6–9, 232–5.
[2] J. L. Dohne, *A Zulu Kafir Dictionary*, p. xv.
[3] N. J. van Warmelo, *Preliminary Survey of the Bantu Tribes of South Africa*, p. 70; J. Laredo, Unpublished MS. 1964.
[4] They are made up as follows:

Xhosa in Republic	3,044,634	*Republic of S. Africa, Population Census, 1960*, Pretoria, 1965, Sample Tabulation 8, p. 94.
Zulu in Republic	2,867,177	
Swazi in Swaziland	229,744	*Swaziland Census, 1956.*
Swazi in Republic	334,310	*1960 Census*, Bureau of Statistics, Sample Tabulation 8.
Ndebele in Republic	294,253	*1960 Census*, Bureau of Statistics, Sample Tabulation 8.
Ndebele in Rhodesia	400,000?	A. J. B. Hughes and J. van Velsen, *The Shona and Ndebele of Southern Rhodesia*, 1955, p. 45.
	7,170,118	

According to the Census figures, 754,290 Africans born in Rhodesia lived in Matabeleland in 1962. These were not all Ndebele, but Ndebele lived also in other parts of Rhodesia (Southern Rhodesian Information Service). All these figures must be taken with reserve.

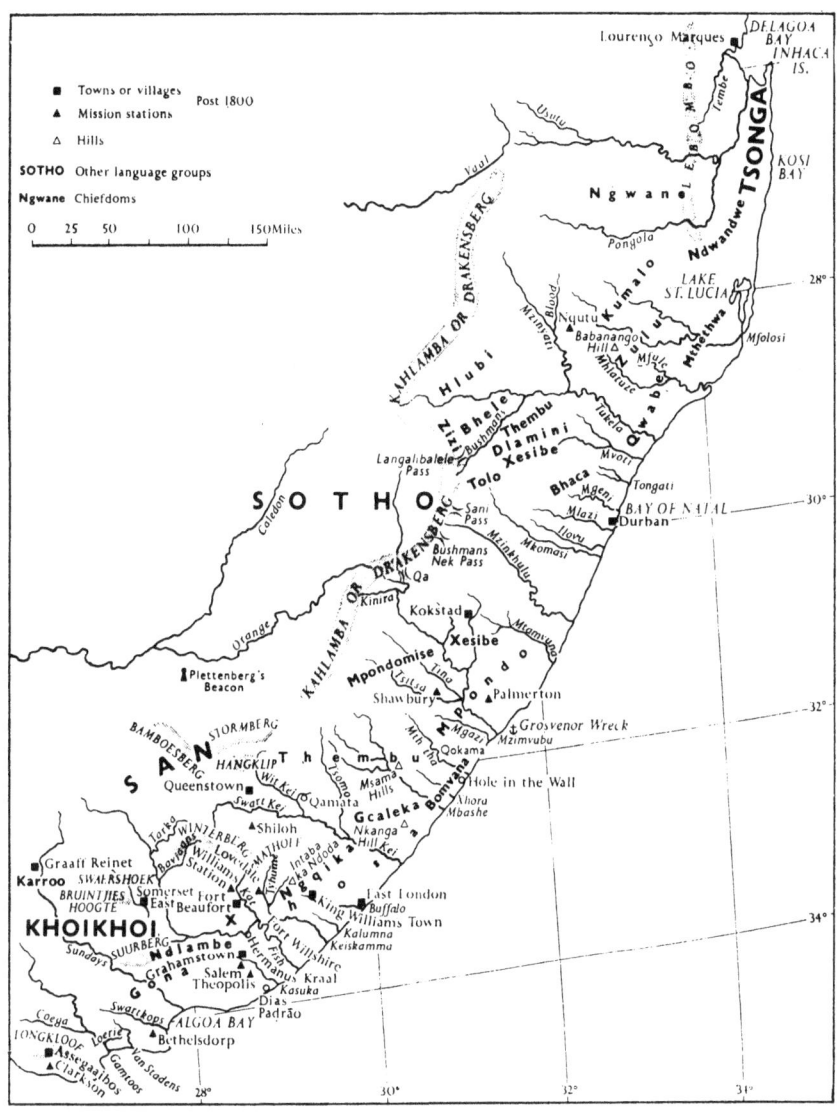

MAP 3. Distribution of Nguni c. 1800. *After M. Pimstone*

Sources: J. Shooter, *The Kafirs of Natal and the Zulu Country*, London, 1857; A. T. Bryant, *Olden Times in Zululand and Natal*, London, 1929; D. Moodie, *The Record*, Cape Town, 1838 (reprinted Cape Town, 1960), 5 parts; *Report and Proceedings of the Government Commission on Laws and Customs*, Cape Town, G. 4-'83, 1883, Map

The earliest Portuguese voyagers to round the Cape encountered at Saldanha Bay, the Cape itself, and Mossel Bay 'swarthy' people[1] who, from later evidence regarding them, may be assumed to have been Khoikhoi. Bartholomew Dias saw no inhabitants at his turning-point, the Infante river (probably the Keiskamma or Kowie),[2] or near Bushman's river mouth where he built a *padrão* in 1488.[3] Vasco da Gama saw 'two men' running along the beach near this *padrão* and 'many cattle wandering about' in 1497, but he did not land there,[4] and though he sighted land—almost certainly the modern Pondoland—and named it Natal, and fished off a point which was probably Durban Bluff, he did not go ashore even to take in water, until he came to the small 'Copper river'. This has not been certainly identified but it was probably north of the Limpopo.[5]

The *first* party known to have travelled along the south-east coast was one of survivors from the wreck of the *São João* in June 1552. They were cast ashore in what is now Pondoland a little way north of the Mzimvubu river, and travelled along the coast until they reached Delagoa Bay in October. At the place of the wreck they were visited by 'seven or eight Kaffirs . . . leading a cow' which they were about to barter for nails when five other men appeared and shouted to the first party not to sell the cow. They kept close to the shore, and though they fought several skirmishes in which 'the Kaffirs were always worsted', they reported no settlements except one group of deserted huts, until they came near the river Lourenço Marques, where a chief 'Inhaca' sheltered and fed them.

They 'went back six leagues on the road they had come' to help Inhaca defeat a 'rebellious Kaffir' and seize his cattle, so apparently they had overlooked some of the settlements they had passed.[6] 'Inhaca' has been convincingly identified as a Tsonga chief, Nyaka, whose descendants live where he lived and still use his name in greeting one another.[7] Already, by 1552, a ship from Sofala was expected annually at Lourenço Marques to buy ivory.

In April 1554 the *São Bento* was wrecked west of the 'River Infante', i.e. the Keiskamma or Kowie, but Theal thought that the men of the

---

[1] *Diário da Viagem de Vasco da Gama*, vol. i of *Livraria Civilização*, Oporto, 1945. Translated and quoted by E. Axelson, *South African Explorers*. The Portuguese text and another translation is in *Documentos sobre os Portugueses ém Moçambique na África Central* (*Documents on the Portuguese in Mozambique and Central Africa*), *1497–1840*, vol. i, 1497–1506.
[2] E. Axelson, *South East Africa, 1488–1530*, pp. 19–20. Appendices II and III.
[3] Professor Axelson found this cross in 1938.
[4] Da Gama, p. 9.   [5] Axelson, *South East Africa*, pp. 37–38.
[6] Theal, *Records*, i. 108–49.
[7] H. A. Junod, 'The Condition of the Natives of South-East Africa in the Sixteenth Century according to the early Portuguese Documents', in *Report of the Eleventh Annual Meeting of the South African Association for the Advancement of Science*, Lourenço Marques, 1913, p. 147.

São Bento had mistaken the Mthatha for the Infante because they 'passed no stream of any importance before they reached the Umzimvubu'.¹ Certainly the wreck was somewhere between the Kasuka and the Mthatha. Before leaving it the survivors saw 'seven or eight . . . Kaffirs, very black in colour, with woolly hair, and . . . naked . . .'. Later they saw 'about a hundred' with 'many wooden pikes with their points hardened in the fire . . . and some assegais with iron points', who spoke 'a language not so badly pronounced as we always heard and was customary on that coast'. And they came to a village of

about twenty huts built with poles and thatched with dry grass, in form and size like a baker's oven, such as is usual among all the people of this coast. They move them from place to place with the seasons, according to the abundance or barrenness of the ground, upon the wild fruit of which they principally subsist.

A large and well-provided village was reported to be close by. Though they were 'constantly followed by Kaffirs' the first food bartered was after twenty-two days' travelling, probably on the Mzimkhulu. There they got 'cakes made of a seed called nacharre' and later a cow and a goat, in exchange for iron, and they learnt from a Bengali, who had been shipwrecked earlier, that 'the country was thickly populated and provided with cattle'. A little further on they stole a large basket of millet, the first they had seen, and thence they were well provided with food until they reached Lourenço Marques. They also met various survivors from the previous wrecks who were living with the people of the country and refused to come on with them.²

The *Santo Thomé* was wrecked in 1589 on the Mozambique coast north of the Nguni area, but the chronicler who wrote of their journey has one comment on the political structure of the people to the south which is of great interest. He says: 'All this land of Fumos [Tsonga country] is under the king called Viragune', south of it is 'another land called Mokalapapa', which

joins another kingdom, that of Vambe, which runs south, where our people also carry on a trade in ivory. From this kingdom, which includes a great part of the land called Natal, to the Cape of Good Hope there are no other kings, but all is in the possession of chiefs called Ancozes, who are the heads and governors of three, four, or five villages.³

Four years later, in March 1593, the *Santo Alberto* was wrecked three days west of the Infante, at a place the inhabitants called Tizombe and the Portuguese 'Penedo das Fontes'. This name was used for the

---

¹ Theal, *Records*, ii, p. xii note. In fact they crossed a large river (i. 230) before they came to the 'river St. Christopher'.
² Ibid. i. 150–285.   ³ Ibid. ii. 164, 199.

promontory to the west of Bushman's river mouth on which Dias built his last *padrão*,[1] but no mention is made in the journal of the *padrão* or of crossing a river close to the wreck, and Theal thought, from the latitude and details given of the country, that the Mthatha was again mistaken for the Infante and that the place was 'Hole-in-the-Wall' near the Mbashe (Bashee).[2] The survivors were greeted by a chief, Luspance, 'with about sixty negroes'. 'He was of good stature, well made, of a cheerful countenance, and not very black. He had a short beard, and long moustaches. . . .' In the Portuguese party was a slave who 'understood the language of these Kaffirs and spoke also that of Mozambique' and another who understood both the latter language and Portuguese, so by means of two interpreters communication was established. The journalist reports that:

> The dress of these Kaffirs is a mantle of ox-hide, with the hair outwards, which they rub with grease to make it soft. They are shod with two or three soles of raw leather fastened together in a round shape, and secured to the feet with straps; in these they run with great lightness. In their hands they carry the tail of an ape or a fox fastened to a thin piece of wood, with which they clean themselves and shade their eyes when observing. This dress is used by almost all the negroes of Kaffraria, and their kings and chiefs wear, hanging to the left ear, a copper ornament made after their own fashion.
>
> These and all other Kaffirs are herdsmen and cultivators of the ground, by which means they subsist. They cultivate millet, which is white and the size of a peppercorn; it is the fruit of a plant of the size and appearance of a reed. Of this millet, ground between two stones or in wooden mortars, they make flour, and of this they make cakes, which they cook among embers. Of the same grain they make wine, mixing it with a quantity of water which, when it has fermented in a vessel of clay and has cooled and turned sour, they drink with great enjoyment.
>
> Their cattle are very fat, tender, well-flavoured, and large, the pastures being very rich. Most of them are hornless, and the greater number are cows, in the abundance of which their riches consist. They use milk and the butter which they make from it.
>
> They live in small villages, in huts made of reed mats, which do not keep out the rain. These huts are round and low, and if any person dies in one of them, the others take it down with all the rest of the village, and remove to another spot, thinking that in a place where their neighbour or relation died everything will be unlucky. And so, to save this trouble, if anyone is ill they carry him into the thicket that if he is to die it may be out of the houses. They surround the huts with a hedge, within which they keep the cattle. . . .
>
> . . . Most of the inhabitants of this land, from latitude 29° and downwards, are circumcised. . . . They obey chiefs whom they call Ancosses.[3]
>
> The language is the same in nearly all Kaffraria, the difference being only

---

[1] Axelson, *South East Africa*, pp. 173–4.   [2] Theal, *Records*, ii, pp. xxvi, 293–4.
[3] So spelt in the Portuguese text.

like that between the different dialects of Italy and the ordinary dialects of Spain. The people never go far from their villages, and thus they know and hear nothing except what concerns their immediate neighbours. . . .
They value the most necessary metals, as iron and copper, and for very small pieces of either they will barter cattle, which is what they esteem most, and with which they trade, exchanging them for other treasures.[1]

The greeting used by Luspance, south of the Mthatha, *Nanhata, nanhata*, was the same as that used north of the Tukela.[2]

The party agreed to travel inland to 'avoid the inevitable hardships of the coast', and indeed they suffered much less than the preceding parties. The chief had brought them 'two large sheep of the Ormuz breed', and they bartered two cows and two sheep for copper before starting. They had guides, and instead of travelling along the very broken coastal belt they followed a route where 'the ground was very good and level, . . . abounding with pasture and water'. Two days after crossing the Infante they passed a village with millet standing in the fields, and went on to visit the chief 'travelling over level ground with rich and abundant pasture'. The next day they came to a village consisting of a few houses around a kraal, in which there were about a hundred cows and a hundred and twenty very large sheep of the Ormuz breed. Here lived an old man with his sons and grandsons, who with great surprise and joy received our people, and brought them gourds full of milk. . . .

The next village belonged to a man, Ubabù, who entertained them with a dance. Then they crossed the Mzimvubu at a cattle ford and met a chief, Vibo, 'accompanied by many others driving some hundred cows', who provided them with two of his sons as guides and two cows for provisions. Villagers gave them 'cakes of millet, which they call sincoà',[3] showing that *isonka*, the Xhosa word for bread or an unleavened cake, was already in use.

Between leaving Vibo and arriving at Lourenço Marques they crossed two belts of country without villages and through which they could not get guides, but otherwise they found it thickly populated and were supplied with food all the way. Their one dangerous encounter was a little way south of Lourenço Marques where they were misled and attacked by men whose chief was 'a great thief named Bambe'. This party was exceptional in that they did not steal provisions or attack anyone, and they were welcomed almost all the way.[4]

In October 1622 the *São João Baptista* was wrecked, probably a little way east of the Fish river (lat. 33°), where the survivors met people

---

[1] Theal, *Records*, ii. 134–5, 293–4.   [2] Bryant, *Olden Times*, pp. 10–12.
[3] Theal, *Records*, ii. 310.   [4] Ibid., pp. 225–346.

'whiter than mulattoes', and though they remained a month and six days they 'could never understand a word these people said, for their speech is not like that of man, and when they want to say anything they make clicks with their mouths at the beginning, middle, and end . . .'. They 'brought as a present an ox, very big and fine, and a leather bag of milk . . .'. They lived upon '. . . shell-fish, certain roots found in the earth, and the produce of the chase', as well as milk and meat from their cattle, and had 'no knowledge of any seed'.[1]

Between them and the next people with cattle lay a 'desert' 'twenty days as the Kaffirs travel, which would be two months at our speed', but they found in it hunters and fishers, and eventually came to a village whose inhabitants could understand some of the slaves in the party. Some way west of the Mthatha (where they met a survivor from the 1593 wreck) they procured cattle and grain, and were welcomed by 'the son of the king . . . with a hundred men all well armed with iron assagais . . . and had with him the most splendid ox we had ever seen, without horns, and he made the captain a present of it'. Further on they saw 'an infinite number of kraals with herds of cattle and gardens', and 'negroes came out bringing vessels full of milk and cows for sale'.[2] After that they found people all the way to Lourenço Marques, only occasionally passing through belts without villages.

In June 1635 the *Nossa Senhora de Belem* went aground between the Mthatha and Mbashe (lat. 32°), perhaps at the Xhora mouth, and the survivors spent six months there building themselves a boat. The people they met used words still used in Xhosa—they addressed the captain as *Umlungo* and *Umkulu*—and their manner of life was that of two centuries later. The journalist reported that:

> The men of this country are very lean and upright, tall of stature, and handsome. They can endure great labour, hunger, and cold; they live two hundred years and even more in good health, and with all their teeth. They are so light that they can run over the rugged mountains as fleetly as stags. They are clothed in skins which hang over their shoulders to the knees; these are cow-hides, but they have the art of dressing them till they are as soft as velvet. There are rich and poor among them, but this is according to the number of their cattle. They all carry sticks in their hands about two spans in length, with a tail at the end like the brush of a fox, which serves them as a handkerchief and fan. They use sandals of elephant's hide, which they carry hanging from their hands, and I never saw them on their feet. Their arms are assagais with broad well-fashioned heads. Their shields are of elephant hide with handles like ours, but made like leathern targets; the richest use others. They all have dogs with ears and tails cropped, with which they hunt wild pigs and stags, as well as buffaloes, elephants, tigers, and lions. . . .

[1] Theal, *Records*, viii. 8-10, 76-78.   [2] Ibid., pp. 86-90.

The kings have four, five, and seven wives. The women do all the work, planting and tilling the earth with sticks to prepare it for their grain, which is millet as large or larger than linseed. They have maize also, and plant large melons which are very good, and beans and gourds of many kinds, also sugar canes, though they brought us very few of these. Cows are what they chiefly value: these are very fine and the tamest cattle I have ever seen in any country. In the milk season they live chiefly upon it, making curds and turning it sour, which was little to our taste. They also eat a certain root which resembles spurge laurel, and they say it is very strengthening. There are others yielding a fine seed, which also grows under ground. They eat this with great enjoyment, and also the gum from the trees. . . .

The women bring no dowry in marriage, on the contrary the husband pays the bride's father with cattle, and they become as slaves to their husbands; they choose six or seven, and take one into their house every moon without any jealousy whatever arising. Even their ornaments go to the men, and the women wear only skins better or worse according to the position of their husbands. Their ornaments are bracelets on their arms and pendants in their ears, of copper or bone.[1]

The survivors of the *Belem* met a man who had been left behind by the 1593 party as a boy, with the chief Luspance, because he was too ill to travel. He 'was now very rich and had three wives and many children'. Through him they were able to buy 219 cattle, many in calf, but they lacked the leadership and discipline of the 1593 party and ended by shooting a chief, as well as several other men.[2]

The survivors of a wreck in 1647 west of the River Infante (which they recorded at latitude $33\frac{1}{3}°$) add little to our knowledge except that[3] on the Infante they found people whom 'no one could understand because they spoke with clicks'. 'They sow no grain, and live only on roots, the produce of the chase, and some shell-fish when they come down to the shore. Their arms are of fire-hardened wood and a few iron assagais.' This party were able to barter cattle some days west of the river where the *Belem* was wrecked in 1635, i.e. probably about the Kei,[4] and they themselves trained some of those they bought to carry their baggage.

The most useful evidence in the seventeenth century comes from the survivors of a Dutch ship, the *Stavenisse*, wrecked in February 1686 seventy miles south of the Bay of Natal (the modern Durban). Forty-seven of the party set off southward to walk to the Cape; others who were ill or wounded remained some time at the wreck, then went north to the Bay of Natal, where, along with the survivors of other wrecks, they built a small vessel, the *Centaurus*, which took them safely to the Cape. When they got there none of the forty-seven who set out to

[1] Ibid., pp. 204–5.   [2] Ibid., pp. 141–235.   [3] Ibid., p. 307.
[4] Ibid., pp. 237–360.

walk from the wreck had arrived, so early in 1688 the *Centaurus* was sent back along the coast to look for survivors. They rescued eighteen of the *Stavenisse* crew and a Huguenot boy, the sole survivor of another wreck, near the mouth of the Kei. A few months later another search expedition rescued two more of the *Stavenisse* survivors at the Bay of Natal, and one at the Buffalo. From these men a great deal was learnt about the country between the Buffalo and the Tukela. Some of them had been living with the Xhosa for nearly three years and had learnt to speak the language. The Huguenot boy had lived under the protection of a Xhosa chief, Sotopa, and Togu was then the senior chief of the Xhosa. Another Xhosa chief, Magamma, was living on the Buffalo.

The people they found along the coast from the wreck southward were 'the Semboes, the Mapontemousse, the Maponte, the Matimbes, the Magryghas . . . and the Magosse [also Magossche]',[1] (i.e. Mbo?, Mpondomise, Mpondo, Thembu, Riligwa (Griqua?), a Khoikhoi people,[2] and Xhosa), or, according to another survivor (south to north), 'the Magoses, the Makrigqas, the Matimbes, Mapontes, and Emboas' (Xhosa, Riligwa (Griqua?), Thembu, Mpondo, Mbo). The country was reported to be 'exceedingly fertile, and incredibly populous, and full of cattle'.[3]

The picture we get, then, is of a *coast* sparsely populated in 1552 and 1554, but with many villages further *inland*. The 1593 party, travelling inland and NNE., were told that they would 'always find villages with provisions in this direction', as indeed they did, and the Bengali met in 1554 north of the Mzimkhulu assured the *São Bento* party that 'the country was thickly populated and provided with cattle'. It is not surprising that a cattle people should have chosen to live in the inland areas, for, at least in Pondoland, there is a strip of very sour veld along the coast whereas further inland the pastures are sweeter;[4] the quality even of the sweet veld is variable,[5] and it is reasonable to suppose that the early distribution of a pastoral people was related to this. A hint is given in the journal of 1622 when a man who had come some distance and brought forty cattle for sale at the coast, west of the Mthatha, was asked to keep most of them near by until those bought had been eaten. 'He replied that there was no good pasture there, and he would make a tour and return in six or seven days', which he did.[6] Still, today, though the population of the Transkei is so heavy, the concentration lies inland of a coastal belt some miles in width, and long stretches of beach are deserted. In March 1960 two survivors from an aircraft

---

[1] Moodie, i. 426–7, 431.   [2] J. H. Soga, *The South-Eastern Bantu*, p. 110.
[3] Moodie, i. 431.
[4] J. P. H. Acocks, *Veld Types of South Africa*, pp. 32–34 and Maps.
[5] E. D. Matthews, *Tukulu*, p. 150.   [6] Theal, *Records*, viii. 98.

which crashed in the sea north of the Mzimvubu 'walked ten miles along the uninhabited coast before they stumbled across a party of campers'. Yet the Transkei has a population density of nearly a hundred to the square mile.[1] As already noted, the 1593 party crossed two belts of 'desert' (*deserto*), i.e. country without villages, between the occupied areas in Natal; another 'desert' is mentioned by the 1622 party west of the Infante;[2] and two are mentioned by the survivors of the *Grosvenor*, in 1782, north of the Kei.[3] Such uninhabited belts between independent political units still existed in the Transkei in 1865[4] and in Tanganyika up to 1938.[5] They are a common feature of small-scale societies so long as the population is not very dense.

The journals of 1552 and 1554 show that what is now the Transkei was already occupied by people who had cattle. They do not make it perfectly clear whether these were Nguni-speaking or Khoikhoi, but the fact that they 'spoke a language not so badly pronounced' suggests that they were neither San nor Khoikhoi, whose clicks later travellers commented on immediately. The journal of 1593 proves that the country was occupied by an Nguni-speaking people at least to the south of the Mthatha and possibly further. The chronicler states specifically that the 'language is the same in nearly all Kaffraria', and the chiefs are called 'Ancosses' (*inkosi*), a word already used in the form 'Ancozes' in 1589. Bryant even goes so far as to argue that the dialect spoken about the bay of Natal was 'Ntungwa Nguni' (Zulu), as distinct from the *tekela* dialect spoken further south and further north (see p. 76).[6] The people practised circumcision (which the Khoikhoi did not),[7] and they both cultivated millet and kept cattle. In the south the units under 'Ancosses' were small as opposed to the kingdoms of the north which were trading with the Portuguese.

How far does oral tradition fit with contemporary records? Genealogies of Nguni chiefs were collected before 1821,[8] and there have been a number of studies of genealogy and tradition since then.[9] The fact

[1] *Cape Times*, 14 March 1960. The area of the Transkei is 16,554 square miles. *Census, 1961*, gives a population of 1,387,682.
[2] Theal, *Records*, ii. 255, 306, 316; viii. 79, 83.
[3] G. Carter and J. van Reenen (eds.), *The Wreck of the Grosvenor*, VRS, 1927, pp. 59–65.
[4] G. Callaway, *A Shepherd of the Veld*, p. 28.
[5] Monica Wilson, *The People of the Nyasa-Tanganyika Corridor*, p. 5.
[6] Bryant, *Olden Times*, p. 12. [7] Schapera, *Khoisan*, p. 71.
[8] G. Thompson, Appendix I, containing John Brownlee's unpublished notes.
[9] Col. Maclean, *Compendium of Kaffir Laws and Customs*, pp. 10; 162–4; John Ayliff and Joseph Whiteside, *History of the Abambo*; C. Brownlee, *Reminiscences*; F. Brownlee, *The Transkeian Native Territories: Historical Records*; Bryant, *Zulu Dictionary*, *Olden Times*, and *Zulu People*; W. D. Cingo, *I-Bali labaTembu*; W. D. Hammond-Tooke, *The Tribes of Mount Frere District*, *The Tribes of Umtata District*, *The Tribes of Willowvale District*, and *The Tribes of King William's*

that it has been written down does not, of course, turn an oral tradition into documentary evidence comparable to the records of eye-witnesses such as those we have discussed, but it is useful to know *when* a tradition was first recorded. The earliest publications all refer to traditions of living within the area now occupied by Nguni peoples. The Xhosa and Mpondomise traditions speak of a river, the Dedesi, an upper tributary of the Mzimvubu, which is not identified today but which is said to have been in what is now Griqualand East, close to a pass into the Kahlamba mountains. There, they say, their earliest chiefs lived, and from there they moved down towards the mouth of the Mzimvubu.[1]

Theal says: 'The legends of all the tribes of importance now living south of the Zambesi river, none of which can be more than a few centuries old, point to a distant northern occupation.' And he continues: 'Those along the south-eastern coast are so closely related to each other in language and customs that they must have formed a community by themselves, or perhaps a single tribe, at no distant time, and as some of them are known to have crossed the Zambesi only a little more than three centuries ago, the others cannot have long preceded them.'[2] However, his only evidence for the dating of the crossing of the Zambezi appears to be the fact that 'a horde of barbarians' suddenly appeared and attacked the Portuguese at Tete and Sena in 1570; they laid the whole country waste, and some of them, turning northward, destroyed Kilwa and part of Mombasa, only being stopped at Malindi; in 1592 two sections of them 'remained on the northern bank of the lower Zambesi. One was called by the Portuguese the Mumbos, the other was the far-dreaded Mazimba.' So much is fact recorded in the Portuguese journals. But Theal makes a wild deduction. He writes: 'The Mumbos of the Portuguese are to a certainty the Abambo of more recent history'; '... A section of the Abambo must have directed its march towards the south some time between 1570 and 1590'; '... The Abambo at length reached the valley of the Tugela river, in what is now the colony of Natal, where they formed settlements.'[3] For all this there is not a shred of evidence. The only *facts* we have are that there were Mumbos on the north bank of the Zambezi in 1592, a kingdom Vambe in Natal in 1589, a great thief named Bambe a little way south of Lourenço Marques in 1593, and Emboas on the Natal coast in

Town District; R. T. Kawa, *I-Bali lama Mfengu*, Lovedale, 1929; Victor Poto Ndamase, *Ama-Mpondo, Ibali ne-Ntlalo*; A. Z. Ngani, *Ibali LamaGqunukwebe*; W. B. Rubusana, *Zemk'inkomo Magwalandini*; J. H. Soga, *South-Eastern Bantu*; T. B. Soga, *Intlalo ka Xosa*; Cape of Good Hope, *Report and Proceedings of the Government Commission on Native Laws and Customs*, 2 parts, Cape Town, G. 4–83, 1883 (hereafter *1883 Report*); Stow; J. Stuart and D. McK. Malcolm (eds.), *The Diary of Henry Francis Fynn* (hereafter Fynn); Van Warmelo, *Preliminary Survey*.

[1] *1883 Report*, ii. 403–7; Soga, *South-Eastern Bantu*, pp. 91–93, 109.
[2] G. M. Theal, *History and Ethnography of South Africa before 1795*, i. 55–56.
[3] Ibid. i. 352–9.

1686 (pp. 81, 84). No one can say whether or not the Mumbos had any connexion with the Vambe kingdom, the chief Bambe, or the Emboas.[1] Theal's speculation—for it was no more than that—was taken as assured fact by Walker and Soga,[2] and has provided a legendary basis for South African history ever since.

The single instance of a tradition of *recent* migration from the north that Theal can cite is that of the Mthethwa, who were said to have been driven over the Zambezi 'In the time of the father of Phunga, the grandfather of Dingiswayo', but there was no Phunga in the Mthethwa lineage and the famous bearer of that name was a brother of Shaka's great-great-grandfather, so Theal's informant was mistaken.[3]

As has already been shown, there were Xhosa-speaking people as far south as the Mthatha river in 1593, and there is no indication that they had only recently arrived there. By their own account Thembu and Xhosa (along with Mpondomise) were on the upper reaches of the Mzimvubu for generations before they came down to the coast. There were also Thembu and Xhosa in Natal, related to the Thembu and Xhosa of the Transkei,[4] and it is possible, though not certain, that the ancestors of all the Transkeian groups were in Natal before travelling southward. Bryant believes that the Nguni people were in the valley of the Vaal (where the Sotho are known to have been) before they travelled eastward to cross the Drakensberg,[5] and his arguments are much more cogent than Theal's mumbo-jumbo.

Bryant, however, makes one unwarranted assumption. He is prepared to assume,[6] without any corroborative evidence, that a people moved in the time of the first ancestor mentioned, and that the period they have occupied their country may be calculated from the number of generations mentioned in the genealogy. This is very doubtful. Where the founding ancestor of a lineage was indeed a Moses who brought his people to a new country the fact is long remembered, as it is by people in Central Africa today, who name the heroes who brought them to their present countries not less than three hundred years ago, and probably before that.[7] The Xhosa genealogies recorded in 1840 and 1858 give twelve and sixteen generations; that of the Mpondomise gives seventeen, and that of the Thembu nineteen generations, yet none of the chiefs named is mentioned as having brought them to the

[1] Junod, 'Condition of the Natives', p. 150 n.; G. M. Theal, *Ethnography and Condition of South Africa before A.D. 1505*, pp. 193–5.
[2] E. Walker, *Historical Atlas of South Africa*, p. 6; Soga, *South-Eastern Bantu*, pp. 49–58.
[3] Bryant, *Olden Times*, pp. 35, 85.
[4] Ibid., pp. 241 ff.; Soga, *South-Eastern Bantu*, p. 84; Bennie, p. 38.
[5] Ellenberger and Macgregor, pp. 17, 18; J. Walton, *African Village*, pp. 25–26; Bryant, *Zulu People*, pp. 3–10, 19–20.
[6] Ibid., p. 22.
[7] Monica Wilson, *Communal Rituals of the Nyakyusa*, pp. 1–16, 80–99, Genealogies.

TABLE II
XHOSA GENEALOGY

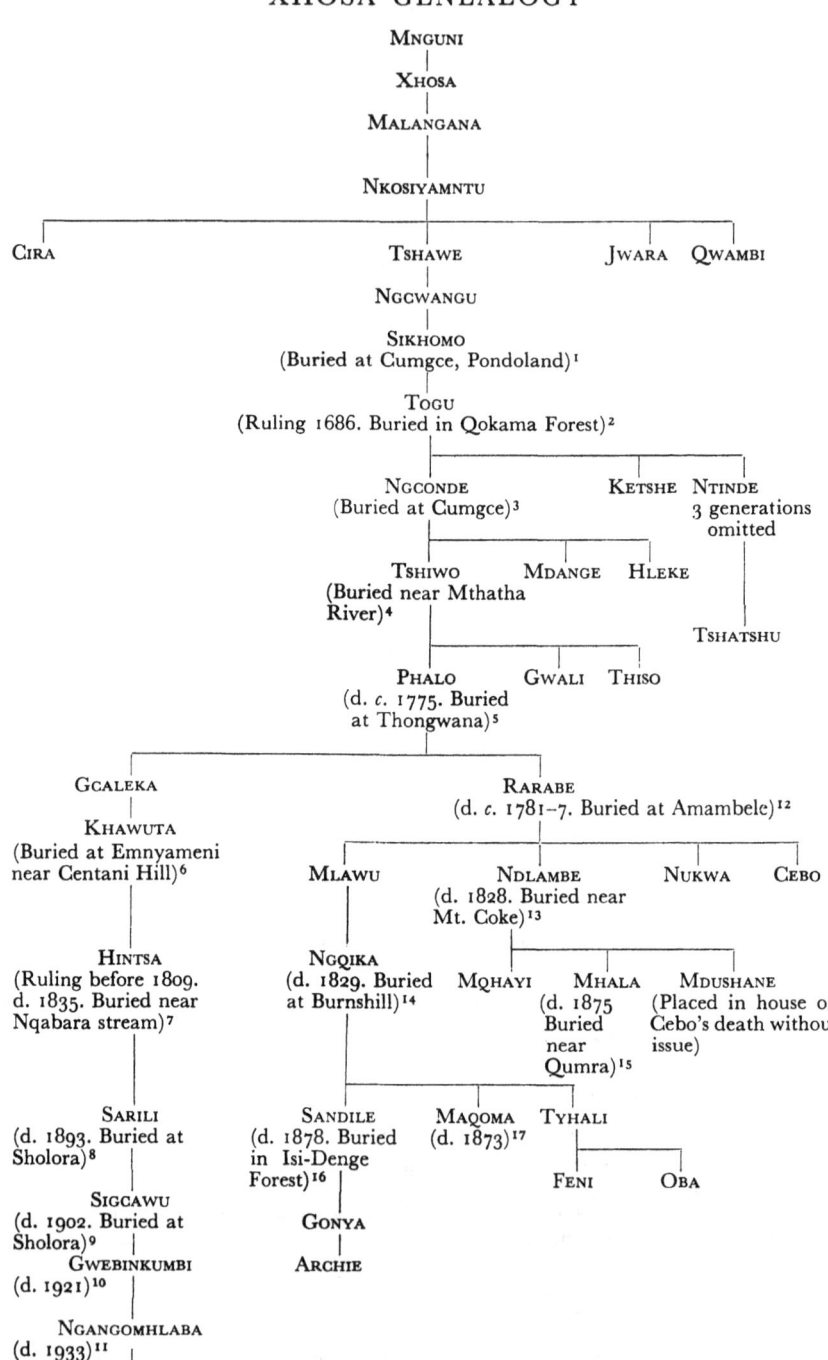

Dedesi.¹ Furthermore, anthropological investigations during the past twenty years have shown that there is a marked tendency towards the telescoping of genealogies.² Preliterate peoples tend to remember the names of only the more important figures among their earlier ancestors so that a genealogy often covers a much longer period than is indicated by the number of generations.

A useful check on the average length of a chief's reign is available from the Xhosa genealogy. Togu was alive in 1686. Let us suppose that he died before 1690. His seventh successor, Sarili (Kreli), died in 1893 (see p. 88). Seven chiefs in 203 years gives twenty-nine years to a reign. It should be noted that this dating is taken from the more recent names in the Xhosa genealogy, and that the telescoping commonly occurs in the *early* generations. Occasionally a chief might rule for over forty years, as, for example, Faku of the Mpondo, who was already chief in 1824 and probably some years earlier, and who only died 'at the age of ninety years' in 1867.³ Bryant postulates eighteen years to a reign but thirty to a generation, and these can be reconciled only by juggling with the figures.⁴ He has, however, demonstrated that the number of names cited as successors in the genealogy of Zulu chiefs varied considerably, and therefore dating from a genealogy alone is precarious.⁵

¹ Maclean, p. 162; W. C. Holden, *The Past, Present and Future of the Kaffir Races*, p. 143.
² E. Peters, 'The Proliferation of Segments in the Lineage of the Bedouin in Cyrenaica', *JRAI*, 90 (1960), 29–53.
³ Fynn, pp. 63–64, 110–14; Bryant, *Olden Times*, p. 258; Blue Book on *Native Affairs, 1885*, quoted Brownlee, *Historical Records*, p. 73.
⁴ Bryant, *Olden Times*, p. 35. Malandela must have lived to 94, and his father to 106, and an elder brother to 97, if Bryant's rules are followed.
⁵ Ibid., pp. 32–33.

REFERENCES TO XHOSA GENEALOGY

¹ J. H. Soga, *The South-Eastern Bantu*, Johannesburg, 1930, p. 102.
² Ibid., p. 102.   ³ Ibid., p. 111.   ⁴ Ibid., p. 114.
⁵ Ibid., p. 125. W. D. Hammond-Tooke, *Tribes of Willowvale*, Pretoria, 1956–7, p. 34.
⁶ G. M. Theal, *History and Ethnography of Southern Africa before 1795*, 4th ed., 1927, iii. 156.
⁷ D. Moodie, *The Record*, Cape Town, 1838, v. 40; Soga, p. 179; Theal, *History of South Africa, 1795–1872*, 4th ed., ii. 112–15; Hammond-Tooke, *Tribes of Willowvale*, p. 40.
⁸ Hammond-Tooke, *Tribes of Willowvale*, p. 46; *Cape Times*, 7 Feb. 1893; E. Rosenthal, *Encyclopedia of Southern Africa*.
⁹ Hammond-Tooke, *Tribes of Willowvale*, p. 47.
¹⁰ Ibid., p. 15.
¹¹ Ibid.
¹² Soga, p. 128; Theal, *History and Ethnography before 1795*, iii. 155.
¹³ Theal, *History of South Africa, 1795–1872*, ii. 50.
¹⁴ Soga, p. 153; Theal, *History of South Africa, 1795–1872*, ii. 51.
¹⁵ Hammond-Tooke, *Tribes of King William's Town*, Pretoria, 1958, p. 26.
¹⁶ Soga, p. 219; Theal, *History of South Africa, 1872–84*, London, 1919, i. 130–1.
¹⁷ Soga, p. 177; Theal, *History of South Africa, 1872–84*, i. 28. For whole genealogy cf. S. E. K. Mqhayi, *Ityala Lamawele*, Lovedale, 1914.

Oral tradition is concerned mainly with the genealogies of clans and location of particular chiefdoms, the details of which are not relevant to this study, but to define the distribution of the Nguni in time and space it is necessary to discuss the genealogies of one or two clans and the whereabouts of particular chiefdoms. The most certain evidence on their position comes from the sites of chiefs' graves. These are remembered for a very long time.

The Zulu founding ancestor, Malandela, probably six generations before Shaka, lived and perhaps was buried on Babanango hill. When his ancestors occupied Babanango, or whence they came, no one yet knows. The only clue is a cryptic reference to their having come down 'on account of the grain-basket, following behind the grasshoppers'.[1] Malandela or his sons moved down the Mhlatuze valley towards the coast, and his younger son, Zulu, together with the later Zulu chiefs, is buried in the Mfule valley, about sixty miles inland: his senior son, Qwabe, and Qwabe's descendants settled thirty miles nearer the coast.[2] Shaka died in 1828 and Bryant dates Malandela's movement to the mid seventeenth century, but either other Nguni speakers preceded them, or they moved at least a century earlier, because the survivors of the *São Bento* in 1554 found the country north of the Mzimkhulu 'thickly populated and provided with cattle' (p. 79).

The Dlamini people, who now are the dominant lineage in Swaziland, once lived in the region about Delagoa Bay. The chief, Ngwane II, built on the north bank of the Pongolo river. 'Here he died, and annual pilgrimages have ever since been made to the cave in the tree-covered hill where he and later kings lie buried in state.'[3] He is seven generations before the Swazi chief, Sobuza, who, in 1966, is still ruling, but twenty-two generations before Ngwane are listed. From this lineage also came the Ndwandwe, Mkize, Gumede, and Bomvana.[4]

Another cluster of related chiefdoms, the Hlubi, Bhele, Zizi, and Tolo, occupied, in the eighteenth century, the country from the upper Tukela westward, along the foothills of the Drakensberg.[5] They, like the Dlamini, were *tekela* speakers, and Kuper and Bryant link them,[6] but Soga does not: he classifies the Hlubi as Lala.[7] Chief Poto carefully notes that it is not known whether Dlamini the Swazi ancestor is the same as Dlamini a Hlubi ancestor.[8] The Hlubi genealogies are long,

---

[1] Bryant, *Zulu People*, pp. 20–21.
[2] Bryant, *Olden Times*, pp. 17–29.
[3] H. Kuper, *An African Aristocracy*, p. 12.
[4] Bryant, *Olden Times*, pp. 312–19; Soga, *South-Eastern Bantu*, p. 360.
[5] *1883 Report*, ii. Sketch Map of Natal before 1812, after Sir Theophilus Shepstone.
[6] Kuper, p. 12; Bryant, *Olden Times*, p. 147.
[7] Soga, *South-Eastern Bantu*, p. 78.
[8] Ndamase, p. 7.

and it might yet be possible to disentangle their movements and connexions if the graves of their chiefs could be located.[1]
Of the Mpondo chiefs, Faku's great-grandfather, Tahle, and five of Tahle's predecessors were buried in what is now eastern Pondoland, between the Mzimvubu and the Mtamvuna; Ncindise (nine generations from Faku) south of the Mzimkhulu; and his father Msiza on the Tukela.

TABLE III
ZULU GENEALOGY

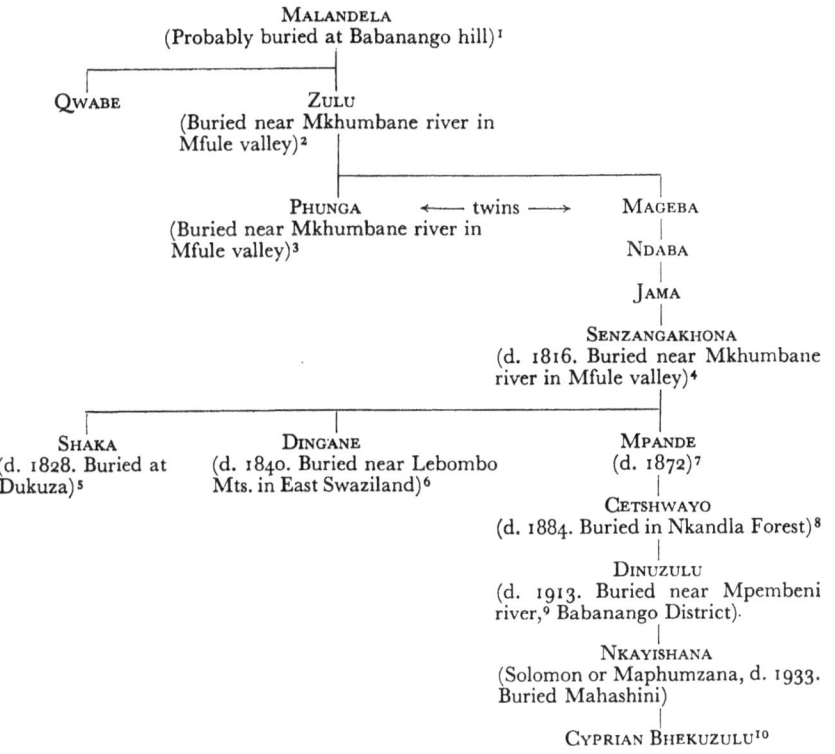

REFERENCES TO ZULU GENEALOGY

[1] A. T. Bryant, *Olden Times in Zululand and Natal*, London, 1929, p. 17.
[2] Ibid., p. 21. [3] Ibid., p. 20. [4] Ibid., pp. 20, 35.
[5] Ibid., pp. 35, 666. [6] Ibid., pp. 35, 325.
[7] Ibid., p. 35; G. M. Theal, *History of South Africa, 1795–1872*, 3rd ed. London, 1919, iv. 178.
[8] Bryant, pp. 35, 681. [9] Ibid., p. 35.
[10] I am much indebted to Chief Gatsha Buthelezi and his mother Princess Magogo, daughter of Dinuzulu and full sister of Solomon, for checking this genealogy and providing additional information.

---

[1] G. W. Stow, 'Intrusion of the Stronger Races', Unpublished MS. Grey Collection, S.A. Public Library, Cape Town.

TABLE IV
MPONDO GENEALOGY

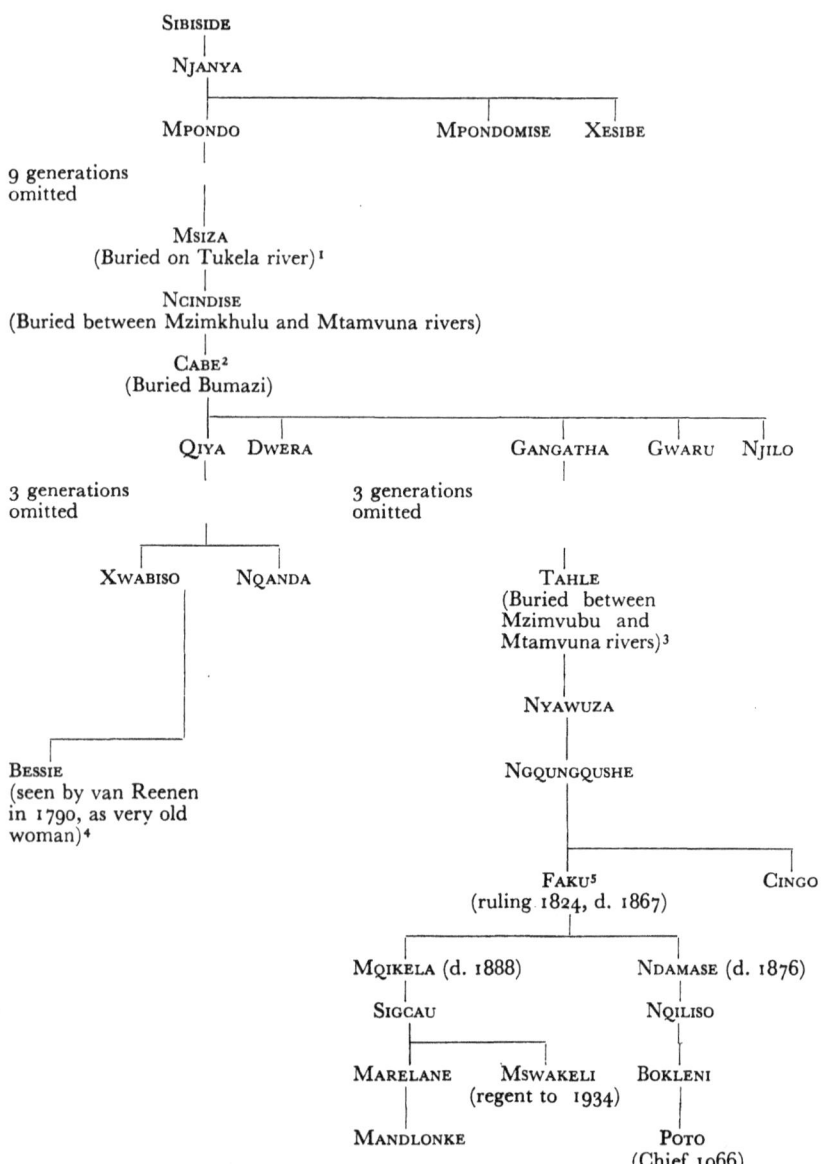

[1] V. Poto Ndamase, *AmaMpondo, Ibali ne-Ntlalo*, Lovedale, n.d., cf. M. Hunter, *Reaction to Conquest*, London, 1936, pp. 397–9.
[2] Ndamase, p. 1. [3] Ibid.
[4] J. van Reenen, Journal in *Wreck of the Grosvenor*, ed. C. Graham Botha, Cape Town, 1927, p. 160; *Diary of Henry Francis Fynn*, ed. J. Stewart and D. McK. Malcolm, Pietermaritzburg, 1960, pp. 110–14. J. H. Soga, *South Eastern Bantu*, p. 379.
[5] F. Brownlee, *The Transkeian Native Territories: Historical Records*, p. 73.

DEMARCATION AND DISTRIBUTION

Msiza is said to have come south from Swaziland on a hunting expedition. Faku died in 1867, as already noted. In 1790 Bessie, a descendant of Msiza in the eighth generation,[1] was seen by van Reenen. She was then an old woman (see p. 233). It is likely, therefore, that Msiza came south *no later* than the mid sixteenth century, and perhaps earlier.[2] The connexion of the Mpondo with the Swazi is remembered also by the Swazi,[3] and there is every reason to accept the traditions regarding the places of burial. The Dlamini, with whom the Mpondo are thus linked, speak a *tekela* dialect (see p. 76) and the Mpondo do not, but there is ample evidence from the nineteenth century to show that speech changed fast when groups moved and mingled with others. Common lineage does not guarantee cultural identity, nor does cultural identity necessitate common origin.

The graves of the early Mpondomise chiefs were at the sources of the Mzimvubu; later chiefs were buried at Latana, near Shawbury, and in the Tina river.[4] But the survivors of the *Stavenisse* referred to 'Mapontemousse' north of the 'Mpontes' on the coast. Mpondo tradition claims that Mpondomise was a twin of Mpondo, and both groups recognize descent from Njanya,[5] so it is possible that they moved southward together. The Mpondomise, like the Mpondo, speak Xhosa and not a *tekela* dialect of Nguni.

Oral tradition, recorded before 1821, asserts that the Xhosa chief Togu, whose name was mentioned by the survivors of the *Stavenisse* in 1686, settled on the Kei, and that his two sons, Ntinde and Ketshe, lived between the Buffalo and Chalumna. 'At that period the Gonaqua [Khoikhoi] . . . had their chief kraals on the coast; but likewise inhabited the country along the Buffalo river, and up to the very sources of the Keiskamma.'[6] This fits exactly with a statement of the *Stavenisse* survivors that there were Khoikhoi (Makrigqas) east of the Xhosa on the Buffalo. Another tradition asserts that Togu was buried further east, in the Qokama forest in Ngqeleni district, about twenty miles from the sea.[7] Togu's senior son was buried on the bank of the Ngwanguba, a stream flowing into the Mthatha,[8] and his grandson Tshiwo died on a hunting expedition 'far to the westward'.[9] It is Togu's father, Sikhomo, who is said to have led the Xhosa from the Dedesi to the sea.[10]

[1] Ndamase, p. 143; Monica Hunter, *Reaction to Conquest*, pp. 396–400.
[2] Soga, *Intlalo ka Xosa*, p. 63.
[3] Bryant, *Olden Times*, p. 314. Soga and Bryant class the Mpondo as *abaMbo* but the Mpondo proper distinguish themselves sharply from certain clans of Eastern Pondoland and Southern Natal whom they call *abaMbo*. Hunter, pp. 58, 380.
[4] *1883 Report*, ii. 403–7.
[5] Ndamase, p. 1; Soga, *South-Eastern Bantu*, pp. 229, 334; Hunter, p. 398.
[6] Thompson, p. 440.   [7] Soga, *South-Eastern Bantu*, pp. 102, 111.
[8] Theal, *History and Ethnography*, iii. 77.   [9] Ibid., p. 78.
[10] Soga, *South-Eastern Bantu*, p. 109.

TABLE V

THEMBU GENEALOGY[1]

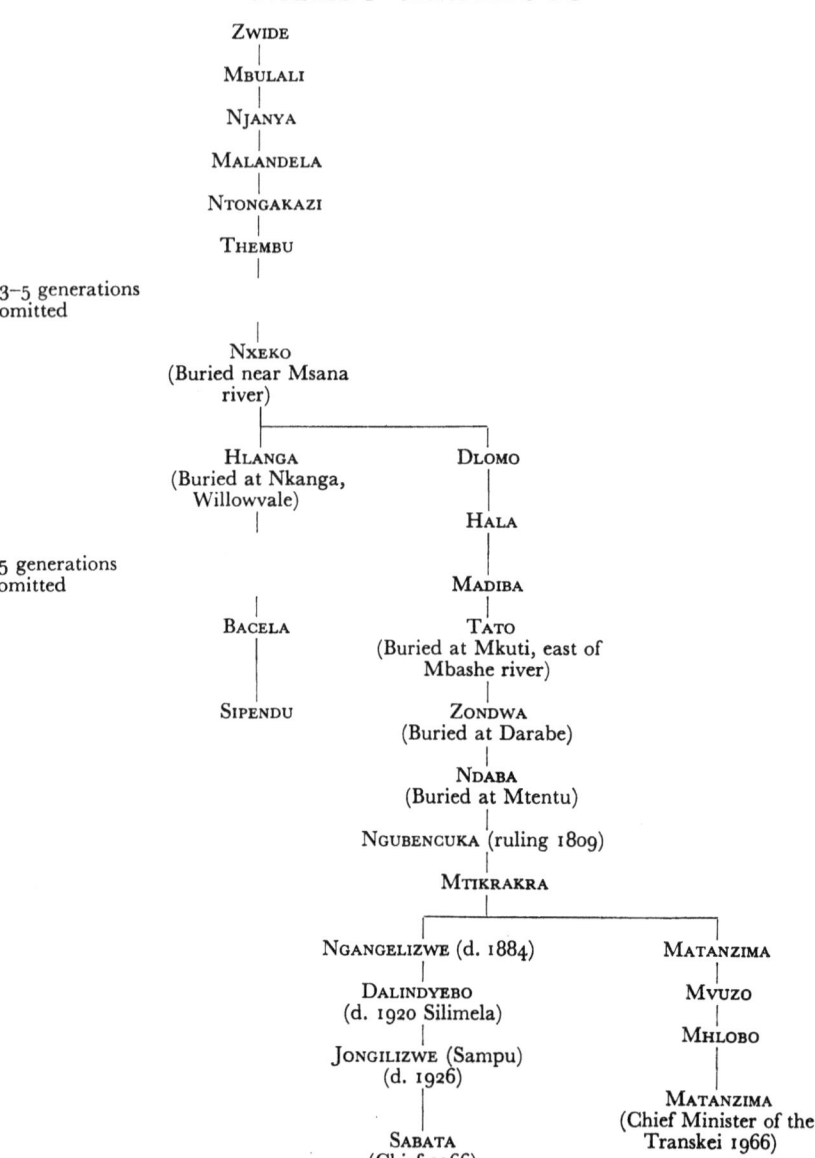

[1] Maclean, *Compendium of Kafir Laws and Customs*, Cape Town, 1866. (Genealogy recorded, 1858), p. 165; J. H. Soga, *The South-Eastern Bantu*, Johannesburg, 1930, p. 466; Archie Mafeje, *Leadership in the Transkei*, unpublished M.A. thesis, University of Cape Town, 1963, p. 51.

There is not agreement as to the order before Nxeko, but most of the same names recur in the lists given by the authors cited.

Njanya occurs in the Mpondo genealogy, Malandela in the Zulu, but connexions are quite uncertain.

DEMARCATION AND DISTRIBUTION

A Thembu chief, Nxeko (Nxego, or Xekwa), before whom the Thembu lineage lists nine chiefs, and after whom there were nine chiefs before 1868 (the last being a minor),[1] was buried on the Msana, a tributary of the Mbashe, and there his sons Hlanga and Dlomo fought for the chieftainship. If thirty years are allowed to a chieftainship Nxeko died before 1620, and the Luspance who welcomed the survivors of the *Santo Alberto* near the mouth of the Mbashe in 1593 may well have been a Thembu. Nxeko's son, Hlanga, was buried at Nkanga (in the modern Willowvale district) and later chiefs on the Mbashe and in the modern Mqanduli district.[2] The Thembu were said to be the senior Nguni line.[3]

According to tradition, chiefdoms and clans known today already existed in the sixteenth century, and were fighting and intermarrying. It is remembered that Tshawe, reputed to be the great-grandfather of Togu (the Xhosa chief ruling in 1686), was given help in battle by the Mpondomise, and that Jwara, the half-brother of Tshawe, took refuge with his mother's people, the Bhele.[4] According to Mpondomise tradition they were together with the Thembu and Xhosa on the Dedesi.

The Mpondo moved slowly westward during three hundred years (1550–1850), and the Xhosa, Thembu, and Mpondomise did so also but in a piecemeal fashion and not consistently, for a chief who had moved westward as a young man might move east again as he grew older, as Rarabe, the Xhosa chief, did after 1770;[5] or his son might settle where his grandfather had been, as Majola, the Mpondomise chief, did. Moreover, a great chief had many homesteads, often far apart: the Mpondomise chief Ncwini (twelve generations back in 1858) is said to have had homesteads on the Mzimvubu, the Kinira, the Tina, the Tsitsa, and the Mthatha.[6]

2. *Relations with Other Groups*

The Nguni have been defined in terms of language, and this is what primarily distinguishes them from the Tsonga on their north-eastern border and the Sotho to the north and northwest. For the language differences to have emerged there must have been both a period of isolation of Nguni from Sotho and Tsonga (as well as Sotho and Tsonga from each other) and different contacts. Evidence from elsewhere suggests that in isolation a language may change little during centuries,

---

[1] Maclean, Genealogy opposite p. 164; cf. Stanford Papers, Jagger Library, University of Cape Town, F(g) 12.
[2] Soga, *South-Eastern Bantu*, pp. 468–70.
[3] Holden, pp. 142–3; Stow, Unpublished MS.
[4] Soga, *South-Eastern Bantu*, pp. 106–8.
[5] Theal, *History and Ethnography*, iii. 90.   [6] *1883 Report*, ii. 403–4.

but once the speakers are mixing with other people it changes fast.[1] We know that one of the divergent influences on Nguni was Khoikhoi (see pp. 103–5).

Matching the cleavages in language there are also marked differences in the kinship systems of Nguni on the one hand and Sotho and Tsonga on the other. Every Nguni child is born into a patrilineal clan and marriage within the clan is a heinous offence, whereas the Sotho and Tsonga observe no such rule and the preferred form of marriage is with a cousin. Differences in their kinship systems are linked with differences in economy. The Nguni clan system interlocks with the ownership of cattle and begins to crumble when men no longer depend upon inherited herds; whereas the descent groups among the Sotho are associated with wild animals[2] and suggest a greater dependence upon hunting. The preoccupation of the Nguni with cattle, and greater dependence of the Sotho and Tsonga on game and crops, is reflected also in the rituals. The reasons for divergence in kinship systems are still very obscure and links with economy have yet to be conclusively demonstrated, but it is along these lines that anthropologists look for explanations.

Nguni are sharply demarcated from Tsonga,[3] as well as Khoikhoi and San, by the fact that they avoid fish,[4] whereas the Tsonga, Khoikhoi, and San[5] relish it. Food taboos commonly express social cleavages: in Europe frog-eaters are distinguished from non-frog-eaters; those who relish horse-flesh or pork from those who abstain; and on the Witwatersrand migrants discussing other language groups speak particularly of peculiar tastes in food.[6] It is reasonable to suppose the Nguni maintained the fish taboo (however it may have originated) partly to *distinguish* themselves from other groups.[7] The taboo applied most stringently to chiefs and other persons of consequence; it was ignored sometimes by the poor living along the coast, who collected shell-fish, or speared fish found in rock pools;[8] but there was no exploitation by

---

[1] e.g. 'Icelanders today speak almost exactly the same language as they spoke in the early Middle Ages 700 or 800 years ago. The language of the Sagas is the language of the present-day farmer and shopkeeper, of children at play and a boy and girl courting.' (P. D. Smith, *The Listener*, 24 September 1964, p. 460).

[2] I. Schapera, *A Handbook of Tswana Law and Custom*, p. 6.

[3] H. A. Junod, *The Life of a South African Tribe*, ii. 84–89.

[4] Lichtenstein, i. 335; P. A. W. Cook, *Social Organization and Ceremonial Institutions of the Bomvana*, p. 162.

[5] Schapera, *Khoisan*, pp. 137–8, 304.   [6] A. Mafeje, personal communication.

[7] Certain pastoral people in East and Central Africa, notably the Somali and Tutsi, to whom fish was accessible, also kept this taboo. (F. J. Simoons, *Eat Not This Flesh*, p. 113; J. Roscoe, *Immigrants and their Influence on the Lake Region of Central Africa*; J. J. Maquet, *Le Système des relations sociales dans le Ruanda ancien*, p. 27.) Nguni living in cities are now fast abandoning it. (M. Wilson and A. Mafeje, *Langa*, p. 24.)

[8] Hunter, p. 96.

the Nguni generally of the enormous resources in fish of the coast and rivers on which other groups had feasted on the south-eastern coast and even some way inland, as we know from the middens remaining. It is likely that the midden people were Khoikhoi or San and that at least some of those Xhosa speakers who relish shell-fish are their descendants who have been absorbed by the Xhosa.[1]

Although Nguni, Tsonga, and Sotho must once have lived apart for their languages to develop so differently, they nevertheless have interacted and influenced one another during the last two centuries or more. According to tradition, the country draining into the Usutu river (now Swaziland) was occupied by Sotho-speaking groups who were conquered and absorbed five generations ago by the Nguni-speaking Dlamini. The Dlamini entered from Lourenço Marques, and some of the Sotho escaped their lordship by moving northward into what is now the Transvaal.[2] Tsonga impinged on Nguni in the neighbourhood of Lake Kosi, and the influence of both is apparent in the *tekela* dialect of Nguni (see p. 76). It is apparent also in Swazi law, which permits the marriage of cross-cousins,[3] which is anathema to Xhosa or Zulu, and in the ancient law of those descendants of the Dlamini or Lala (the Bhele, Zizi, Tolo, and Hlubi) who later fled south to take refuge with the Xhosa, who are less rigorous than the Xhosa in prohibiting marriage into the mother's clan.[4] And it seems likely that the rite of circumcision was learnt by Nguni from Sotho, because the lodge is still known as *isutu* and the first boy circumcised is called *usoSotho*.[5]

Nguni groups have been absorbed by the Sotho and Sotho by Nguni, as movement back and forth along their common frontier—the Drakensberg—has occurred through centuries;[6] other groups which crossed the range retained their language and cultural identity. As yet we know very little about *why* some were absorbed and others were not, though this is a question fundamental to any understanding of social change in Africa.

The most conspicuous fact about Nguni history, as opposed to the history of most other groups in South Africa, is the *absence* of clear links

---

[1] J. Hewitt, 'Notes relating to aboriginal Tribes of the Cape Province', *SAJS* (1915), 306–7. In 1622 the survivors from the *São João Baptista* found a fishgarth and traps in a river, probably east of the Kei. It is possible, but not certain, that the fishermen spoke a Bantu language. In 1686 there was a Khoikhoi group *east* of the Xhosa, see p. 84 (C. R. Boxer, ed., *The Tragic History of the Sea, 1589–1622*, p. 208).

[2] Kuper, *African Aristocracy*, pp. 11–14.

[3] H. Kuper, 'Kinship among the Swazi', in *African Systems of Kinship and Marriage* (ed. A. R. Radcliffe-Brown and D. Forde), p. 104.

[4] M. Wilson et al., *Social Structure*, vol. iii of *Keiskammahoek Rural Survey*, p. 77.

[5] Ibid., p. 215.

[6] Bryant, *Olden Times*, pp. 311–12; Ellenberger and Macgregor, pp. 19, 21–30, 44–48; P.-L. Breutz, *The Tribes of Rustenburg and Pilansberg Districts*.

in language or tradition with any group further north other than those which split from the Nguni south of the Drakensberg and travelled *northward*. The Sotho, Venda, and even the Tsonga fit into an ancient pattern of relationships between the Limpopo and the Zambezi: the Nguni do not. Their only demonstrable connexions are with Koni, Ndebele, and Ngoni, who came from the south. The Transvaal Koni are thought to have moved northward from Swaziland in the seventeenth century, and they now speak Sotho,[1] but two groups of Ndebele in the Transvaal, also ancient offshoots of the main Nguni stock, and long surrounded by Sotho, still speak an Nguni dialect. According to oral tradition the founding hero of the southern Ndebele group, Msi or Musi, the third in a list of twenty-eight successive chiefs, lived just north of where Pretoria now stands. One tradition refers to his father having lived on the Tukela: others speak of the Mzimvubu and the Orange. What is certain is that the Ndebele have long lived between the Vaal and the Limpopo, and that their linguistic and cultural affiliations are with the Ntungwa—Xhosa and Zulu proper.[2]

A third group of Ndebele—and the name derives from a Sotho term for Nguni people[3]—crossed the Drakensberg only in 1823. They were led by a Zulu headman, Mzilikazi, of the Kumalo clan, and numbered between two and three hundred warriors.[4] Small fugitive bands of Zulu joined them, and in the Transvaal they raided numerous Sotho villages 'capturing their women, impressing their young men into his [Mzilikazi's] own service . . .'.[5] Pursued by Shaka, Mzilikazi laid waste the country behind him, and this scorched earth policy continued to characterize Ndebele movements.[6] In 1829 he was visited by the missionary, Robert Moffat, on the upper Apies river near where Pretoria now stands,[7] and in 1838, after clashing with the Voortrekkers, he crossed the Limpopo and built his great place, Bulawayo. The number of Mzilikazi's followers increased as he travelled. Moffat refers to 1,400 warriors at the capital in 1829, and 'thousands dancing'.[8] By 1836 there is reference to 5,000 warriors.[9] The Ndebele still (1966) speak a dialect of Zulu and use Zulu books in the senior classes of their schools,

---

[1] N. J. van Warmelo, *The Bakoni of Maake, The Bakoni of Mametsa, passim*; J. D. Krige, 'Traditional Origins and Tribal Relationships of the Northern Transvaal', *BS*, 2 (1937), 346–50.

[2] H. C. M. Fourie, *Amandebele van Fene Mahlangu*, pp. 30–31; N. J. van Warmelo, *Transvaal Ndebele Texts, passim*; van Warmelo, *The Ndebele of J. Kekana*; van Warmelo, *Preliminary Survey*, pp. 87–89.

[3] Van Warmelo, *Preliminary Survey*, p. 87.   [4] Bryant, *Olden Times*, p. 423.
[5] Ibid., p. 423.   [6] Bryant, *Zulu Dictionary*, p. 52.
[7] R. Moffat, *The Matebele Journals of Robert Moffat*, i. 13.
[8] Ibid. i. 13, 21.
[9] W. C. Harris, *The Wild Sports of Southern Africa*, p. 92; D. J. Kotzé (ed.), *Letters of the American Missionaries*, VRS, 1950, p. 166.

RELATIONS WITH OTHER GROUPS 99

though some are now writing a language which reflects the modifications in speech which have resulted from the close association with Sotho and Shona.

Other parties of Nguni warriors had fled, like Mzilikazi, from Zululand. One, under Zwangendaba of the Jele clan, and another under Nqaba[1] or Nxaba[2] of the Kumalo clan became known as Ngoni. There are differing accounts of the relationship between these parties,[3] but it is likely that, after raiding and fighting over a great area in Mozambique, the Transvaal, and north of the Limpopo, they reached the Zambezi independently, the one under Zwangendaba crossing near Zumbo on 20 November 1835 (there was an eclipse of the sun that day)[4] and the other destroyed by the Kololo near Senanga.[5] Zwangendaba's Ngoni travelled up through Malawi, some of them eventually reaching Lake Tanganyika and approaching Victoria. Burton heard much of them in Unyanyembe and Ujiji in 1858.[6] Nqaba's party, now under Ngwana, travelled on the east of Lake Malawi towards Songea.[7]

Like the Ndebele, the Ngoni absorbed women from the conquered groups as wives, and young men as warriors. Social position depended largely on descent and knowledge of Zulu. A distinction was made between those clans which were true Swazi (for the Ngoni stress that their origin was Swazi rather than Zulu), those which originated before crossing the Zambezi, and those which emerged later in the journey up to Lake Victoria.[8] Zulu was still in common use in 1878 when missionaries arrived among the Ngoni living to the west of Lake Malawi, around Ekwendeni. With the missionaries was William Koyi, a Xhosa from Lovedale on the eastern frontier. He could converse freely with the Ngoni,[9] and education began in Zulu,[10] but by 1935 Zulu was not spoken as a home language except by a very limited group,[11] and it was not taught in any of the schools attended by Ngoni children. The languages of the people among whom the Ngoni had settled—Tumbuka, Cewa, Ndendenule—had absorbed that of their conquerors.[12]

[1] Bryant, *Zulu Dictionary*, p. 53*.   [2] Bryant, *Olden Times*, p. 454.
[3] Ibid., pp. 454, 458–72; J. Barnes, *Politics in a Changing Society*, p. 18.
[4] Ibid., pp. 3, 16.   [5] Bryant, *Olden Times*, p. 471.
[6] R. F. Burton, *The Lake Regions of Central Africa*, ii. 76, 156.
[7] M. Read, *The Ngoni of Nyasaland*, p. 9.   [8] Ibid., pp. 4–5.
[9] W. A. Elmslie, *Among the Wild Ngoni*, pp. 191 ff.; Robert Laws, *Reminiscences of Livingstonia*, p. 73.
[10] D. Frazer, *Winning a Primitive People*, p. 30: 'Although the proportion of men and women who had come from south of the Zambesi, or were their descendants, was very slight, the language used on all public occasions, and indeed generally in village life, was Chingoni, a slightly modified Zulu. It was this language the missionaries spoke, and in it all the education was conducted.' This apparently refers to the early years of the mission. Frazer himself went to Ekwendeni in 1897.   [11] Read, *The Ngoni*, p. 22.
[12] For this reason no Ngoni are included among Nguni speakers on p. 76.

Yet another Nguni offshoot was that established by Soshangane of the Gaza house of the Ndwandwe. He had fled from Shaka's tyranny in 1820 or 1821, a little earlier than Mzilikazi, with a party 'probably not more than a hundred strong',[1] and he raided through Mozambique as far as the Savi river. Soshangane established himself as overlord of the Tsonga, and his sons succeeded him, breaking up his Gaza kingdom, but though Soshangane and his followers left their mark on the Tsonga language, they never taught the Tsonga to speak Zulu.

This account of the dispersal of Nguni people anticipates events described more fully later in their chronological context, but reference to the nineteenth-century movements has been necessary here in order to define the boundaries of the Nguni in space and time, to show that Nguni-speaking groups north of the Drakensberg indeed came from south of the mountains, and to demonstrate certain historical possibilities. In peering into the distant Nguni past we may be guided by what is known to have happened within historical times. One outstanding fact is the enormous area over which Nguni people dispersed within thirty-five years. People with the same clan, praise, or family names scattered from Natal, reaching the Fish river in the south and Lake Victoria in the north. These are over 2,000 miles apart, as the crow flies. The similarity in the names of the refugees from Natal who settled on the eastern Cape frontier in 1835, and of the Ngoni of Malawi and Tanzania, is conspicuous: Nguni (or Ngoni) is a praise name still used by a lineage in the Tyhume valley; Jele, the clan name of the Ngoni leader Zwangendaba,[2] is also the praise (in the form Jili) of the famous Jabavu family, long linked with Fort Hare; and the names Mzimba and Mbeya, townships in Malawi and Tanzania in the areas once dominated by Ngoni, are familiar family names on the Tyhume.

This rapid dispersal involved not only warriors but also women and children. Bryant described 'the armed warriors going on ahead, the women bearing the household goods and the boys driving the cattle behind'[3] as Mzilikazi moved into the Transvaal, and Moffat describes beer coming from Mzilikazi's mother[4] when he visited Mzilikazi near where Pretoria now stands. Some Ngoni used pack and riding oxen: Burton (quoting Arabs) described them south of Lake Victoria in 1858:

> They wander from place to place camping under trees, over which they throw their mats, and driving their herds and plundered cattle into the most fertile pasture-grounds. . . . On their forays they move in large bodies, women as well as men, with the children and baggage placed on bullocks, and their wealth in brass wire twisted round the horns.[5]

---

[1] Bryant, *Olden Times*, p. 448.
[2] Ibid., p. 278. Bryant notes that the Jele are an offshoot of the Tolo.
[3] Bryant, *Zulu Dictionary*, p. 52*. [4] Moffat, i. 86. [5] Burton, ii. 77.

But the Ndebele appear to have carried their own luggage. Moffat remarked that 'the Matebele never ride their oxen nor even pack them, like other nations'.[1] The Tshangane and Ngoni raided along the Mozambique coast and up the Limpopo valley, and the Ngoni crossed the Zambezi, so all the parties are likely to have passed through tsetse areas, but they remained cattle people, acquiring new herds if they lost their own. Their essential habit of life as pastoralists survived.

As has already been noted, the migrants also took their language with them, and in Rhodesia it survived, whereas in Malawi, Tanzania, and Mozambique it did not. It is apparent from the history of various groups in Africa that children commonly learn the language of their mothers, and the mother tongue prevails, but how the Ndebele, who absorbed many Sotho and Shona women, as well as incorporating Sotho and Shona men in their regiments, succeeded in establishing a form of Zulu as their language, when the Ngoni and Tshangane failed to do so, is not certain. Two factors were important: the proportion of Zulu-speaking mothers, and the status of the foreign women incorporated. We lack any precise figures on the proportions of Nguni and foreign stock in the three groups, but the Ndebele under Mzilikazi were a larger group to start with than the followers of Shoshangane, or those of Zwangendaba and Nxaba (see above, pp. 98–100), and climate was in their favour. The Ndebele occupied healthy highlands and did not suffer the ravages of malaria and dysentery in the manner which decimated the followers of Shoshangane (and a Zulu army) in Mozambique,[2] and the Ngoni in parts of Malawi and Tanzania. So the proportion of Nguni-speakers who survived, and the fertility of Nguni women, were probably greater. According to Livingstone[3] malaria reduced the fertility of Kololo (Sotho) women on the Zambezi. Secondly, Nguni continued to be spoken in the Transvaal when Sotho women were taken as concubines, but not when they had the full status of wives,[4] and Mzilikazi's army incorporated Sotho and Shona women as war captives rather than wives for whom marriage cattle were given.

Nowhere did the migrants find unoccupied country, but they established themselves as rulers (Ndebele, Ngoni, Tshangane) or as subordinates of other Nguni or Sotho groups (Bhele, Zizi, Tolo, Hlubi) forming more or less stratified chiefdoms in which status was related to origin. After a hundred years the migrants still have detailed traditions of their journeyings. These are most lively and explicit where the strangers established themselves as rulers, as among the Ngoni, and the traditions

---

[1] Moffat, i. 30.
[2] Bryant, *Olden Times*, p. 452.
[3] D. Livingstone, *Missionary Travels and Researches*, p. 162.
[4] B. H. Dicke, 'The Northern Transvaal Voortrekkers', *AYB*, 1941, i. 102–4.

are the charter for high status,[1] but they are still alive even among those who arrived as refugees.[2]

All this has important implications for early Nguni history. Firstly, migrants may move fast and far, scattering over 2,000 miles in a generation. The Ngoni had travelled half-way from Zululand to Merowe in the Sudan (whence iron spread through much of Africa) in thirty-five years. Secondly, a cattle people could cross the Zambezi and move along the coastal belt, retaining cattle in spite of tsetse in that area. Thirdly, connexions in language long survive even when the original migrants are few in number, and the absence, north of the Drakensberg, of any language closely related to Nguni (other than the Transvaal and Rhodesian Ndebele, Ngoni, and Tshangane just mentioned) suggests that the Nguni migration southward is indeed a very ancient one. Fourthly, detailed traditions of migrations easily survive a hundred years, and the name of a leader in a migration twenty-five generations back is remembered by the Ndebele of the Transvaal. As already indicated, the absence of any such detailed traditions or the name of any Moses who brought the people south supports the view that the Nguni have occupied the country south of the Drakensberg for many centuries.

We turn now to the relations of the Nguni with the Khoikhoi and San. The earliest records mention small groups speaking a click language or languages on the coast at Mossel Bay, near the Infante river, and further east, probably about the Kei mouth.[3] The survivors of the *Stavenisse* wrecked in 1686 speak of 'Magryghas' or 'Makriggas' *east* of the Xhosa who were settled on the Buffalo.[4] Traditions refer to a Khoikhoi group, the Gona living near Togu's grandson of the senior line, Tshiwo. Soga says they were on the Mngazi river,[5] but John Brownlee, writing a hundred years earlier,[6] says Ntinde and Ketshe, younger sons of Togu, were settled on the coast between the Buffalo and Kalumna, and the Gona were on the Buffalo near the coast, and on the Keiskamma up to its source. Brownlee's evidence fits exactly with the reports of the survivors from the *Stavenisse*. According to tradition, Ntinde's mother and two of his wives were Khoikhoi.[7] There is also a circumstantial account of how a number of persons accused of witchcraft and condemned to death were helped to escape by Khwane, a councillor of Tshiwo, took refuge with the Gona, and married Gona

---

[1] M. Read, 'Tradition and Prestige among the Ngoni', *Africa*, 6 (1936), 453–83.
[2] Kawa, *passim*.   [3] Boxer, p. 198 (1622).
[4] Moodie, i. 426, 431. They have been identified by some as *Griqua*, but the main body of Griqua was then in the Western Cape (Moodie, i. 429).
[5] Soga, *South-Eastern Bantu*, p. 116; Ngani, pp. 9–10.
[6] Thompson, pp. 439–40.   [7] Theal, *History and Ethnography*, iii. 78.

women. Later, they were brought back to Tshiwo by Khwane and as the Gqunukwebe formed a section of his chiefdom which later, under Khwane's descendants, made some pretension of independence.[1] They were not a clan but a territorial unit under a sub-chief.

There is ample evidence, from the seventeenth century, of continual interaction between Xhosa and Khoikhoi in the country between the Kei and the Gamtoos rivers. According to tradition Gwali, Tshiwo's right-hand son, fled to the Little Fish river about the end of the seventeenth century and took refuge there with a Khoikhoi chief, Hintsati, and their people mingled.[2] Rarabe, a later Xhosa chief, defeated another Khoikhoi leader at the lower Kei drift, and gave his widow Hoho many cattle for the right to occupy the Mathole mountains.[3] In 1772 Thunberg found Xhosa living intermingled with Khoikhoi on the Gamtoos river: 'Hottentots and Caffres lived promiscuously near this river, as on the frontier of the two countries, the real Caffraria beginning several miles farther up in the country.'[4] The immediate ancestors of a group of 'Gunjemans Hottentots' living near the Zwartkops river had, by their own account, moved eastward from the Cape after the Dutch settlers had occupied their country[5]—the slopes of Table Mountain and Constantia—but the Gona had lived at least from the seventeenth century in groups interspersed with Xhosa and had been considerably influenced by them.[6] The Gona (ǂgona) still spoke Khoikhoi as distinct from Xhosa,[7] but Thunberg notes in 1772 when he came to van Stadens river—the first camp of Gona he met—that 'our Hottentots from the Western Cape no longer perfectly understand'.[8] Moreover, the Gona like the Xhosa and unlike other Khoikhoi were circumcized, and wore calf-skin and not sheep-skin cloaks. Some of them cultivated sorghum. Le Vaillant's portraits of Nerina and other Gona show people of negroid physical type.[9]

Interaction between Xhosa and Khoikhoi of the west as distinct from Gona must, however, have been restricted, since their breeds of cattle were 'very easily to be distinguished' in 1774.[10] Whether Gona cattle resembled those of the Xhosa or those of the west is nowhere explicitly stated, but it seems likely that the differentiation came where forest and karroo combined placed a barrier to the easy movement of stock—i.e. between Mossel Bay and the Gamtoos. Contact between

---

[1] Cowper Rose, *Four Years in Southern Africa*, pp. 148–50.
[2] Soga, *South-Eastern Bantu*, pp. 121–2; Theal, *History and Ethnography*, iii. 79–80.
[3] Theal, *History and Ethnography*, iii. 81.
[4] Thunberg, i. 203.   [5] Sparrman, ii. 335.   [6] Thompson, p. 440.
[7] L. F. Maingard, 'The Lost Tribes of the Cape', *SAJS* (1931), 504. Stow thought the Gona were San, but on linguistic grounds they are classed as Khoikhoi.
[8] Thunberg, ii. 83.
[9] F. Le Vaillant, *Collection of Cape Aquarelles*, South African National Gallery, Cape Town.
[10] Moodie, iii. 24.

Nguni and Khoikhoi began before the seventeenth century, for the speech of Zulu, who were far removed from seventeenth- and eighteenth-century meetings between the Buffalo and the Gamtoos, as well as the speech of Xhosa proper, who mingled with the Khoikhoi then, shows indisputable evidence of Khoikhoi influence. The Nguni and Khoikhoi languages are not genetically related as the Bantu languages are, but Nguni has a number of sounds, including three clicks, as well as many words which have come from Khoikhoi.[1]

To the historian the most significant connexions are in the words for cattle and sheep, but here the relationship is not confined to Khoikhoi and Nguni; it includes also Sotho, Tsonga, and Venda. The words for cow (*komu), fat-tailed sheep (*gú), and milk (*pi) in Bantu languages south of the Limpopo are not from the common Bantu stems (though there is an archaic Sotho word from the Bantu stem for cow), but they are from the same roots as the Khoikhoi terms.[2] The probable implication is either that the southern Bantu got their cattle from the Khoikhoi or that they and the Khoikhoi both drew from the same, non-Bantu-speaking, source.[3] The word for goat, on the other hand, in both Nguni and Sotho languages is from the common Bantu root *budi, and distinct from the Khoikhoi root *biri; and the word for dog, inja in Nguni, is also from the common Bantu root. Did the Nguni, if not the Sotho, separate from the main Bantu stem *before* they acquired cattle? Or did the cattle they acquired from the Khoikhoi direct, or from a common source, differ from the stock they had already, and so come to be called by a different term?[4] It is relevant to note that one new term from Khoikhoi, *igusha*, and another derived from Dutch and filtered through Khoikhoi, *ibokwe*, came into Xhosa in the eighteenth or nineteenth century for the merino sheep and the new breed of goat introduced by whites. These are still in common use as well as the ancient words *imvu* and *imbuzi* for older breeds.[5]

The intermingling of Nguni and Khoikhoi languages is ancient: so too are certain techniques and peculiar ritual observances. For example, the Nguni style of hut and homestead plan from the sixteenth to the nineteenth century resembled that of the Khoikhoi rather than that of

---

[1] H. D. Anders, 'Observations on Certain Sound Changes in Xhosa Derivatives from Khoisa', *SAJS* (1937), 921–5.

[2] E. O. J. Westphal drew attention to this very important point. 'The Linguistic Prehistory of Southern Africa', pp. 253–6. I am indebted to Professor Westphal also for information on the archaic Sotho word. L. F. Maingard, 'Linguistic Approach to South African Prehistory and Ethnology', *SAJS*, 30 (1934), 132–8.

[3] The common source is not connected with the Malagasi words but might come from Iranian or Old Persian roots (Westphal, p. 256).

[4] There are many puzzling points, for connexions between Shona and Venda are certain, but Shona uses the common Bantu root *ŋòmbè*, and Venda the Southern root *komú*.

[5] A. Kropf, A *Kaffir-English Dictionary*, i-gusha, i-bokwe, im-vu, im-buzi.

the Sotho or Tsonga, and the Xhosa or Mpondo manner of killing a sacrificial animal by breaking the aorta and wearing the inflated gall bladder in the hair[1] is similar to that observed in 1622 and 1779 for Khoikhoi groups.[2] In dress the Xhosa resembled the Khoikhoi more closely than they did their Zulu kinsmen.

The Xhosa word for Khoikhoi, *ilawu*, has derogatory connotations, implying someone without customs, and it seems to have already had this implication by the early nineteenth century,[3] but it is unlikely that it was so in the eighteenth century when a number of Xhosa chiefs married Khoikhoi women as principal wives. The condemnation by most white South Africans of racial intermixture has been projected on to the early cultural mingling of Bantu-speakers with Khoikhoi and San, as well as to intermarriage between these groups. Thus Bryant speaks of a time when 'the Nguni blood and speech and life were still pure—save for some linguistic Bushman taint', and of their being 'doomed to suffer still further damage to their speech by the infliction of two other root-clicks', though 'successfully resisting all temptation to intermarriage'.[4] But symbols of 'purity' and 'contamination' in this context perhaps stem from white South African traditions rather than black.

And what of the relation between Nguni and San, or Twa as the Nguni called them? As has already been shown, small groups of hunters who painted, and who made stone tools, have been very widely distributed through southern Africa, and their area of occupation included the country between the Drakensberg and sea (map 2). In the eighteenth and nineteenth centuries the 'Chinese Hottentots' who spoke a language distinct from Khoikhoi[5] were found living in the mountains between the Tsomo (a tributary of the Kei) and the Sneeuberg, and in this area—particularly down the Kei and in the Queenstown district— quantities of paintings have been found. Two sorts of people are depicted: one with tiny feet armed with bows and arrows, and the other with large feet armed with shields and spears. The San artist fastened on characteristic differences between bush-boskop and negroid-physical types and exaggerated them.[6] San were still painting in the nineteenth century: Stow reports a portrait of van der Kemp in a cave

[1] Hunter, pp. 243, 248, 250.
[2] Theal, *Records*, viii. 76; Wikar (1779), pp. 83, 87.
[3] Thompson, pp. 196, 450.   [4] Bryant, *Olden Times*, pp. 7–8.
[5] Sparrman, i. 242; ii. 157–8, 377–80. Barrow notes that several Colonists, having had San nurses, spoke the language 'as fluently as the natives' (Barrow, i. 290). Professor Westphal states that the San language spoken in the Eastern Cape was akin to that of the Western Cape (personal communication).
[6] G. W. Stow and D. F. Bleek, *Rock Paintings in South Africa*, Plate 17; E. Rosenthal and A. J. H. Goodwin, *Cave Artists of South Africa*, Plates 9, 24, 25, 26; A. R. Willcox, 'Who made the Rock Art of South Africa and When?', *SAJS*, 62 (1966), 8–12.

near Whittlesea, and he met an old man with his paint pots at his belt on the Kei in 1869,[1] and there are numerous paintings depicting horses and Europeans, and one of a commando.[2]

It is a gross error to suppose that Nguni and San—any more than Nguni and Khoikhoi—were mutually exclusive. There is evidence to show that Nguni and San long occupied the same territories, living side by side in some sort of symbiotic relationship. The Mpondo and Mpondomise depended upon the San as rainmakers, paying them in cattle and a share of the crops.[3] The Xhosa and Mpondo traded with them, buying ivory, feathers, and egg-shell beads in exchange for iron, grain, and later tobacco; and the Thembu used them as woodcutters for their smelting furnaces[4] near the Tsomo river. Thembu and Mpondomise intermarried with San, and such marriages cannot have been despised in the sixteenth century, since the mother of the Mpondomise chief Cira (ten generations back in 1883), who became the most popular of three brother chiefs, is remembered to have been a San woman.[5] Sotho traditions tell of the sons of a Fokeng chief and a San woman who, with their followers, crossed the Drakensberg and joined the Thembu, and the mixture in physical type is reflected in Le Vaillant's portraits of 'Tamboeki'.[6] Stanford reports a marriage between Thembu and San as late as 1874, but by then the mother of the groom looked upon it as a mésalliance.[7] The custom, practised in some Mpondo, Thembu, Xhosa, and Zulu families, of amputating one joint of the finger of a child who is ailing was a San rather than an Nguni ritual,[8] and was sometimes taken as evidence of San descent.[9]

But there were periods when Nguni and San were at war, the San raiding Nguni stock and the Nguni seeking to exterminate them. This again is reflected in the paintings[10] and recorded by the survivors of the *Stavenisse*. In the eighteenth century the San killed the favourite ox of the Xhosa chief, Rarabe, near the Kei, and he ordered their extermination.[11] The Xhosa were then moving westward, and so were the Thembu, who shifted first across the Tsomo and then across the Kei into land previously occupied by the San alone. Perhaps conflict occurred as population increased and there was competition for grazing and hunting grounds,

---

[1] Stow, pp. 200–1.
[2] A. R. Willcox, *Rock Paintings of the Drakensberg*, Plates 38, 45, 46, 47.
[3] *1883 Report*, ii. 409.
[4] Sparrman, ii. 158–9.
[5] *1883 Report*, ii. 403, Genealogy; Ellenberger and Macgregor, p. 19.
[6] Le Vaillant, *Cape Aquarelles*, 37, 38, 39.
[7] W. Stanford, *The Reminiscences of Sir Walter Stanford*, VRS, 1958, i. 45–46.
[8] Barrow, i. 289.
[9] Stow, pp. 129, 170; Hunter, pp. 264–5.
[10] Stow and Bleek, Plates 17, 28, 36; Rosenthal and Goodwin, Plates 24, 25.
[11] Brownlee, *Reminiscences*, p. 182.

and the Nguni pushed out the San by sheer weight of numbers because their food supply was more secure. Sparrman remarks that the San, armed with poisoned arrows, were more than a match for the Nguni at a distance. Generally speaking the San flourished in the more arid areas and the high mountain grasslands where buck abounded, whereas the Nguni sought the better watered and less frost-bitten grass and forest land suitable for cultivation, as well as grazing. The San could not use their bows in rainy weather,[1] and van der Kemp noted that they 'avoid woods', whereas the Xhosa 'prefer a woody situation'.[2] It is likely that the whole Nguni area was at one time largely forest country;[3] their westward boundary coincided closely with an ecological boundary; they settled neither beyond the hills, Bruintjieshoogte, that mark the eastern boundary of the dry Karroo, nor on the very sour veld west of the Gamtoos. Indeed, refugees from Shaka's wars who were settled near the edge of the Tsitsikamma at Clarkson suffered much because their cattle did not thrive on the very sour grass, and the soil was not productive.[4] The areas that were in dispute between Xhosa, Gona, San, and Dutch settlers in the late eighteenth century were the transition areas between well-watered grassland, arid land, and very wet and sour forest country.

3. *Economy*

As quotations from the Portuguese chroniclers have shown, the Nguni people were herders and cultivators, as well as hunters. They kept mainly cattle and dogs, but also goats and a few sheep 'of the Ormuz breed'.[5] In the early nineteenth century the cattle population is estimated as far exceeding the human population: Colonel Collins writing in 1809 put Hintza's herds at twice the number of his followers.[6] Bannister estimated that the Xhosa, west of the Mbashe, who numbered about 100,000,[7] kept 360,000 cattle.[8]

The cattle are described by the Portuguese as large, 'very tame', and often 'without horns',[9] and they were distinguishable from Khoikhoi cattle in the eighteenth century.[10] According to modern veterinary reports the Zulu breed was of lyre-horned Sanga cattle with a cervico-

[1] Campbell, *1813*, p. 147.
[2] J. T. van der Kemp, *Transactions of the Missionary Society*, i. 437 (Vanderkemp in original).
[3] Acocks, Map 1.
[4] Cape Archives, Dispatches from Lieut. G. W., 1836–66, G. H. 8/7, No. 1, 10 Oct. 1838 (Enclosure to Dispatch 61/1838); G. H. 8/5, No. 325.
[5] Theal, *Records*, ii. 292, 301 (refers to 1593); Moodie, i. 432 (refers to 1686); I. L. Mason and J. P. Maule, *The Indigenous Livestock of Eastern and Southern Africa*, pp. 100–4, 116. Sparrman, Barrow, and Lichtenstein reported that the Xhosa had *no* sheep in 1776, 1797, and 1803.
[6] Moodie, v. 42–43.
[7] Thompson, p. 196.
[8] S. Bannister, *Humane Policy*, p. 133.
[9] Theal, *Records*, ii. 301.
[10] Moodie, iii. 24; Barrow, i. 203.

thoracic hump and a circular cross-section of the horn, distinct from the Afrikander type with an oval cross-section of the horn kept by the Khoikhoi.[1] Afrikander cattle with wide horns captured north of the Drakensberg by Dingane's army from Mzilikazi in 1837 were the first of that type that the Zulu had seen.[2]

The Nguni were skilful cattle-men, shifting their stock from one pasture to another so long as land was plentiful, and using the new growth on sour mountain grassland (burnt in winter) for spring grazing. They lavished care on their cattle, each man training his herd to respond to whistles, bending the horns of oxen in shapes regarded as beautiful,[3] displaying them at dances, making up poems about them, and identifying himself with a favourite ox; but, so far as our evidence goes, it was chiefly the southern Nguni who trained them as riding, pack (*iqegu*), and racing animals, and this they may well have learnt from the Khoikhoi with whom they were in contact. The Portuguese survivors of the wreck of 1647 trained pack-oxen themselves (see p. 83), and no mention is made of the Xhosa riding in the detailed accounts of them dating from 1686 (though they gelded animals),[4] therefore it is likely that they learnt the art of riding after that date. Barrow speaks of the chief, Ngqika, of the Xhosa returning from his cattle-post in the mountains in 1797, 'riding an ox in full gallop',[5] and the illustration opposite dates from 1850. The Ndebele, even when on the move, did not use pack-oxen (see p. 101), and there is little evidence of the Zulu training cattle for riding,[6] though the Ngoni had learnt to do this by the time they reached Tanzania. Soga gives a vivid description of Xhosa cattle-racing (*uleqo*),[7] and there is some evidence of it also among the Mpondo and Bhaca,[8] but no references to it in ancient Zululand have been found, nor are the words for a pack-ox and cattle-racing in the Zulu dictionary.

The use of pack and riding oxen had a distribution[9] which coincided in southern Africa with the distribution of Afrikander cattle, except that the Xhosa acquired these techniques while their cattle were still distin-

---

[1] H. H. Curson and R. W. Thornton, 'A Contribution to the Study of African Native Cattle', *Onderstepoort Journal of Veterinary Science and Animal Industry* (1936), 672; Mason and Maule, pp. 40–46. Strictly, the Afrikander breed is *derived* from Khoikhoi cattle, but it is convenient to use the term also for the parent stock. R. Singer and H. Lehmann, 'The Haemoglobins of Afrikander Cattle', in *Man and Cattle* (ed. A. E. Mourant and F. E. Zeuner), pp. 119–25.
[2] Bryant, *Zulu Dictionary*, p. 53*; *Olden Times*, p. 309.
[3] Theal, *Records*, ii. 324; Barrow, i. 203.
[4] Moodie, i. 432.   [5] Barrow, i. 193.
[6] Cetshwayo had a white riding ox, set aside for the purpose. I am indebted to Revd. A.-I. Berglund for this information.
[7] J. H. Soga, *The Ama-Xosa; Life and Customs*, pp. 221, 371–6; S. Kay, *Travels and Researches in Caffraria*, p. 128; Bennie, p. 27.
[8] Hunter, pp. 68, 366–7; W. D. Hammond-Tooke, *Bhaca Society*, p. 23.
[9] H. G. Lindblom, *The Use of Oxen as Pack and Riding Animals in Africa*.

guishably of another strain, but it is significant that the spread of the Afrikander breed and techniques of training cattle did *not* coincide with the spread of Nguni people whose language was modified by Khoikhoi, nor did it coincide with still larger areas within which words for 'cow' and 'milk' come from similar roots which are not common Bantu roots.

Horses, pigs, woolled sheep, and a new variety of goat were introduced by white settlers. Fowls were mentioned in 1498 at the Copper river[1] in the Tsonga area, and in 1593 and 1622 in Natal,[2] but were absent in at least part of the Nguni area in the sixteenth century, and they play no part in Nguni ritual, whereas among the Tsonga and peoples further north they play an essential part.

The traditional crops were two varieties of sorghum, *amabele* (*sorghum caffrorum* Beauv.)[3] and *imfe*,[4] pumpkins (*amathanga*), calabashes (*amaselwa*) and melons (*imixoxosi*), a bean[5] (*intlumayo*), the coco yam, *colocasia antiquorum* (*idumbi*),[6] and possibly another root crop *umhlaza*.[7]

The Portuguese survivors from wrecks speak of 'crops of millet' (*sementeiras de milho*) in 1554,[8] in Natal, and in 1593 about the Mthatha.[9] The Portuguese *milho* is doubtless one or other variety of sorghum, which is repeatedly called 'millet' by later writers. Melons, calabashes, and beans are mentioned in 1593,[10] 1622,[11] and 1635.[12] In 1686 there were 'beans, pumpkins, water melons, and such like, in abundance' among the Xhosa, and other survivors from the *Stavenisse* reported: 'They cultivate three sorts of corn, as also calabashes, pumpkins, water melons and beans, much resembling the European brown beans; they sow annually a kind of earth nut, and a kind of under-ground bean, both very nourishing. . . . Tobacco grows there wild. . . .'[13]

The 'three sorts of corn' perhaps included maize, to which there is a probable reference in 1635[14] and which was seen growing in Pondoland in 1790,[15] but sorghum was still the main crop in 1821.[16] Tobacco is reported at the Cape in 1601, and at least by 1800 it was cultivated 'in great quantities' by the Xhosa.[17] Wheat (*inqholowa*), sweet-potatoes

[1] Da Gama, pp. 10–11. [2] Theal, *Records*, ii. 318; iii. 104.
[3] Sparrman, ii. 11, calls it *holcus sorghum*. The Xhosa proper use the word *amazimba* for the grain called *amabele* by Zulu, Hlubi, and others. I am indebted to the Botanical Research Institute, Pretoria, for identifying a specimen of *amazimba*.
[4] *Sorghum dochna* Snowden. [5] Kropf, *Dictionary*. [6] Bryant, *Zulu Dictionary*.
[7] Ibid. [8] Theal, *Records*, i. 237.
[9] Ibid. ii. 240, 267, 299, 310, 329.   [10] Ibid. ii. 304.
[11] Ibid. viii. 86. [12] Ibid. viii. 168, 216.
[13] Moodie, i. 427, 431.
[14] '*Tamben o ha de macaroacas*' (Theal, *Records*, viii. 157, 205). No convincing evidence for the view that the Nguni grew maize before they came to Natal has yet been published (cf. E. H. Brookes and C. de B. Webb, *A History of Natal*, p. 2 n.).
[15] Carter and Van Reenen, p. 160. [16] Thompson, p. 452.
[17] Van der Kemp, i. 438; W. Paterson, *A Narrative of Four Journeys into the Country of the Hottentots and Caffraria*, p. 94; cf. Moodie, v. 41.

(*ubatata*), potatoes (*amatapile*), and new varieties of beans (*imbotyi*) and peas (*iertyisi*) were also introduced, the names of the last three being derived from Dutch. In the traditional rituals it was beer brewed from sorghum, and in a lesser degree calabashes, pumpkins, and stems of sweet sorghum (*imfe*), that played a part, along with milk and the flesh of cattle and goats. Maize came to be used for ritual beer in place of sorghum. Contrary to Barrow's statement beer was brewed by the Xhosa as well as other Nguni, but van der Kemp notes that the Xhosa were 'moderate' in their drinking.[1]

John Brownlee[2] and others describe the Xhosa scattering seed on grassland and dibbling it in, but at least some Mpondo and Xhosa select forest land for fields when possible, since it offers much higher yields than the grass veld, and there is good reason to suppose that the Nguni have long cultivated at the edges of forest or bush, pushing it back and back, and utilizing the ash from the trees that were burned as fertilizer.[3] Since the seventeenth century they, like the whites, have much reduced the forests in the areas they occupied.[4] The Nguni never carried dung to their fields, but old cattle byres were planted with tobacco.

Although the Nguni were pastoralists and cultivators and had such a deep attachment to cattle, they depended also for food on hunting and collecting, and, at least until the nineteenth century, for clothing. Hunting also provided the most important article for export—ivory— and the wealth and power of chiefs came to depend upon control of it. Above all, hunting was a sport. John Brownlee notes that the Xhosa,

> though not, like the poor Bushmen, impelled to the chase to provide for their subsistence, they are passionately fond of it, as an active and animating amusement. They generally go out to hunt in large parties; and when they find game in the open fields, they endeavour to surround the animals, or drive them to some narrow pass, which is previously occupied by long files of hunters, stationed on either side, who, as the herd rushes through between, pierce them with showers of assagais.[5]

Brownlee goes on to describe how elephant, rhino, hippo, buffalo, and lion were hunted and killed with assagais, dogs playing an important part in the lion hunt. A great battue, organized like a military expedition,[6] always marked the end of mourning for a chief, and a small hunt the purification after mourning for the head of a homestead.

The relative dependence upon milk, or grain, or game, or wild produce clearly varied from one group to another and changed with time. The Xhosa on the frontier seem to have depended largely on milk and game—particularly during the frontier wars—whereas the Lala in Natal

---

[1] Lichtenstein, i. 335; van der Kemp, i. 419.   [2] Thompson, p. 453.
[3] Hunter, p. 73, and other direct observation.   [4] Acocks, Map I.
[5] Thompson, p. 454.   [6] Cf. E. A. Ritter, *Shaka Zulu*, pp. 205–15.

were more assiduous cultivators, and Mpondo men certainly shared with their women in the work of cultivation when they lost most of their cattle in Shaka's raids.[1] Wild greens and roots and fruit have probably always played an important part in the diet of Nguni women and children, but were eaten by men only during times of famine. Whatever the local or temporary conditions, however, herding and hunting were regarded as honourable occupations, worthy of a man, whereas cultivation was women's work in which men participated only from necessity, or as a service to their chief. The contrast, in this regard, with some of the peoples of Central Africa, such as the Nyakyusa or Lozi, is marked.

The Nguni lived in scattered homesteads. Among commoners each was composed of two to forty huts, disposed in a semi-circle if the number were sufficient, with a circular cattle byre made of brushwood in the open segment of the arc. There is consistency in the reports, from 1554 when the survivors of the *São Bento* already quoted (p. 79) came to a village of 'about twenty huts' to 1797 when Barrow 'passed a number of villages containing from ten to thirty huts each'[2] and 1830 when Boyce visited the Mpondo and saw 'a hundred kraals, each of which contained from twenty to forty houses'.[3]

Homestead sites were on ridges, and wherever the lay of the land permitted the huts faced eastward to catch the early sun. Each married woman had her own hut, and the disposition of huts was important, for polygyny was approved and the status of each wife was reflected in the placing of her hut. The mother of the head of the homestead occupied the 'great hut'[4] at the centre of the arc which faced the gate of the cattle byre. If she were dead, or living elsewhere, his senior wife occupied this position and his junior wives and wives of the other men of the homestead were disposed in order of rank on both sides.

Chiefs' homesteads everywhere tend to be larger than those of commoners, and with the development of the military power of the Zulu barracks were built at certain royal homesteads that might contain altogether a thousand huts,[5] and perhaps twice as many persons, but it is doubtful whether before this military concentration chiefs' homesteads exceeded that of Khawuta, a minor Xhosa chief who, in 1779, lived in a homestead of 'about fifty houses' with 'three hundred inhabitants'.[6]

There is no question that a radical difference existed in the degree of concentration of Nguni and Sotho, the Sotho peoples generally living in

---

[1] Hunter, pp. 73–74.   [2] Barrow, i. 192; Moodie, v. 43.
[3] A. Steedman, *Wandering and Adventures in the Interior of Southern Africa*, ii. 268.
[4] Hunter, pp. 15–16.
[5] Capt. A. F. Gardiner, *Narrative of a Journey to the Zoolu Country*, drawing of Umgungundlovu, and pp. 56, 62, 143; R. C. Samuelson, *Long, Long Ago*, pp. 128–9, gives a diagram of Ulundi, Cetshwayo's great place.
[6] Paterson, p. 90.

large compact villages, and the Nguni in scattered homesteads. Both in the form of their homesteads and in their style of building the Nguni resembled the pastoral and nomadic Khoikhoi rather than the Sotho. The San were again quite different, with tiny huts each 'about three feet high and four feet wide and the ground in the middle was dug out like the nest of an ostrich'. There was no cattle byre, but 'a small circular trodden place around their huts for dancing'.[1]

The traditional Nguni style of hut was a circular framework of saplings bent across in a dome and tied with bark, and the frame was covered either with woven reed mats or else with grass bound with a net of rope. The hut was ten feet in diameter,[2] the doorway very low—three feet or less—and the interior might or might not be mudded over. This 'mouse's house' (*indlu yempuku*), as it is called in Xhosa, required a large number of straight saplings and much tall grass or reeds, but given the materials it was quickly made, and where mats were used it was easily packed up and moved. Moffat notes that some of the Ndebele north of the Drakensberg used mats in this way,[3] and the style indeed reflects the needs of a pastoral people who moved readily. As the Nguni became more settled, and saw other types of dwelling, successive changes occurred: wattle and daub walls with a domed roof replaced the older grass structure, and later on sod or brick or stone walls sheltered with a pitched roof, thatched in 'Dutch' style, became common. Rectangular houses, subdivided into rooms, spread slowly in the country because they afford less privacy and are less easy to roof with local materials, but they are common enough where timber and corrugated iron are bought. Two hundred years of change in Nguni housing can be traced in styles still being built, and the old grass 'mouse's house' appears annually in the lodge built for boys newly circumcised.

The cattle byres were of brushwood or logs, always circular, with the entrance facing the arc of huts. Circular stone and mud cattle byres were probably also built long ago (as they are today) by Nguni living in tree-less country. Allen Gardiner saw such byres and 'the circular site of . . . perishable dwellings' in 1835, in grassland east of the Mkomasi river, and he was told that the area had been 'well inhabited' before Shaka's army swept through. Shepstone showed the area occupied before 1812 by a number of small Nguni groups.[4]

The Xhosa and other southern Nguni do not surround their villages with any palisade, nor is there any record of this in traditions or early journals, other than one reference in 1593 (see p. 80), but the Zulu and some Khoikhoi did build such a palisade.[5] The reasons for its absence

---

[1] Barrow, i. 275, 284.   [2] Ibid. i. 200.   [3] Moffat, *Matabele Journals*, i. 25.
[4] Gardiner, pp. 307–8; *1883 Report*, Map I.
[5] G. Angas, *The Kafirs Illustrated*; Gardiner, p. 167 and Plate 2.

among the Xhosa remain obscure. Neither Zulu nor Xhosa wall off each wife's courtyard as the Sotho and Swazi do, to ensure privacy.[1]

Grain was stored in flask-shaped pits dug (if the type of soil permitted) in the cattle byres, plastered with mud and cow dung inside, and sealed with a stone. Such pits (first noted in 1686,[2] and still in use in 1931)[3] might hold ten to twenty-eight bushels.[4] This technique of storing grain distinguished the Nguni from the Sotho, but flask-shaped pits like those of the Nguni are reported from Venda country.

Women made clay pots, using the coiled technique, and firing them with ordinary wood. They were used for cooking, drawing water, and brewing beer, but the Nguni pottery—so far as we know it—is mostly coarse and not decorated except sometimes with a slip of red ochre and thumb-nail notching round the mouth.[5] Milk pails, spoons, and neck rests were carved out of wood, but there can be no doubt that both in pottery and carving as well as in smelting the Nguni were less skilled and less productive than the Tswana. The ubiquitous clay oxen were made by children in a stylized form with exaggerated humps and wide horns. These were toys.

Clothing was of both cow-hide and the pelts of wild animals—the Xhosa women in the late eighteenth century favoured buck-skin for caps,[6] and Zulu men wore strips and tails of various wild cats as kilts, but skirts and shields were of cow-hide, and some cloaks also. Leopard-skin cloaks were the insignia of chiefs, and other differences in status, as between married and unmarried women, young and mature men, or, in the late eighteenth century, between regimental affiliations, were reflected in dress and hair styles. Ornaments included copper and iron beads and ear-rings, ivory bracelets, shells, feathers, and trade beads and buttons. Fashions change even in the most isolated societies and clothing and ornaments varied in both space and time, local styles distinguishing chiefdoms or groups of chiefdoms, and sometimes changing from one reign to the next, because the mourning for a chief, when men and women shaved and put off all ornaments, was an occasion for change in styles.[7]

The ancient Nguni weapons were iron throwing spears and wooden clubs, and they used hide shields. Survivors from the *Stavenisse* note of the Xhosa that: 'They are armed with shield and assagai with which they oppose their enemies, the Makanaena [Khoikhoi or San] who use the bow and arrow and do them great injury, for they not only steal

---
[1] H. Beemer, 'The Swazi', in Duggan-Cronin, *The Bantu Tribes of Africa*, vol. iii, section IV, p. 16 and Plates CXXIII and CXXIV.
[2] Moodie, i. 431.   [3] Hunter, p. 86.   [4] Thompson, p. 453.
[5] Hunter, p. 100 and Plates IX and X.   [6] Van der Kemp, i. 440.
[7] Hunter, p. 400.

their cattle, but they do not spare women and children, inhumanly murdering them.'[1] A long-bladed stabbing spear with a short handle replaced the throwing spear among the Zulu, in Shaka's time.

Certain groups were famous as smiths and bartered their products to others. North of the Mzimkhulu the Lala were pre-eminent as iron-workers, and one section of them, the Zizi, exchanged metal weapons and implements for cattle across the Drakensberg.[2] The Zulu smelted iron ore, but the brass and copper they worked were obtained elsewhere.[3] Though the Xhosa themselves could smelt in 1686[4] and there was said to be ore in their country,[5] they were exchanging cattle for iron from the Thembu a hundred years later.[6] But the resources in metal of the Nguni area are much more limited than the resources north and west of the Drakensberg,[7] and there is no evidence of smelting copper and gold, as there was to the north. The copper ornaments the Xhosa wore were obtained from the Tswana (Kwena), and probably some of their weapons were also.[8] John Brownlee, writing before 1821, reported that

> At Hintza's kraal we found a few people residing, who had come from a tribe lying to the north-west of Lattakoo. They had been a good while in this country; and from the great similarity both of their personal appearance and their language to that of the Caffers, it is evident they are originally of the same race; but I could not clearly ascertain whether they belong to the Bechuana or Damara tribes.[9]

We do not know how far the trade network extended at any given time, but it is clear that regular markets, such as were common further north in Africa, did not exist among the Nguni, and the trade in metal must have been small because even iron remained so scarce until the nineteenth century. As we have seen, survivors from the wreck of 1554 found the people they met partly armed with iron spears and partly with wooden pikes with points hardened in the fire. Iron and copper were the goods most sought after from survivors from wrecks, and in 1686 iron or copper gave 'inducement to the murder of those who have them'.[10] Lichtenstein refers to the Xhosa burning the grass after a hunt that they might recover the blades of assagais.[11] Such iron as was available was used by the Xhosa and Mpondo for ornaments and spears. Even as late as the nineteenth century[12] they cultivated with wooden digging sticks or hoes, though the Zulu had iron hoes.

---

[1] Moodie, i. 417. [2] Ellenberger and Macgregor, p. 26.
[3] N. Isaacs, *Travels and Adventures in Eastern Africa*, VRS, 1937, ii. 269–70; Fynn, p. 270.
[4] Moodie, i. 427.
[5] J. W. D. Moodie, *Ten Years in South Africa*, ii. 260; Ndamase, p. 118.
[6] Barrow, i. 203.
[7] Geological Survey, *The Mineral Resources of South Africa*, Mineral Map.
[8] Lichtenstein, i. 368. [9] Thompson, p. 461. [10] Moodie, i. 431.
[11] Lichtenstein, i. 332. [12] Thompson, p. 453; Hunter, p. 74.

Medicines, cosmetics, and ornaments also passed from one group to another, in exchange for stock or grain, and later tobacco, but again the quantities were small. The main circulation of wealth occurred at marriage, when the groom's lineage offered cattle for a bride and feasts were exchanged. Lichtenstein comments: 'The trade which the Koossas [Xhosa] keep up with other Caffre tribes is very insignificant; the tribes of Beetjuan [Tswana] are in this respect much before them, since they carry on a far brisker trade.'[1]

A great development in crafts and trade coincided with the growth of the kingdom in Dingiswayo's reign.

In the first year of his chieftainship [about 1795] he opened a trade with Delagoa Bay, by sending 100 oxen and a quantity of elephants' tusks to exchange for beads and blankets. Prior to this a small supply of these articles had been brought to that country from Delagoa Bay by the natives. The trade thus opened by Dingiswayo was afterwards carried on, on an extensive scale, though the Portuguese never in person entered his country. The encouragement held out to ingenuity brought numbers around him, liberal rewards being given to any of his followers who devised things new and ornamental. His mechanical ingenuity was displayed in the carving of wood. He taught this art to several of his people.

Milk dishes, pillows, ladles of cane or wood, and snuff spoons were also produced. . . . A kaross manufactory was also established, a hundred men being generally employed in that work.[2]

Men travelled even when they did not trade. Alberti met at Ngqika's great place, between 1802 and 1806, two men whom he concluded came from near Delagoa Bay, since their people were selling ivory to whites and they were familiar with boats. They spoke a dialect not immediately intelligible to a Xhosa-speaker, but understandable after two days' conversation.[3] Their presence west of the Keiskamma makes nonsense of the argument that Dingiswayo *could not* have visited the Cape as Shepstone thought he had,[4] though Fynn's account of Dingiswayo's sojourn with the Hlubi[5] is a more probable version of his adventures (see p. 339). How common such travel was we do not know. The Portuguese chronicler of the wreck of 1593 reported that 'The people never go far from their villages' (see p. 81), but the dispersion, before the period of Shaka's wars, of sections of one clan or chiefdom shows that movement occurred. For example, Thembu who travelled from the Cape to near Durban with a missionary were welcomed as kinsmen by Thembu whom they found there.

These details regarding breeds of stock and crops; patterns of settlement; techniques of building and of storing grain; and some account of

---

[1] Lichtenstein, i. 369.
[2] Fynn, pp. 8, 10.
[3] L. Alberti, *Description physique et historique des Caffres*, p. 9.
[4] *1883 Report*, p. 415.
[5] Fynn, pp. 2–8.

weapons, clothes, ornaments, and toys, and of trade and travel, are included here because it is from such detail that the archaeologist and ethnologist must piece together evidence of the distribution in space and time of particular economies and material 'cultures', and of interaction between peoples. This evidence concerns mode of subsistence and artefacts, and gives few clues to social structure and none regarding language. From documents, and more tentatively from oral tradition, it is possible to show connexions between a particular economy and the language spoken, or the type of social structure at a particular period, but of course these links are not indissoluble. Since 1800, for example, the Nguni have changed their settlement patterns, and style of building and clothing, without radically changing their language.

4. *The Structure of Nguni Society*

Some indication has already been given of Nguni social structure; it remains to formulate it more systematically and in greater detail. The Nguni lineages, referred to earlier, were rooted in territories. Each homestead was occupied by a man with his wives, his unmarried daughters, his sons, and their children, and any poor people who might have attached themselves to him. In the early nineteenth century three generations living in one homestead appears to have been the widespread pattern, and in 1931 elderly Mpondo men spoke of twenty married men in one homestead having been usual,[1] but tiny homesteads with two huts also occurred.[2] Attachment of unrelated men was probably frequent in the homestead of a chief, but infrequent among commoners. Homesteads could and did split, and near kinsmen were likely to build in the same neighbourhood—commonly on one ridge in broken country—forming a unit under the leadership of their senior kinsman. The local group was not necessarily and exclusively a kinship group, however: an unrelated man might choose to build his homestead among friends, so on one ridge or hillside, even more often than within a homestead, a distinction could be drawn between kinsmen and neighbours. A number of local groups made up a chiefdom. These differed considerably in size, and fluctuated in time, splitting as rivalries grew, or coalescing under a popular leader.

A *lineage* consisted of all the descendants of a common ancestor in the male line. Lineages varied in span from the three generations which often lived together in one homestead to six or more generations of the living and dead, who claimed to be able to trace their exact connexions. A clan was composed of a number of lineages whose members claimed

---

[1] This section is based partly on my own field work. [2] Moodie, v. 43.

THE STRUCTURE OF NGUNI SOCIETY

descent from a common ancestor and who did not intermarry. Clans varied considerably in size, probably numbering something over five hundred and under four thousand living persons who traced descent from an ancestor four to ten generations back.[1] At some unspecified point a clan would split, intermarriage beginning between two lineages within it. The formal division was marked by the marriage of a chief to a girl of another lineage in his clan. Thus clusters of clans were formed with a recognized common origin. This process still continues. Membership of lineage and clan depended upon birth, a child taking the clan of its mother's husband or, should the mother have been unmarried, that of the mother herself.

In any local area one clan, that of the local leader, predominated, and in any chiefdom the clan of the chief was pre-eminent in prestige and in numbers, but neither in local area nor in chiefdom is there evidence of exclusive occupation by men of one clan. Bryant suggests that there was 'at least in very early times', but his own evidence contradicts this, for he refers to 'a servant of another clan' living with the widow of Malandela, six generations before Shaka, and repeatedly mentions splinter groups from foreign clans being received and settled by Mthethwa, Ndwandwe, Zulu, and other clans,[2] long before the disruption of Shaka's wars. Moreover, the age-mates of a young chief formed his following when he set up a homestead of his own (see p. 119), and those included men of clans other than his own. Probably the coincidence between locality and clan was higher a hundred years ago than it is today, but it is unlikely that it was ever absolute. In 1949, in one neighbourhood investigated among the Bhaca, the men of half the homesteads were of one clan; in three adjoining neighbourhoods the proportion was between a quarter and a half.[3] Even in the eighteenth century men of the same clan were often dispersed in several chiefdoms, as is plain from the division of Xhosa chiefdoms between brothers. At the present time the more conservative people lay greater stress on ties of kinship, while the less conservative stress ties of locality,[4] and it is likely that this shift in emphasis has been going on for a long time: it was conspicuous during the development of kingdoms early in the nineteenth century; but even when land was ample and groups mobile a leader numbered among his followers unrelated people. At least from the sixteenth century onwards Nguni society permitted the absorption of strangers: an appreciable number of survivors

---

[1] Bryant, *Olden Times*, pp. 3 note, 82; Hunter, pp. 58, 398–9.
[2] Bryant, *Olden Times*, pp. 57–58, 184, 259, 398–9.
[3] Hammond-Tooke, *Bhaca*, p. 56.
[4] A. Mafeje, 'Leadership in the Transkei' unpublished M.A. thesis, University of Cape Town, 1964. Hammond-Tooke noted the difference but attributed it partly to a divergence in tradition between Mpondomise and Mfengu. 'Kinship, Locality, and Association', *Ethnology* (1963), 307.

from shipwrecks and refugees from the Cape were absorbed (see pp. 233–4), some being provided with cattle by the chief they acknowledged.

Though it is improbable that *exclusive* occupation of large areas by men of a single clan ever existed, Nguni nomenclature is couched in terms of kinship, so that localities of varying size are referred to by the clan name of the leader of the locality, and his followers are addressed by his name or that of one of his ancestors. The distinction between membership of a clan and adherence to the leader of a local group or chiefdom emerges, however, as soon as questions of marriage or property, or the celebration of rituals, come up. Marriage within a clan was excluded, but not between neighbours of different clans. Inheritance was within the agnatic lineage and sacrifices to the shades were the sole concern of members of a lineage, except when a chief sacrificed to his shades seeking fertility for the whole chiefdom. Women were never completely absorbed into the clans of their husbands, but retained legal and ritual ties with their own, returning 'home' to share in sacrifices to their own ancestors, to mourn a kinsman, or to discuss the division of his property. Thus a network of kinship links bound neighbouring clans.

A great deal of confusion has arisen because one writer after another has used *clan* both for the exogamous group claiming common descent, and for a local group under a subordinate leader. In this book it is used in the first sense only.

By chiefdom is meant a political unit, occupying a defined area under an independent chief. Sometimes such chiefdoms were sub-divided under subordinate leaders who were also addressed and referred to as *inkosi* but who acknowledged the authority of a superior chief: in 1809, for example, Hintsa, the Xhosa chief with 10,000 followers, had eleven sub-chiefs under him.[1] Independent chiefs acknowledged the *seniority*, and right of precedence in ritual, of related chiefs whose political authority they did not recognize, and often it is very difficult to determine whether a particular chief was subordinate to another or merely acknowledged his seniority. This was a common ground of conflict between Nguni chiefs themselves, and a source of confusion in their relation with whites on the frontier. The marks of subordination were: admission of right of appeal to the court of the superior chief, payment of a portion of death duties and fines collected to him, and attendance at his capital for a council, or an army review, or to fight, when called upon by him.[2] Seniority of another chief was acknowledged by giving him the royal salute, but this did not necessarily imply recognition of his authority.

Until the late eighteenth century Nguni chiefdoms remained small. A Portuguese chronicler of the sixteenth century quoted above specifically contrasts Natal, where 'chiefs called Ancozes'[3] were the heads of

---

[1] Moodie, v. 42–43. [2] Hunter, pp. 378–9. [3] Portuguese spelling.

'three, four, or five villages', with the large chiefdoms north of the Lourenço Marques,[1] and only in the time of Dingiswayo did the consolidation of chiefdoms begin in Natal. How kingdoms developed there, and why they never extended south of the Mzimvubu, will be discussed in later chapters; here it suffices to note that the Xhosa chiefdoms of the early nineteenth century probably ranged between 1,000 and 35,000 persons and could muster between 150 and 6,000 fighting men.[2]

The small size was maintained because chiefdoms split. Among the Nguni the common line of cleavage was between the followers of the eldest son, known as the 'right-hand son', and those of the senior son, who was the legal heir born of the 'great wife' (see p. 126), and often considerably younger than his half-brother of the 'right hand'. A chief was expected to marry many wives and they did not all live in one homestead. The 'right-hand wife' had her own establishment, often at a considerable distance from the 'great place' where the 'great wife' lived, and when the 'right-hand son' grew up he had a following composed of men from his mother's homestead and neighbourhood, and of his own immediate contemporaries from other parts of his father's chiefdom who had been circumcised with him. Dugmore noted in 1847 that 'the youths, generally a large number, who are circumcised at the same time with a young chief of rank became his retinue'.[3] With these men—and their wives and children—he often moved still further from the 'great place', and might establish his independence even in his father's lifetime, or the move might take place later, after a battle between the brothers. Study of tradition shows that among the Xhosa-speaking people it was very often the 'right-hand son' who pioneered, occupying new territory to the west. A division of the chiefdom in each generation was not a constitutional requirement among the Nguni, as it was among the Nyakyusa in Tanzania, but it occurred very frequently where land was plentiful. It was probably linked also with a continuing increase in population (see pp. 253–4).

When a chiefdom divided the common ancestry of the sections was still acknowledged, and clusters of chiefdoms were referred to by the name of their common founding father. Thus the Xhosa comprised at least two (Gcaleka and Ngqika) and possibly nine chiefdoms[4] by 1800; the Thembu showed signs of splitting in 1851, but the conflict was not decided before they came under the colonial Government. Whether or

---

[1] Theal, *Records*, ii. 199.
[2] Moodie, v. 20, 42, 50; Steedman, i. 248; ii. 268. [3] Maclean, p. 155.
[4] Soga, *South-Eastern Bantu*, pp. 120–79; Maclean, pp. 8–22, 162–4. Ndlambe, Ntinde, Gwali, Jinqi, Dange, Mbalu, and Gqunukwebe were incipient chiefdoms, not clans, each marrying within the group. W. D. Hammond-Tooke, 'Segmentation and Fission in Cape Nguni Political Units', *Africa* (1965), 143–66, admirably demonstrates detailed relationships, though certain of his conclusions as to which were independent chiefdoms may be questioned.

not they did split is still a political issue.[1] The Mpondomise formed two chiefdoms from about 1825;[2] the Mpondo two (Qawuka and Nyanda) before 1867,[3] the Bhaca three after 1875.[4]

It is generally supposed that *all* Nguni groups must at some point be related by descent as well as marriage. Links between some have already been noted (pp. 90, 93), but the genealogical connexions between such clusters as Xhosa, Thembu, Zulu, Hlubi, Swazi, Mthethwa, Bhaca, Xesibe (pp. 90, 95), and others remain a matter of argument.[5] What is certain is, first, that in 1686 Xhosa, Thembu, Mpondo, and Mpondomise groups already existed, and there is reference in oral tradition to them as well as to Mpondomise, Bhele, and Zizi, long before Togu, the Xhosa chief alive in 1686. Secondly, inter-marriage between the chiefs' families of neighbouring clusters—as Bhele and Mpondomise—is mentioned as occurring before Togu. Such affinal links were particularly strong between Xhosa and Thembu.

Within a chiefdom members of the royal clan had greater prestige than other people, and in Nguni law a higher fine for murder, assault, seduction, or adultery was levied if the injured party was of the chief's lineage, and more marriage cattle were given for a girl of his lineage than for a commoner, but this extended only to a lineage of three generations, not to a whole clan.[6] Members of clans related to the royal line were also distinguished from those of foreigners, but they had no peculiar legal privileges. The incorporation of foreigners—even those who differed in colour—occurred again and again, and can be traced in the clan salutations. For example there are two clans, the Lungu and Mholo, still living on the Transkei coast who trace descent from the survivors of shipwrecks, and whose appearance and ritual practices support this claim.[7] Similarly, there are clans known to be of Mpondomise and Xesibe descent among the Thembu and Mpondo.

There was also a system of clientship whereby a poor man sought from a chief or wealthy neighbour cattle on loan.[8] These he herded, drinking the milk and being recompensed after a year or more with some of the increase. In return he was expected to carry out certain services for his benefactor, assisting in any heavy work, such as building a byre or fencing the fields, and attending him on a journey, at a court case, and in war. The system worked because some men possessed 'several hundreds' or 'above a thousand' cattle[9]—herds so large that

---

[1] Blue Book on *Native Affairs*, 1885; A. Mafeje, unpublished M.A. thesis. University of Cape Town.   [2] *1883 Report*, p. 407.
[3] Hunter, pp. 379–80. More familiar in the locative forms *eQawukeni* and *eNyandeni*.
[4] Hammond-Tooke, *Bhaca*, p. 7.
[5] W. C. Holden, Genealogy opposite p. 147; Rubusana, pp. 226, 290; *1883 Report*, Genealogy opposite p. 422.   [6] Hunter, p. 376.
[7] Ibid., pp. 6–7; see p. 233.   [8] Van der Kemp, p. 436.   [9] Ibid., p. 460.

they and their families could neither tend them nor use the milk—and prestige depended largely on the distribution of wealth. A stingy chief lost followers; a generous man attracted them.

The stress on rank was probably considerably greater in the kingdoms formed in the early nineteenth century than in the small chiefdoms which preceded them: in Shaka's day many men of conquered kingdoms were compelled to do menial tasks for the conquerors, but they were also incorporated into regiments as citizens. And the Nguni differed from many peoples further north in this: they neither traded in slaves among themselves nor (except on one recorded occasion) sold slaves to foreigners. In Nguni law a kinsman was never handed over in fulfilment of a debt, as commonly happened in Central Africa, and although a ready market for slaves existed on their frontiers in Mozambique and the Cape, there is only a single reference to Zulu or Xhosa having sold as slaves even men taken in war. Survivors from the *Stavenisse* who had walked from the Bay of Natal to the Buffalo and lived with the Xhosa reported in 1689: 'It would be impossible to buy any slaves there, for they would not part with their children, or any of their connexions for any thing in the world, loving one another with a most remarkable strength of affection.'[1] White farmers were said to have seized Xhosa and Bhaca children as slaves, but there was never any suggestion that a chief had sold them.[2] Dingiswayo sent cattle and ivory to market at Delagoa Bay but not slaves, though at that time many slaves were exported from Inhambane in Mozambique.[3] The Zulu exception is in a report by Captain Robert Drury that in 1719, at the Bay of Natal, he 'traded for slaves with large brass rings or rather collars and several other commodities. In a fortnight we purchased 74 boys and girls',[4] and there is a tradition that in 1854 Swazi, in response to a demand by Boer farmers, raided his Tsonga neighbours for some boys and girls.[5] Only among those Nguni who raided north of the Limpopo did the regular practice grow up of selling war captives into slavery (see pp. 346–7).

What struck the survivors from the *Stavenisse* who lived for nearly three years among the Xhosa was the rule of law and the extent of hospitality.

Revenge has little or no sway among them, as they are obliged to submit their disputes to the king, who, after hearing the parties, gives sentence on the spot, to which all parties submit without a murmur; but should the matter in dispute be of great importance, and when he cannot rely upon his own judgment, he refers the parties to an older king in his neighbourhood.

[1] Moodie, i. 431.
[2] Lichtenstein, i. 385, 389; G. M. Theal, *The Republic of Natal*, pp. 19–20.
[3] S. Kay, *Travels and Researches in Kaffraria*, p. 396; Philip D. Curtin and Jan Vansina, 'Sources of the Nineteenth-Century Atlantic Slave Trade', *JAH* (1964), 205.
[4] Robert Drury, *Madagascar*.   [5] A. T. Bryant, *A History of the Zulu*, p. 9.

When a father beats his son so as to draw blood, and complaint is made to the king, he must pay the king a cow, as a fine.[1]

Already then, in 1686, as in later Nguni law, every man was regarded as 'a shield of the chief' and any assault on him was treated as an injury to the chief himself, and the fine went to the chief and not to the kinsmen of the injured, as it did among many other African people. And the practice was established of a sub-chief referring a difficult case to his superior. The procedure in such a case is brilliantly described by a Xhosa bard who drew on tradition in 'The Case of the Twins'.[2] The chief's court, at which disputes were tried publicly, and every adult man had the right to attend and speak, was the pivot of the legal and political structure.

In 1686 a traveller among the Xhosa was secure:

One may travel 200 or 300 *mylen* through the country, without any cause of fear from men, provided you go naked, and without any iron or copper, for these things give inducement to the murder of those who have them. Neither need one be in any apprehension about meat and drink, as they have in every village or kraal a house of entertainment for travellers, where these are not only lodged, but fed also; care must only be taken, towards night fall, when one cannot get any further, to put up there, and not to go on before morning.[3]

Booty and game went to the chief:

When the Magossche have a dispute with any of their enemies, and declare war, the booty of cattle taken from the enemy is divided between the King and other great men; but, the iron and copper is worn as a mark of bravery by those who get it. . . . No one must presume to barter any thing to a stranger, without the King's consent. On going to hunt, and killing any game of value, they bring the same before the King, who keeps it, rewarding the bringers by slaughtering an ox.[4]

In 1809 Colonel Collins, a British officer, was astonished at the security of Hintsa's country, where two hundred head of cattle were left overnight in charge of a boy of eight, and he notes that the chief, during his reign, had never ordered an execution.[5] An Nguni chief was traditionally below the law, and could be tried and fined by his own privy council.[6]

His power depended upon the number of his followers; he had rivals in his own half-brothers and neighbouring chiefs who were seeking to build up followings of their own; and men were scarcer than land; so if a chief became unpopular his following melted.

Van der Kemp, the first missionary to the Nguni, reported in 1800, of the Xhosa chief Ngqika:

[1] Moodie, i. 431. [2] S. M. Mqhayi, *Ityala Lamawele*.
[3] Moodie, i. 431. [4] Ibid. i. 427–8. [5] Ibid. v. 44. [6] Kuper, pp. 63–64.

he has his counsellors who inform him of the sentiments of his people, and his Captains admonish him with great freedom and fidelity, when he abuses his authority to such a degree, that there is reason to fear that the nation will shew him their displeasure. This is done if he treats the admonition with contempt, not by way of insurrection, or taking up arms against him, but most effectually, by gradual emigration. Some kraals break up, and march towards the borders of the country, and there they stay, keeping themselves ready to emigrate to another country; they are successively followed by others, and this seldom fails to have the effect wished for; I have myself been a witness to these proceedings, but I know of only one instance of the nation taking up arms against their sovereign. . . .[1]

According to the German professor, Lichtenstein, who visited the Xhosa in 1805,

Vanderkemp twice saw this method pursued, one time when Geika [Ngqika] had made a law against private revenge, forbidding a man, who had detected his wife in infidelity to the marriage bed, taking away the life of the seducer; and the second, when he would have made the king heir to all his subjects who died without heirs in a direct line. He was required to retract both; that however relating to private revenge was established, the other was set aside.[2]

Records of the eighteenth and nineteenth centuries among the Xhosa and Mpondo, and the eighteenth century in Natal, thus depict a society in which disputes were settled in court, trade regulated, and the power of the chief himself bridled. But the records also show that there was a lively belief in witchcraft and sorcery; those accused were often tortured to obtain a confession (for the life of the victim was held to depend partly on such confession); and those convicted were killed. Long before the disturbance of frontier wars survivors of the *Stavenisse* reported:

When any one dies, and another, either man or woman, is accused of having killed the deceased by poison (for they deem themselves immortal unless the thread of life is thus severed, therefore, on getting sick they become suspicious, and are very distrustful); the suspected culprit is laid on the ground, his hands and feet extended and tied to four stakes, he is then severely beaten with sticks, and to double the pain, they lay on the patient's breast, nostrils, and privates, the nests of red ants . . . and if a person is only sick or indisposed, and any one is laid hold of on that account, the torture is renewed until either the sick person recovers, or both die.[3]

Accounts by one traveller after another of actual cases of accusation of witchcraft and torture leave no doubt that these occurred, and were not rare. The one security was escape to another chiefdom, and van der

[1] Van der Kemp, i. 436. [2] Lichtenstein, i. 353. [3] Moodie, i. 427.

Kemp suggests that those condemned were sometimes deliberately allowed to escape.[1] The tradition of Gqunukwebe origin already related (pp. 102–3) confirms this.

In spite of witch trials the society described in 1686 and in the eighteenth and early nineteenth centuries by van der Kemp, Lichtenstein, Barrow, Collins, and others was orderly and democratic, and contrasts with the violence and tyranny of Shaka in Zululand and Mzilikazi across the Vaal. North of the Tukela, a radical change in the relations between chief and people came at the end of the eighteenth century with the emergence of kingdoms. This coincided with a change in the manner of warfare. By all accounts warfare in the seventeenth and early eighteenth centuries was limited: young men raided cattle and the warriors of one chiefdom fought those of the next, but women and children were not killed.[2] Indeed, a challenge might be issued and a day fixed for the fight, and women came to urge on their men.[3] This pattern continued into the nineteenth century among the southern Nguni. But Shaka established a much more ruthless pattern of destroying all those he raided, save for the young men and women, who were incorporated into his regiments and harems, and this sort of total war was practised also by Mzilikazi and the Ngoni.

Another important change in the manner of warfare took place in Dingiswayo's time. Among all the Nguni the military organization was traditionally based on local organization, the men from each homestead joining with those from neighbouring homesteads at the great place of their local chief, and thence marching as a local detachment to that homestead of his superior, the ruler of the chiefdom, to which they were assigned. Among the Mpondo, at least, adjoining local detachments were assigned to different homesteads, so that the whole regiment did not come from one locality,[4] but large sections within each regiment were locally based, and the men of each homestead fought side by side. Dingiswayo instituted the system of age regiments, calling up the young men of an age group from all over the chiefdom, and forming them into a regiment. Thus fathers and sons, elder brothers and younger brothers joined different regiments, and regimental loyalties cut across both local and kinship ties. Regiments based on age have been common enough further north in Africa and had probably long existed among the Tswana and Pedi, but they were an innovation among the Zulu in the late eighteenth century and never extended south of the Mzimkhulu to the Mpondo, Xhosa, or Thembu, or even to the Bhaca who had fled before Shaka. It has been suggested that age regiments are used for attack, and

[1] Van der Kemp, i. 468. [2] Bryant, *Olden Times*, p. 79.
[3] Bryant, *Zulu Dictionary*, p. 35*; cf. Hunter, pp. 408, 410–13.
[4] Ndamase, p. 54; Hunter, pp. 400–1.

defence is always organized on a local basis.¹ Certainly the Zulu regiments emerged during a period of conquest. However this may be, it is clear that the new military structure greatly increased the power of the chief, because the tendency to splitting on territorial and kinship lines, hitherto so marked among the Nguni, was offset by regimental loyalties.

Before Dingiswayo's time the practice of circumcision, which had been general among the Nguni, was dropped among the Zulu and Swazi,² as it was among the Mpondo fifty years later,³ but it continued among the chiefdoms further south—Mpondomise, Xhosa, and Thembu—and among the refugees who fled south from Shaka. Contemporaries from one locality are circumcised together, and it is considered appropriate that they should be led by the son of a chief, but it is doubtful whether all the candidates of a chiefdom ever gathered for a single celebration among the southern Nguni.⁴ In the north, the ancient pattern of age groups formed for circumcision was transformed: the physical operation was dropped and the boys from all the localities of a chiefdom were enrolled in a single regiment. The reasons why circumcision was dropped by the northern Nguni and clung to so tenaciously by their southern neighbours remain obscure, but it is certain that in Pondoland the prohibition came from the chiefs, and it is possible that circumcision lapsed as the authority of chiefs developed in kingdoms, and continued where their authority remained less. Some anthropologists interpret initiation rites as the assertion of authority by an elder generation where it is insecure.

Initiation for a girl among the Nguni was always an individual affair, carried out at the home of her father, and not a group ritual as among the Sotho. It involved seclusion—in a hut built some distance apart before 1811⁵—sacrifices and dances offered to the shades, a treatment with medicines, and anointing with red ochre. Its object was to ensure her fertility after marriage.⁶

Marriage was marked by a gift of cattle (or something symbolizing cattle) from the groom to the bride's father. Without this *lobola* no legal bond was established and any children remained under the authority of the bride's lineage; once cattle had passed, however, children belonged to the lineage which gave the cattle even if the mother were divorced. Polygyny was approved and chiefs had four or five wives, as well as concubines.⁷ A rich commoner might have several wives also. The effect of polygyny of this sort was to permit the rapid increase in numbers of those lineages which controlled cattle, at the expense of those which had few, and whose sons therefore married late and monogamously. Births

---

¹ E. E. Evans-Pritchard, 'Political Structure of Nandi-Speaking Peoples', *Africa*, 10 (1940), 260–7.
² Bryant, *Olden Times*, p. 99.   ³ Hunter, pp. 165, 396.   ⁴ Cook, p. 52.
⁵ Alberti, p. 76.   ⁶ Hunter, pp. 165–74.
⁷ Moodie, i. 427; van der Kemp, i. 439.

were carefully spaced, three hoeing seasons apart, and the prohibition against a woman continuing to bear children after the marriage of a daughter limited the period of conception.[1]

Each wife had her own 'house'—a dwelling and property—and houses differed in rank. Among commoners the first wife married was the senior (except among the Swazi), but a chief's first wife formed the 'right-hand house', and his 'great wife'—'the mother of the country' for whom the marriage cattle were given by the leading men of the chiefdom—was only selected later. Within one house a younger brother showed deference to his elder brother, a younger sister to her elder sister, and the distinction was marked in language. This extended to houses, the son of a junior wife calling the son of a senior wife 'my senior brother', irrespective of their relative ages, and the principle of seniority between generations, between siblings, and between houses permeated the whole social structure. A second principle, complementary to this, was that whereby a younger brother took the place of an elder brother who was dead or absent, a younger sister the place of an elder sister; the brothers and sisters of a man's parents were in some measure parents to him, and the children of his brothers as his children, but the children of his sisters fell into a different category. All this was precisely reflected in the kinship terminology.

Political and kinship structures interlocked as has been indicated, and both were expressed in and reinforced by ritual. The Nguni chief not only exercised practical authority but also partook of the nature of divinity. A chief was 'born not made', and his position as senior kinsman of a senior lineage made him the mediator between his people and his ancestors, who were thought of as exercising power over the country they had once ruled. It has been shown how, among the Swazi, the strength and fertility of the nation were thought to be bound up with the strength and virility of the chief. Annually, at the summer solstice, a great ritual was celebrated at which the chief and his army were treated with medicines to make them strong, and the new green vegetables offered first to the ancestors, then tasted by the chief, and each of his sub-chiefs in order of rank. Only after that might the common people eat of the new crops. It was an occasion when criticism of the chief was openly expressed and the anger men felt against him confessed.[2] This *incwala* (or *ingxwala*) ritual was at one time celebrated by all the Nguni chiefdoms. During a drought further rites were celebrated and sacrifices offered by the chief on behalf of his country.

[1] *1883 Report*, ii. 72; Hunter, pp. 158–9.
[2] Kuper, *African Aristocracy*, pp. 197–225; M. Wilson, *Divine Kings and the 'Breath of Men'* pp. 11–14.
[3] Hammond-Tooke, *Bhaca*, pp. vii, 179–97, 312; Hunter, pp. 404–6; Soga, *Ama-Xosa* p. 153; *1883 Report*, ii. 409.

Commoners sacrificed to their own ancestors, the descendants of a common great-grandfather, or occasionally a whole clan, gathering to partake of the sacrificial meat and beer. It was held to be very important that on such occasions all the kinsmen should meet, and that they should be in love and charity one with another, admitting openly any quarrels that existed, and seeking reconciliation,[1] for it was thought that the shades were angered not only by neglect of themselves, and disrespect shown by junior to living seniors in the lineage, but also by quarrels within the lineage, and that they showed their anger in inflicting sickness and sterility.

The rituals reflect the preoccupation of the Nguni with cattle. These provided the most usual and most acceptable sacrifice, at puberty and at marriage, in sickness and at death. They were offered by a commoner to the shades of his lineage or a chief on behalf of his people. Goats were used as a substitute only by poor men, or on lesser occasions, such as the purification of a woman after the birth of a child. Cattle were so closely identified with the clans of their owners that milk was drunk only at the homesteads of fellow clansmen, or clansmen of one's mother or grandmother—those with whom one could not marry—or at the great place of the chief himself.[2] Colonel Collins, travelling across the Kei in 1809, noted that his guide refused milk from a strange homestead.[3] An essential part of the marriage ritual was the formal offering of curds to the bride—*ukudlisa amasi*—after which she might begin to drink the milk of her husband's clan. Until then she drank only that of her parents' clans. Elaborate taboos surrounded women in their relations with cattle and milk, reflecting the symbolic association of women's reproductive functions with the cattle of the lineage,[4] and indeed the two were directly linked, for cattle were given in exchange for nubile women. There were two shrines: the gate of the cattle byre, where sacrifices were offered and the head of the homestead buried, and the inner portion of the great hut, where sacrificial beer stood to mature, and this expresses the dual dependence upon cattle and grain. A further association existed between the royal line of a chiefdom and a particular natural feature. Among the northern Nguni it was with certain caves or woods in which past chiefs had been buried; in the southern chiefdoms the connexion was more often with a river, or a particular pool in a river, where a chief had been buried and sacrifice was made.[5]

Evil was personified in myths of witchcraft: certain persons were believed to have innate powers which they used directly, or through

---

[1] Hunter, pp. 240–68; Wilson *et al.*, *Social Structure*, pp. 163–7, 194–8.
[2] Hunter, pp. 48, 52–53. [3] Moodie, v. 41.
[4] Hunter, pp. 46, 200–1; Alberti, p. 76.
[5] Kuper, *African Aristocracy*, p. 12; Hunter, pp. 256–64, 488; *1883 Report*, ii. 403.

familiars—hyenas, baboons, snakes, or the fabulous *tikoloshe* and lightning bird—to injure their neighbours; and other evilly disposed persons were thought to use poison. The beliefs were rooted in nightmares and the awareness of anger, lust, and envy in men. These realities were interpreted in material form—envy became a baboon sent by a poor man to suck dry the cows of his rich and stingy neighbour, and lust a demon lover. Hence the 'smelling out' and torture of supposed witches and sorcerers.[1] Three differences in the technique of divination distinguish the Nguni from peoples further north: the Nguni used neither bones nor a poison ordeal, nor drums in divination, but there were diviners who, after a period of illness, seclusion, and initiation, were believed to reveal the will of the shades and the identity of evildoers.[2] These men and women—and more women than men were initiated—were thought of as called by the shades to a special vocation.

The values of Nguni society were vividly realized by some of the survivors of the *Stavenisse* in 1686. They speak of the hospitality and courtesy of the Xhosa among whom they lived: of their respect for their chiefs, and for the rule of law (see pp. 121-2). The concern for kinship and seniority, and the preoccupation with cattle, have also been described. One traveller after another mentions the gaiety and good humour of the women[3] and the good manners of the men.[4] Nothing has yet been said of the feeling for poetry and oratory, and the great development of dance and song, yet these have also endured through time, for some of the praises of chiefs and songs peculiar to particular clans are ancient,[5] and there is mention in tradition of the reputation of men for their power as orators in chiefs' courts.

One of the dominant values of Nguni society was respect for traditional customs: as so commonly in small-scale societies piety and conservatism were identified, and the chief obligation of the living was to carry out the *amasiko*, the ritual observances sanctioned by the shades. It is therefore not surprising that both contemporary documents and oral tradition bear witness to the slow pace of change among the Nguni during 200 years—from the late sixteenth to the late eighteenth centuries—and to the persistence of much of the ancient way of life for a third century and more. Not only the symbolic idiom, but minute details of ritual observances, of marriage and family relationships, and of law[6] described from the sixteenth century onwards are familiar to

---

[1] Hunter, pp. 275-95.
[2] Revd. Canon Callaway, *The Religious System of the Amazulu*, pp. 259-374; Hunter, pp. 320-41; M. Wilson, 'Witch Beliefs and Social Structure', *American Journal of Sociology* (1951), 307-13; Rubusana, *passim*.
[3] Alberti, p. 32; Barrow, i. 168; Lichtenstein, i. 309.   [4] J. W. D. Moodie, *Ten Years*.
[5] Ndamase, pp. 58-75; Rubusana, *passim*; Bryant, *Olden Times*, pp. 39, 45, 69-70, 663-5.
[6] Theal, *Records*, ii. 293-4; viii. 204-5; Moodie, i. 427-8; 431-3.

THE STRUCTURE OF NGUNI SOCIETY 129

anyone acquainted with the conservative section of Mpondo or Xhosa even as late as 1930. For example, it was reported in 1622 that Nguni boys at circumcision

clothe themselves from the waist downwards with the leaves of a tree like the palm, and rub themselves with ashes till they look as if they were whitewashed. They all keep together in a body, but they do not come to the village, their mothers taking food to them in the bush. These boys have the duty of dancing at weddings and feasts which it is customary to hold, and they are paid with cows, calves, and goats where there are any.[1]

Even the manners of 1686 are those of the same countryside nearly three centuries later.

In their intercourse with each other, they are very civil, polite, and talkative, saluting each other, whether male or female, young or old, whenever they meet; asking whence they come, and whither they are going, what is their news, and whether they have learned any new dances or tunes. . . .[2]

Periods of radical and rapid change have occurred, as in Zululand and Natal in the time of Dingiswayo and Shaka, and among the Xhosa after the cattle killing of 1857, and again throughout the Nguni area since 1938, but there have also been periods of remarkable stability. Certain of the values and customs of contemporary Nguni society, most conspicuously the stress on *ubuntu*—humanity— have roots which can be traced back three centuries, and which doubtless extend much further.

Though the pace of change varied, however, there is one consistent trend from the sixteenth century onwards, that from isolation to wider interaction. This had implications in economy, political and kinship structures, and religion which will be pursued in later chapters.

There are many tantalizing questions about Nguni history which cannot yet be answered. We do not yet know when they first established themselves south of the Drakensberg, though there is indisputable evidence that they were on the coast, and speaking an Nguni dialect, by 1593, and by their own traditions Xhosa, Thembu, and Mpondomise were on the upper Mzimvubu for generations before that. We do not know where they crossed the Drakensberg and whether it was in one party or many. The Mpondo came from Swaziland and the Thembu have kinsmen in Natal, but Thembu and Xhosa might well have come through the mountains from the country between the Orange and the Vaal by several passes. There has been much speculation on the meaning of the word *eMbo*, which is variously interpreted by Bryant, Soga, and Mpondo.[3] The one consistent meaning is 'to the north-east', the

---
[1] Boxer, p. 217.   [2] Moodie, i. 431.
[3] Braynt, *Olden Times*, pp. 7, 158, 232, 312-17; Soga, pp. 49, 65-67; Hunter, pp. 58, 380; Ayliff and Whiteside, pp. 1-5.

application varying with the position of the speaker; and it contrasts with *ebuNguni*,[1] 'to the west', so AbeNguni lived west of AbaMbo, but *where* is not specified. Bryant identifies Nguni and Koni and supposes that Nguni and Tswana were once one people. He also suggests that the Lala were an offshoot of the Kalanga, a Shona group north of the Limpopo.[2] Both hypotheses may be correct, but evidence is lacking. The diverse physical types among the Nguni, as well as fragmentary traditions, suggest that there may well have been successive migrations and layers of population which fused.

The Nguni show marked similarities in economy, local grouping, law, ritual, and symbolism with the cattle people of the Sudan, Uganda, and Kenya borderlands.[3] The identification of a man with a particular ox in his herd, the poetry in praise of cattle, the shaping of cattle horns, the association of the shades with river pools, the forms of divination and prophecy are alike. So, too, is the dispersion of homesteads, each occupied by a cattle-owner with his wives, and sons, and grandchildren, and the forms of marriage whereby cattle may even be given on behalf of a dead son so that seed may be raised in his name. Each item taken alone has little significance, but when there are many one begins to speculate on what ancient movements of people linked the Sudan with the Transkei, for it is unlikely that the whole pattern has been twice invented. It is noticeable, first, that the similarity between the extremities of the cattle-owning peoples is greater than with cattle-owners in the centre of Africa, such as the Nyakyusa; and secondly, that the similarity is a very partial one. The cattle-keepers of whom we speak north of the Equator have no chiefs, an institution which characterizes the south, and their languages are not of the Bantu family. There has long been a very complex interaction of cultural traditions and of people in Africa. Something of the process since the sixteenth century has been recorded, but we can still only speculate as to the ancient history that produced a Bantu language so deeply influenced by Khoikhoi; a people spread along the coast who avoided fish; and a nation of warriors who revered their chiefs but rejected slavery.

[1] Kropf, *Dictionary*.
[2] Bryant, *Zulu Dictionary*, p. 26; *Olden Times*, pp. 5–9.
[3] E. E. Evans-Pritchard, *The Nuer*; P. H. Gulliver, *The Family Herds*, London; L. Marshall Thomas, 'The Herdsmen', in *The New Yorker*, 1, 8, and 15 May 1965.

IV

THE SOTHO, VENDA, AND TSONGA[1]

THERE are three peoples in South Africa, the Sotho, the Venda, and the Tsonga, whose homes (so far back as there is evidence) lay to the north of the Nguni. Their languages and traditional histories differ radically and therefore they are treated separately, but since one of them, the Sotho, is very much larger than the other two, the greater part of this chapter relates to them.

1. *The Sotho*

(a) *Distribution in Space and Time*

The Sotho people are demarcated by language. The name is used in this book in a wide sense to include those who speak 'southern Sotho', 'northern Sotho' or Pedi, and Tswana. There is some tendency to confine it to the first group—or those of them who live in Lesotho (Basutoland)—but the chief Moshweshwe, who formed Lesotho a century ago, was of the same stock and spoke the same language as the Tswana and Pedi, differing only in dialect. Traditionally, the Sotho were distinguished also by dress. Very early tales make reference to the skins which they wore and which distinguished them from Nguni men, and the name Sotho itself is thought by some to be derived from an Nguni jest about their clothing.[2]

In 1965 there were five million Sotho speakers scattered throughout southern Africa.[3] A hundred and fifty years ago they were concentrated between the Limpopo and the Orange rivers, north and west of the

---

[1] I am indebted to Mr. C. C. Saunders, who worked with me as a research assistant on this chapter, and to Professor L. M. Thompson, Professor Eileen Krige, Mr. R. R. Inskeep, and Mr. Archie Mafeje for helpful criticism of an early draft.

[2] Ellenberger and Macgregor, p. 34; cf. Bryant, *Olden Times*, pp. 309-10.

[3] In Republic: 971,427 (Pedi), 1,282,544 (Moshweshwe's), 1,148, 599 (Tswana). *Republic of South Africa, Population Census, 1960*, Pretoria, 1965, Sample Tabulation 8, p. 94.

In Lesotho, 638,857. *Basutoland Population Census 1956*, Maseru, 1958, p. 19.

In Bechuanaland about 440,000 (total African population). *Bechuanaland Protectorate Report for the year 1963*, London, 1965, p. 18.

In Barotseland, 378,000. What proportion of these speak Lozi (Kololo) is not known. It was estimated at 67,193 in 1934 by Moffat Thompson. *Republic of Zambia, Monthly Digest of Statistics*, xii (March, 1965), Lusaka, p. 1.

In Southern Rhodesia and South West Africa, 1,700. I. Schapera, *The Tswana*, p. 11.

Drakensberg, with some across the upper reaches of the Limpopo. In 1824 a party under Sebetwane struck north and established themselves on the Zambezi, as the rulers,[1] and other groups spilled south and eastward over the Drakensberg into what is now Natal and the Transkei.

The traditional distribution of the Sotho was related to the distribution of tsetse fly, which carried a deadly cattle disease, and probably also to the distribution of malaria.[2] A wide tsetse belt once stretched along the curve of the Limpopo river and cut off the foothills of the Drakensberg from the coast. The area of infection contracted in the nineteenth century, retreating eastward from the Crocodile and upper reaches of the Limpopo (map 4). This contraction was possibly related to the spread of firearms and the destruction of game; it was accelerated by the rinderpest epidemic of 1896, but it had begun well before.[3] In the eighteenth century the Tswana moved northward through the fly-free corridor between the desert and the Limpopo,[4] a corridor which the whites used after them. It is possible that the Sotho had also come southward by this route,[5] but there is no evidence of that. The distribution of tsetse fly changes in time and the Limpopo valley may not always have been dangerous to cattle. Moreover, skilled herdsmen, such as the Tswana were, knew how to move their stock with a minimum of danger. They knew and avoided the patches of bush in which fly lurked;[6] they travelled by night when the fly does not bite; they gathered their cattle over smoky fires during the heat of the day;[7] and they were careful to fire the grass at certain seasons so that the encroachment of bush, and therefore the fly, might be limited.[8] The movements of the Ngoni, already described, are certain evidence that a tsetse belt was no absolute barrier to the passage of a cattle people.

But cattle-keepers could not settle in heavily infected areas, and the concentration of early Sotho occupation was in fly-free country. Traditions point to the well-watered and well-wooded Magaliesberg, named after the Kwena founding ancestor Mogale; and to the watershed between the Limpopo, the Molopo, and the Harts as the area of earliest Sotho occupation and the centre of dispersion.[9] A flat-topped hill,

[1] Livingstone, *Missionary Travels*, pp. 84–85.
[2] V. Ellenberger, 'Di Robaroba Matlhakola—Tsa Ga Masodi-a-Mphela', *TRSSA*, 25 (1937–8), 36.
[3] C. Fuller, *Tsetse in the Transvaal and Surrounding Territories, passim*.
[4] I. Schapera, 'The Native Inhabitants', in *CHBE*, viii. 36; J. Mackenzie, *Austral Africa*, i. 23; Ellenberger and Macgregor, pp. 15–16, 31.
[5] B. H. Dicke, 'The Tsetse Fly's Influence on South African History', *SAJS*, 29 (1932), 792–6.
[6] Livingstone, *Missionary Travels*, pp. 79–83, 177.   [7] Wilson, *Good Company*, p. 34.
[8] P. A. Buxton, *The Natural History of Tsetse Flies*, p. 307; C. F. M. Swynnerton, 'The Tsetse Flies of East Africa', *Trans. Royal Entomological Society*, 89, 1931, 513.
[9] Ellenberger and Macgregor, pp. 31–37; Stow, pp. 432, 490, 521, 544–6; S. M. Molema, *The Bantu Past and Present*, pp. 40–57.

THE SOTHO 133

Ntsuanatsatsi, between the modern Frankfort and Vrede in the Orange Free State was occupied by settlers from Magaliesberg, and it is the hill of origin to the ruling lineage of Lesotho. According to tradition, it was once fringed with wild olive trees[1]—'olives of endless age'. Desiccation of the country has long been going on, the rivers diminishing, pastures eroding, and the boundary of the Karoo and Kalahari moving eastward, so the western portion of the Sotho area was once considerably better watered, wooded, and grassed than it is now.[2]

Among the Sotho several layers of population can be traced, and it seems that each new wave of immigrants established themselves as rulers, and either absorbed the earlier inhabitants, or forced them to move westward into the desert.[3] Cattle-keepers and cultivators absorbed both hunters and other cattle-keepers and cultivators. People of at least three physical types have mingled. First, a short, black, negro physical type has existed from the Limpopo valley and Mujaji's mountain in the lowveld to the fringes of the Kalahari, and into South West Africa. These negroes (Kattea, or Khiogá, or Ngona, or Berg Dama) speak, in the twentieth century, only the language of the people among whom they live—that is, one or another dialect of Sotho, or Venda, Nama, or Herero.[4] Secondly, the bush-boskop physical type is conspicuous, and though many of this stock were absorbed by the Sotho speakers, others, the Sarwa, have remained distinct physically, and speak as their home language not Sotho but a Khoikhoi dialect.[5] The third type is tall and dark, distinct from either negro or bush-boskop, and it is these people who are the earliest Sotho speakers. Some of them, the Kgalagadi, retreated towards the desert as other Sotho lineages, more recent immigrants to the south, established themselves.

Oral traditions are largely concerned with the splitting of lineages and the genealogical connexions between chiefs. The genealogies of successive waves of immigrants are distinguished. Those of the earliest Sotho speakers—the Kgalagadi and Fokeng—are disconnected. That of the second wave—the Rolong and their offshoot the Tlhaping—ramifies and includes twenty-one generations before 1900; and that of the third wave—the Hurutshe—has numerous offshoots and seventeen generations

---

[1] Ellenberger and Macgregor, p. 17.
[2] Acocks, *Veld Types of South Africa*, pp. 12-18. Maps 1-5; Moffat, *Missionary Labours*, pp. 329-33; Livingstone, *Missionary Travels*, pp. 110-12; L. F. Maingard, 'The Brikwa and the Ethnic Origins of the Bathlaping', *SAJS*, 30, 1933, 599.
[3] Stow, pp. 420-59; Molema, *The Bantu*, pp. 36-41.
[4] F. Elton, 'Exploration of the Limpopo River', *Proceedings of the Royal Geographical Society*, 16, 1872, 95; Krige, 'Origins', 325; E. J. and J. D. Krige, *The Realm of a Rain Queen*, p. 6; B. H. Dicke, *The Bush Speaks*, p. 10; P.-L. Breutz, *Tribes of Kuruman and Postmasburg District*, pp. 24-30; Vedder, 'Berg Damara', pp. 39-41.
[5] Westphal. It has long been supposed that Sarwa was a click language akin to a San language. Professor Westphal has demonstrated its links with Nama and Kora.

(see p. 136). Furthermore, some link the Hurutshe with the Rolong line. The Hurutshe genealogy includes the famous chiefdoms of Kwena, Ngwato, Ngwaketse, Tawana, Kgatla, Pedi, and Tlokwa, as well as that of Moshweshwe.[1] But some Sotho chiefdoms—notably the Lobedu and Phalaborwa of the lowveld, and the Birwa of the northern Transvaal—have not been linked to either of the major lineages or to the Kgalagadi or Fokeng. Their identity with other Sotho rests on similarity of language and custom alone.

The Hurutshe lineage has

a tradition to the effect that in the land whence their remote ancestors came the sun shone on the opposite shoulder . . . indicating a shadowy recollection of the remote period when their forefathers were still north of the equator. . . . Before coming from the north, the place whence the first people came was the east, some indefinite place towards the sun-rising. . . . This is the reason why in burying their dead they place the face of the deceased person in that direction. . . .[2]

Some features in Lobedu and Pedi ritual confirm a north-eastern origin, and suggest links with the lake chiefdoms north of Malawi (see pp. 169–71). The Hurutshe also claimed in 1822 that there was, in their country, a hole 'out of which the first men came, and their footmarks are still to be seen there'. 'The cattle also came from the same hole',[3] indicating that they thought of themselves as aborigines in the country. Two such contradictory traditions of origin suggest a fusion of earlier inhabitants and immigrants.

Ellenberger and Macgregor, working on genealogies and oral tradition, thought that the Sotho crossed the Zambezi during the eleventh or twelfth century and were in 'Bechuanaland', where the Hurutshe and Kwena separated, . . . 'about the thirteenth or fourteenth century';[4] Breutz thinks the Kwena and Hurutshe 'arrived in South Africa between 1300 and 1400'.[5] Casalis showed that Sotho south of the Caledon had been in possession of their country for five generations before 1833,[6] i.e. probably from about 1670, and their traditions indicate a sojourn at Ntsuanatsatsi and north of the Vaal long before that. Schapera's conclusion that 'all that can safely be said is that the Sotho were in possession of the eastern half of their present habitat by about 1600 A.D.'[7] seems

---

[1] Ellenberger and Macgregor, pp. 15, 331–94. I. Schapera, *The Ethnic Composition of Tswana Tribes; A Short History of the BaKgatla-bagaKgafela of Bechuanaland Protectorate*; 'A Short History of the Bangwaketse', *AS*, 1 (1942), 1–26; and, with D. F. van der Merwe, *Notes on the Tribal Groupings, History and Customs of the BaKgalagadi*. Krige, 'Origins'; van Warmelo, *Preliminary Survey*. [2] Stow, pp. 432, 545.

[3] Campbell, *1813*, p. 192; Campbell, *1820*, i. 303, 306; Moffat, *Missionary Labours*, p. 263.

[4] Ellenberger and Macgregor, pp. 15, 333.

[5] P.-L. Breutz, *The Tribes of Mafeking District*, p. 24.

[6] E. Casalis, *Les Bassoutos*, p. 200. [7] Schapera, 'The Native Inhabitants', p. 36.

unduly conservative even in the light of oral tradition, and still more so when recent archaeological evidence is considered.

In Rolong tradition their founding ancestor, Morolong, was born near the present Zeerust twenty-one generations before 1900,[1] indicating the thirteenth or fourteenth century, though of course dating from genealogies is precarious. Archaeological evidence shows that iron was worked at Melville Koppies in the period 1060±50,[2] and in Phalaborwa during the period 770±80 A.D.[3] We do not know what language these early iron-workers spoke, but it is significant that Morolong was celebrated as 'the forger' who 'danced to iron' (see p. 145). Whether (as so often happens) the genealogy has been telescoped, or whether the Sotho iron-workers arrived in an area in which smelting was already practised, is uncertain. There can be no doubt that the Sotho speakers came from the north, and we have some indications of their date of arrival and route, but no conclusive evidence. Similarities between Sotho pottery and that at Uitkomst have already been noted (p. 38), and the clustering of both Uitkomst and Buispoort sites in the areas to which Sotho oral traditions point (pp. 34, 35, 38).

Written records by eye witnesses start much later for the Sotho than for the Nguni, but the first Dutch settlers at the Cape heard reports of a people living north of the Orange whom we can identify as Sotho. *Brijckje* were mentioned by Nama to explorers travelling northward in 1661,[4] and again by Nama who visited the Cape in 1681.[5] Explorers heard of them again in 1682[6] and 1689.[7] The Brijckje were the Tlhaping.[8] The earliest reports containing any detail are those of Hendrik Hop and Brink in 1761,[9] Roos and Marais in 1761-2,[10] and Wikar in 1778-9,[11] but all these spoke from hearsay.[12] The first eye witness account of the Sotho is that of 1801 when the British Government at the Cape sent an expedition under Truter and Somerville north to seek cattle. Daniell, the secretary of the expedition, painted what he then saw at Dithakong

[1] Ellenberger and Macgregor, pp. xviii–xix, 394.
[2] Mason and van der Merwe, 'Radio-carbon Dating of Iron Age Sites in the Southern Transvaal', 142.
[3] M. Stuiver and N. J. van der Merwe, 'Radio-carbon Chronology of the Iron Age in Sub-Saharan Africa', *Current Anthropology*, 9, 1 (1968), 56.
[4] *VRJ*, iii. 343; E. C. Godee-Molsbergen, *Reizen in Zuid-Afrika*, i. 62.
[5] Moodie, i. 386.
[6] O. Bergh and I. Schrijver, *Journals of the Expedition of Olof Bergh and Isaq Schrijver*, VRS, 1931, p. 121.
[7] Ibid., p. 234; Moodie, i. 437.
[8] Maingard, 597; Schapera, *The Early Cape Hottentots*, p. 37 n. 46.
[9] C. F. Brink and J. T. Rhenius, *The Journals of Brink and Rhenius*, VRS, 1947, p. 31.
[10] Godee-Molsbergen, ii. 53–54.
[11] Wikar, pp. 145–69.
[12] The evidence is reviewed by C. C. Saunders, 'Early Knowledge of the Sotho', *Quarterly Bulletin of the South African Public Library*, 20 (1960), 59–70.

TABLE VI
PUTATIVE GENEALOGY OF SOTHO ROYAL LINE

(After D. F. Ellenberger and J. C. Macgregor, *History of the Basuto*, London, 1912. Dates from Ellenberger and Macgregor. Cf. G. W. Stow, *The Native Races of South Africa*, London, 1905, pp. 559–61, who gives two generations before Masilo.)

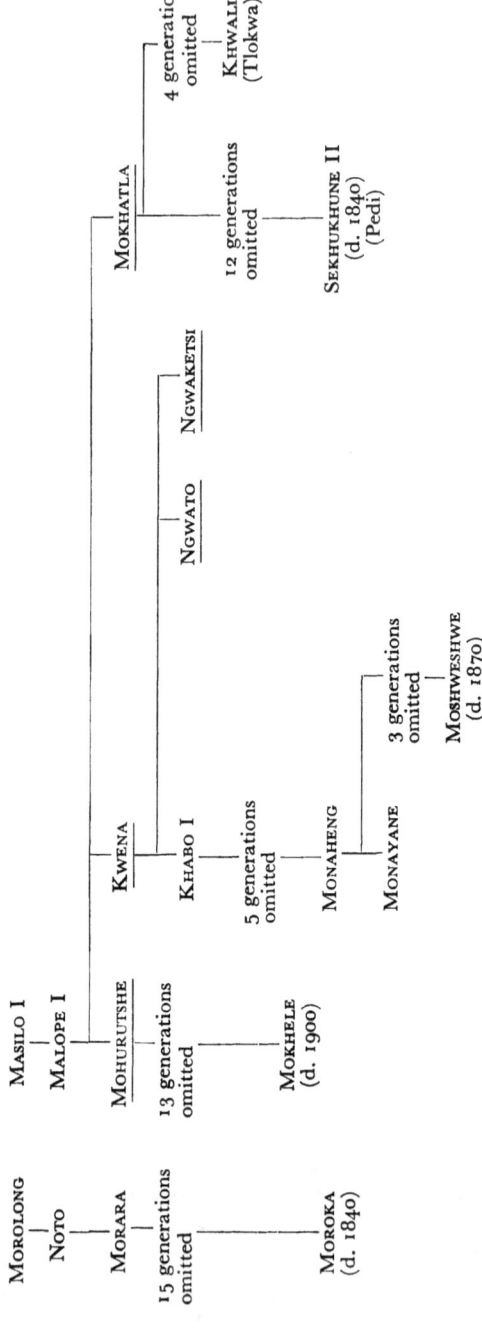

Names of chiefs from whom chiefdoms took their title are underlined.
Only Pedi and Tlokwa chiefdoms do not appear in the genealogy as names of former chiefs.

('Old Lattakoo'),[1] Borcherds, the assistant secretary, left a written record,[2] and Barrow recorded what the members of the expedition told him.[3] After 1801 travellers and missionaries in Sotho country were numerous, and a number of them left detailed journals.[4] Oral traditions were recorded from early in this century,[5] and there is a magnificent body of detailed ethnographical material on the Tswana, collected by Isaac Schapera,[6] which is unmatched elsewhere in southern Africa. There is also substantial material on the Lobedu and southern Sotho,[7] and a little on the Pedi.[8]

Map 4 shows the extent of the dispersion of Sotho-speaking people according both to oral tradition and to eye witness report before 1822, and between 1822 and 1839. Such gaps as there are may be due to the absence of early travellers or detailed ethnographic study in the

[1] Samuel Daniell, *African Scenery and Animals*.
[2] P. B. Borcherds, *An Autobiographical Memoir*, pp. 77–87, 123–34.
[3] J. Barrow, '*Voyage to Cochinchina . . . to which is annexed an account of a Journey . . . to the Residence of the Chief of the Bootchuana*.
[4] Lichtenstein; Burchell; Campbell, *1813*; Campbell, *1820*; S. Kay, *Travels and Researches in Caffraria*, pp. 215–36; S. Broadbent, *A Narrative of the First Introduction . . .*; Thompson; Moffat, *Missionary Labours*; R. Moffat, *Apprenticeship at Kuruman*; Andrew Geddes Bain, *Journals*, VRS, 1949; *The Diary of Dr. Andrew Smith*, VRS, 1939–40; T. Arbousset, *Voyage d'exploration au nord-est de la colonie du Cap de Bonne-Espérance*; Backhouse; Livingstone, *Missionary Travels*; Casalis.
[5] J. C. Macgregor, *Basuto Traditions*; Ellenberger and Macgregor; S. M. Molema, *Chief Moroka*; Z. K. Matthews, 'A Short History of the Tshidi Barolong', *Fort Hare Papers*, 1 (1945), 9–28.
[6] I. Schapera, 'The Social Structure of the Tswana Ward', *BS*, 9 (1935), 203–24; *A Handbook of Tswana Law and Custom*; *Married Life in an African Tribe*; 'The Political Organisation of the Ngwato of Bechuanaland Protectorate', in Fortes and Evans-Pritchard (ed.); *Ditirafalô tsa Merafe ya BaTswana*; *Native Land Tenure in the Bechuanaland Protectorate*; *Tribal Legislation among the Tswana of the Bechuanaland Protectorate*; 'Notes on the History of the Kaa', *AS*, 4, 1945, 109–21; 'Some Features in the Social Organization of the Tlokwa', *SwJA*, 2, 1946, 16–47; *Migrant Labour and Tribal Life*, 'The Tswana Conception of Incest', in M. Fortes (ed.), *Social Structure*; 'Kinship and Marriage among the Tswana', in Radcliffe-Brown and Forde; *The Tswana*, 'Should Anthropologists be Historians?', *JRAI*, 92, 1962, 143–56; 'Agnatic Marriage in Tswana Royal Families', in Schapera (ed.), *Studies in Kinship and Marriage*; 'Kinship and Politics in Tswana History', *JRAI*, 93, 1963, 158–73; and *Praise Poems of Tswana Chiefs*. See also p. 134 n. 1; Z. K. Matthews, 'Marriage Customs among the Barolong', *Africa*, 13, 1940, 1–24. Also F. J. Language, 'Herkoms en Geskiedenis van die Tlhaping', *AS*, 1, 1942, 115–33; *Stamregering by die Tlhaping*; 'Die Verkryging en Verlies van Lidmaatskap tot die Stam by die Tlhaping', *AS*, 2, 1943, 77–92; 'Die Bogwera van die Tlhaping', *Tydskrif vir Wetenskap en Kuns*, 4, 1943, 110–34. Also B. A. Pauw, *Religion in a Tswana Chiefdom*; 'Some Changes in the Social Structure of the Tlhaping of the Taung Reserve', *AS*, 19, 1960, 49–76.
[7] E. J. and J. D. Krige, *Rain Queen*; 'The Lobedu of the Transvaal', in D. Forde (ed.), *African Worlds*; E. J. Krige, 'Property, Cross-Cousin Marriage, and the Family Cycle among the Lobedu', in R. Gray and P. Gulliver (ed.), *The Family Estate in Africa*, pp. 155–92; E. H. Ashton, *The Social Structure of the Southern Sotho Ward*; *The Basuto*; P. Duncan, *Sotho Laws and Customs*.
[8] C. L. Harries, *The Laws and Customs of the Bapedi and Cognate Tribes of the Transvaal*; D. Hunt, 'An Account of the Bapedi', *BS*, 5, 1931, 275–326; G. Pitje, 'Traditional Systems of Male Education among the Pedi and Cognate Tribes', *AS*, 9, 1950; C. V. Bothma, *Ntshabeleng Social Structure*; N. J. Van Warmelo, *Ethnological Publications* 10–22.

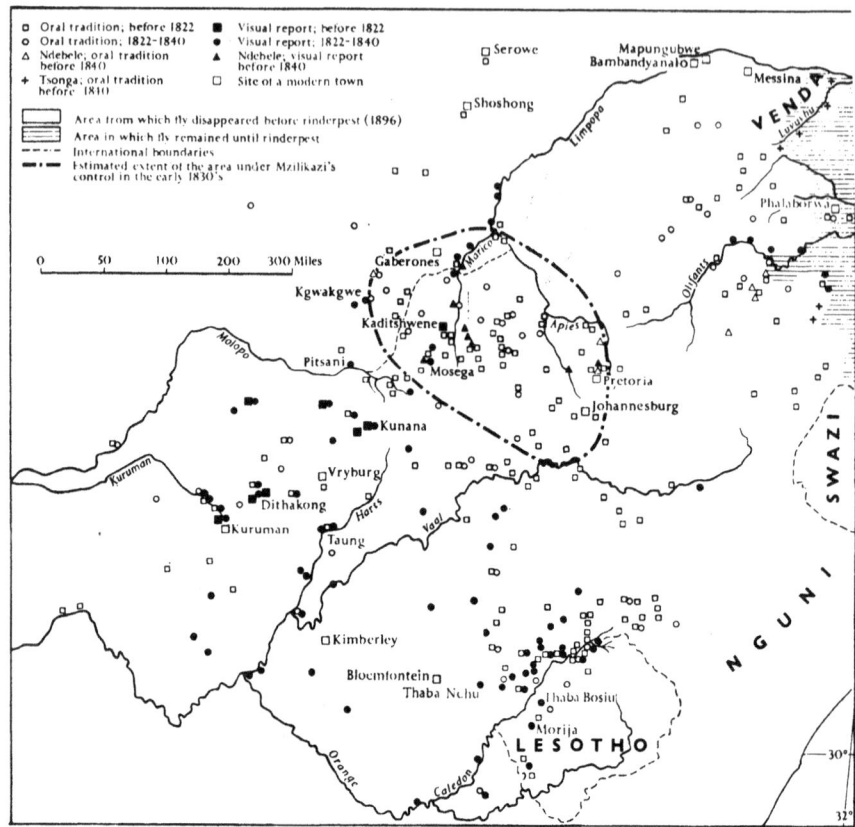

MAP 4. Distribution of Sotho before 1822 and 1822–40, also the Tsetse zone in the Transvaal. *After C. C. Saunders* (References are filed in the University of Cape Town). Tsetse distribution after C. Fuller, *Tsetse in the Transvaal and Surrounding Territories*, Pretoria, 1923.

THE SOTHO

area, rather than to the absence of any Sotho-speaking group before the devastating wars of 1822–38.

A further source of evidence is to be found in the remains of stone buildings which are widely distributed over the areas the Sotho occupy. These include large settlements with stone hut foundations, byres, and enclosing walls; and small, scattered, corbelled, stone huts. There is lively debate whether all of these were, or were not, built by the ancestors of the modern Sotho. Mason, the leading Iron-age archaeologist of the Transvaal, is convinced that they were.[1] P.-L. Breutz, who has made a number of ethnographic studies, is insistent that they were not,[2] though his own evidence confounds him. It is therefore necessary to set forth the evidence in some detail. Daniell painted homesteads in Dithakong (Lattakoo) in 1801 and showed huts with mud walls and courtyards fenced with wood or reeds;[3] Burchell described this in detail in 1812 and drew cross-sections.[4] Members of the 1801 expedition, however, reported that the houses of Dithakong were 'walled up with clay and stones, to the height of about five feet'.[5] Campbell, who had described the mud and wood walls of Dithakong in 1813, visited another Tswana town, Kaditshwene, in 1820 and reported: 'We were led ... to an extensive enclosure surrounded by a stone wall, except at the gate by which we entered. . . . Every house was surrounded, at a convenient distance, by a good circular stone wall. Some of them were plastered on the outside and painted yellow.'[6] And commenting on the 'ancient cattle inclosures built of stone' near Dithakong, he says the Hurutshe 'build their inclosures of stone exactly in the form of these ancient ruins'.[7]

In some Tswana groups there is a tradition that they did not build the stone walls in the area they occupy, but there is an equally explicit tradition among others that they did. Borcherds noted in 1801 that the Tlhaping did not build the stone ruins at Dithakong and did not know who had built them, but 'the habitations were circular in shape, and the walls of stone, about four or five feet high, resembling the houses in the inhabited town'.[8] Ellenberger records a tradition that another Sotho-speaking group, the Hoja (Lihoya), had built them,[9] and Moffat noted

---

[1] Mason, *Prehistory*, pp. 378–81; R. J. Mason, 'The Origin of South African Society', *SAJS*, 61, 1965, 255–67.
[2] e.g. Breutz, *Tribes of Kuruman and Postmasburg*, p. 24. Breutz makes an inexplicable error in stating that 'Campbell's descriptions and drawings of the Hurutshe twin capital Tshwenyana and Kaditshwene indicate nothing in the way of stone structures', *The Tribes of Marico District*, p. 15.
[3] The Fehr Collection, Rust en Vreugd, Cape Town.
[4] Burchell, ii. 360–71; Kay, p. 227.   [5] Barrow, p. 391.
[6] Campbell, *1820*, i. 223–4; Kay, p. 227.
[7] Campbell, *1820*, i. 126.   [8] Borcherds, pp. 84–85.
[9] Ellenberger and Macgregor, pp. 52–53.

that they were 'supposed to have been built in the days of Tlou, the greatest of the Barolong kings, whose power extended from the Bahurutsian mountains to the Hamhana hills, a distance of two hundred miles'.[1] Schapera records a tradition that Moleta, a Ngwaketse chief of the late eighteenth century, 'surrounded his new village with stone walls' on a hill overlooking Lobatsi, and Makaba built walls on Kanye hill.[2] And P.-L. Breutz, despite his conclusions (p. 139), reports that: 'According to the tradition of the baKwena ... the extensive ruins at Moedwil and Selouskraal ... were built by chief Sekano ... who lived about 1730–40.'[3] Moffat saw the stone walls of 'towns of former generations' in 1835 and supposed them to have been built by the Hurutshe:

> Innumerable vestiges remain of towns, and some very large ones. Some are miles in circumference, which must have cost immense labour, being entirely built of stones, that is the fences and folds; also the lower part of the houses, the upper part of which there are but few vestiges, having been built of clay mixed with cow dung.
>
> [And further on:] The country was formerly thickly inhabited with many tribes of Bakueans [Kwena] and innumerable ruins are scattered under all the mountains and on every hill. They built their fences with stone.[4]

Cornwallis Harris noted that 'extensive stone walls marked the site of a once flourishing Bamaliti town, now destroyed',[5] and Bain in 1834 'passed the ruins of a very extensive Bechuana town, its numerous stone kraals being still in a good state of repair, though it was forsaken by its inhabitants on the irruption of the Mantatees about twelve years ago'.[6] Andrew Smith, after meeting Mzilikazi on the Tolane, passed 'immense ruins of stone kraals formerly inhabited by the aborigines, principally Bapuroo, a tribe of Baquana [Kwena]'.[7]

Arbousset reported in 1836 'des murailles de pierre, bâties en cercle, à la hauteur d'environ quatre pieds, où les naturels de ce fertile pays renfermaient autrefois leurs heureux troupeaux' near the source of the river Enta (Vals),[8] and the Revd. John Bennie, travelling in 1834 near the Sand river, describes both the ruins of an extensive settlement similar to those already mentioned and, elsewhere, corbelled stone huts.[9] Ellenberger,[10] and recently A. C. Myburgh,[11] record clear oral traditions that the Sotho built these corbelled huts as a protection against lions.

[1] Moffat, *Missionary Labours*, p. 375, n.
[2] Schapera, 'Bangwaketse', pp. 3–4.
[3] P.-L. Breutz, 'Stone Kraal Settlements in South Africa', *AS*, 15, 1956, 170.
[4] Moffat, *The Matabele Journals*, i. 99–100, 137.
[5] Harris, *The Wild Sports of Southern Africa*, p. 143.
[6] Bain, p. 138.   [7] Smith, ii. 75.   [8] Arbousset, pp. 298–9.
[9] J. Bennie, *An Account of a Journey into Transorangia and the Potchefstroom-Winburg Trekker Republic in 1834*, pp. 10–11.
[10] Ellenberger and Macgregor, p. 71.
[11] A. C. Myburgh, *Die Stamme van die Distrik Carolina*, pp. 45–49.

The Sotho are still building in stone, as is apparent to any traveller in Lesotho. Walton has demonstrated, with admirable diagrams, that the plan of homesteads now built is similar to that of ancient stone ruins.[1] The building of stone huts and byres, as well as miles and miles of stone walling, has in fact continued through a wide area. Livingstone noted the presence of Tswana migrant labourers building stone walls for farmers in the Clanwilliam area before 1856,[2] and stone walls, byres, and huts have been and still are being built for white farmers by Africans in the Queenstown, Tarkastad, and Cathcart districts. They are also being built in Reserves, notably around Qamata in the Transkei (where stone hut walls are sometimes completely mudded over, within and without) and Nqutu in Zululand. Stone contour-walls to hold soil and water were still, in 1966, being built by Lobedu where they hoed steep slopes.[3]

There can therefore, be no doubt that the modern (1966) Sotho built in stone and that their ancestors did so from at least 1801 onwards. In their ground plan, in their concentration, and in their location on 'hill slopes and hill crests' the Iron Age settlements studied by archaeologists resemble very closely those of Sotho-speakers described by eye witnesses. Moreover, the areas of dense settlement as revealed in air-photo surveys of Iron Age sites are exactly the areas to which oral traditions and eye witness records point as the areas of early Sotho settlement. The population must have been very considerable: Mason reports 998 settlements in 971 square miles in the Magaliesberg.[4] This population cannot have vanished into thin air. The other known occupants of the Transvaal, the Venda, were few in numbers and according to their own tradition never penetrated south of Pietersburg. There is an overwhelming presumption that the Sotho were the main body of early stone builders in the Transvaal.

The questions at issue are these:

(i) Was the technique of building used in Dithakong and Kaditshwene before 1820 exactly similar to that in the widely dispersed settlements of which remains are found between the Vaal and the Limpopo? Can it be distinguished from the technique used by the Venda (p. 174) or is it identical?
(ii) Were the large settlements with stone walling and the corbelled stone huts built by the same or different peoples?
(iii) Which of the techniques of stone building and walling still in use are traditional and which are modern?

[1] Walton, *African Village*, pp. 32–51, Plates 87–89.
[2] Livingstone, *Missionary Travels*, pp. 32–33.
[3] E. J. Krige, 'The Place of the North-Eastern Transvaal Sotho in the South Bantu Complex', *Africa*, 11 (1938), 270 and personal communication.   [4] Mason, 'Origin', 258–60.

A systematic investigation of ancient dwelling-sites and of stone huts, byres, and walls is an essential first step to understanding early South African history.

(b) *Economy*

In the early nineteenth century the Sotho were hunters, herders, and cultivators, much as the Nguni were. They, too, herded cattle, goats, and a few sheep, and set no store by fowls,[1] but they used sheep in rituals[2] (which the Nguni did not) and associated them with chiefs. They, too, depended largely on game for meat, using their cattle for milk and transport rather than as slaughter stock. They too grew sorghum and sweet reed, kidney beans, pumpkins, sweet melons, and gourds.[3] Maize was unknown to the Taung and Hoja until 1822,[4] and the Pedi, after obtaining seed in 1838, rejected it after one season's trial,[5] so, on the high veld, the addition of this important crop came considerably later than it did along the coast. Grain was sometimes offered for exchange: some of the Thamaga, of Kgalagadi stock, sowed no grain, but Campbell noted in 1820 that 'With the skins of the animals killed they are able to purchase grain from the neighbouring nations',[6] and at a later date large quantities of grain were brought from Lesotho for sale to whites.[7] But often it was scarce. In 1812 Burchell could buy none in Dithakong,[8] and the Voortrekkers sometimes obtained it only by force.[9]

From the time travellers first visited them Sotho were using cannabis (dagga, bang) and tobacco,[10] and these were most important as articles of barter with the Khoikhoi and San, who had such a craving that they smoked 'wild hemp' (*leonotis leonoris*).[11] Campbell reported of the Hurutshe in 1820 that 'They grow much tobacco, both for their own consumption and as an article of trade'.[12]

The Tswana and Pedi cattle were the long-horned Sanga type, distinguished from Nguni, Shona, and probably Khoikhoi cattle, but in Lesotho there was an early intermixture with Nguni stock.[13] Pack oxen[14]

---

[1] Campbell, *1813*, pp. 218–19.
[2] Ellenberger and Macgregor, p. 248; Krige, *Rain Queen*, pp. 45, 237, 274, 276–8.
[3] Moffat, *Matabele Journals*, i. 8; Burchell, ii. 368, 379–80, 413–14.
[4] Ellenberger and Macgregor, p. 54.   [5] Arbousset, p. 342.
[6] Campbell, *1820*, ii. 7–8.   [7] Theal, *Basutoland Records*, ii. 438.
[8] Burchell, ii. 293.
[9] Thomas Baines, *Journal of a Residence in Africa*, ii. 171.
[10] Ellenberger and Macgregor, pp. 8, 71; Burchell, ii. 230, 414; Casalis, pp. 182–3.
[11] Campbell, *1813*, pp. 143–4.
[12] Campbell, *1820*, i. 276.
[13] Livingstone, *Missionary Travels*, p. 49; H. H. Curson and R. W. Thornton, 'A Contribution to the Study of African Native Cattle', *Onderstepoort Journal of Veterinary Science and Animal Industry* (1936), 672, Figs. 68–82; Mason and Maule, pp. 34–36, 41–43, 47; Singer and Lehmann, 'The Haemoglobins of Afrikander Cattle'.
[14] A. Sekese, *MeKhoa le maele a Basotho*, p. 59.

were constantly used for bringing in grain from the fields and transporting household goods and articles for trade—one gets the impression from the literature of a considerably more widespread use of pack animals than among the Nguni. According to Moffat[1] neither the Rolong nor the Ngwaketsi rode 'even on oxen' in 1824, and the Makololo 'had never attempted to ride oxen' until Livingstone advised them to do so in 1851. Livingstone adds: 'The Bechuanas generally were in the same condition until Europeans came among them',[2] but Lichtenstein reported in 1805 'Beetjuans' bartering ornaments for riding oxen with the Kora at Witwater,[3] so the Tlhaping learnt to ride from the Khoikhoi.

The main distinction between the economy of the Sotho and that of their neighbours was the skill of the Sotho as craftsmen.[4] They mined and smelted iron, copper, and tin, and carried on an extensive trade in metal goods. Eye witness evidence on this trade begins with Wikar's journal of 1778–9. He found Khoikhoi on the Orange river using a barbed spear and metal knives, and wearing massive armlets of copper, and ear-rings, and was told that these were made by the Tlhaping ('Bliqua'). He was told, also, how the Tlhaping dug ore from the mountains, two days' journey from their main village,[5] but he did not reach Tlhaping country himself. Borcherds describes the heavy copper and iron ornaments worn by the Tlhaping in 1801, and Daniell painted ornaments and tools. Their weapons were spears and battle-axes, and shields of ox-hide shaped like an hour-glass, quite distinct from those of the Nguni.[6] Borcherds notes that each man wore round his neck a 'pointed knife, sharpened on both sides, and resembling a small flat dagger, carried in a sheath made of ivory or wood, beautifully carved and ornamented with figures of animals', and the Tlhaping rejected trade knives as not being as good as their own. The 'earrings and earplates . . . of red and yellow copper' which they wore were obtained from the Rolong.[7] Campbell thought that, in 1813, the Tlhaping bought both iron and copper from the Hurutshe, though they manufactured tools and ornaments from these metals themselves,[8] and Burchell says that in 1812 there was only one smith at work, and he had just begun,[9] so Wikar (quoted above) may have been misinformed. However that may be, there is no question that the Hurutshe mined and smelted. Campbell on his second journey in 1820 visited Kaditshwene and reported: 'The rainmaker took us to see one furnace, in which they smelted the iron.' This Campbell drew.

[1] Moffat, *Missionary Labours*, p. 393. [2] Livingstone, *Missionary Travels*, p. 182.
[3] Lichtenstein, ii. 318. [4] Kay, pp. 227–31; Burchell, ii. 415–20.
[5] Wikar, pp. 145, 149, 155.
[6] Campbell, *1820*, i. 259–60; Burchell, ii. 404, 422; Stow, Plates 14, 19; Moffat, *Missionary Labours*, pp. 533, 535.
[7] Borcherds, pp. 83, 124. [8] Campbell, *1813*, pp. 186–7, 213, 217.
[9] Burchell, ii. 308 Illust., 340–1, 420–1.

And later he 'stopped at two smiths shops... and procured some samples of the iron they had been smelting'. This was 'found to be equal to any steel'. But he was never allowed to see the copper furnaces which 'were behind the houses of some of their captains'.[1] Robert Moffat was shown by a Hurutshe coppersmith how to draw copper wire,[2] and this man was careful to explain that coppersmiths were distinct from iron-workers. Livingstone found a Fokeng chief 'busily engaged in drawing copper wire and manufacturing ornaments'.[3] Phalaborwa were pre-eminent as iron-workers,[4] and in Pedi country 'Le fer abonde', wrote Arbousset in 1842: 'Les naturels en forgent des houes deux fois aussi pesantes et bien meilleures que celles des autres tribus béchuanas et caffres de nous connues.'[5]

Livingstone wrote of the Kgatla settlement near Mabotsa in 1843: 'The manufactory of iron seems to have been carried on here uninterruptedly from a very remote period.'[6] Travelling eastward through the Transvaal he came to 'Bagalaka' (of Transvaal Ndebele stock), who, he reported, 'smelt iron, copper, and tin, and in the manufacture of ornaments know how to mix the tin and copper so as to form an amalgam. Their country abounds in ores.'[7]

A section of the Lete[8] acquired their stock by selling iron implements. They

'moved ... to the valley of the Taung River ... and settled along the string of pans or vleis ... where they carried on an extensive manufacture of iron implements and ornaments; the traces of their occupation, in the shape of furnaces and slag-heaps, hut foundations, grindstones, pottery, and graves, being visible to this day.... Mokgosi's people had no cattle when first they settled at Rabogadi, but they built up a big trade in iron implements, supplying the BaRolong, the BaTlhaping, the BaNgwaketsi, and the Ba-Hurutse with axes, spears, hoes, bracelets, etc., in return for goats and later for cattle. Four hoes purchased a cow, three an ox. The iron implements were loaded on to pack-oxen and taken to the tribes mentioned above, and when they had been disposed of the Ba-ga-Malete returned home with the goats or cattle they had acquired.[9]

This occurred after the wars (about 1843), but it reflects a pattern established in the traditional society, not one introduced by whites.

[1] Campbell, *1820*, i. 228, 244–5, 275, 277, Plate opposite p. 276; Burchell, ii. 308.
[2] Moffat, *Missionary Labours*, pp. 466–8.
[3] Livingstone's *Missionary Correspondence, 1841–56*, p. 95.
[4] C. M. Schwellnus, 'Short notes on Palaborwa smelting ovens', *SAJS*, 33 (1936), 904–12; E. J. Krige, 'Note on the Phalaborwa and their Morula Complex', *BS*, 11 (1937), 362, and verbal communication. [5] Arbousset, p. 349.
[6] Livingstone, *Missionary Correspondence*, p. 35. [7] Ibid., p. 97.
[8] The Lete (Baga-Malete) were of Nguni origin but absorbed by Sotho. For spelling of the name cf. note by Professor Cole, in A. Sillery, *The Bechuanaland Protectorate*, p. 160.
[9] V. Ellenberger, 36, 44.

THE SOTHO

So there is indisputable evidence of Sotho-speaking people smelting at places widely scattered through what is now the Transvaal and Botswana. Oral tradition credits the founding lineage with the art of smelting, and an ancient ritual of dancing in honour of the totem associated with the lineage (see p. 162) confirms this.

The Barolong dance in honour of a hammer and of iron. Established in the neighbourhood of Mosika (or Mosiga), where there is much iron, one of their chiefs, expert in the art of Vulcan, took to forging it. He was in consequence called *Morolong*, i.e. blacksmith.... This name ... comes from an old word, *rola* 'to forge'. His son Noto—that is, the hammer—also bore the name of the iron instrument which took the place of the primitive flint. Father and son from that time were able to forge much; and were justly celebrated among the tribes for the agricultural instruments and weapons which they made. It is from this that the Barolong (smiths), whose emblem was at once the iron (*tsepe*) and the hammer (*noto*), took their name. The genealogy of the Barolong, however, does not carry us any farther back than about the end of the fourteenth century to Morolong, the smith of Mosika. Their more remote ancestors, therefore, must have borne another name, before the birth (in the neighbourhood of Zeerust) of him from whom they take their present one.[1]

The contrast between the Xhosa, to whom metal was a temptation to murder in 1686 (see p. 122), and the Tlhaping, who preferred knives of their own and their neighbours' manufacture to trade knives in 1801, is obvious, but not all Sotho were metal-workers. In Lesotho it was the Zizi who were the first smelters and the Sotho learnt from them. Before the whites came hoes were few and costly.[2] The art of smelting was already practised at Phalaborwa from the eighth century and at Melville Koppies from the eleventh century (see pp. 34–35, 38), but elsewhere also iron remained very scarce for nine centuries after the technique was first practised.[3] An examination of the distribution of mineral resources in South Africa suggests that the development of skill was related to accessibility and quality of ore. With the exception of Ntsuanatsatsi and Lesotho, the areas of early Sotho occupation were areas in which iron ore was plentiful. It is noticeable that the large Tswana settlements of Dithakong, Kuruman, and Ramoutsa lie along the line of iron ore deposits.[4]

Not only are the techniques of smelting similar over a wide area in Africa and through centuries—the Melville Koppies hearth is similar to that of the Hurutshe in 1820—but the associated symbolism is similar

---

[1] Ellenberger and Macgregor, pp. xviii–xix, quoting from the Revd. P. Lemue, missionary of Mothito in 1843.
[2] Ellenberger and Macgregor, pp. 26, 255.
[3] Wilson, *Peoples of the Nyasa-Tanganyika Corridor*, pp. 15–16.
[4] Geological Survey, *The Mineral Resources of South Africa*, Pretoria, 1959, Mineral Map; Government of Bechuanaland, *Mineral Resources of the Bechuanaland Protectorate*, H.M.S.O., London, 1965.

also, from the Zulu and Sotho in the south to the Shona in Rhodesia, and Nyiha and Nyakyusa in Tanzania. Among all these people the process of smelting is identified with the reproductive cycle in women, and there are rigid taboos on women, and sometimes married men, approaching a furnace or forge.[1] Livingstone wrote of the Kgatla foundry: 'They always refuse admittance to those who have had intercourse with the other sex since the period of the year when they annually commence smelting, lest they should bewitch the iron.'[2] Detailed associations recur. These are no foreign symbols but are deep-rooted in Bantu-speaking Africa, and it can hardly be doubted that the art of smelting spread from one common source.

The question is not whether the Sotho mined, but whether it was they who were chiefly responsible for the extensive mining and metal trade between the Limpopo and the Orange. The Shona and the Venda were pre-eminent as miners, but the Venda number only 246,000 (1960), and oral tradition places them in their present habitat, with only minor incursions further into the Transvaal. Their special skill was the mining and working of gold.[3] Of Sotho working in gold there is no evidence, though gold was mined in the Transvaal, and Campbell saw both gold and silver ornaments in Kaditshwene in 1820. They were obtained, he was told, from the north.[4]

Skeletal remains at Mapungubwe and Bambandyanalo classified as bush-boskop,[5] and the evidence of the use of gold there, have led some to suppose that the chief metal-workers of the Transvaal were men of bush-boskop physical type, and Breutz suggests that they were the Kora or other Khoikhoi.[6] Such a hypothesis does not fit with the evidence from oral tradition or eye-witness report, which leaves no doubt that the Sotho were adept craftsmen in iron and copper working, whereas most of the Khoikhoi certainly did not smelt.[7] Nama were reported by eye-witnesses to be smelting copper in 1762,[8] but, according to Wikar, in 1778 it was not the Nama themselves who smelted; they employed Dama—a negro people—to smelt for them, at the astonishingly high fee of a she-goat for one day's work.[9] As has been shown, other Khoikhoi bartered metal from the Tlhaping.

---

[1] Monica Wilson, *Rituals of Kinship among the Nyakyusa*, pp. 141–2; C. Bullock, *The Mashona and Matabele*, p. 110; B. Brock, 'Iron Working among the Nyiha of Southwestern Tanganyika', *SAAB* (1965), 99, 105; Ritter, *Shaka Zulu*, p. 27; Stow, Plates 15 and 16.
[2] Livingstone, *Missionary Correspondence*, p. 15; V. Ellenberger, p. 44.
[3] Fouché, p. 123.   [4] Campbell, *1820*, i. 270.
[5] Fouché, pp. 127–74; A. Galloway, *The Skeletal Remains of Bambandyanalo*, pp. xvii, 118–25, passim.   [6] P.-L. Breutz, *The Tribes of Vryburg District*, p. 14.
[7] A. J. H. Goodwin, 'Metal Working among the Early Hottentots', *SAAB*, 11 (1956), 46–51.
[8] O. F. Mentzel, *A Complete and Authentic Geographical and Topographical Description of the ... African Cape of Good Hope* VRS, 1944, iii. 297.
[9] Wikar, pp. 77–79.

THE SOTHO 147

Moreover, such skeletons as have been described from iron-working settlements between the Limpopo and Vaal other than Mapungubwe and Bambandyanalo have been classed as 'negro' with bush-boskop admixture.[1] Culturally, the archaeologists regard Mapungubwe and Bambandyanalo as outposts of Zimbabwe,[2] and this view is confirmed by tradition and ritual. The Venda and Lemba who worked in gold were closely linked with the Shona (see pp. 169, 172). The weight of evidence indicates that it was indeed the ancestors of the Sotho who were the chief miners of iron and copper in the Transvaal, but the ancient gold-miners were perhaps people linked with the Shona, such as the Venda and Lemba.

The Sotho were craftsmen in metal: they were also highly skilled in leather-work, and in carving in wood and ivory, and they made ostrich-feather parasols which caught Daniell's eye. Wikar speaks in 1778 of skins 'as soft as chamois leather' obtained by Khoikhoi on the Orange from the Tlhaping. He brought back an old specimen, but 'did not have enough to pay for a new one',[3] and still, in 1966, the Sotho kaross, made of jackal pelts beautifully tanned and stitched, was a staple of the luxury 'curio' trade in Cape Town, costing up to R70.

Tanning and sewing were the work of men, and in their initial stages they were a co-operative activity, a number of men taking hold of a hide and manipulating it together to soften it.[4] Men of high status occupied themselves stitching karosses. At Kaditshwene Campbell found 'the Regent busy sewing a skin cloak'[5] between a feast and court case. The poor wore antelope skin, the rich fur, and a fine fur cloak required forty skins[6] meticulously pieced together. The display and comfort of the rich, and the trade with other peoples, depended, therefore, on hunters bringing in pelts, and to supply jackal and cat pelts was a main function of the Sarwa and other men without cattle.[7] Undressed pelts were also an article of trade, used to obtain grain or even cattle.[8] From the time traders' wagons first penetrated into 'the interior' they brought back

[1] R. A. Dart, 'Report on the Vechtkop Skeletal Material', *JRAI*, 67 (1927), 230–4; P. W. Laidler, 'The Archaeology of Certain Prehistoric Settlements in the Heilbron Area', *TRSSA*, 23 (1935), 58–63; T. R. Jones, 'Prehistoric Stone Structure in the Magaliesberg Valley, Transvaal', *SAJS*, 32 (1935), 319–33; E. J. Haughton and L. H. Wells, 'Underground Structures in the Caves of the Southern Transvaal', *SAJS*, 38 (1942), 319–33; R. A. Pullen, 'Remains from Stone-Hut Settlements in the Frankfort District, O.F.S.', *SAJS*, 38 (1942), 334–44. (I am indebted to my colleague, Professor L. H. Wells, for these references and helpful discussion.) D. R. Brothwell, 'Evidence of Early Population Change in Central and Southern Africa: Doubts and Problems', *Man*, 63 (1963), 132.
[2] R. Summers, 'Proto-Historic Cultures of Rhodesia and South Africa', *Systematic Investigation of the African Later Tertiary and Quaternary*.
[3] Wikar, pp. 143, 149.
[4] Borcherds, p. 126; Burchell, ii. 416; Campbell, *1813*, p. 185.
[5] Campbell, *1820*, i. 235.   [6] Campbell, *1813*, p. 187; Lichtenstein, ii. 411.
[7] Livingstone, *Missionary Travels*, p. 50.   [8] Campbell, *1820*, ii. 7–8.

karosses, as well as ivory and ostrich feathers, but long before that the Sotho had been selling cloaks to their Khoikhoi neighbours,[1] and perhaps even sending them to the coast. Livingstone wrote in 1857:

> During the time I was in the Bechuana country between twenty and thirty thousand skins were made up into karosses; part of them were worn by the inhabitants and part sold to traders: many, I believe, find their way to China. The Bakwains [Kwena] bought tobacco from the eastern tribes, then purchased skins with it from the Bakalahari, tanned them, and sewed them into karosses, then went south to purchase heifer-calves with them. . . .[2]

No doubt there was a great development of trade in the nineteenth century, but the fact that fragments of Sung celadon ware from between the twelfth and fourteenth centuries have been found at Mapungubwe[3] shows that some tenuous communication between the Limpopo and China was already established long before the whites arrived.

The other men's craft was carving in wood and ivory. They made utensils, and hafts for metal tools, sometimes beautifully ornamented.[4] The women's craft was pottery. Earthen jars for storing grain which held ten to twelve bushels were in regular use.[5] Stone pipes, and baskets or mats made of rushes, are also mentioned as articles of trade,[6] and some of the Sotho made a great rush basket—*sesiu*—for storing grain, a technique which distinguished them from most of the Nguni.[7] Ivory, in the form of tusks, was relatively plentiful and was pressed on the first travellers who were seeking rather to buy cattle and corn.[8] Livingstone even notes ivory rotting near Lake Ngami,[9] and it had been used there to fence cattle byres.[10] Therefore there cannot have been a ready market for ivory near Lake Ngami, or even on the upper reaches of the Limpopo, before Hume and other whites arrived with wagons to buy and transport it, though the Ngwato sent some to Delagoa Bay.[11]

What the Sotho did not sell was men. Livingstone stated categorically: '. . . never in any one case, within the memory of man, has a Bechuana chief sold any of his people, or a Bechuana man his child',[12] and the Hurutshe in 1820 'knew of no nation who sold men'![13] Tswana chiefs and certain leading families had Sarwa families attached to them, who owed obligations in labour, as will be shown, but Sarwa could not be bought

---

[1] Campbell, *1813*, p. 232. [2] Livingstone, *Missionary Travels*, p. 50.
[3] Fouché, pp. 26, 44, Plate XVI.
[4] Wikar, p. 149; Burchell, ii. 404–5; Stow, Illusts. 17, 18.
[5] Borcherds, p. 124; Campbell, *1820*, i. 244.
[6] Campbell, *1820*, i 276. [7] Arbousset, p. 251; Burchell, ii. 288.
[8] Livingstone, *Missionary Travels*, pp. 68–69; Burchell, ii. 286, 288.
[9] Livingstone, *Missionary Travels*, p. 69.
[10] Sillery, p. 26. [11] Moffat, *Matabele Journals*, i. 18.
[12] Livingstone, *Missionary Travels*, p. 31. The only exceptions reported were *post* and probably *propter* the wars. Moffat, *Apprenticeship*, p. 131; Broadbent, pp. 97, 107.
[13] Campbell, *1820*, i. 242.

and sold. Moffat, giving evidence in 1824, said of the Tswana: 'They have a servile class but no slaves.'[1] Sebetwane on the Zambezi only began to sell captives in 1850.[2]

There are, however, some scraps of evidence which suggest that employment for wages in kind occurred among the Sotho before whites settled north of the Orange. Campbell met in 1820 '... a party of poor people from Mashow [Masweu], both men and women, with four pack-oxen. They were travelling to the nations in the north, seeking for employment in thrashing out their corn.'[3] And Eileen Krige notes that among the Lobedu: 'In the old days an orphan usually hired out his services to carry salt or iron ore from far countries in order in this way to acquire marriage hoes or cattle.'[4]

Moffat says of the Sarwa: 'They are generally spoken of in the same light as pack oxen and are actually used for that very purpose',[5] but references to Sarwa porters for anything other than meat are few. It will be shown (p. 235) that the existence of animal transport distinguished South from Central Africa, and obviated the need for great caravans of porters through much of the country. The Tswana used pack-oxen in their metal and grain trade (see pp. 143-4), and even the earliest white traders and missionaries travelled with wagons. Transport on foot occurred, but it appears that only the Tsonga, who were cut off from the interior by tsetse, regularly worked as porters, carrying Portuguese goods inland and returning with metal and ivory. Lobedu country abutted on one of the Tsonga paths and that may be why poor Lobedu took to carrying also.

We know little of trade routes in Sotho country. Wikar reported in 1779[6] that the Tlhaping travelled on foot, annually, down the Orange to exchange metal goods and karosses for cattle with the Khoikhoi.

The Blip [Tlhaping] come each year to the tribes living along this river to trade, bring with them tobacco, ivory spoons, bracelets, copper and iron beads, glass beads, copper earrings and bracelets, knives, barbed assegais and also smooth axes and awls. This is the way they trade: for a heifer they give eight assegais, an axe and an awl, a small bag of tobacco and a small bag of dagga, and for a bull or an ox, five assegais plus all the other things as for a heifer. They also bring soft, well tanned skins of hartebeest with the grain removed....

The regent of Kaditshwene with whom Campbell talked in 1820 said that:

---

[1] *Papers relative to the conditions and treatment of the Native inhabitants of Southern Africa within the Colony of the Cape of Good Hope*, Printed for the House of Commons, 1835, Part I, p. 128.
[2] Livingstone, *Missionary Travels*, pp. 91–92.   [3] Campbell, *1820*, i. 282.
[4] Krige, 'Property, Cross-Cousin Marriage, and the Family Cycle', p. 173.
[5] Moffat, *Apprenticeship*, p. 126; *Missionary Labours*, p. 9.   [6] Wikar, p. 149.

He had heard of a nation to the N.E. called Mahalaseela, who use elephants as beasts of burden;[1] beads came from them, and they lived near the Great Water. He had heard also of a people called Matteebeylai to the eastward, who also lived near the Great Water, and have long hair; and of another nation to the N.E., who bring beads to the Boquains, called Molloquam; pointing to many beads on his arms, he said he got them by means of a servant whom he sent to the Boquains with an elephant's tooth.[2]

The fact that the people of Kaditshwene knew how to vaccinate also suggests that they had some contact with the coast.[3]

The upper tributaries of the Limpopo ran through Sotho country, and long reaches of the Limpopo are navigable during a wet season. When the Crocodile river is flowing—and it flows only intermittently—canoes can travel down it from Hartebeest Poort to its confluence with the Marico, and on two hundred miles (interrupted by one major waterfall) to 'Zanzibar'. Then follow fifty miles of rapids, and a hundred miles of navigable water past Mapungubwe, to the Tola Azime falls, near Beit Bridge. Below that there are forty miles navigable, thirty-two miles of rapids, and navigable water from Pafuri to the coast (maps 4, 5). The evidence suggests that a hundred years ago the Limpopo had considerably more water in it than it does now.[4] Nevertheless, most of the Sotho were certainly not river men—the Kololo learnt to manipulate canoes only after they arrived on the Zambezi.[5] 'At a great distance north or north-east of the Bamangwato, people came up rivers with boats who exchanged ivory and Khotlo (a name given to any yellow metal or copper).' This statement was made to Moffat in 1829 at Mzilikazi's place near where Pretoria is now. It might, therefore, refer to the Limpopo, but more probably to the Save and Zambezi.[6] What is certain is that Vasco da Gama found Africans with 'much copper' which they wore 'on their legs and on their arms and in their much curled hair', and tin which they used 'on the hilts of the daggers', at the mouth of an unidentified river, a little way north of Delagoa Bay—i.e. near the Limpopo mouth—in 1498;[7] and both copper and tin were sold in Delagoa

---

[1] M. Shinnie, *Ancient African Kingdoms*, p. 36, shows a picture of a Meroitic king riding an elephant. The elephant is African not Indian. Campbell was mistaken in believing that African elephants were never trained. I am indebted to Sir Robert Birley for evidence on African elephants in classical times. Jan H. van Linschoten. *Itineraria, 1579–1592*, p. 49, refers to Prester John, as Abyssinian King, riding an elephant.

[2] Campbell, *1820*, i. 240–1: cf. Campbell, *1813*, p. 216.

[3] Campbell, *1820*, i. 236.

[4] I am much indebted for information to Major R. J. Horsham, who knows the whole length of the Limpopo and has canoed down it: cf. Elton, 89–101; W. Ranke, 'Down the Limpopo', *South African Geographical Journal*, 15 (1932), 35.

[5] Livingstone, *Missionary Travels*, p. 88.

[6] Moffat, *Matabele Journals*, i. 18.

[7] Da Gama, p. 11; Axelson, *South East Africa, 1485–1530*, p. 38 n.

Bay in 1723.¹ In 1731 the tin bought amounted to 213 lb.² We know also that copper was mined at Messina, tin in the Randberg (Malepo range),³ and iron at Thabazimbi, all of which lay near the Limpopo or its tributaries. The suggestion that metal might have been brought to the coast down the Limpopo by canoe is not confirmed by any direct evidence, but it is a possibility.

Metal may also have been brought along the footpath which Dicke mentions:

Past Levanga, skirting the Wolowedo range on its eastern point, led the great communication route, the inland short cut, between Delagoa Bay and Southern Rhodesia (Mashona and Manica land). Along this road, only a native footpath . . . the Magwamba traders with their porter columns came from Delagoa Bay to compete with the traders from the mouth of the Limpopo, from Inhambane, from Sofala. For centuries the native traders of the Thonga [Tsonga] tribes, to which the Magwamba belong, had been using this route from Delagoa Bay through the Northern Transvaal lowveld before the inland regions through which they passed had become inhabited. . . . The path crosses the Limpopo near its junction with the Limvubu.⁴

The Pedi showed Trichardt another path in 1838. Arbousset says of them: 'They used to procure copper articles of hardware and cloth at Lorenzo Marques, and barter them in the interior for ivory, horns, cattle, and skins.'⁵ And van Warmelo says: 'The arid flat mopani country between the Zoutpansberg and the Limpopo . . . up to the second half of the last century . . . provided the route for the constant stream of travellers going to and coming from the copper mines at Messina, where they bartered for the precious metal.'⁶

Another path ran from the salt-pan on the Brakriver past the copper mine of Messina.⁷ These were well trodden when the Voortrekkers reached the Transvaal, but how ancient they were we do not yet know. Dicke notes that 'There were no Sofala (Sabie) traders operating south of the Zoutpansberge, or south of the Limpopo',⁷ but Potgieter's party travelled in 1836 from the Soutpansberg across the Limpopo to the Nuanetsi, and came on a people, 'knopneuse', trading with the coast. To these Tsonga the inhabitants of the Soutpansberg were sending iron which they smelted, in exchange for beads and other wares.⁸ It seems certain, therefore, that a trade route linked Sofala with the Soutpansberg.

¹ Theal, *Records*, i. 413–17, 497.
² H. C. V. Leibbrandt, *Précis of the Archives of the Cape of Good Hope: Journal, 1699–1732*.
³ P. J. van der Merwe, *Nog Verder Noord*, pp. 38, 170.
⁴ B. H. Dicke, 'The Northern Transvaal Voortrekkers', *AYB*, 1941, i. 150; *Bush Speaks*, pp. 4, 17.   ⁵ Ellenberger and Macgregor, p. 33.
⁶ N. J. van Warmelo, *The Copper Miners of Musina and the Early History of the Zoutpansberg*, p. 4.
⁷ Dicke, 'Transvaal Voortrekkers', i. 150.
⁸ Van der Merwe, pp. 38–43, 164–6, 173–4.

Paths also existed between Lesotho and Zulu country. Arbousset wrote that: 'Un petit sentier à peine tracé, qui va de Bossiou à Mococoutlouse, résidence de Dingaan, nous servit de fil conducteur à travers ce labyrinthe de montagnes.'[1] When Sotho first penetrated south of the Caledon the Zizi brought iron weapons and tools from the coast up the mountain passes, and much later Moshweshwe sent cattle and feathers to Shaka. By what means copper ornaments and iron weapons or tools percolated from the Sotho to the Xhosa in the eighteenth century we do not know, but it is conceivable that the people 'who had come from a tribe lying to the north-west of Lattakoo' mentioned as visiting the Xhosa chief Hintsa before 1821 were itinerant traders (see p. 114) who had crossed the Drakensberg and reached the Mbashe valley by yet another path.

Campbell makes a tantalizing remark about individuals in Kaditshwene and Dithakong having 'marts' (*maats*?), 'a particular connection with a person belonging to another nation',[2] which suggests the possibility of trading partners, and later he says: 'Our Lattakoo friends, who travelled with us, having "marts" at Mobatee, were well received into their houses.'[3] 'Mobatee' was a Kora settlement on a tributary of the Harts. No further evidence on 'marts' has been found, nor is there any evidence of regular markets such as occurred elsewhere in Africa. As we have seen, Campbell 'stopped at two smiths' shops' in Kaditshwene to obtain samples of metal-work.[4] The Portuguese are known to have traded gold at three inland 'fairs' in Rhodesia to the north of Zimbabwe,[5] but none is mentioned south of the Limpopo. Why did no regular markets emerge among the Sotho, when it is abundantly clear that at least some of them were craftsmen, as well as miners and hunters, and that they sold tools, utensils, and sewn karosses, together with ivory, and ingots of copper and iron? Trade was controlled by the chiefs, who insisted that they should be the first to see imported goods for sale,[6] and communication with the outside world was hampered by the attempt of one chief after another to prevent traders from outside reaching the next chiefdom.[7] This, however, is no complete explanation for the absence of markets, for chiefly monopolies occurred also in the kingdom of Monomotapa, and in other parts of Africa where markets existed.

The imported goods most desired were beads, which Campbell calls

[1] Arbousset, pp. 125–6, Map.
[2] Campbell, *1820*, i. 274: Dutch *maats* = English *mates*.
[3] Ibid. ii. 23.
[4] Ibid. i. 244–5.
[5] E. Axelson, 'Portuguese Settlement in the Interior of South East Africa in the Seventeenth Century', *Congresso Internacional de Historia dos Descobrimentos*, Actas v. I am much indebted to Professor Axelson for help on this and other points.
[6] Burchell, ii. 280; Campbell, *1820*, i. 268, 316.
[7] Harris, p. 136; Borcherds, p. 85; Campbell, *1813*, p. 193; Campbell, *1820*, i. 145; Livingstone, *Missionary Travels*, p. 77.

'the only circulating medium or money in the interior of South Africa',[1] and it is from a study of the distribution and dating of beads that the trade routes are likely to be plotted.

(c) *Social Structure*

The Sotho were distinguished from their neighbours not only by their skill as craftsmen, but by the fact that most of them lived in large settlements rather than scattered homesteads. The Commissioners who made direct contact with Sotho in 1801 were astonished to enter Dithakong (Lattakoo), a settlement with 3,000 huts and 10,000 to 15,000 inhabitants and a dependent village, Patani, with 1,500 to 2,000 inhabitants.[2] In 1817 the Tlhaping chief moved to a new town on the Kuruman river, which later travellers thought had a population of 4,000 to 10,000,[3] but almost the same number remained near the old site.[4] Kaditshwene, the Hurutshe settlement, had between 13,000 and 16,000 inhabitants in 1820–1;[5] Masweu (Mashaw) 10,000 to 12,000 inhabitants in 1820;[6] Taung 1,300 to 1,400 in 1824, but nearly 20,000 by 1836;[7] and Kgwakgwe, where Moffat visited the Ngwaketse chief in 1824, 'covered a vast extent so that the population must have been great compared with that of the towns of South Africa generally'.[8] There were others too: Phitshane, on the Molopo river, had a population of 'upwards of 20,000' in 1824,[9] and Thaba Nchu was estimated by Backhouse in 1839 as having 9,000 inhabitants.[10] Campbell heard in Kaditshwene in 1820 of many large settlements to the eastward,[11] seldom more than a day's journey apart, which were not seen by any literate visitor before they were destroyed in war, and similar settlements have continued in Botswana.[12]

Each large settlement was a capital in which an independent chief lived with most of his followers, and each was surrounded by cattle-posts at which stock were kept under the care either of young bachelors from the capital or else of dependants of the stock-owners.[13] Small groups of hunters, clients of the chief and leading families, occupied areas distant from the capital and cattle-posts. Moffat remarks that 'poor Bechuanas who belonged to the Barolongs'...'inhabit those parts of the country where neither towns nor cattle-posts can be fixed'[14]—i.e. desert, or tsetse country. The poor, according to Moffat, 'vastly preferred' the liberty of the

---

[1] Campbell, *1820*, i. 246.   [2] Borcherds, pp. 85, 88, 130.
[3] Campbell, *1820*, i. 122; Thompson, p. 93.
[4] Campbell, *1820*, i. 67; Thompson, p. 121.
[5] Kay, p. 325; Campbell, *1820*, i. 181, 277.   [6] Ibid. i. 181.
[7] Moffat, *Missionary Labours*, p. 591.
[8] Ibid., p. 398.   [9] Ibid., p. 388.   [10] Backhouse, pp. 411–12.
[11] Campbell, *1820*, i. 241, 271, 313; Kay, p. 225.
[12] Schapera, *The Tswana*, pp. 35–36, and *Tswana Law*, p. 8.
[13] Schapera, *Ethic Composition*, p. 3.
[14] Moffat, *Apprenticeship*, pp. 83, 125.

country to 'a kind of vassalage in the towns',[1] and sought to live as hunters.

Many of the settlements were on hill-tops. Kay describes Kaditshwene as standing 'on the very summit of a mountain, on every side of which access is extremely difficult',[2] situated exactly like Thaba Bosiu, and Maseu was on 'an eminence'.[3] The cultivated fields spread around the capital, sometimes covering 'several hundred acres', 'at least twenty miles in circumference' in the valley below,[4] and during sowing and reaping families might camp on their fields, but their huts might be burned if they failed to return to the capital when the work in hand was done.[5] Pack-oxen were used to bring home the grain, for some fields were twenty-five miles from the owner's homestead.[6]

Such concentration was inconvenient for cultivators, herdsmen, and hunters, and we must ask ourselves *why* the Sotho should have lived in such large settlements. First, it must be noted that concentration was not uniform over the whole Sotho area: it was conspicuous towards the west and north, and much less in the east and south, but even in Lesotho the average village is much larger than an Nguni homestead. In 1936 the average size of a village in Lesotho was 30–50 *families*, whereas the average for a Swazi[7] commoner homestead was 7·2 *persons* and 22·5 in the homestead of a 'prince' or chief. And even in Lesotho it varied with group tradition. Ashton noted: 'The Koena [Kwena] prefer to have large compact villages whereas the Tlokoa [Tlokwa] and Fokeng prefer small family groups.'[8] It has also changed in time; the Tlhaping once lived concentrated in Dithakong and Kuruman, but now live scattered,[9] and the Tawana, who were once concentrated, also scattered. It has been suggested that concentration was due to shortage of permanent water, but settlements *moved*, showing that there was more than one spring in their territory, and each cattle-post had some water supply. In fact concentration results in long queues of women waiting for water at the wells, a problem which might be obviated if settlements split up. Moreover, the largest of the ancient settlements recorded, Kaditshwene, was in well-watered country. The argument that concentration was for defence is more plausible, particularly since many settlements were on hill-tops and difficult of access, but this alone can hardly be the explanation. The most valuable and most vulnerable property—cattle—was mostly kept at cattle-posts, not at the capitals. Also, it is repeatedly asserted that the Sotho were less warlike than the Nguni, who have lived scattered during most of their own history. Concentration among the

---

[1] Moffat, *Missionary Labours*, p. 8. [2] Kay, pp. 215, 226.
[3] Campbell, *1820*, i. 171. [4] Ibid. i. 64, 169, 177, 181, 220.
[5] Schapera, *Land Tenure*, pp. 99, 112–13. This relates to a later date but was traditional law.
[6] Schapera, *Tswana Law*, p. 11 n. [7] Kuper, *An African Aristocracy*, pp. 37–38.
[8] Ashton, *Basuto*, p. 21. [9] Pauw, *Tswana Chiefdom*, p. 6, Map B.

Nguni occurred over a short period during the existence of military kingdoms, but the large capitals, in essence army barracks, disappeared with the collapse of the military organization. None of the Sotho were organized in military kingdoms comparable to that of the Zulu, and concentration has continued in Botswana until the present day, though not in the Republic or Lesotho. Concentration in Botswana is explicitly linked with the authority of chiefs, and the scattering of the Tawana from their capital, Maun, has been attributed to the 'inefficiency and misrule' of their chiefs over thirty years.[1]

What distinguished almost all the Tswana who lived in large settlements, both from the Sotho of Lesotho and from the Nguni, was the degree of stratification. All the Sotho chiefdoms, like those of the Nguni, had a nucleus of kinsmen, members of a royal lineage, from which the chief came. Some lineages claimed a common descent with the royal line, but others were admitted to be strangers—adherents who had been accepted into the chiefdom at a more or less distant date. The proportion of nuclear stock to strangers varied from one chiefdom to another: it was less than one-tenth among the Lobedu and about one-fifth among the Ngwato,[2] but considerably larger in others. The relative status of 'foreign' lineages varied also: that of Shona (Kalanga) in Serowe was high; that of Sarwa low.

Among all cattle-owners in South Africa some form of clientship tended to develop, poor men without cattle herding for the wealthy in return for a portion of the progeny (see pp. 63, 120–1), but among the Tswana the system developed much further than among the Nguni or in Lesotho. Tswana clients received dogs as well as cattle, and they hunted and brought meat, and above all pelts, to their patrons. The Tswana trade in cured and sewn karosses was dependent upon the supply of raw pelts by Kgalagadi and Sarwa clients. A symbiotic relationship existed between cattle-owners living in large settlements and hunters and collectors who scattered in small family groups in arid or tsetse country, but who returned periodically to the capital to hand over to their patrons pelts, ivory, and meat, and receive in return iron weapons, tobacco, grain, and beads.[3] According to Moffat the Sarwa were never permitted to own cattle,[4] but the Kgalagadi were cattle-owners who had lost their cattle to later invaders, and those who were employed as herdsmen might gradually acquire a portion of the progeny and start a herd of their own. The Ngwato Regent, Tshekedi, claimed in 1935 that some Sarwa also were being transformed into cattle-owners. He described how his father, Khama, had placed cattle with certain Sarwa families

---
[1] Schapera, *Land Tenure*, pp. 25, 271–2.
[2] Krige, *Rain Queen*, p. 85; Schapera, *Ethnic Composition*, p. v.
[3] Campbell, *1813*, p. 219.   [4] Moffat, *Missionary Labours*, p. 9.

and allowed them some of the calves. Sarwa were not at first compelled to serve any patron, Tshekedi claimed, and he described how a Sarwa family with whom Khama had placed cattle brought them back and then took to the desert. The Sarwa returned after sixteen years saying 'they were hungry and came back to herd the cattle'.[1] Livingstone commented on the ease with which a man who was dissatisfied could move to another chiefdom.[2]

The relationship between Tswana patron and Sarwa client was similar to that so vividly described by Turnbull as existing between negroes and pygmies in Ituri,[3] and it is clear that in some cases it was acceptable to both parties, the client gaining hunting dogs and a valued supply of food and tobacco, the patron pelts and the services of herds. In other cases it was felt to be intolerable, and the opportunity of Sarwa to escape obligations diminished as hunting areas grew more and more circumscribed. Sarwa were not admitted into Tswana regiments, and could not bring cases to court themselves: they could be heard only through their patron. Marriage of a Tswana with Sarwa was strongly disapproved.[4]

The political unit was a chiefdom, which included one large settlement, the capital; a number of cattle-posts; outlying villages; and scattered bands of hunters. The office of chief was hereditary, passing from father to senior son, and the fiction was maintained that the chief was the senior kinsman of the ruling lineage. But every chiefdom included members of many lineages. Schapera has shown (in a model study) that members of all totem groups—and the totem indicates descent—were included in the various Tswana chiefdoms.[5]

Chiefdoms split repeatedly, and the conflict commonly appeared as a rivalry between the chief and a close agnatic kinsman, or between potential heirs to the chieftainship. Each protagonist was supported by personal followers, and the upshot was commonly the establishment of a new chiefdom. The disputes were couched in terms of personal rivalries and were similar to disputes in commoner families over inheritance and status.[6] But it is not clear how these personal rivalries were linked to other cleavages within the chiefdom. In Sotho and Nguni history the institution of chieftainship was never questioned, and conflicts were always expressed as rivalries between claimants to the office of chief; nevertheless the rivals might themselves epitomize divergent social policies. Indeed, during the years 1960–5 conflicting parties, separated by fundamental issues of policy, have become involved in ancient dynastic quarrels. Each party has used the leader of a lineage to express

[1] London Missionary Society, *The Masarwa (Bushmen), Report of an Inquiry*, pp. 2–18.
[2] Livingstone, *Missionary Travels*, p. 186.
[3] C. M. Turnbull, *The Forest People*, passim.
[4] Schapera, *Tswana Law*, pp. 31–32, 66, 121, 250–3; *Ethnic Composition*, p. v.
[5] Ibid., *passim*. [6] Schapera, 'Kinship and Politics', 59–72.

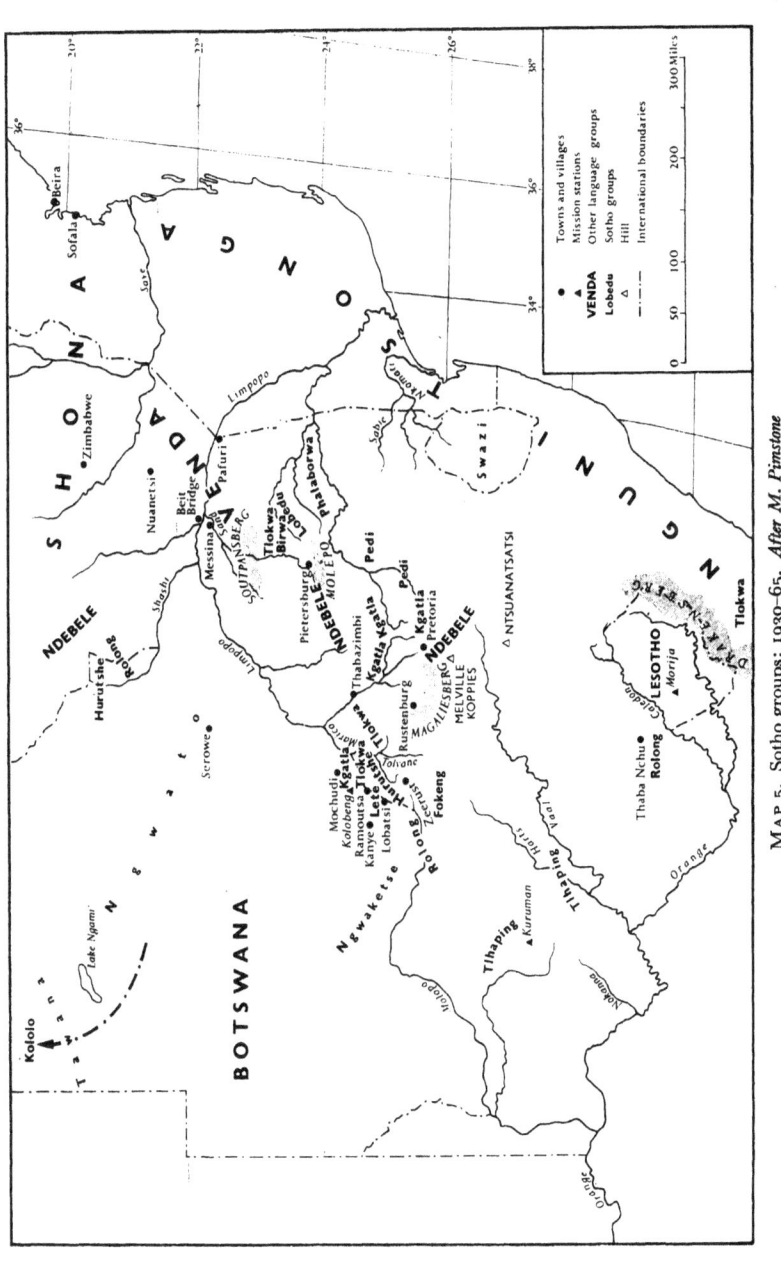

MAP 5. Sotho groups: 1930-65. *After M. Pimstone*

Sources: I. Schapera, *The Tswana*, Ethnographic Survey of Africa, ed. D. Forde, London, 1953; C. M. Doke, *The Southern Bantu Languages*, London, 1959; N. J. van Warmelo, *A Preliminary Survey of the Bantu Tribes of South Africa*, Pretoria, 1935

its differentiation from and opposition to the other. Cleavages were traditionally expressed in terms of opposition between lineages, but they were not necessarily comprehended by such opposition. Much of traditional history is concerned with tracing splits and showing the links between the ruling lineages of existing chiefdoms, but we know little about the underlying causes of fission.

The independence of a chief was asserted by the leader moving away with his followers and establishing himself in a territory which might or might not overlap with that claimed by the chief whom he left. He also asserted the independence of his court, no cases being sent on appeal to any other authority. But seniority in ritual was still recognized, and Livingstone notes that none would eat of the first fruits until the Hurutshe chief's son had done so,[1] for the Hurutshe were the lineage from which others had sprung. Independence did not imply isolation. Emissaries from independent chiefs attended at the Hurutshe capital, Kaditshwene, when Campbell visited there in 1820, and emissaries were exchanged between other Tswana chiefdoms also.

The Tswana, like the Nguni, were characterized by a great development of law, and a respect for the courts. The *kgotla* (which means both a courtyard and a court of law) was the centre, physically and metaphorically, of every capital. The first travellers found both the chief in Dithakong and the regent in Kaditshwene sitting in the *kgotla* with counsellors, settling disputes. And not only did every capital have its *kgotla*: every lineage which occupied a section of the capital had its own central courtyard—its *kgotla*—and there disputes between members of a lineage were either settled by arbitration, or sent on to the chief's court.

All the courts were concerned with reconciling the disputants and their families, rather than enforcing a legal code, but a distinction existed between the Tswana chiefdoms and that of the Lobedu. Among the Tswana (as among the Nguni) certain offences—murder, assault, witchcraft, and slander—were treated as attacks on the chief, who represented the state, and the fine in such cases went to the chief; but among the Lobedu even murder and assault were treated as offences against the kinsmen of the injured party, and only witchcraft was clearly an offence against the state.[2] The chief was beneath the law and among Rolong and Kgatla could be tried by his own counsellors.[3] None of the Sotho chiefdoms was a military kingdom in which authority was maintained by force: order was secured rather through negotiation and compromise, and early travellers noted that the freedom of criticism of authority (the chief) in public assembly was much greater than was then permitted in Europe.[4]

---

[1] Livingstone, *Missionary Travels*, p. 45.
[2] Schapera, *Tswana Law*, p. 46; Krige, *Rain Queen*, p. 201.
[3] Schapera, *Tswana Law*, p. 84.   [4] J. Philip, *Researches in South Africa*, ii. 132–6.

THE SOTHO 159

The Sotho differed radically from the Nguni not only in the pattern of settlement but also in the rules of marriage. The Sotho marry cousins of all sorts, whereas the Nguni totally prohibit such marriages. The only exception among the Nguni are the Swazi and ancient Hlubi, who permit marriage between cross-cousins, and this may be explained by the fact that they lie or lay on the boundary of Sotho and Nguni areas and have roots in both cultures (see p. 97). The rules of marriage vary somewhat from one Sotho area to another: all the Tswana approve marriages between the children of brothers, and between cross-cousins, whereas the Lobedu do not, and their ideal is marriage with the daughter of a *particular* mother's brother—he who received cattle for the groom's mother. But despite detailed differences the principle is accepted among all the Sotho that the girl 'born to be your wife' is the daughter of a kinsman. She will be your great wife whomever else you marry, and the higher the status of the family the more rigidly cousin marriages are insisted upon.[1] Why this cleavage in the rules of marriage existed between Nguni and Sotho peoples who were, in other respects, very similar has not yet been explained, but it is noticeable that they both stress the importance of lineages in marriage, the Nguni prohibiting marriage within one's own or a linked lineage, the Sotho preferring it. This is characteristic of herdsmen in South Africa. Hunters, who are not much concerned with inherited wealth, are not organized in property-owning lineages and neither prohibit nor prescribe marriage within such groups.

Among the Sotho the members of a lineage occupied a defined section of the settlement, but, where this was large, each ward commonly contained more than one lineage.[2] The composition of lineage units and wards in a Tswana capital therefore corresponded closely to the composition of Nguni homesteads and sub-districts, and the arrangement of dwellings round a byre was similar,[3] but the Sotho lived compactly, whereas the Nguni scattered.

Age-groups were of great importance among the Sotho and were directly linked with political authority. Both boys and girls were initiated after puberty into groups which were coterminous with the chiefdom. The men's groups were regiments with military and political as well as economic functions, and the women's groups had certain communal responsibilities also. There was no individual initiation of girls at puberty, such as still exists among the Nguni. For the boys, besides a physical operation, there was a period of hardship and very rigorous discipline in a place of seclusion. Great secrecy still surrounds the schools where they

[1] Schapera, *Married Life*, pp. 41–42, 'Kinship and Marriage', 140–65, and 'Agnatic Marriage', 103–13; Krige, *Rain Queen*, pp. 142–4.
[2] Schapera, *Tswana Ward*; Ashton, *Southern Sotho Ward*.
[3] Hunter, *Reaction to Conquest*, pp. 15–17, 61–64; W. D. Hammond-Tooke, *Bhaca Society*, pp. 33–62; Walton, Figs. 55, 56.

continue. One reason for secrecy was the traditional practice of treating the male novices with powder from the medicine horn of their chief. One ingredient of the medicine horn was commonly human flesh, and the treatment was thought of as strengthening the novices, and transforming them from boys to men. This use of the chief's horn is comparable to the annual treatment of the army at the 'time of the first fruits' among the Nguni, rather than to any rite at Nguni initiation, and it underlines the fact that Sotho chiefs controlled initiation schools, whereas among the Nguni they were locally organized. The Mthethwa chief, Dingiswayo, deliberately separated military organization from circumcision: the Sotho did not. It was possible, among the Sotho, for a boy to run away and join the regiment of another chief, but this implied transferring his allegiance to another chiefdom.

Schools were held at irregular intervals of four to seven years, and all those who had passed puberty since the last school were summoned to attend. It was held essential that the schools should separate brothers, and thus cut across kinship loyalties. Mr. Godfrey Pitje notes that traditionally two full brothers could not be initiated at the same time: the younger must wait.[1] The schools enshrined traditional values which were inculcated partly through songs and riddles in which novices must become word perfect, partly through ritual dramas in which the novices, after being terrified, were invited to view the old men who mimed the shades, and partly through the rigid discipline which constantly asserted the authority of seniors and the obligation of obedience to them. A secret language, learnt in the school, identified initiates to each other, and emphasized their distinction from members of the other sex, from children, and from foreigners.[2] Once initiated, a youth was accepted as an adult man and a woman as marriageable in any other chiefdom. Before initiation neither was eligible for marriage. And a fugitive from another chiefdom was 'directed to the mopato (regiment) analagous to that to which in his own tribe he belongs, and does duty as a member'.[3] Ellenberger and Macgregor draw attention to the fact that the boys with whom a chief's son was circumcised

go through life with him as counsellors, officers, messengers—his eyes and ears among the people. They would marry about the same time, and their children would be about the same age; and when the eldest son of one chief came to undergo the rite in his turn, the eldest sons of his father's mates would go with him, and remain his till death. The second son would be accompanied by the second sons of the father's mates, and so on. Thus it came about that at an early age every son of a chief of any importance had the nucleus of a following, which increased according to his popularity, his father's favour, or other circumstances.

---

[1] Pitje, 28.   [2] Ibid. 37.   [3] Livingstone, *Missionary Travels*, p. 148.

Age-groups, which, in East Africa, themselves controlled administration, therefore functioned among the Sotho as subsidiary groups buttressing chieftainship.[1]

Initiation leads us directly to a consideration of the shades. It could, indeed, be argued that the principal rituals of the ancestral cult among the Sotho were those celebrated at initiation, when initiates were shown mysteries—masked dancers and drums which represented the shades.[2] Most of the Sotho lived in dry, hot country, and a major function of the chief was to procure rain, either directly, through the power of his shades, or through a doctor who was a specialist in rain medicines. A breach of taboo by one individual was thought likely to cause drought to the whole community, and therefore favourable weather was linked with right living. All the people of a chiefdom were 'members one of another' in so far as the rain and their crops depended upon the observance by all of certain moral rules, such as completion of mourning before remarriage.[3] Disorder in the physical universe was held to reflect disorder among men.

It was thought, also, that sterility, sickness, or other misfortune afflicted individuals who incurred the anger of their senior kinsmen, living or dead. Hence the rite, celebrated on many occasions, of spitting out water as an expression of good will, of cleansing oneself of angry thoughts—'with the expectorated spittle whatever feelings of hurt or evil that may be in the heart will be expelled, and so the curse removed from the sick person'.[4]

The chief gave the order for each activity of the agricultural cycle to begin; hoeing, planting, weeding, reaping, and threshing were initiated in the 'tribute' land (*masotla*) cultivated by each community for their chief; and a day for thanksgiving appointed. He tasted the new green vegetables—cucurbits—first, as the Nguni chiefs did, but his leadership in cultivation was not confined to that, as it was among most Nguni. This participation by the chief suggests that among all the Sotho (and not only the Lobedu, who had few cattle)[5] cultivation was of greater importance traditionally than it was among the Nguni. Where the chief initiated an activity every family had to start with him and keep in step,[6] so the laggards were forced to work. The importance of this in a community in which those who lack food expect to be fed by those who have it is obvious.

Animal sacrifices are (and apparently were traditionally) less common among the Sotho than among the Nguni. They use sheep as well as cattle

---

[1] Ellenberger and Macgregor, pp. 264, 272.   [2] Krige, *Rain Queen*, pp. 134-40.
[3] Campbell, *1820*, ii. 205-6; J. T. Brown, *Among the Bantu Nomads*, pp. 130-1.
[4] Ibid., p. 158; Ellenberger and Macgregor, p. 269.
[5] Krige, *Rain Queen*, pp. 20, 42-44.
[6] Schapera, *Land Tenure*, pp. 184-97.

and goats in sacrifice, which the Nguni do not, but offerings of the flesh of domestic animals play altogether a lesser part,[1] and milk, so important in Nguni ritual, is never mentioned. By contrast, links between certain lines of descent and certain species of wild animals were recognized. Each major line venerated an animal or object with which its founding ancestor was associated, and by which members of the line might be known, as the Lobedu were called 'the wild pigs' and the Kwena were known after the crocodile (*kwena*) they venerated. These 'men of the crocodile' might neither kill nor touch a crocodile; they scrupulously avoided the flesh and skin; they swore by it; and they used a sign representing it to mark their stock, shields, and utensils.[2] So with the men of the lion, or elephant, or eland. As lineages expanded and split a section might express its identity and distinctness from the parent group by venerating some new-chosen animal in honour of which, in the traditional phrase, they *danced*—perhaps a hint of the dances miming wild animals, so familiar among the hunters, or the miming of a favourite ox among the Nguni. The various groups danced in honour of the crocodile, the lion, leopard, hippopotamus, elephant, and buffalo; the kudu, hartebeest, reedbuck, duiker, eland, and impala; the wild pig, ant-bear, hare, porcupine, meercat, civet-cat, wild dog, and hyena; the owl and bustard; the locust and lizard; and the ape and baboon.[3] As already noted (p. 145) one of the founding lineages, the Rolong, 'dance in honour of a hammer and of iron' (*tshipi*). All this was unknown to the Nguni. The nearest parallel among them was the identification of certain species of snakes as ancestors of certain lineages. One can hardly escape the conclusion that the ancient Sotho rituals reflect the life of a people for whom hunting was more important than cattle-keeping, and some of whom, in the distant past, recognized the smelting of iron as their major resource. It seems likely, also, that the rites associated with wild animals and with iron have vanished *because* the Sotho have ceased to depend upon hunting and smelting. If this argument is valid, the rituals point to an ancient Sotho economy dependent primarily on hunting, cultivation, and iron-smelting, to which herding was added; whereas the Nguni economy was based on cattle.

Some hints confirming this interpretation may be found in the forms of marriage. Both Nguni and Sotho kinship systems reflect the importance of cattle as symbols of status: it is the passage of cattle at marriage which determines the affiliation of children, who belong to the group which has given cattle for their mother. But in a Tswana marriage the bride

---

[1] Brown, p. 150; Pauw, *Tswana Chiefdom*, pp. 25, 161, 213–15.
[2] Ellenberger and Macgregor, pp. 240–5.
[3] Schapera, *Ethnic Composition*, passim. *One* Sotho group honoured cattle. Some at least of these cattlemen were of Nguni origin.

commonly lived with her own people until the birth of a child, her husband visiting her there. The number of marriage cattle given by commoners was small (two to four)[1] and they were not returnable if the marriage broke up, whereas among the Nguni a bride was required to join her husband's homestead immediately the marriage took place, the number of cattle ordinarily given was larger (five to ten),[2] and most of them were returned if divorce occurred. Among the Tswana also 'considerable store is set' on the groom performing services for his in-laws such as 'bringing them loads of fire-wood or earth, building fences at their fields, or ploughing with them' during the period of betrothal.[3] This obligation, together with the uxorilocal stage, and the relatively small and non-returnable marriage gift, suggests that Tswana marriage was perhaps once closer to the pattern of a hunting and agricultural people with labour service than to that of a dominantly pastoral people like the Nguni. But such an interpretation must remain uncertain unless supported by other evidence.

(d) Relations with Other Groups

It has been argued that the Sotho were notable craftsmen, particularly in metal-work and stone building. The Shona of Rhodesia were the great miners and stone builders of Central Africa,[4] so it is pertinent to inquire into Sotho connexions with them. The types of relationship we may consider are cultural similarities in techniques, language, and ritual; trade; and traditions of common descent or intermarriage.

No detailed comparative study has yet been made of Sotho and Shona metal-work, stone building, and pottery. In general terms the similarities are close, as they are also in language and in ritual, but much detailed work is necessary before continuities and discontinuities are made clear. Traditions of common descent can also be traced between certain Sotho and certain Shona groups, notably the Lobedu, Phalaborwa, and Birwa of the northern Transvaal,[5] and the Rozwi, a Shona people who are said to have preceded the Karanga in the country between the Limpopo and the Zambezi.[6] The Lobedu claim descent from a Mambo, one of the sons of Monomotapa,[7] and they cherish, as sacred, certain beads similar to those found in the layer at Zimbabwe now dated to c. A.D. 400–1000.[8]

[1] Schapera, *Married Life*, pp. 82–92. Lobedu give eight cattle, seven to eight goats, and £10 cash. Krige, *Rain Queen*, p. 150.
[2] Wilson et al., *Social Structure*, pp. 85–87.   [3] Schapera, *Married Life*, p. 66.
[4] D. P. Abraham, 'Ethno-history of the Empire of Mutapa', in *The Historian in Tropical Africa*, ed. Vansina, Mauny, and Thomas, pp. 104–19.
[5] Van Warmelo, *Preliminary Survey*, pp. 32, 113; Krige, 'Origins', pp. 325, 336, 352.
[6] Abraham, p. 107.
[7] Krige, 'Origins', p. 325.
[8] C. van Riet Lowe, 'Beads of the Water', *BS*, 2, 1937, 367–9; G. Caton Thompson, 'Zimbabwe, All Things Considered', *Antiquity*, 38, 1964, 100.

The Lobedu also have certain ritual characteristics, notably the seclusion of the queen and her ritual suicide, the sacred drums, the death of her sons before reaching maturity, the extinction of fire at the accession of a chief, and a myth that the chiefs brought fire to a people who ate their food raw, which suggest links both with the Shona and with a people far to the north—the Nyakyusa-Ngonde of Tanzania and Malawi. It is significant also that the Lobedu called themselves 'wild pig'—Golove—and were light in colour, and the ancestor of the Nyakyusa-Ngonde chiefly lineage was also called 'the wild pig'—*Ngulube*—and he was 'pale'.[1] Moreover, the Lobedu chiefs, like those who spread around the great lakes, chose to settle in wet, hilly country, clothed in forest. But these features which link the Lobedu with a northern people distinguish them from most other Sotho,[2] and one can but suppose that certain ritual observances, the title *Golove*, and the preference for misty forest country were brought by one lineage from the north, and fused with the language and customs of a small section of the ramifying Sotho-speaking people. Such similarities in title, myth, and ritual are but straws, and each taken alone has little significance, but they indicate a possible line of connexion which can now be most fruitfully pursued by archaeologists.

The northern neighbours of the Lobedu, the Venda, speak a different language, but they also came from the Rozwi kingdom, following after the Lobedu movement southward, and the Venda share some of the characteristics which suggest lacustrine connexions (see below, pp. 169–72).

Lobedu links with the Tsonga of the east coast were not traditionally so close. They were long separated by a tsetse belt (see maps 3, 4), and Tsonga settlers only moved into what is now the Transvaal under the pressure of Nguni raids in the early nineteenth century.[3] But there was an ancient footpath which ran from Delagoa Bay past the Lobedu mountain, past Phalaborwa, and across the Limpopo to Shona country, and this Tsonga ('Magwamba') traders had used for unknown generations before Shaka (see p. 151).

Contacts between Sotho and Nguni have already been touched upon (pp. 97–98). Some Sotho living in the Lebombo mountains (in the modern Swaziland) fled north when the Dlamini conquerors came; others remained and were absorbed; and some Nguni groups who crossed the Drakensberg on to the highveld kept their language and customs while others did not. Links were close along the mountain range, where an ancient trade between Zizi and Sotho is remembered (see p. 152).

As noted earlier (see p. 63) relationships between groups depended largely on possession of cattle: those without cattle became clients of

[1] Krige, *Rain Queen*, pp. 2–3, 91, 126–8, 166–8; G. Wilson, *The Constitution of Ngonde*, p. 10.
[2] Krige, 'North-Eastern Transvaal Sotho', pp. 266–8, 286–7.
[3] Krige, 'Origins', pp. 355–6.

those with cattle, often herding for them, or bringing in pelts, in return for food and tobacco. It is in terms of co-operation between cattle-owners and hunters that the relationship between Sotho and San is to be understood. It was profoundly modified when bands of Coloured people (descendants of Khoikhoi and whites), armed with muskets and mounted on horses, began hunting on a hitherto impossible scale.

By their own account, the Sotho found San hunters in much of the country they occupied,[1] notably between the Vaal and the Orange and in the mountains of Lesotho, where independent San communities survived into the nineteenth century.[2] In 1820 Campbell met Makoon, 'the captain of the Bushmen on the Malalareen' (Harts). Makoon had been born on the Harts and some years previously had had 'about a hundred people in his kraal'.[3] The Fokeng lineage, which led the Sotho advance southward, lived in small, scattered communities, intermingled with San, and a click language has had an appreciable influence on the southern dialect of Sotho.[4] It is also asserted by the Sotho that they learnt from the San to circumcise.[5] Considerable intermarriage took place, a Fokeng chief at Ntsuanatsatsi even marrying a San girl as his great wife. Much of this fusion appears to have been acceptable, but there were occasions when San origin was treated as degrading. One reproach brought against the San was that the whole family slept in one hut,[6] whereas the Sotho, like the Nguni, were rigid about privacy within the family, each married couple having their own hut, and the children sleeping elsewhere. Perhaps the status of the hunters diminished as the Sotho increased in numbers, but the tradition is that Sotho and San lived in peace until the continuous Kora raids and Zulu invasions between 1822 and 1833.[7]

The Tswana were (and still are) in close relations with hunters, the Sarwa, who are commonly spoken of as 'Bushmen', but whose language is Khoikhoi.[8] As has been shown, many of them became clients of Tswana cattle-owners, but intermarriage with them, at least since the late nineteenth century,[9] has been strongly disapproved. Tswana, however, intermarried with Khoikhoi herdsmen along the Orange, where Wikar found a mixed group which could speak both languages in 1778,[10] and Campbell visited the 'Tammaha', who 'speak the Bootshuana language ... but many of them can also speak the Corranna and Bushmen languages', between Dithakong and Kaditshwene.[11] The mother of Mothibi, a

[1] Ellenberger and Macgregor, pp. 18, 56; Walton, pp. 26-31.
[2] *Basutoland Records*, ii. 424-7.   [3] Campbell, *1820*, ii. 28-32.
[4] V. Ellenberger, *La Fin tragique des Bushmen*.
[5] Ellenberger and Macgregor, pp. 7, 280; S. M. Guma, 'Some Aspects of circumcision in Basutoland', *AS*, 24, 1965, 241.
[6] Ellenberger and Macgregor, pp. 10-11, 19.   [7] Ibid., p. 13.
[8] Westphal, p. 249.   [9] Schapera, *Tswana Law*, p. 127.
[10] Wikar, p. 143.   [11] Campbell, *1820*, ii. 6-8.

Tlhaping chief at Dithakong, was a Kora, and he could speak Kora.[1] We do not know for how long such interaction had been going on. The Kora, who drove the Tlhaping from Nokana about 1790 and attacked them at Dithakong before 1801, had trekked northward from the Cape.[2] The Kora were already a people of mixed Khoikhoi and white descent— Coloured in later terminology—who understood Dutch and were armed with guns and mounted on horses, and relations between them and Sotho must have been considerably different from the relations of Khoikhoi and Sotho a century earlier. Because of their arms and mobility a handful of Kora could tip the balance of power between warring Sotho chiefs, and they were indeed said to have combined with the Tlhaping to defeat the Rolong in a battle in which the great Rolong chief, Tau, was mortally wounded, in about 1760.[3] The Nama had straddled the Orange and had some tenuous contact with the Tlhaping (Brijckje) at least from the mid seventeenth century (see p. 149), but the main body of the Nama was separated from the Sotho by the Kalahari. The Nama had one outstanding skill which the Tlhaping had begun to learn by 1805 (possibly earlier) and which other Sotho acquired only later. That skill was riding: they trained oxen to the saddle. It is therefore unlikely that the Sotho, generally, were in long and close contact with Khoikhoi-speaking riders (such as the Nama) before 1800.

Piecing together evidence from a variety of sources (pp. 55–57, 108, 135, 142) we may conclude that there were Khoikhoi-speaking riders, with Afrikander cattle, on the south coast by 1497 and on the lower Orange at least by 1661. The Xhosa learnt from them to ride after 1686 and the Tlhaping probably about the end of the eighteenth century. Other Bantu-speaking cattle-owners in South Africa lacked any knowledge of riding, and therefore the Khoikhoi riders must have been isolated. It is unlikely that they were in the western Cape for any long period before 1500 (see p. 30). Whence and when they came to the south coast we do not know. The nearest point in time and space at which other riders are known to have existed was at Sofala in the tenth century. Did a small group travel southward, keeping their skill to themselves until the eighteenth century?

It is significant that, though the Khoikhoi language had a profound influence on Nguni, it has not, so far as has been demonstrated, appreciably influenced Sotho. It seems likely, therefore, that marriage on an equal basis between Khoikhoi-speakers and Sotho-speakers was limited. Marriage with Sarwa was disapproved, and even if cohabitation occurred the language of the offspring was likely to be Tswana. Where women come from a group treated as grossly inferior, the general rule that children learn the language of the mother no longer holds.

---

[1] Burchell, ii. 282.
[2] Maingard, p. 599.
[3] Molema, *Chief Moroka*, p. 2.

In another respect, however, some Sotho are closer to the Khoikhoi and San than the Nguni are: some of them eat fish. Many Sotho avoid it,[1] as the Nguni do, and as the Shona (Karanga), with whom the Sotho have ancient links, do also. The songs of the circumcision schools assert traditional rules. One heard in the Leribe district runs:[2]

Nna ha ke je hlapi	I do not eat fish
Hlapi ke noha	A fish is a snake
Noha ya metsi	A water snake
E ya nkudisa.	It makes me ill.

David Livingstone described fish left to rot when the River Kolobeng in Botswana ran dry, even though the Kwena were very hungry at the time. So many fish were killed that the hyenas from the whole country round collected to feast and were unable to finish the putrid masses.[3] On the other hand, Arbousset[4] and others have recorded Sotho in Lesotho eating fish, and according to oral tradition the Tlhaping abandoned the taboo during a period of scarcity. Their name—'the fish people'—underlines the change.[5]

It has been argued that maintenance of a taboo on fish among the Nguni was an assertion of their distinction from their fish-eating neighbours, the San and Khoikhoi (see above, p. 96). If this is true, the Sotho cannot have maintained such a sharp separation with *both* peoples. The evidence of economy, language, and ritual combined indicates a more intimate association between Sotho and San than between Sotho and Khoikhoi.

2. *The Venda*

Like the Nguni and Sotho, the Venda are defined in terms of language. Their speech has close affinity with Shona (spoken over the greater part of Rhodesia) and clear connexions also with Sotho, but is nevertheless distinct.[6] They occupy the Soutpansberg, a range running east and west,

[1] Livingstone, *Missionary Travels*, p. 72.
[2] I am much indebted to my colleague Mr. J. R. Masiea for this song.
[3] Livingstone, *Missionary Travels*, pp. 20–21. [4] Arbousset, pp. 158–9.
[5] Molema, *The Bantu*, p. 38; Breutz, *Tribes of Kuruman and Postmasburg*, p. 38.
[6] Doke, *The Southern Bantu Languages*, pp. 154, 205. Shona is here used, as Doke uses it, to mean Karanga, Kalanga, Rozwi (including Korekore and Lilima), Zezuru, Manyika, and Ndau.

Mr. Abraham stresses the distinction between Karanga and Rozwi but he is not always consistent in his usage. (D. P. Abraham 'The Early Political History of the Kingdom of Mwene-Mutapa, 850–1589', in *Historians in Tropical Africa, Leverhulme Conference, Proceedings*, Salisbury, 1962, p. 14.)

Some authorities link Venda with Rozwi, others with Kalanga (not specifying whether this includes Rowzi or not) or Karanga. See H. A. Stayt, *The Bavenda*, p. 15; G. P. Lestrade, 'Some Notes on the Ethnic History of the BaVenda and their Rhodesian Affinities', *SAJS*, 24, 1927, 487–8; Van Warmelo, *Copper Miners*, p. 23, and *Contributions towards Venda History, Religion and Tribal Ritual*, p. 9.

south of the Limpopo. At one time an outlying group stretched further into the Transvaal, where their influence on the Lobedu is plain. There are still Venda-speakers north of the Limpopo, in the Nuanetsi district of Rhodesia,[1] but the well-watered and wooded mountains are their chosen home.

In numbers the Venda are insignificant—246,000[2] compared with 7,000,000 Nguni and 5,000,000 Sotho. They are of interest to the historian because they form a link between the empire of Monomotapa (and perhaps the lacustrine chiefdoms of Central Africa) and the peoples south of the Limpopo; they participated in the great copper trade from Musina (Messina); and their artefacts are similar to those in the upper layers at Mapungubwe and Bambandyanalo (see pp. 33–34).

Documentary evidence which indisputably relates to the Venda only begins with the arrival of the Voortrekkers in the northern Transvaal in 1836, but an account of the gold trade by Vasco da Gama's Arab pilot in 1530 points in the direction of Venda country,[3] and in the Dutch accounts of trade in copper and tin in 1723, 1725, and 1731–2 chiefs are mentioned who *might* be Venda.[4] There is no certainty. However, oral tradition is rich.

The Venda are a fusion between a lineage of incoming chiefs[5] and the Ngona and other aborigines. The Ngona occupied both the Soutpansberg and the Lobedu mountain.[6] They are described as being 'short, slight, dark, and flat nosed', or short, broad-shouldered, heavy-jawed, with round heads, and dark,[7] and they

did not know how to drill fire with sticks, and lived like wild beasts. They were taught by us [the chiefs] how to make fire. They wanted to fight with those who came from Vhukalanga [Shona country], but the latter set the countryside alight, and the others fled, for the fire was something strange to them.[8]

---

[1] Van Warmelo, *Copper Miners*, p. 23; Stayt, p. 1; Doke, p. 154; Krige, 'Origins', pp. 324–6; Krige, *Rain Queen*, end Map.
[2] Republic of South Africa, *Population Census, 1960*, Sample Tabulation 8, p. 94.
[3] 'The mine of gold farthest to the south is called Vadijuria; the last city is Saiha. From the mine to this city is a month of journey towards the north-east; the inhabitants are heathens' (Ahmad Ibn Madjid, *Tres Roteiros Desconhecidos*, Moscovo Leninegrado, 1957; Portuguese translation by Professor Myron Malkiel Jirmounsky, Lisbon, 1960). I am indebted to my colleague Professor Eric Axelson for drawing my attention to this and translating it from the Portuguese.
[4] Theal, *Records of South Eastern Africa*, ii. 407–20; F. R. Paver, 'Trade and Mining in the pre-European Transvaal', *SAJS*, 30, 1933, 603–11.
[5] Van Warmelo, *Copper Miners*, pp. 4, 10, 71–80.
[6] Krige, *Rain Queen*, p. 6. It is not certain whether the earlier inhabitants spoke Sotho, or an archaic Shona: G. P. Lestrade, 'Some Notes on the Political Organization of the Venda-speaking Tribes', *Africa*, 3, 1930, 307; Van Warmelo, *Copper Miners*, pp. 7, 74.
[7] Stayt, p. 11, but cf. Van Warmelo, *Copper Miners*, p. 79; Dicke, *Bush Speaks*, p. 10.
[8] Van Warmelo, *Contributions*, p. 9.

The chiefly lineage crossed the Limpopo and came to the Soutpansberg from Shona country. According to their own account they sojourned there for some generations and married Shona girls:[1] certainly Venda language and customs show very close links with Shona. But tradition points to an earlier home from which they had travelled southward for a month before reaching the first Shona chiefdom.[2]

The original BaVenda were led southwards from a place which was near the sea, and situated in 'a land of many rivers which all join and in one body rush to the sea. ... Our ancestors have told us that it was a warm climate, warmer than the Njelele (in the Zoutpansberg) and that not far to the east were long pools of silent waters, they are unlike the sea because of their silence.'[3] [It was] a country of great rivers and lakes . . . a country overflowing with water and with many forests and fruit, of bananas growing in many groves and of tubers and pea-nuts in great variety.[4]

All this suggests an area to the west of Lake Malawi or Lake Shirwa, for Tanganyika or Kivu or Victoria would be more than a month distant from Shona country. Stayt notes that Chief Senthumule insisted (about 1930) that the ancestral home was in 'Nyasaland',[5] and similarities between pottery from Nkudzi (Malawi) and Venda pottery support this (see p. 37).

The linguistic evidence, according to that meticulous scholar G. P. Lestrade, shows that in grammatical structure and phonology Venda is akin to Shona (Karanga), but in vocabulary the largest number of words are akin to Sotho, a smaller number of roots are Shona, and a third, still smaller, group 'have their closest affinities with the East African group of Bantu languages'.[6] No detailed comparison has yet been published of this 'residue' in Venda vocabulary and the Nyakyusa language or its Ngonde (Konde) dialect, but such a comparison might prove instructive, for origin of their royal lineage in the ancient kingdom of Ngonde, to the north-west of Lake Malawi, would not only fit with the topographical, climatic, and botanical details given in Venda oral tradition, but would also account for the very close similarities in ritual and symbolism of Venda and Ngonde.

According to tradition, the Venda chiefs brought with them not only the art of making fire, but also a magic drum, Ngoma-lungundu, which caused the collapse of their enemies, 'for when the drum of the gods sounded all the enemies lay down in a deep sleep'.[7] In Shona country 'Tshilume beat the drum of death: Nduu! Straightway the men of Thivi

---

[1] Van Warmelo, *Copper Miners*, pp. 17–23; *Contributions*, p. 6. These two accounts do not agree on the period spent in Shona country.
[2] Van Warmelo, *Copper Miners*, p. 17.   [3] Lestrade, 'Ethnic History', 489–90.
[4] Van Warmelo, *Copper Miners*, p. 10.   [5] Stayt, p. 14.
[6] Lestrade, 'Ethnic History', 487–8.   [7] Van Warmelo, *Copper Miners*, p. 19.

fell to the ground in a deep sleep and knew no more.' And when the chiefs crossed the Limpopo

The VhaNgona became very alarmed, because they had heard what had been done to the VhaKalanga of Tshivhi who had all been laid down in sleep by the drum of Mwali, the ancestor spirit of the VhaSenzi, the drum of which the sound made people other than its masters faint in fear and lie down as in death. In this way the owners of the drum could do what they liked with their enemies, whether it be to bind them or slay them, everything was in their hands. Many people in their fear of the drum, hearing that the VhaSenzi were coming, immediately made way for them and fled further southwards or westwards or eastwards. A great flight ensued from the country of the VhaNgona, villages were left in ruins and gardens were left unreaped.[1]

Both peoples associate the chief with lion and leopards which guarded the sacred groves;[2] and link earthquakes with their founding heroes. In Nyakyusa myth 'the earth rumbled as they walked',[3] and in Venda myth 'when their ancestor spirit had ceased speaking, the countryside shook with an earthquake for a little while, and clouds gathered in the sky'.[4]

Among the Nyakyusa all the old fires in the country were extinguished at the coronation of a chief, and new fire taken by all the people from that lighted by the new chief. This was explicitly linked, by Nyakyusa informants, with the account of chiefs bringing fire to a barbarous land. It is 'because of old ... we chiefs came with fire, the commoners had not yet got it, they ate raw food only. ... Men were astonished. ... They were burned so they said "These are chiefs because they brought this fire".'[5] The Venda also extinguished the old fires and lighted a new one for the new chief at his coronation, and he distributed fire to his people.[6] No one supposes that the inhabitants of Venda country in the seventeenth or eighteenth century, or of Nyakyusa country in the sixteenth, were without fire, but the myth symbolizes a reciprocal relationship between two stocks: the chiefs were pictured as chiefs *because* they came as benefactors.

The story of the chief beating a drum which caused his enemies to flee is also familiar near Lake Malawi. The first Kyungu climbed Mbande hill and there 'beat his drum and the men of Simbobwe heard it and fled'.[7] There are many other similarities in the institution of chieftainship among the Nyakyusa-Ngonde and the Venda. The details cannot all be catalogued here, but the following points are conspicuous: the seclusion of both Venda chief and the Kyungu of Ngonde in a capital, built on a hill, surrounded by a palisade;[8] the ritual death by strangling or

---

[1] Van Warmelo, *Copper Miners*, p. 23.   [2] Wilson, *Communal Rituals*, p. 58.
[3] Ibid., p. 7.   [4] Van Warmelo, *Copper Miners*, p. 25.
[5] Wilson, *Communal Rituals*, p. 53.   [6] Stayt, p. 207.
[7] G. Wilson, *Constitution of Ngonde*, p. 10. Mbande hill closely resembles Mapungubwe.
[8] Ibid., pp. 11–13, 18; Van Warmelo, *Copper Miners*, pp. 10–11, 14–15.

smothering, and the form of burial;[1] the stones planted at the marriage of a chief,[2] the sacred spears, the use of otter skins as royal emblems, the taboos surrounding the drum, in particular the taboo on its touching the earth,[3] the use of the poison ordeal to discover witches.[4] The manner in which a Venda girl greets respectfully is exactly that in which a Nyakyusa girl greets,[5] and the ritual washing of hands and catching the water used described by Dicke, and implied to be a marriage rite,[6] is similar to the Nyakyusa ritual washing of husband and wife, which marks the marriage union.[7] The patterns in clay on the interior walls of Nyakyusa huts are similar to those on the door of a Venda chief's hut.[8]

The Shona also have a tradition that their chiefs brought fire, and the rite of extinguishing all old fires in the chiefdom and taking new fire from that lighted by the ruler was recorded by early Portuguese travellers.[9] Many other features of the Shona ritual of kingship resemble that of the Venda and Ngonde. Furthermore, Shona (Rozwi) traditions of origin also point northward, to an area east of Lake Tanganyika where a Shona (Karanga) group are said still to live.[10]

It is improbable that such complex ritual and symbolism should have been invented thrice independently, and since explicit traditions link Venda, Shona, and Ngonde to the lacustrine area there is an overwhelming presumption that these ideas have a common origin. It has already been argued elsewhere that the Nyakyusa-Ngonde people are a southern outpost of the royal lineages which spread round the lakes.[11] It is likely that Venda ideas of chieftainship, if not the ancestors of the royal lineage itself, also came from the same source.

The choice of the lush and wooded Soutpansberg, which was preferred as being warmer and more like 'the homeland of our ancestors' than the plateau further south,[12] is significant. Migrants tend to choose a climate

[1] Wilson, *Communal Rituals*, pp. 22, 41; Van Warmelo, *Copper Miners*, pp. 25, 35–36.
[2] Among the Nyakyusa a stone was planted at the marriage of a chief between the memorial trees, beside which he was later buried, and which became his sacred grove. The stone *was* the chief, and sacrifices to him were made there. Similarly, among the Venda, stones were identified with the shades, and sacrifices made to them. The stone illustrated by Stayt, Plate VII, is identical with that planted at the marriage of the Nyakyusa chief, Mwanyilu. Wilson, *Communal Rituals*, p. 56; Stayt, pp. 7–8, 243–4, 256, Plate XXXVIII; Van Warmelo, *Contributions*, pp. 153–4, 159–60.
[3] Wilson, *Communal Rituals*, pp. 10, 12, 45, 52.
[4] Stayt, p. 282; Wilson, *Good Company*, pp. 115–18.
[5] Stayt, Plate XXXII; Dicke, *Bush Speaks*, pp. 60–61, 345, Plate opp. p. 332.
[6] Dicke, *Bush Speaks*, pp. 346, 348.   [7] Wilson, *Rituals of Kinship*, p. 90.
[8] Monica Wilson, 'Nyakyusa Art', *SAAB*, 19 (1964), 61; Stayt, Plate XVI.
[9] Theal, *Records of South Eastern Africa*, vii. 484.
[10] Abraham, 'Early Political History', p. 14. Walton's argument for a Congo origin of the Rozwi people, as distinct from the metal gongs they use, is unconvincing: J. Walton, 'Some Features of the Monomotapa Culture', in *3rd PAC*, pp. 350–5.
[11] Wilson, *Nyasa-Tanganyika Corridor*, pp. 48–50.
[12] Van Warmelo, *Copper Miners*, p. 23.

and environment with which they are familiar. In the nineteenth and twentieth centuries white settlers moved up the backbone of Africa, choosing the healthy highlands from the Transvaal to Kenya, and there is reason to think that Bantu-speaking groups moving south did the same. There are similarities in custom between the people of Rwanda, Kilimanjaro, Rungwe (where the Nyakyusa lived), Inyanga (in eastern Rhodesia), the Soutpansberg, and Lobedu mountain which cannot be explained by environment alone. In Africa some migrants moved from mountain to mountain, as in Oceania they crossed from island to island. Other settlers, such as those from Indonesia, probably moved up river valleys, preferring the hot, humid climate to which they were accustomed.

Tracing such connexions is a fascinating pursuit, and it can give us some notion of the movement of peoples and the spread of ideas and customs in space and in time, but it reveals little about the *process* of change in societies. The crucial fact is that in the mountains south of the Limpopo a *new* culture emerged which, though it shows links in language and ritual with that of Shona, Nyakyusa-Ngonde, and Sotho, was distinct from any of them. What are the factors which make for the creation of a new language and distinctive culture? About this neither anthropologist nor historian can yet tell us very much, but we can note certain reasons for the acceptance of new rites or institutions. The Venda only began to practise circumcision in the early nineteenth century. They learnt from their Sotho neighbours, rather than from the Lemba who lived among them and had long practised the rite; and they adopted it because travel for an uncircumcised man through Sotho country was dangerous, but one who was circumcised could claim the hospitality of contemporaries circumcised with him.[1] The attraction of the rite was therefore its practical value in securing acceptance as a member of a wider community. This hypothesis has yet to be confirmed by detailed comparative studies, but it fits the Venda evidence.

Secondly, we know from eye-witness accounts, as well as from many local traditions, that an incoming group better armed, or bringing domestic animals, new crops, or new techniques, or thought to have magic for rain or fertility, or a combination of several of these, has repeatedly established itself as a chiefly lineage.[2] The Venda tradition emphasizes the magical element—the terrifying drum—but when the Venda travelled a little further south the Pedi 'did not fear' the drum.[3] Perhaps the Ngona who fled were less well armed than the Venda, who used bows and poisoned arrows, battle axes, and spears.[4] The Venda chiefs brought with them an endogamous group of Lemba, who were

[1] Stayt, p. 127; Van Warmelo, *Contributions*, p. 125.
[2] A. Southall, *Alur Society*, pp. 181–228; Wilson, *Nyasa-Tanganyika Corridor*, p. 59.
[3] Van Warmelo, *Copper Miners*, p. 23.   [4] Stayt, pp. 69–70.

conspicuous as craftsmen—workers in iron, copper, and gold, potters, and weavers. The circumcised Lemba referred to the Venda chief's lineage as *VhaSenzi*, a form of the word Swahili-speakers use for pagans of the bush, and the Lemba were careful to avoid pork and cut the throat of any animal slaughtered. They were not explicitly Moslem, and they spoke among themselves an archaic Shona, not Swahili, but they were traders as well as craftsmen, and it can hardly be doubted that they, and the Venda through them, had some tenuous links with the coast.[1]

The Ngona already had a few cattle when the incoming chiefs arrived. These were short-horned, small, humped cattle, similar to those kept by the Shona, the Toka on the middle Zambezi, and the Nyakyusa-Ngonde,[2] and unlike those of the Nguni and Sotho. The immigrants had lost their cattle on their journeys, the mountains were surrounded by tsetse areas, and cattle were scarce. Nevertheless, they were used for sacrifice, and by those who had them in marriage. The commoners gave hoes at marriage.[3]

The economy was based on cultivation, hunting, and metal-working. Young boys fished in the rivers, but adults avoided fish as rigidly as any Nguni or Sotho.[4] The Venda made their fields on the fertile fringes of the forests which once covered much of the Soutpansberg, planting their traditional grain, eleusine, for beer, and in the forest they hunted with the great dogs 'like calves' which their chiefs had brought with them. The chiefs' dogs were distinguished by a wisp of cotton twisted round their necks, for (as in Ngonde) woven cotton cloth was one of the emblems of chieftainship. Only the chiefs and their wives, and the wives of the Lemba weavers, might wear it.[5] There is no indication, in the traditions, that cotton was cultivated (as it was among the Shona),[6] but wild cotton grows between Ngamiland and Mozambique. This cotton is thought to be ancestral to one of the most ancient cultivated strains in India,[7] and so it is of particular interest to find cotton from this area celebrated in African rituals.

The Venda forged iron hoes for themselves, and bartered them to the Tsonga.[8] They participated in the copper trade from Musina (Messina), and the Lemba among them worked in gold, but it was not they who organized the copper mines. According to oral tradition the Musina mines were organized by a lineage which came from Tsonga country

[1] Lestrade, *Africa*, 3, 1930, 307; Fouché, pp. 121, 124; Stayt, pp. 52, 58–59; Van Warmelo, *Copper Miners*, pp. 63–67.
[2] Curson and Thornton, 655–62, Map II, Plates 39–40, 62–63; Livingstone, *Missionary Travels*, p. 192; Wilson, *Communal Rituals*, Plate 1.
[3] Stayt, p. 37. [4] Ibid., pp. 47, 80–81.
[5] Ibid., p. 24; Van Warmelo, *Contributions*, p. 9.
[6] Mackenzie, i. 33.
[7] C. Wrigley, 'Speculations on the Economic Prehistory in Africa', *JAH* (1960), 192–3.
[8] Junod, ii. 138; Stayt, p. 61.

(Mpfumu) via Phalaborwa, and they established trade with Mpfumu importing black cloth which they wore, and selling copper. They worked deep shafts and *employed* Venda, Sotho, Nguni, and Shona as miners. They neither kept cattle nor cultivated, but bought their food with copper,[1] and, typically, they were people who ate alone: 'When strangers came they gave them no food.' However, the Musina lineage intermarried with the Tshivula (who were closely related to the Venda) and learnt their language.[2]

The Venda were stone builders, The capital Dzata, built by the incoming chiefs, though in ruins by 1930, clearly showed stone walling of two types,[3] and some of the mountain villages had stone walls and passages 'built by the veterans still living in them'.[4] In 1931 Professor Kirby watched the building of a new capital for Sibasa, the Venda chief, with stone retaining walls for terraces and stone stairways and walls enclosing passages. The village's plan was 'a kind of maze in which a stranger could easily lose his way', and the walls had breast-high loopholes through which spears could be thrust.[5]

Stayt draws attention to stone pillars set upright on walls, and long narrow stones set in the ground; to signs of ancient irrigation, and to terracing.[6] These features confirm the relationship with the Shona and with the Nyakyusa-Ngonde[7] already postulated. What has not yet been demonstrated is whether the techniques of building in stone, and settlement plans of Dzata and other Venda villages, are basically similar to, or differ consistently from, the techniques of Sotho building and plan of settlement. Walton has presented a considerable body of evidence but not sufficient to reach a final conclusion on this point.[8] In one minor point, significant to the archaeologist, the Venda did differ from the Sotho. They stored some of their grain in underground pits below the cattle byre, just as the Nguni did.[9]

Venda villages (so far back as evidence goes) were built in inaccessible places for protection, and they were much the size of those of the southern Sotho. In 1930 two chiefs' villages had about two hundred inhabitants each. Traditionally, villages were larger,[10] but there is no evidence that Dzata, the most famous settlement, was ever the size of a Tswana capital.

The pots the Venda use in their rain ritual, and which are acknowledged to be of ancient pattern, resembled the many-mouthed pots found

---

[1] Cf. Evidence of full-time iron workers among the Shona (Kalanga): J. T. Bent, *The Ruined Cities of Mashonaland*, p. 45.
[2] Van Warmelo, *Copper Miners*, pp. 5, 81–93.
[3] Fouché, pp. 45–46. [4] Stayt, pp. 6–7, 30, 31.
[5] P. R. Kirby, 'The Building in Stone of a New Kraal for the Paramount Chief of the Venda', *SAJS* 52 1956 167–8.
[6] Stayt, pp. 5–8, Plates VI and VII.
[7] Wilson, *Good Company*, p. 7; *Communal Rituals*, p. 56.
[8] Walton, *African Village*, passim. [9] Stayt, pp. 36–37. [10] Ibid., p. 29.

at Bambadyanalo.[1] The beads they treasure as heirlooms are like those from Mapungubwe,[2] and some resemble those from the c. A.D. 400–1000 level at Zimbabwe.[3] Venda spindle whorls may also resemble those excavated, but the evidence is inadequate for exact comparison.[4]

Traditionally, all Venda pottery was made by the Lemba who lived among them, and the Lemba alone were the weavers, so the artefacts indicate links between the ancient settlements and Lemba craftsmen, rather than Venda. But burials on the ancient sites have wider parallels. The Venda and Shona (Karanga) dehydrated the corpse of a chief and then buried the bones, and the Ndali branch of the Nyakyusa sometimes exhumed and reburied their dead. Moreover, a cow was buried with a chief.[5] Therefore the collections of human bones, sometimes in association with animal bones, found buried at Bambandyanalo (p. 33) have a parallel in contemporary or recent past practice. And further, the Venda build cairns of stones, where a chief's cortège stopped, like those found at Mapungubwe.[6]

In social structure the Venda are very similar to the Sotho people already described. They are patrilineal and virilocal and share with the Sotho the form of preferred cousin marriage which distinguishes the Sotho from Nguni.[7] Their system of chieftainship, though differing in detail, was again not radically different from that of the Sotho. It resembled that of the southern and eastern Sotho rather than the Tswana, for the incoming chiefs fused with the Ngona and did not form a stratified society as the Tswana did.

The lineage of Venda chiefs certainly arrived south of the Limpopo later than any of the other peoples previously discussed. On the basis of genealogies Lestrade puts their arrival in the Soutpansberg 'about the end of the seventeenth, or the beginning of the eighteenth century',[8] and Stayt (without discussing the grounds) gives this date also. But the Ngona and other early inhabitants, possibly speaking a form of Shona, were there ahead of them. Some Mapungubwe artefacts dated 1370±60 resemble those of the Venda. Either the Venda chiefs arrived much earlier than has been supposed, or craftsmen like the Lemba long preceded the chiefs, or the artefacts came from further north. The Ngonde line, from which it is suggested the Venda chiefs sprang, probably occupied the Karonga plain on Lake Malawi in the fifteenth century.[9]

[1] Fouché, Plates XXIV, XXV, XXX, pp. 121–2. [2] Ibid., pp. 36–61, 113, 121–4.
[3] Van Riet Lowe, 'Beads of the Water', 367; Caton Thompson, 100.
[4] Van Warmelo, *Copper Miners*, Plate VII; Fouché, Plate XV, 5, p. 26.
[5] Van Warmelo, *Contributions*, pp. 134–5; Wilson, *Rituals of Kinship*, pp. 249–50; *Communal Rituals*, pp. 54–55; Abraham, 'Early Political History', pp. 13–14.
[6] Stayt, p. 206; G. A. Gardner, *Mapungubwe*, ii. 8.   [7] Stayt, p. 175.
[8] Lestrade, 'Ethnic History', 490; Stayt, p. 12.
[9] Wilson, *Communal Rituals*, Genealogies; *Nyasa-Tanganyika Corridor*; K. R. Robinson, 'A Preliminary Report on the Recent Archaeology of Ngonde, Northern Malawi',

3. The Tsonga

The Tsonga occupy the coastal belt, stretching from Kosi Bay to the Save (Sabi) river, a little way south of the ancient port, Sofala. They number something over one and a half million.[1] Several dialects (Tonga, Ronga, Tswa, Hlengwe, and others) are included under Tsonga,[2] the people are known by a variety of names (Thonga, Tonga, Gwamba, Knop Neuse, Tshangane, or Shangaan), and they have often been confused with other Tonga groups such as the Tonga enclave around Inhambane, where a language totally different from Tsonga is spoken,[3] the Tonga of Mazabuka and the Zambezi valley, and the Lake-shore Tonga of Malawi. The root of the word probably means *east*,[4] and scholars are wary of such 'easterners'. Those with whom we are concerned are described in Portuguese journals dating from 1498 onwards, and in an anthropological classic, *The Life of a South African Tribe*, by the Reverend H. A. Junod. This was published originally in French in 1898, and it was the first detailed study of an African people. Oral tradition confirms that the Tsonga have long lived on the coast between the Save river and Kosi Bay, and they once stretched considerably further south, beyond Lake St. Lucia, until they were driven out by the Mthethwa. One chief's lineage claims to have moved some centuries ago into the Limpopo plain from what is now Zululand, and Chief Libombo moved to Nkomati from the Lebombo hills before 1554, indicating a movement from the south into Tsonga country. Several lineages came from the north-west and claim links with the Shona (Kalanga), and one of them, the Tembe, have a tradition that they came down by river. Another lineage is related to the Pedi section of the Sotho. The earliest inhabitants are said once to have been without fire, and to have eaten their food raw.[5]

The Tsonga were conquered by one of Shaka's warriors, Soshangane (Manukosi), in 1820–1, as described elsewhere (p. 346), and they were deeply influenced by the language and customs of their conquerors—so much so that many call themselves Tshangane or Shangaan after Soshangane—but their traditional culture was distinct from that of the Nguni and it largely remains so. Zulu and Tsonga are not mutually intelligible. One of the effects of the nineteenth-century wars was to

---

JAH, 7, 1966, 176. A radiocarbon date for Mbande hill gives A.D. 1410±80 (J. D. Clark, personal communication).

[1] Mozambique, 1960, 1,258,000 (estimate by 'local authorities'); Republic of South Africa, 511,093, *Population Census 1960, Sample Tabulation*, 'Shangaan'.
[2] Doke, p. 180.   [3] Junod, i. 291.   [4] Ibid. i. 15.
[5] Ibid. i. 21–27, 357; H. A. Junod, 'The Condition of the Natives of South East Africa in the XVIth Century, according to the Early Portuguese Documents', *SAJS* (1913), 147–52; A. W. Lee, *Charles Johnson of Zululand*, p. 141; D. Earthy, *Valenge Women*, pp. 3–10; C. E. Fuller, 'Ethnohistory in the Study of Culture Change in Southeast Africa', in *Continuity and Change in African Cultures* (ed. W. R. Bascom and M. J. Herskovits), pp. 116–26.

THE TSONGA 177

drive many Tsonga westward, so that they came into much closer contact than they had been previously with Sotho and Venda. This movement was facilitated towards the end of the century, by the contraction of tsetse belts which had separated Tsonga from Venda and Sotho,[1] but some tenuous contacts had long been established, for the Tsonga bartered hoes from the Venda in return for cloth from the coast; copper from Sotho smiths at Phalaborwa; ivory, rhino horn, gold, and furs.[2] The trade was partly by river. The Tsonga used canoes, and both the Nkomati and the Limpopo, which run through their country, are navigable; in the wet season Pafuri, three hundred miles inland on the Limpopo, can be reached by canoe. The coastal people sold amber.

From 1498 (and probably long before that) the Tsonga traded with the outside world. Vasco da Gama found the people of the 'Copper river' ready to 'give much copper' for linen cloth (see p. 78), and the Tsonga were the middlemen of the eighteenth-century metal trade (see p. 151). They commanded one route from the middle Limpopo to Sofala, and all the approaches to Lourenço Marques, a port from which ivory was shipped at least from 1552 onwards (see p. 78).

The sixteenth- and seventeenth-century records show that in Tsonga country the population was considerable, food plentiful, and (to the comfort of the shipwrecked) fish and fowl readily available.[3] In economy they differ radically from Nguni, Sotho, and Venda: they are fishermen and have long sought much of their food in the coastal lagoons and rivers, using fish-weirs in the sea and traps in the rivers. When the lakes and ponds are drying up they organize great battues, with a crowd of fishermen driving the fish into the traps.[4] The Tsonga also kept fowl traditionally, and used them in rituals,[5] as other Bantu-speakers in Central Africa do. In this, again, they differ from the Nguni, Sotho, and Venda. Their chief grain was sorghum—maize was recognized as an introduction—and goats were the common domestic animal. Cattle existed but were scarce in the tsetse-ridden[6] lowlands, and milk was not a staple food as with the Nguni.[7] Their weapons were 'very great bows and arrows',[8] and assagais of iron.

The local group consisted of a man together with his sons and grandsons, and their wives and children, with possibly one or two unrelated people who had sought his protection. There were no concentrations of population as with the Tswana, but scattered homesteads with perhaps seven married men. Huts were built in an arc surrounding a byre, the position of each depending upon the status of the occupant in terms of

[1] Krige, 'Origins', p. 322. [2] Junod, ii. 138, 140–7.
[3] Da Gama, pp. 10–12; Theal, Records, i. 238; viii. 119, 345, 353.
[4] Junod, ii. 86–87. [5] Ibid. i. 42, 58; ii. 51–52.
[6] Missão de Combateas Tripanossomiases, Relatoria Anual de 1954, Mapa 1, 3.
[7] Junod, ii. 48, 61. [8] Da Gama, p. 11.

the kinship structure. The whole settlement was surrounded with a fence, and the courtyard of each woman's hut was enclosed,[1] but with a lower wall than among the Tswana.

Either hoes—forty or fifty—or cattle were given at marriage,[2] and once they had been handed over, a wife was taken to her husband's homestead and any children she bore belonged to his group. Thus marriage was virilocal and descent patrilineal, but in other respects the kinship system differed from those already described. The Tsonga neither had exogamous clans like the Nguni nor preferred cousin marriage like the Sotho; their one obligation was to avoid marrying the descendant of a common grandfather. And their form of inheritance differed also, for a man's heir was his younger full-brother, and property went to his son only after the death of all the full-brothers in a house, whereas among Nguni and Sotho property descended directly from father to son.[3] In this again the Tsonga resemble many of the peoples of Central Africa.

The Tsonga had a lively belief in their dependence upon their ancestors and made offerings to them of sorghum, beer, fowls, and goats.[4] The altar was a tree or forked pole in the courtyard of the homestead, not the byre, as elsewhere (p. 127).[5] Lineages did not identify themselves with particular animals, as among the Sotho,[6] but they practised circumcision, traditionally, just as the Sotho did. Some dropped it before the Nguni conquest, others after it.[7]

As among the Nguni, Sotho, and Venda, births were carefully spaced at least three hoeing seasons apart,[8] so population was in some measure controlled. Indeed, increase may have been very slow, for Tsonga country was so ridden with malaria and dysentery that large numbers of Zulu warriors (who came from more healthy country) died there.[9]

Before the Zulu conquest the Tsonga lived in small independent chiefdoms, each with a population of perhaps six to eight thousand.[10]

Each chief sat in court and settled disputes independently of his brother chiefs. Three hundred years of trade with the Portuguese, and earlier trade with Arabs, had not stimulated the growth of any Tsonga kingdom. What it had stimulated was slave-trading. At least from the time of the Nguni conquest, and probably long before, women taken as prisoners of war were sold at Lourenço Marques.[11]

---

[1] Junod, i. 310–19.   [2] Ibid. i. 108, 275.   [3] Ibid. i. 202–3, 211, 410–13.
[4] Ibid. ii. 50–51, 324.   [5] Ibid. i. 313, 323, 341, 567.   [6] Ibid. i. 363.
[7] Ibid. i. 71–73.   [8] Ibid. i. 56–57, 60–61.
[9] Bryant, pp. 452, 627; W. C. Holden, *The Past and Future of the Kaffir Races*, pp. 35–36; Junod, i. 28; Brownlee, *Reminiscences*, p. 82.
[10] Junod, i. 358–9. Junod refers to them as *clans* but makes it clear that they included unrelated people.
[11] Ibid. i. 283. Tonga (of Inhambane) were sold at Inhambane: P. D. Curtin and J. Vansina, 'Sources of the Nineteenth Century Atlantic Slave Trade', *JAH*, 5, 1964, 205.

4. Conclusion

Certain tentative conclusions emerge from this analysis. So far as our evidence goes, the Rolong and Hurutshe, who are regarded by most other Sotho groups as their founding fathers, lived in large settlements, and their society was stratified. Cattle-owners had clients who herded for them, and who collected jackal pelts which their patrons tanned and sewed. Iron and copper were mined extensively, and certain specialists smelted and fashioned weapons, tools, and ornaments which were traded, along with skin cloaks and wooden utensils. The large settlements, the stratification, and the trade were linked. The clients were attached only to the chief and his immediate kinsmen, thus the wealth in skins and in stock that accrued to a patron was mainly in the hands of the chief. He was also entitled to one tusk of every elephant killed, and the skins and pads of certain royal game, such as leopards. This was an important source of wealth after the wagons of white traders crossed the Orange, and in a lesser degree before that. There is no evidence that the chief also gained specifically from the metal trade, but analogy with peoples further north suggests that he would,[1] and he controlled all barter. Indeed, the Ngwaketse chief claimed a monopoly of barter.[2] The wealth coming to the chief from skins and ivory, and probably from the metal trade, enabled him to distribute wealth. Livingstone reported[3] that when goods

> are brought into the kotla, Sekelutu [the Kololo chief] has the honour of dividing them among the loungers who usually congregate there. A small portion only is reserved for himself. The ivory belongs nominally to him too, but this is simply a way of making a fair distribution of the profits. The chief sells it only with the approbation of his councillors, and the proceeds are distributed in open day among the people as before. He has the choice of everything; but if he is not more liberal to others than to himself, he loses in popularity.

Thus a chief attracted followers to him, and residence in the capital was secured not primarily by force, but because a chief's followers gained by living there: they got some share of the wealth coming to the capital through trade.

This hypothesis—and it is no more than a hypothesis—gains support from the fact that there is a coincidence between the distribution of large settlements and the trade in worked skins, ivory, and metal. Dithakong, Kaditshwene, Kanye, Serowe, all lie both where metal was accessible, and near the boundary between the desert and the sown. The desert

---

[1] Mgr. Lechaptois, *Aux Rives du Tanganyika*, pp. 94, 259.
[2] Campbell, *1820*, i. 316.
[3] Livingstone, *Missionary Travels*, p. 198.

continued to supply pelts long after they were scarce elsewhere among the Sotho, and ivory was brought across the desert from Ngami.[1] The Sotho who were least concentrated—the Fokeng—were not metal-workers but bought iron from the Zizi (pp. 145, 152). The fact that large settlements existed in the more arid areas to the west has long been noted but never convincingly explained.[2] For example, *why* did the Tlhaping concentrate and *why* did they choose Dithakong when richer pastures lay to the east? Neither metal-working nor trade alone led to concentration, for (so far back as our evidence goes) the Venda metal-workers and Tsonga traders lived in much smaller settlements than the Tswana. The system of clientship (which flourishes where people of different physical type, economy, and language come into relationship) did not lead to concentration in Rwanda, but in Botswana it was probably a factor in creating concentration, through increasing the wealth of the chiefs, and producing goods for barter. It is suggested that concentration occurred where metal, ivory, and furs, important to trade, were all accessible, and clients were available to labour.

The word 'town' is not used here of Tswana settlements, because there is no evidence that any substantial section of the population lived by craft or trade: the inhabitants were all cattle-owners and cultivators or their dependents, though it is possible that some full-time craftsmen existed, as they did at Musina and among the Shona. It is significant, however, that crafts and trade, which are the hall-mark of the growth of towns, were of such importance in Dithakong, Kaditshwene, and the other great Tswana settlements. Elsewhere towns have grown out of ritual centres,[3] and the earliest travellers commented on the celebration of girls' initiation rituals in Dithakong, but, although these were communal, not individual, it cannot be shown that they were dependent on concentration. The most that can be argued is that concentration encouraged their corporate, as opposed to individual, character.

This chapter can conclude only with questions: was the Sotho pattern of stratification and settlement an isolated phenomenon, or was it part of a traditional culture that embraced the mining kingdoms of central and southern Africa? What was the distribution of ancient settlements with more than five thousand inhabitants? Did true towns exist in Monomotapa's kingdom apart from those on the coast? Did they exist on the ancient copper mines of Katanga? Linyanti, the Kololo capital on the Chobe, a tributary of the Zambezi, had between six and seven thousand inhabitants in 1853.[4] Lunda, Kazembe's capital on the margin

---

[1] Livingstone, *Missionary Travels*, p. 45.
[2] Schapera, *Land Tenure*, p. 269; Van Warmelo, *Preliminary Survey*, p. 103.
[3] R. J. Braidwood and G. R. Willey (eds.), *Courses towards Urban Life*, p. 350.
[4] Livingstone, *Missionary Travels*, p. 178.

of Lake Mofwe (in the modern Zambia), was described as 'two miles across, and its streets are wide, straight and very clean' in 1831. Kazembe's army of five or six thousand men could assemble in the central square.[1] Lunda was no new growth, and already, in 1798, the ruling Kazembe was trading with both east and west coasts.[2] Did any Lozi or Lunda settlements contain a class no longer directly dependent on farming? If they did not, just where, moving north and westward, did trading towns like Kano begin?

Then, how far did Sotho trade extend? There is good reason to suppose that they were the chief metal-workers of the Transvaal, and supplied the coast (see pp. 145–7, 150–1). Were they also linked with the trading empire of Monomotapa? The evidence of the Hurutshe chief in 1820 (p. 150) suggests that they were, though the link was tenuous.

Another set of questions relates to dates. *When* did the first Sotho ancestors cross the Limpopo? The Sotho, unlike the Nguni, have demonstrable connexions with one people to the north of them, the Shona, and possible links with the lacustrine people (see p. 171). It is likely that at least some of them came from north of the equator and east of the Rift (see p. 134), but the dating of their movements is still uncertain. Conscious identity, as pictured in tradition, goes back to the twelfth or thirteenth century: iron-working to the eighth century. If the Sotho were indeed the chief metal-workers supplying the coast, the descendants of Rolong the Forger, or those in Phalaborwa who spoke their language, must have been organizing production of copper for trade overseas before 1498. If they were Venda who commanded this trade then they must have crossed the Limpopo more than two centuries earlier than is supposed. It is highly improbable that the Shona sent copper for export so far south as the 'Copper river', and the Tsonga were middlemen, not miners.

We know that hunters occupied much of the area later settled by Sotho. Some of these spoke languages peculiar to hunters, others still speak a Khoikhoi language. There is also evidence of Khoikhoi cattle-keepers on the Orange river in the seventeenth century, and in the eighteenth century, when they had acquired fire-arms and horses, they penetrated northward across the Vaal. There is no certain evidence of Khoikhoi-speaking pastoralists north of the Vaal before that. It has been shown that the Sotho were metal-workers and stone builders, whereas most (if not all) the Khoikhoi were not. Who, if not the Sotho, built and mined between the Limpopo and the Vaal, and what has happened to their descendants?

In considering dates it should be noted that though traditions generally indicate an origin in the north, among all the people discussed some

[1] A. C. P. Gamitto (trans. I. Cunnison), *King Kazembe*, ii. 17, 19, 110.
[2] F. J. M. Lacerda (trans. R. F. Burton), *The Lands of Cazembe*, passim.

sections have a tradition of having moved *from* the south, and with Nguni and Tsonga such movements almost certainly began before 1550 (pp. 98, 176).

Finally, though it is possible to distinguish clearly in language and custom between Nguni, Sotho, Venda, and Tsonga groups, and they must have lived in relative isolation to grow so different, there was some movement between them. It can be shown in detail how each absorbed remnants of the others. The political unit, the chiefdom, was always made up of people of diverse descent, and strangers, even those who spoke another language, were readily accepted. Differences in law and ritual were tolerated on the ground that 'such is the custom in their lineage'. In their intellectual system, as expressed in language and material symbol, ritual and law, there is a great similarity between Nguni, Sotho, Venda, and Tsonga. Details varied in grammar and vocabulary, in the rules of marriage and rituals celebrated, but the framework was constant. People thought in categories of kinship; they assumed the dependence of the living upon their dead ancestors, who might be propitiated by prayer and sacrifice, and who were angered by quarrelling among their descendants; they assumed the existence of chiefs and some relationship between the health of the chief and the fertility and well-being of his people; they assumed the rule of law and thought the primary function of a chief was to settle disputes, to achieve reconciliation between conflicting parties; they assumed a moral order intrinsic in the universe.

V

WHITE SETTLERS AND THE ORIGIN OF A NEW SOCIETY, 1652–1778

'ALL the sins of the past . . of omission and . . . commission, can now be wiped out as with a damp sponge, with one stroke of the pen all the old contentions can be blotted out and forgotten; and on the clean white page may be written the new Charter for this settlement, framed with wisdom, mildness and discretion':[1] so wrote J. A. U. de Mist to the Batavian Republic's Department of Indian Affairs in his memorandum on the Cape in 1802. His views could not be tested, for most of the Batavian Republic's reforms lapsed when the Cape became a British possession in 1806. But de Mist's faith in the ease and efficacy of planned, drastic action is interesting, because its serene rationalism is in such striking contrast to the crisis and confusion at the Cape at the turn of the eighteenth century.

The emergence of turbulence in Cape public life indicated that the society which had imperceptibly developed during the past century and a half was under considerable stress. Its characteristic attitudes and expectations were confronted by new challenges, epitomized by two events of 1779. While the *Kaapse Patriotte*, a western Cape settlers' organization, demanded political and economic reforms from the Netherlands East India Company (VOC),[2] which ruled the Cape, on the northern and eastern frontiers the San and Xhosa were resisting the advance of white occupation. These circumstances mark a boundary between an epoch of uneventful maturation and one of turmoil. The government of the Cape could no longer be conducted on the assumption that it was essentially a refreshment station: the problems of a multi-racial colonial society had become too pressing to be ignored. The turning-point came in the 1770s because the frontiersmen could no longer cope alone with war against San and Xhosa simultaneously. Government intervention became necessary. In extending its authority for the first time over the frontier regions the government was gradually faced with the grievances of landless detribalized non-white servants

[1] J. A. U. de Mist, *The Memorandum of Commissary J. A. de Mist*, VRS, no. 3, 1920, p. 172.
[2] *Vereenigde Nederlandsche Ge-Octroyeerde Oost-Indische Compagnie* (United Netherlands Chartered East India Company) in abbreviated form.

against their white stock-farmer masters (whose attitudes of white superiority stemmed from the slave-owning traditions of the western Cape), because the extension of the colonial frontier against the Xhosa was impossible without the loyal aid of the coloured frontier population.

The problems of the Cape in the late eighteenth century stemmed from the emergence of a new society, which arose after Europeans first became permanently established there, when the VOC occupied Table Bay as a refreshment station in 1652. In order to provision its ships as cheaply and conveniently as possible, the VOC tried to stimulate agricultural production by white settlers. By 1700 the Cape could no longer absorb white immigrants on any scale. The existing white settler population grew rapidly by its own increase, and found the means of survival in semi-subsistence stockfarming, conducted on a very extensive scale, which led to the rapid dispersal of white settlement. By 1778 this process was checked by aridity in the north, near the Orange river, and by warfare with the cattle-keeping Xhosa tribes beyond the Bushmans river in the east. By that time the white settler community, very largely isolated from European influences, had developed a distinctive culture and spoke a local variation of Dutch, the *taal*, which became the Afrikaans language.

The presence of white settlers determined the composition of the new society at the Cape. Slaves were imported on a small scale from the beginning of the settlement, but became an important and permanent element in the new society, once private agriculture became established in the south-west Cape towards the end of the seventeenth century. The indigenous herding and hunting societies had largely disappeared as autonomous entities by the late eighteenth century. The Khoikhoi exchanged their sheep and cattle for European goods, white settlers occupied their grazing lands, smallpox and other epidemics caused great mortality; some groups retreated inland, others remained and their chiefs accepted VOC staffs of authority; many broke up altogether. The San, too, lost their hunting land and retreated with the game, but guerrilla warfare between settlers and the San on the Cape's northern fringes grew so intense after 1715 that the San were systematically exterminated. During the process of the displacement and destruction of the indigenous societies, many Khoikhoi and some San were incorporated into the new society as servile dependants of white farmers, working for barely more than their keep as herdsmen, domestic servants, or agricultural labourers. In the course of time cultural barriers between the various elements in Cape society broke down, partly as a result of widespread miscegenation between whites, slaves, Khoikhoi, and San, which foreshadowed the emergence of the Afrikaans-speaking Cape Coloured people.

The new Cape always remained a genuinely colonial society, which could not achieve the autonomy and self-sufficiency of the San and Khoikhoi societies which preceded it. The settlers provided both the impetus for its growth and the measure of its dependence. The birth of the settler community was linked with the economic value to Europe of the Cape's resources, a harbour with fresh water where fresh vegetables and meat could be produced for passing ships. The existence of the 'Tavern of the Seas', the town of De Kaap and its hinterland of corn and winefarming in the south-western Cape, was always dependent on its usefulness to Europe, expressed in the size of the Cape market constituted by the garrison and the visiting ships. Even the frontiersmen, who had gone far in achieving economic self-sufficiency, could not survive without European guns and ammunition, and never lost the taste for coffee, tea, sugar, simple ironmongery, crockery, and cloth, which could be obtained only by exchange. Cape society was also politically dependent on Europe, partly because of the strategic importance of Table Bay harbour, partly because of the settler community's weakness in numbers, financial resources, and political maturity. In the eighteenth century the frontiersmen begged a slow-moving, reluctant central government to extend its control over them. Even when that control was rejected in the revolts at Graaff-Reinet and Swellendam at the turn of the eighteenth century, as much through frustration over endless, apparently fruitless, frontier warfare as through dissatisfaction with government from above, the frontier republics soon collapsed, because they were not viable economically, politically, or in military terms.

Many of the most important features of the emergent new society at the Cape were moulded by the policies of the VOC, which ruled the Cape as a minor part of the Dutch Eastern Empire from 1652 to 1795.

The VOC was an amalgamation of several fiercely-competing Dutch trading companies which sprang up after 1598, when the Dutch successfully invaded the Portuguese monopoly of Eastern trade, particularly spices. Its six chambers (*kamers*), each managed by Directors, were represented on the VOC's executive committee, the Chamber of Seventeen, roughly in proportion to their contribution to the VOC's working capital. Its charter, issued by the Netherlands States-General in 1602, and renewed periodically until 1796, granted it the monopoly of Dutch trade and navigation between the Cape of Good Hope and the Straits of Magellan, where it could make treaties, wage war, administer stations, and appoint military and civilian officials. Its extensive political powers were subject to the States-General. All employees swore loyalty to the States-General, all important VOC appointments had to receive its confirmation, and the VOC had to submit regular reports to it. In practice, since the merchant class of Holland was firmly entrenched both in the State and in the Company, the VOC became practically sovereign. The States-General prevented shareholders from suing Directors in Dutch courts, and underpinned the VOC's authority by promulgating the conditions of service in the VOC army, navy, and civil service, in the *Artikelbrief* (1601).[1] Although the Charter stipulated that as few foreigners as possible should be recruited by the VOC, in 1691 one-third of its army and civil service were foreigners, of whom half were German, while in 1778 two-thirds were foreign, almost all German.[2] In 1644 the Seventeen informed the States-General that their 'places and strongholds . . . in the East Indies should not be regarded as national conquests but as the property of private merchants, who were entitled to sell [them] . . . to whomsoever they wished, even . . . to the King of Spain, or to some other enemy of the United Provinces'.[3]

Confident in its freedom from State interference, the Seventeen met three times a year to decide important matters relating to the VOC's trade and the government of its Eastern possessions. The capital of the Dutch Eastern Empire, and the VOC's 'head office' (*hoofd comptoir*) in Asia was Batavia in Java, the seat of the Governor-General and Council of India, which regulated Dutch trade and government in Asia, subject to the control of the Seventeen. Subordinate to Batavia were 'branch offices' (*buiten comptoiren*) ruled by Governors: Amboyna, Banda, the Moluccas, Malacca, Ceylon, Macassar, the north-east coast of Java and the Cape (after 1699), controlling lesser stations, under a director, commander, *opperhoofd* or regent, depending on their importance.[4]

This system of authority in Asia originated in the need to exert control in varying degrees, so as to secure a monopoly of trade in various Asian goods, notably spices. By linking the vast network of VOC trading posts in the East it provided the framework for the realization of the essential purpose of the Company, the profitable exchange of European and Asian goods by means of its fleets, of which three left the Netherlands for Batavia every year, and two returned home.[5]

---

[1] Cf. F. Valentijn, *Beschrijving van Oud en Nieuw Oost-Indieen*, i. 186 ff.; C. R. Boxer, *The Dutch Seaborne Empire 1600–1800*, pp. 22–24, 44–47, Ch. II; G. Masselman, *The Cradle of Colonialism*, pp. 62 ff.; Clive Day, *The Policy and Administration of the Dutch in Java*, p. 87; H. R. Hahlo and Ellison Kahn, *The Union of South Africa, The Development of its Laws and Constitution*, pp. 11–12; H. T. Colenbrander, *Koloniale Geschiedenis*, ii. 208–9; E. C. Godée-Molsbergen, *De Stichter van Hollands Zuid Afrika, Jan van Riebeeck, 1618–1677*, Appendix XII.
[2] Colenbrander, ii. 216.
[3] Quoted in *Dutch Seaborne Empire*, pp. 45–46.
[4] Colenbrander, ii. 212.
[5] *Dutch Seaborne Empire*, Ch. IV, *passim*, and p. 197.

1. *The Foundation of the Cape Station*

On 20 March 1651 the Seventeen approved a proposal discussed for twenty months in various committees[1] that 'to provide that the . . . East India ships, to and from Batavia . . may . . . [procure] . . . herbs, flesh, water, and other needful refreshments—and by this means restore the health of their sick—. . . a general rendezvous be formed' at the Cape of Good Hope.[2] On 7 April 1652 an expedition of about ninety men, under Jan van Riebeeck, went ashore at Table Bay.

The *Cabo de Boa Esperance* had then been known to Europeans since its discovery by Bartholomew Diaz in 1488. The Portuguese, pioneers of the Cape maritime route to Asia, monopolized it from 1498 to 1595, without showing interest in the Cape. Like the Arabs they crossed the Indian ocean on the south-west monsoon on their voyages from Lisbon to Goa or Cochin, usually stopping at Mozambique on the way out, St. Helena or the Azores on the way home.[3] The Cape, with its small groups of Khoikhoi, having only cattle and sheep to barter, could not compare commercially with the Congo, Angola, the East African ports and Zambesia, where the Portuguese had vast commitments. Even without its unsavoury reputation, derived from d'Almeida's fatal skirmish with some Khoikhoi in 1510, the Portuguese had no reason to frequent the Cape.

When Dutch and English interlopers broke the Portuguese monopoly of the Cape route, they aimed for the South-East Asian spice-producing areas where the Portuguese were weakest. This caused a south-eastward shift in European trade with Asia. The two most important national monopolistic East India companies, the Dutch and the English, became based in Java and India respectively. In 1611 a VOC captain discovered a new direct route to the Straits of Sunda, using the westerlies and the deflected south-west monsoon.[4] The Cape, almost midway on this new longer route, was visited increasingly frequently by Dutch, English, French, and other East-Indiamen, especially after the Dutch failed to capture Mozambique in 1609–10, so that by the 1620s ships even left messages for one another under special 'post office' stones.

Although the Portuguese, English, and Dutch[5] all considered establishing themselves at the Cape, nothing was done until 1652, since

---

[1] G. M. Theal, *Chronicles of the Cape Commanders* . . . , p. 23.
[2] '1651, March 25. Instructions . . .', in Moodie, parts i, iii, v, photographic reprint, i. 7.
[3] C. R. Boxer (ed.), *The Tragic History of the Sea, 1589–1622*, p. 6.
[4] *Dutch Seaborne Empire*, p. 197; N. C. Pollock and Swanzie Agnew, *An Historical Geography of South Africa*, p. xvii.
[5] Cf. Sir Charles Lucas, *Historical Geography of the British Colonies*, vol. iv: *South Africa—Part I: History to 1895*, Ch. I; I. D. MacCrone, *Race Attitudes in South Africa, Historical, Experimental and Psychological Studies*, p. 14.

all the East India Companies already maintained many costly factories and the Cape could offer nothing except 'water and a little scurvy grass'.¹ Moreover, its inhabitants were reputed to be savage.² Furthermore, East-Indiamen did not automatically stop there. Although outward-bound ships often did, St. Helena was the main port on the return voyage. Thus the limited usefulness of the Cape would not justify the expense of permanent occupation.

By the late 1640s, however, the wild pigs and goats on St. Helena had been almost exterminated. Henceforth Dutch ships would find only 'a few herbs . . . apples and lemons . . . How severely it will be felt by the crews, to come home without touching at any place of refreshment is sufficiently known . . . and thus the Company's ships, in the event of great sickness and many deaths, would encounter no small danger.'³ Thus argued the *Remonstrance*, presented to the VOC in July 1649, '. . . in which is briefly . . . explained, the service, advantage and profit . . . [of] making a Fort and Garden, at the *Cabo de Boa Esperance*'.⁴ The *Remonstrance* followed the wreck of the *Haerlem*, in Table Bay in March 1647. The survivors remained until March 1648 and discovered Table Valley had fertile, well-watered soil, where a very great variety of vegetables and fruit could be grown, including citrus, known to be effective against scurvy. The *Remonstrance* recommended making a garden at Table Bay, which should become a compulsory stop for VOC ships to and from Batavia. The consequent prevention of sickness, the reduced provisions necessary on board, and the shorter voyage involved in by-passing St. Helena would entail great savings. Fresh water could be obtained more easily by building pipes or a pier, and accidents prevented by those on shore guiding ships into harbour. The *Remonstrance* denied the assertion that the natives were cannibals. They responded to kindness, learnt Dutch easily, and might become servants and be taught Christianity. Finally, the *Remonstrance* warned the VOC that, if the Cape was not occupied by the Dutch, it might be used by 'our public enemies the Spanish and Portuguese' as a base for attacking Dutch ships.⁵

Boxer has shown that the Cape's greatest advantage was that it was a temperate area, without tropical diseases, where Europeans could safely grow fruit and vegetables effective in preventing shipboard diseases like scurvy. Though the death-rate from scurvy apparently fell towards the mid seventeenth century, it was still high.⁶ Scurvy might cause the illness or death of so many sailors that a ship could not

---

¹ 'Remonstrance. . . .' by Janz and Proot, in Moodie, i. 1.
² Ibid. i. 3.   ³ Ibid. i. 2.   ⁴ Ibid. i. 1.
⁵ Ibid. i. 1–4, *passim*.
⁶ C. R. Boxer, 'The Tavern of Two Seas . . .', *History Today*, June 1964, p. 393.

be sailed properly, and it might even founder. At best, 'the hospital at Batavia, to the [VOC's] great cost and injury . . . is crowded with invalids, who often lie there for months without doing any work, but drawing wages notwithstanding'.[1]

To minimize these hazards on voyages normally lasting five-and-a-half to seven months or more, the VOC occupied the Cape as a refreshment station.[2] Van Riebeeck was ordered to build a lodge and a fort near a freshwater stream running into the harbour, and to select suitable land for gardens, pasture, and cattle breeding.[3]

The refreshment station started operating remarkably quickly, owing to the energy and ability of van Riebeeck, who was trying to reinstate himself in his first VOC post since his dismissal in 1648 for private trading.[4] He faced great difficulties. When he arrived

On . . . a parched, poor soil without a dwelling place, and only some light material . . . to build . . . a fort . . ., work had to be started with about 90 persons . . . just from a sea voyage, and suffering from scurvy. They were as raw as the whole world had ever seen . . . [and he had] to work himself as engineer, digger, gardener, farmer, carpenter, mason, smith, etc., so . . . that . . . after 10 months the Company's return fleet . . . which . . . remained . . . between 6 and 7 weeks was abundantly supplied with refreshments, [including] . . . cattle obtained by barter from the natives.[5]

When van Riebeeck left, in 1662, the Cape establishment was on its feet.[6] Round the fort were the hospital, workshops, a mill, a corn granary, houses, and stables for cattle, sheep, and horses, and vegetable and fruit gardens near by. A jetty completed in 1659 allowed passengers to disembark directly on to dry land. Ships' water barrels were rolled along it to a freshwater pond.[7] The VOC construed its aims so narrowly that van Riebeeck was told in 1657 'that . . . not too much work should be taken in hand, but . . . the Cape establishment should be kept as confined and . . . small . . . as possible'.[8] Partly for this reason, partly to guard against Khoikhoi thieving, the Directors seriously contemplated building a canal from False Bay to Table Bay to turn the Cape peninsula into an island, and van Riebeeck in fact planted a hedge enclosing an

---

[1] Moodie, i. 2.
[2] *Dutch Seaborne Empire*, p. 198.
[3] Moodie, i. 7–8.
[4] *VRJ*, Introduction.
[5] Van Riebeeck to the XVII, 5 Mar. 1659, H. C. V. Leibbrandt, *Letters Despatched* . . . *1652–1662*, iii. 73–74.
[6] Cf. H. M. Robertson, 'The Economic Development of the Cape under Jan van Riebeeck', *SAJE*, 1–4, 1945.
[7] H. Déhérain, *Études sur l'Afrique*, 2 ième série, *Le Cap de Bonne-Espérance au XVIIe siècle*, pp. 25–26.
[8] *Letters Despatched* . . . *1652–1662*, iii. 20. Cf. Dispatch from the XVII, 23 Aug. 1661: 'of what use would a large colony . . . be to us if we must always support it from abroad; besides the men are more useful to us in India . . .'. Moodie, i. 240.

area of about 6,000 acres, which was considered the right size for the settlement.[1] The *Remonstrance* had claimed that a VOC station at the Cape would make the Eastern voyage less costly. But the Cape base was unsatisfactory in many ways, and very expensive to maintain, though its advantages always outweighed its disadvantages.

The VOC's somewhat lukewarm attitude towards the Cape is indicated by the steps it took to defend the Cape, and thus to remain master of it. During the Second and Third Anglo-Dutch Wars (1665-7, 1672-4) the stone Castle was built to replace the original mud fort, badly sited and collapsing since 1660. Though better placed to protect the anchorage, it was open to attack from behind, from Devil's Peak, which remained unfortified till 1782, and most of Table Bay was beyond the range of its cannon. Between 1715 and 1744 new fortifications were built along the inner rim of Table Bay. But the defence of the rest of the peninsula remained inadequate, despite the work of the French (who forestalled an English attack in 1780) and the Cape government. In particular, False Bay remained unfortified. The English landed there in 1795, and captured the Castle from behind. Furthermore, the numerous cannon were badly maintained and there was insufficient gunpowder. The garrison, though rigidly disciplined, was kept well below its necessary strength, because the VOC hoped the burgher militia could substitute for regular troops; about half were artisans or unskilled labourers, and the genuine soldiers were inadequately trained. In 1722 the Governor thought the Castle could be captured in twenty-four hours.[2]

The Cape's defences were inadequate, not only because the Directors were loath to spend money, but also because of its defects as a port. Outward-bound ships had to go off course to reach it. Van Riebeeck, on the Seventeen's instructions, sent several unsuccessful naval expeditions to find more suitable refreshment stations.[3] To counteract the time lost the VOC limited the stay of East Indiamen at Cape Town.[4] Calling there was also dangerous, because of northerly and north-westerly gales in May and June, and south-easterly winds between December and February.[5] So many shipwrecks occurred off Table Bay,

---

[1] *Letters Despatched . . . 1652-1662*, iii. 247; cf. Moodie, i. 50.

[2] Cf. P. E. Roux, *Die Verdedigingstelsel aan die Kaap onder die Hollands -Oosindiese Kompanjie (1652-1795)*, pp. 1-21, 29, 71-107; Anna Boëseken, 'Die Nederlandse Kommissarisse en die 18de eeuse Samelewing aan die Kaap', in *AYB, 1944* (hereafter called Boëseken (1)), pp. 94-99, 243; O. F. Mentzel, *Life at the Cape in the mid-eighteenth century . . . R. S. Allemann* (1785), VRS, no. 2, 1921 (hereafter called *Allemann*), pp. 149, 151-2, 157; Barrow, ii. 212, 217; *The Reports of De Chavonnes . . . correspondence*, VRS, no. 1, 1918 (hereafter called *Chavonnes*), pp. 143-5; Déhérain, pp. 15-25.

[3] *Letters Despatched . . . 1652-1662*, iii. 202-3.   [4] *Dutch Seaborne Empire*, p. 244.

[5] *Letters Despatched . . . 1652-1662*, iii. 29.

THE FOUNDATION OF THE CAPE STATION 191

especially among returning vessels, that in 1743 ships were ordered to use False Bay from mid May to mid August. An attempt to protect the Bay by a breakwater failed,[1] and in 1766 ships leaving Batavia after 1 December were advised to avoid Cape harbours altogether.[2] Nevertheless, after 1652 all VOC fleets usually called at the Cape.[3] One advantage was that the sick were disembarked and sent to hospital, and vacancies filled by taking on men who had recovered. It is doubtful whether cures were induced by hospitalization or merely by the effect of fresh food and water in Cape Town's healthy climate after the overcrowded unhealthy conditions on the ships. Mentzel's comment that 'conditions at the hospital more often send a person to his grave than the ravages of his disease'[4] seems valid, except, possibly, between 1717 and 1750.[5] Van Riebeeck's hospital was small and exposed to the southeasters. A better-situated, larger one, started in 1694, was completed only in 1699.[6] By 1766 its doors and windows were rotting, but its yet larger replacement was begun only in 1773, took twenty years to complete, and cost half a million guilders.[7] Hospital administration was generally poor and elementary rules of hygiene were ignored,[8] but at least it helped to relieve the pressure on the Batavian hospital.

Another advantage of the Cape station was that captains could careen their vessels, remove barnacles, effect repairs,[9] and obtain equipment and stores from the VOC warehouse there.[10] One commodity that was always needed by homeward-bound ships was firewood, since there was insufficient space to load enough at Batavia. Wood was very scarce in the western Cape, despite many tree-planting schemes. Local supplies were supplemented by imports from Europe and Asia until 1787, when wood from the Knysna and Tsitsikama forests was shipped to Cape Town.[11]

But the greatest needs of calling ships were fresh water, vegetables, fruit, and meat. In supplying these the Cape establishment amply justified its existence. The refreshment station was sited at Table Bay, rather than any other Cape inlet, partly because a freshwater stream ran into the harbour.[12] Van Riebeeck's watering-place allowed water to

---

[1] *Chavonnes*, p. 131.   [2] *Dutch Seaborne Empire*, p. 244.
[3] Ibid., p. 198.
[4] O. F. Mentzel, *A Geographical and Topographical Description of the Cape of Good Hope*, VRS, nos. 4, 6, 25, 1921, 1925, 1944 (hereafter called *Description*), i. 4, 113.
[5] Boëseken (1), pp. 146–7.
[6] C. Graham Botha, *Collected Works*, i. 196–7.
[7] Boëseken (1), pp. 147–8.
[8] Ibid., pp. 146–7; *Description*, i. 113.
[9] Van Imhoff's recommendation in 1743, *Chavonnes*, p. 132; cf. Barrow, i. 13.
[10] *Description*, i. 142.
[11] Ibid., p. 108, *Chavonnes*, p. 136; Boëseken (1), p. 20; *Bel. Hist. Dok.* i. 23–25.
[12] Pollock and Agnew, Fig. 17, p. 38; *Bel. Hist. Dok.* i. 16.

be obtained conveniently,[1] and complaints of its foulness ceased in the later seventeenth century.[2]

As for fresh foodstuffs, by 1659 each Dutch ship was given sufficient fresh vegetables and fruit for two meals a day during its stay, and '6 or 8 oxen and 10 or 12 sheep'. It left with 'at least a 12 or 14 days' supply of carrots, beet, parsnips, turnips, cabbages etc.',[3] and about 15 live sheep.[4]

This was a remarkable achievement, particularly at the beginning of the settlement, when the establishment was very small, as most VOC ships called between February and May.[5] On average 33 Dutch ships a year arrived between 1652 and 1699, 46 from 1700 to 1714, 68 from 1715 to 1739, 52 from 1740 to 1759, and 51 from 1760 to 1779.[6]

2. Agriculture and Immigration

Initially the Company itself produced fruit and vegetables, bartered sheep and cattle from Khoikhoi herders, and attempted to increase its flocks and herds by breeding. Khoikhoi labour was virtually unobtainable, so the garrison did everything—wood-cutting, collecting shells for lime, brickmaking, building, and guard duty. Naturally they worked unwillingly and carelessly. To escape the perpetual hard labour under iron discipline, often on short rations, many deserted.[7] Though vegetable and fruit gardening succeeded, stockrearing, which required more individual attention, suffered because the men knew they would be paid whatever happened.[8] Worse still, the summer south-easters made wheat-growing in Table Valley impossible. Though sheltered land behind the Cape mountains along the Liesbeeck river was soon discovered,[9] it was too far from the fort to be farmed on any scale by soldiers who needed strict supervision. The Netherlands and Batavian authorities thought the Cape was absorbing too many men, and costing far too much, especially as the rice imported from Batavia to feed the men took up valuable cargo space.[10]

The long-term answer to the 'overwhelming expenditure' at the Cape was to find sources of revenue, preferably in exports, to counterbalance expenses.[11] Van Riebeeck tried hard to diversify the economy

---

[1] Déhérain, p. 26.
[2] *Bel. Hist. Dok.* i. 16; Anna Boëseken, *Nederlandsche Kommissarissen aan de Kaap 1657–1700* (hereafter called Boëseken (2)), pp. 26–28.
[3] *Letters Despatched . . . 1652–1662*, iii. 83–84.   [4] *Description*, i. 171.
[5] *Letters Despatched . . . 1652–1662*, iii. 251.
[6] F. C. Dominicus, *Het huiselik en maatschappelijk leven van de Zuid Afrikaner in de eerste helft der 18de eeuw*, p. 86; C. Beyers, *Die Kaapse Patriotte, 1779–1791*, Appendix G.
[7] See *VRJ*, i–iii, *passim*.   [8] Ibid. i. 346.
[9] Ibid. i. 350.   [10] Moodie, i. 90.   [11] Ibid. i. 8.

AGRICULTURE AND IMMIGRATION

by starting sealing, whaling, fishing, viticulture, olive growing, and other activities,[1] and he dispatched several expeditions inland, among whose aims was always the discovery of valuable products like 'honey, wax, ostrich feathers, elephant tusks, silver, gold, pearls, tortoiseshell, musk, civet, amber, any fine pelts, or anything else'.[2] But despite his efforts and those of his successors the only Cape exports before 1778 were a trickle of hunting products (ivory, pelts, ostrich feathers, and so on),[3] and wheat, wine, and brandy in the eighteenth century.[4]

But these were long-term solutions. Meanwhile the Cape government had to reduce its responsibilities. In 1654 van Riebeeck stopped issuing food to women and children, and offered married employees private gardens to grow vegetables and keep poultry and pigs.[5] He also transferred other activities to private hands. In 1655 the Company's cows were leased to the gardener's wife, who was allowed to sell milk and butter privately after van Riebeeck's household was supplied.[6] Later, tavern-keeping, milling, woodcutting, hunting, fishing, tailoring, and even medical practice were delegated to freed servants,[7] usually as licensed monopolies.

But the Cape still had to produce enough grain to become independent of Batavian rice. Also, because so few sheep and cattle were obtainable by barter in 1653 and 1654,[8] stock-breeding had to be increased.

Only two weeks after the party arrived (21 April 1652) the writer of the Cape official journal noted that industrious Chinese could be even more successful as cultivators there than at Formosa. A week later 'some married Chinese, Mardykers[9] or even Hollanders' were wistfully referred to.[10] The Batavian government tried unsuccessfully for over ten years to get Chinese or Mardykers 'by fair measures' to emigrate to 'that remote and solitary Cape'.[11] Van Riebeeck dared not suggest Dutch colonization, because of the Seventeen's intention of limiting the Cape to a refreshment station only.[12] But in April 1655, in response to their query about colonizing Hout Bay, he recommended colonization near Table Bay, where 'a thousand families' could grow corn and rear livestock. Since freemen in Asia had shown that they only wanted to

[1] *VRJ*, i–iii, *passim*, and index.
[2] Instructions for van Hoesem's expedition (Feb. 1659) to the Namaquas. *VRJ*, iii. 12–13.
[3] S. D. Neumark, *Economic Influences on the South African Frontier, 1652–1836*, pp. 27–32, 64–67.
[4] Boëseken (1), Ch. XI, and Appendices 7 and 8.
[5] *Chronicles of the Cape Commanders* . . ., p. 64.   [6] *VRJ*, i. 345–9.
[7] Company employees whose period of service had expired could either sign on again, or take out letters of freedom (*vrybrieven*), which entitled them to the privileges of freemen (*vryburghers*).
[8] Cf. *VRJ*, i, *passim*.
[9] Liberated Indonesian slaves or their descendants.
[10] Ibid., pp. 33, 35.   [11] Moodie, i. 262 n.   [12] MacCrone, p. 28, n. 2.

get rich by tavern-keeping and return to Europe, married men should be bound to remain for ten years and their children for twenty, so that they would 'in time . . . come to regard this country as their Fatherland'. The Company should support settlers until their lands were cultivated, not tax them immediately, provide slaves 'to place them the sooner on their legs', and eventually abandon agriculture to allow them a livelihood. In return they must sell their produce to the Company only, which 'should be the master in every way'. But since settlers would not come 'upon vague hopes', he suggested starting with a few employees accustomed to the country and willing to become freemen.[1] The Directors approved,[2] and nine freed servants were settled along the Liesbeeck, on conditions signed on 21 February 1657, and improved a little later by Commissioner[3] Rykloff van Goens, who wanted as many free farmers as possible, to reduce the salaried employees necessary. Under the final conditions each settler-farmer would get about twenty-eight acres in freehold, to be farmed with cereals for twelve years before it could be sold. In future only Dutch or German married men of good character, who must remain for twenty years, would get land. The Company would supply rations and tools at cost on credit, and oxen, cows, and sheep at fixed prices, and would buy wheat at a fixed price in repayment of debts. Vegetables could be sold to ships three days after they arrived, provided the Company's needs were first satisfied. To encourage stock-rearing, which the Directors regarded as an important justification for allowing free agriculture,[4] van Goens authorized freemen to barter stock with Khoikhoi, provided they bought all trade goods from the Company and did not outbid it. Freemen must sell cattle, sheep, and wheat to the Company only. They must perform military service to help reduce the garrison. To safeguard their interests, a respectable freeman would be selected to participate in criminal trials of freemen.[5]

Clearly in 1657 the VOC did not envisage colonization as an end in itself. It merely wished to substitute limited private farming for state production to reduce its expenditure. It therefore signed new contracts with some ex-employees, which, from its own point of view, were generous.[6] But this did not make private agriculture attractive or successful. The establishment of settlers in the Liesbeeck valley on Khoikhoi grazing ground provoked the first war (1658–60) which retarded progress. The first slaves, from Guinea and Angola, were very intractable and many absconded. The freemen, fearing for their lives,

[1] Van Riebeeck to the XVII, 28 Apr. 1655, Moodie, i. 60–62.
[2] XVII to Van Riebeeck, 30 Oct. 1655, ibid. i. 75.
[3] See below, pp. 214–15.   [4] Moodie, i. 75.
[5] *Letters Despatched . . . 1652–1662*, iii. 260–3; cf. Boëseken (2), Ch. iv.
[6] Cf. Van Riebeeck's Instructions to Wagenaar, *Letters Despatched . . . 1652–1662*, iii. 238.

returned most of them to the Company. Above all, the free farmers resented the conditions imposed on them. In 1658 they staged the first 'strike',[1] declaring 'it is too hard that they are compelled to plant ... this or that, ... to refrain from following their own bent, [and] from bartering all sorts of things from the natives ... to sell ... to the ships' and 'we will not be slaves to the Company'.[2] Some decamped, leaving their debts unpaid.[3] Very few burghers wanted to farm, preferring tavern-keeping or cattle-barter.

In 1661 Van Riebeeck was ordered 'to make no more freemen ... at the Fort or the Town ... corn growers however may be multiplied'.[4] But by 1662 there was hardly any space left, on the land encompassed by the hedge, suitable for grain-growing, and van Riebeeck advised his successor, Wagenaar, not to grant land beyond, as it would cost too much to protect.[5] In 1666 Wagenaar said only three or four farmers could afford white employees (*knechts*). The others were too poor, or too lazy and dissolute, to succeed. Some, he said, 'have abandoned all hope, all inclination for farming and all enterprise ... and requested to be received back into the Company's service, or at least to be permitted to earn their subsistence in some other way, or to set up houses ... for the sale of brandy'.[6] As time went on, Cape dispatches still lamented the freemen's drunkenness, their preference for tavern-keeping, their 'spoiling the Hottentot trade' by offering more money than the Company, and their illegal private trade in farm products, which fetched far more than the Company's fixed price.[7] Meanwhile the VOC authorities complained that far too many employees were retained at the Cape, which 'has brought us no other advantage than refreshments to the shipping, and you would make us purchase those at a high rate'.[8]

But if the garrison were reduced, the Company's 'chief strength and dependence here must consist in the *burgers* and *boers*' (farmers) whose welfare depended on agriculture, which, if successful, would make the Cape independent of imported food. Therefore the government must abandon official farming on the Liesbeeck river, begin experimental grain farming beyond the Cape flats at Hottentots Holland, and then settle freemen there. Meanwhile private grain-farming must be encouraged by raising the fixed price. These recommendations by Commissioner van den Brouck in May 1670[9] were approved in May 1671.

---

[1] Walker, *A History of Southern Africa*, p. 39.
[2] *Letters Despatched ... 1652–1662*, iii. 65, Van Riebeeck to the XVII, 5 Mar. 1659, and *VRJ*, ii, 23 Dec. 1658, pp. 391–403.
[3] Cf. Van Riebeeck to Batavia, 30 Nov. 1658, *Letters Despatched ... 1652–1662*, iii. 53.
[4] Van Riebeeck ... to Wagenaar, *Letters Despatched ... 1652–1662*, iii. 237.   [5] Ibid.
[6] Moodie, i. 293–4, Memorandum ... by Wagenaar ..., 24 Sept. 1666.
[7] Ibid. i. 300–4.   [8] Ibid. i. 302 n., 299.
[9] Ibid. i. 307.

The Seventeen stressed that official production should be abandoned wherever possible, and transferred to freemen.[1] In 1676 Commissioner Verberg stated 'as a matter of course . . . a good Dutch colony shall be planted and reared here'. He recommended more slaves, as the few colonists could not produce enough grain for the Cape's needs, and that the colonists' justifiable dissatisfaction should be reduced by less rigid Government control.[2] Again the Directors approved.[3]

This change in sentiment reflected a general desire to promote colonization throughout the Eastern Empire,[4] reinforced by fear of an English capture of the Cape in the Third Anglo-Dutch War (1672-4). But the colonization policy could not be fully implemented, partly owing to scarce numbers, partly because the Second Khoikhoi War (1673-77) delayed the extension of white settlement beyond the Cape flats. Nevertheless, between 1672 and 1679 the free white population increased from 168 to 259, partly through freeing suitable VOC employees, partly through the excess of births over deaths, and to a minor degree through immigration.[5] By 1677 there were 38 farmers at the Cape, compared with 13 in 1663.[6] After 1679 new settlements were founded beyond the Cape flats—at Stellenbosch in the Eerste river valley (1680) where 30 families were living by 1683, and at De Paarl on the Berg river in 1687.[7] In 1685 there were 30 families in Cape Town, engaged in inn- and tavern-keeping and vegetable gardening, compared with 24 in Table Valley up to the Steenberg mountains, and 99 in Stellenbosch, all farmers.[8]

Up to this time there were few European immigrants, except some orphan girls and a few families arriving between 1670 and 1679. Desirable immigrants of sound Protestantism and of Dutch or German extraction were with difficulty attracted to settle at the Cape.[9] But the revocation of the Edict of Nantes sent large numbers of Huguenot refugees to the Netherlands, and enabled the Directors to initiate the only large assisted immigration scheme to the Cape during the VOC period. After 1688 about 200 Huguenots arrived and were 'partly settled in the Cape district, and partly at Stellenbosch, but chiefly at Drakenstein'.[10] To facilitate their rapid assimilation, the Cape government interspersed Huguenots among Dutch farmers, and made Dutch the only medium of instruction in public schools. The French language soon began to disappear and the Huguenots,[11] who regarded the Cape

[1] Moodie, i. 299-300.   [2] Ibid. i. 340.
[3] Ibid. i. 344 n. Dispatch from XVII, 21 Oct. 1676.   [4] Boëseken (2), p. 54.
[5] MacCrone, pp. 59-64.   [6] Moodie, i. 251 n., 358 n.
[7] E. A. Walker, *CHBE*, viii: *South Africa*, pp. 132-3.   [8] *Bel. Hist. Dok.* i. 28.
[9] H. C. V. Leibbrandt, *Rambles through the Archives . . . of the Cape of Good Hope, 1688-1700*, p. 10.
[10] Simon van der Stel to the XVII, 12 June 1690, Moodie, i. 446.
[11] Cf. *Rambles*; C. G. Botha, *The French Refugees at the Cape*.

AGRICULTURE AND IMMIGRATION

as a permanent refuge, intermarried with other burghers. This helped to stabilize the free white population. By the end of the seventeenth century the crystallization of a distinction between 'Afrikaners', burghers who regarded the Cape as a permanent home, and 'Europeans', largely Company servants who were only temporary residents, was already under way.

By the late seventeenth century the Company's limited economic aims in promoting free agriculture were in sight of success. The Cape was becoming self-sufficient in cereals, as the first export of wheat in 1684 showed; after 1707 wheat was fairly regularly exported to Batavia.[1] Though initially settlers grew vines reluctantly, later viticulture was combined with cereal-growing on many farms, which helped to offset the low fixed grain prices, and provided wine for local consumption.[2] The Company encouraged stock-keeping in conjunction with agriculture to provide trek oxen, manure, and meat, and bought livestock from colonists to promote stock-breeding and augment its own supplies. Although private stock-barter with Khoikhoi was prohibited in 1658, the most severe regulations could not prevent such lucrative transactions. The colonists' flocks and herds increased rapidly, and in 1700 the government was successfully petitioned to allow grazing outside the existing settlement.[3] In 1695 the Seventeen wrote, 'The cultivation of wine and corn, and the breeding of cattle by the Company have long ago . . . gone against our grain, for we think that this work would better suit the colonists who would earn their living by it; to say nothing of the number of Company's servants, who, with the slaves, are used for the purpose. We . . . order you to . . . [gradually] get rid of the whole, and leave it to the colonists',[4] starting with the vineyards. In 1699 the Seventeen cancelled the local law prohibiting private cattle-barter, so that the Government could envisage abandoning cattle-keeping when existing herds were exhausted.[5] As a consequence, the Company sold or leased most of its farms.[6] Its gardens at Table Bay, Rondebosch, and Newlands became botanical gardens, but continued producing vegetables and fruit for the Governor, the VOC fleets, and the hospital.[7]

By the end of the seventeenth century the Cape had reached a crossroads in its economic development. Since 1680 the VOC had tried to guarantee itself cheap provisions by establishing agriculture, particularly

---

[1] *Dutch Seaborne Empire*, p. 250; Boëseken (1), pp. 155–69.
[2] Moodie, i. 188; H. C. V. Leibbrandt, *Letters Despatched, 1696–1708*, p. 41; C. G. Botha (ed.), *Collectanea*, VRS, no. 5, 1924, p. 12; M. W. Spilhaus, *The First South Africans . . .*, p. 100.
[3] MacCrone, pp. 92–94.
[4] H. C. V. Leibbrandt, *Letters Received, 1695–1708*, p. 61.
[5] Ibid., p. 205.   [6] Spilhaus, p. 8.   [7] Sparrman, i. 11.

wheat farming, in the fertile valleys behind the Hottentots Holland mountains, through settling white immigrants there in compact groups on freehold farms of about 120 acres. Simon van der Stel (1679–99), who successfully undertook this colonization policy, ardently advocated close settlement as a means of checking illegal cattle barter, and obtaining an easily mobilized militia.[1] The question was whether planned development based on white immigration could be continued.

In June 1700 the Seventeen authorized the constituent VOC chambers to send emigrants to the Cape on free passages,[2] and it enquired whether the Cape Government wanted more freemen, 'what number ... could find a living ...: what kind of persons would be most serviceable ...'.[3] The Governor replied that all the fertile land within the settlement had 'so to say' been occupied; newcomers would have to go far inland, and would not easily succeed, being inexperienced and poor. Many recent immigrants were already a burden on the poor fund. However, 'the Cape promises to grow by the increase of its own people, who, not knowing another fatherland, will not ... again depart'. The government had allowed them to spread inland and they had received, 'as being born here, a helping hand from friends and relations'.[4] Consequently Company-sponsored Huguenot immigration was stopped, although Zeeland emigration continued.[5]

However, it soon became clear that the vital issue affecting immigration was not only lack of suitable land near the market, but the smallness of that market compared with the Cape's productive capacity. From the beginning of the eighteenth century the problem was no longer inadequate production, but over-production in terms of a market limited virtually to Cape Town and the ships. During W. A. van der Stel's rule (1699–1707) the free farmers were faced with unfair competition from the Governor, five other senior officials, and Simon van der Stel, the ex-governor, and his son Frans, both burghers. Despite a VOC regulation of 1668 forbidding officials to farm or trade privately, Cape officials did so with impunity. Indeed, visiting Commissioners made generous land grants to them. In the seventeenth century, when it was essential to establish agricultural production, official farmers like van Riebeeck and Simon van der Stel had benefited the colony by initiating new crops, and the burghers had never objected. But matters changed by the early eighteenth century, when the market became 'hopelessly oversupplied',[6] and when officials farmed on such a scale that rumours circulated that they could soon supply the market themselves and 'no free burghers would be required'.[7]

---

[1] *Collectanea*, p. 16. [2] *Letters Received, 1695–1708*, p. 468. [3] Ibid., p. 250.
[4] *Letters Despatched, 1696–1708*, p. 164. [5] Walker, *History*, p. 53.
[6] *CHBE*, viii. 139. [7] Ibid. 138–41.

AGRICULTURE AND IMMIGRATION

A crisis occurred in 1705 when the Governor took steps to corner the market. The system of distribution at the Cape consisted of monopolies in the main articles of consumption, which the government leased out at auction for fixed periods. The leaseholder (*pachter*) contracted to supply the Company's requirements in a commodity at a low fixed price. In exchange he obtained the monopoly of purchasing and retailing it after supplying the Company. The most important were the meat and the wine contracts. By manipulating them, and arranging for his agents to hold them, W. A. van der Stel put himself in a position to control the market.

The protest movement of the free farmers of the south-west Cape against W. A. van der Stel in 1705–6, led by Henning Huising, an erstwhile meat contractor and a very rich burgher, his nephew Adam Tas, and others, is too well known for detailed exposition.[1] Its consequence was that the Directors, on 30 October 1706,[2] redressed the main grievances of the free farmers: they recalled the chief officials involved, again prohibited private farming or trading by officials (and enforced it pretty effectively by 1722),[3] and re-allocated the wine and meat contracts. Finally, they ordered the Cape government to take care that any one freeman should not get so much land that two or three could subsist on it, for they intended that all colonists should be able to earn an honest living, but none should rise too prominently above his fellows. This has been interpreted[4] as alluding to Huising, but it seems equally applicable to Simon and Frans van der Stel, both very rich burghers. It seems consistent with wanting to prevent any individual or small group from monopolizing the market, and with continuing the close settlement policy which increased the Cape's defensive potential. Every freeman between sixteen and sixty had to enrol in the burgher militia,[5] which by 1708 had 513 men[6] and favourably impressed J. Simons. Both he and other Commissioners agreed that the militia was a far better means of defence than 'making the Castle ... impregnable ... at great expense'.[7]

The settlers' movement of 1705 did not necessarily 'confirm ... [the Directors] in their aversion to all colonising experiments'.[8] True, in 1707 they cancelled free passages to the Cape, despite the Zeeland Chamber's plea that the matter should be further considered.[9] But in June 1716, 'having had under consideration the question as to whether

[1] Cf. Leo Fouché, *The Diary of Adam Tas (1705–6): with an enquiry into the Complaints of the Colonists against the Governor W. A. van der Stel*; H. C. V. Leibbrandt, *The Defence of Willem Adriaan van der Stel*; G. M. Theal, *Willem Adriaan van der Stel and other Historical Sketches*.
[2] *Letters Received, 1695–1708*, pp. 432–6.   [3] Boëseken (1), pp. 26–29.
[4] *CHBE*, viii. 145.   [5] Roux, p. 54.   [6] *Collectanea*, pp. 44–45.
[7] *Chavonnes*, pp. 142–3; Boëseken (1), p. 55.   [8] *CHBE*, viii. 145.
[9] *Letters Received, 1695–1708*, pp. 468–9.

it would be . . . [desirable] to add to the population at the Cape', they submitted searching questions to the government, including the queries whether more white immigrants could be absorbed, 'whether European farm hands and agriculturalists would be less expensive than slaves', how many artisans were needed, and whether, if existing industries could not support new immigrants, some new ones could be devised.[1]

The answers of the Cape government were discouraging. Only Captain D. P. de Chavonnes recommended white immigration, and favoured substituting white farmhands for slaves, starting with 100 to 150 bachelors, indentured at fixed wages. He argued that though white labour appeared more expensive than slave labour, in the long run it was not, as two Europeans could do as much as three slaves. While money spent buying slaves was 'dead money', which left the country permanently and burdened the country districts with debt, the wages of white labourers would circulate within the colony. Employing whites would increase consumption, revenue, and the potential military force. Moreover, a larger white population might stimulate greater subdivision and better land-use, and provide the inducement to find new means of subsistence.[2] But the other senior officials[3] agreed that the Cape could not absorb white immigrants. Few artisans were needed. Immigrants could not succeed as grain or wine farmers, as fertile land within economic reach of the Cape Town market was scarce, and the population already so dispersed that those furthest away hardly found it worth while bringing crops to market. Poverty was increasing and 'not 30 families . . . can be regarded as wealthy'. The rest had all mortgaged their property and had no hope of clearing it or becoming wealthy.[4] Substituting white farm labourers for slaves would be unwise. They would cost far more, be more insubordinate and prone to drink, and would increase the housing shortage. Also, certain work was felt to be fit only for slaves; white labourers would not, or could not, do all unskilled work. Various possible new industries suggested by the Directors were considered, including coffee, sugar, indigo, olives, tobacco, flax, cotton, hop, and silk production, but each had disadvantages—the climate was unsuitable, or the market too small, or the production costs too high. The underlying objection seemed to be that farmers were too poor to experiment, 'even if they had the necessary knowledge and could hope to gain profits in . . . time'.[5] Four officials[6] suggested that free trade between the Cape and areas like Mauritius, Madagascar, and the East African coast might improve the economy, but as employees of a com-

---

[1] *Chavonnes*, p. 85.   [2] Ibid., pp. 103-8.   [3] Ibid., pp. 87-128, *passim*.
[4] (Cranendonk.) De la Fontaine thought only eighteen families were free of debt (ibid., pp. 93, 116).
[5] Ibid., p. 94.   [6] Cranendonk, D. de Chavonnes, van Beaumont, Cruse.

pany wedded to mercantilist principles, including the need for the mother country to monopolize colonial trade, they did not stress this point.

These strong opinions against white immigration decided the Directors to allow the Cape to continue importing slaves. In this sense, 1717 was a turning-point in South African history. But the VOC's interest in white immigration continued. In December 1750 the Cape government asked the local boards to consider the practicability of white immigration. All agreed that it was 'absolutely impossible' and 'would, if anything, bring ruin upon the Cape, and merely add to the very serious state of poverty which already exists'.[1] In Cape Town opportunities for making a living from passing ships were reported to be much reduced. In Stellenbosch and Drakenstein many could only subsist very frugally through agriculture and stock-farming. Others were in debt. Soil-fertility was deteriorating, which forced people further inland. Although the country was vast, fertile well-watered land was scarce and the existing population was growing fast, so that even in Swellendam, three weeks' journey from Cape Town, it was difficult for anyone to apply for new land without prejudicing others.[2]

Thus the consensus of Cape opinion was that a white immigration policy was impossible. Limited markets, capital, and skills; few incentives to improve production methods in existing industries or experiment with new crops; inadequate, slow, and expensive transport; the wide dispersal of population outside the peninsula and the south-west Cape; a low living-standard in outlying areas; and constricted trade, were all interlocking causes and effects that apparently made economic backwardness inevitable. It seemed obvious that since the existing white population, fed by a trickle[3] of ex-VOC employees and others, was multiplying rapidly (to increase from 1,265 to 9,721 between 1701 and 1778),[4] new immigrants could not be absorbed unless economic circumstances changed.

The Company alone was capable of initiating improvements. It acted on the suggestion to experiment with new crops and even sent experts to examine the possibilities of olives, tobacco, indigo, Persian sheep, cotton, and silk. But nothing was achieved,[5] and wheat-farming, viticulture, and stockraising continued to be the main economic activities.

Another possibility mooted by Cape officials in 1717 was allowing private trade between the Cape and other areas to enlarge the market

[1] Ibid., p. 150.   [2] Ibid., pp. 149–54.
[3] Just over 300 founders of families arrived between 1706 and 1750. S. F. N. Gie, *Geskiedenis van Suid-Afrika of Ons Verlede*, Deel I—*1795*, p. 165.
[4] Beyers, Appendix H.
[5] Walker, *History*, p. 86.

for Cape produce, a request repeated by burgher representatives in 1718, 1751, and 1779.¹ Such concessions might not, in fact, have helped the Cape, since the smallness of its market was mainly due to its geographical isolation and the relatively high cost and low quality of its produce, a situation merely exacerbated by commercial restriction. Also, such concessions might not have been used sufficiently to improve matters. In the early eighteenth century private capital available for investment in foreign trade was lacking at the Cape.² Even towards the end of the century, although some wealthy men lent money at interest, and many merchants speculated in trade, there was no bank or stock exchange and bills of exchange and promissory notes were apparently not used.³ Nevertheless, Cape contraband trade with Europe and Asia and nearby foreign dependencies, like Madagascar and Mauritius, through Dutch and foreign ships, flourished in the eighteenth century,⁴ and might have increased if it had been legalized. But private export of Cape produce would have raised the prices obtainable by farmers and made it difficult, if not impossible, for the VOC to buy provisions at a low fixed price, thus endangering the essential purpose of the station. The VOC refused to abandon its monopoly of external trade, except for limited concessions in 1785 and 1792 which had no effect on Cape economic development.⁵

Alternatively, the VOC could consider the Cape a genuine colony and improve its economic potential by capital investment, particularly in its transport. Numerous unnavigable rivers, liable to flood, and mountain ranges with few and dangerous passes, meant that the sturdy and easily dismantled, but slow and cumbersome ox-wagon was the only means of transporting goods. High transport costs and the time involved in getting to market reduced the profits of distant producers. Wine was produced for sale only two or three days' journey from Cape Town, grain somewhat further afield.⁶ Beyond, only cattle and sheep (which could walk to Cape Town), and their by-products, became profitable to sell. Conversely, transport difficulties helped reduce the demand for all but necessities, and encouraged the development of a frontier economy with tenuous market ties. But contemporary attitudes were not consistent with a policy of capital investment. The VOC regarded the Cape essentially as a refreshment station, to be run as economically as possible. Thus the VOC only provided capital for

---

¹ Boëseken (1), p. 174; *Chavonnes*, p. 150; Beyers, pp. 30–31.   ² Spilhaus, p. 160.
³ *Description*, ii. 75–99, *passim*. But M. H. de Kock, *Selected Subjects in the Economic History of South Africa*, pp. 65–66, argues that the preference of Cape officials for payment in Holland suggests a demand for bills of exchange on Holland by Cape merchants engaged in contraband trade.
⁴ *Description*, ii. 75–99, *passim*.   ⁵ Cf. Beyers, *passim*; Boëseken (1), Ch. XII.
⁶ Beyers, pp. 108, 110.

fortifications and other public works associated directly with its shipping. Local authorities were allowed to levy local taxes for roads and bridges, and made some small improvements.¹ But even in the 1770s there were no bridges and only two ferries, while long-distance roads were beaten tracks which frequently disappeared altogether.² Coastal traffic was attempted only in 1786, when grain was shipped from Mossel Bay to Table Bay, but ceased after a few years.³

In the eighteenth century, as in the seventeenth, the Company was convinced that the Cape was a source of great loss. The public accounts seemed to substantiate this: in 1743 the annual deficit was said to have long been about two-and-a-half times the annual revenues;⁴ from 1757 to 1777 it was probably over one-and-a-half times as large.⁵ These enormous deficits were partly a function of the accounting system, which reflected the view that the Cape station was an adjunct to the Company's shipping, rather than a separate administration in its own right. Thus expenses and revenues in selling merchandise from VOC stores were included in the Cape government's accounts. Even expenses on behalf of VOC ships, and regiments temporarily billeted at the Cape *en route* to other areas, were charged against the Cape government.⁶ Consequently, the Company tried to increase its revenues wherever possible, and otherwise took the path of least resistance, so long as its fleets were provisioned cheaply, and not too many demands, particularly financial ones, were made on it.⁷

The main sources of Cape revenue, apart from profits on imported goods (which provided the bulk of government revenues until well into the eighteenth century),⁸ were monopolies in retail trade, rents, and taxes. Rents on grazing farms leased annually by the government provided growing sums in the eighteenth century. When tithes on all grain and wine produced proved impossible to collect, a 10 per cent tax on grain, and a duty on wine brought into Cape Town were levied instead. Stamp duties and transfer duties on sales of fixed property were also levied.⁹ The government benefited indirectly, too, from allowing some officials to charge fees, thus saving itself the cost of higher salaries.

¹ P. J. Venter, 'Landdros en Heemrade (1682–1827)', *AYB, 1940*, part ii, pp. 86–106.
² Sparrman, i. 53, 126, 221; Thunberg, i. 176.
³ Beyers, p. 110. Sparrman (i. 262–7) pleaded passionately for coastal traffic to improve the Cape economy.
⁴ Up to 1743 the annual deficit had been 300,000 guilders, while the revenues were scarcely 120,000 or 130,000 guilders annually (*Chavonnes*, p. 146).
⁵ Profits and revenues in 1757 and 1777 were between 160,000 and 200,000 guilders, the expenditure in 1757 and 1777 was 433,000 and 454,000 guilders (De Mist, p. 180).
⁶ *Description*, i. 167–75, *passim*; De Mist, p. 181.
⁷ Preamble to increase of taxes 20 Feb. 1732. South Africa, Union Archives Commission, *Kaapse Plakkaatboeke*, ii. 152.
⁸ Trading profits were 102,000 guilders in 1725, 131,000 guilders in 1750, and 145,000 guilders in 1794 (M. H. de Kock, p. 78). ⁹ Ibid., pp. 78–83.

Thus an important aspect of the settlers' image of the Cape government was that of a landlord and tax-collector, who only reluctantly gave them anything in return. Nevertheless, as de Mist remarked, 'A commercial Government . . . regards its colonists as those who use a mail route regard the inn-keeper in whose stables their postillions refresh themselves and their horses; self-interest forces them to protect him.'[1] While in the seventeenth century the Company assisted settlers by granting them freehold land and advancing them food, clothes, tools, and trek-oxen at low cost, to stimulate production, in the eighteenth century self-interest induced it to provide settlers with cheap labour and cheap, abundant land on the frontier.

The main demand for labour by Cape settlers was for more slaves. Slavery had become well established in the seventeenth century. Soon after van Riebeeck landed he recommended importing slaves to relieve the work of the garrison: when freemen were introduced, it was thought essential to provide them with slaves. Khoikhoi were erratic, unreliable servants, unaccustomed to continuous physical exertion; although many worked occasionally for tobacco, brandy, or European food, their flocks and herds gave them a method of obtaining these luxuries alternative to permanent employment. *Knechts*, soldiers loaned to farmers, were expensive and insubordinate. Since slaves were used throughout the Dutch Empire, they were naturally considered for the Cape. The first slaves in any numbers were two shipments from Angola and West Africa in 1658 and 1659, but they were intractable, many absconded, and eventually nearly all were returned to the Company. During the 1660s the Company could not supply sufficient slaves for the Cape's needs, and in 1672 the burghers owned only 53 slaves. Importations increased in the 1670s, and became larger still after 1691, when agriculture became established in the south-western Cape. By 1711 the burgher population of 1,756 souls owned 1,781 slaves, and the Company 440 in 1710.[2]

Many slaves and Khoikhoi died in the smallpox epidemic of 1713. The resulting labour shortage was probably the most important reason why the Directors considered substituting whites for slaves in 1716. The opinions of the Cape government indicate how firmly rooted slavery had become. Slaves were considered much cheaper than white labourers, and some officials thought it was more fitting for slaves to do menial work.[3] One even dismissed the suggestion to switch to white labour as 'useless', adding 'they should carefully consider in what way the work is done, throughout the whole of India, all the Colonies, the

---

[1] De Mist, p. 168.
[2] MacCrone, pp. 28–33, 59, 74 ff.; Beyers, Appendix H; Valentijn, v, Bk. x, 145.
[3] See above, p. 200.

West Indies, Suriname etc.'[1] The only official who approved of the proposal did not think it could be effected immediately: he suggested the Company should first sell its slaves to the colonists, and then stop further importations, so that colonists would gradually become used to employing white labourers.[2]

As a result of this strong preference for slaves, the Company allowed importations to continue. Most Cape slaves were Africans, obtained mainly from Madagascar and East African slaving centres, including Delagoa Bay, where the Company maintained a slave depot from 1720 to 1730.[3] Some slaves also came from the Bay of Bengal, Indonesia, and other Asian areas until 1767.[4] In time, despite a great discrepancy between the sexes throughout the eighteenth century,[5] more and more Cape slaves were local-born children of slave mothers and slave, Khoikhoi, and white fathers. Although the Company used many white employees in skilled and unskilled work, and sub-contracted a few to burghers as *knechts* (estate-managers and overseers) or schoolmasters,[6] during the eighteenth century slaves constituted the predominant source of labour. The Company tried to limit its slaves to 450, but there were usually 600 to 800, 'stevedores, bricklayers, builders, millers, potters, dairymen, grooms, hospital-nurses, bookbinders, gardeners, thatchers etc.'[7] But the vast majority were privately owned. In 1778 the census indicated 11,107[8] burgher-owned slaves, but these figures are certainly understatements,[9] and excluded slaves privately owned by officials.[10] Although slaves were used throughout the Cape, they were concentrated in Cape Town and the western Cape, where they were domestic servants, skilled tradesmen and petty retailers (whose masters often hired them out, or allowed them to earn their own living on payment of certain sums), and farm labourers or herdsmen.[11]

Since the wheat and wine producing areas were most dependent on slave labour, it seems reasonable to suppose that the Company's willingness to allow the Cape to import slaves after 1717 was connected with developments in those industries.

[1] Pietersoon, *Chavonnes*, p. 126.   [2] Ibid., p. 104.
[3] *CHBE*, viii. 266; C. G. Coetsee, 'Die Kompanjie se besetting van Delagoabaai', *AYB*, *1948*, ii.
[4] *Description*, ii. 125.
[5] In 1701 there were 7 men to every woman among burgher-owned slaves; by 1778 there were 3½ to 1 (Beyers, Appendix H).
[6] *Description*, i, Chs. VI, VII; Beyers, Appendix H; Spilhaus, pp. 121–3.
[7] *Dutch Seaborne Empire*, p. 260.
[8] Beyers, Appendix H.
[9] A *placaat* of 4 Oct. 1776 denounced the inaccurate returns submitted by burghers, including slave returns (ibid., p. 111).
[10] *Description*, ii. 124.
[11] Cf. Victor de Kock, *Those in Bondage: An Account of the Life of the slave at the Cape in the days of the Dutch East India Company*; Spilhaus, pp. 123–32.

Wheat production increased considerably during the eighteenth century. Although the annual returns were unreliable, since they were used to assess certain taxes,[1] a comparison between the 1701 figures (646 muids wheat sown, 3,868 muids harvested) and those of 1778 (2,951 muids sown, 17,350 muids harvested)[2] roughly indicates the actual increase in wheat-growing. Demand increased correspondingly. The government estimate of the annual wheat consumption by the official establishment and the fleets was $5,774\frac{1}{2}$ muids in 1720, 5,000 in 1740, 8,000 in 1747, and 12,000 in 1787.[3] Population growth also increased local demand. The burghers and their slaves increased from about 2,000 to about 21,000 between 1701 and 1778, according to the census;[4] Cape Town alone was estimated at some 1,200 houses in 1786 compared with 254 in 1714.[5] Visiting foreign ships also enlarged the internal market: their numbers fluctuated widely, especially between 1700 and 1770, depending on war and peace between the European powers. On average 20 to 25 foreign ships called annually between 1700 and 1723, under 10 between 1724 and 1742, 15 to 20 between 1743 and 1766, 25 or more from 1767 to 1770, about 65 from 1771 to 1781, and usually 100 or more from 1782 to 1793.[6] They provided a lucrative source of contraband trade, and although, obviously, no statistics are available, an important proportion of Cape wheat production apparently found its way into foreign ships.[7] In the eighteenth century the Dutch Eastern Empire also demanded more and more Cape wheat. The Directors had to force Batavia to take small cargoes of Cape wheat from 1696 to 1718, but Batavian demand grew so large thereafter, when Javanese ricefields were destroyed in the wars of 1704–55, that the Cape could not always supply it. Between 1758 and 1780 the Cape government exported on average about 12,000 muids of wheat annually to Batavia.[8] Ceylon also took a little Cape wheat after 1710, and roughly 1,000 muids annually between 1758 and 1780, while Cochin, Bengal, and Coromandel also imported small quantities in the 1770s. Thus the Cape supplied the whole Eastern Empire with wheat until 1781, when the war with England (1780–4) made this impossible. Between 1773 and 1780 the Cape government also exported approxi-

---

[1] Valentijn, v, Bk. x, 144–5. Beyers (pp. 111–12) considers the annual average production of 17,370 muids between 1787 and 1791 grossly underestimated, since the 1786 harvest alone was estimated at 70,000 muids, excluding the amount used by the farmers themselves for seed corn and bread.

[2] Beyers, Appendix H. The muid varied according to the commodity weighed. One muid corn (Amsterdam measure) was 175 lb.; Cape farmers had to deliver some 10 lb. more per muid (Spilhaus, p. 168).

[3] Boëseken (1), pp. 158, 161, n. 70; Beyers, p. 112.

[4] Beyers, Appendix H. [5] Valentijn, v, Bk. x, 13; *Description*, i. 136.

[6] Beyers, Appendix H. [7] Boëseken (1), p. 160.

[8] Boëseken (1), pp. 155–61, Appendix 7.

mately 15,000 muids annually[1] to the Netherlands, since the scarcity from other sources raised the price sufficiently to make Cape wheat competitive.[2]

Cape wine production also expanded considerably during the eighteenth century, particularly between 1776 and 1786, when it actually doubled.[3] Wine and brandy were not exported much, since, apart from Constantia wine, the quality remained poor, probably because of crude manufacturing techniques.[4] There was little incentive to improve quality, because the Company paid low prices for a limited quantity of wine and brandy, and levied dues on volume brought into Cape Town for sale without taking quality into account, and officials sometimes forced farmers to sell better wines for the same price as ordinary wine.[5] Also, there was such a demand for wine from the Cape Town taverns and boarding-houses, and ships, that it was often consumed before it had been given time to mature.[6] The government profited from domestic consumption, since the sale of the wine monopoly constituted an important source of revenue, although it always suffered from smuggling.[7]

Thus, in view of the almost permanent shortage of other suitable labour, the expansion of wheat and wine production in response to increased demand was facilitated because the Company allowed settlers to increase their investment in slaves, and subsidized that process in so far as it allowed them to buy slaves from the government on credit. Many regulations regarding slaves, though sometimes differently motivated, helped to increase servile labour. For example, the provision that Christian, Dutch-speaking slaves, the offspring of Dutch fathers and slave mothers, could claim their freedom once they reached adulthood, brought it about that only those slave children whose fathers wished them to be free were baptized.[8] Again, from 1721 slave owners in outlying areas demanded the unpaid labour of children of slave fathers and Khoikhoi mothers, brought up on farms, in recompense for maintaining them; in 1775, on the ground that escaped slaves were pretending to be 'bastard Hottentots', the government decreed that these children should be apprenticed from the age of eighteen months to twenty-five years to the owner of the farm on which they lived[9]. Apprentices received food and clothing but no wages. Similarly, in

---

[1] Boëseken (1), p. 161, Appendix 7.
[2] In the later seventeenth century the cost price of Cape wheat was twice that of Netherlands wheat (*Dutch Seaborne Empire*, p. 250).
[3] Ibid., p. 251; Boëseken (1), pp. 170-1.
[4] *Description*, iii. 174-87; Sparrman, i. 31.   [5] Beyers, pp. 108-9.
[6] Sparrman, i. 40; Spilhaus, pp. 98-105.   [7] Spilhaus, pp. 98-105.
[8] Sparrman, i. 284-5.
[9] Walker, *History*, p. 96; Theal, *History of South Africa [1691-1795]*, p. 226.

1774 the government approved instructions to commandos[1] about to attack the San, authorizing them to release women captives, but to distribute adult and young males 'in proportions among the poorest of the inhabitants there ... to serve them for a fixed and equitable term of years, in consideration of their receiving proper maintenance'.[2] This became common practice on the frontier.[3] As P. J. van der Merwe observes, the number of these captives (mainly children) was never very large, and he argues they were kept mainly out of sheer kindheartedness.[4] Yet in at least one instance capturing a 'little one' was regarded as a reward of commando service,[5] and the effect of apprenticing captives was to increase supplies of cheap, docile labour on the frontier.

3. *Pastoral Farming*

During the eighteenth century the Company allowed grazing land to be acquired easily and cheaply. Consequently it was forced to acquiesce in the rapid dispersal of white settlement east and north of the south-west Cape, in consequence of the extension of grazing into country already explored by hunters.

From the beginning of white settlement legal and illegal expeditions penetrated the interior to hunt and to barter stock.[6] These expeditions were largely financed by well-to-do settled farmers, and undertaken mainly by '*eenlopende persone*—unanchored men . . . [with] no settled position on the land and in society'.[7] They prepared the way for a more rooted occupation of the country by stockfarmers. Originally, the Company encouraged stock-rearing by settlers to provide sources of meat alternative to the erratic, unreliable Khoikhoi supplies, in the hope that it could eventually abandon stock-keeping itself. It even allowed settlers to barter stock with Khoikhoi from 1657 to 1658, from 1700 to 1702, and from 1705 to 1727,[8] and could not prevent wide-

[1] See below, pp. 226–7.
[2] Moodie, iii. 29, 31–32. Commandos had captured San women and children since 1715 (Boëseken (1), p. 81).
[3] Moodie, iii. 38–39, 40, 82.
[4] Actions prompted by kindheartedness sometimes had unexpected results. In 1794, to prevent the wholesale extermination of the San, the government offered a 'premium' of 15 rixdollars in cash per adult and 10 rixdollars per child under seven, taken alive. This led 'to a sort of trade in Bushmen'. One Petrus Pienaar applied for permission to form a commando at his own expense, to deliver 'Bushmen' to the government at that price. His offer was refused (Boëseken (1), p. 87).
[5] P. J. van der Merwe, *Die Noordwaartse Beweging van die Boere voor die Groot Trek (1700–1842)*, Ch. V, pp. 161–7.
[6] P. J. van der Merwe, *Trek, Studies oor die Mobiliteit van die Pioneersbevolking aan die Kaap*, pp. 10–42.
[7] W. K. Hancock, 'Trek', *Economic History Review*, 2nd Series, vol. x (1957–8), p. 332.
[8] W. A. van der Stel prohibited private stock barter in 1702, because, he alleged, all the

spread illegal trade at other times. At first private stock-keeping was subordinate to agriculture and was conducted with it, although even before 1679 some colonists were pastoralists exclusively.[1] In the 1680s and '90s the attempt to keep the settlement compact and to promote agriculture was undermined because some preferred to be hunters or graziers rather than agriculturalists. Illegal trekking far beyond the boundaries to hunt, barter, and graze stock was so prevalent during Simon van der Stel's rule that he imposed severe penalties against it.[2] In his memorial to his son in 1699 he observed that farmers were pleading soil-exhaustion as an excuse to move to new land, where they only sowed enough for themselves and made a living by stock-barter: 'should you be weak enough to give way to such sinister tricks, the whole of Africa would not be sufficient to accommodate and satisfy that class'.[3]

By the turn of the eighteenth century, therefore, pastoralism was already separate from agriculture. Although throughout the century many stock-owners lived permanently in the agricultural areas, and used distant land for pasture only, more and more became *trekboeren* (graziers), who lived permanently on grazing farms, migrating seasonally for pasture, or moving on altogether as land became exhausted. Some led such nomadic lives that they never settled down anywhere and lived in ox-wagons.[4] During the first two decades of the eighteenth century the agricultural depression in the western Cape caused by overproduction gave a special impetus to full-time stock-farming. But throughout the century, when the white population increased rapidly and capital and skills were scarce, only pastoralism could take advantage of the Cape's abundant land by using it extensively, easily overcoming the variations in fertility and the transport difficulties that impeded agriculture.[5] It also needed fewer labourers than agriculture, and both the Khoikhoi and San made excellent herdsmen, who were employed for little more than their keep.[6] The adventurous frontier life, free from the petty exactions of Cape Town officials, attracted colonial-born children, who mostly could not afford to become traders or lodging-house keepers in Cape Town, or vegetable, wine, or grain farmers in the western Cape, and were too ill-educated to enter the

---

colonists were implicated in incidents in which Khoikhoi cattle were taken by force. The colonists denied this. Private stock-barter was again sanctioned by the XVII in 1704 and took effect in March 1705. (Spilhaus, pp. 34–36, 84–87).

[1] P. J. van der Merwe, *Die Trekboer in die Geskiedenis van die Kaap Kolonie*, p. 22.
[2] *CHBE*, viii. 134–6; Leibbrandt, *Rambles*, pp. 58–61.
[3] Ibid., p. 8.
[4] Hancock, pp. 334–6; cf. Leo Fouché, *Die Evolutie van die Trekboer*; E. A. Walker, *The Frontier Tradition in South Africa*, and *The Great Trek*, Ch. II; P. J. van der Merwe, *Noordwaartse Beweging, Trekboer*, and *Trek*; Neumark, *passim*.
[5] M. H. de Kock, p. 31.
[6] *Noordwaartse Beweging*, pp. 159–61; Boëseken (1), p. 77.

limited ranks of the Civil Service or the professions, and too proud to become farm-hands or artisans. It was possible to make a living as a grazier, since there was a constant demand for mutton,[1] trek-oxen for transport and ploughing, and pastoral by-products like soap, butter, and tallow. After 1713, when the Khoikhoi were decimated by smallpox and their stock attacked by disease, the Cape market for pastoral products was supplied mainly by white graziers, who moved ever further afield.

After the beginning of the eighteenth century the government no longer resisted the development of full-time sheep and cattle farming, because it realized that 'The spreading out of the inhabitants with their cattle is the principal reason that meat can be delivered so cheaply to the Company and private individuals.'[2] Moreover, the government profited from this development by tightening up the regulations respecting grazing-farms. In the later seventeenth and early eighteenth centuries, although grazing-land was sometimes granted in freehold, it was usually leased for from three months to a year by licences,[3] which roughly indicated the area of the grant and stipulated that the Company should receive one-tenth of the agricultural produce reaped. By the second decade of the eighteenth century, when graziers were increasing rapidly, many used grazing-land for crops without paying tithes. So in 1714 the government again claimed tithes from grazing-farms, and levied *recognitiegeld* (recognition money), of 1 rixdollar per month, or 12 rixdollars a year,[4] for annual licences for grazing-land. In 1732 *recognitiegeld* became 24 rixdollars.[5]

Recognitiegeld provided an increasingly important part of Cape revenues until about 1780, as *leeningsplaats* (loanplace) tenure became universally used in outlying areas. Alternative tenures, the *erfpacht* (1732) and the *leeningseigendom* (1743), were introduced to encourage improvements on the land by giving greater security, but they involved higher charges for much smaller areas, and were not popular.[6]

The *leeningsplaats* was ideal for the stock-farmer. He could occupy land without any capital outlay, at a low rent, and move away when he pleased without financial loss. Neither the seventeenth-century nor the

---

[1] H. B. Thom (ed.), *Willem Stephanus van Ryneveld se Aanmerkingen . . . 1804*, VRS, no. 23, 1942, pp. 55-71.
[2] Cape Government to XVII, 21 Jan. 1730, quoted in *Trekboer*, p. 136.
[3] Boëseken (1), p. 110; cf. *Trekboer*, pp. 63 ff., for transition from communal to individual grazing rights.
[4] The rixdollar was equivalent to 4s. 6d. until the 1770s: it fell rapidly thereafter until it was fixed at 1s. 6d. in 1825.
[5] Botha, 'Early Cape Land Tenure', *Collected Works*, ii. 81-100; H. M. Robertson, 'Some Doubts concerning Early Land Tenure at the Cape', *SAJE*, June 1935, pp. 158-72; *Kaapse Plakkaatboeke*, ii. 31, 152.
[6] M. H. de Kock, pp. 32-33; Boëseken (1), pp. 110-12.

eighteenth-century grazing-licence specified exact limits to the *leeningsplaats*. In practice the occupier could use as much land as he liked if he did not come into conflict with his neighbours. In cases of trespass, the farm's size and shape were measured by walking a horse for half-an-hour in all directions from the *opstal* (homestead), which created a roughly circular farm of about 6,000 acres. Its greatest disadvantage, theoretically, was insecurity. The licence had to be renewed annually, and the government could revoke it and reassign the land, compensating the licensee for the *opstal* alone. But the government seldom refused to renew licences. Again, though loanplaces could not be bequeathed they were actually held in families for generations. The stipulation that the *opstal* alone, not the land, could be sold was similarly ignored, since farms were sold with impunity for prices much greater than their *opstal* value.[1] Another disadvantage was that a fixed rent was levied indiscriminately on all farms, irrespective of size or fertility. Although the rent was low and was sometimes taken in kind,[2] poorer graziers living close to subsistence level found it burdensome, but petitions for lower *recognitiegeld* (in 1732, 1745, 1758, and 1779) were ignored. The administrative apparatus remained primitive even though graziers rapidly moved further away from Cape Town where rents had to be paid,[3] so that many fell in arrears with rents or even occupied land without applying for licences. The system broke down completely in the 1780s, when Cape Town officials stopped keeping lists of defaulting debtors, since they knew that some had not paid rents for twenty, even forty years, and had not been punished. The 1791–2 revenue derived from *leeningsplaatsen* was almost half that collected ten years before, and only about one-fifth of what should have been received.[4] By the late eighteenth century most stock-farmers occupied land for nothing.

For most of the eighteenth century, climate and geography alone affected the rate and direction of the extension of the Cape grazing frontier. In 1700 the settlement was a rectangle, with Table Bay in the south-east, and Tulbagh in the north-west. Later the grazing frontier proceeded eastward along the south coast, and northward along the west coast. About 1730 thick forests beyond the Great Brak river diverted the eastward trek over the first coastal ranges, through the Little Karoo and Longkloof, to spread along the Gamtoos and Sundays rivers to reach Camdeboo just before 1770. Here it joined the main northerly stream similarly diverted by about 1730 by aridity beyond the Olifants-Doorn river junction into the interior plateaux (the Warm and Cold Bokkeveld) along the mountains skirting the Great Karoo. In

---

[1] *Allemann*, pp. 77–78; *Trekboer*, pp. 79 ff., 106–12, 114–17.
[2] Boëseken (1), pp. 112, 201.   [3] Pollock and Agnew, p. 59.
[4] Boëseken (1), pp. 112, 200–1; *Trekboer*, p. 113.

the 1770s stock-farmers held land between the Gamtoos and Fish rivers, and occupied the present Somerset East district by 1779. The main advance between 1730 and 1780 followed the distribution of grassland around the Great Karoo. A slower and more dispersed northerly occupation also occurred. By 1778 there were even two farmers living near the Orange river. Although aridity limited permanent occupation in the far north, a wide area between the Orange and the Riet and Sak rivers was used for communal grazing by farmers living further south.[1]

The government periodically proclaimed boundaries beyond which settlement was illegal, partly to prevent illegal trading and conflict with indigenous peoples, partly to secure maximum revenues from grazing-licences, which theoretically had to be obtained for grazing-land within the colony.[2] There were only two administrative districts, the Cape district (from the Cape peninsula to Saldanha Bay and Malmesbury, then called Zwartland) and Stellenbosch (founded 1682), until the northward and eastward extension of Stellenbosch resulted in the creation of Swellendam district (1743) from Worcester to the Great Brak river. But the continuing dispersal of *trekboers* beyond the borders made it necessary to extend the eastern frontier to the Gamtoos (1770), the Upper Fish-Bushmans river (1778), and finally the entire Fish river (1780). The north-west remained open, but the north-east boundary was successively fixed at Bruintjes Hoogte (1774), the middle Fish (1775), and finally at a point near Colesberg, marked by a beacon during van Plettenberg's tour in 1778[3] (see maps 2, 3).

By the 1780s the Cape's northern limits were fixed by extreme aridity in Namaqualand and the areas behind the Roggeveld and Nieuweveld mountains. Further north-east, expansion was halted by increasingly ferocious warfare between *trekboers* and San hunters. After 1715 *trekboers* encroached further into 'Bushman country'. By the 1770s conflict was so intense that *trekboer* commandos[4] systematically exterminated the San, while San raids forced *trekboers* to abandon farms in the Nieuweveld and Sneeuberg, and endangered *trekboer* occupation in the Tarka region, in the 1780s.[5] In the east, Xhosa tribes constituted an even more formidable barrier than the San. Although private cattle barter with Xhosa was prohibited in 1737, by the 1770s a beaten track from Swellendam to the Fish witnessed to its frequency.[6] By 1778 some

[1] *Noordwaartse Beweging*, pp. 1–7; E. A. Walker, *Historical Atlas of South Africa*, pp. 11–12, Maps V, VII.
[2] *Trekboer*, pp. 148–9; cf. 1770 *Plakkaat* making the Gamtoos river the Eastern boundary (*Kaapse Plakkaatboeke*, iii. 76–78).
[3] *Atlas*, notes to Map VII; Lucas, pp. 80–84; J. S. Marais, *Maynier and the First Boer Republic*, pp. 2–6.
[4] See below, pp. 226–7.
[5] Moodie, iii, *passim*; *Noordwaartse Beweging*, Chs. I, II; J. S. Marais, *The Cape Coloured People, 1652–1937*, pp. 13–19. [6] *Trekboer*, p. 148; Walker, *History*, p. 97.

trekboers were living among Xhosa pastoralists in the Zuurveld (between the Bushmans and the Lower Fish rivers), and in 1779 the long series of 'Kaffir wars' began. Because the burgher officers in charge of commandos could not force *trekboers* to perform military service simultaneously against the San and the Xhosa, the government formed a new district, Graaff-Reinet (1785), on the eastern border, under a *landdrost* with the authority of the government behind him. For the first time, the eastern frontier became subject to the dictates of the distant Cape Town government.

By the early eighteenth century the Cape's white settler community had become African-based and self-perpetuating, knowing no other Fatherland.[1] The bird-of-passage mentality of the early freemen, mostly bachelors who hoped to get rich quickly and leave, had been replaced by that of Company-sponsored immigrant families, who intended to remain permanently. The Huguenots probably helped cement this attachment to the Cape, since their emotional links with France had been weakened by persecution, and the French language almost disappeared after the first generation died. The Company's aim of a firmly based settler population, which would produce cheap food and constitute a defence against attack, had proved successful. But would this developing community consider its own future to be bound up with VOC administration? The answer would depend ultimately on the government provided by the VOC. While 'just and humane government' might secure 'the happiness of the settlers, the advantage of the Motherland and the prosperity of the . . . [VOC's] trade',[2] corrupt and inefficient rule would not promote VOC interests and might weaken the links between government and subject, without providing a basis for effective Cape self-government.

4. *VOC Government at the Cape*

The Cape was simultaneously a remote branch of a very large business concerned primarily with profits, and a sprawling Dutch Colony containing the largest population of white settlers in the Dutch Eastern Empire, with many of the rights of freemen in the mother country. The Cape Constitution from 1652 to 1778 reflected this dualism. Although colonists were encouraged to participate in local administration, they did not share in policy making, and remained politically retarded. Until 1778 they did not demand representation on the central government, to secure redress of economic grievances, or for its own sake. Even in their struggle against W. A. van der Stel, although officials used government powers to protect their private interests and

[1] See above, p. 198.   [2] De Mist, p. 183.

crush opposition,[1] the colonists did not demand constitutional changes, but concentrated on attacking unfair official competition. When political demands were made for the first time by the *Kaapse Patriotte* (1779–91) they were comparatively modest.[2] From 1657 to 1778 there was almost no progress towards democracy in the central government, and a visible list towards anarchy and contempt for the law in the *platteland*.

The Cape station fitted into the over-all political structure of the Dutch Eastern Empire. Its government was subject to the instructions and veto of both the Chamber of Seventeen in the Netherlands and the Governor-General in Council at Batavia. It corresponded directly with both and sent them copies of all its transactions.[3] The Batavian government sent the Cape copies of laws passed by the States-General, orders of the Seventeen, and Batavian laws applicable to all the *buiten comptoiren*, subject to the approval of the Seventeen. The codified Batavian statutes, notably the 1642 code ('Statutes of India'),[4] were an important source of Cape law—many Cape *placaaten* (ordinances) were modelled directly on Batavian ones, and after 1715 Batavian statutes were used to interpret Cape law.[5] Appeals from Cape courts received final judgement in the Batavian High Court of Justice. After 1734 the Batavian authorities ceased to veto Cape transactions, and much previous confusion arising from contradictory orders from Holland and Batavia was thenceforth avoided,[6] but the other links with Batavia remained.

The routine control of the Netherlands and Batavian authorities over the Cape was supplemented by visiting commissioners, who took command during their stay, made inspections, left instructions for Cape government, and reported to the Directors. Although the Batavian government was directed in 1632 to inspect all its dependencies regularly, this practice soon lapsed.[7] Only the Cape was so visited by commissioners, probably partly because all homeward fleets called there, partly because of its importance to VOC shipping. Twenty-six commissioners arrived between 1656 and 1699, including all return fleet admirals of rank equal or superior to that of the Cape commander and certain special commissioners, like Commissioner-General H. A. van Rheede tot Drakensteyn, who arrived in 1685 while inspecting all VOC possessions (1683–91). In the seventeenth century their regular visits produced a crop of instructions, which were all assumed to be equally binding, but were in many cases inconsistent with each other and with orders from Holland or Batavia. Van Rheede's criticisms of this led to visits being suspended from 1685 to 1698 and there were only sixteen between 1700 and 1794.[8] When after 1723 visiting com-

---

[1] See below, pp. 217, 221–2.   [2] Beyers, *passim*.   [3] Botha, *Collected Works*, iii. 117–19.
[4] Ibid. ii. 71–72.   [5] Ibid. ii. 44–45.   [6] *Description*, i. 137.
[7] Colenbrander, ii. 212; Boëseken (1), p. 1.   [8] Ibid., Introduction.

missioners were given specific duties,[1] their instructions were generally more useful, but since they could not get much first-hand knowledge during their short stay, and relied heavily on official information, they became correspondingly less impartial.[2] Commissioners nevertheless helped to prevent misgovernment at the Cape. They introduced constitutional changes. Van Goens arranged that a burgher should participate in burgher criminal trials. Van Rheede reorganized the Councils of Policy and Justice and appointed a *landdrost* at Stellenbosch in 1685. They also helped to reveal abuses. Commissioner Douglas in 1716 reported that officials were farming illegally on a large scale and that Governor Chavonnes was granting land to burghers without the Council of Policy's knowledge. The Seventeen specifically forbade these abuses.[3] Simons in 1708 gave detailed criticisms of the administration, especially of justice, and suggested remedies.[4] Although commissioners sometimes colluded in illegal practices, as did Heyns (1698) and Valkenier (1700) in granting land to Cape officials against VOC regulations, it is probably significant that the most serious misgovernment at the Cape occurred in 1705 and 1706 when no commissioners called.

But essentially, the quality of day-to-day government would depend on the effectiveness of the local constitution. The Cape, like all VOC dependencies, was governed by a Council of Policy, an adaptation of the Broad Council on all VOC ships or fleets, consisting of the commanding officer and his senior subordinates, which decided all important matters at sea. The Council of Policy was intended to prevent the head of a dependency using his powers arbitrarily or at variance with VOC interests. At the Cape the Council of Policy represented the 'dignity and authority' of the VOC and the 'majesty of the State'.[5] Its overriding aim was 'protecting and supporting the commercial interests' of the VOC.[6] It administered the Cape as a provisioning and hospital station, punished offences, and filled vacancies which occurred south of the Equator on Batavia-bound ships.[7] As an ancillary function it governed the colony, acting as a combined legislature and executive.

The Council of Policy legislated for all who participated in the Cape polity, VOC servants, burghers (including a few 'free blacks', liberated slaves and their descendants),[8] and slaves. As far as the indigenous peoples were concerned, the Dutch did not clearly distinguish between Khoikhoi ('Hottentot') and San ('Bushman') people, and tended to refer to San in conflict with whites as 'rebellious Hottentots'.[9] In the

[1] Ibid., p. 3.   [2] Ibid., pp. 6–7, 34.   [3] Ibid., pp. 27–29.
[4] *Collectanea*, pp. 31–32.   [5] *Description*, i. 144.
[6] *Reports of the Commissioners of Inquiry*, I: *Upon the Administration of the Cape of Good Hope* . . . May 1827, Br. Parl. Pap. XXI (282), p. 5.
[7] *Description*, i. 145.   [8] MacCrone, pp. 70–73.
[9] Boëseken (1), p. 79.

seventeenth century those who were Christian, Dutch-speaking, and had become 'assimilated' were subjected to Cape laws: for example in 1672 the body of such a woman, who had committed suicide, was dragged through the streets, then put into quicklime.[1] All others were assumed to be under the jurisdiction of their own rulers. In the eighteenth century, however, the Cape government claimed jurisdiction over all Khoikhoi within its boundaries, even those in tribal communities, whose captains were given VOC staffs of office. It directed that 'Hottentot' servants must receive wages and redress for ill-treatment, and Cape courts even judged cases in which Khoikhoi had injured one another.[2]

The Council of Policy levied taxes on burghers and fixed prices for produce which they must sell to the Company. Burghers did not participate directly in legislation or levying taxes, since they were not represented on the Council of Policy, but the burgher councillors (the white burghers chosen to sit on the Council of Justice to help try cases involving burghers) were traditionally consulted on matters affecting burghers, although the Council of Policy was not obliged to follow their advice.

The Council of Policy appointed and dismissed all VOC servants at the Cape, except those few appointed by the Seventeen, and directed their operations. It also appointed burghers to various administrative boards, using the 'double list' system whereby vacancies were filled from a list presented by the sitting members containing twice the number of names to be chosen. All incoming dispatches had to be opened and read by the Governor at a full meeting of the Council of Policy[3] and the Council drafted outgoing dispatches.

The extent to which the Council of Policy could control the Governor was determined by its constitution. After its reorganization by van Rheede in 1685[4] it consisted of the Governor and the seven most senior officials, three 'upper-merchants' and four 'merchants'. Decisions were taken after discussion and voting (the Governor having an extra casting vote as chairman), and noted by a secretary as resolutions signed by the members present.[5] Unlike those of Batavia, where Governors-General often ruled without their Councils,[6] Cape governors never tried to dispense with them altogether, although de Chavonnes successfully granted land without his Council's knowledge or consent in 1714.[7] But Governors could easily persuade their Councils to be co-operative and seldom overruled them with the formula 'Ik neem haet op mij'.[8]

[1] Moodie, i. 315 n. 1.
[2] Boëseken (1), pp. 76–79.
[3] Botha, *Collected Works*, iii. 117.
[4] *Bel. Hist. Dok.*, i. 46.
[5] Ralph Kilpin, *The Parliament of the Cape*, . . . , pp. 8, 21–23.
[6] Day, p. 92.
[7] Boëseken (1), p. 29.
[8] Walker, *History*, p. 32.

Governors effectively controlled all local patronage,[1] and their normally long tenure of office (thirteen years on average, twenty-one in Simon van der Stel's and Ryk Tulbagh's cases) increased their real power. Only the upper-merchants, who were appointed by the Seventeen, the *Secunde* (Vice-Governor), the Captain, and the Independent Fiscal could afford to cross the Governor, and 'they can make his life very bitter . . if they combine against him'.[2] But the only official whose power approached that of the Governor was the Independent Fiscal, who, in addition to acting as public prosecutor in criminal trials, preventing smuggling, and controlling the police, was in 1688 given vast powers (abolished elsewhere in the Dutch Empire in 1711) to punish officials for dereliction of duty, including the right to report the Governor to the Seventeen, with whom he corresponded directly.[3] But in practice strong governors did not encounter much opposition and their subordinates abetted their illegal practices. The most flagrant example is W. A. van der Stel's administration, when all the main officials engaged in illegal farming and trading sided with van der Stel against the colonists, and used the public powers of the executive to protect their private interests. Under VOC rule, government by this narrow official oligarchy was carelessly inefficient and corrupt, although the strictures about Batavia (the 'respectable reformatory')[4] were not applied to the Cape administration, where Eastern opportunities for large-scale fraud did not exist. The Cape often obtained the best men from passing ships and, despite nepotism,[5] allowed rapid promotion by merit.

Many commissioners complained of the slackness of the Cape bureaucracy. The Council of Policy's records were not properly kept, answers to letters were long delayed, and departments like the Hospital and Orphan Chamber were shamefully neglected. The tremendous increase of the official establishment (120 in 1662, 1,016 in 1732, 1,695 in 1769, and 2,039 in 1794,[6] of whom the majority in the eighteenth century were underpaid civil servants) did not improve efficiency, since members of the Council of Policy were only collectively responsible for the administration as a whole, not individually responsible for particular departments. Visiting commissioners could only expose glaring faults; their visits were too short for extensive reforms, which in any case went beyond their powers. As Commissioner Simons observed, the real responsibility rested with the Netherlands and Batavian authorities for

---
[1] *Description*, i. 144.   [2] *Allemann*, p. 123.
[3] Botha, *Collected Works*, ii. 140–5; De Mist, p. 237; Beyers, p. 138.
[4] Coen, quoted by Day, p. 97.
[5] *Allemann*, pp. 36–37; *Description*, ii. 68 f.
[6] *Letters Despatched, 1652–1662*, iii. 303–5; *Journal, 1699–1732*, p. 335; Boëseken (1), p. 136, n. 103.

not providing Cape officials with adequate instructions. Though he recommended in 1708 that Coen's regulations for the Indian Empire should be sent to the Cape, in 1792 when Commissioners-General Nederburgh and Frykenius arrived to institute thoroughgoing reforms, they found that the Cape government still did not conform with Batavian standards. They simplified the Cape administrative system and made each member of the Council of Policy ultimately responsible for specifically demarcated duties; but little improvement resulted, partly because there were so few officials on the Council that they found their tasks overwhelming.[1]

Corruption was endemic to the whole VOC service, since officials were deliberately underpaid. Although Cape officials were in some ways better off than Batavian officials, for example in having fewer deductions, and in receiving higher pay immediately on promotion instead of only after serving their full enlistment period, the lower ranks led hard lives, especially compared with more senior functionaries, whose duties were often light, and whose incomes were supplemented by fees and perquisites of office.[2] A tone of petty extortion characterized the whole administration. The fiscals, who should have ensured honest administration, were among the chief offenders, and were so hated and feared by the burghers that the predatory butcher-bird was called 'fiskaal' in Afrikaans.[3] Although official malpractices harmed the Company, the burghers were the chief sufferers, whence the tension between officials and burghers exemplified in the saying that officials were the 'legitimate' and burghers the 'illegitimate' children of the Company.[4] This tension became explosive in 1705 when a group of burghers by-passed the Council of Policy altogether, and protested against illegal farming and trading by Cape officials directly to the VOC authorities in Batavia and Holland, threatening to go to the States-General if necessary.[5] This galvanized the VOC into vigorous action. The Governor and other offending officials were recalled, and some were ultimately dismissed. Official farming and trading were again prohibited and the prohibitions were finally enforced after 1721.[6] Thus the burghers, not the Council of Policy, acted as the guardians of public morality at the Cape. But despite their great victory in 1706, they were not capable of extirpating 'the extortions of greedy officials'.[7] Although Governors like Ryk Tulbagh (1751–71) tried to eliminate malpractices and individuals were punished, permanent reform was never attempted, for the chain of

---

[1] Boëseken (1), Chs. VIII–X.
[2] *Allemann*, p. 162; *Description*, i. 138–45, 163; ii. 61–71.
[3] Botha, *Collected Works*, ii. 140–5; Boëseken (1), pp. 126–30; Beyers, 132–9.
[4] *Diary of Adam Tas*, p. 193.
[5] Ibid. *passim*; *CHBE*, viii. 139 ff.
[6] Boëseken (1), p. 29.   [7] *Collectanea*, p. 31.

corruption extended throughout the VOC service to the very Directors themselves.¹ All the VOC did was to allow certain officials to charge fees, thus setting legal limits to previously illegal practices. In effect the general public had to make up the salaries of Company servants.

Another yardstick by which the quality of VOC rule at the Cape could be judged was the administration of justice. The Cape judicial system was defective in two main respects: the superior court of the colony consisted overwhelmingly of officials, very largely the same officials who, as members of the Council of Policy, made and executed the laws, and the quality of justice dispensed by the court was unsatisfactory.

The members of the Council of Policy were the only judges until three military officers were added to help try cases involving soldiers in 1656, and in 1657 one burgher (two in 1658, three in 1675), selected on the 'double list' system, was appointed to participate in cases involving burghers.² In 1685 van Rheede laid down that seven of the eight officials comprising the Council of Policy should be included among the nine officials serving the Council of Justice.³ Although in 1732, to avoid concentrating all the powers of government in the same hands, the Seventeen forbade the senior officials in the VOC's dependencies to participate in the administration of justice, and accordingly, at the Cape, after 1734 the Governor ceased to sit on the Council of Justice and the *Secunde* became merely its titular president,⁴ all the other Council of Policy members remained, and until 1783 the Council of Justice was never truly differentiated from the Council of Policy.⁵ At the same time, the burgher councillors were always heavily outnumbered by senior officials. Cape senior officials tended to regard Cape burghers as mere liberated VOC servants, instead of genuine freemen entitled to the same rights as those in the mother country. The first burghers were in fact VOC servants, who were granted letters of burghership that allowed them to own property and to trade, but they could be forcibly taken back 'if the exigencies of the service demanded it', or if they misbehaved. This was sometimes done.⁶ But by the later eighteenth century the Cape burgher population was large, and was descended from free immigrants as well as from VOC servants. Yet in 1781 Boers, the Independent Fiscal, contemptuously contrasted the position of Cape burghers with those of the Netherlands, saying that there was 'a most important distinction between those Burghers whose ancestors owed their independent freedom to their Arms, and out of whose Bosoms the sovereignty of our Republic itself flowed forth, and ... those to whom

¹ *CHBE*, viii. 144–5.   ² Botha, *Collected Works*, i. 239.
³ *Bel. Hist. Dok.*, i. 46.   ⁴ Colenbrander, ii. 215; Hahlo and Kahn, p. 200.
⁵ *CHBE*, viii. 862.   ⁶ Botha, *Collected Works*, iii. 121.

permission was granted, as a favour upon their request, to remain resident in a country which had been taken possession of in the name of our Sovereign, as Farmer, Tailor, Shoemaker or Saddler'.[1] The *Kaapse Patriotte* demanded that burghers should be represented equally with officials on the Council of Justice, and that these officials should not be members of the Council of Policy. In 1783 the Seventeen created a new High Court of Justice, of six burghers and six officials under the chairmanship of the *Secunde*, and directed that the *Secunde* and the Fiscal were to be the only officials of higher rank than under-merchant on this court.[2]

The Council of Justice sat in Cape Town and was the superior court of the colony. It had jurisdiction over criminal and civil cases, and heard appeals from the inferior courts—the Court of Petty Cases in Cape Town and the district courts in Stellenbosch and Swellendam. The Batavian Council of Justice was the final court of appeal from its judgements. The members of the Cape Council of Justice were appointed by the Council of Policy, subject to the approval of the Seventeen. The only necessary qualifications were that judges must be members of the Dutch Reformed Church and not closely related to one another.[3] No legal qualification was expected. The Fiscal was usually a trained lawyer,[4] but he might be the only judge with legal knowledge. The judges were not paid for their judicial work, although the Fiscal received fees and a share of fines and forfeitures, and other official judges were usually given additional minor posts to supplement their salaries.

Cape law was based on Roman-Dutch law, the common law of the province of Holland, modified by statutes—Cape *placaaten*, extended where necessary by relevant *placaaten* of Batavia, the Netherlands States-General, and the States of Holland.[5]

The Cape superior court followed the court procedure of Holland and Batavia. Its members acted as judges and jury combined, deciding cases in closed court on the basis of written documents. Judgement was based on a majority vote. It was pronounced in open court, but no grounds were given. The Fiscal was public prosecutor in criminal cases unless they had occurred in the country, when a district official, the *landdrost*, arrested the criminal and arraigned him before the Council of Justice in Cape Town. Since the death penalty could not be inflicted without absolute proof of guilt, torture was very frequently used to obtain confessions. Neither in criminal nor in civil cases did a party automatically have the right to be represented by counsel.[6]

---

[1] Boers' answer to the burgher petition of 1779, Beyers, p. 39.
[2] Ibid., pp. 29, 47, 55. [3] Botha, *Collected Works*, iii. 125. [4] Ibid. ii. 162-3.
[5] Cf. *CHBE*, viii. 857-62; Botha, *Collected Works*, ii. 42-49.
[6] Ibid. ii. 101-17, 129-48; iii. 126-9.

Cape justice in the VOC period is open to considerable criticism, because the laws were unsatisfactory and the judges lacked legal training. Commissioner Verburg (1676) described Cape laws as 'too minute, and in some respects rather too rigid, and if acted upon to the letter without connivance, the inhabitants would be subject to constant penalties so severe as often to produce their ruin',[1] while Commissioner Simons (1708) referred to the 'meaningless, useless and odious placaaten' in force.[2] Also, though Cape law was difficult to master, as it derived from many sources, the government did not cancel obsolete or unsatisfactory legislation, or consolidate the laws.[3] Thus the judges might not know all the laws to be enforced and, because they were untrained, were often ignorant of legal procedure and jurisprudence. Commissioner Ryklof van Goens regretted that judges ignored legal formalities, gave free rein to passion, and resorted to inappropriately severe punishments.[4] Simons recommended putting an extract of procedural rules in the court-room to guide judges, and compiled a list of textbooks as a nucleus for an official law library,[5] but in 1739 the Council of Justice had only ten lawbooks.[6] Consequently, the arguments used in deciding cases were sometimes irrelevant. The Bible was frequently quoted, although it was not part of Roman-Dutch law.[6] The rule of law could not be said to apply when even the judges might not know what the law was, and what the consequences of breaking it might be, let alone the ordinary citizen.

In another sense, also, the rule of law did not apply. Before 1783 the executive and the judiciary were in practice synonymous. This made an independent bench impossible. When the governor gained the support of his senior officials there was no check on the executive. In fact, the judiciary could easily be used to bolster up executive powers even when officials were acting illegally.

Governor W. A. van der Stel's actions in 1706 show how easily the executive could dominate the judiciary and stage-manage court proceedings. In 1705 a group of colonists drew up a memorial against official malpractices and it was smuggled to Batavia. When van der Stel discovered the conspiracy, the leaders were arrested and a special commission was set up to try thirteen and extort recantations. All its members were interested parties, directly or indirectly.[7] The Governor was not a member but he stood behind the door 'some twelve feet from the table', and constantly intervened in the interrogations.[8] The prosecutor was not the Independent Fiscal, who should have taken charge,

[1] Moodie, i. 340.
[2] *Collectanea*, p. 29.
[3] Ibid., p. 30; *Report of Commissioners of Inquiry* . . . *1826*, p. 10; Beyers, pp. 27–28, 47–48.
[4] *Collectanea*, p. 30.   [5] Ibid., pp. 31–32.   [6] Botha, *Collected Works*, ii. 160.
[7] *Diary of Adam Tas*, pp. 227–8.   [8] Ibid., pp. 229–37.

but the Stellenbosch *landdrost*, who had organized a counter-memorial praising van der Stel.[1] He falsified the record of one interrogation, in the presence of the prisoner and the Secretary.[2] Imprisonment without bail, threats of banishment, and torture were used to get the Governor's opponents to retract.[3] Although nearly all eventually signed confessions, the Governor falsified the record of the trials sent to Holland.[4]

Clearly no force in the Constitution was strong enough to uphold justice against the illegal proceedings of the Governor and his clique. Even the Independent Fiscal, whose office was intended as an independent focus of power, was ousted from his proper functions without protest.[5] The Independent Fiscalate did not guarantee that the executive would respect fundamental rights of the individual, such as freedom of speech or freedom from arbitrary arrest, without which justice in cases involving the individual against the state is difficult to achieve. Indeed, a powerful fiscal might become as tyrannical as a powerful governor, as the burghers' complaints against successive fiscals in the later eighteenth century show.[6]

The executive also possessed two major prerogatives which might be exercised against the individual without recourse to the courts. These were the power to summarily banish undesirable individuals to Batavia by forcibly taking them into the Company's service,[7] and the power to revoke loanplace leases. Twenty persons were deported between 1738 and 1770, eighteen between 1771 and 1778.[8] The summary banishment of the burgher Carl Buitendag in 1778 prompted the dispatch of the *Kaapse Patriotte* petition to the Netherlands.[9] The power to revoke loanplace leases was not often used, but was obviously potentially dangerous to the security of the individual. The *Kaapse Patriotte* petitioned that both powers should be limited and controlled by the courts.[10]

Much of the Cape administration was entrusted to Councils on which burghers served. The VOC was anxious to associate burghers with officials in routine administrative duties which affected the burghers.[11] In Cape Town two Councils—the Matrimonial Council and the Orphan Chamber (each with an equal number of nominated officials and burghers selected by 'double list', with another official as chairman)—

[1] *Diary of Adam Tas*, pp. 211–17, 237, 253.
[2] Ibid., pp. 255–7.
[3] Ibid., pp. 239–43.
[4] Ibid., pp. 261–3, 267 ff.
[5] Ibid., pp. 227, 253.
[6] Beyers, pp. 132–9; Boëseken (1), pp. 126 ff.
[7] Any VOC servant could be summarily transferred to another station without redress.
[8] Theal, *History of South Africa* [*1691–1795*], p. 230.
[9] Beyers, pp. 134–5.
[10] The governor confiscated three loanplaces belonging to one of the burgher representatives who went to Holland to plead for changes in the Cape Constitution (Beyers, pp. 27, 50, 54 n. 2, 115).
[11] Boëseken (1), pp. 38–39.

administered aspects of civil law for the whole colony. The Matrimonial Council (founded 1676) certified proposed marriages as legally valid before the banns were called.[1] The Orphan Chamber (founded about 1673) administered orphan and intestate estates, registered wills and deaths, and provided loans.[2]

In local government the only administrative agencies were Councils in which unpaid burghers predominated. The burghers selected to attend the Council of Justice constituted the Burgher Council, Cape Town's municipality. Though it had no legal existence as such, it was recognized *de facto* by the government.[3] It was in charge of roads, streets, bridges, civic police, sanitation, fire precautions, weights and measures, and food prices in Cape Town. To defray expenses it levied local taxes authorized by the Council of Policy.[4]

Councils consisting of a full-time paid official (*landdrost*) and four part-time unpaid *heemraden*, locally resident burghers selected annually by 'double list', administered outlying districts. Stellenbosch district (founded 1682) was originally under four *heemraden*, appointed mainly to settle land disputes. But as they lacked authority they were conjoined with a minor official (*veldwagter*) and finally with a *landdrost* (1685).[5] Drakenstein was subordinate to Stellenbosch, though its deputy *landdrost* was associated with *heemraden* (one in 1697, two in 1704) and it had its own treasury. Swellendam, constituted in 1743, was subordinate to Stellenbosch until 1745.[6] No other districts existed until Graaff-Reinet (1785) was created to cope with the eastward dispersal of *trekboers* from Stellenbosch and Swellendam.[7]

These local boards combined judicial and administrative functions. Like the Cape Town Court of Petty Cases (founded 1682) they settled minor cases between burghers, who had a right of appeal to the Council of Justice. Matters likely to harm the Company were brought directly before this superior court.[8] Though this division of duties corresponded roughly to the modern distinction between civil and criminal cases, these district courts settled burgher cases, like assault, which were strictly speaking criminal, by imposing fines and awarding compensation. Only very serious offences were regarded as crimes to be tried by the Council of Justice in Cape Town, which alone could impose criminal penalties on burghers (lashes, torture, and the death penalty).[9] The distinction between civil and criminal matters was vague, because the original instructions of the central government to the colleges were not rigorously framed, and were only revised in the late eighteenth

---

[1] Botha, *Collected Works*, ii. 50–52. [2] Ibid. iii. 131–5. [3] Boëseken (1), p. 39.
[4] Botha, *Collected Works*, i. 154, 157–63. [5] Venter, pp. 13–17.
[6] Ibid., pp. 19–22. [7] Walker, *History*, p. 123. [8] Venter, p. 19.
[9] Ibid., pp. 34–36.

century. The competence of the Stellenbosch and Swellendam colleges was only 25 guilders (£2. 1s. 8d.) and their sentences were sometimes not enforced because the cost involved was greater than the fine. Swellendam's jurisdiction was increased to 25 rixdollars (£5. 12s. 6d.) in 1779 for this reason. It was equally difficult to serve summonses on outlying inhabitants. Even in cases heard by the superior court, the colleges sometimes sent letters instead. Such letters and summonses were often ignored, either through ignorance, or because offenders were seldom punished. The colleges, even the law itself, tended to be held in contempt—a tendency already noticed in the ignoring of loanplace rents. Slack law enforcement in outlying areas helped to foster resentment against authority, and allowed individuals to assert private interests over community ones, as when they refused to pay local taxes, or to undertake commando service.[1]

In contrast to these limited and laxly asserted powers over burghers, the district courts had extensive powers over slaves. Slave law mainly served to maintain the master's authority, while preventing gross ill-treatment of the slave. Owners were given great latitude in punishing slaves themselves, but 'domestic correction' excluded prolonged whipping. Nevertheless, on the bare word of the owner that a slave had been impertinent or had absconded the *landdrost* could impose severe penalties, like lashes, without informing any higher authority. Until 1794 district courts could execute slaves on trial for capital crimes, who had attempted to commit suicide, without bringing them to trial. Thus slaves had a status inferior to that of their masters in the courts. Many owners were prosecuted and punished for ill-treating slaves, but the fact that *landdrosts* and *heemraden* were themselves slave-owners and without legal training affected their attitude in slave cases. Masters' crimes tended to be judged more leniently than slaves' crimes. In a case of 1685, in which a master was tried for murdering his slave, the Stellenbosch *landdrost* quoted Exodus xxi. 20–21 (which distinguished between freemen, servants, and slaves) to support the argument that the criminal's status, rather than the crime itself, should determine the punishment.[2]

In 1748 Commissioner Nolthenius instructed the Cape government that 'Hottentots' should be allowed to lay complaints about whites before the courts, and this occurred on occasions.[3] But local prejudices also affected the colleges' attitude to the Khoikhoi. Thus, in a Stellenbosch case of 1797, where a 'Hottentot' man had summoned a white woman to appear before the court, the *heemraden* were doubtful whether he had the right to do so, since it might make the Khoikhoi think they

[1] Venter, pp. 22–28. See p. 226 below for conditions of commando service.
[2] Ibid., p. 38, n. 82.
[3] Boëseken (1), pp. 76–78.

were equal to burghers; the *heemraden* were reluctant to agree with the *landdrost* that all were equal before the law.[1]

The ignorance and prejudice of members of district courts sometimes affected criminal justice, since they performed preliminary investigations connected with post-mortems and viewing wounds, to decide whether a crime had in fact been committed. If they so decided, the *landdrost* took preliminary statements and sorted out details in what amounted to a hearing, before going to Cape Town to explain the case and act as public prosecutor before the Council of Justice. But in cases where the local authorities decided a crime had not been committed, the matter never went to court at all. For example, in 1750 the Swellendam *landdrost* ruled unfounded a slave's accusation that his master had beaten another slave to death, and there were no further proceedings. Similarly, in 1752, when a white woman shot a Khoikhoi dead, it was ruled that the circumstances made it legal.[2] In the light of such examples it is easy to understand why the white inhabitants felt so outraged when the 1812 'Black Circuit' court found that allegations that whites had ill-treated slaves and Khoikhoi were unsubstantiated: they felt these cases should never have come to court at all.

As administrative agencies the district colleges executed central government policy and reported on local events.[3] They provided the Council of Policy with information on land settlement to enable it to decide on applications for land. Such applications were sometimes made directly to the colleges instead of the central government. Although the Council of Policy took the final decisions, the local boards could influence land policy by their reports. The colleges also inspected and measured farms to resolve conflicting land claims. After 1788 they also took over the annual census of production (*opgaaf*), on which assessment for taxes was based, formerly conducted by Commissioners of the Court of Justice.[4] They built, inspected, and repaired roads and bridges, and paid out 'lion and tiger money', a reward offered by the government for exterminating wild animals.[5]

Although the district colleges performed many important duties, the central government never gave them direct financial aid. All the expenses of local administration, except the salaries of the *landdrost* and his clerk or clerks, were borne by the district itself. The Swellendam college even paid the cost of building its *drosdy* (the building in which the college sat). The colleges were authorized to levy local taxes, usually on cattle and sheep, which varied in amount and were often

[1] Venter, p. 38.   [2] Venter, pp. 38–40.
[3] In 1708 the Stellenbosch 'local board proceeded to Cape Town, to report to . . . [Commissioner] Simons on the state of the district'. (P. B. Borcherds, *An Autobiographical Memoir*, p. 144).
[4] Venter, pp. 70 ff.   [5] Ibid., pp. 90–142.

insufficient to cover expenses. The colleges had to borrow on their own account. Loans, from the Orphan Chamber or private individuals, were usually negotiated by the unpaid *heemraden*.[1]

A similar attitude characterized the central government's policy on the defence of the interior. After 1672 all adult male burghers between sixteen and sixty had to undertake military service and annual training. The burgher corps was first formed in 1659. As the numbers enrolled increased, it was divided into several companies of infantry, largely manned by Cape Town burghers, and cavalry, by burghers from outlying districts. The men elected their officers, and each district had a council of war (*Burger Krygsraad*) of senior officers, who appointed junior officers and supervised the militia. Burgher companies were controlled by the *landdrost*. The VOC intended that the militia should serve with regular troops against European invaders as well as indigenous enemies.[2] But inevitably the VOC concentrated its defence efforts against possible attack by European powers, so that military measures against indigenous enemies had to be undertaken increasingly by the local inhabitants, particularly in the later eighteenth century, when the VOC was becoming bankrupt. Thus the central government's role in the defence of the interior was limited to building frontier posts manned by a few regulars, and even this gradually ceased after about the middle of the eighteenth century.[3]

In the 1670s the commando, a new institution for frontier warfare, began to evolve. In its final form it consisted of quasi-military, quasi-police action against indigenous enemies by mounted burghers and their servants—'Bastards and Hottentots whose help was essential for the success of the undertaking'[4]—under the command of burgher officers. The government provided ammunition for the white and guns for the coloured members of the commando. In the seventeenth century 'official commandos' were punitive expeditions of regulars, burghers, and coloured servants under an army officer, or later, the Stellenbosch *landdrost*. By the beginning of the eighteenth century very few regular soldiers participated. In 1715 a turning point occurred when the Council of Policy allowed a group of volunteers under two burgher officers to proceed against San hunters and keep part of the booty. Later these expeditions were commonly led by *veldkorporaals* (burgher officers in charge of a group of men from a ward), whose importance was shown by a change of name (to *veldwagmeester*) and an increase in status in 1774. At the same time they were forbidden to resign their office except for very good cause. These changes reflected the inability of the small, loosely organized commandos to deal with the increased intensity of

---

[1] Venter, pp. 141 ff.   [2] Roux, pp. 50–55, 64–65.   [3] Ibid., Ch. VI, *passim*.
[4] *Noordwaartse Beweging*, p. 29.

the conflict with the San in the 1770s. The need for a more highly organized military force was recognized in 1774 when the government granted the request of Stellenbosch frontiersmen, and appointed one of the *veldkorporaals* as *veldkommandant*, to co-ordinate the activities of commandos. He had to report to the *landdrost* in writing every four months, and in person twice a year.[1] In 1774 a 'general commando' of 'about 100 "Christians" and 150 Bastards and Hottentots'[2] from all the wards on the frontier under Veldkommandant Opperman proceeded against the San. The government provided guns and ammunition. In 1780 the government, at the burghers' request, appointed two *veldkommandants*, one for the northern frontier and one for the eastern frontier, where skirmishing with Xhosa had begun in 1778.[3] Although the commando system proved fairly adequate in the north against the San, it was much less effective in the east. Consequently, the government created a new district, Graaff-Reinet, in 1785. Here, as in Swellendam, the strain of undertaking military expeditions against two different groups of enemies created a serious rift between the white farming community and the *landdrosts* representing the central government. Many of the eastern frontiersmen, who suffered directly, pressed for an aggressive eastern frontier policy, but this was impossible, since the *landdrosts* had no military force except commandos. The central government advocated a peaceful Xhosa policy, and concentrated military operations against the San. At the same time, it began to regain control over frontier areas, particularly in the administration of justice. This led to revolts by the white farmers, and the temporary establishment of republics at Swellendam and Graaff-Reinet at the turn of the eighteenth century, in an attempt to achieve full local self-government on the frontier.[4]

During the eighteenth century Cape burghers participated to a considerable extent in aspects of government which did not involve policymaking, especially in local government. The government deliberately encouraged this, to reduce its own administrative burden and to obtain the co-operation of 'competent subjects' in matters directly affecting burghers. Although burgher councillors and *heemraden* were not freely elected and usually belonged to a rather narrow circle, they came to be regarded by the burghers as their representatives. For example, in 1716 the Burgher Councillors presented a burgher petition to Commissioner Douglas without first going through the Council of Policy.[5] Several times in the eighteenth century *heemraden* presented petitions from the burghers in their districts asking the government to reduce taxes or

---

[1] Roux, pp. 139–57; *Noordwaartse Beweging*, pp. 25–65.
[2] *Noordwaartse Beweging*, p. 28.   [3] Roux, pp. 158–62.   [4] *Maynier, passim*.
[5] Boëseken (1), p. 39.

recognitiegeld, or to raise fixed agricultural prices.[1] The Burgher Councillors and the Stellenbosch *heemraden* figured prominently in the *Kaapse Patriotte* movement of 1779–91. In 1779 they presented a memorial including demands that burghers should have equal representation with officials on the Councils of Policy and Justice, and that burghers on the various councils should be freely elected, subject to the approval of the Governor and the sitting burgher representatives. In 1791 they demanded that the Burgher Council should be recognized as a separate body in law, pointing out that it had been so recognized in fact for a century. These demands were not fully met, but in 1783 the reorganized Council of Justice consisted of six burghers and six officials; a commission, of three burghers and three officials, was created in 1785 to fix official prices for agricultural surpluses, and in 1793 the status of the Burgher Council as a separate entity was officially recognized.[2]

Although the memorials of the *Kaapse Patriotte* included many demands which affected the whole burgher population, the movement was limited to the western Cape; the Swellendam and Graaff-Reinet *heemraden* did not join the Stellenbosch *heemraden* and the Cape Town Burgher Councillors in presenting memorials to the Directors or the States-General. It was difficult for burghers from the western Cape to combine politically with those from frontier areas. This was partly because of the dispersal of whites in the hinterland, and also because, while the inhabitants of Cape Town and the western Cape agricultural areas were vitally concerned with Company policy on internal and external trade and the behaviour of VOC officials (matters which predominated in the *Kaapse Patriotte* memorials), the frontier *trekboers* did not share these grievances, since their contact with the Cape Town market and the officials there was far less important to them.

5. *The White Colonial Community*

But despite differences in economic and political orientation between the western Cape and the frontier areas, the white colonists were essentially a single community with a common heritage. Widely ramifying kinship ties, confirmed in family gatherings where people of very different circumstances assembled, helped emphasize the closely-knit character of this community, very largely descended from seventeenth-century settlers, into which the occasional outsider, usually an ex-VOC official, was easily incorporated, often by marriage. Family feeling extended to all whites and was expressed by the use of familial terms (like 'grandfather', 'uncle', 'aunt', 'nephew') in addressing any other

---

[1] Venter, pp. 178 ff.
[2] Boëseken (1), pp. 38–45; Beyers, pp. 28–29, 37, 49–50, 76–82; Venter, pp. 185–6.

white person of a different generation. The experience of VOC political institutions, particularly in local government, formed part of this heritage. But the strongest unifying institution, both emotionally and intellectually, was provided by the Dutch Reformed Church in its spiritual and social aspects.[1]

The doctrine of the Dutch Reformed Church, 'primitive Calvinism as embodied in the Heidelberg catechism and the decrees of the Synod of Dort... with its emphasis upon the Old Testament and predestination ... was peculiarly suited to the taste of the white community ... struggling to survive in a stern environment and accustomed from birth to treating nonwhite peoples as slaves, or serfs, or enemies'.[2] The Dutch Reformed Church was the Cape's State Church, and no other denomination was officially tolerated until 1780, when the Lutherans received freedom of public worship. In its temporal aspects it was a branch of government. The VOC received *predikanten* (ministers) ordained by the Classis of Amsterdam into its service, and appointed them to churches. To exclude undesirables from *kerkraden* (Church Consistories), the government in VOC possessions (in contrast to the Netherlands practice and the decrees of the Synod of Dort) also appointed the two deacons by double list. The four elders were elected by the congregation, subject to government approval.[3] A lay official, the political commissioner, was supposed to attend the meetings of each *kerkraad* and report matters of interest to the government, though at the Cape he confined himself almost entirely to meetings held in Cape Town.[4] But even though ministers tended to regard themselves as VOC officials and to side with other officials against the burghers in conflicts between the two groups, the Cape Church never became identified with VOC authority, partly because the government interfered in spiritual matters only to enforce the Classis of Amsterdam's authority (as in 1759 forbidding the holding of synod meetings representing all Cape congregations),[5] and partly because the Church's Presbyterian organization allowed considerable participation by the congregation in church affairs, and in each Cape *kerkraad* two officials and four burghers held the posts of elders and deacons.

The Cape white population tried not to lose touch with the Church. Baptism, though often delayed in remote areas, was not neglected, and

---

[1] C. Spoelstra, *Bouwstoffen voor de Geschiedenis der Nederduitsch-Gereformeerde Kerken in Zuid Afrika*; S. P. Engelbrecht, *Geschiedenis van de Nederduits Hervormde Kerk in Zuid-Afrika*; A. Moorrees, *Die Nederduitse Gereformeerde Kerk in Suid Africa*; B. Booyens, 'Kerk en Staat, 1795-1843', in *AYB, 1965*, ii, pp. 13-21.
[2] L. M. Thompson, 'The South African Dilemma', being Ch. VI in Louis Hartz, *The Founding of New Societies...*, p. 187.
[3] *Description*, i. 149; Booyens, p. 15.
[4] Booyens, p. 19.   [5] Engelbrecht, i, pp. 5-6.

people trekked great distances to attend *nagmaal* (communion). But though outlying inhabitants frequently petitioned the government to establish more churches,[1] before 1792, when the Graaff-Reinet church was founded, there were congregations at only five centres, all in the western Cape—Cape Town (1666), Stellenbosch (1685), Drakenstein (1691), Roodezand (Tulbagh) (1743), and Zwartland (Malmesbury) (1745).

The Church was the main instrument of culture and education[2] at the Cape in the eighteenth century, since it insisted that communicants should be able to read. By the late eighteenth century the only schools in the colony were elementary schools[3] run by the parish clerks. The only other education available locally was given by itinerant *meesters*, usually VOC servants employed by farmers to teach their children.[4] Cape education did little more than prepare children for confirmation and impart an elementary knowledge of reading, writing, spelling, and arithmetic. There was so little demand for higher education that a Latin school (high school) started in 1714 was closed in 1742 for lack of pupils. As Mentzel commented, 'what use could anyone make of the learning acquired there in a land where life is still primitive and Company rule is law?'[5] Although there was considerable illiteracy in remote areas, the Bible, collected sermons, and hymns provided a background that all could share.[6]

But, intellectually, the Cape remained a backwater. 'To the end of the eighteenth century the Afrikaners produced no literature, no painting, no music. The one distinguished art form . . . was the architecture of some . . . public and private buildings . . . designed by [visiting] Europeans . . . and executed by slave artisans. . . . There was nothing approaching an intellectual circle.'[7] The public library contained only Latin works, apart from some very old books in modern languages, and was hardly ever used except by foreigners. There were no journals or newspapers (since there was not even a government printing press), no theatre, and the only recreations besides hunting were eating, drinking, dancing, music, cardplaying, and gossip.[8] Educated visitors commented on the ignorance and lack of scientific curiosity even of the best-

---

[1] Boëseken (1), pp. 49–50.
[2] E. G. Malherbe, *Education in South Africa, 1652–1922*; P. S. du Toit, *Onderwys aan die Kaap onder die Kompanjie, 1652–1795*.
[3] For a delightful, but idealized, picture of an eighteenth-century elementary school see Borcherds, pp. 18–21.
[4] *Description*, i. 165–6. [5] Ibid. ii. 109.
[6] Malherbe, p. 26; P. J. Idenburg, *The Cape of Good Hope at the Turn of the Eighteenth Century*, p. 112.
[7] Thompson, in Hartz, pp. 188–9.
[8] C. de Jong, *Reizen naar de Kaap de Goede Hoop . . . 1791 to 1797*, i. 115, 130–1; Barrow, i. 47–48, 76–78.

educated local inhabitants, and were sometimes shocked by their insularity.[1] But it was probably this very isolation from the outside world, particularly in the country districts, which provided the feeling of community among the nascent Afrikaner people. The feeling was cemented by the growth of a local variant of Dutch, the *taal*, with a simplified grammar and a vocabulary incorporating Portuguese, Malay, and Khoikhoi words, which became increasingly divergent from the language spoken in the Netherlands, and was the ancestor of modern Afrikaans.[2]

By the 1770s a social and cultural transformation had occurred at the Cape. It involved two immigrant populations, Northern European Protestants (largely of Dutch, German, and French extraction)[3] and slaves (mainly pagan Negroes from East Africa, with a significant minority of Malays[4]—Mohammedans from the East Indies), and the indigenous Khoikhoi and San peoples. The focal point of the new society thus created was the white settler community. Boxer has described the Cape as 'a colony *sui generis*', because this community had grown large enough to acquire its own identity, and, in becoming rooted at the Cape, had incorporated peoples of diverse cultural traditions into a new society with a predominantly Dutch stamp—a process which occurred nowhere else in the Dutch Eastern Empire.[5] Indeed, the spread of white occupation into the interior, which was crucial in developing the distinctive features of the emergent Afrikaner people, resulted in Dutch Calvinism and a language of Dutch cast taking root far beyond the original settlement.

But though, in this sense, the Cape settler community was a 'fragment'[6] of its parent society, it also differed from it fundamentally, whether because the Cape burghers sprang largely from 'elements which had failed to prosper in the free, competitive society of the Netherlands ... the peasant and unsuccessful townsman',[7] or because, in an African environment, under the over-regulated, but weak and inefficient rule of the VOC, many traits of Dutch society could not survive. The seventeenth-century Dutch Republic was a highly complex society, dominated by a rich merchant class, whose commercial triumphs had made the Netherlands the most advanced country in Europe, where political liberty was cherished, and art, science, and philosophy

[1] Cf. Sparrman, i. 47–49.
[2] Cf. P. Ribbinck, *Gids tot die publikasies in en oor Afrikaans*; J. J. Smith, 'Recognition and Evolution of the Afrikaans Language', in *Union Yearbook No. 8*; C. M. van den Heever and P. de V. Pienaar (eds.), *Kultuurgeskiedenis van die Afrikaner*, ii.
[3] Cf. Idenburg. p. 111 and n. 19 for discussion of various estimates of the composition of the Cape white settlers.
[4] I. D. du Plessis, *The Cape Malays*, Ch. I.
[5] *Dutch Seaborne Empire*, pp. 245–7, 267.
[6] Cf. Hartz, *passim*. [7] Ibid., p. 182.

flourished—industrious, prosperous, self-confident, and secure. The eighteenth-century Cape burgher community received its most distinctive features from the fact that most whites were farmers (*boers*). Apart from a few hamlets in the south-west Cape, Cape Town was the only urban centre, and its white inhabitants were almost all small retailers or boarding-house keepers, who indulged in feverish petty smuggling and speculation when ships arrived. Otherwise the Cape white settlers were a rural community in which virtues such as hospitality, frugality, candour, and simplicity of dress and manners developed side by side with an ignorant complacency and insularity, a positive enjoyment of quarrels with neighbours, and an overwhelming individualism.[1] The dispersal of the population over vast distances tended to create a series of atomized families. Even the south-west Cape farms resembled large patriarchal estates where many family needs were supplied by slaves, and self-sufficiency was even greater in the frontier regions. According to C. de Jong, the further people lived from Cape Town, the more rough and uncivilized they became.[2] Class distinctions, in the European sense, did not apply within the white community,[3] but by the late eighteenth century the distinctions between Christians and non-Christians, free and non-free, were giving way before the growing gulf in social status between white and non-white.[4] Although to many Europeans the Cape settlers appeared to lead much more prosperous and secure lives than the peasants in Europe,[5] as de Jong observed, even in Cape Town 'the apparent prosperity and wealth is just tinsel',[6] and the apparent security was always tinged with the fear of violence from slaves.[7]

Cape society in the late eighteenth century rested on two main assumptions: that whites should be allowed to deal with slaves and other non-white dependents more or less as they saw fit, without government interference, and that all whites were entitled to as much land as they wanted without paying for it. These assumptions were to be put to the test in the period after 1778.

[1] Idenburg, pp. 11–18, 107–8; *Description*, i. 11; iii. 22, Ch. VII.
[2] De Jong, i. 99.   [3] *Description*, ii. 104–8.   [4] MacCrone, *passim*.
[5] Cf. Kolb, ii. 8; Sparrman, i. 50.   [6] Quoted in Idenburg, p. 18.
[7] Sparrman, i. 38–39, 73.

VI

CO-OPERATION AND CONFLICT: THE EASTERN CAPE FRONTIER[1]

1. *The Beginnings of Interaction*

THE eastern Cape frontier is a vaguely defined area lying eastward of the Gamtoos river. It is important in South African history because it was here that black Africans, speaking a Bantu language, first encountered white settlers (as distinct from traders and missionaries), and it was here that policies which have had a profound influence on southern Africa were first formulated and applied. It was a cultural frontier between warring states, and it has many of the characteristics of frontiers elsewhere.[2]

The Nguni people encountered men of other races as survivors from shipwreck in the sixteenth century, and there is evidence that they absorbed some individuals into their society. Survivors of wrecks in 1554 and 1635 met men from previous wrecks who refused to accompany them on their journey up the coast.[3] In 1705 an expedition sent to Natal to look for timber found an Englishman living there with African wives, and so well satisfied that two of the crew deserted to join him.[4] Two other men who survived from an early eighteenth-century wreck on the Mpondo coast became the progenitors of a clan still known in 1965 as the Lungu (Abelungu), i.e. the whites, and a girl wrecked with them was later married by the Mpondo chief, Xwabiso (Xwebisa).[5] Her daughter, Bessie, was seen by Jacob van Reenen in 1790, as an old woman.[6]

---

[1] I am particularly indebted to Professor Hobart Houghton, Mr. Leo Marquard, Dr. Rodney Davenport, Mr. Archie Mafeje, and Professor L. M. Thompson for helpful criticisms of a draft of this chapter, and to Mrs. M. Pimstone, who worked as research assistant. I thank also the University of California, Los Angeles, for an invitation as Visiting Professor in the Fall term of 1963, when an early draft of this chapter was discussed at a graduate seminar. However I, alone, am finally responsible for the argument and selection of material.
[2] Cf. W. K. Hancock, *Survey of British Commonwealth Affairs*, ii, parts I and II.
[3] Theal, *Records of South-Eastern Africa*, i. 235; viii. 217.
[4] Theal, *History and Ethnography*, ii. 421–2.
[5] Soga, *The South Eastern Bantu*, pp. 376–83; W. Shaw, *The Story of my Mission in South Eastern Africa*, pp. 489–95, 498–9; Hunter, *Reaction to Conquest*, p. 399.
[6] J. van Reenen, *Journal*, in *The Wreck of the Grosvenor*, VRS, p. 160; Soga, *South Eastern Bantu*, p. 379.

A second category who were absorbed into Nguni chiefdoms were refugees from the colony: escaped slaves and 'apprentices'; deserters from the army or navy; and convicts.[1] In the eighteenth century, when the gibbet, the wheel, and the rack were still publicly displayed at the Cape and flogging with up to a hundred lashes was a regular punishment for soldiers and sailors,[2] the rule of a Xhosa chief was mild by comparison. The frontier records are full of references to parties of farmers riding into 'Caffreland' to recover slaves, as Willem Prinslo did in 1773,[3] and in the Governors' parleys with Xhosa chiefs demands that they return runaway slaves and deserters were repeatedly made.[4]

From the beginning of the eighteenth century a regular traffic in cattle and ivory developed. Expeditions left Stellenbosch and remained away for eight or nine months. They returned loaded with ivory. The members were reticent about the routes they had followed, but in 1702 a scandal broke. A party of forty-five young white men, from Stellenbosch, each with a Khoikhoi servant, rode eastward and fought with a party of five or six hundred Xhosa whom they met near where Somerset East is now. They got no cattle from the Xhosa, but lifted cattle and sheep from Khoikhoi encampments. Trade in cattle was a Government monopoly, and travel east of the Gamtoos was forbidden, hence the scandal. It received further publicity at the impeachment of the Governor, Willem Adriaan van der Stel, four years later, when he was accused of being privy to the expedition.[5] The occasion is important because it is the first evidence of a party of whites from the settlement at the Cape making contact with the Xhosa.

By 1736 two expeditions had crossed the Keiskamma, one of four colonists with six wagons trading ivory with the Thembu, and the other of thirteen wagons and eleven white men under Heupenaer. Each wagon took a load of 800 to 900 kilograms of ivory. Heupenaer was killed with most of his men as they crossed the Kei. According to Thunberg and Sparrman,[6] writing in 1773 and 1776, the Xhosa wanted the iron from the wagons: according to a Xhosa chief in 1752[7] misunderstanding had been caused by the Khoikhoi interpreter.

These were not the only trading parties. Farmers came and went without there being any record in Cape Town of their movements, and by 1752, when Ensign Beutler was sent by the Government to inquire into the possibility of trade, he found that elephant hunters were

---

[1] Van Reenen, *Journal*, pp. 162–4; Moodie, *Record*, v. 41; Lichtenstein, i. 362.
[2] Sparrman, i. 54–55; Moodie, *Record*, i. 252–4.
[3] Ibid. iii. 19.   [4] Lichtenstein, i. 385–6; Moodie, *Record*, v. 56.
[5] H. C. V. Leibbrandt, *Archives of the Cape of Good Hope*, Précis of The Defence of Willem Adriaan van der Stel, pp. 15–17, 53, 133–5; *Diary of Adam Tas*, pp. 335–7.
[6] Thunberg, ii. 94; Sparrman, ii. 166.
[7] Theal, *History and Ethnography*, iii. 151.

already familiar with the headland *Intaba ka Ndoda*,[1] near the present village of Debe Nek. In 1770 a regular wagon-road led to Hermanus Kraal (the present Fort Brown) on the Fish river; and in 1776 Sparrman met a farmer, travelling alone, who had just bought several tusks in Xhosa country.[2] A cattle-trading party of six farmers and ten Khoikhoi servants was detected in 1778.[3]

The wagon-road to the frontier has profound significance. South Africa differed radically from the greater part of Africa to the north in this one respect: the facility of transport. Horses flourished, and south of the Vaal there was no tsetse fly to impede the movement of stock to the coast, or prevent ox transport. The most lucrative trade was in cattle, and these were driven to market. Every hunting and trading party was mounted, and many of them were accompanied by ox-wagons which carried metal, beads, and tobacco to exchange, and brought back ivory. The implications of this were far reaching. Horses and ox-wagons gave a mobility to the colonists which was absent further north, and it made possible the development of trade without dependence on slavery. On Lake Malawi until the late nineteenth century ivory was of little value without slaves to carry it to the coast,[4] but, except from Lourenço Marques, the safari with head-loads was rare in the south. Instead, there was the ox-wagon. Trade seven hundred miles from the Cape was thus profitable, and whole families, not only single men, could move readily.

As colonists, seeking hunting and grazing land, moved eastward across the Gamtoos, Xhosa moved westward across the Fish, seeking exactly the same things.[5] The farmers lived on game so far as they could,[6] and sold butter and cattle to victual ships at the Cape.[7] The Xhosa hunted for meat and clothing and, though prodigal of game, sometimes killing more than they ate or even skinned, they were very sparing in their use of cattle.[8] Milk, along with venison, was their staple food. Dependence upon hunting was not solely due to poor soil and uncertain rainfall: as on the Canadian frontier, it was a *preferred* way of life,[9] which became impossible as the population grew larger.

---

[1] Ibid. iii. 153; V. S. Forbes, *Pioneer Travellers in South Africa*, p. 16. Theal's identification is the more probable.
[2] Sparrman, ii. 167.   [3] Moodie, *Record*, iii. 73–74.
[4] David and Charles Livingstone, *Narrative of an Expedition to the Zambesi and its tributaries*, pp. 140–1.
[5] J. S. Marais, *Maynier and the First Boer Republic*, pp. 23–24.
[6] Lichtenstein, i. 285.
[7] Sparrman, i. 285.
[8] Lichtenstein, i. 284–5, 330.
[9] In 1857 on the Red river (now Manitoba) 'many . . . preferred the excitement of the buffalo-hunt to the humdrum drudgery of tilling the rich land . . .' (Irene M. Spry, *The Palliser Expedition*, p. 37).

From the time the struggle for land on the eastern Cape frontier began, in the early eighteenth century, there has been argument about who occupied certain areas, and at what date. Xhosa, Khoikhoi, San, and white have mingled between the Kei and the Gamtoos for nearly three centuries. The record of the survivors of the *Stavenisse* shows that in 1686 the Xhosa were living on the Buffalo, and there were also Khoikhoi and San groups in the neighbourhood (see p. 93).[1] In 1689, when Schryver's party travelled down the Long Kloof, it was occupied by Khoikhoi with cattle, and groups of San without cattle.[2] He met no Xhosa. According to Xhosa tradition Tshiwo's son, Gwali, was received by a Khoikhoi chief, Hintsati, who lived at Nojoli, where Somerset East is now,[3] and it was near there that the party from Stellenbosch encountered the Xhosa in 1702.[4] In 1772 Thunberg met Xhosa mingled with Khoikhoi on the Gamtoos, and he described the characteristic Xhosa dancing and 'javelins which they knew much better how to manage than the Hottentots did'.[5] By 1809 the official view was that the Xhosa who met Governor Plettenberg in 1778 had come from beyond the Keiskamma, but an eyewitness later insisted that they had come from Naude's Hoek (now Somerset East).[6] The exact disposition of Xhosa in the eighteenth century became a matter of bitter argument. John Brownlee, who wrote before 1820 and drew his information from Xhosa born in the mid eighteenth century, described the distribution of Xhosa and Khoikhoi on the Buffalo and Keiskamma, and the movement of Xhosa into land on the Suurveld previously occupied by Khoikhoi.[7] One small group of Xhosa, or Xhosa and Thembu,[8] who lived north of the Orange was noted by Borcherds, in 1801, and by Lichtenstein in 1805.[9] They had recently left the eastern Cape.[10] Other groups were seen by Paravicini in 1803 in the Nieuweveldsbergen, where they had been for eight years;[11] by Lichtenstein in the Roggeveld in 1806;[12] and by Thompson in 1824 east of the Sak river near the Karee mountains, where they had been for about fifteen years.[13] The Gqunukwebe under Cungwa ('Congo' or 'Kongo') lived for a time in the Long Kloof[14] (see map 3).

---

[1] Moodie, *Record*, i. 424–7. [2] Ibid. i. 435–7.
[3] Theal, *History and Ethnography*, iii. 144; Soga, *South Eastern Bantu*, p. 113.
[4] Leibbrandt, p. 133.
[5] Thunberg, i. 203–4.
[6] Moodie, *Record*, v. 9–10; Sir Andries Stockenström, *Autobiography*, i. 45.
[7] G. Thompson, *Travels and Adventures*, pp. 439–41.
[8] P. B. Borcherds, *An Autobiographical Memoir*, p. 93.
[9] Lichtenstein, ii. 283–4. [10] Moodie, *Record*, v. 14.
[11] W. B. Paravicini di Capelli, *Reize in de Binne Landen van Zuid Africa*, VRS, 1965, pp. 186–7, 265.
[12] Lichtenstein, ii. 219–21.
[13] Thompson, p. 23. [14] Moodie, *Record*, v. 60.

THE BEGINNINGS OF INTERACTION

The San lived in dispersed groups and were particularly conspicuous in the valleys of the Kei and Fish, and north of the Mathole range[1] which separates the coastal plain from the inland table-land. The competition for land, and the market for meat in Cape Town, led, very early, to raiding for stock. The party of 1702 from Stellenbosch stole Khoikhoi cattle, and this was one of the reasons why they were so bitterly attacked by the Governor. The San raided Xhosa and Thembu cattle and drew pictures of their raids, and they stole cattle, sheep, and occasionally horses from the white farmers.[2] The Xhosa raided cattle and horses from the farmers, and the farmers retaliated, not troubling greatly whether the cattle recovered were all originally their own or not. In 1793 Maynier from Graaff-Reinet raided as far east as the Buffalo[3] (Qonce, 'Kognie'), and in 1798 fighting bands of Xhosa raided farms in the Long Kloof and along the coast as far west as Plettenberg Bay. In 1799 they destroyed buildings in Knysna.[4]

Successive governments sought to avoid conflict by limiting interaction between Xhosa and white. The Dutch East India Company also sought to maintain its monopoly of the cattle trade. In 1774 a burgher was imprisoned for bartering cattle with the Xhosa, and an order was issued that all 'Kafir cattle' in farmers' kraals were to be handed over to the government. These cattle were 'very easily to be distinguished',[5] but the trade continued.[6] Farmers were forbidden to settle east of the Gamtoos. In 1770 the furthest farm was Uytkomst on the Camdeboo mountains, thirty-three hours on horseback from the Fish,[7] but by 1772 Willem Prinslo was beyond Bruintjieshoogte in the valley of the Fish.[8] Even in 1770 cattle belonging to farmers were grazed on the Loerie, van Stadens, and Coega rivers.[9]

In 1778 Governor Plettenberg set up beacons marking the boundary of the colony beyond which no white man might pass. He met some Xhosa near Bruintjieshoogte and admonished them not to move west of the beacons (map 3). The Xhosa paid little attention, and raid and counter-raid continued in 1779.[10] In 1781 a commando drove the Xhosa out of the Suurveld East over the Fish. This campaign was marked by blatant deception. The white leader, Adriaan van Jaarsveld, scattered tobacco and then, as the Xhosa stopped to pick it up, he gave the order to fire on them.[11] The occurrence is remembered by the descendants of the Xhosa concerned.[12] Thirty years later, Landdrost Andries Stockenström the elder and fourteen men were killed when

[1] Ibid. v. 32, 38; Stow, pp. 198–212. [2] Moodie, *Record*, iii. 77, 79, 81–89.
[3] Ibid. v. 11; Marais, pp. 46–47.
[4] Lichtenstein, i. 242–3; Paravicini, pp. 39, 288. [5] Moodie, *Record*, iii. 24.
[6] Ibid. iii. 76. [7] Ibid. iii. 2. [8] Ibid. iii. 15, 50 n.
[9] Ibid. iii. 3. [10] Ibid. iii. 89–101. [11] Ibid. iii. 110.
[12] W. D. Hammond-Tooke, *The Tribes of the King William's Town District*, p. 103.

they were amicably smoking with a Xhosa leader.[1] 'From that day all Kafirs who resisted were shot; their kraals burnt down; and their cattle seized. No prisoners were made and the wounded and infirm were left to perish.'[2]

For nearly a century before the British took the Cape in 1795, communication between Xhosa and colonists had been growing, and the Company's government had failed to stop it. The reasons for increasing interaction were of four sorts: economic,[3] religious, aesthetic, and political. Trade began because it was profitable. The cattle trade providing fresh meat for passing ships was particularly lucrative, and farmers were constantly seeking to breach the Company's monopoly in this. The trade in ivory was likewise rich when elephant abounded and tusks might be bought for tobacco. The Xhosa, for their part, wanted metal and beads, and later blankets, and brandy, and tobacco, and above all muskets and horses. Barrow noted in 1797 that the staples of trade were copper sheets, brass wire, knives, looking-glasses, flints, tinder boxes, tobacco, and glass beads.[4]

Furthermore, employment was profitable. Farmers wanted herdsmen —they were perpetually short of servants[5]—and the Xhosa wanted the things which service with farmers could buy—particularly horses. In 1803 the Xhosa chiefs Ndlambe, Cungwa, and others told the Governor, General Janssens, that 'there could be no true peace, if people might not have intercourse with each other, besides the colonists were such rich people that they should be glad to come among them and gain a day's wages now and then'.[6] Nevertheless the prohibition on farmers employing them continued.[7]

The second reason for interaction was religious. To preach the gospel to every man, without qualification of colour, was an obligation which pressed on some, notably on the Hollander J. T. van der Kemp. Ex-army officer, medical doctor, and theologian, van der Kemp came to the Cape as a missionary of the London Missionary Society in 1799. During 1799 and 1800 he spent eighteen months with the Xhosa chief Ngqika, preaching, making a garden, and defending himself against the attacks of those who blamed him for the drought.[8] In 1801 he visited

[1] T. Pringle, *Narrative of a Residence in South Africa*, pp. 99–103.
[2] Moodie, *The History of the Battles and Adventures of the British, the Boers, and the Zulus etc.*, in *Southern Africa*, i. 186.
[3] H. M. Robertson, '150 Years of Economic contact between Black and White', *SAJE*, 2, 1934, 403–25; 3, 1935, 3–25. This paper gives a brilliant account of the growth of economic contact.
[4] Barrow, i. 197; Lichtenstein, i. 387.
[5] Moodie, *Record*, v. 10, 11; Marais, pp. 15, 17, 32.
[6] Lichtenstein, i. 386.
[7] Paravicini, pp. 97, 242; Moodie, *Record*, v. 56, 60.
[8] J. T. van der Kemp, *Transactions of the Missionary Society*, i. 374–431; Lichtenstein, i. 312.

the site where Shiloh mission was later built, and in 1803 he established a station at Bethelsdorp (near the present Port Elizabeth) where the son of a Xhosa chief, Tsatsu, came to learn. Joseph Williams, an L.M.S. missionary, set out from Bethelsdorp in 1816 to establish the first regular mission station within Xhosa country, on the Kat river,[1] and he was followed by John Brownlee, and then William Thomson, and John Bennie of the Glasgow mission, who began work in the Tyhume (Tyumie, Chumie) valley.[2] Between 1823 and 1845 a chain of seven Methodist stations was established stretching from Salem through to Palmerston in eastern Pondoland.[3]

Preaching involved learning the language, writing it, and printing the gospels, and teaching converts to read these for themselves. By 1823 there was a printing press in the Tyhume and village schools, and eighteen years later a seminary for the training of teachers at Lovedale.[4] The missionaries were among the first whites to learn Xhosa—farmers and travellers mostly used Khoikhoi or Coloured interpreters—and missionaries were the first to write the language and to teach an Nguni people to read. The shift had begun from a preliterate tribal society, isolated from the outside world, to a 'peasant society' in which some people could read and write, and which traded with towns (see vol. ii, chapter II).

The missionaries preached something else also: the gospel of work.[5] They pressed on the Xhosa the advantages of settling down as cultivators and craftsmen, in substantial houses rather than grass huts, and they begged them to wear more clothes. They made irrigation furrows[6] —almost every mission station has one, often still in use—and taught men to plough with oxen. The need for this sort of teaching was formulated by van der Kemp, though he was bitterly criticized for the 'idleness' of the Khoikhoi at Bethelsdorp,[7] and it was explicit in the work of John Brownlee, William Chalmers, John Ross, and the other Scots and Methodists who spread through Nguni country. James Stewart insisted on 'daily manual labour' for all pupils at the Lovedale seminary. 'They are engaged in making roads, cutting water-courses, constructing dams, or at work in the fields and gardens about the place. The object is not the value of their labour but the principle that Christianity and idleness are not compatible.'[8] *Men* began to cultivate, in place of

[1] B. Holt, *Life of Joseph Williams*, pp. 40–42.
[2] R. Young, *African Wastes Reclaimed*, pp. 10–12.
[3] Shaw, pp. 337–64, 468–518. [4] Young, pp. 12–13.
[5] Ibid., pp. 30–31, 82; W. C. Holden, *The Past and Future of the Kaffir Races*, pp. 420–2; Brownlee, *Reminiscences*, p. 179.
[6] Holt, p. 44; Kay, *Travels and Researches in Caffraria*, p. 421.
[7] Moodie, *Record*, v. 21; J. Philip, *Researches in South Africa*, i. 73–74, 92, 94, 99.
[8] J. Stewart, Paper read at the General Missionary Conference, London, 22 Oct. 1878, in *African Papers*, I (ed. J. Stewart).

women, and to buy clothes they had to enter employment or sell cattle, so farmers and traders viewed these missions with less disapproval than they had van der Kemp's Bethelsdorp.

The third reason for interaction was pleasure. Adventure beckoned. Young burghers rode eastward, exploring, hunting, love-making, raiding. Xhosa walked westward, as far as Cape Town, viewing the marvels of a strange culture and visiting their friends in the employment of farmers. Coenraad de Buys, a farmer, became the lover of Chief Ngqika's (Gaika's) mother,[1] who, as a widow, could choose the man with whom she lived; Ngqika claimed that de Buys had promised him a daughter in marriage.[2]

De Buys had fled to Xhosa country after participating in the rebellion in Graaff-Reinet in 1799,[3] and other Dutch farmers took refuge in the Bamboesberg. Slaves, Khoikhoi servants, deserters, and criminals continued to cross the frontier seeking to escape from their former masters or the authorities.[4] A few refugees crossed the frontier the other way also: those accused of witchcraft customarily fled to another country, and during the frontier wars Christian converts left their own people and sought security with the missionaries either on the mission stations or in the colony.[5] So refugees of one sort or another formed an important link between the two communities, white and Xhosa.

When successive governments—Dutch, British, Dutch, and again British—failed to stop interaction they sought to regulate it. Some sort of government is a condition of trade, as Sir Keith Hancock has shown, for trade depends upon a modicum of security: continuing trade compels the establishment of some sort of order.[6] Ensign Beutler was sent to negotiate with Xhosa chiefs in 1752 after illegal private trade in cattle and ivory had begun, and both the Secretary, John Barrow (in 1797), and Governor Janssens (in 1803) visited Ndlambe, Cungwa, Ngqika, and others, and discussed with them boundaries, the return of deserters, and trade,[7] as well as reiterating the demand that interaction with whites other than government officials should cease.

Reluctantly, Cape governments assumed responsibility for their frontiersmen. They tried to maintain order between groups competing for hunting and grazing lands, and to stop raiding from both sides for cattle. The Xhosa, for their part, fought bitterly to retain their land and independence, and between six and nine wars followed over a hundred years—the number depends at what point raiding and retaliation may be termed war. During this time the frontier moved

[1] Lichtenstein, i. 259, 365.
[2] Paravicini, pp. 17, 82–83, 223.
[3] Marais, pp. 98–100.
[4] Moodie, *Record*, v. 98.
[5] J. A. Chalmers, *Tiyo Soga*, pp. 36, 40, 58, 352, 373; Brownlee, pp. 26–28, 180.
[6] Hancock, ii, part II, pp. 162–72.
[7] Barrow, i. 174, 193, 195–6; Lichtenstein, i. 385–7, 397–402; Paravicini, pp. 123–7.

THE BEGINNINGS OF INTERACTION 241

eastward and the whites, who were better armed (since they traded with the outside world) and members of an organized state, conquered a people much more numerous, but ill-armed, and without any central authority. On this frontier the whites encountered, for the first time, a sedentary, or would-be sedentary, population, and one much more numerous and closely settled than the nomadic bands of San and Khoikhoi hordes who occupied the western Cape. Moreover, the Xhosa had chiefs with authority, which the Khoikhoi and San had not. Nevertheless, resistance was limited because, in the early nineteenth century, the Xhosa comprised a number of tiny independent chiefdoms which continued to split (see p. 119).

In their attempt to limit interaction between Xhosa and colonist the British Government at the Cape introduced one new technique and extended an old one. In 1817 they established a bi-annual fair for trade at Grahamstown, and Xhosa were permitted to enter the territory defined as the colony to attend it. By 1824 the fair was held thrice weekly, and it had shifted to Fort Willshire (Wiltshire) on the Keiskamma.[1] Ordinance 49 of 1828 provided for the entry of Xhosa seeking work in the colony, and the system of passes, already established by the Dutch Government for the Khoikhoi, was extended so that those Xhosa who crossed the frontier, whether to attend a fair or to seek employment with a farmer, must carry a written permission from the white officer in charge of a frontier post. Permission to employ Xhosa was of importance to frontier farmers, since their prosperity depended upon securing labour. George Thompson noted in 1826 that 'The distribution of some hundreds of refugee Mantatees among the most respectable families, as servants and herdsmen, has been a great advantage'.[2]

As already indicated, the fact which dominates the history of the frontier from 1702 onwards is the *failure* of successive white governments in their attempts to stop interaction between white colonists and black Africans. Trade between white and black Africans grew steadily; the number of blacks in white employment increased, and so did the number of missionaries at work across the frontier. It was characteristic of the eastern Cape that Xhosa women, as well as men, sought employment,[3] and missionary wives, who accompanied their husbands into Xhosa country, took Xhosa girls as household servants.[4] They also, from the very beginning, taught sewing classes, that the women might make clothes for themselves.[5] Though the total number of blacks and whites thus interacting was small, the implications were profound.

[1] Robertson, 409–10; G. M. Theal, *Records of the Cape Colony*, xviii. 179–80.
[2] Thompson, p. 349.   [3] Pringle, p. 168.
[4] Una Long, *Index to Authors of Unofficial, Privately-owned MSS., 1812–20*, London, 1947, pp. 211, 220, 234.
[5] Holt, pp. 43, 46.

After a fair at Fort Willshire was established in 1824 the price of ivory paid to the Xhosa rose steeply,[1] and by 1831 Grahamstown was exporting annually £50,000 of goods of which £27,000 was in hides and £3,000 in ivory,[2] and the Xhosa were acquiring not only the regular trade goods—blankets, beads, and metal—but also horses and guns. By 1832 there were 'traders all over Kafirland',[3] at least as far as the Mthatha (Umtata).[4] They numbered about two hundred men, and many had their families with them.[5] In 1839 it was reported that many Xhosa had obtained 'large numbers of muskets, first by smuggling and indeed now openly by traders', and were 'becoming more bold and expert in the use of them. . . .' 'Not many years ago the Kaffir . . . looked upon a horse as a strange animal which few of them would venture to mount. Now they are becoming bold horsemen, are possessed of large numbers of horses stolen from the Colony. . . .'[6] By 1846 Chief Sandile attended a meeting accompanied by about 3,000 men, 'for the most part mounted'.[7] Some of the horses the Xhosa acquired were earned: others were stolen. Stock theft remained the unresolved problem of the frontier, with raid and counter-raid embittering relationships between white and black.[8]

Enormous herds of cattle were sometimes taken and retaken, and since many families on both sides of the frontier depended largely on milk for sustenance the loss of their stock implied starvation. In 1781 the farmers' commando took herds totalling about 5,500.[9] They claimed to have lost 65,327 horned cattle, 11,000 sheep, and 200 horses.[10] In 1818 the colonial forces took 23,000 cattle from Ndlambe.[11] In 1835 over 14,000 cattle were captured by the colonial forces from the Xhosa within a month,[12] and the Governor reported that a total of 60,000 had been taken.[13] In the campaign against the Gcaleka in 1877 the booty was reported to be not less than 15,000 cattle and 20,000 sheep.[14]

The farmers who lost their stock, and whose homesteads were burnt, spoke of the Xhosa as barbarians, but warfare with them (as opposed to San hunters) was limited, and certain conventions were respected by both sides. Women and children were not intentionally killed.

[1] Long, p. 218.
[2] *South African Almanac and Directory* (compiled by G. Greig), p. 188.
[3] Long, pp. 236, 237.
[4] Andrew Smith, *Andrew Smith and Natal*, VRS, 1955, p. 15.   [5] Pringle, p. 334.
[6] *Despatches from Lieutenant Governor, 1836–66*. G.H. 8/8 No. 43, 21 Aug. 1839.
[7] Ibid. 8/15 No. 9, 31 Jan. 1846.
[8] Marais, pp. 39–63, 80, 93, 95, 97–98, 121–3, 141–3; Moodie, *Record*, iii. 91, 93, 97, 110–12; v. 57–59; Pringle, pp. 243–4, 286, 288, 293, 311–12, 353; Stockenstrom, *passim*.
[9] Moodie, *Record*, iii. 111–12.   [10] Theal, *History and Ethnography*, iii. 282.
[11] Pringle, p. 295.   [12] Moodie, *Battles*, i. 306–10.
[13] *Despatches to Secretary of State, 1833–8*, G.H. 23/11 No. 20, 7 Nov. 1835.
[14] Moodie, *Battles*, ii. 177.

THE BEGINNINGS OF INTERACTION 243

Lichtenstein wrote: 'Any one who falls unarmed into the hands of the enemy is never put to death: the women and children equally have never anything to fear for their lives; they are universally and without exception spared.'[1] The attack was on soldiers—and all men except missionaries were assumed to be fighting men—and on property. This was as true in the early eighteenth century as in 1850, when the soldier settlers in the Tyhume were killed, but their wives and children, and the missionaries together with their families, unharmed. Property was seized and mission houses burnt, but the missionaries themselves survived.[2] Even a lone pacifist in Salem was left uninjured in the bitter war of 1834–5.[3] The security of women was recognized[4] in each succeeding war. In 1880 Walter Stanford forbade W. J. Webb to go to the rescue of his wife (who had refused to leave her home), saying: 'The Xhosa and Thembus in warfare ... do not injure women and children, but you they will kill before your wife's eyes.'[5] The contrast with the total war practised in the Zulu kingdom and by the Matiwane, Ndebele, and other raiders who emanated from it is marked[6] (see pp. 98, 343).

The continuing failure of successive governments to limit interaction was reflected in changing frontier policies.[7] The first phase was one of annexation of land, expulsion of the Xhosa, and the maintenance of an unoccupied strip of 'neutral territory' separating colonist and Xhosa. As the Xhosa were pushed back the 'neutral territory' shifted, until in 1835 Sir Benjamin D'Urban annexed land as far east as the Kei, and proposed expulsion of all Xhosa living west of it. At that point a new policy was devised. It was shown that disorder was inevitable if the whites took the land occupied by a large population: that the just claims of the Xhosa had been ignored, and that annexation was costly.[8] D'Urban's annexation policy was reversed and Lord Glenelg at the Colonial Office through Andries Stockenström, entered into treaties with the Xhosa chiefs between Keiskamma and the Kei.[9] This policy also failed to achieve order, and raid and retaliation continued. The third phase was annexation and rule of the Xhosa population through their chiefs. The concern of Sir Harry Smith, after the annexation of 'Kaffraria' in 1848, and of his successors was to bridle the power of the chiefs and use them as 'agents', 'advised' by white magistrates. The shift from the

[1] Lichtenstein, i. 344; Thompson, p. 446.
[2] Chalmers, pp. 56–57; Brownlee, pp. 31–39.
[3] Moodie, *Battles*, i. 269–70; H. E. Hockly, *The Story of the British Settlers of 1820 in South Africa*, pp. 121–3.
[4] Long, p. 233.   [5] Stanford, i. 124–5.
[6] Moodie, *Battles*, i. 242.
[7] Marais, *Maynier*; J. S. Galbraith, *Reluctant Empire*; J. S. Bell and W. P. Morrell, *Select Documents on British Colonial Policy, 1830–60*; W. M. Macmillan, *Bantu, Boer and Briton*.
[8] P.P. 1836, XXXIX (quoted Bell and Morrell, pp. 463–77).
[9] Ibid. 1851, XXXVIII (quoted Bell and Morrell, pp. 477–86).

rule of hereditary chiefs to rule through paid headmen was largely achieved west of the Kei by 1858.

In addition to an unoccupied strip separating Xhosa and colonist, British Governments sought to maintain a belt of dense settlement to hold the frontier. The first such experiment was of 4,000 British settlers who were established in 1820 in Albany district to the west of the Fish river, and in the valley of one of its tributaries, the Baviaans. Grahamstown developed as their centre—administrative, commercial, and religious. These settlers encountered many difficulties: few of them were bred to farming;[1] grazing rather than cultivation was the profitable activity of the frontier, but their land grants were deliberately made too small for them to be graziers, since the aim was to establish a close settled community;[2] their first wheat crops were blighted with rust,[3] and cattle-raiding continued.[4]

War with the Xhosa broke out fourteen years after the arrival of these settlers, and three times within thirty years (1834–5; 1846–7; 1850–1) their homesteads were burned, crops destroyed, and cattle lifted.[5] But many of them stayed on the frontier, and they made a notable economic contribution in developing wool farming and trade. They were quick to establish schools, libraries, and churches, and they maintained, for a hundred years, much closer relations with the main stream of European culture than did the majority of Afrikaners. But they and their descendants also became South Africans. When they arrived they were brought to the sites allocated them in the wagons of Afrikaner frontiersmen (called out and paid for by the government),[6] and friendly relationships were established between Dutch and English-speaking farmers who, however different their background, shared common problems and a common piety. Some of the settler parties were based on identity of religious belief,[7] and, to most of them, religion was vital, as it was to the Afrikaner colonists.

Although the settlement of 1820 failed to secure the frontier, the plan of establishing close-knit groups to guard it was repeated. In 1829 a Coloured community was established in the Kat valley (see p. 248); in 1835 Mfengu were placed along the frontier from Keiskamma mouth to the Tyhume valley, and later north of the Mathole mountains (see p. 249); and in 1857 German legionaries were settled west of the Kei.

[1] Pringle, p. 110.
[2] Ibid., pp. 50–51, 220–1; Hockly, p. 85.
[3] Pringle, pp. 66, 111, 219.
[4] Ibid., pp. 233 ff., 308–9, 311; Moodie, *Battles*, i. 248–52. See also: G. M. Cory, *The Rise of South Africa*, ii. 114–15, 143–5; iii. 54–55; T. Phillips, *1820 Settler, His Letters*, passim; J. M. Bowker, *Speeches, Letters and Selections from Important Papers (1836–47)*, passim.
[5] Moodie, *Battles*, i. 248–74; ii. 6–67; Cory, iii. 63–73; v. 312–19.
[6] Pringle, pp. 22, 111.
[7] Ibid., pp. 18–19.

One of the problems of the frontier was the lawless behaviour of 'border ruffians', particularly their treatment of Coloured and African servants. The Dutch East Indian Company administration sought to deal with one such ruffian, Ferreira, by exiling him from the frontier. 'To prevent him from disturbing the peace again by cruelties that cry to high heaven, committed against the original inhabitants of the land, driving them to desperation and now disturbances, it was decided to banish him and his family from Algoa Bay, and send them to Swellendam to live there under the eye of the Landdrost.'[1] The succeeding British Government was driven to hanging five men who resisted arrest. The conflict in both cases was primarily over the treatment of Coloured servants,[2] but it was exacerbated in the second case by the rebellious burghers seeking the aid of the Xhosa chief, Ngqika.[3]

A radical disagreement with the administration over the treatment of Coloured people and Africans was one of the factors that led to the exodus of parties of Afrikaner farmers from the eastern frontier in 1836 (see pp. 310, 408). None of the English-speaking settlers trekked with the Dutch, but they wished them well, presenting Jacobus Uys' party with a Bible before they left Grahamstown,[4] and in their attitudes towards Coloured and African people many English settlers came to share the views of the Afrikaner farmers.

The administrative and military officers who negotiated with the Xhosa chiefs treated them with formal courtesy and repeatedly invited them to their tables: Governor Janssens invited Ngqika and his mother to dine with him at his table,[5] and Sir Harry Smith similarly invited Hintsa;[6] Stockenström the younger dined at a Methodist mission house with the chiefs.[7]

Intermarriage occurred: van der Kemp had 'gone among the Caffres, wearing their clothes and eating their food',[8] and he and two other L.M.S. missionaries, Read and Ullbricht, married Coloured wives;[9] two Methodist missionaries married Xhosa women,[10] and Tiyo Soga, the son of a Xhosa councillor, who was an ordained minister of the Free Church of Scotland, married a Scots woman.[11] The lineages of frontier families indicate that both marriage and concubinage of farmers

---

[1] Paravicini, p. 236.
[2] Pringle, pp. 67–77; Marais, pp. 29–32.
[3] Pringle, pp. 71–73; Marais, p. 102.
[4] Moodie, *Battles*, i. 384.
[5] Paravicini, pp. 124, 248.
[6] Harry Smith, *The Autobiography of Sir Harry Smith*, ii. 35–36.
[7] Kay, p. 255.
[8] Macmillan (quoting Philip), p. 77.
[9] J. Philip, *Researches in South Africa*, i. 137; *Transactions of the London Missionary Society*, ii. 166; iii. 199; J. du Plessis, *Christian Missions in South Africa*, p. 118.
[10] B. E. Seton, 'Wesleyan Missions and the Sixth Frontier War', unpublished Ph.D. thesis, University of Cape Town, 1962, p. 68.
[11] Chalmers, pp. 93–94.

and traders with Coloured and African women occurred.¹ Some of the offspring of these unions were absorbed into the Xhosa community; others swelled the numbers of the Coloured community on the frontier.

2. *Intermediaries*

The Khoikhoi (Hottentots) played a crucial part in the early interaction between Xhosa and white. They were the interpreters and intermediaries, for some of them could speak Xhosa. Every hunting and trading expedition of colonists, whether with riding and pack horses only, or with wagons drawn by oxen, was accompanied by Khoikhoi or Coloured servants. All the Khoikhoi were intelligible to one another, and although the Gona dialect was somewhat different they could still communicate with men from the Cape. Thunberg reported in 1773 that across the Gamtoos were 'inhabitants whose language our Hottentots now no longer perfectly understood',² but yet they communicated. The Gona, for their part, had lived in such close association with the Xhosa, from the late seventeenth century and perhaps earlier (see pp. 102–3), that some of them, at least, spoke Xhosa.³

Each of the young men of Stellenbosch who rode east in 1702 had a Khoikhoi servant with him, and it was these servants who established communication with the leaders of Khoikhoi encampments which they visited or raided. A Khoikhoi leader gave them word of the Xhosa, but there is no evidence of conversation with the Xhosa at this time, only fighting. Heupenaer's trading party in 1736 had Khoikhoi interpreters;⁴ so did Ensign Beutler in 1752, Barrow when he visited the Xhosa chief, Ngqika, in 1797, and Janssens in 1803.⁵ Van der Kemp, the first missionary to the Xhosa, preached in Dutch and his Khoikhoi servant interpreted. A number of the villagers in Bethelsdorp understood Xhosa and could translate it into Dutch. The pupils, indeed, included Jan Tsatsu, heir to the Ntinde chief, who later became interpreter to Williams, the missionary who settled with his family among the Xhosa in 1816.⁶

Khoikhoi and Coloured servants were not only cooks, herders, and labourers, wagon drivers, and interpreters; they were also, very often, fine shots and horsemen.⁷ They hunted for their masters and they were sent as soldiers on commando against San and Xhosa. In 1778 many Coloured men—'Basters'—were going to Namaqualand to avoid serving

---

¹ Personal field work.   ² Thunberg, ii. 83.
³ Sparrman, ii. 7, 29, 255–6; Thunberg, i. 203, 205; ii. 80.
⁴ Theal, *History and Ethnography*, iii. 151.
⁵ Barrow, i. 146; Lichtenstein, i. 375.
⁶ Holt, pp. 32–33, 40; Maclean, pp. 132–3.   ⁷ Pringle, p. 114.

on commando.¹ By 1808 nearly a hundred men from the village of Genadendal—with a population of about eight hundred—were serving as recruits in the Cape Regiment,² and they sometimes out-numbered whites on commando.³ In 1818 a party of Coloured buffalo-hunters from Theopolis helped to tip the balance in the battle of Grahamstown,⁴ and in 1820 it was small contingents of Coloured farm servants, and of the Cape Corps, that were sent to protect the Scots settlers on the frontier.⁵ Khoikhoi and Coloured were 'found to be by far the most efficient troops for dealing with the Kaffres'.⁶

The Khoikhoi were so important to the farmers as servants that there was bitter opposition, after the mid eighteenth century, to their living free. The conflict was most obvious on the frontier. In 1797 Barrow noted that Graaff-Reinet district had 10,000 Khoikhoi and Coloured servants, and there were 15,000 in the Colony.

> Twenty years ago, if we may credit the travellers of that day, the country beyond the Camtoos river, which was then the eastern limit of the colony, abounded with kraals or villages of Hottentots, out of which the inhabitants came to meet them by hundreds in a group. Some of these villages might still have been expected to remain in this remote and not very populous part of the colony. Not one, however, was to be found. There is not in fact in the whole extensive district of Graaff Reynet a single horde of independent Hottentots; and perhaps not a score of individuals who are not actually in the service of the Dutch.⁷

John Philip and other missionaries made themselves bitterly unpopular by their battle to establish legal rights for the Khoikhoi and Coloured, a battle which culminated in the passing of Ordinance 50 in 1828 (see pp. 304–5).

There was great fear lest the Khoikhoi and Coloured people should ally themselves with the Xhosa in the frontier wars. Between 1798 and 1802 they did so, and the combined force destroyed farm houses on the Gamtoos and down the Long Kloof.⁸ Andries Stockenström reported in 1808 that 'During the disturbances under the former English Government the Kaffirs were courageously assisted by some rebellious Hottentots who with their firearms made the conflict much more dangerous.'⁹ Colonel Collins, as a military officer, was concerned that Bethelsdorp, a mission station occupied by Khoikhoi who were mostly 'connected with the Caffres either by relationship or otherwise', was too near the frontier. Theopolis was criticized for the same reason.¹⁰ In 1847 the Xhosa chief, Maqoma, even hoped that the Coloured soldiers in the

---

¹ Moodie, *Record*, iii. 77.   ² Ibid. v. 36.   ³ Marais, p. 68.
⁴ Pringle, pp. 300–1.   ⁵ Ibid., pp. 44–45, 79.
⁶ J. W. C. Moodie, *Ten Years in South Africa*, ii. 304.
⁷ Barrow, i. 143–4.   ⁸ Pringle, pp. 251–2; Marais, pp. 105–9.
⁹ Moodie, *Record*, v. 60.   ¹⁰ Ibid. v. 20–22.

Cape Corps would deliver Fort Willshire, a frontier post, to him. He employed a Gona to communicate with them.[1] The missionary Joseph Williams was strictly limited in the number of Khoikhoi or Coloured people he might take with him when he crossed into Xhosa country to establish a mission on the Kat river in 1816, and he was scolded by the Governor for not intervening to return Khoikhoi deserters who took refuge at the mission, and with the Xhosa, from their former masters.[2]

At what point Khoikhoi merged into Coloured on the frontier is never clear. The literature refers chiefly to 'Hottentots', and only occasionally distinguishes 'Basters', but, as has been shown (p. 207), slaves often married Hottentot women, and their children, though 'apprenticed' until the age of twenty-five, became free. Whites also cohabited both with slave and with Khoikhoi women. The San captured as children and 'apprenticed' mingled with slaves, Khoikhoi, and whites, so that on farms as well as in Cape Town and the smaller 'dorps' a mixed population emerged. Their language was Afrikaans. Khoikhoi and San were spoken on the frontier in the eighteenth century, and many whites learnt one or other as children from their nurses,[3] but by 1834 Gona, the Khoikhoi dialect spoken on the frontier, was being replaced by Xhosa and Afrikaans. Boyce, a Wesleyan missionary, began a study of Gona, but abandoned it 'on account of its apparent inutility'.[4] Thomas Pringle notes that in 1820 the Dutch language was 'universally spoken by the colonial Hottentots'.[5]

In 1829 land in the Kat river valley, from which Ngqika's son, Maqoma, had been evicted, was granted to 250 Coloured and Khoikhoi families. Preference was given to property owners and men who had served in the Cape Corps. They received four- to five-acre allotments (with the possibility of an additional allocation if they made good use of what they had), and rights in common pasture. Furrows were dug to irrigate gardens, and within the second year a surplus of barley was produced. Two ministers worked among them and schools were established.[6] Despite criticism from the Colonists, the men were armed to protect themselves against Xhosa attack. For twenty years the settlement flourished, and productivity increased.[7] It reached a total of 4,000 souls with 700 muskets.[8] Then, in 1851, some of the Kat river men joined the Xhosa in their attack on the colonists,[9] and the subsequent war was bitter.

[1] Brownlee, pp. 23–24.   [2] Philip, *Researches*, ii. 176–9.
[3] Thunberg, ii. 56; Moodie, *Record*, v. 38; Sparrman, i. 243; Barrow, i. 162, 290. Cf. p. 105, n. 5 above.
[4] J. Archbell, *A Grammar of the Bechuana Language*, p. xii; Maingard, 'The Lost Tribes of the Cape', 501.   [5] Pringle, p. 48.   [6] Ibid., pp. 269–80.
[7] Macmillan, pp. 63, 71, 72 n., 90, 245, 262.
[8] Pringle, pp. 274, 278.   [9] Macmillan, p. 283.

After this Coloured and Khoikhoi people played a much smaller part on the frontier: direct contact between white and Xhosa had been established; many whites had learnt to speak Xhosa; and Mfengu refugees from Natal partly took the place of Coloured contingents as auxiliary troops. The Coloured people remained on the frontier as 'marginal men' in certain specific types of employment. A few became transport-riders with their own wagons and teams, or employed by a contractor, and they were the butchers and cleaners in all the small towns. They played an important part in the building of frontier farms and towns as independent craftsmen: sawyers (working the yellow-wood forests of Loerie, Suurberg, Alexandria, and the Kat and Tyhume valleys, and the olive wood of the Kei);[1] builders; and carpenters. They also left their mark on the social patterns established, as is shown below (p. 262).

The Mfengu were refugees, mostly from the Hlubi, Bhele, and Zizi chiefdoms of Natal, who arrived in Xhosa country from about 1822 onwards. John Ross talked to a Zizi in the Tyhume in 1824 who had been driven from his home by war seven years before,[2] and in 1825 these 'marauders' (*fecane*) defeated the Thembu near Hangklip, west of the White Kei.[3] In language and custom the Mfengu were close to the Xhosa, and they attached themselves in the customary way to wealthy men as clients. They occupied a subordinate position in Xhosa chiefdoms, but certainly were not 'slaves'[4] when, at the close of the Frontier War of 1835–6, 17,000 of them crossed the Kei at the invitation of the governor and were established in the Colony. They arrived driving 22,000 head of cattle, and were settled on land which had formerly been occupied by Xhosa.[5] The Mfengu sought a place to build in security, and graze their cattle and cultivate; the whites looked for allies and frontier guards in their long-drawn-out struggle with the Xhosa, and the Mfengu supported the whites in the wars of 1846 and 1850.[6] But since the fundamental issue was competition for land, the settlement of newcomers exacerbated the conflict rather than solved it. The War of 1878 was an attempt by the Gcaleka to regain land from which they had been ousted and which was occupied by Mfengu.

[1] Field Work, N. J. Merriman, *Cape Journals*, VRS, 1957, p. 225; Moodie, *Battles*, i. 281; Pringle, p. 96.
[2] Long, pp. 212, 216.
[3] Pringle, pp. 231–2; Thompson, pp. 208–15.
[4] T. B. Soga, *Intlalo ka Xosa*, pp. 108–10.
[5] Ayliff and Whiteside, pp. 26–34; Galbraith, p. 114; R. T. Kawa, *Ibali lama Mfengu*, passim; Maclean, p. 138; *Report and Proceedings of the Government Commission on Native Laws and Customs*, G. 4–83, 2 parts (hereafter *1883 Report*), ii. 367–77.
[6] Moodie, *Battles*, ii. 153–8.

3. *Fragmentation and Pressure on Land*

All the Nguni were organized in small chiefdoms until the end of the eighteenth century (see pp. 118–19). On the eastern Cape frontier the whites continually sought for a 'supreme chief' with whom they might negotiate, and who might be required to control all the Xhosa, but they did not find any such chief. Ngqika acknowledged the seniority of the Gcaleka chief,[1] Hintsa (see pp. 88, 118), but acted independently of him, and actually fought him over hunting lands in 1848. Ngqika was also unable to exercise effective authority over his father's brother, Ndlambe, or over the Dange, Ntinde, Gwali, Mbalu, or Gqunukwebe,[2] all of whom lived for long periods west of the Fish, and whose occupation of country Ngqika claimed (after they had been driven eastward by the whites), embittered Xhosa relationships. The Xhosa chiefs sought again and again to secure solidarity among themselves, and alliance with Thembu, Mpondo, and Sotho neighbours, but they failed in both aims.[3] Zulu, Swazi, and Sotho kingdoms were created to the east and north, and their emergence (like that of similar kingdoms elsewhere) has been related to the development of trade under control of the chief;[4] pressure on land;[5] and opposition to a common enemy (see pp. 340–1). All these factors were conspicuous on the frontier, but they did not lead to the growth of a Xhosa kingdom. Why?

The chiefdoms first on the frontier—Ntinde, Dange, Mbalu, and Gqunukwebe—were conspicuously weak. Three of the chiefs were 'right-hand' sons, who had been pushed westward, and the fourth was of commoner stock (see p. 88). Furthermore, the frontier chiefdoms were in process of absorbing the culturally different Khoikhoi,[6] who had no tradition of strong chieftainship. How far the disorder that existed in them was due to the fact that they were on a frontier on which white and Coloured graziers, such as Prinslo (white) or Ruyter (Coloured), virtually maintained their own law,[7] and how far it was due to the fact that Ntinde, Dange, Mbalu, and Gqunukwebe chiefs had never established their authority, is not clear. There certainly was a contrast between the degree of order within the frontier chiefdoms and that obtaining with the Gcaleka of the Kei, where Hintsa maintained 'perfect security of life and property without ever condemning any person to death'.[8]

---

[1] Tiyo Soga, a Ngqika, still recognized Hintsa's heir, Sarili, as 'head of the Gaikas [Ngqika] as well as the Galekas' in 1867 (Chalmers, p. 379). A word for senior chief, *ukumkani*, existed.

[2] Maclean, pp. 8–22, 162–4; Moodie, *Record*, v. 8–10; W. D. Hammond-Tooke, 'Segmentation and Fission in Cape Nguni Political Units', *Africa*, 35 (1965), 159–61.

[3] Brownlee, *Reminiscences*, pp. 129–56, 169; Stockenström, i. 115.

[4] G. Wilson, *The Constitution of Ngonde*, Rhodes–Livingstone Papers, 1939, *passim*.

[5] Gluckman, 'The Kingdom of the Zulu', p. 193.   [6] Moodie, *Record*, v. 54.

[7] Sparrman, ii. 167–8.   [8] Moodie, *Record*, v. 44.

The ruthlessness whereby potential rivals, whether adult or infant, were sometimes eliminated elsewhere,[1] was conspicuously absent among the Xhosa—there was no attempt to limit the number of living sons born to a chief, and Ngqika freed his most dangerous rival, his father's brother Ndlambe, when he was in Ngqika's power.[2] But magnanimity did not bring reward to Ngqika as it later did to Moshweshwe.

Trade was traditionally through the chiefs (see p. 122) and Ngqika exercised his right to a portion of the profit on sales at the Fort Willshire fair,[3] but whether chiefs got regular dues when many colonists came to buy cattle and ivory in 'Caffreland' is not clear. Certainly no one chief succeeded in concentrating trade in his own hands as the Kyungu did in Ngonde, and as Dingiswayo appears to have done in Natal (see p. 115). Had *one* chief acquired guns and horses when other chiefs did not, frontier history might have been very different. Ndlambe secured 'several guns' and 'a number of horses' before Ngqika, and this enabled him to defeat Ngqika in 1818,[4] but he did not retain a monopoly. The weapons and animals acquired were dispersed between seven or more chiefs, even Hintsa across the Kei obtaining them.[5] Elsewhere a chief who was already strong took control of increasing trade (as Shaka and Dingane did in Natal),[6] and this added to his strength in relation to other chiefs. What is not so clear is how one chief, an equal among others, initially got control. In Ngonde the geographical position of the Kyungu was all-important;[7] in Natal trade was canalized through two ports, first Lourenço Marques and later Port Natal (Durban); but in the eastern Cape it was dispersed. Farmers seeking cattle and ivory might cross a hundred-mile frontier anywhere between Swaershoek and Algoa Bay. The weakness of white authority on the frontier, which failed to enforce the law prohibiting private trade, itself contributed to the rivalries of Xhosa chiefs. Disorder bred disorder and in this, as in everything else, white and black reacted to one another.

After Ntinde, Dange, Mbalu, Gqunukwebe, and Ndlambe had been driven eastward over the Fish, Ngqika's chiefdom was on the frontier, and his 'right-hand' son, Maqoma, 'by all allowed to be the greatest politician and best warrior in Kaffraria' (1835),[8] came nearest to forming an effective military alliance against the whites; but he, too, failed. The chiefs did not all combine. Sarili, Hintsa's heir, in his turn sought to create unity, but he pinned his faith on the shades and brought starvation to his people (see pp. 256–9). What factors are decisive in

[1] H. Kuper, *An African Aristocracy*, p. 102; G. Wilson, p. 13.
[2] Moodie, *Record*, v. 60. [3] Steedman, i. 8–10.
[4] Thompson, p. 444. [5] Moodie, *Record*, v. 43.
[6] A. F. Gardiner, *Narrative of a Journey to the Zoolu Country*, p. 74.
[7] G. Wilson, p. 9.
[8] Maclean, pp. 129–30; Galbraith, p. 160.

creating unity is a problem that still eludes those who study the growth of government.

The Xhosa lost the greater part of their land to the whites, a little to the Coloured people, and some to the Mfengu refugees, who became allies of the whites. They fought bitterly to retain it but the inequality in arms (most Xhosa fought with spears and all whites with firearms); the fact that the whites were mounted, whereas the Xhosa mostly fought on foot; and above all the power of an organized state as opposed to fragmentary chiefdoms, outweighed superiority of numbers. Twelve thousand Xhosa warriors crossed the Fish in 1834,[1] but they were defeated within five months. After the diamond fields provided employment, from 1867 onward, Kimberley became the centre of an enormous gun trade, and many more Xhosa acquired guns,[2] but by then their power was broken, and the war of 1877 was short. On four occasions (1811, 1819, 1835, 1850) war began about the summer solstice, the season of the year at which a raid on a neighbouring chiefdom commonly took place in independent Nguni chiefdoms, and traditional custom as well as military considerations may have affected the *timing* of Xhosa attacks.[3] The frontier wars, however, differed from the raids described in oral tradition, or early records, in that they were more prolonged and more devastating. The Xhosa were fighting not *primarily* for booty, but for survival as an independent people.

During a hundred years the boundary shifted eastward, and sometimes (notably in 1822, 1854, and 1864) it was suspected that war was fomented by whites seeking farms.[4] Outbreak of war can be linked to drought when the farmers looked to the better-watered eastern areas and the Xhosa were most conscious of land shortage.[5] In 1772 some Xhosa, mingled with Khoikhoi, were living on the Gamtoos;[6] in 1806 the boundary was the Fish, and in 1811 Ndlambe, with 20,000 followers, was pushed across it. In 1819 the country between the Fish and the Keiskamma was declared neutral; by 1824 it was partly occupied by whites. In 1847 the boundary shifted to the Kei; in 1858 to the Mbashe (Bashee); in 1878 to the Mthatha; and in 1894 Pondoland, between the Mthatha and Mtamvuna, was annexed (map 3). East of the Kei little land was allocated to whites; west of it the greater part fell to them.[7] Some farms were occupied by newly arrived British and German

[1] Moodie, *Battles*, i. 227.
[2] A. Wilmot, *History of the Zulu War*, p. 37.
[3] Kuper, *African Aristocracy*, pp. 201, 225; E. J. Krige, *The Social System of the Zulus*, p. 267; Hunter, *Reaction to Conquest*, pp. 404–6; Moodie, *Battles*, i. 367.
[4] Pringle, pp. 309–10; J. Rutherford, *Sir George Grey*, pp. 309–10; Chalmers, pp. 305–9.
[5] Macmillan, pp. 245–7, 281–2.
[6] Thunberg, i. 203–4.
[7] Walker, pp. 153, 155, 286, 372, 433; F. Brownlee (ed.), *The Transkeian Native Territories: Historical Records*, pp. 1–80.

settlers (see pp. 280-3), and some by colonists who had long coveted the good grazing land occupied by the Xhosa.

Such a history of dispossession on a frontier by settlers better armed and organized is not unique. A 'Trail of Tears' forms part of the history of many nations,[1] and dispossession had, indeed, already occurred in South Africa as Bantu-speakers pressed on San.[2] What distinguished the Xhosa was that they did not diminish in numbers as the Khoikhoi and San and other preliterate people have done in defeat. They were probably already increasing before interaction with whites began, and they continued to increase.

The history of the splitting of chiefdoms and the distribution of graves of successive chiefs indicate that Nguni people were spreading towards the coast and westward during the sixteenth, seventeenth, and eighteenth centuries, and it is likely (though we have no direct evidence) that, in spite of the wide spacing of children (p. 126), the population was growing. Lichtenstein wrote of the Xhosa in 1806: '. . . an increasing population is very often a cause of their wars: it creates a want of increase of territory, and that leads to encroachments upon their neighbours, which the latter must resist.'[3] Such increase may have been linked to the introduction of a new crop, maize, which had been grown in Pondoland from at least 1790 and probably before 1635 (see p. 109). Maize matures in five months, while sorghum (as grown by Xhosa and Sotho) takes eight to nine,[4] and maize is not devastated by birds as sorghum is, so larger yields may have encouraged growth of population. A shift to maize may also have caused more frequent movement, since maize planted continuously leaches the soil faster than sorghum. The Nguni economy presupposed ample land, and where that existed fields and pastures remained in good heart, because when productivity fell, a field was abandoned and cattle moved to new pastures. Sparrman noted as early as 1785 the adverse effects on Cape pastures of continuous grazing, and contrasts the practice of white farmers with the less destructive use by the Khoikhoi.

In direct contradiction to the custom and example of the original inhabitants, the Hottentots, the colonists turn their cattle out continually into the same fields, and that too in a much greater quantity than used to graze there in the time of the Hottentots; as they keep not only a number sufficient for their own use but likewise enough to supply the more plentiful tables . . . of Cape Town . . . as well as for the victualling of ships. . . .

In consequence of the fields being thus continually grazed off . . . grasses and herbs . . . are prevented . . . from thriving . . . the rhinoceros bush which the cattle always pass by and leave untouched is suffered to take root. . . .[5]

[1] B. de Voto, *The Course of Empire*, passim. [2] Stow, pp. 232-48. [3] Lichtenstein, i. 302.
[4] Ellenberger and Macgregor, *History of the Basuto*, p. 255; direct observation.
[5] Sparrman, i. 267-8.

The same thing happened as the Xhosa population grew more dense. The unoccupied belts between chiefdoms, to which reference has been made (p. 85), were used as hunting lands, and as these strips shrank in size so the game diminished. Barrow noted in 1799 that there was almost no game left in the Suurveld, where white and black both hunted,[1] though twenty-five years earlier, when Sparrman travelled through the same area,[2] there were great herds of buck; as well as buffalo, rhinoceros, and lion. Alberti notes that by 1802–6 buck were scarce east of the Kei, though still plentiful between Kei and Keiskamma.[3] By 1833 game was 'exceedingly scarce' in 'Kafferland'.[4] The rapid disappearance of game in the nineteenth century made the dependence of the Xhosa on other foods increasingly greater. Sparrman, who advocated the domestication of indigenous animals, was then a voice crying in the wilderness: 'The animals which occur only in Africa are, in my opinion, as much designed for the plants peculiar to this climate as the plants are for the animals. . . . The African colonists ought to take it into serious consideration whether by extirpating the game they are not in reality laying waste their country.'[5] One of the effects of heavy grazing by cattle, and the disappearance of elephant and various types of buck which were browsers, was the increase in scrubby bush as opposed to grass.[6] The elephant fed on mimosa roots, and uprooted the bushes.[7]

There was another factor, however, more important than any new crop, the destruction of game, or even the loss of land. In South Africa during the nineteenth century a condition that stringently limits population disappeared: isolation, in any absolute sense, ceased. Communications were established over a wide area, so that drought or flood in one part of the country did not *necessarily* mean starvation for its inhabitants. So long as a group remains isolated, starvation follows ill weather, unless it can migrate; once wider communication has been established, the corn of Egypt may supply the need of Israel, and men multiply. In the catastrophe of 1857 about a fifth of the Xhosa population died, in spite of some supplies coming from the Colony (see p. 258); but since then acute periods of shortage have been mitigated by supplies from outside.

The early estimates of population were almost certainly too low. Van der Kemp, on the basis of the homesteads he had seen, estimated

---

[1] Barrow, i. 187; cf. Pringle, pp. 27, 79, 91–92, 109.
[2] Sparrman, ii. 80–84, 90–96.
[3] L. Alberti, *Description physique et historique des Caffres*, pp. 23–24.
[4] Kay, p. 134; J. W. C. Moodie, *Ten Years in South Africa*, ii. 269.
[5] Sparrman, i. 269–70; Moodie, *Record*, v. 32.
[6] The increase in bush is reported by the Hon. Mr. C. M. van Coller, Mr. E. H. Matthews, and others in the eastern Cape. Verbal communications.   [7] Pringle, p. 124.

FRAGMENTATION AND PRESSURE ON LAND 255

the Xhosa west of the Kei at 38,400 'male inhabitants' in 1800.[1] Colonel Collins, writing in 1809, thought this 'little less than the total amount of all description of inhabitants', and he estimated Hintza's people between the Kei and the Mbashe at 10,000.[2] Fifteen years later Thompson estimated all the Xhosa from the Keiskamma and Tyhume to 'the river Bashi or St. John' at 100,000 souls[3]—twice Collins's estimate. In 1848 Colonel Maclean took a detailed census of the Xhosa west of the Kei, and on that basis, along with other information, estimated the Ngqika (including Ndlambe's people) at 70,000, and the Gcaleka (between Kei and Mbashe) at 70,000, nearly half as much again as Thompson's estimate. In addition, Maclean estimated the Thembu at 70,000, and Steedman put Faku's immediate followers among the Mpondo at not less than 20,000.[4] The differences are probably due to increasing accuracy in estimation as well as increasing population.

Thompson's estimates of population and area give seven persons to the square mile; and he wrote of the Xhosa:

Having been recently dispossessed of the territory between the Keiskamma and the Fish River, their kraals are now crowded upon one another, in such a manner that there is scarcely sufficient pasture for their cattle; and, unless they borrow from the Colony the advantage of an improved mode of agriculture, famine must occasionally prevail, till their numbers are again reduced to the limits which the country can support on their present system. Until some such change takes place, it will perhaps scarcely be practicable even by an improved system of defence, altogether to repress depredations upon the Colony.[5]

Grey estimated the population of Kaffraria at 33·5 to the square mile in 1855; Godlonton at 10.[6] King William's Town District was overcrowded and overstocked.[7] By 1865 the Mfengu locations west of the Kei were also crowded, and 30,000 to 40,000 Mfengu were settled on land from which Sarili had been driven, between the Kei and Mbashe.[8] Beyond the Mbashe 'The whole country was dotted with small villages, as far as the eye could see, tier above tier of Kafir huts on every hillside', and Sarili was complaining bitterly of being crowded.[9] In 1875 the Gcaleka were estimated at 60,000, the Thembu at 70,000, the Bomvana at 20,000, and all the Mpondo at 200,000.[10]

[1] Van der Kemp, i. 435. [2] Moodie, *Record*, v. 8, 42.
[3] Thompson, p. 196.
[4] Maclean, pp. 142-4. Dugmore's estimate of Xhosa and Thembu together was 300,000, as opposed to Maclean's 210,000 (ibid., p. 7); A. Steedman, *Wanderings and Adventures in the Interior of Southern Africa*, ii. 268.
[5] Thompson, p. 196.
[6] *Correspondence between H.E. Sir George Grey and Secretary of State for the Colonies, 1855-7*, p. 155.
[7] CGH Blue Book on *Native Affairs, 1875*, G. 21-'75, p. 59.
[8] W. Govan, *Memorials of the Rev. James Laing*, p. 250; Brownlee, *Reminiscences*, p. 172.
[9] Chalmers, pp. 304-5. [10] Blue Book on *Native Affairs, 1875*, G. 21-'75, p. 131.

The density of population in areas occupied by whites was much lower, as Thompson noted: 'Xhosa country is far more densely peopled than any district of the Colony or than even the Bechuana country.'[1] Frontier farms to support one white family were 6,000 acres in size—over nine square miles—and they lacked labourers to work them. As their land shrank, Xhosa were driven into still closer association with whites. The one commodity they had to sell was their labour.

4. *The Pagan Reaction*

The pagan reaction to military defeat, loss of land, growing pressure of population, and penetration by Christian churches and schools was to seek supernatural aid. The Xhosa turned to their shades. They listened to diviners or 'prophets' who urged purification from witchcraft and sacrifice to the shades. In the War of 1819 Makanda ('Makanna' or Nxele), a diviner, was the Xhosa leader. He led 9,000 or 10,000 men in an attack on Grahamstown, and, that having failed, he gave himself up. His return was long awaited, though he was drowned when trying to escape from the prison on Robben Island in 1820.[2] In the 1840s a young man, Mlanjeni, built up a reputation as a witch-finder and pressed men to purge themselves of witchcraft and sorcery. He commanded the sacrifice of dun- and cream-coloured cattle throughout Xhosa country. He received deputations from Faku and Moshweshwe.[3] Finally, he convinced men that he, the war-doctor (*itola*)[4] had power to make them invulnerable, to fill the white men's guns with water, and to drive the whites out of the country, provided that each Xhosa warrior would sacrifice to his shades and wear the medicines he gave him.[5] All this was strictly in accordance with traditional custom: purification from witchcraft; sacrifice to the shades; and the treatment of the army by a war-doctor were part of the ancient system of ritual and belief. Mlanjeni was discredited in the War of 1851–3 but the ideas he preached lived on.

Rumours of the Crimean War were current in Xhosa country from 1854, and 'the remark was frequently made: "The Russians are black people like ourselves, and they are coming to assist us to drive the English into the sea." '[6] In March 1856 Mhlakaza, councillor of the Xhosa Chief, Sarili, was told by Nongqause, his brother's daughter,

---

[1] Thompson, p. 196.
[2] Theal, *History of South Africa from 1795–1872*, i. 329–41; Pringle, pp. 296–307; Moodie, *Battles*, i. 196–200; Thompson, pp. 36, 445.
[3] Brownlee, *Reminiscences*, p. 169.
[4] J. H. Soga, *The Ama-xosa, Life and Customs*, p. 173.
[5] Chalmers, pp. 51–54; Brownlee, *Reminiscences*, p. 169; Govan, p. 119.
[6] Chalmers, p. 102.

that she had 'seen strange people and cattle'.¹ On going to investigate he 'was directed by these strangers to return to his kraal, to purify himself for three days, and on the fourth to offer an ox in sacrifice and then return to them'. He did so, and on his return saw a number of black people among whom he recognized his brother some years dead. He was told by these people that they had come from across the water; that they were the people—the Russians—who had been fighting against the English with whom they would wage perpetual warfare; and they had now come to aid the Kafirs, but before anything could be done for them they were to put away witchcraft, and as they would have abundance of cattle at the coming resurrection, those now in their possession were to be destroyed.²

Mhlakaza was a man of importance, 'the most renowned of Kafir seers',³ who was 'looked upon very much as Mlanjeni'⁴ had been. Girls who saw visions were taken seriously in Xhosa society; they became initiated as diviners and filled an accepted role. Moreover it was customary that a novice should be supervised by a senior diviner as Nongqause was by Mhlakaza. Much of her vision was in familiar idiom. She saw 'the horns of beautiful oxen peeping from beneath the rushes'⁵—in Xhosa myth men and cattle emerged from a bed of rushes —and the insistence on purification, on renouncing witchcraft, and on sacrifice was all part of a traditional pattern. Witchcraft was thought of as the cause of death: once it was destroyed men were immortal,⁶ and sacrifices nourished the shades.

But it was sacrifice with a difference: men were bidden to kill *all* their cattle; to destroy their grain; and to refrain from sowing. If they did so, Nongqause (and others who prophesied confirming her message)⁷ said the heroes would rise and the living be restored to youth; the choicest of English cattle would fill the byres; the grain pits would overflow; wagons, clothes, guns, and ammunition would appear in abundance; and a great wind would sweep the whites into the sea.⁸ Some of the heroes had been 'seen' on horseback—the Chief Sarili

---

¹ Information is drawn from the official report of Charles Brownlee, who was the administrator most immediately concerned, and very close to the people (Chalmers, p. 293); from an account written by his wife; from Revd. A. Kropf of the Berlin Mission, the author of a superb Xosa dictionary; and from comments of Tiyo Soga, who returned from Scotland as an ordained minister during the famine. Tiyo's father was a Xhosa councillor who opposed the killing. Kropf's and Soga's comments and Mrs. Brownlee's account in its fullest form appear in Chalmers. There is no record from anyone who favoured the movement.
² Brownlee, *Reminiscences*, pp. 128-9.
³ Chalmers, p. 103; Brownlee, *Reminiscences*, p. 126.
⁴ Chalmers, p. 109.   ⁵ Ibid., p. 105.
⁶ Moodie, *Record*, i. 427; Chalmers, p. 104.
⁷ CGH, *Annexures to Votes and Proceedings of the House of Assembly, 1858*, G. 5-'58, p. 1.
⁸ Chalmers, pp. 103-4.

himself had a vision of a famous horse, long dead.[1] Unbelievers would be destroyed with the whites, and for the Mfengu (see p. 249) 'there was no message'. They were like white men.[2]

The prophecies created bitter conflict between chiefs, between chief and councillor, and in families. Sarili, the senior Xhosa chief, pressed men to obey; Sandile his junior was hesitant, while Sandile's mother, Sutu, aged about seventy, urged him on, saying: 'It is all very well for you, Sandilli; you have your wives and children; but I am solitary: I am longing to see my husband, and you are keeping him from rising and me from being restored to all the freshness and vigour of a blooming maiden.'[3]

Charles Brownlee sought desperately to stop the killing. He scoured the countryside on horseback, urging wisdom, and earned the name *Napakade*—'Never'—from his reiterated reply to the prophecies.[4] He bought up what grain he could—1,000 bags—but it was against the prophet's orders for the Xhosa to sell either grain or cattle: they should sacrifice all. The money they got from selling hides and horns was spent forthwith on coffee and sugar.[5]

In October it was announced that all cattle must be killed within eight days, and on the eighth day the dead would rise. When prophecy proved false the unbelievers who had not killed were blamed, and further slaughter went on. At least 150,000 to 200,000 cattle were killed.[6] By February 1857 the whole countryside was starving. Relief was provided at a number of mission stations, at the newly established Grey hospital in King William's Town, and in frontier towns like Grahamstown. The Bishops of Cape Town and Grahamstown organized a 'Kafir Assistance Society' to distribute food and nurse the sick.[7] Thousands of families moved into the Colony to take employment with whites, while others scattered among their neighbours to the east and north who had not killed.[8] The population of certain chiefdoms between the Kei and Fish was estimated to have dropped from 104,721 in January 1857 to 37,697 in December[9]—a loss of over 67,000. Brownlee estimated that of these 20,000 had died, and 30,000 moved into the Colony for employment.[10] Some went as migrant labourers and returned. Others settled on farms of the eastern Cape, and their descendants have remained there as farm servants ever since.[11] Nongqause herself was said to be living on a farm in Alexandria District in 1905.[12]

[1] Brownlee, *Reminiscences*, p. 127.
[2] Ibid., p. 140.
[3] Chalmers, pp. 113, 142.
[4] Brownlee, *Reminiscences*, p. 127.
[5] Chalmers, pp. 112-13, 119.
[6] Brownlee, *Reminiscences*, p. 138.
[7] Rutherford, p. 369.
[8] Chalmers, pp. 123-8, 138, 142-4, 373.
[9] Maclean, Table opp. p. 164.
[10] Brownlee, *Reminiscences*, p. 138.
[11] Hunter, p. 505.
[12] Stanford, i. 5; Soga, *South Eastern Bantu*, p. 247, says she died in King William's Town in 1897.

The question the whites all asked was: 'Is this a deep-laid plot to bring about war?' Brownlee thought at the time that it was. He noted that there was no public discussion—no debate in Sarili's council—as there should have been on a matter of public importance, before Sarili began killing, and that Sarili was alleged to have said 'Everyone will fight now'.[1] Nonkosi, a little girl of nine, who prophesied near Fort Murray, was said to have been put up to doing so on the orders of Chief Umhala.[2] Many of the Thembu were involved also, and messages came and went to Moshweshwe in Lesotho, and Faku in Pondoland.[3] The prophecies coincided with crisis in Lesotho, and the governor believed the two to be linked. Walker assumes that a 'plot' was proved.[4] But Brownlee himself began to doubt as years passed and no evidence of a concerted plan emerged,[5] and Stanford was sceptical of any plan for invasion.[6] Horses—so important in war—were not killed, but Tiyo Soga noted that guns and assagais were sold to whites and Mfengu, along with ornaments.[7]

Some writers are now asking whether it was a white plot to destroy Xhosa military power, whether the 'strangers' whom Nongqause saw were sent by whites.[8] For that there is absolutely no evidence, and a close study of Brownlee suggests that he was indeed a man of integrity who battled to save a people he loved from self-destruction. Tiyo Soga thought that rumours of war were spread by land-hungry whites who wished to precipitate war (see p. 252), but neither he nor any other eyewitness of the period has suggested that Mhlakaza was a tool of any whites.

The similarities between the 'cattle-killing' and happenings elsewhere indicate that it was a spontaneous reaction rather than one deliberately manipulated by any person. In South Africa there is a popular belief, curiously enough, still repeated by serious historians,[9] that the 'cattle-killing' was a unique event. It was not. It was foreshadowed by the sacrifices made on Mlanjeni's order, and followed by a movement in Zululand and Natal during 1905–6,[10] and by the Wellington movement in the Transkei in 1921, when men were ordered to destroy all pigs and white fowls, and they looked for salvation from American aeroplanes manned by negroes.[11] It has been paralleled again and again elsewhere.

[1] Brownlee, pp. 128, 140–2. [2] CGH, *Annexures*, G. 5–'58, pp. 4–5.
[3] G. M. Theal, *Basutoland Records*, ii. 184, 229–31, 247–8.
[4] Walker, p. 289. [5] Brownlee, *Reminiscences*, p. 142.
[6] Stanford, i. 5. [7] Chalmers, p. 142.
[8] Mnguni, *Three Hundred Years*, pp. 87–88; N. Majeke, *The Role of the Missionaries in Conquest*, p. 73.
[9] A. E. du Toit, 'The Cape Frontier', in *AYB*, 1954, p. 99.
[10] J. Stuart, *A History of the Zulu Rebellion, 1906, and of Dinizulu's Arrest, Trial and Expatriation*.
[11] Hunter, pp. 570–2.

Three outstanding features of the cattle-killing were purification from witchcraft, chiliastic expectations, and the destruction of wealth *in order that* the millennium might come. The millennium implied the resurrection of the dead and the disappearance of death; a return to youth for the living; wealth without labour for the elect; and the destruction of unbelievers and foreigners. Witch-finding movements have recurred repeatedly in Europe and America as well as in Africa, and millenary expectations with the hope of resurrection, lasting youth, wealth, and justice are similarly widespread. Woroka, prophet of the American Indian 'Ghost Dance' in 1889, promised his followers much what Nongqause promised.[1] What is less common is the destruction of property in order to bring about the millennium, but this also has occurred repeatedly in Melanesia. In the 'Cargo Cults' property has been destroyed and cultivation abandoned in the expectation that the heroes would live again; the righteous and the damned be separated; youth be renewed for the faithful; and plentiful cargoes arrive.[2] Perhaps the self-flagellation that was explicitly undertaken in medieval Europe to hasten the millennium[3] was comparable to the sacrifice of cattle and pigs in other places at other times.

The cattle-killing was clearly, in one aspect, a 'resistance movement', in which people participated in the hope of getting rid of the whites and recovering their land. It was also a 'revivalist' movement involving purification from witchcraft; and it was a fusion of old and new religious ideas. The symbolism was rooted both in ancient notions of the shades and revelation through diviners, and in Christian teaching of the apocalypse.[4]

5. *Civilization by Mingling*

After the devastating war of 1850–3,[5] and rule by a governor who was a soldier—Sir Harry Smith—a new governor arrived with other ideas. Sir George Grey had also begun his career as a soldier, but he had been horrified by his early experience of collecting tithes by military force, and searching for stills among Irish peasants who were landless and bitterly poor. He had experimented in New Zealand with a policy of 'civilizing' rather than fighting the indigenous inhabitants, and he sought to apply that policy to the South African frontier.[6]

---

[1] J. Mooney, 'The Ghost Dance Religion of the Sioux Outbreak of 1890', in *Fourteenth Annual Report of the Bureau of Ethnology to the Smithsonian Institute, 1892–93*, passim; L. P. Mair, 'Independent Religious Movements', *Comparative Studies in Society and History*, vol. i, no. 2, 1959, 113–36; S. L. Thrupp (ed.), *Millennial Dreams in Action*.

[2] P. Worsley, *The Trumpet shall Sound*, pp. 52–54, 99, 111, 139, 151, 154–5, 167, 202, 213–15.   [3] N. Cohn, *In Pursuit of the Millennium*, p. 135 ff.

[4] M.-L. Martin, *The Biblical Concept of Messianism and Messianism in Southern Africa, passim*.

[5] Godlonton and Irving, *passim*.   [6] Rutherford, pp. 6, 221–87.

Schools had begun in Xhosa country more than thirty years before his arrival (see p. 239): Grey nourished the existing school at Lovedale with grants of money and land, providing for an industrial department, with instruction in the trades most urgently needed on the frontier: wagon-making, blacksmithing, masonry, printing, and bookbinding.[1] He established the principle, new in African education, that the government might pay teachers' salaries,[2] and he also provided the money for missionaries to start new schools at Healdtown, St. Matthew's, St. Mark's, Salem, Peelton, Mount Coke, and in Grahamstown. Three of these offered industrial or agricultural training,[3] and one school, Lovedale, continued it for a century.

Lovedale was a mixed school. It started in 1841 with eleven Africans and nine whites,[4] and it deliberately continued mixed until 1926. In 1878 James Stewart wrote: 'The institution is non-sectarian and undenominational, though it is supported financially by the Free Church of Scotland. All colours, white and black, and brown and yellow, are to be found among the pupils. These represent nearly all the tribes of South Africa. There are Kafirs, Fingoes, Hottentots, Pondos, Bechuanas, Basutos, Zulus, English, and Dutch.'[5] Lovedale was not peculiar in this: Zonnebloem began with white, Coloured, and African pupils; in the western Cape it was common for the poorer white children to attend mission schools along with Coloured children; and mixed schools were tolerated even in Bedford and Uitenhage on the frontier and, for a time, in Ugie. In 1883 there were 6,000 whites in the same class rooms as 32,000 Coloured children, and in 1891 a third of the total number of white children at school in the Cape Colony attended mission schools in which there was no colour bar.[6] More than one mission school in Natal was mixed. Backhouse visited Swellendam in 1838 and found there a flourishing 'school for white and coloured children', and an African librarian who, 'having received the advantages of a civilized education', was 'as competent in his post as if he had been born in civilized society'.[7] Even the Theological Seminary at Stellenbosch (with a Scots professor) admitted one or two non-whites, including an African, Daniel Gezani.[8]

[1] J. Stewart, *Lovedale Past and Present*, p. ix.
[2] Govan, p. 155; Rutherford, p. 320.
[3] Ibid., pp. 318-20; Holden, pp. 447-9.
[4] Stewart, *Lovedale*, p. viii; Govan, pp. 74-75.
[5] J. Stewart, *General Missionary Conference*, pp. 8-9.
[6] D. Ross, *Preliminary Report of the State of Education in the Cape of Good Hope*, G. 12. '83, 1883, p. 11; *Education Commission 1892: First Report*, G. 9. '91, pp. 151-2; CGH, *Report of Sup. Gen. of Educ.*, Cape Town, 1910, p. 6. My attention was drawn to this material by a former colleague, Mr. Graham Watson. J. Backhouse, *Narrative of a Visit to the Mauritius and South Africa*, p. 169.
[7] Backhouse, pp. 105-6.
[8] J. Mackinnon, *South African Traits*, pp. 60-68.

The schools were mixed, not only in the sense that they included different racial groups, but also in that they accepted girls as well as boys, and the girls willingly came to school. This can only be understood in relation to the position of women in South African society. On farms and villages in the Colony female slaves, and Khoikhoi or Coloured women, either 'apprenticed' or free, worked as domestic servants, and in Xhosa country, as nowhere else in black Africa, women as well as men took employment with whites. Sometimes this was under duress,[1] but often it was of choice. From the early nineteenth century domestic work was done on the frontier by Xhosa women rather than Xhosa men.[2] This was possible partly because the marriage age of Xhosa girls was well after puberty—not before it, as in parts of Africa—but it was also encouraged by the pattern of Khoikhoi and Coloured women before them. The implications were profound. When mission schools were established girls attended:[3] Backhouse found seventy-five females and fifty-four males in school in the Tyhume in 1839,[4] and girls with some education found ready employment, first as domestics, then as teachers, and later as nurses, and in industry. By 1868 the seminary at Lovedale had ten girls as boarders,[5] and two of the new schools for which Grey provided were girls' boarding schools,[6] so the disparity between the education of men and of women, which has been so marked in East, Central, and West Africa never emerged. Because education for girls led to jobs, parents were less reluctant to send their daughters to school than they were elsewhere, and the girls themselves early grew to value education as a means to earning. The contrast was apparent in Livingstonia (Malawi), where the same mission as that in Lovedale, even when working among Ngoni people (see p. 99), had considerable difficulty in establishing women's education above the elementary level.[7] Where boys are occupied as herders girls may have more leisure to attend school than their brothers, but it does not necessarily follow that they will do so. Among various cattle-keepers in Central Africa boys far outnumbered the girls in school before 1939. Boys would work in shifts or combine herds to enable them to attend school, while their sisters gossiped at home.[8] Mixed schools contributed much to South Africa, and Lovedale in particular includes on its register of past students men and women, both white and black, who laboured to build a civilized society.[9] It includes teachers and nurses, academics and administrators, clergymen and medical doctors, a

---

[1] Pringle, p. 15.   [2] Long, pp. 214, 220.   [3] Ibid., p. 217; Govan, p. 60.
[4] Backhouse, p. 212.   [5] Stewart, *Lovedale*, p. 397.   [6] Rutherford, pp. 319-20.
[7] According to Dr. Agnes Frazer, it was easier to get Ngoni than girls of other language groups to continue with schooling. Personal communication.
[8] Hunter, pp. 175, 177; Wilson, *Good Company*, p. 56.
[9] Stewart, *Lovedale, passim*.

Minister of Agriculture, a General Manager of de Beers, a judge, and two Chief Justices of South Africa. Lovedale attracted pupils—white as well as black—because it provided such a good education. The founder, William Govan, and his successors cherished academic standards, and already in 1878 Stewart was talking of the possibility of a university.[1]

Besides providing for frontier schools Grey brought forty sons of chiefs to Cape Town to be educated at Zonnebloem (started by Bishop Gray), and maintained them for some months at his own expense; he also founded schools in Port Elizabeth and Bloemfontein for white boys.

Sir George Grey not only encouraged schools, but he provided for a hospital at King William's Town which, under an inspired and devoted superintendent, J. P. Fitzgerald, had seven hundred cases a month within two years of its establishment. It accommodated both white and African, who were treated identically,[2] and Fitzgerald (unlike most whites) was careful to cultivate traditional diviners whom he received as 'colleagues', and invited to view his hospital.[3] He had worked with Grey in New Zealand and had treated the Maori also as intelligent human beings.[4]

Settled farming by Africans was encouraged in every possible way. Ploughs and irrigation furrows first introduced on mission stations were fostered by the administration.[5] Charles Brownlee, the administrator, who worked very closely with Grey, even bought sheep at his own expense to distribute among the Xhosa, because he believed that with sheep they would be less mobile, and therefore less inclined for war, than as cattle owners. They could not 'fly about with sheep'.[6] By 1863 four Africans in Glen Grey District owned 1,400 sheep.[7] Individual, as opposed to communal, tenure was established in a number of areas west of the Kei occupied by Africans,[8] and the holdings of white and black were deliberately mingled.[9] Many Africans were reluctant to take up individual tenure, and those who did so, and their heirs, tended to treat the land as a lineage holding rather than as individual property,[10] but the legal principle of individual holding was established.

The power of the Xhosa chiefs had diminished with successive defeats and loss of land. The Mfengu refugees who had been settled in the Colony in 1835 were broken remnants of people without hereditary chiefs of their own, though certain leaders were recognized and established as headmen.[11] Individual tenure, as opposed to communal tenure,

---

[1] Stewart, *General Missionary Conference, passim*, p. 14.   [2] Rutherford, p. 323.
[3] Ibid., p. 323.   [4] Ibid., pp. 216–18.   [5] Shaw, p. 419; Young, p. 47.
[6] Brownlee, p. 9.   [7] Chalmers, p. 262.   [8] *1883 Report*, ii. 366–79.
[9] M. E. Elton-Mills and M. Wilson, *Land Tenure*, vol. iv of *Keiskammahoek Rural Survey*, p. 3.
[10] Ibid., pp. 50–58.
[11] Chalmers, pp. 320–1.

involved a further diminution in chiefly power, because a freeholder or quit-rent holder was not dependent on any leader for land, in the way in which those who shared communal tenure were dependent.¹ Mission land might also lie outside the jurisdiction of chiefs, and this was a burning issue.²

Grey deliberately set out to diminish the power of the chiefs by persuading them to take salaries in place of their right to court fines, and by appointing paid headmen to serve as a police force.³ In his policy of destroying chieftainship he had the support of at least some of his subordinate administrators. J. C. Warner, the Government 'agent' stationed among the Thembu, wrote in 1856:

the political and religious governments of the Kaffir tribes are so intimately connected, that the one cannot be overturned without the other,—they must stand or fall together.... As so many untoward events have happened in our intercourse with these people, and so many clashing interests now exist; and as the Kaffir tribes have now become so thoroughly imbued with hatred to the 'white man', and appear so resolutely determined on his destruction, or to lose their political existence in the struggle, and above all as they have so resolutely and so perseveringly refused to give to the Gospel even an attentive hearing, it seems to me that the sword must first ... break them up as tribes, and destroy their political existence; after which, when thus set free from the shackles by which they are bound, civilization and Christianity will no doubt make rapid progress among them....⁴

The chiefs in fact never fully recovered their power after the cattle-killing of 1857, and Grey seized the opportunity to increase the power of the magistrates;⁵ nevertheless, as late as 1878 the Revd. John Buchanan reported:

The evils of the old traditional policy of maintaining and subsidizing the chiefs within the colonial territory having at last culminated in the miserable war now raging, the whole Cape Colony seems to be inspired with one over-mastering wish and determination to have no more of this mischievous mixture of authorities—, this *imperium in imperios*,—but to have the whole population of the country placed, as speedily and as thoroughly as possible, under one law and one administration.⁶

Other missionaries and their sons held similar views.⁷

In the traditional society the centre of social life as well as of government was the 'great place', the capital. A chief had a number of homesteads in different parts of his country, and all of them were social and

¹ Elton-Mills and Wilson, p. 134.　　　　² Chalmers, p. 372.
³ Rutherford, pp. 333–6, 356.　　　　⁴ Maclean, pp. 103–6.
⁵ Rutherford, pp. 380–1.
⁶ J. Buchanan, 'Lovedale, South Africa', Report in Free Church General Assembly, May 1878, *African Papers*, i (ed. J. Stewart), n.d., 19.
⁷ Holden, pp. 436–40; Hahn, *Tsuni-//Goam*, p. 76.

CIVILIZATION BY MINGLING 265

administrative centres, but the capital was pre-eminent. Gradually, in the nineteenth century, the centre of activity shifted to the trading and administrative centres established by whites, and the mission schools and churches. The small market towns and the traders' stores became the centres at which people gathered to gossip and see their friends as well as transact business,[1] and the school and church became a focus for those who accepted a new way of life. Mission stations were burned again and again during the frontier wars, but the missionaries themselves were not attacked and they persistently returned. Converts repeatedly refused to fight on the Xhosa side, and some took refuge with missionaries.[2] They were caught between two loyalties: one to their own chiefs and communities, and the other to the white missionaries who taught them. Tiyo Soga found himself pressed to read for his chief messages captured from white soldiers, and this he refused to do.[3] Brownlee reported that during the war of 1850–3 1,500 from mission stations refused to join their chiefs and assembled at King William's Town. From this conflict of loyalties sprang a cleavage between the pagan or 'red' people, who continued to anoint themselves with red clay, and the Christian converts, who attended school and wore a European pattern of clothes. It was adumbrated in 1818 in the opposition between Makanda the diviner and war-doctor, and Ntsikana, who called men to worship with a chant he composed; and in 1853 in the conflict between Mlanjeni, also a diviner and war-doctor, and Tiyo Soga, the teacher and Christian minister.[4] The cleavage has been deeper and more persistent among the Xhosa-speaking than in any other community in Africa, and its roots lie in the hundred years of war.[5] It was exacerbated by the conflict between the Xhosa and the Mfengu refugees, who allied themselves with the whites, and who accepted Christian teaching and schools much more readily than the Xhosa. Not all Mfengu became 'school people' and many individual Xhosa were baptized—Tiyo Soga among them—but 'mission work went much faster among the Mfengu'.[6] By 1882 one-fifth of the King William's Town District, with both Xhosa and Mfengu, was 'school'.[7]

As elsewhere in Africa, in the earliest stages of mission work, converts were settled on land allocated to the mission, and withdrawn from the jurisdiction of chiefs.[8] Mission stations became places of refuge, not only during war, but also for those accused of witchcraft,[9]

[1] Hunter, p. 10.　　[2] Brownlee, p. 180.　　[3] Chalmers, p. 58.
[4] Ibid., p. 51.　　[5] Hunter, pp. 6–7, 377, 534.
[6] J. Lennox, *The Story of our Missions in South Africa*, p. 25; Chalmers, pp. 397–8; Govan, pp. 109, 118.　　[7] *1883 Report*, i. 173.
[8] R. Oliver, *The Missionary Factor in East Africa*, pp. 58–65, 172–9; Wilson, *Good Company*, pp. 40–43; *Communal Rituals of the Nyakyusa*, pp. 166–76.
[9] Chalmers, p. 352; Steedman, i. 229–33.

and some people thought for other evildoers. The policy presented many difficulties, because the missionary became, in one sense, the rival of the chief, and there was endless argument as to whether or not the missionary should exclude from mission land those who failed to live a Christian life.[1] In some areas the practice of mission as landowner, with converts as tenants, has continued. But by 1865, east of the Kei, an alternative policy was established. Tiyo Soga, when planning missions there, wrote: 'The native Christians . . . are to remain where they have been located by their chiefs, without being congregated in masses on so-called mission lands.'[2]

Acceptance of Christian teaching implied a radical change in the manner of life of converts; the Christian gospel has been a yeast fermenting change in societies for two thousand years. The writing of the vernacular, the translation of the Bible, and teaching converts to read it (which for Protestant missionaries was fundamental to their mission) was in itself revolutionary. Family relationships and the political structure were radically changed by the condemnation of polygyny, and the insistence that death was not caused by witches. It could not have been otherwise. But the missionaries were also mostly from Britain, and they were Victorians imbued with a conviction of the value of their whole manner of life—a conviction matched since 1918 only by Communists—and they pressed all sorts of peripheral changes which later generations have questioned. Not only did they preach the Protestant gospel of work, but they expected their converts to wear a Western style of clothing; to build square houses rather than round ones; to settle in a village round the church and school rather than in scattered homesteads; to change the division of labour between men and women;[3] and to abandon ancient festivals, such as the traditional initiation dances, which were judged by whites to be lewd, and became illegal west of the Kei.[4] Sir Harry Smith, the administrator, roundly condemned 'the sin of buying wives', and demanded that the chiefs abandon *lobola*: i.e. he demanded that they should abandon the legal form of marriage,[5] just as, a hundred years later, Communists prohibited *kalym*, the Kirghiz form of marriage with stock. The nub of Sir Harry's objection to *lobola* was that it precipitated cattle raiding, for the desire of young men for marriage cattle induced them to raid.[6] Later generations of missionaries and administrators have been doubtful of the value of such peripheral changes—the 1883 Report reflects views on *lobola* very different from those of Smith,[7] but the fact that the Gospel is potentially revolutionary

[1] Chalmers, pp. 264–9.   [2] Ibid., p. 316.   [3] Govan, p. 201.   [4] Maclean, p. 96.
[5] Walker, p. 250; Theal, *A History of South Africa from 1795–1872*, iii. 61.
[6] Smith, *Autobiography*, ii. 92; cf. A. W. Lee, *Charles Johnston of Zululand*, pp. 19–20, 'without cattle and consequently without raids and warfare the young men could not marry . . .'.
[7] *1883 Report*, Minutes of Evidence.

CIVILIZATION BY MINGLING

in any society cannot be doubted. Neither the traditional kinship system nor the traditional economy of the Xhosa could survive unchanged. Inevitably converts were drawn from isolation into wider interaction. Tiyo Soga saw 'civilization alone', without Christianity, as destructive of the traditional society, but at the same time he pressed for greater economic opportunity for the Xhosa: 'I see plainly that unless the rising generation is trained to some of the useful arts, nothing else will raise our people, and they must be grooms, drivers of waggons, hewers of wood, or general servants. . . .' The Colonists 'do not like the elevation of the natives, whom they would fain keep down as men and maid-servants'.[1]

Stewart of Lovedale stated his policy explicitly: 'Merely to civilize can never be the primary aim of the missionary. . . . But among barbarous races a sound missionary method will in every way endeavour to promote civilization by education and industry, resting on the solid foundation of religious instruction.'[2]

The difficulties of missionaries were increased by the fact that both white governments and African chiefs tried to use them as political agents. The earliest missionaries among the Xhosa, van der Kemp and Williams, jibbed at being asked to 'return deserters';[3] but more than one missionary was appointed for a time as a government 'Agent'. Tiyo Soga found Chief Oba and later Sarili determined to use him,[4] and, willy-nilly, many missionaries became negotiators between chiefs and the Colonial Government, for it was often they who had the closest links with both sides.[5] Some critics, both African and white, see the missionaries as agents of the conquest, and interpret their preaching as activated by 'the expansion of capitalism',[6] or 'cultural imperialism'.[7] That missionaries brought Western culture as well as the Christian Gospel cannot be doubted. In the nineteenth century most Christian missionaries in Africa were as convinced of the supreme value of their own culture as Communist missionaries working in Soviet Asia in the mid twentieth century are of theirs, and individuals (such as the administrator, J. C. Warner, quoted above) scarcely differentiated between the spread of the Gospel and the spread of the British Empire or, at least, of white rule.[8] But the force compelling the Christian to action was religious conviction, not cultural chauvinism. The lives of men like van der Kemp, Robert Moffat, Eugene Casalis, or James Stewart are not intelligible on any other hypothesis. 'The story of the

---

[1] Chalmers, pp. 249, 288, 313.
[2] J. Stewart, *Lovedale, South Africa*, p. 4.
[3] Moodie, *Record*, v. 20; Holt, pp. 65–67.
[4] Chalmers, pp. 294, 305, 328.
[5] Moodie, *Battles*, i. 243–4.
[6] N. Majeke, p. 1 *et passim*; Mnguni, pp. 69–72.
[7] K. Knorr, *British Colonial Theories, 1570–1850*, p. 381.
[8] M. Warren, *The Missionary Movement from Britain in Modern History*, p. 42 *et passim*.

missionary movements can record countless missionaries who were resented as bringing with them an alien and uncongenial culture. Not infrequently this led to their suffering violence. Often they were in fact "offered". But their own self-offering was not in the name of their culture. It was in the name of "Him who had died for *them*".[1]

Civilization by mingling and the pagan reaction were opposite trends, and so they have been discussed separately, but they were contemporary rather than successive in time. The pagan reaction started at least as early as 1818, with the preaching of Makanda; civilization by mingling, though intensified after 1854 by Grey, had begun with Williams's mission on the Kat river in 1816, and it continued.[2]

It was between 1818 and 1854 that raiding and wars were most bitter, but it was during this period also that raid and punitive commando were finally contained. Effective authority of the central government was established as far as the Kei by 1858, and it gradually extended eastward, linking with Natal in 1894. The development of farming, of roads and transport, and of trade, employment, and government, all tended to draw the Xhosa into closer and closer interaction with whites. The wider-scale community came into being on farms, and military and administrative posts, as well as in market towns and on mission stations.

6. *Conflicting Attitudes*

The basic fact of frontier history is the conflict between black and white over the occupation of land—fertile land. Linked with it was competition for the possession of stock over a hundred years during which no government was able to secure property rights on the frontier. The strong raided the weak and in turn were raided. There were also radical differences between black and white in their ideas about land tenure, labour, marriage, and the causes of disease.

Six times, after war, the boundary moved eastward and more farms were taken up by whites. Sometimes it was alleged that one chief or another had agreed to granting land. But no chief 'owned' land in the European sense, nor could he dispose of it;[3] he could only grant right of occupancy. Further, it was assumed by the Xhosa that every man had the right to the use of land just as he had a right to breathe the air,

---

[1] M. Warren, *The Missionary Movement from Britain in Modern History*, p. 44 *et passim*.

[2] F. Flemming, *Kaffraria and its Inhabitants*, p. 25.

[3] Kay, p. 266; S. Bannister, *Humane Policy or Justice to the Aborigines of New Settlements*, pp. 73–81; Pringle, p. 313.

and the notion of exclusive rights of individuals, which could be sold, over land that was neither a building site nor under cultivation, was foreign.

The popular white view was that African men did no work and left all heavy labour to their women (see pp. 111, 239–40). Employers and administrators, as well as missionaries, stressed the moral value of labour (pp. 239, 267), though in fact the white grazier, having servants, did rather less for himself than the African grazier.[1]

A deep conflict of values appeared in the attitude towards polygyny. It was accepted in traditional Xhosa society as right and proper for a chief and a wealthy man, but its incidence was limited. Lichtenstein remarked that 'most Kaffirs have only one wife, and chiefs four or five'.[2] Hintsa himself had nine wives—no great harem.[3] With the increase in the circulation of cattle, however, polygyny increased,[4] as it has elsewhere in the early stages of black–white contact. Most missionaries and administrators stressed monogamy, and polygyny has virtually disappeared under religious and economic pressures,[5] but for a hundred years it was a burning issue.

There was conflict also in ideas about the causation of disease, and the law regarding accusations of witchcraft. The Xhosa believed that all disease, or virtually all, was due to witches—murderers who acted through 'familiars' such as baboons, wild cats, snakes, or a fabulous hairy animal, the *tikoloshe*. They depended on diviners (*amagqira*) to discover the witches (*amagqwira*), and torture was used to extract confessions (see pp. 123–4). The whites denied the reality of accusations of witchcraft, and ridiculed them, though belief in witchcraft in England was scarcely dead. The missionaries and administrators were convinced that witchcraft accusations among the Xhosa were deliberately levelled against the wealthy. Sir Harry Smith (with typical exaggeration)

> soon discovered that might was right, that the damnable forgery of sorcery and witchcraft was the *primum mobile* of oppression and extortion, and that under the cloak of punishment for this offence there was committed oppression of so barbarous and tyrannical a kind as it was hardly to be conceived that beings endowed with reason could perpetrate on one another.... Whenever any individual renders himself obnoxious to the chief or any of his family or influential men, he is accused of bewitching either the chief, his wife, or child, or cattle, or any other thing, but no one is ever considered capable of this sort of sorcery but a man rich in goods, viz. cattle.[6]

Less partial observers also thought it was the rich who were attacked.[7]

---

[1] Sparrman, ii. 164–9.   [2] Lichtenstein, i. 322; Van der Kemp, i. 439.
[3] Cowper Rose, *Four Years in Southern Africa*, p. 185.
[4] *1883 Report*, ii. 72.
[5] Wilson et al., *Social Structure*, pp. 56, 93.
[6] Smith, *Autobiography*, ii. 74.   [7] Chalmers, p. 397; Govan, pp. 20–22.

Under Colonial law imputation of witchcraft became a punishable offence, and diviners were treated almost as if they, themselves, were witches. *Igqira* and *igqwira*, detective and murderer in Xhosa thought, were 'witch-doctor' and 'witch' to whites, and by many all but identified:[1] men like Dr. Fitzgerald at the Grey Hospital in King William's Town, who treated diviners as 'colleagues', inviting them in to see his wards,[2] were rare. There was a fundamental cleavage in thought between those who accepted impersonal causes of misfortune and those who asked, and still ask: 'Granted that typhus is carried by lice, *who sent the louse?*'[3] The contradictions about causation were dramatically apparent in the attitude towards drought. Repeatedly, missionaries were held responsible for having *caused* drought;[4] occasionally, they were credited with having brought rain.[5] Many of the early missionaries in South Africa felt obliged to 'pull down the fanes' rather than purify them as Pope Gregory the Great, twelve centuries earlier, had instructed the missionaries in England to do.[6] Sacrifices to the shades and the use of medicines for protection and cure tended to be lumped together as 'witchcraft'. Traditional initiation rituals were condemned as immoral.[7]

These differences in ideas and values made communication between black and white more difficult, and increased the mutual fear and distrust generated in the fight for land and cattle.

But the cleavage between white and black was not monolithic. There was diversity and contradiction within each group. Among the whites there were cleavages between Afrikaner and English; between colonist and administrator; settler and missionary; or most farmers on the one hand and most missionaries and administrators on the other. There were radical differences in the white group as to whether there should be equality before the law for white and Coloured and African, and mingling or separation in church and school. In the period during which Lovedale developed as a mixed school, Stellenbosch theological seminary admitted non-whites, and 1820 settlers in Glen Lyndon welcomed Coloured people at their services,[8] opposition to Coloured worshippers attending Dutch Reformed churches grew. In 1801 churchgoers in Graaff-Reinet had objected to van der Kemp preaching to Coloured people in their church,[9] and in 1857 the Synod of the Dutch Reformed Church in the Cape resolved to start separate congregations for non-whites 'because of the weakness of some'.[10]

---

[1] Kay, pp. 164–72, 208, 420–1.   [2] Rutherford, p. 323.   [3] Hunter, p. 274.
[4] Van der Kemp, i. 419, 423; Steedman, ii. 282; Livingstone, *Missionary Travels*, pp. 22, 23; Kay, pp. 208–9; Govan, pp. 69–70.
[5] Van der Kemp, i. 427; Kay, p. 211; Chalmers, p. 322; Govan, p. 68.
[6] Haddon Stubbs, iii. 30; Bede, *Ecclesiastical History*, i. 30, quoted E. K. Chambers, *The Medieval English Stage*, i. 95–96.   [7] Chalmers, p. 264–9.   [8] Pringle, pp. 115–16.
[9] Marais, p. 127.   [10] B. B. Keet, *Whither South Africa?*, p. 37.

'The weakness referred to was of course the colour consciousness and colour prejudice that would make living together as members of the same congregation difficult.'[1] Even among English-speaking missionaries there were marked differences in the views of Wesleyans who were closely linked to the 1820 settlers, and those expressed by members of the Scottish and London Missionary Societies who worked primarily with African and Coloured people. Individual missionaries varied considerably in their attitudes towards traditional custom, Bishop Colenso even maintaining that, in the circumstances of Zululand, polygyny should be no absolute bar to baptism.[2]

On the African side the cleavage between conservative and radical— 'red' and 'school'—and between Xhosa and Mfengu has already been described (pp. 249, 258, 265), but the cleavage was never absolute. Marriage between Xhosa and Mfengu had begun before 1857 and continued despite war,[3] just as marriage between Afrikaans and English-speaking people has done.

Conflict was also *within* individuals who pursued incompatible ends. The most obvious incompatibility was between maintaining separation of white and black and trading with Africans, employing them as labourers, and preaching the Gospel. The same people, in the white group, supported separation and interaction: they talked about maintaining the frontier, but themselves employed African labourers and travelled in Xhosa country buying cattle and ivory. The Xhosa, for their part, wanted *both* the goods of civilization and to maintain traditional custom. The whites sought chiefs in control of their subjects with whom to negotiate, and at the same time they broke the power of the chiefs because they were a military threat.[4] They spoke of the Xhosa as barbarians, but in fact counted on warfare being limited.

In its widest sense the conflict was between isolation and wide-scale interaction: between a tribal outlook and a universal one; between an exclusive interpretation of 'Who is my neighbour?' and a Christian one; and the cleavage did not coincide exactly with differences in race or language.

---

[1] Ibid., p. 37.
[2] P. Hinchliff, *John William Colenso*, pp. 64, 81, 192.
[3] Maclean, p. 134.
[4] Young, p. 76; Chalmers, p. 194.

VII

THE CONSOLIDATION OF A NEW SOCIETY: THE CAPE COLONY

DURING the century between 1778 and 1870 there were four simultaneous developments of major importance in the history of the Cape Colony, to each of which a section of this chapter is devoted. First, the cultural pattern of Colonial life became much more diverse. The population increased at least eight-fold. English and Xhosa were added to its spoken languages, the former replacing Dutch as the main language of official communication, and both together interrupting the trend towards linguistic uniformity. Education made significant strides, to a great extent outside the control of the kind of people who had set the tone of eighteenth-century Cape thought. Religious toleration was extended to include non-Reformed, non-Protestant, and even non-Christian creeds; it led into a movement for the disendowment of all churches; and there was some dilution of the Calvinist outlook of the early settlement. The old contrast between the capital and its environs on the one hand, and the pastoral farming areas of the interior on the other, still remained and by 1870 had grown both more and less marked. More, because the urban areas tended to become predominantly English-speaking, whereas Afrikaner dominance of the rural areas remained fairly intact save in the south-east. Less, because of developments in the economic field, the second main area of change.

The removal of mercantilist restrictions on trade, together with improvements in communications and the development of new forms of productive activity from the 1830s onwards, brought more wealth to the settlement, in turn encouraged further immigration, and drew the farmers of the interior so much within the range of a market economy that they found their cultural isolation much harder to maintain. The social basis of economic life was altered, though in the first instance productivity seems to have been interrupted, by the emancipation of the Khoikhoi and slaves between 1828 and 1838; but in economic terms emancipation involved not much more than the replacement of unfree labour by cheap labour.

In the third place, great progress was made towards securing the liberty of the subject, with the removal of arbitrary forms and differential standards of justice, together with the legal emancipation of subject groups. A by-product of these developments, though an important one, was that long before 1870 the barbaric forms of deterrent punishment thought necessary in Company days for the maintenance of public order, which shocked visitors like Sparrman and Barrow, had given place to gentler methods of law enforcement. But the habit of class and colour differentiation in the outlook of the socially dominant groups, and the tendency towards abjectness on the part of those accustomed to bondage, could not be legislated out of existence, and survived as social attitudes liable to be reasserted in times of stress.

Finally, the political institutions of an authoritarian trading company gradually gave place to new ones operating on the principle of government by consent, under a franchise based on reasonably low qualifications, which conveyed political power to men of all races on equal terms but, because it was a racially stratified society, not in equal proportions. A period of unsettlement in the political control of the Cape underlay these changes, for it changed hands three times between 1795 and 1815. In September 1795 the Dutch East India Company lost the Cape to the British, who kept it until February 1803. In terms of the Treaty of Amiens, it was then restored, not to the Dutch Company, which had ceased to exist, but to the new Batavian Republic, which had been established in the Netherlands at the time of the exile of the House of Orange in 1795. But after the resumption of the Napoleonic War Batavian rule was ended by a second British attack at the beginning of 1806, and the Cape was confirmed in British hands in 1815. Meanwhile the borders of the Colony continued to move out northwards and eastwards, with the result that when the time arrived to talk about self-government, one of the main difficulties was the devising of a constitution to take account of divergent regional interests.

1. *The Diversification of Culture*

The development of the Cape Colony during the hundred years before the discovery of diamonds was slight by comparison with that of the following century; but when measured against the first hundred years after van Riebeeck, it was immense. The increase of population gives some idea of the scale of growth, though the figures must be treated with caution. In 1773 there were 20,621 people living in the Colony, of whom 2,165 were Company officials and sick seamen, 8,554 were white settlers, and 9,902 were slaves.[1] The Khoikhoi, however, were not counted. Between 1806, when they were included, and 1865, which was the year of the last census in the period covered by this chapter, the total population of the Colony grew from 77,075 to 566,158.

[1] Moodie, *Record*, iii. 16.

By 1819 white settlers numbered 42,217. They increased to 111,956 in 1855 and 187,439 a decade later.[1] There had been an improvement in the official capacity for counting heads, which was linked with the extension of government into the interior; but immense population growth cannot be doubted. Asian immigration stopped with the abolition of the slave trade from 1807; but any tendency for the European population in the Colony to increase proportionately to the non-European was more than checked by the incorporation of Nguni people, along with their territory, within the eastern borders of the Colony, notably 17,000 Mfengu settled by Sir Benjamin D'Urban in 1835, and 64,000 Xhosa who became Cape Colonials when British Kaffraria was annexed to the Cape in 1865.

Cape society was very diverse in its cultural origins. As late as 1792 the Commissioners Nederburgh and Frijkenius, wishing to ensure that a trading regulation should be properly understood, instructed that it should be published 'not only in Dutch, but also in the Malay, Javanese and Chinese languages'.[2] More Germans than Dutchmen entered the Colony during the eighteenth century. But the pressure towards cultural uniformity was as strong then as it had been in the experience of the Huguenots in the seventeenth, and a common language was developing among the inhabitants in general. Burchell, writing of the 'Dutch part of the community' in 1810, described them as 'Africaanders, whether of Dutch, German or French origin'—a definition which would still commend itself to first-generation Afrikaner nationalists in the 1870s;[3] and if language had been his sole criterion, Burchell could have extended his definition to the Coloured population as well.[4] The Afrikaner people, as a distinctive amalgam of several strains, existed before the great immigration of the nineteenth century began. But the nineteenth-century immigrants, most of whom were British, assimilated far less readily to the Afrikaner norm than did their predecessors, chiefly because English was made the official language of the settlement, and also because of the greater sophistication of the newcomers, who imported new standards and grafted them on to the Colonial rootstock, as in their architecture, or planted new seeds and watered them, as in literature and education.

In the century covered by this chapter a succession of new influences was brought to bear on the Colony. As the strategic value of the Colony grew in the context of the eighteenth-century colonial wars, a larger and larger proportion of the ships to visit the Cape was of other than Dutch origin—French, British, Danish, American in many cases, always

---

[1] Thompson, ii. 426; CGH annual Blue Books; C. G. W. Schumann, *Structural Changes and Business Cycles in South Africa, 1806-1936*, pp. 37-39.
[2] *Kaapse Plakkaatboek*, iv. 162.
[3] Burchell, i. 21; S. J. du Toit and others, *Die Geskiedenis van ons Land in die Taal van ons Volk*.
[4] See also pp. ix, 66, 70, 248.

more foreign than Dutch after 1772. During the Anglo-Dutch War of 1780–3 a French fleet under Admiral de Suffren made a strong if transitory impact on the life of the capital. After the British military occupation of 1795 British manners governed life at the castle, where monthly balls at the court of Lady Anne Barnard helped to 'reconcile the Dutch by the attraction of fiddles and French horns'.[1] The new régime had some impact on contemporary modes: it brought the Adam influence into the architectural tastes of the Cape Town community, where continental classicism had already begun to take a hold. But on the whole the government stood aloof from the local population in the capital, and was involved for much of its time in the suppression of revolts by Dutch and Khoikhoi in the interior,[2] while the writings of John Barrow, the governor's secretary, alienated colonists whom Lady Anne had mellowed. Many Cape Dutch kept their distance, and some refused to take the oath of allegiance.[3]

With the arrival of the Batavians the atmosphere changed. Dutch once again became the sole official language; officials who had served under the British were in a number of cases replaced by men who had not; and a goodly proportion of the English merchants who had arrived since the conquest now moved out. The new régime under Commissioner-General J. A. de Mist and Governor J. W. Janssens planned reforms in the spirit of the European Enlightenment, especially in the fields of religion and education.

During the Company period the control of religious activity at the Cape had been vested immediately in the Company and ultimately (though informally) in the Amsterdam *classis* of the *Nederduitsch Gereformeerde Kerk*.[4] They had permitted the Lutherans to worship in public only from 1778.[5] The British authorities during the first occupation had allowed the right of public worship for the first time to the Cape Malay community,[6] and de Mist's *Kerkenordre* of 1804 granted the protection of the law on equal terms to 'all Religious associations which for the furtherance of virtue and good conduct respect a Supreme Being'.[7] This included the Roman Catholic Church, which quickly

---

[1] Lady Anne Barnard, *South Africa a Century Ago*, p. 144.
[2] Marais, *Maynier and the First Boer Republic*, pp. 90–91, 101–8.
[3] *Kaapse Plakkaatboek*, v. 87–89.
[4] A. Moorrees, *Die Nederduitse Gereformeerde Kerk in Suid-Afrika, 1652–1873*, pp. 51–53; S. P. Engelbrecht, *Geskiedenis van de Nederduits Hervormde Kerk in Zuid-Afrika*, p. 21; A. Dreyer, *Boustowwe vir die Geskiedenis van die Nederduits-Gereformeerde Kerke in Suid-Afrika*, iii. 262. (J. A. Truter's Report.)
[5] Moorrees, pp. 240–64, esp. pp. 250 ff.
[6] Br. Parl. Pap. 50 of 1835, pp. 207–10, esp. evidence of Imam Ackmat.
[7] Dreyer, iii. 8–23: Text of the *Kerken-Ordre* of 25 July 1804, of which Cap. I, art. 1, reads: 'Alle Kerkgenoodschappen, welke ter bevordering van deugd en goede Zeden een Hoogst Wezen eerbiedigen, genieten in deze Volksplanting eene gelyke bescherming der Wetten.'

availed itself of the opportunity, and the small Jewish community, which apparently did not.[1] The Batavians also departed from local tradition by authorizing the secular solemnization of marriages.[2] A Dutch captain, de Jong, who frequently visited the Colony in the 1790's and displayed no animus against the colonist, found lack of education to be 'one chief cause of his shortcomings'.[3] Itinerant schoolmasters of various origins and qualifications, often men who had served on the Company's ships, imparted the rudiments of learning to farmers' children on the *platteland*.[4] In Cape Town proper, as well as in some outlying centres such as Stellenbosch and Paarl, organized schools existed and carried on their work in the spirit of Chavonnes's instruction of 1714, and, as Borcherds shows, with the strong religious emphasis of that document.[5] Because of growing dissatisfaction over the lack of good schools, two Dutch Reformed clergymen, Serrurier and Fleck, appealed for funds in 1791 in order to improve them. They raised f. 60,000 (£4,000) 'wholly . . . from the inhabitants of European descent, not 5000 in all, in the Cape division', and proposed with the money to set up what they termed 'Dutch' schools to give elementary instruction in the three R's, 'French' schools, where some history, geography, Italian book-keeping, and the French language were to be taught, and a 'Latin' school for the training of candidates for overseas university entrance. In the view of the Education Commission of 1863, the first British occupation of the Colony seriously hampered these plans.[6] Janssens and de Mist resumed the task where Serrurier and Fleck had been obliged to leave off, and were strongly influenced by the Dutch society *Tot Nut van 't Algemeen*, whose school in Cape Town trained many prominent Cape Colonials between 1804 and 1870.[7] In a school ordinance of 1805, de Mist laid down a constitution for a school commission, and devised an elaborate educational system embracing primary schooling, secondary schooling, and teacher training, together with a plan for the education of girls, all on a non-confessional basis.[8] But as with the earlier attempt, the promulgation of de Mist's plan was forestalled by

---

[1] W. E. Brown, *The Catholic Church in South Africa*, p. 6; L. Herrman, *A History of the Jews in South Africa*, pp. 67, 114, 192, 249, for salient facts concerning the Jewish community, which had no synagogue until 1841, and only totalled some sixty families in 1860.
[2] Dreyer, iii. 47–59 (*Huwelikswet*).
[3] Idenburg, *The Cape of Good Hope at the Turn of the Eighteenth Century*, pp. 14–15; De Mist, para. 41.
[4] e.g. Thompson, p. 299; Burchell, i. 143, ii. 82.
[5] P. B. Borcherds, *An Autobiographical Memoir*, pp. 18–22; Lichtenstein, ii. 122. For Chavonnes's instruction see *Kaapse Plakkaatboek*, ii. 35–38.
[6] G. 24–'63, pp. ix–xi.
[7] De Mist, paras. 35–41; Idenburg, p. 83 (Janssens's views); see Borcherds, pp. 244–5; T. N. Hanekom, *Die Liberale Rigting in Suid-Afrika: 'n Kerkhistoriese Studie*, pp. 194–202.
[8] Dreyer, iii. 31–46: De Mist's School Ordinance, Dutch text; G. 24–'63, Appendix V, pp. 10–21 (English translation).

the return of the British, and it was consequently abandoned.[1] Enough had been done, however, to shatter the monolithic Calvinism of Company days. The Batavians, through their policies for religion and education, had started new trains of thought which would secure wide adoption in the Colony during the following half century, because the Church in the Netherlands, whose ties with the State had been broken in 1795, and whose ties with the Cape Church were not broken even after 1806, itself moved in a liberal direction. Under the influence of scholars like Opzoomer at Utrecht and Scholten at Leiden, through whose universities most of the trainees for the Cape ministry passed prior to the establishment of the Stellenbosch Seminary in 1859, the Cape Church, though generally suspicious of *nuwighede* (new-fangled notions), acquired a nucleus of clergymen who kept in step with modernist scholarship in Europe.[2] But the Batavians had come too late to make an impact on the farming communities of the interior and their pastors, for these were already isolated from the intellectual influences of the capital and held fast to the theology of a pre-liberal age.[3] A clash eventually took place between the latitudinarian and the strict Calvinist sections of the *Kerk*. This reached its peak with the trial for heresy of three unorthodox clergy in the early 1860s, and resulted in the defeat, but not the elimination, of the liberal section, whose impact was still strong enough to prevent a return to the literal acceptance of all Calvin's teachings, as was shown by the failure of the *Kruiskerk* movement in the closing years of the century.[4] The fact that such a clash took place must be attributed in the first instance to the Batavian rulers at the beginning of the century, for they created an intellectual division within the Cape Dutch community on top of, but not necessarily corresponding with, the political rift between '*Jacobijnen*' and '*Anglomannen*' which had arisen out of the circumstances of the European war.[5] To attribute the ideological clashes of the Cape Colony in the nineteenth century simply to a conflict between Boer and Briton is therefore to overlook a most important background factor—the conflict between the Calvinist fundamentalism of the frontier and the Christian or secular humanism of the Enlightenment, whether in its Batavian or its British form.

The British administration which took over the Cape in 1806 was immediately faced with the problem of managing people who spoke a

[1] G. 24–'63, pp. xv–xvi.
[2] Hanekom, pp. 278–307; Moorrees, pp. 881 ff.
[3] B. Spoelstra, *Die 'Doppers' in Suid-Afrika, 1760–1899*, pp. 12–32.
[4] Moorrees, pp. 889–1001; S. P. Engelbrecht, *T. F. Burgers*, pp. 29–63; J. H. Hofmeyr, *Life of J. H. Hofmeyr ('Onze Jan')*, pp. 44–64; J. A. S. Oberholster, *Die Gereformeerde Kerke onder die Kruis in Suid-Afrika*.
[5] See below, p. 313.

different language, lived under a different system of law, and for the most part adhered to an established religion which differed from that of the English governing class. To some extent the government would be able to profit from the British experience in governing French Canada, which had revealed the wisdom of interfering as little as possible with existing institutions; but, since it intended to keep the Cape on account of its strategic value and its commercial potential, it was bound to try to impose its own image on its new possession, and it was bound to meet some opposition from the resident population as it did so. Yet the actual resistance encountered was less intense and slower to develop than might have been expected, and for this several explanations may be offered. The Cape Dutch were divided in their loyalties on account of developments in the Netherlands, so that there were not lacking colonists whose attachment to the Stadtholder enabled them to serve or support the British régime with a clear conscience.[1] The Cape Dutch had almost no experience of a Dutch government which had their material interests at heart, and found the British yoke appreciably lighter, and prosperity under the British greater, than they had ever known before. The Cape Dutch had already lost many of their cultural bonds with the Netherlands, and in the absence of any regular instruction of the youth in their own language and literature, they were malleable clay for a régime bent on moulding them in its own image.

The British Government encouraged the settlement of English-speaking people at the Cape, but the 1820 settlement in Albany was primarily an attempt to buttress an insecure frontier at a time when Whig demands for a reduction of the army estimates were growing, when there was much unemployment in Great Britain, and when, after Makanda's attack in 1819, that frontier badly needed defending.[2] The settlement of white colonists on the eastern frontier had been suggested periodically since 1809.[3] In 1817 Benjamin Moodie arrived with fifty Scottish labourers, but left the bulk of his party in Cape Town and himself settled in the region of Swellendam.[4] The same year Lord Charles Somerset, the Governor of the Cape, began to urge the settlement of the Suurveld, describing it in his dispatches as a 'succession of parks' where the soil was 'well adapted to cultivation' and 'peculiarly fitted for cattle and pasturage', and the climate 'the most healthy in the universe'.[5] The hazards were not advertised by the British Government when, in September 1818, it offered free passages and land at the

[1] e.g. W. S. van Ryneveld and J. A. Truter.
[2] For the 1820 Settlers, see especially I. E. Edwards, *The 1820 Settlers in South Africa*; H. E. Hockly, *The Story of the British Settlers of 1820 in South Africa*; Cory, esp. vol. ii.
[3] *RCC*, vii. 101–4: Report of Col. R. Collins; x. 206–8.
[4] Edwards, pp. 41, 48–49; E. H. Burrows, *Overberg Outspan*, pp. 209–28.
[5] *RCC*, xi. 303–9, 425–31; Edwards, *1820 Settlers*, p. 44.

THE DIVERSIFICATION OF CULTURE 279

rate of 100 acres per settler to men who recruited parties which included ten or more men, and would deposit £10 per head until the settlers were established on the land.[1] Some 4,000 settlers arrived at the Cape early in 1820, of whom about 2,400 were males. They came from all four countries of the British Isles,[2] and included farmers and artisans and a sprinkling of professional men, military, medical, and clerical.[3] Another 1,000 followed on the heels of the organized parties. Some parties were recruited and paid for by single wealthy leaders, who brought groups of indentured servants; other parties were 'independent', each member paying his own deposit and receiving title to land on arrival.[4]

The independent parties fared best in face of the initial hazards which beset the young settlement—three successive harvest failures, and disastrous floods in 1823. Many indentured retainers of the larger proprietors, unused to working on the land, defied the pass system imposed to keep them to their contracts, and went to Grahamstown and other centres to seek a better living from the practice of their trades.[5]

There were human difficulties too. Lord Charles Somerset, who had been allowed much discretion in the planting of the colony, returned to England on leave before the settlers arrived, and left authority in the hands of a newcomer to the Cape, Sir Rufane Donkin, whose sympathy for settler needs led him to abandon some of the main principles of Somerset's policy.[6] Thus he permitted a regulated trade with the Xhosa at Fort Willshire, and established an extensive military colony for veterans of the discredited Royal African Corps, previous defenders of the frontier, at Fredericksburg, which was within the 'neutral belt' demarcated by Somerset in his questionable arrangement with Ngqika of 1819.[7] Donkin's insubordination, heightened by a quarrel between him and Colonel Henry Somerset, the governor's son, led after Somerset's return in 1822 to a bitter quarrel between the governor and his deputy,[8] during which the governor's image became tarnished in

---
[1] See the contemporary circular printed in *RCC*, xii. 225–7, Cory, ii. 11–13, and Hockly, pp. 26–27.
[2] Bathurst had suggested that the English, Scottish, Irish, and Welsh parties should be kept apart. The Scots were accordingly sent to the Baviaans river, north of Albany, to act as a shield for Graaff-Reinet; the Welsh (with some English) were sent to the upper reaches of the Rivier Zonder Eind near the present Caledon, the Irish to the Olifants river valley (the present Clanwilliam); but these last two groups found the sites allotted inadequate, and subsequently took up land in Albany.
[3] Hockly, pp. 31–32, 202–52; Edwards, *1820 Settlers*, pp. 171–6 (based on less complete data).
[4] Edwards, *1820 Settlers*, p. 56; *RCC*, xxi. 281–2.
[5] *RCC*, xxi. 303. The Commissioners of Inquiry sent out in 1823 to examine the state of affairs at the Cape had no doubt that the independent parties fared best.
[6] Edwards, *1820 Settlers*, p. 60.   [7] Macmillan, *Bantu, Boer, and Briton*, pp. 79–84.
[8] A. K. Millar, *Plantagenet in South Africa: Lord Charles Somerset*, pp. 135–42, 246–8; *RCC*, xxiv. 156 ff.: Report of the Commissioners of Inquiry on the dispute.

the eyes of settlers who lionized Donkin, and much general backbiting ensued.[1]

From 1824, however, the settlers' fortunes improved. An inspector appointed by Somerset to review their position recommended the extension of land grants in order to facilitate pastoral farming.[2] Donkin had allowed this in the Fredericksburg settlement, which had, however, collapsed under Somerset's pressure,[3] and more beneficially among the Scottish settlers on the Baviaans river.[4] Greater prosperity, but also greater exposure to border cattle raids, followed this change of emphasis in settler farming which, by reducing the intensity of the settlement, also undermined its military effectiveness. Visiting the eastern frontier in 1825, Somerset further alleviated the settlers' lot by disbanding the Albany Levy, a conscript militia set up in October 1822.[5] Thenceforward the main burden of frontier defence was to fall on regular troops, assisted by volunteer Colonial units, both white and Coloured (until the latter were disarmed after the grant of responsible government in 1872).[6] Somerset also abandoned finally the fiction of a neutral territory by permitting the settlement of colonists beyond the Fish.[7] He helped to remove the handicap under which settlers lived through not being permitted to own slaves, by allowing the seven-year apprenticeship of refugee 'Mantatis'.[8] He persuaded Bathurst to write off arrear settler debts,[9] and in the interest of private traders reverted to Donkin's policy of frontier fairs under strict control at Fort Willshire, and closed down the Government-owned Somerset Farm, which became the village of Somerset East.[10] Thereafter the settlement flourished.

The arrival of the 1820 Settlers resulted in at least a doubling of the English-speaking population at the Cape, and the establishment of a bridgehead in the east to balance that which was growing in the capital itself, from which British culture, and more particularly the characteristics of British urban civilization, with its retail shops, its newspapers, debating societies, horse-racing, and cricket matches, would radiate into the villages of the interior. The Settlers, though in many cases of humble

[1] For the notorious cases of [Mr.] Bishop Burnett, William Parker, and others, see Theal's *Records*.
[2] Edwards, *1820 Settlers*, pp. 122–3; *RCC*, xvii. 340–50: Hayward's instructions; xxi. 289–90: Somerset's view on inadequacy of original land grants.
[3] Edwards, *1820 Settlers*, pp. 72–73; *RCC*, xiv. 220, 275–6.   [4] *RCC*, xxi. 304.
[5] *RCC*, xv. 14–16, 51, 108, 200; Edwards, *1820 Settlers*, pp. 73–74; Hockly, p. 80: Albany Levy; Edwards, p. 123; *RCC*, xx. 354: Proclamation of 1825 disbanding the Levy.
[6] Hockly, p. 124; Marais, *Cape Coloured People*, pp. 131–4.
[7] Edwards, *1820 Settlers*, p. 123; Macmillan, *Bantu, Boer, and Briton*, pp. 83–89; *RCC*, xxv. 230–1: Proclamation of 1825, in which the expression 'neutral ground' still appears.
[8] *RCC*, xx. 405–6, Somerset to Bathurst, 31 Mar. 1825.
[9] Edwards, *1820 Settlers*, p. 124, quoting C.O. 48/68, Somerset to Bathurst, 31 Mar. 1825; *RCC*, loc. cit.
[10] Hockly, pp. 103–4.

origin, were an articulate community, by contrast with the relatively unlettered boers among whom they were placed. Their role in the struggle for press freedom, in the establishment of a South African literature, in the planting of schools and libraries,[1] was especially noteworthy. A few achieved reputations in the field of science.[2] Their architecture introduced a distinctive British idiom, whether in their farm buildings, which often reproduced British rural styles, or in the Georgian town houses that gave a special character to the streets of Grahamstown, and matched the new styles beginning to appear in Cape Town.[3] Finally, the Settlers became frontiersmen, active like their boer counterparts in the defence of their material goods, attempting to cling to the values of the civilization they brought with them, even under extreme provocation,[4] succumbing sometimes to excessive violence in word or deed,[5] but providing from their ranks people who were prepared to move and live among the neighbouring Xhosa to impart their Christian religion,[6] or to trade, or simply to employ them as their servants. But although they soon identified themselves with the land of their adoption, the Settlers remained to a large extent a separate community, encouraged to retain their distinctiveness by the fact that the language they spoke had been made the language of official communication and to a large extent the language of the schools. Neither the Huguenots before them nor the German settlers who came after them were given such a strong incentive to remain apart. To some extent the exclusiveness of the Settler community was broken down by intermarriage with Afrikaners; but however frequently this happened among the Settlers generally, it was not a common occurrence in those families whose histories have been published.[7]

Just as the consolidation of Albany was the main reason for introducing the British Settlers of 1820, so the need to consolidate British Kaffraria lay behind the British Government's decision in 1856 to

[1] Hockly, pp. 151-8. Even a literary primitive like Jeremiah Goldswain could write a journal of immense humanity and charm: see VRS, vols. 27, 29 (ed. Una Long).
[2] Mary E. Barber and W. G. Atherstone, for example.
[3] R. Lewcock, *Early Nineteenth Century Architecture in South Africa: A Study of the Interaction of two Cultures, 1795–1837*, pp. 79–109, 131–90, 201–14. The relatively unsung British Settlers of the western Cape, who were the real builders of the Colony's export trade in the first half of the century, are given some prominence in R. F. M. Immelman, *Men of Good Hope*. See below, p. 294.
[4] e.g. W. A. Maxwell, *Random Reflections on the Study of History in South Africa* (inaugural lecture, Rhodes University, Grahamstown, 1956), p. 23: the anguished prayer of a plundered settler, asking to be saved from 'infidelity and unbelief' after 'those wicked caffers' had robbed him of all his carefully trained oxen and milch cows.
[5] J. M. Bowker, *Speeches, Letters and Selections from important Papers*, p. 125 (the celebrated 'springbok' speech).   [6] e.g. the Revds. J. Ayliff and H. H. Dugmore.
[7] I. and R. Mitford-Barberton, *The Bowkers of Tharfield*; E., M., and J. Pringle, *Pringles of the Valley*. Professor F. G. Butler let me see a copy of the Collett family tree.

establish a settlement of Germans.[1] Germans were selected, in the first instance, because British military pensioners had not responded to the invitation to settle, and because the British Foreign Legion (or 'British-German Legion', as it came to be known), which had been recruited for service at the time of the Crimean War, was a burden on the War Office once that war was over. Sir George Grey, Governor of the Cape in 1854–61, desired to promote the settlement of Kaffraria, partly to protect the trade route from East London through Queenstown to the north, and partly to encourage the Xhosa to adopt European ways by interspersing European settlers among them. The German legionaries were offered free passages for themselves and their families, free rations for a year, free building lots and gardens, and (if officers) the right to purchase public land at a discount, in return for an undertaking to serve under the colours for seven years at military rates of pay. Some 2,872 settlers arrived under these conditions, of whom only 343 were women and 178 children. Although over a thousand of the legionaries left to help in the suppression of the Indian Mutiny in 1857, of whom less than 400 returned, the imbalance between the sexes brought disciplinary difficulties, and led Grey to decide on the introduction of German peasant families in the interest of social stability. He accordingly made contact with the firm of Godeffroy in Hamburg, who agreed to recruit some 4,000 settlers of this type and transport them for the cost of £50,000. The Colonial Office, jibbing at the expense, preferred the introduction of single women—Irish girls were suggested—and required Godeffroys to limit their passages to 1,600. These settlers duly arrived in 1858–9, and were in fact, as laid down in the Cape Government's regulations, 'chiefly composed of persons who have been engaged in agricultural pursuits'.[2] Heads of families were granted free building lots and entitled to buy land at £1 per acre, at the rate of twenty acres per married couple, ten for a single man, and two for each child. If immigrants disliked the land allotted to them, they could buy alternative land on privileged terms at public auctions.

Like the Huguenot settlers of the seventeenth century, the Germans were dispersed among settlers of another language, in this case mainly English-speakers, but in small nuclei rather than on isolated farms. Like the Huguenots, too, they gradually lost their cultural distinctiveness, for German speech tended to disappear from the children of later

[1] Br. Parl. Pap. 2202 and 2352 of 1857, and 389 of 1858; E. L. G. Schnell, *For Men must Work: an Account of German Immigration to the Cape*; J. F. Schwär and B. E. Pape, *Germans in Kaffraria, 1858–1958*; J. Rutherford, *Sir George Grey: a Study in Colonial Government*.

[2] Br. Parl. Pap. 389 of 1858, pp. 20–21; Schwär and Pape, pp. 48–62. Of 448 heads of families listed in the latter work, about four-fifths were described as peasants, and a very low proportion were distributed among the various crafts—tailors, masons, carpenters, shoemakers, weavers, locksmiths, millers, etc.

generations, usually in favour of English, which was the home language of many of their brides. Other factors aided the process. The Legion, which was disbanded in 1861, did not hold together as a community. It contained Poles, Frenchmen, Belgians, and Italians as well as Germans, and Roman Catholics in substantial numbers as well as Lutherans.[1] German place names like Berlin, Potsdam, and Hamburg mark the sites of military posts from which the legionaries dispersed. The peasant small-holders remained, as patterns of industry to their neighbours, but sending their children to schools and attending churches (especially German Baptist churches) where English rapidly became the language of communication.

The overriding importance of the public use of its language if a cultural group was to preserve its identity was well illustrated in the case of the British settlers, who succeeded, and the German settlers, who failed. That the British authorities saw the importance of language is apparent from the steps periodically taken to compel the public use of English.[2] They applied pressure first in the schools; they extended it by proclamation to the courts from the late 1820s onwards; in 1853 they made English the exclusive language of Parliament; and by the close of our period they appeared to be triumphing on all fronts. By the middle 1870s the Chief Justice, J. H. de Villiers, could tell an audience that although 'the time is still far distant when the inhabitants of this Colony will speak and acknowledge one common mother-tongue', it would come at last, and 'when it does come, the language of Great Britain will also be the language of South Africa'.[3] But the resistance of Afrikaners had already started, and in the early 1880s would achieve its first legislative successes.

When the British took control of the Cape, de Mist's School Commission remained in being. Its early reports show that its activity was limited to the neighbourhood of Cape Town, and that in accordance with British policy some attempt was being made to establish English-medium schools.[4] From 1812 the Government tried to accelerate this trend. Cradock's proclamation of that year, which took public education into the country districts for the first time, offered a bonus to competent teachers who undertook to teach in English.[5] In the following year the replacement of de Mist's School Commission by a Bible and

---

[1] Schwär and Pape, pp. 21–22, quoting a report by Major Follenius of August 1857, which listed 1,250 Protestants, 805 Roman Catholics, and eight Jews in the Legion. Contrast Schnell, p. 240, where the Catholic element is minimized.

[2] *RCC*, xiv. 183–5: Memorandum of Henry Ellis; 452–3: Somerset's language proclamation of 5 July 1822, which laid down a time-table for the adoption of English as sole language of the courts and public records.

[3] E. A. Walker, *Lord de Villiers and his Times: South Africa 1842–1914*, p. 146.

[4] G. 24–'63, Appendix V, pp. 21–33.   [5] Ibid., pp. 36–38; Scholtz, pp. 6–11.

School Commission was an attempt to enlist the support of the churches behind public education, and it attracted sufficient contributions to make free public schools possible.¹ Free public schools giving organized instruction through the English language were set up at Graaff-Reinet, Uitenhage, George, Tulbagh, Stellenbosch, and Caledon in 1822. They reported to the Bible and School Commission, but drew their funds direct from the Colonial Treasury. By 1827 there were twenty-six free schools in the country districts, in nearly all of which English, or English and Dutch jointly, were taught, many of them run on the monitorial system of Lancaster and Bell, which was cheap. There were also some twenty Dutch fee-paying schools established under Caledon's reform of 1812. When the English schools were first established, several of the Dutch schools lost pupils and had to close down, so that P. J. Truter, a commissioner of the court of justice who carried out an inspection in 1824, came to the conclusion that the 'Government had entirely accomplished its design, in the establishment of English schools, to make that language the general one among the inhabitants'.² But the early promise of Somerset's schools was not sustained.³ The system did not generally satisfy the rural population and, quite apart from the language difficulties, children came to resent the irrelevance of much of the syllabus to their circumstances in the veld.⁴ Enthusiasm for free schools consequently declined and the Government decided in 1843 to extend to third-class rural schools the system of grants-in-aid which had been started two years earlier in respect of the largely, but not exclusively, Coloured mission schools.⁵ Langham Dale, the Superintendent-General of Education, told the Watermeyer Commission in 1863 that, although English was well understood in the government schools, of the sixty-one aided schools he had inspected, containing 3,305 scholars aged five to seventeen, only about eleven per cent. could read English 'with tolerable accuracy and intelligibly', and another ten per cent. 'very imperfectly'.⁶ This was no basis for the building of an English-speaking community, and the Education Act of 1865, which flowed from the Commission's report, was an attempt to make good its deficiency: English was made the medium of instruction in all first- and second-class schools, and its use was to be required in the third-class schools after one year.⁷ The near-extinction of Dutch as a medium of instruction in

---

¹ G. 24–'63, Appendix V, pp. 39–43.
² Ibid., pp. 44–51: Report on the State and Progress of the Government Schools in 1824.
³ Ibid., pp. 52–55: Memorandum by Col. Bell, Aug. 1837.
⁴ Idenburg, p. 121, quoting E. G. Malherbe.
⁵ E. G. Malherbe, *Education in South Africa, 1652–1922*, p. 88; J. du P. Scholtz, *Die Afrikaner en sy Taal, 1806–1875*, pp. 64–66.
⁶ G. 24–'63, Minutes of Evidence, Q.222; cf. evidence in Scholtz, pp. 163–6, for the period 1860–75.   ⁷ Malherbe, pp. 95–97; contrast the emphasis in Scholtz, pp. 110–12.

secondary education and in the larger towns resulted from this measure, even *Tot Nut van 't Algemeen* being compelled to shut down in 1870. But Dutch survived because the 1865 Act, as applied to the third-class aided schools, was largely a dead letter, and the number of such schools grew remarkably—from ten in 1850, to twenty-six in 1855, to sixty-one in 1863, and to 168 in 1887.[1] It was to these rural primary schools that the *Genootskap van Regte Afrikaners*, a society established in Paarl in 1875 to fight for the rights of Afrikaans-speakers, directed the bulk of its textbooks and educational propaganda.[2]

It was in the courts of law that the Afrikaner felt the effects of anglicization most profoundly, and this chiefly for two reasons: in the first place, even if he understood no English, he was not excused jury service; and secondly, the court interpreter on whom he depended was not infrequently a coloured person, whose normal subordination to the white man was reversed in such a situation.[3] At the official level, the use of English does not appear to have been harshly enforced. It was in the interest of the government to see that the law was understood by all, so that proclamations, ordinances, and acts of parliament were as a matter of course gazetted in Dutch as well as English throughout the century, even though the constitution of 1853 laid down that 'all debates and discussions, . . . journals, entries, minutes and proceedings' of the legislature should be in English.[4] It was not normal, on the other hand, to publish bills in Dutch, while there are signs that the policy of translating official documents into Dutch was growing more slipshod during the Wodehouse era. When Sir George Grey opened Parliament in April 1857, his speech was gazetted in both languages; but when Sir Philip Wodehouse opened the session of 1870, his speech was given only in English.[5] There are signs, too, that Afrikaners resented the obligatory use of English in Parliament from the early days of representative government.[6]

A policy of thoroughgoing anglicization would have required the capture of the Afrikaner's cultural citadel, his church. After an unsuccessful attempt had been made to recruit Dutch clergy in 1814, Lord Charles Somerset appointed three Scots clergy, who spoke Dutch and had studied in the Netherlands, to vacant pulpits in the *N.G. Kerk* at Caledon, Cradock, and Beaufort West in 1817–18. In 1820 he prevailed on one of these, George Thom, to recruit more Scots clergy and schoolmasters.[7] But if this was an attempt at cultural conquest, it was not

[1] Malherbe, p. 88. [2] See vol. ii.
[3] See T. R. H. Davenport, *The Afrikaner Bond: the History of a South African Political Party, 1880–1911*, pp. 8, 117 and n. 8.
[4] Constitution Ordinance, 1853, s. 89.
[5] *Government Gazette*, 10 Apr. 1857, 28 Jan. 1870.
[6] Scholtz, pp. 96–98. [7] Dreyer, iii. 363–4; Moorrees, pp. 499–509.

seriously pressed. Some of the Scots clergy married into Afrikaner families and adopted the way of life of their congregations;[1] they did not, on the whole, constitute a liberal wing (theologically speaking) in the *N.G.* synod, though their ascendancy in that synod, especially in the year 1837, has been adversely noted in some Afrikaans writings;[2] and their arrival marked no more than a temporary break in communications between the Dutch and the Cape Churches. The English language came to be used with growing frequency in services of the *N.G. Kerk*, especially in the Groote Kerk, Cape Town, and this would call forth some expressions of resentment among Dutch Reformed churchmen during the 1860s. The use of English, like the use of the Groote Kerk building by the Anglican clergy in the early years of the century, had originated through the courtesy of the *N.G.* clergy; but its continuance reflected the subtle pressures of an increasingly dominant culture.[3]

The British occupation of the Cape tended to confirm the traditional dominance of the State over the Church which had characterized the Company period and remained essentially undisturbed during the Batavian. But the term 'Church' now included the full range of confessions which enjoyed the right of worship in Great Britain, though there were signs of minor intolerance towards the sects in the early decades after the conquest. The fact that the 'State' was now an alien power from the point of view of the majority of churchmen also tended to attract attention to the officer through whom state control was exercised, the political commissioner. The office was ancient, it had been allowed to lapse in the eighteenth century, and was revived in 1793; but opposition to it during the first three decades of the nineteenth century led to its abolition by Governor Napier's Ordinance 7 of 1843;[4] and this in turn precipitated a movement for the disendowment of all churches. Saul Solomon's campaign for the 'Voluntary Principle', which he launched in 1854, did not triumph until 1875, largely on account of the opposition it encountered from Dutch Reformed quarters, where the notion of the separation of Church and State was repugnant, and the idea of mutual co-operation in their respective spheres (*soewereiniteit in eie kring*) was preferred.[5]

---

[1] Notably the Revd. Andrew Murray of Graaff-Reinet.

[2] e.g. Engelbrecht, *Ned. Herv. Kerk*, p. 32; Hanekom, pp. 432–3. Hanekom's list of 'liberal' clergy in the *N.G. Kerk* during the controversies of the mid 19th century does not include a single Scottish name.

[3] Idenburg, pp. 127–8; Engelbrecht, *Ned. Herv. Kerk*, pp. 34–35 (English services); Dreyer, iii. 148–62 (use of Groote Kerk by Anglicans).

[4] For the political commissioner, see Moorrees, pp. 64–65 (the office dated to the 17th century), 467–70; *Kaapse Plakkaatboek*, iv. 223–4 (its revival in 1793); Dreyer, iii. 22, 87–108, 119–37, 169, 207–68: documents relating to the office under the Batavian and British régimes. For Ordinance 7 of 1843, see Moorrees, pp. 664 ff.

[5] W. E. G. Solomon, *Saul Solomon*, pp. 34–47, 173–9.

2. The Diversification of the Economy

During the last two decades of the eighteenth century the economic power of the Dutch East India Company declined, but the fortunes of its Cape *buitencomptoir* oscillated in accordance with the changing relationships between the European powers. In war time they improved with the presence of visiting troops. In peace time the settlement was usually required to tighten its belt, and the free burghers felt the pinch of Company control, as was shown in the Burgher Petition of 1779. This petition, the legal and political aspects of which are handled elsewhere,[1] contained a long list of economic grievances, some of which were concerned, as in the time of Adam Tas, with the privileged position of the Company officials in the exploitation of a limited market: their right to trade on their own account; their position as middlemen in dealings between the burghers and the Company. Others concerned the need for access to better markets, where the burghers might buy their needs and dispose of their wares, above all to markets outside the Colony. The burghers also pressed for the denial of trading rights to foreigners, and the institution of better prices—a guaranteed forty rix-dollars per leaguer for wine, together with better opportunities for storage and a fixed payment to the Company; but they wanted to pay *recognitie* at *ad valorem* rates for loan farms in place of the fixed sum.[2] Renewed prosperity during the visit of the French fleet under Suffren, followed by an era of substantial building during the governorship of van der Graaff, covering the years 1780–91, removed much of the urgency from these complaints; but enforced economy during the early 1790s, when the Commissioners Nederburgh and Frijkenius slashed expenditure at the Cape in a vain bid to stave off the Company's financial collapse, resulted in a renewal of old dissatisfactions, which are well illustrated in the address of a frustrated concessionaire, J. F. Kirsten, to the occupying power in 1795.[3] Kirsten's grievances were mainly concerned with the inability of the burgher to find a market for his wares, above all his meat, his wheat, and his wine, for which he blamed the private and public monopolies; but he added two new complaints which had not troubled the earlier petitioners. The first was against the inflated value of coin, consequent upon the introduction of paper money in 1782, which was linked with an actual shortage of both specie and paper, and had led to a decline in trade with foreign nations because

---

[1] See below, pp. 298, 311–12.
[2] Burgher Petition, 1779, section III, quoted in C. Beyers, *Die Kaapse Patriotte, 1779–1791*, pp. 26–30.
[3] C. F. J. Muller, *J. F. Kirsten oor die Toestand van die Kaapkolonie in 1795: 'n kritiese studie*; *RCC*, i. 167–75 (inferior text of the same document).

they were unwilling to accept the Company's notes.[1] He also resented the attempt of the Company to call in the substantial arrear *recognitie* payments on loan farms, totalling some 376,360 rix-dollars, about seven times the annual amount due.[2]

It was politically imperative for the British military rulers in 1795 to meet the burghers' grievances, and they hastened to inform the inhabitants that they intended to abolish all monopolies and restrictions on internal trade. Burghers could forthwith 'set up a brewery or any other manufacture not under a general prohibition, ... possess boats, ... fish, or ... trade from any harbour of the Colony to another'.[3] An Imperial order-in-council of December 1796 threw the external trade of the Colony open to friendly nations on a basis of imperial preference; but a monopoly of trade with the East, and of the re-export of eastern goods, was given to the English East India Company.[4] Having emancipated the local producers and given them theoretical access to the outside world, the government then attended, like the Company before it, to the difficult task of procuring food supplies for the Cape Town market at reasonable prices, and protecting its treasury, and those licencees who were permitted to continue, against the enterprise of local smugglers.[5]

The Batavians followed on similar lines, keeping a tight hold on wheat supplies, which were scarce, but endeavouring to find markets for Cape produce in the Netherlands, and permitting trade with the West Indies and America. The Council for Asiatic Possessions, however, maintained a monopoly on goods produced in the East, especially tea and spices, while de Mist prohibited direct trade with England and her eastern colonies, or with any part of Europe save the mother country. The Batavians showed a great deal of interest in developing the Colony commercially in its own right as a colony of settlement.[6] A certain G. C. van Hogendorp planned a settlement in 1803 in order to develop the resources of the Tzitzikama coast, whence timber for building had been reaching Cape Town since the 1780s.[7] Other evidence of Batavian enterprise can be seen in the enthusiasm of de Mist, and in the stimulus given to meat and merino wool production by the report of W. S. van Ryneveld, inspired by the efforts of enterprising farmers in the Hantam and the south-western districts.[8] Their interest matched that of the

---

[1] Muller, pp. 62–63; *Kaapse Plakkaatboek*, iii. 155–8, iv. 38.
[2] Muller, p. 64; P. J. van der Merwe, *Die Trekboer in die Geskiedenis van die Kaapkolonie*, p. 113.
[3] *Kaapse Plakkaatboek*, v. 1–5.   [4] Ibid., 78–79.
[5] Ibid., 55–66, 68–73, 151–2.
[6] J. P. van der Merwe, *Die Kaap onder die Bataafse Republiek*, pp. 320–39.
[7] For van Hogendorp, see Idenburg, pp. 62–73; and for the timber industry Lichtenstein, i. 232; Thompson, p. 417; Lewcock, p. 10.
[8] De Mist, paras. 5, 45 ff., 104 ff.; Van Ryneveld; Lichtenstein, i. 103, 114; E. H.

THE DIVERSIFICATION OF THE ECONOMY 289

Englishmen, Barrow and Thompson,[1] which suggests that, had the Batavians remained at the Cape they might well have developed its resources on the lines attempted under British rule. But the absence of adequate communications or of adequate harbours along the southern coast, the presence of internal lawlessness and troublesome frontiers, and the realization that the defence of the Colony against acquisitive foreigners was likely to be beyond their resources, caught the Batavians in two minds. Baron van Pallandt, who accompanied de Mist, undermined the effect of the latter's propaganda in the mother country;[2] the Pensionary Schimmelpenninck in Holland was frankly defeatist;[3] while even van Hogendorp expected that the Cape, if developed, would break away from its parent, like the United States.[4] In 1806 the Colony's resistance to the second British invasion lacked real determination.

There was a certain continuity in British designs for the economic development of the Cape Colony as between the first and the second occupations. One aim was the establishment of an entrepôt where vessels from Europe and America could purchase goods delivered from the East. Such an idea was limited by the need to placate the English East India Company, which had an exclusive interest in the trade and was confirmed in its monopoly through the re-issue of the order-in-council of December 1796 at the beginning of Britain's second period of rule.[5] In 1813, however, the East India Company lost nearly all its trading monopoly, which opened the door to fresh speculation. Lord Charles Somerset revived the entrepôt idea, which gained support after 1814.[6] But such a policy never worked. The East India Company opposed it, and held fast to its surviving monopoly of the tea trade;[7] the regulations were so complex that they actually deterred Cape merchants from participating in the scheme; British merchants preferred to work through the established agency houses in Calcutta, while foreign vessels were still prevented from trading in eastern goods at the Cape.[8]

The gradual relaxation of British tariff policy during the first half of the nineteenth century affected very closely the development of

Burrows, *Overberg Outspan*, pp. 87-115; H. B. Thom, *Geskiedenis van die Skaapboerdery in Suid-Afrika*, pp. 267-89.
[1] Barrow, i. 17-19; Thompson, ii. 180 ff.
[2] A. van Pallandt, *General Remarks on the Cape of Good Hope, 1803*.
[3] *RCC*, v. 218-22.   [4] Quoted in Idenburg, pp. 68-69.
[5] V. Harlow and F. Madden, *British Colonial Developments, 1774-1834: Select Documents*, pp. 307-8. The privileges of friendly powers were withdrawn in October 1811, but substantially restored by Orders-in-Council of 1814 and 1820 (*RCC*, viii. 157-8, x. 188-91, xxxv. 231-2).
[6] M. Arkin, 'John Company at the Cape: A History of the Agency under Pringle (1794-1815), based on a Study of the *Cape of Good Hope Factory Records*', in *AYB*, 1960, ii, p. 307. See also *RCC*, i. 23-26, and Harlow and Madden, pp. 313-15, for similar arguments in 1795 and 1819.
[7] Arkin, p. 301; Immelman, pp. 81-85.   [8] Arkin, pp. 308-9.

productive activity at the Cape. Emancipated on the one hand from the worst pressures of the Navigation Acts, the Colony also profited at first from imperial preference, above all where its wine industry was concerned.[1] The elimination of continental competition during the Napoleonic Wars, combined with the enjoyment after 1813 of preferential duties on the British market, gave the Cape exporters a profitable trade. But owing to the ease of marketing, little effort had been made to produce a competitive export wine, so that when Britain began to withdraw the preferences she had given to the Cape, by two stages in 1825 and 1831, the trade took a serious knock. A further crisis came with the Cobden Treaty of 1860, which abolished imperial preference on wines and subjected the Cape producers to all the disadvantages of the long haul and the conveyance of their product through the tropics. Thompson's hope that wine would remain 'the staple commodity of the Colony' was consequently disappointed.

The gap was to be filled by wool; but the development of the wool industry involved the abandonment of the indigenous fat-tailed sheep which had played so important a part in the economy of the eighteenth century. Spanish merinos gradually took their place. The first of these had been imported through the good offices of the *Tot Nut van 't Algemeen* Society and the enterprise of Colonel R. J. Gordon in 1789. At the end of the Batavian period less than 8,000 of the one and a quarter million sheep in the Colony were wool-bearing, while Thompson, writing in the middle 1820s, stated that the merino breed had been confined for the most part to Government farms, and that the production of wool had been handicapped on account of sand-clogging and 'small decayed vegetable substances' which diminished its value in manufacture. After 1820, however, useful experiments were carried out by Andries Stockenström at Graaff-Reinet and by Major Pigot, a settler, in Albany, and the Sneeuwberg and Nieuwveld ranges in the Karoo proved to be good sheepwalks.[2] From the middle 1830s the export of wool began to increase significantly. The demand was created in Britain by the application to the wool industry of mechanical manufacturing techniques which had been applied to cotton several decades earlier, and although the Cape never achieved the profits realized by Macarthur's merinos in Australia, the value of its wool exports rose fairly steadily from £16,186 in 1835, to £176,741 in 1845, to £634,130 in 1855, to £1,680,826 in 1865, and to the peak figure of £3,275,150 in

---

[1] *RCC*, ix. 42–44 (1813 preferences); xxv. 259–64: *Report of Commissioners of Inquiry upon the Trade of the Cape of Good Hope*; Thompson, pp. 321–2; C. L. Leipoldt, *Three Hundred Years of Cape Wine*, p. 93, quoting Sir J. E. Tennent's *Inquiry into the Operation of the Wine Duties on Consumption and Revenue* (1855).

[2] Thom, *Skaapboerdery*, p. 63; H. J. Mandelbrote in VRS 25 (Mentzel), p. 211 n.; Thompson, pp. 412–13.

1872, after which it fluctuated.¹ Wool was thus the Colony's main answer to its balance-of-payments problem between the age of the vine and the age of diamonds, and accounted for nearly three-quarters of its income from exports in 1862–9.² The feather industry, by contrast, was of little significance before the late 1860s.

The early decades of the nineteenth century witnessed important developments in land policy. At the beginning of the century the loan farm system (*leeningsplaatsstelsel*) was the normal form of tenure in the country districts.³ Control over the use of land had hitherto been largely beyond the resources of the Government; but the attempts made in the 1790s to call in arrear *recognitie* payments, and the detailed regulations of the Batavian régime to determine the boundaries of farms, indicated that the old informality was coming under fire.⁴ The argument that the loan farm gave inadequate security of tenure, used by Fiscal J. A. Truter in support of the transition to perpetual quitrent tenure in 1812,⁵ had not so far troubled the frontiersman, in the view of P. J. van der Merwe, because it was possible in practice to do what one wanted with one's loan farm.⁶ Ownership of the *opstal* led, by association, to the assumption that the occupier had a continuing claim to the grazing and could not be evicted; sales of loan farms took place, and in 1790 they were loosely subjected to a 2·5 per cent. transfer duty;⁷ loan farms could even be surreptitiously subdivided, without any change of title. What was even more startling, land was occupied on an enormous scale without any title at all: the *trekboer* was as much a part of the scene in the early nineteenth century as he had ever been.⁸ The chief inconveniences of such a lax system from the Government's viewpoint were that it was impossible to control the spread of settlement, with all the disadvantages this had for the proper farming of the land, the raising of revenue, and the prevention of crime. In 1813 Governor Cradock offered the alternative of perpetual quitrent at *ad valorem* rentals; but the response was

---

¹ Thom, *Skaapboerdery*, pp. 198–9; S. D. Neumark, *Economic Influences on the South African Frontier*, pp. 165–71.
² J. A. Henry, *The First Hundred Years of the Standard Bank*, p. 13.
³ See Ch. V.
⁴ *Kaapse Plakkaatboek*, iv. 41, 73–75; *Ordonnantie raakende het Bestier der Buitendistrikten . . . aan de Kaap de Goede Hoop, 1805*, art. 267.
⁵ *RCC*, viii. 91–107: J. A. Truter to Col. C. Bird, 28 June 1811, the report on which Cradock's policy of perpetual quitrent tenure was based.
⁶ P. J. van der Merwe, *Die Trekboer*, pp. 107–30.
⁷ *Kaapse Plakkaatboek*, iv. 40: '. . . dat voortaan, wanneer eenige zogen [aamde]leeningsplaatsen, ofte eigentlyk den opstal derselver, 't zy publiequelyk, 't zy onder de hand, zullen worden verkogt, ofte veraliëneert de kopers ofte veraliëneerders als dan verplicht en gehouden zullen weesen, van 't waare koopsbedraagen van voorsch[reven] leeningsplaatsen aan de Ed. Compagnie te betaalen den veertigsten penning . . .'.
⁸ Lichtenstein, ii. 83; H. A. Reyburn, 'Studies in Cape Frontier History: I. Land, Labour and Law', in the *Critic*, Oct. 1934, pp. 41–42.

sluggish, as might have been expected in view of the boers' attachment to the loan farm system, and the Government did very little in practice to encourage acceptance of its offer.[1]

The Great Trek, in one of its aspects, was a continuation of the *trekboerdery* which had become part of the rhythm of *platteland* life, and which Cradock's Proclamation of 1813 had failed to prevent.[2] The slowing down of eastward expansion once contact had been made with the Xhosa,[3] and the allocation of much of the available land on that frontier to the Albany settlers in 1820, meant that land-seekers had to look elsewhere. By the mid 1820s seasonal trekking across the Orange river from the north-eastern parts of the Colony had become a normal event, and some boers began to settle in Transorangia.[4] Some of the Voortrekkers left the Colony before the frontier hostilities of 1834 had unsettled frontier minds, because they were short of land.[5] Professor Eric Walker has suggested that those parties included squatters who feared displacement through an impending auction of Crown lands, though there was no hint in the proclamation that land under actual occupation was liable to be expropriated.[6] The economic origin of the Trek lay, not in the shortage of land alone, but in land shortage together with the shortage of labour which followed Khoikhoi (and possibly slave) emancipation,[7] the insecurity of frontier life on account of stock thefts, and the fluctuations of British policy after the frontier war of 1834–5. The Great Trek was no ordinary trek: it involved the abandonment by

[1] *RCC*, viii. 268–80: J. A. Truter's argument in favour of transition to perpetual quitrent, 11 Feb. 1812; ix. 203–8: Proclamations of 23 July and 6 Aug. 1813, announcing the perpetual quitrent offer and explaining procedures; x. 215–16: Proclamation by Somerset, 23 Dec. 1814, extending the time limit for conversion on account of the meagre response; x. 279–80: a list of 64 quitrent leases issued in 1814, giving the rates for various regions. See also L. C. Duly, 'The Failure of British Land Policy at the Cape', *JAH* (1965), 357–71.

[2] See below, p. 310, for the ideological background to the Great Trek. On its origin see Galbraith, pp. 176–81; Walker, *Great Trek*, pp. 59–105; C. F. J. Muller, *Die Britse Owerheid en die Groot Trek*, pp. 50–80. M. Nathan, *The Voortrekkers of South Africa*, is weaker analytically than the above works, but is a well-documented account of the movement as a whole.

[3] See above, pp. 235–44, 252–3.

[4] P. J. van der Merwe, *Die Noordwaartse Beweging van die Boere voor die Groot Trek*, pp. 241–321; Macmillan, *Bantu, Boer, and Briton*, pp. 53–70; Marais, *Cape Coloured People*, pp. 51–53.

[5] Muller, *Britse Owerheid*, p. 53, quoting G. B. A. Gerdener, *Sarel Cilliers*, p. 131, and correspondence between the Voortrekker leader, Piet Uys, and Sir B. D'Urban.

[6] Walker, *Great Trek*, p. 84, and in *CHBE*, viii. 326, quoting the Cape *Government Gazette*, 18 May 1832.

[7] The importance of slave emancipation as a part cause of the Great Trek has sometimes been underplayed, in view of the fact that most of the Voortrekkers came from the eastern districts, whereas most of the slaves had been held in the west. It is clear, however, that some Voortrekkers lost substantial property in slaves as a result of emancipation (see H. B. Thom, *Die Lewe van Gert Maritz*, pp. 60–61, for Maritz's personal holding of twelve slaves valued at £1,540; and G. Preller (ed.), *Dagboek van Louis Trigardt, 1836–1838*, p. lxxiii, for Trigardt's holding of ten), and that those who did not lose slaves were not likely to draw too fine a distinction between slaves and free Coloured, whose emancipation certainly affected the labour supply in the eastern districts.

THE DIVERSIFICATION OF THE ECONOMY 293

the Voortrekkers, often at a loss, of homes they had built up over years, and to which they did not intend to return. This meant in some cases a considerable sacrifice of wealth, in others the translation of fixed property into liquid assets.[1] There were plenty of aspirant white landowners left in the Colony to take over the land which the Voortrekkers abandoned, and one consequence of the Great Trek was to extend the pressure on the land into the regions north of the Orange river to the east and west of its confluence with the Vaal, regions settled to a large extent by the Griqua under the guardianship of the London Missionary Society.[2] The discovery of diamonds would eventually precipitate a lawless scramble for claims, but a land speculator like David Arnot could be very active some years before any mineral wealth was thought to exist there.[3]

Another change at the Cape during the middle years of the nineteenth century was the transition from slavery and other forms of bond-labour to free labour based on contract. But no great change in economic relationships ensued, for the Coloured labourer did not acquire much bargaining power. Since the end of the eighteenth century the rural Khoikhoi had been virtually a landless people, very few possessing land titles recognized by the Government.[4] Forced to abandon their traditional pastoral life, they were obliged to seek new employment in the service of farmers, or in the Colonial armed forces, or to enter the mission reserves, or to repair to *platteland* village locations, or to emigrate beyond the Colonial borders.[5] A twentieth-century commission which examined conditions in Coloured locations in the Cape found a great deal of squalor, and endemic tuberculosis. Equally noticeable were the ravages of liquor, whether purchased in the 'canteen' or distributed by white employers as truck.[6] The ex-slave urban artisans, however, presented a contrast to the emancipated Khoikhoi. Throughout the period covered by this chapter they retained their hold over the traditional crafts—shoe-making, tailoring, wagon-making, building, and many others—which they had practised earlier as slaves.[7]

The era of commercial agriculture and free labour was also an era of

[1] See Thom, *Maritz*, pp. 81-83; G. Preller, *Andries Pretorius*, pp. 20-21; Muller, *Britse Owerheid*, pp. 52-55. There is some evidence for a decline in land values on the frontier at the time of the Trek.
[2] Marais, *Cape Coloured People*, Ch. II.
[3] J. A. I. Agar-Hamilton, *The Road to the North*, pp. 38-42.
[4] For illustrations of the manner of Khoikhoi dispossession, see D. G. van Reenen, VRS 18, pp. 82-87 and Mentzel, VRS 4, p. 36. For examples of land grants to Khoikhoi see Thompson, p. 308; *RCC*, x. 279-80.
[5] H. A. Reyburn, 'Studies in Cape Frontier History', in the *Critic*, Oct. 1934, pp. 44-48; Marais, *Cape Coloured People*, pp. 109-54; Macmillan, *The Cape Colour Question*, pp. 27-28.
[6] Marais, *Cape Coloured People*, pp. 256-9, 266-8.
[7] Ibid., pp. 259-60.

developing private business. This began with the Batavians, whose establishment of a *Kamer van Commercie* in 1804, on the initiative of Hollanders like R. G. van Polanen and R. A. de Salis, was the first attempt to put private business on an organized footing.[1] By 1811, but perhaps owing as much to British as to Batavian enterprise, there were forty-two small retail shops in the mother city. Businessmen were meeting at George's Coffee House in Berg Street by 1817. There was a Commercial Exchange with its own impressive building by 1822—a revival of the Batavian *Kamer*, which had gone defunct.[2] One of the early achievements of the Commercial Exchange was to establish and maintain relations with a Cape of Good Hope Trade Society in London, through which negotiations with the Imperial Government over its contentious wine duties of 1825 were conducted, and with the aid of which the East India Company's tea monopoly at the Cape was brought under heavy pressure and eventually abandoned in 1834.[3] The Commercial Exchange kept a close watch on the arrival and departure of shipping, and on the development of new commercial enterprises such as the export of horses to India from the 1820s. It looked after Table Bay's interests in the export of wool, especially after the beginning of competition from Port Elizabeth from about 1850. Its members were active in the exploitation of Namaqualand copper after 1854 (the first serious attempt to exploit resources which had been known to exist since the days of Simon van der Stel).[4] Known as the Cape Chamber of Commerce from 1861, it was the elder brother of similar organizations to spring up at Port Elizabeth in 1864, East London (1873), Graaff-Reinet (by 1875), Pretoria and Pietermaritzburg (1884), Johannesburg (1890), and other places. Chambers of commerce presupposed business houses, and these began in the second quarter of the nineteenth century to penetrate the *platteland*, where for some years still the *smous* (itinerant trader, often but not always Jewish) and the shopkeeper would subsist side by side.

Trade required improved communications, and although the South African railway age falls outside the scope of this chapter, the development of the Cape road system during the Colonial Secretaryship of John Montagu (1842–52) was of immense importance.[5] Telegraphic communication between Cape Town and Grahamstown was opened in 1864.

[1] Immelman, pp. 23–25; J. P. van der Merwe, pp. 338–9.
[2] Immelman, pp. 29–42; Lewcock, pp. 77–78.
[3] Immelman, pp. 58–60, 83–85.
[4] CGH, *Correspondence upon . . . the Discovery of Metals in Namaqualand*, 1854, esp. Lt. Govr. C. H. Darling to Newcastle, 23 Feb. 1854.
[5] J. J. Breitenbach, 'The Development of the Secretaryship to the Government at the Cape of Good Hope under John Montagu, 1845–1852', in *AYB, 1959*, vol. ii.

THE DIVERSIFICATION OF THE ECONOMY

The growth of the Colonial monetary system over the same period was rapid. Like the American colonies on the eve of independence, the Cape in the 1780s and 1790s travailed under the uncertainties of paper money (first printed in 1782) and lack of specie. The Company did its best to redeem its paper issues, and had recalled nearly all its first notes by 1789; but by 1795 over a million paper rix-dollars were in circulation again. The British printed another half-million, but left behind an equivalent value in military stores. The Batavians recalled all paper and issued fresh, and although they were faced with a trade recession they left the rix-dollar at about its par value of four shillings when they departed in 1806. Then, however, serious inflation began. Finding two million rix-dollars in circulation on their arrival, the British authorities were encouraged by the success of the wine trade to issue another million between 1810 and 1815, with the result that, aided by the post-war depression and the collapse of the St. Helena trade after the death of Napoleon in 1821, the value of the rix-dollar dropped steadily.[1] This might have passed largely unnoticed but for the Imperial Treasury's decision to convert the foreign currencies of annexed colonies to sterling in 1825.[2] When this was done, the rix-dollar had fallen to 1s. 6d. As it was commonly taken for granted that it had maintained its par value in relation to sterling, the outcry among Colonial creditors was great, and the Government felt obliged to leave the rix-dollar as legal tender until 1841 (though naturally without restoring its exchange value) in order to cushion the shock.

Conversion to sterling and the revaluation of the rix-dollar, however, were not the only developments of note. The organization of commerce required the organization of finance, and this was marked, on the one hand, by the appearance of insurance companies from the 1830s,[3] and on the other by the growth of banking. The Lombard (Loan) Bank, established in 1793, was the earliest bank, and its discount branch accepted loans from the public from 1808. Between 1837, when the first commercial bank, the Cape of Good Hope, was founded, and 1863, nearly every village in the Colony acquired its own local bank, with an initial capital of between £10,000 and £120,000.[4] The expansion of credit made possible by these institutions enabled the large commercial organizations in the seaports to offload their wares in the country districts, thus bringing the farmers well into the exchange economy.

---

[1] Arkin, p. 285; Schumann, pp. 64–65; E. H. D. Arndt, *Banking and Currency Development in South Africa, 1652–1927*, pp. 5–43. The Commissioners of Inquiry (in *RCC*, xxii. 130–53) and Thompson (at pp. 395–405) appear to lay too much blame on the Batavians for the depreciation of the rix-dollar.

[2] *RCC*, xx. 123, xxi. 5; Arndt, pp. 44–68.   [3] Immelman, pp. 110–11.

[4] Arndt, pp. 11–12, 178, 235–52; C. G. W. Schumann, *Die Kredietmark in Suid-Afrika*, pp. 109–10.

They were, however, hazardous enterprises, vulnerable to the fluctuations of the money market (especially when only a fraction of their capital was paid up and when their note issue was inadequately controlled),[1] and nearly every district bank either came to grief in the depression of the mid sixties or was devoured by one or other of the larger 'Imperial' banks which opened houses in the Colony from 1860 onwards. The relative strength of these new leviathans, which had the great advantage of being able to draw on the London money market, is shown by the fact that in 1863 the paid-up capital of the Standard and of the London and South African Banks together amounted to £1 million, which was only a fraction less than that of the twenty-seven district banks together.[2] Not even stronger assets necessarily made for greater security, however. Imperial banks also fell victims to their lack of caution, especially after the discovery of diamonds removed the ceiling on speculative risks. Thus the London and South Africa Bank, incorporated in 1860 with a share capital of £400,000, with headquarters at Port Elizabeth and branches at Grahamstown, Cape Town, Graaff-Reinet, Colesberg, Fort Beaufort, Uitenhage, King William's Town, Durban, and Pietermaritzburg, was bought out by the Standard in 1877, when it became known that it held £175,000 in overdue bills.[3] Yet the existence of such an enterprise is itself astonishing when we recall the rudimentary state of financial organization only fifty years earlier.

Although the salient feature of the Cape's economy during the early nineteenth century was expansion, the rate of expansion was uneven, and subject to a variety of hazards. Over-confidence in the closing stages of the Napoleonic Wars led to inflation and the sharp retrenchment of the 1820s. The slow build-up of productive farming in the late 'twenties and early 'thirties was followed by the emancipation of slaves, as a result of which labour became irregular for a few years, some land values dropped, and some farmers suffered capital losses. The 1850s, in which copper flared and fizzled, saw a steady growth in wool production and the influx of thousands of hungry Xhosa labourers to the Colonial farms, at a time, before the age of railways, when competitors for their labour outside farming were still relatively few. The Cape could now afford to pay for representative government and to indulge in the lavish public spending which marked the governorship of Sir George Grey. But in the mid 1860s a severe depression hit the Colony, mainly on account of the collapse of wool prices on the international market at the end of the American Civil War.[4] The depression reacted sharply

---

[1] Schumann, *Kredietmark*, pp. 112–13.   [2] Arndt, p. 259.   [3] Ibid., pp. 255–6, 279.
[4] Henry, pp. 13–23. For the political events referred to in this paragraph, see section 4 of this chapter.

THE DIVERSIFICATION OF THE ECONOMY 297

on the Colony's political structure, and produced the agitation against the Wodehouse régime which led to the adoption of responsible government at the beginning of the diamond era.

3. *The Extension of Freedom under Law*

The rule of law did not exist at the Cape during the Company period. The discretionary authority of the Governor and Council of Policy was vast, the authorities to whom they reported were far distant, and the Independent Fiscal, who was supposed to watch the Government in the Company's interest, was usually far from regarding the protection of the subject as lying within his province.[1] Freemen and Company servants had access to the courts, but those whose status was servile *de facto* or *de jure* had not. Members of the executive government, sitting as a court of law, administered justice behind closed doors. The law was to a large extent certain, for the Roman code and the Roman-Dutch common law prevailed wherever local *placaaten* and the statutes of India (or Batavia) did not cover the issue in question; but it was uncertain in so far as the burghers were consciously ignorant of it in particular respects, and had no ready means of finding out. The law was not uniform, for the severity of sentences depended, as the authorities openly admitted, largely on the legal status of the offender or the person offended against.[2] The law was not fully impartial, for the local courts were controlled mainly by white farmers, the central by Company officials, and they tended to protect the interests they represented. Nor were the judges trained men, which was a fact of great significance in the administration of criminal justice, where the Roman code left considerable discretion to the court in the imposition of sentences, and where the absence of systematic case records helped to encourage not only a Gilbertian attitude to crime and punishment, but also the idea (as explained by the Council of Justice to Major-General Craig when he proposed the abolition of torture in 1796) that it was desirable 'to aggravate the severity of capital punishments, in order to diminish the frequency of crimes'.[3]

---

[1] On the office of Independent Fiscal see L. Fouché, *The Diary of Adam Tas*, pp. 197, 220–3, 308–9, 316–17: Fiscal Blesius and the affair of W. A. van der Stel, 1705–7; Beyers, pp. 13–16, 132–9; and S. C. Naudé, 'Willem Cornelis Boers', in *AYB, 1950*, vol. ii: Fiscal Boers and the affair of Carel Buytendag, 1779; Boëseken (1), *AYB, 1944*, pp. 126–30: investigation by Commissioners Nederburgh and Frykenius of the dispute between *ad interim* Fiscal Baron van Lijnden and the cellarer le Sueur, leading to the abolition of the Fiscal's independence in 1792; *RCC*, i. 242 ff.: account by Fiscal W. S. van Ryneveld of the duties of his office; xxxiii. 62–70: report on the office by the Commissioners of Inquiry, 1827.

[2] See *RCC*, i. 302–9.

[3] Ibid., i. 306.

White settlers of Cape Town, Stellenbosch, and Drakenstein resisted Company authority in defence of the rule of law over the case of a free burgher, Carel Buytendag, in 1778-9.[1] This man's violent manner and his maltreatment of Coloured people in his employ had led the *landdrost* and *heemraden* of Stellenbosch to recommend his banishment. Governor van Plettenberg, reacting to this request, compelled Buytendag to move to Cape Town; but in January 1779, on the initiative of the Fiscal, W. C. Boers, it was decided to impress him into the military service of the Company and draft him to Batavia. Buytendag was then forcefully arrested by armed 'caffers'[2] and exiled, all without court process. The Batavian authorities subsequently let him return, but he died on the voyage back.

The maltreatment of Buytendag was not the spark which kindled the 'Patriot' movement, for the holding of secret conclaves and the spread of anonymous pamphlets had preceded this episode, and these showed that there was a good deal of political and economic discontent in addition to popular anger over arbitrary justice. But the affair brought public anger to the boil, and highlighted some of the worst features of the general situation—among them the imposition of excessive fines and the fact, admitted by Boers himself in his defence, that the exile of burghers, whether free-born or emancipated from the Company's service, had often happened in the past.[3] That this Fiscal had little respect for the free burghers as a class appeared, moreover, from the comparison which he chose to draw between the founding fathers of the Dutch Republic, on the one hand, and 'such as are named burghers here, who have been permitted as a matter of grace to have residence in [this] land', on the other.[4]

In their petition of 1779 the *Patriotte* asked for justice for Buytendag, and, arising from his case, that the fiscal should be limited in his powers of apprehension to criminals caught *in flagrante delicto*, and be made to employ only white men to arrest white burghers.[5] They also asked for the right to appeal to the Netherlands instead of to Batavia against sentences imposed locally, giving delays and—strangely—distance as their reason. They sought equal representation on the Council of Justice with Company officials, and asked that their senior burgher councillor should be made its vice-president. Finally, they asked for

[1] Beyers, pp. 135-7.
[2] The term 'caffers' here refers to employees of the Fiscal's department, normally Asians, sometimes slaves, who lived in the slave lodge and were employed in the apprehension of criminals. See *RCC*, i. 243-4.
[3] Beyers, p. 137. Idenburg, pp. 25-26, gives the number of people deported to the East Indies by W. C. Boers as 18 in less than 8 years—an 'abnormally large number'.
[4] Cit. Beyers, p. 39: 'soudanige Burgeren . . . aan wien als eene gratie op hun versoek gepermitteerd word om in (deze) land . . . te mogen blijven'.
[5] Ibid., pp. 26-27.

greater certainty with regard to the law: that the Seventeen should 'stipulate precisely according to what general laws . . . people at the Cape will henceforth have to live, whether the written Statutes of India or the Placaat of . . . the States General'; and that 'authentic copies may be put into [the hands of *heemraden*] of all special placaaten, or particular statutes and resolutions in force at the Cape which concern the burghers', or alternatively, 'that . . . a Company printing-house and printer should be established' so that copies of the law could be made available to all, and the Fiscal and *landdrosts* thus be prevented from extorting 'any more arbitrary fines'.

The appointment of burghers to official bodies which dealt with their affairs was normal Company practice, and Governor van Plettenberg regarded some of the burgher demands as reasonable. Therefore the Seventeen adopted the recommendation of the Chambers of Amsterdam and Zeeland in December 1783 for equal burgher representation on the Council of Justice, though they would not budge on the question of appellate procedures. They conceded the point as to the uncertainty of the law, not by sanctioning the establishment of a printing press, which the Company always resisted, but by authorizing the drafting of a general *placaat* at the Cape which would have to be first approved by the authorities in the Netherlands and Batavia. This was apparently done, but not very effectively, and the fact is generally unnoticed.[1] The *Patriotte* were not fully satisfied with the Seventeen's response, and decided in November 1784 to appeal directly to the States-General. A further deputation in 1785 therefore reiterated their demands respecting the administration of justice; but the States-General would not enlarge on the concessions already made, and the deputation returned frustrated.[2]

They had, however, blazed a trail, and within a few years of the fall of the Company in 1796 their aims were substantially realized. The Commissioners Nederburgh and Frijkenius abolished the independent status of the Fiscal in 1792, thereby starting a process which would end with the abolition of the office itself in 1827, the Batavians having first realized that the demise of the Company had made the continuance of

---

[1] Ibid., pp. 47–48, 77–78. See also J. L. W. Stock, 'The New Statutes of India at the Cape', *SALJ*, 32, 1915, 328–37. This writer seems to have identified an alphabetical edition of the 1752 revision of the Statues of India, for which he has proposed a Cape origin and a date between 1784 and 1790, suggesting 'that it was made in response to the demands of the petitions against van Plettenberg's rule'. See also C. 76, pp. 319–21, and C.J. 2488 (Cape Archives): Council of Policy resolution of 25 May 1784, and instruction from the Council of Policy to the Council of Justice dated 11 Jan. 1785, ordering the consolidation of the law, as instructed by the XVII in response to the request in the Burgher Petition at III. 7. Significantly, de Mist (paras. 87–89) was entirely unaware that any attempt had been made to provide a 'lawbook for the Colony'.

[2] Beyers, pp. 59–62, 70–71, 76–82; Idenburg, pp. 21–32.

an official who combined judicial and mercantile responsibilities an anachronism.[1] The coveted appeal to the Netherlands, which the *Patriotte* had failed to win, was granted in principle by the Batavians, but the break in communications caused by the war prevented its effective exercise.[2] The British alternative of vesting appellate jurisdiction in the governor, with assessors, which was applied to civil appeals in 1797 and to civil and criminal in 1807–8, was not a desirable alternative in theory for it retarded the creation of a professional appeal court; but, once a professional bench was established in 1827, justice stood to gain from the speed and relative cheapness of appellate jurisdiction on the spot.[3]

The reforms mentioned above effectively extended the civil liberties of all who were free under the law, but they had little relevance for two elements in Cape Society, namely the slaves, who had no legal standing, and the Khoikhoi, who could be sued in, but had no effective access to, the courts. The next significant stage in the evolution of the Colonial legal system, therefore, was its enlargement to include all men under its protection.

The status of slaves at the Cape was, with minor variations derived from the Statutes of India and Cape *plakkate*, essentially that defined in the Roman law. This was confirmed by Fiscal Denyssen in 1813, when he referred to the Roman code for his assertion that

slaves have not any of those rights and privileges which distinguish the state of the free in civil society; they cannot marry, they do not possess the right of disposing of their children, even if they be minors, they cannot possess any money or goods in property, they cannot enter into any engagements with other persons, so that they can compel them to the fulfilment of such engagements, they cannot make a will, and they are therefore considered in the civil law as not existing.[4]

For the obligation on Christian slave-owners to bring up their slaves in the Christian faith, and for general rules regarding domestic correction, Denyssen looked to the Statutes of India; and for the crop of particular rules, like the ban on slaves' carrying weapons or lighted pipes in the street, which were designed to promote the security of Europeans, he looked mainly to Cape *placaaten*. Certain restrictions on the power of the master over his slave gave the latter a shadowy form of protection:

---

[1] Boëseken (1), pp. 126–30; J. P. van der Merwe, p. 82.
[2] *Kaapse Plakkaatboek*, vi. 136–43; J. P. van der Merwe, pp. 82–83.
[3] *RCC*, ii. 126–8; *Kaapse Plakkaatboek*, v. 94–96: establishment of an appeal court in civil cases, first British occupation; Eybers, pp. 102–3; *RCC*, vi. 262–3: revival of civil and creation of criminal appeal courts, second British occupation.
[4] *RCC*, ix. 143–61: Denyssen to Cradock, 16 Mar. 1813, enclosing a 'Statement of the Laws of the Colony of the Cape of Good Hope regarding Slavery', of which paras. 1–8 and 25–30 have special relevance.

arbitrary manacling and confinement were prohibited, for example, and the murder of a slave by a white man was an offence as such, though the penalty was light if intention to kill was not proved. All in all, slavery was a legally rightless state.

The inferiority of the Khoikhoi, by contrast with that of the slave, derived not from his lack of standing in law, for he was never technically enslaved, but from his inability to resist the arbitrary assertion of authority over him by the white employer to whom circumstances obliged him to attach himself.[1]

Behind the British movement for the emancipation of subject peoples stood a combination of new forces. Chief among these were the Protestant evangelical missionaries, who attempted to put across the Christian doctrine of the equal value of all men in the eyes of God. In a complementary but essentially subordinate role, though they commanded considerable voting strength in the House of Commons, were the representatives of new business interests, who queried the efficiency of slavery as a productive institution and wished to replace it with free labour.[2] Such influences operated on both sides of the Atlantic Ocean and on both sides of the English Channel, though where the Cape Colony was concerned the new ideological impact was almost exclusively a British one, because the Batavian authorities, whose views on slavery were in step with the growing humanitarianism of contemporary Europe, were not in control of the Colony for long enough to implement their policies.[3] The impact was mainly British, in the second place, because the English common law proved more adaptable to the new ideological perspectives than did the Roman-Dutch. Before Mansfield's celebrated judgement in 1772, the English courts had tended to assume that the existence of slavery in England was legal, and they had no doubt that it was legal if practised by Englishmen outside their own country.[4] But once the status had been declared repugnant to English and Scottish law in the cases of Somerset (1772) and Knight (1778) respectively, political action of necessity followed. The slave trade was abolished in the British Empire in 1807. This led into a campaign for the amelioration, and subsequently the abolition, of slavery itself (1823–38), and it was accompanied by closely parallel movement for the improvement of the living conditions of subject coloured races throughout the British Empire, and for the overhaul of British legal and social institutions—the criminal law and the prisons, the poor law, and the factory system in particular. Slavery and the Cape Colony were thus only aspects of a movement which

[1] Marais, *The Cape Coloured People*, p. 111, quoting *RCC*, xxiv. 372, xxxv. 310–12.
[2] See G. R. Mellor, *British Imperial Trusteeship*, p. 424.
[3] De Mist, para. 116.
[4] Holdsworth, *History of English Law*, iii. 505; T. F. T. Plucknett (ed.), *Taswell-Langmead's English Constitutional History*, p. 183 and note; Mellor, p. 37.

covered a much wider area thematically and geographically. The movement was, however, resisted in South Africa for two reasons: it threatened, as in Britain, to undermine an already established order with fixed social assumptions and behaviour patterns, and its doctrine of equality was repugnant to the prevailing legal system. Thus, though the movement took root at the Cape, there was no Cape Colonial equivalent to the East Indian sugar planters with their interested clamour for the freeing of slaves (unless the 1820 Settlers, who 'for the most part readily acquiesced in the prohibition of slavery', filled this role),[1] and there was no Colonial-born Thomas Clarkson, while in the nature of the case a Colonial Mansfield would have been an impossibility.

The crux was the removal of inequalities from the law; but although some of the legal reforms of the second British occupation were clearly related to the equalization of rights, others were as clearly concerned with the transformation of a Roman-Dutch into an English legal system for reasons of empire.[2] Circuit courts were instituted in 1811, and special care was taken to see that they were made accessible to all.[3] The sessions of all courts were thrown open to the public in 1813.[4] Criminal process was brought into conformity with English standards, though not necessarily with English procedures, with the introduction in September 1819 of the Crown Trial.[5] Trial by jury was instituted under the first Charter of Justice in 1827, though without adequate attention to the advice of the Commissioners of Inquiry (who recommended the system) as to its dangers in cases involving people of different races.[6] An English magisterial system replaced the local boards of *landdrost* and *heemraden*.[7] All in all, however, the Roman-Dutch civil law was left largely intact, and the inequalities under the criminal law were removed by specific legislative action.

[1] I. E. Edwards, *Towards Emancipation*, p. 69.

[2] See, for example, the Report of J. T. Bigge on the courts of justice, 6 Sept. 1826, in *RCC*, xxviii. 1–111, especially his assumption at p. 13 that the adoption of English law was desirable, together with the English language, as 'the great basis of improvement', and his proposal at p. 17 to anglicize the bench and the magistracy.

[3] *CGH Proclamations, 10 Jan. 1806 to 2 May 1825*, pp. 153–9; Eybers, pp. 103–4.

[4] *CGH Proclamations, 1806–25*, pp. 259–63; Eybers, p. 105.

[5] *CGH Proclamations, 1806–25*, pp. 709–32, and W. W. Bird, *State of the Cape of Good Hope in 1822*, pp. 249–81 (text of the Proclamation of 2 Sept. 1819); J. W. Wessels, *History of the Roman-Dutch Law*, pp. 364, 381–4.

[6] *RCC*, xxviii. 24–25 (Bigge's Report, 6 Sept. 1826); xxxiii. 112–23 (Report of the Commissioners of Inquiry on the Criminal Law, 18 Aug. 1827), recommending the introduction of trial by jury under certain safeguards; xxxii. 274 ff. (Charter of Justice, 1827), laying down jury trials in criminal cases (Art. 22); Eybers, pp. 114–19 (Charter of Justice, 1832), laying down jury trials in criminal cases (Art. xxxiv). For illustrations of miscarriage of justice under the jury system, see Edwards, *Towards Emancipation*, pp. 126–35; D. P. Faure, *My Life and Times*, pp. 69 ff.

[7] Ordinance 33 of 19 Dec. 1827, in Eybers, pp. 109–12.

THE EXTENSION OF FREEDOM UNDER LAW 303

The removal of the disabilities of Coloured persons reached an important stage with the Earl of Caledon's proclamation of 1 November 1809,[1] though it owed something to the pioneering efforts of landdrosts Stockenström senior and Maynier in regulating labour conditions in the Swellendam and Graaff-Reinet districts before and after the Khoikhoi rebellion of 1799, and to Batavian legislation.[2] Caledon wanted to induce Coloured people to enter the service of the whites, and laid down that they, like other people, should have fixed places of abode officially registered. If they were unable to produce a certificate of residence, or a pass if travelling on their masters' business, they could be convicted of vagabondage. Landowners who took into their employ work-seekers who could not show that their previous employment had terminated were made liable to a heavy fine, under proclamations of 1795–7 directed against the harbouring of white vagrants and deserters.[3] Any service contract of over a month's duration had to be written and officially recorded. Masters were required to provide board and lodging for their servants and their families, to release their servants promptly on the expiry of their engagements, and to refrain from various enumerated subterfuges sometimes used as a means of binding them beyond the contractual period.[4] Provision was made for appeal to the board of *landdrost* and *heemraden* by the servant if his wages were withheld, or if he had any other legitimate complaints. The master, for his part, could arraign his servant for unsatisfactory conduct, while the court would protect him against 'wanton or malignant' accusations by the servant.

The measure brought the Coloured people under discipline; but it gave them much greater protection than they had had before, and although the restrictions on vagrancy attracted the fire of humanitarians, chiefly on the ground that they were discriminatory, an experienced frontier administrator like the younger Stockenström could defend them.[5] Less defensible, however, was the provision in a further proclamation of 23

[1] *CGH Proclamations, 1806-25*, pp. 119–21; *RCC*, vii. 211–16.
[2] Marais, *Maynier*, pp. 70–73, 117–19; *RCC*, iv. 294–5; C. W. Hutton (ed.), *Autobiography of Sir Andries Stockenström*, i. 282–3; *Kaapse Plakkaatboek*, vi. 24–25.
[3] *Kaapse Plakkaatboek*, v. 13–14, 106–7 (Proclamations of 16 Oct. 1795 and 19 (not 17) Oct. 1797); B.O. 61, p. 453 (Cape Archives).
[4] For example, making advances in clothing or liquor and using them as a lever in wage disputes; paying wages beyond the expiry date as an excuse for retaining a man's services beyond that date; preventing the widow or children from leaving on the death of the wage-earner, or making them leave without their property.
[5] Macmillan, *Cape Colour Question*, pp. 164–5, has roundly condemned Caledon's Proclamation, as the Revd. John Philip condemned it, on three grounds: first, for not making room for Khoikhoi land ownership; second, for allowing the *landdrost* too much discretion in determining the time limit within which an ex-servant was required to find a new master; third, for not giving the servant sufficient security, even under written contracts. Contrast H. A. Reyburn in the *Critic*, Oct. 1934, p. 51 (supported in Marais, *Cape Coloured People*, pp. 121–2), who has argued that the Proclamation 'gave [the Khoikhoi] only a lowly status in society, . . . but . . . defended them in it'.

April 1812, which empowered any farmer, with the permission of the *landdrost*, to apprentice children reared on his farm for ten years from the age of eight.[1] To tie the children in such a way was to tie their parents, whatever the terms of the contracts to which they had agreed.[2]

That the Coloured people needed legal protection was amply attested by the findings of the Circuit Commissions of 1812 and 1813, which, although they heard numerous charges by Coloured servants that could not be substantiated, at least revealed a considerable amount of violence in master and servant relations.[3] The London Missionary Society conducted a campaign on behalf of the Coloured people, of which Philip's *Researches in South Africa* formed a part.[4] On 15 July 1828 Sir George Murray, the Secretary of State, accepted a Commons motion for an address to the Crown to ask for uniform liberties for all in South Africa. Two days later the Advisory Council at the Cape put the final touches to Ordinance 50, a law which embodied the principle agreed to by Murray, and reflected certain suggestions made to Lieutenant-Governor Bourke in April by Andries Stockenström, who had urged 'the enactment of a law placing every free inhabitant in the Colony on a level in the eye of the law, as to enjoyment of personal liberty and the security of his property'. Stockenström, himself a member of the Council, with whom Philip had agreed 'remarkably well' in 1825, had also wanted 'strict prohibitions against ... an abuse of the liberty generally conceded', and suggested the carrying of passes by all persons when away from their home districts, to be asked for only 'upon well-founded suspicion of criminality'. The Council did not incorporate this suggestion in its Ordinance, but Bourke announced his intention of preparing a draft vagrancy law to meet the situation likely to arise from the passage of Ordinances 49 and 50, the former of which relaxed the restrictions on immigration across the frontier.[5] No vagrancy bill appeared, however, until 1834, Bourke having meanwhile left the Cape, and the measure then was disallowed.

[1] *RCC*, viii. 385-7. This Proclamation did, however, require the *landdrosts* to make detailed annual census returns of Khoikhoi living in their districts, on information which farmers were required to supply to the field-cornets. Further proclamations governing the Khoikhoi were issued on 9 July 1819 (text in *RCC*, xii. 249-50) and 23 May 1823 (text in *CGH Proclamations, 1806-25*, pp. 607-8).

[2] See Marais, *Cape Coloured People*, pp. 127-9; Macmillan, *Cape Colour Question*, pp. 167-8.

[3] See Reyburn, in the *Critic*, Oct. 1934, pp. 53-56. The name 'Black Circuit' refers to the Commission of 1813 which investigated complaints in the Districts of George, Uitenhage, and Graaff-Reinet. The Slagters Nek Rebellion resulted indirectly from its proceedings.

[4] Macmillan, *Cape Colour Question*, pp. 217-18.

[5] On Ordinance 50 and its background see CGH *Government Gazette*, 25 July 1828, and Br. Parl. Pap. 50 of 1835, pp. 169-73 (text of the Ordinance, given also in abbreviated form in Eybers, pp. 26-28); Hutton, *Stockenström*, i. 286-91 (Stockenström's memorandum, which is comparable with his earlier memorandum of February 1827 in *RCC*, xxxiv. 378-81); Macmillan, *Cape Colour Question*, pp. 209-19; Marais, *Cape Coloured People*, pp. 155-7; Advisory Council Minutes, 16, 17 July 1828 (Cape Archives).

THE EXTENSION OF FREEDOM UNDER LAW 305

Ordinance 50 was for the most part consolidating legislation. But it limited the power of employers still further by prohibiting contracts of more than one year's duration, and by forbidding the apprenticeship of children without their parents' consent. It deprived the magistrates of the power to administer corporal punishment. It also abolished the obligation on Coloured people to carry passes. This last provision almost certainly resulted in an increase in vagrancy and rural crime, as Stockenström and others feared it would,[1] though the establishment of the Kat River Settlement in 1829 was a partial answer to this problem.[2] On the side of legal principle, Ordinance 50 went a stage closer to the realization of equality of all men before the law, though, as Philip protested, it was still specifically directed to 'Hottentots and other free persons of colour'. Its substance, however, was later taken over into master and servant legislation from which all references to racial groups were excluded.

The emancipation of slaves at the Cape belongs, in all its phases, to the period of the second British occupation. The manumission of individual slaves who had worked for thirty years, learnt Dutch, and been converted to Christianity (or, in the case of Mohammedan-owned slaves, Islam) was a long-standing tradition at the Cape;[3] but in spite of the effective stopping of slave importations after the abolition of the trade in 1807,[4] it never came near to being a solution to the total problem. There is some evidence that manumission had become harder to obtain in the eighteenth century,[5] and although there was an increase in the number of manumissions as the day of general emancipation drew nearer, despite an increase in slave prices,[6] these did not keep pace with the natural increase of the slaves.[7] So effective had the ban on the sale of Christian slaves been, as a deterrent to slave baptism, that it was withdrawn by Cradock in 1812.[8] When manumission was

---

[1] Macmillan, *Cape Colour Question*, p. 221; but see also Marais, *Cape Coloured People*, pp. 180–1, referring to Br. Parl. Pap. 538 of 1836 (Aborigines Committee Report), pp. 644, 729, and other sources.

[2] For the Kat River Settlement, see Marais, *Cape Coloured People*, pp. 216–45; Hutton, *Stockenström*, i. 352–71.

[3] Edwards, *Towards Emancipation*, pp. 28, 151; Br. Parl. Pap. 50 of 1835, pp. 207–10. There is conflict of evidence as to whether the Mohammedan slave was automatically emancipated on the death of his Mohammedan owner.

[4] *RCC*, xv. 212–13; Marais, *Cape Coloured People*, p. 163.

[5] Edwards, *Towards Emancipation*, pp. 28–29, quoting *plakkaaten* of 1708 and 1783.

[6] Burchell, *Travels*, i. 28; Thompson, p. 321; Marais, *Cape Coloured People*, p. 163; A. F. Hattersley, 'Slavery at the Cape', in *CHBE*, 1963 edn., viii. 270; J. T. Bigge in *RCC*, xxiv. 427.

[7] Figures for manumissions are given in *RCC*, xxvi. 112–13, xxvii. 239–40, xxxii. 136–49, and analysed in Edwards, *Towards Emancipation*, p. 153, and Marais, *Cape Coloured People*, p. 167. For the increase of the slave population see *RCC*, xi. 438; Thompson, p. 490; Thom, *Maritz*, pp. 58–59.

[8] *RCC*, ix. 130–2. That this was inspired largely by a desire to prevent slaves' adopting the Mohammedan religion is suggested by Marais, *Cape Coloured People*, pp. 168–73, and Edwards, *Towards Emancipation*, pp. 113–14.

withdrawn from the discretionary authority of the master in 1826, and put within reach of slaves who had acquired the means to pay their assessed price, there was strong opposition among the masters to this infringement of their property rights.[1] It was therefore no matter for surprise that the various proposals made in the late 1820s for abolishing slavery by emancipating female slave children failed to satisfy either humanitarians or slave owners.[2]

Nor did amelioration prove an efficient way to grasp the nettle. Foreshadowed by Cradock's clarification of the slave's status, and by Somerset's institution of a Slave Registry in April 1816,[3] the purpose of which was to check the importation of new slaves or the enslavement of free blacks, a policy of amelioration was first deliberately applied in 1823. On 18 March that year Somerset issued a proclamation designed to facilitate the admission of slaves to the Christian Church and their marriage by Christian rites, to validate the oath of a Christian slave in a court of law, to ensure proper food and clothing, to limit working hours, restrict the severity and frequency of punishments, and protect the slave from maltreatment and the master from 'unfounded or frivolous' complaints.[4] The proclamation took the interests of slave-owners fully into account, and it anticipated by two months a resolution moved in the Commons by Canning on 15 May in favour of ameliorating measures for the slave population in British colonies.[5] Bathurst censured Somerset on 10 August for not waiting for a general Order-in-Council, but the governor claimed to have been ignorant of the Imperial Government's intentions when he framed his proclamation.[6] It is not clear from the printed records that he had in fact stolen a march on the English humanitarians in order to 'stave off [a] more comprehensive programme', though this has been suggested.[7]

Bathurst treated the March proclamation as an act of evasion, and insisted on the introduction at the Cape of a new ordinance based on an Order-in-Council drawn up in 1824 for the island of Trinidad.[8]

[1] Marais, *Cape Coloured People*, p. 167 n. 5; Edwards, *Towards Emancipation*, pp. 152–5; *RCC*, xxvii. 98.
[2] Edwards, *Towards Emancipation*, pp. 157–64.
[3] Hattersley, in *CHBE*, viii. 270–1; Edwards, *Towards Emancipation*, p. 53; *RCC*, xi. 102–5.
[4] Text in *RCC*, xv. 336–42.
[5] Canning aimed to defeat a move by Fowell Buxton to enforce child emancipation. See Harlow and Madden, p. 560 (text of Commons resolution of 15 May 1823); *H. of C. Deb.* ix. 274, 285–6 (Buxton's and Canning's motions).
[6] Harlow and Madden, pp. 566–7; *RCC*, xvi. 180, xvii. 42–44.
[7] Edwards, *Towards Emancipation*, p. 91; but see Somerset's explanation of his action in *RCC*, xv. 354–6.
[8] Edwards, *Towards Emancipation*, pp. 96–97; *RCC*, xx. 2 (Bathurst to Somerset, 8 Feb. 1825); Harlow and Madden, pp. 567–73 (draft Trinidad Order-in-Council).

THE EXTENSION OF FREEDOM UNDER LAW

Ordinance 19 of 19 June 1826 was therefore promulgated by Somerset's successor, Major-General Richard Bourke.¹ Sir John Truter, the Chief Justice, who drew it up, was alive to the different circumstances of the Cape and the West Indies, and made some significant changes, omitting, for example, the compulsory keeping of punishment record books for quarterly inspection by the magistrate, on account of the inconvenience of such a rule in relation to South African distances.² Bathurst accepted the revision but insisted that the new regulations should issue in local legislation and not in an Imperial Order-in-Council.³ The Advisory Council resisted passively.⁴ Slave-owners from all parts of the Colony, together with the Burgher Senate in Cape Town, protested vigorously against the new provisions, particularly those which interfered with the owner's discretionary authority over his slaves.⁵ A constitutional difficulty arose over the question of whether the governor was competent, in the absence of support from his council, to enact a law on his sole authority, and the ordinance remained in abeyance for three years, until the Imperial Government, 'wearied by colonial obstruction' in the West Indies and at the Cape, decided in February 1830 to issue its own consolidated Order-in-Council, based on the Trinidad ordinance, and applying to the West Indies and the Cape equally, thus imposing on the Cape the inconveniences and irrelevancies which Truter had expunged from the measure in 1826.⁶ Cape resistance intensified, this time with greater cause, and a minor outbreak of violence occurred at Stellenbosch in June 1831.

By this time, however, the policy of amelioration was no longer being taken seriously in Britain. As early as 1820 it had been decided that the British settlers on the Cape eastern frontier would have to do without slaves (though the magistrates in their midst, and the Dutch colonists around them, were subject to no such limitation, and the area in which the ban on slaves operated was interpreted as narrowly as possible by the Colonial authorities).⁷ Even Somerset, in his apologia to Bathurst of 31 March 1823, had professed to look forward to 'the abolition of Slavery entirely in this Settlement', and toyed with the idea of the

---

¹ Text in *RCC*, xxvi. 468–91: an ordinance of 50 clauses, as against the 42 of the draft Trinidad order.
² Edwards, *Towards Emancipation*, pp. 97–100.
³ Ibid., p. 101; *RCC*, xxvi. 37–38 (Bathurst to Somerset, 20 Feb. 1826).
⁴ Advisory Council Minutes, 5 June 1826.
⁵ Ibid., 3, 24 July 1826; Edwards, *Towards Emancipation*, pp. 101–2, quoting Burgher Senate minutes, 30 June 1826; *RCC*, xxviii. 271 (Bourke to Bathurst, 25 Oct. 1826).
⁶ Edwards, *Towards Emancipation*, pp. 89, 102–4; Harlow and Madden, pp. 567–73 (excerpts from the draft Trinidad ordinance).
⁷ Edwards, *Towards Emancipation*, pp. 65–77; Hattersley, in *CHBE*, viii. 271; *RCC*, xiii. 135–6, xv. 347–8 (ban on Settler ownership of slaves). For the geographical limits of the ban, see Edwards, pp. 71–74.

emancipation of slave children at birth,[1] an idea which would be taken up by the Philanthropic Society of Cape Town, established in July 1828.[2] Fowell Buxton, on whose shoulders the leadership of the British movement fell in 1823, had then set his eyes on gradual abolition, and nothing that happened afterwards inclined him to change his mind.

Amelioration was largely barren of results. Somerset's expectation that the reforms of 1823 would stimulate the Christianization and the education of slaves proved far too optimistic. It was generally assumed from an ambiguous phrase in the 1823 proclamation that education was intended only for Christian slaves, not the slaves of Christian masters.[3] The Guardian of the Slaves (appointed in 1826, and renamed 'Protector' in 1830) was unable adequately to fulfil his role owing to difficulties of distance, shortage of staff, and lack of co-operation from the slave-owners, who resented in particular the quarterly presentation of punishment books for inspection and the loss of disciplinary powers over their 'property'. 'As time passed,' writes Dr. Isobel Edwards, 'resistance stiffened . . . The result was a progressive falling off in the returns of punishment records'—seventy-six returns for the Cape and Stellenbosch from 3,024 slave-owners in June 1831, two returns for the whole Colony in June 1832.[4] Slaves had been given access to the courts, but at all levels the courts tended to show severity towards the slave and leniency towards the master, while the Protector himself found it necessary on occasion to connive at irregularities and maltreatment.[5]

It was partly for these reasons that the complaints of the Cape slave-owners were not listened to in British philanthropic circles, and partly because the eyes of the philanthropists were fastened on the large-scale plantation slavery of the West Indies rather than upon the less onerous domestic slavery of the Cape. Therefore, instead of the withdrawal of the 1830 Order-in-Council for which the Cape owners had pressed, the Imperial Government put out a revised Order in November 1831, which withdrew none of the 1830 provisions and tightened up on other details, more particularly Sunday work, diet, and the authority of the Protector.[6] The new *Zuid Afrikaan* fumed; Koeberg farmers met in angry protest; Governor Cole banned contentious gatherings and threatened to deport troublemakers. Only then did the Colonial Office yield to Cape pressure, and modify its rules, for example by removing the obligation on farmers to keep record books if they lived more than twenty miles

---

[1] *RCC*, xv. 355-6.   [2] Edwards, *Towards Emancipation*, p. 157.
[3] Ibid., p. 92; *RCC*, xv. 337: Proc., Art. 4: 'Christian slave proprietors . . . are . . . to send their slave children . . . to the established free school.'
[4] Edwards, *Towards Emancipation*, pp. 120-1.
[5] Ibid., pp. 126-7.
[6] Ibid., pp. 108-10.

from Cape Town or Grahamstown.[1] This was, however, a mere interim measure, for with the appearance of new resolution in the Anti-Slavery Society, encouraged by accounts of the Jamaica slave Rebellion of December 1831 and of the owners' retaliatory action, and by the appearance of a more favourable balance of forces in the reformed House of Commons, Parliament reached the point of voting for abolition in May 1833: all slaves in the British Empire were to be set free on 1 December 1834, but apprenticed thereafter to their former owners for periods of four to six years, with the intention that there should be as little dislocation as possible, and that by the end of their apprenticeship they should be in a position as freemen to fend for themselves.[2] Owners were to be compensated for their loss of property.

The Act of 1833, like the Order-in-Council of 1830, was drafted with the West Indies rather than the Cape Colony in mind. Many of the administrative details were left for the colonial governments to determine, but not all. The compensation payable to slave-owners was eventually calculated at about one-third of the assessed value of the slaves; it had to be collected in London, which was in general much easier for the West Indian magnates than for the Cape Boers, who had to employ agents and found that they demanded large commissions.[3] It was natural that they should grieve, especially when they reflected that in owning slaves they had broken no law, and that the external authority which had changed the law had itself previously connived at slavery.

The freeing of the Coloured people and the slaves effected a major revolution in the legal system of the Cape Colony, which would bear immediate fruit in the field of master and servant legislation. The master and servant Ordinance of 1841 was the Council's response to the release of the ex-slaves after their period of compulsory apprenticeship to their previous owners, which ended in December 1838. This law brought Coloured, ex-slaves, and white servants under common rules without distinction of race, laying down criminal sanctions for breach of contract, as had been the case under Ordinance 50 (the substance of which was incorporated in the new law), and as was the case in the West Indies.[4] After the Colony received representative government in 1853, the masters increased their authority over their servants by an Act of 1856, which would itself be liberalized by a further amendment in 1873.[5]

[1] Ibid., pp. 164–6; Advisory Council Minutes 19 July, 7, 13 Aug. 1832: Council's reaction to the Order-in-Council of 2 Nov. 1831; 6 June 1832: *Zuid Afrikaan* and the Koeberg meeting.
[2] 3 & 4 Will. IV, *cap.* LXXIII; K. N. Bell and W. P. Morrell, *Select Documents on British Colonial Policy, 1830–1860*, pp. 389–95.
[3] Hattersley, in *CHBE*, viii. 275; Edwards, *Towards Emancipation*, pp. 187–95.
[4] Marais, *Cape Coloured People*, pp. 199–208; Macmillan, *Cape Colour Question*, pp. 255–7; S. T. van der Horst, *Native Labour in South Africa*, pp. 35–38.
[5] Acts 15, 1856 and 18, 1873; Solomon, *Saul Solomon*, pp. 141, 147.

310   THE CONSOLIDATION OF A NEW SOCIETY

The extent of the humanitarian revolution whereby, in Marais's words, the 'Cape Colony turned a sharp corner', should not, however, be exaggerated. The white Colonial's insistence on privileged treatment *vis-à-vis* the coloured man, of which there had been strong indications in the 1779 Burgher Petition, came into clear focus again with the shooting of Frederik Bezuidenhout in 1815, the prelude to the tragedy of Slagters Nek, when a frontier rebellion was provoked by the use of coloured troops to apprehend a white man.[1] It is extremely doubtful whether Slagters Nek had any material influence in precipitating the Great Trek;[2] but the explanations which some Voortrekkers offered for their decision to emigrate from the Colony included the refusal to accept the idea of equality before the law[3]—a refusal which would manifest itself further in the constitutions of the Voortrekker republics,[4] and find clear expression in a judgement in the Appeal Court after Union.[5] Nor should it be assumed that boers who did not go on trek necessarily identified themselves with the legal changes which had taken place in the Colony. The social assumptions of debates in Afrikaner Bond congresses (on topics such as master–servant legislation, stock theft, and squatting) during the last two decades of the century would be recognizably those of Retief's Manifesto.[6]

Furthermore, legal equality for the Coloured man did not necessarily imply equality in other fields. He remained a proletarian, though a free man and a voter. He was still expected to show deference to white people, as to social superiors, and do his business at the white man's back door rather than in his living room.[7]

There was another limitation, this one affecting immigrant Xhosa who were not domiciled in the Colony. Such people received no protection under Ordinance 50, though Ordinance 49 of 1828 had authorized their movement into the Colony. 1857, the year of the cattle killing among the Xhosa, saw also the passage of a 'Kaffir Employment Act', which, until its repeal in 1867, treated the 'native foreigner' in a special category for labour purposes.[8] The same 'native foreigner' would

---

[1] On both occasions an outcry followed the use of black men to apprehend whites. See p. 298 above, and, for Slagters Nek, H. C. V. Leibbrandt, *The Rebellion of 1815, generally known as Slachter's Nek*; H. A. Reyburn, 'Studies in Cape Frontier History', in the *Critic*, Jan., Apr. 1935; F. A. van Jaarsveld, *The Awakening of Afrikaner Nationalism*, pp. 21, 226.
[2] Muller, *Britse Owerheid*, p. 50.
[3] See Eybers, p. 143 (Retief's Manifesto), p. 153 (Memorial of Port Natal Emigrants); G. Preller (ed.), *Voortrekkermense*, ii. 30–31 (Anna Steenkamp); *Dagboek van Louis Trigardt*, p. 347.
[4] Eybers, pp. 286, 364.
[5] J. A., Beyers, in *Ministers of Posts and Telegraphs* v. *Rassool*, S. A. Law Reports, A.D. 1934, 167.
[6] Davenport, *The Afrikaner Bond*, Ch. VII.
[7] D. P. Botha, *Die Opkoms van ons Derde Stand*, pp. 90–91; J. H. Hofmeyr, *Life*, p. 309.
[8] Van der Horst, pp. 32–35; Act 27, 1857.

also find himself discriminated against in the matter of passport regulations, which was unexceptionable but for the fact that by degrees the passport grew into a pass. An Act of 1857 'for preventing Colonial Fingoes and certain other subjects of Her Majesty from being mistaken for Kafirs, and thereby aggrieved', was superseded in 1867 by one to 'amend the law relating to the issue of passes to, and contracts of service with Natives, and to the issue of certificates of citizenship, and to provide for the better protection of property'.[1] Persons entitled to require a 'native foreigner' to produce his pass under the latter Act included all officials and 'any owner or occupier of land'.

4. *The Move towards Responsible Government*

The autocratic powers of the government at the Cape evoked little protest before the last quarter of the eighteenth century for three main reasons. In the first place, free burghers had always been led to understand that the interests of the Company—the 'Proprietor Octroyé of the Colony', in Fiscal W. S. van Ryneveld's phrase—were paramount. Secondly, malcontents could, and often did, remove themselves to those regions of the interior where the Company's writ failed to run: escape was hazardous, but less dangerous than opposition, on account of the severe punishment inflicted on political offenders. Thirdly, the absence of a popular press meant that organized political opposition was slow to develop. At the end of the eighteenth century, however, against the background of the Company's commercial collapse, direct and vocal opposition emerged, first among the inhabitants of the Cape District in the 1770s and 1780s, and subsequently in the frontier districts in 1795.

The first of these movements drew direct inspiration from the propaganda of opposition which had begun to emerge in western Europe and the British colonies in North America, as shown in anonymous pamphlets which began to circulate among the burghers, of which *De Magt en de Vrijheden eener Burgerlijke Maatschappij* was the most substantial.[2] It led to the drafting of the Burgher Petition of 1779, which not only laid great emphasis, as already noted, on economic grievances and on civil liberty, but also sought a political remedy for various ills—the appointment by the Seventeen of seven burghers to the Council of Policy 'whenever the affairs of the burghers and of the community (*gemeenebest*) of the Cape Colony are discussed', these councillors to be freely nominated and chosen by a majority of votes, and to be permitted to report annually

[1] Acts 24, 1857, and 22, 1867.
[2] i.e. 'The Power and the Liberties of a Citizen Association.' Text in Beyers, *Kaapse Patriotte*, pp. 203-13. Authorities quoted included Puffendorf, Grotius, and Locke. Idenburg, pp. 22, 109, attributes most of the document to Elie Luzac, a Leiden lawyer and uncle of Jean Luzac, editor of the *Leydsche Courant* and friend of John Adams.

to the Seventeen.[1] Representation on the policy-making body was not conceded by the authorities; but the directors, having allowed equal representation for the burghers on the Council of Justice, subsequently set up a committee of that council, consisting of three burghers and three Company servants, with a wide range of responsibilities in the field of local government, including roads, local taxation, police, licences, and food supplies. This committee in due course developed into the Burgher Senate.[2]

The burgher deputation which went to the Netherlands in 1784 established direct links with Joan Derk van der Capellen, the leader of the *Patriot* party, whose own political ideas had developed from a reading of Dutch, English, and American philosophers.[3] This was not surprising, for by the 1770s new conditions were making it possible for the Colony to break out of its ideological isolation. The ideas of the Enlightenment travelled through the barriers of censorship, while the slogans of the French Revolution later found their way into the interior, where they served as rallying cries for an incipient opposition movement in the frontier districts, with a different motivation from that of the malcontent farmers of Paarl.

The republican movement in the frontier districts of Graaff-Reinet and Swellendam, which emerged several months before the first surrender of the Colony to British forces in 1795, and cannot therefore be dismissed simply as patriotic resistance to an alien invader, made particular use of Jacobin jargon. The members addressed each other with such titles as 'citizen (*burger*) *Landdrost*', 'citizen *Predikant*', they denounced their opponents as 'aristocrats', recited a 'prayer of liberty', and sported the tricolour cockade. But H. C. D. Maynier, *Landdrost* of Graaff-Reinet, against whom the frontiersmen rebelled, also acquired a reputation at the hand of hostile critics for attempting the doctrinaire application of Revolutionary theories to the conditions of frontier life.[4] This contradiction shows that the slogans of the frontier need to be interpreted, not at their face value, but, as has been demonstrated by Professor Marais, as the catchwords of a harassed community determined to resist the imposition of any control, whether over their occupation of land or over their relationships with Khoikhoi, San, and Nguni people in the border regions.[5] At the time of the British invasion in 1795,

[1] Burgher Petition, 1779, III. 9, 10.
[2] C. 76: Resolutiën, Raad van Politie, pp. 314–53, 25 May 1784 (Cape Archives): response of the Seventeen and of the Council of Policy to the Burgher Petition of 1779; *RCC*, i. 244–5: van Ryneveld on the duties of the 'commissarissen uit den raad van Justitie', as defined on 13 July 1792.
[3] Beyers, pp. 179–81.
[4] Marais, *Maynier*, pp. 35–37, 88–90, and (less critically) P. A. C. Wieringa, *Oudste Boeren Republieken*, pp. 32–50; Burrows, *Overberg Outspan*, pp. 34, 46 (Swellendam terminology).
[5] De Mist, para. 36: the Graaff-Reinet rebellion ascribed to 'a complete collapse of their

however, the Swellendammers turned out to defend not the hated Company, which was now defunct, but the distant Batavian Republic, which they expected would defend their liberties, against an alien and—so it was argued—Orangist attack.[1] Within a few years it became customary to describe the Batavians' supporters as '*Jacobijnen*' and their opponents as '*Anglomannen*'.[2]

The British military government of 1795–1803 suspended the Council of Policy, but sought to reach accord with the burghers by laying stress on the continued protection of rights, privileges, creeds, and peculiar institutions. It also reduced the membership of the Council of Justice from thirteen to seven, and turned the committee of the Council of Justice into a nominated Burgher Senate of six members, with some increase in its responsibilities.[3]

The Batavian régime was more interested in administrative efficiency than in the extension of popular institutions, though de Mist toyed with the democratization of the Burgher Senate, now called the *Raad der Gemeente*.[4] This was clearly linked in de Mist's mind with his educational reforms, one object of which was to force up the standard of local secondary education in order to train people for responsible civil positions.[5] Local government in the country districts was decentralized with notable thoroughness, through the placing of new *drostdies* at Uitenhage and Tulbagh, and the creation of a new local official, the *veld-kornet*, who was to operate under the supervision of the *landdrost*.[6] Where central government was concerned, de Mist poured scorn on an accounting system which drew no clear line between revenue from taxation and net trading profits, and on a governmental system which, six years after the demise of the Company, was still structured as if the profit motive were the main incentive behind administration.[7] His reduction of the Council of Policy to four members—two Hollanders and two members of the old Council who had not served under the British—

moral sense'; C. F. J. Muller, *J. F. Kirsten*, p. 59, and Burrows, pp. 30–32, 41–43: the outbreaks attributed primarily to economic grievances; Marais, *Maynier*, pp. 69–73, 87–88: the Graaff-Reinet risings seen primarily as a reaction against a humane policy towards the Xhosa and the Khoikhoi. See also Lichtenstein, ii. 87–89, for a good illustration of a confused frontier idealist.

[1] Wieringa, pp. 46–47, 107 n. 100; *RCC*, i. 344. See also Burrows, pp. 36–57 (Swellendam resistance); Marais, *Maynier*, p. 86 (Graaff-Reinet indifference).
[2] *Bel. Hist. Dok.* iii. 191–2; Wieringa, pp. 64–65.
[3] *RCC*, i. 127 (terms of capitulation). For the Burgher Senate, see *Kaapse Plakkaatboek*, v. 18–29, 94–96; *RCC*, i. 244–5, xxvii. 390–7.
[4] De Mist, paras. 79–80; *RCC*, v. 178–85, but also 208–15; J. P. van der Merwe, pp. 91–98 (*Raad der Gemeente*).
[5] De Mist, para. 40; J. P. van der Merwe, pp. 171–94, esp. pp. 176–7.
[6] *Ordonnantie raakende het Bestier der Buitendistricten . . . aan de Kaap de Goede Hoop, 1805*, 23 Oct. 1805; De Mist, paras. 82–86; J. P. van der Merwe, pp. 120–60 (local government reform).
[7] De Mist, para. 66. Cf. Mentzel, VRS 6, pp. 34–49.

followed from this criticism, as did the introduction of a *Rekenkamer* (Accounts Office) and the (temporary) replacement of the fiscal by an attorney-general.[1]

Reversion to British rule, following the reconquest of the Cape in 1806, brought a return to autocratic control,[2] as was normal in Britain's colonies of conquest. The governor in fact took the advice of men with official experience at the Cape; but it was war time, and the future status of the Colony as a British possession was not firmly determined until the Convention of 1815.[3] He governed by proclamation, and was able to make important changes in the law on his own authority and without reference to London, as shown by the introduction of circuit courts in 1811.[4] With supreme authority over all branches of government, and with his 'political commissioner' attached to the synod of the Dutch Reformed Church, he really held all reins in his own hand. For autocratic governors like Lord Charles Somerset (1814–26/7), such an arrangement was satisfactory. But after 1815, when British ownership of the Colony was internationally recognized and began to be followed by British settlement, the live political issues which unsettled the England of the 'old Tories' began to stir the depths of Cape Colonial public life, and eventually destroyed the autocracy.

The Cape Colony had had no experience of a free press or of freedom of assembly. On 21 July 1800 Sir George Yonge licensed two individuals to set up a press and publish a weekly newspaper, the *Cape Town Gazette and African Advertiser*, but the same proclamation held a thousand rix-dollar fine over the head of anybody else who attempted to publish. No such permission would have been needed in Britain; but it was required in terms of eighteenth-century *plakkate* in force in the Colony.[5] Even de Mist, who approved of a printing press at the Cape, insisted that it should be controlled: the pamphleteering of the 1770s, followed later by Baron van Pallandt's critical account of Batavian policy at the Cape, had reinforced the caution of the authorities.[6] Where the right of

[1] De Mist, para. 73; J. P. van der Merwe, pp. 71–81.

[2] See *RCC*, vi. 6–19 (Caledon's Instructions); and cf. *RCC*, xv. 347–50: views of the Commissioners of Inquiry on the autocracy.

[3] *RCC*, x. 170–6 (text of the Anglo-Dutch Convention); E. A. Walker, *History of Southern Africa*, pp. 139–40; V. T. Harlow in *CHBE*, viii. 214–16; M. A. S. Grundlingh, in van der Walt, Wiid, and Geyer, *Geskiedenis van Suid-Afrika*, i. 230–2: commentary on the cession of the Cape to Great Britain. [4] *CHBE*, viii. 203.

[5] Advisory Council Minutes, 7 Feb. 1826, and App. R. 18–21: *placaaten* of the Estates of Holland dated 1702, 1726, and 1744, enforced at the Cape prior to 1800; *Kaapse Plakkaatboek*, v. 210 (Yonge's Proclamation). For the position in England, where the Licensing Act had lapsed in the 1690s, and the chief limitations on press freedom were a high stamp duty and the law of criminal libel, see W. H. Wickwar, *The Struggle for the Freedom of the Press, 1819–1832*.

[6] De Mist, para. 44; A. van Pallandt, *General Remarks on the Cape of Good Hope, 1803*: J. P. van der Merwe, pp. 235–7.

THE MOVE TOWARDS RESPONSIBLE GOVERNMENT 315

assembly was concerned, in 1823 Fiscal Denyssen unearthed a list of proclamations, culminating in Lord Charles Somerset's of 24 May 1822, which banned all meetings 'for the discussion of public measures and political subjects' without the sanction of the governor or (in remote districts) his representative.[1]

The 1820 Settlers, who had left England in the era of Peterloo, Richard Carlile, and the Six Acts, had little expectation of major concessions from an old-school Tory. But Somerset had lent his name to law reform, and it was from Somerset that Thomas Pringle, who was soon to initiate the campaign for a free press, received an appointment to the S.A. Public Library. Pringle invited a fellow-Scot, John Fairbairn, to help found a school and promote 'the English language and literature in South Africa'. He also associated with Abraham Faure, a Dutch Reformed clergyman and educator.[2] Pringle and Faure applied in January 1823 for permission to publish a monthly periodical, in which they undertook to avoid 'the discussion of all controversial or agitating topics'; but Somerset refused, explaining to the Secretary of State, Earl Bathurst, that Pringle was an '*arrant Dissenter*'.[3] George Greig, a printer recently arrived at the Cape, applied for permission to publish a non-political 'literary and commercial magazine' soon afterwards but was side-stepped by the governor.[4] Pringle and Faure then reopened their own project with the Commissioners of Inquiry, who arrived in the Colony in July 1823, and through them approached the Colonial Office.[5] They received permission, and began to publish their *Journal* and *Tijdschrift*. Greig reapplied on his own behalf, and by January 1824 he was publishing the *S.A. Commercial Advertiser* under the editorial management of Pringle and Fairbairn.[6]

Within the next few months first Blair, the Collector of Customs, and shortly afterwards the Governor himself, were injured parties in prosecutions for libel. A certain Edwards, who by general acceptance, including Pringle's, was a rogue, appeared as defendant in each

[1] *RCC*, xiv. 376–7 (Somerset's Proclamation), xvi. 438–40 (Fiscal Denyssen to Commissioners of Inquiry, 18 Nov. 1823); *Kaapse Plakkaatboek*, v. 199–200, vi. 53, 177; L. H. Meurant, *Sixty Years Ago, or Reminiscences of the Struggle for the Freedom of the Press in South Africa*, pp. 10–11.
[2] T. Pringle, *Narrative of a Residence in South Africa*, pp. 188 ff.; Edwards, *1820 Settlers*, pp. 88–89.
[3] A. M. L. Robinson, *None daring to make us afraid: A Study of English Periodical Literature in the Cape Colony from its Beginnings in 1824 to 1835*, pp. 26 (facsimile reproduction) and 246; *RCC*, xvi. 322–3 (incorrectly dating the document). For Somerset's opposition, see Meurant, p. 14; Pringle, p. 192; Robinson, pp. 17–18; *RCC*, xv. 266–7.
[4] Meurant, p. 17.
[5] *RCC*, xv. 241 (Bathurst's Instructions to J. T. Bigge and W. G. M. Colebrooke, H.M.'s Commissioners of Inquiry, 18 Jan. 1823), xvi. 203 (Pringle to Commissioners of Inquiry, 19 Aug. 1823). See also Edwards, *1820 Settlers*, pp. 192–3.
[6] Pringle, p. 194; W. M. MacMillan, in *CHBE*, viii. 257–8.

case.[1] Greig reported the first case fairly.[2] When the second case came up, the government, anxious to avoid the kind of publicity which might cause damage to the governor and his office, decided to insist on pre-publication censorship.[3] Rather than submit to this, Greig closed his paper down.[4] The governor then turned his attention to Pringle, who did likewise.[5] There followed the drafting of a petition to the king in favour of a free press, which Somerset cheaply derided.[6] Though they had denounced 'the arbitrary system of government' in their paper, Pringle and Fairbairn were much more temperate in their criticism of the governor than he was in his criticism of them. It was, indeed, in character that he should have crowned his attack on them by proscribing their Literary and Scientific Society, founded in August 1824, because 'it might have a tendency to produce Political discussion'.[7]

It took four years from the suspension of the *Advertiser* and the *Journal* before the main issues concerning the freedom of the press were settled. The question turned largely on whether permission to publish necessitated the submission by the applicant of a prospectus in which he imposed limitations on himself. Greig, who carried on his campaign in London, and Fairbairn, who re-entered the lists in 1825 with plans for a *New Organ* (Pringle having meanwhile returned to Britain), fought for full press freedom without administrative restriction.[8] They did not get it until Bathurst left the Colonial Office in 1827, and Goderich, his successor, laid down general principles as Fairbairn had insisted.[9] Henceforth publishing licences were not in the first instance to be

[1] Pringle, p. 197; *RCC*, xvii. 268-71; xviii. 441-2, 494.

[2] See *RCC*, xvii. 177-209, and Meurant, pp. 33-48 (extracts from the *Advertiser's* report on the trial); *RCC*, xvi. 113-16 (Fiscal Denyssen's observations on the charge).

[3] Br. Parl. Pap. 470 of 1827, no. 1 (Warrant for the suppression of the *S.A. Commercial Advertiser*, 8 May 1824).

[4] See Greig's *Facts concerning the Stopping of the 'South African Commercial Advertiser'*, 10 May 1824, facsimile reprint, Cape Town, 1963; Meurant, pp. 56-57; Robinson, pp. 28-31; Millar, pp. 183-4; *RCC*, xvii. 306-7.

[5] *RCC*, xvii. 312; Meurant, pp. 21-23; Pringle, pp. 201-4; Cory, ii. 288-91: Pringle's confrontation with Somerset.

[6] Robinson, pp. 34-35 (petition to the King); *RCC*, xviii. 56-59: Somerset to Bathurst, 3 July 1824, dismissing the 'cabal' who had organized the petition with irrelevant and derogatory comments on their status.

[7] Pringle, pp. 205-8; *RCC*, xviii. 285-97.

[8] Br. Parl. Pap. 470 of 1827, pp. 12, 13, 17-19; *RCC*, xix. 502-3, xx. 127-34, 355; Advisory Council Minutes, 4 Aug. 1826, 13 Mar. 1827; Br. Parl. Pap. 470 of 1827 (Bathurst to Bourke, 3 Dec. 1826).

[9] *RCC*, xxxii. 230-2, Goderich to Bourke, 28 July 1827. The core of Goderich's instruction was 'that any person intending to set up a Newspaper should be required to obtain for that purpose a Licence from the Governor, which upon the production of such an explanatory Prospectus, and of satisfactory testimonials to the respectability of his own character, he should be entitled to receive. If having received such a Licence (which it should in the first instance be obligatory on the Governor to grant) the Newspaper should thereafter contain matter which should be deemed libellous, the matter complained of should be submitted to the ordinary Tribunals of the Country by indictment for libel.'

refused. Publishers remained subject to prosecution for libel, but they could defend themselves in the courts (which were now independent of the executive), and the conditions were broad enough for even the argumentative Greig to qualify.[1]

The successful conclusion of the press struggle brought public policy within the scope of general debate. By the early 1830s, newspapers in Cape Town and Grahamstown were starting to lead public opinion in the major issues of the day. By 1860 local papers in the English language were common in the country towns.[2]

Freedom of assembly did not at first accompany freedom of the press. Permission to hold public meetings was often given, but could be refused, as on the occasion in March 1827 when the Council prohibited a meeting to discuss the banning of the *Advertiser*, or in 1831 when Cole obtained an ordinance threatening banishment for agitators during the slavery disturbances in the western Cape; but Sir Harry Smith's Council repealed Somerset's restrictive ordinance in December 1848, having decided that 'there is nothing in the state and condition of this Colony which requires or justifies the continuance of a restraint, so inconvenient and invidious, upon the liberty of speech and freedom of discussion which Her Majesty vouchsafes to regard as the birthright of Her Subjects'.[3]

The Colonial Office, fully aware that the political storms of the early 1820s made some control over the executive desirable, appointed a Commission of Inquiry in January 1823 to examine 'the general administration of the country, and the immediate control exercised by the Governor himself', as well as other questions.[4] Without waiting for the Commission's report, it gave Somerset his first Council in February 1825.[5] This consisted of six officers appointed by the Secretary of State, over whom the governor was to preside, and in consultation with whom he was normally to act. They were to debate only such topics as he placed before them, and he was empowered to overrule them on any matter, though members of the Council could, and occasionally did, record in the minutes their individual dissent from any decision, and the governor was required to explain to the Secretary of State any decision he took to diverge from his Council's advice. The introduction of the Council was followed by a tightening up of legislative procedure.

[1] Advisory Council Minutes, 16 July 1828.
[2] The *Eastern Province Herald* (Port Elizabeth) was established in 1845, the *Port Elizabeth Telegraph* in 1848, the *Graaff-Reinet Herald* in 1852, the *Cradock Register* in 1858, the *Queenstown Free Press* in 1859, and the *Burghersdorp Gazette* in 1860.
[3] Advisory Council Minutes, 13 Mar. 1827; Edwards, *Towards Emancipation*, pp. 164–5; Eybers, pp. 44–45.
[4] *RCC*, xv. 237–42; W. M. Macmillan, in *CHBE*, viii. 250–1.
[5] *RCC*, xx. 7–11; Harlow and Madden, pp. 111–14 (Additional Instructions to Somerset, 9 Feb. 1825); R. Kilpin, *The Romance of a Colonial Parliament*, pp. 33–51.

The ordinance of Governor-in-Council, drafted by the Fiscal and approved by the Chief Justice, now became the standard form. The competence of the governor to legislate without his Council was actually questioned in 1826, but not put to the test.[1] Reserve powers were vested in the Crown, without whose sanction no local ordinance could come into force save in cases of urgent local necessity. This Advisory Council was similar in function to the old Council of Policy after the Batavians had remodelled it.[2] Its establishment in 1825 anticipated by over a year the recommendations of the Commissioners of Inquiry, who considered the use made of it too limited and its power to control the governor insufficient, and recommended a reduction in the governor's meagre-enough patronage in favour of the Crown.[3] After 1834, when its executive functions were assigned to a new Executive Council, some of its deficiencies were made good. The Cape Executive of 1834-53 was strong by standards set elsewhere in the British Empire, above all in its control over the making of policy (no longer rigidly limited to the governor, as in 1825-34), and in the power wielded through it by the local Colonial Secretary—an office remarked upon by the Commissioners of Inquiry in 1826, which acquired great political importance in the period of John Montagu (1842-52), and still had it during the tenures of R. W. Rawson and Richard Southey (1854-72).[4]

Administrative competence, however, of whatever quality, could not extinguish a feeling, detected by the Commissioners of Inquiry in the 'younger portion of the community', of 'honest pride in the advancement of their native country, and a laudable desire to participate in it'.[5]

At the level of local government, important changes, both destructive and constructive, were soon brought about. As part of a calculated attempt to alter local tradition, the Burgher Senate was abolished in 1828, and the boards of *Landdrost* and *Heemraden* replaced by Civil Commissioners and Resident Magistrates (two offices normally held by the same person, with the magisterial function predominating).[6] But to relieve the central government of responsibility for trivia, elective

---

[1] Edwards, *Towards Emancipation*, p. 103. See *RCC*, xxxii. 282, for the relevant section of the 1827 Charter of Justice, on which the case against the Governor's discretionary legislative authority was made to depend.
[2] A. K. Fryer, 'The Government of the Cape of Good Hope, 1825-54: the Age of Imperial Reform', in *AYB*, *1964*, i. 29-34.
[3] *RCC*, xxvii. 342-97, esp. pp. 362-7.
[4] *RCC*, xxvii. 353-5; Fryer, pp. 39-40, 55-59; J. J. Breitenbach, 'The Development of the Secretaryship to the Government at the Cape of Good Hope under John Montagu, 1845-1852', in *AYB*, *1959*, ii, esp. pp. 177-84.
[5] *RCC*, xxvii. 375.
[6] *RCC*, xxvii. 377-80, 387-97: the Commissioners of Inquiry recommend the abolition of *Landdrosts* and *Heemraden* and the Burgher Senate; Macmillan, in *CHBE*, viii. 260.

municipal boards were created in 1836,[1] Cape Town got its municipality back in 1839, and road boards with the power to levy rates could be set up under an ordinance of 1843.[2] The authority of these and other bodies in the rural areas was eventually brought under elective divisional councils from 1855.[3] There was no legal colour bar; the Coloured people in due course acquired a small degree of representation on some municipal councils, and their enfranchisement in the Constitution of 1853 would owe something to this precedent of 1836; yet the establishment of elective local institutions also had much to do with the failure of Coloured people to advance their interests after emancipation, for the householder franchise in the towns and the Lower-House qualifications which operated in the divisional councils ensured white control of both. Coloured people came to realize that more was to be had from 'the beneficent administration of enlightened magistrates' than from the elected representatives of their 'lords and masters'.[4]

Where central government was concerned, repeated petitions for more local control were made from the mid eighteen-twenties. When the Burgher Senate refused to publish the Slave Ordinance of 1826 until Bourke threatened that it would be 'held responsible ... for any mischief that might result', three of its members resigned, and their resignation prompted a well-signed petition for the future election of Burgher Senators. The Council, however, rejected this demand, and Bourke opposed a subsequent petition for a representative assembly which went before the Commons in June 1827.[5] In July 1828 four hundred people met in the Cape Town Commercial Hall to consider another such petition, and received support from Albany.[6] Further petitions reached Britain in 1830 and 1842; but at a time when Great Britain was herself only beginning to move towards democratic government, and when the lessons of the Durham Report of 1839 still lay in the future, all were unsuccessful.[7] The arguments advanced in Downing Street changed as the years went by. In 1827 Wilmot Horton argued against representative government because the Cape was a colony of conquest under a non-British system of law, because the Commissioners of Inquiry had not finished their investigations, because some other colonies had not got

---

[1] Eybers, pp. 78–81; K. S. Hunt, 'The Development of Municipal Government in the Eastern Province of the Cape of Good Hope, with special reference to Grahamstown, 1827–1862', in *AYB, 1961*, esp. pp. 137–47 and documentary appendixes.
[2] Eybers, pp. 81–83. [3] Act 5 of 1855; Eybers, pp. 83–85.
[4] Macmillan, *Cape Colour Question*, pp. 268–9.
[5] Walker, *Southern Africa*, p. 165; Edwards, *Towards Emancipation*, pp. 101–2; *RCC*, xxvii. 89–90, 207–8: Bourke's conflict with Burgher Senate; xxviii. 452–5, xxxi. 443–9 (petition to the Commons).
[6] Immelman, *Men of Good Hope*, pp. 47–48; Walker, *Southern Africa*, p. 167.
[7] Eybers, pp. 30–38, 41–43; Br. Parl. Pap. 400 of 1846, pp. 1–7; Bell and Morrell, pp. 47–53.

representative government, and because the governor of the Cape had advised against it. Speaking against the 1830 petition, Sir George Murray raised the slavery issue, which he insisted should be resolved first, the smallness and geographical spread of the population and its general cultural backwardness, and the danger of division in the white population along cultural lines. Stanley's reflective dispatch of 1842 reiterated those objections of Murray's which still applied, but showed greater concern for actual constitutional mechanics: how to achieve the balanced representation of very different cultural groups, if justice were to be done both to the 'wealthy, active and intelligent class', on the one hand, and to the numerical majority, on the other; and how to set up a single legislature without offending regional interests when a partial *Ausgleich* of the Eastern Province under its own Lieutenant-Governor had already begun to take place.[1]

Though unwilling to concede a representative legislature, however, successive British governments had agreed to introduce an unofficial element. Two Colonists had been added to the Advisory Council in 1827.[2] After the passage of the Reform Bill of 1832 Sir Benjamin D'Urban had been instructed to set up a Legislative Council of five officials and five to seven unofficial members, selected by himself from 'out of the chief landed proprietors and principal merchants' of the Colony.[3] This 'constitution' was a step in the direction of government by consent, but it proved to be unsatisfactory in practice. It was promulgated by Letters Patent, and could be, and was, amended by the same process when successive governors were appointed, and therefore lacked stability.[4] It left a great deal of discretionary authority in the hands of the governor—the right to initiate legislation in certain fields, the right of veto, the right of appointing (or of not appointing) unofficial members. It placed a number of important topics outside the competence of the legislature—constitutional amendment, the Civil List, and the granting of Crown Land, for example, while reservation of all laws was automatic until 1846. The unofficial element, who never reached the maximum permitted strength and sometimes fell below the minimum,[5] proved an ineffective foil to the better co-ordinated executive team. Governors tended almost invariably to choose the unofficial members from the western Cape, largely because there were few in the east who could afford to be away from home for long periods; but this tended to stimulate eastern separatist feelings. Finally, the Council did not satisfy Colonial opinion because it contained no elective element.

[1] Eybers, pp. 39–41.
[2] Harlow and Madden, p. 115; *RCC*, xxxii. 6.
[3] Harlow and Madden, pp. 115–19; Kilpin, *Romance of a Colonial Parliament*, pp. 53–80.
[4] See H. J. Mandelbrote, in *CHBE*, viii. 367–75, and Fryer, pp. 7–10, for illustrations of this defect.   [5] See the Chart in Fryer, p. 143.

THE MOVE TOWARDS RESPONSIBLE GOVERNMENT 321

When the Whigs returned to power in Great Britain in 1846, their minds now more attuned to the constitutional theories of the Colonial Reformers, British objections to the principle of representative government at the Cape were removed. Earl Grey, Colonial Secretary, told Governor Sir Henry Pottinger in November that Her Majesty's Government entertained 'the strongest prepossessions in favour of' representative government, reminded him that his predecessors had allowed the dialogue to lapse at the point where Stanley had left it in 1842, and went on to hint that 'on a question of this nature, some difficulties may be wisely encountered, and some apparent risks well incurred' in the interest of 'intrusting the remote dependencies of a metropolitan state with the largest powers of self-government, in whatever relates to their internal and local affairs'.[1] When Grey wrote, most of the earlier objections raised against representative government no longer held; but its realization was delayed through the appearance of unexpected causes of division within the Cape community.

First came the dispute about convicts. Grey decided in August 1848 to send Irish ticket-of-leave convicts to the Cape, hoping thus to help the Colony overcome its labour shortage, but he failed to anticipate the public opposition of which he got wind only after the convicts had sailed.[2] An Anti-Convict Association was quickly formed in Cape Town, and although Sir Harry Smith undertook not to land convicts from the *Neptune* before receiving fresh instructions from the Secretary of State (which were tardily dispatched in November 1849 and arrived in February, whereupon the ship was ordered away), the Association organized a boycott of those who attempted to supply the *Neptune* with provisions.[3] The episode demonstrated that Cape Colonists could have strong political opinions, that they could express them in a semi-violent way, and that the Government, when confronted with coercive actions by a pressure group, could resist the temptation of resorting to arbitrary methods. Its main contribution, however, was to bring the Dutch-speakers and the English liberals together, help them to bury the antagonisms which had divided them since slavery days, and thus create the setting in which a popular party could emerge. It also destroyed the unofficial element in the Legislative Council, for all but one of them resigned rather than undergo the 'physical, moral and economic' pressure to which they had been subjected by the Association.[4]

[1] Br. Parl. Pap. 1137 of 1850, pp. 92–93.
[2] Fryer, pp. 13–19, quoting J. F. Gobregts, 'Die Anti-Bandiete Agitasie aan die Kaap', unpublished M.A. thesis, University of Stellenbosch, 1937; W. P. Morrell, *British Colonial Policy in the Age of Peel and Russell*, pp. 403–6; Mandelbrote, in *CHBE*, viii. 377; Breitenbach, p. 255.
[3] Kilpin, *Romance of a Colonial Parliament*, pp. 69–76; R. W. Murray, *South African Reminiscences*, p. 3; D. P. Faure, *My Life and Times*, pp. 7–11; Bell and Morrell, pp. 312–14.
[4] Mandelbrote, in *CHBE*, viii. 378; Fryer, pp. 15–18.

Next came a major controversy over the membership of the Legislative Council, which Smith attempted to reconstitute after the unofficial members had resigned, by inviting the municipal and road boards to submit nominations. Following the unofficial elections which they organized, he appointed Christoffel Brand, Andries Stockenström, F. W. Reitz, and John Fairbairn, who had headed the poll; but in place of the fifth favourite, J. H. Wicht, he chose the reluctant Robert Godlonton, who was lower on the list, because he was an influential easterner and leader of Grahamstown separatist opinion. Smith's choice was quite lawful, and sensible in view of his need to have a proper geographical spread of Colonial opinion for the consideration of the proposed constitutional changes. His selection of councillors equalized east and west, English and Dutch. But the men who had headed the unofficial poll, probably failing to realize that their actions would delay self-government, resigned from the Council and formed themselves into an opposition pressure group in association with the Cape Town municipality. They drew up their own constitutional proposals, to rival those that would go forward in the name of the rump of the Legislative Council, which Smith had meanwhile hastily reconstituted as a 'commission'.[1]

A third storm arose, which could easily have scotched the movement for constitutional reform, but in the end did not do so. This was the outbreak of the Kat River rebellion of 1851, which followed on the 1850 frontier war, and in due course gave rise to rumours of unrest among the Coloured levies returning to the west, as a result of which a near-panic seems to have developed in some white farming communities. These developments would encourage Smith's conservative advisers to work for high rather than low franchise qualifications, but did not result in the limitation of the vote either to white men or to rich men. An agitation for the abandonment of high franchise qualifications actually emanated in part from western Dutch farmers, whose desire for a low franchise, when coupled with their fear of Coloured hostility, is not easy to explain. The political interest of the Coloured people, whose performance during the constitutional debates was on the whole passive, was safeguarded by Downing Street's insistence on non-racial qualifications, and at the Cape by the stand of the popular party, made up of a handful of English-speaking liberals, like Fairbairn, and the still predominantly Dutch population of the capital.[2] Fairbairn regarded

---

[1] Mandelbrote, in *CHBE*, viii. 380–1; Fryer, pp. 19–20; Hutton, *Stockenström*, ii. 297; Breitenbach, pp. 257–8, 260–1; B. le Cordeur, 'Robert Godlonton as Architect of Frontier Opinion, 1850–1857', in *AYB, 1959*, ii. 84–89, 156; A. H. Duminy, 'The Role of Sir Andries Stockenström in Cape Politics, 1848–1856', *AYB, 1960*, ii. 106–8, 165.

[2] Marais, *Cape Coloured People*, pp. 208–15, 239–45; S. Trapido, 'The Origins of the Cape Franchise Qualifications of 1853', *JAH*, v, 1964, 37–54. See also the evidence in Br. Parl. Pap. 1362, 1581, and 1636 of 1851–3, cited by Marais.

THE MOVE TOWARDS RESPONSIBLE GOVERNMENT 323

racial qualifications for the franchise as irrelevant, while the Dutch hoped that a low qualification would enable them to contain their main rivals, the English-speaking business community of east and west.

The Cape Colony took up Grey's invitation to ask for representative government in July 1848, when Sir Harry Smith replied to the offer and enclosed his advisers' views.[1] The Executive Council and the judges had agreed over bicameral representative government (having firmly rejected responsible), with an upper house consisting of life nominees and an elective assembly. With regard to the franchise, all agreed with Montagu that it should be 'based on such a moderate qualification as will enable the intelligent and industrious man of colour to share with his fellow colonists of European descent in the privilege of voting for the representatives of the people'. Montagu himself wanted to apply the existing property qualifications under the municipal and road board ordinances, Porter to give some representation to tenants-at-will, and although the Committee of the Board of Trade and Plantations, to whom the documents were referred, expressed approval of the 'Attorney-General's Draft' (as a revised draft by Porter came to be known), they sided with Montagu on the franchise question. In the light of this response, Porter made a compromise proposal for a £25 occupational qualification, which prevailed in the long run, despite the outbreak of the frontier war and the campaign of the popular party.

Stockenström and Fairbairn, who took their rival draft of sixteen articles to London in 1851, were determined to place the strongest possible limitations on the powers of the Secretary of State and the Colonial Executive. They therefore pressed for an elective upper house, chosen on a low franchise and with a relatively low membership qualification (£1,000 against Porter's £2,000), the removal of the governor's right to dissolve one House without dissolving the other, and something like responsible government. These proposals were turned down in England, however, in favour of Porter's revised draft of ninety-four articles, which had been approved by the Commission of the Legislative Council. It was debated in a new Legislative Council in the early months of 1852, in an atmosphere of some tension on account of the racial conflicts on the frontier in the previous year, which had stimulated a reaction against the earlier low franchise proposals. In April the Legislative Council reverted to a £50 occupational qualification. But Porter's influence prevailed on Lieutenant-Governor Darling after Smith's departure, and was reflected in a return to the £25 franchise, together with

[1] For the constitutional debates leading to representative government see the works by Mandelbrote, Kilpin, Breitenbach, le Cordeur, Duminy, Trapido, and Fryer already referred to, and also J. R. Putzel, 'William Porter and Constitutional Issues at the Cape, 1839–1873', unpublished M.A. thesis, University of Cape Town, 1942. The main documents are in Br. Parl. Pap. 1137 of 1850, 1362 of 1851, 1427 and 1581 of 1852.

a £50 income qualification, when the ordinance was confirmed by Order-in-Council in March 1853, to take effect from 1 July.[1]

The 1853 constitution was, on the whole, well received, though some would soon regard it as no more than an interim measure. Opposition to it during the early years was focused, not, as might be expected, on its franchise provisions, which were not seriously challenged in the period covered by this chapter, but on its answer to the political tensions between east and west.

Separatism was the banner under which the residents of distant parts of the Cape Colony challenged the political supremacy of Cape Town and the west, and the word carried a variety of meanings. At one extreme, it meant the complete constitutional separation of east and west as distinct colonies, an ambition which was realized in the case of Natal in 1856, for a short while in the 1860s attracted people in British Kaffraria, and sometimes found supporters in the eastern Cape.[2] Alternatively, it might find expression in a desire to move the centre of government of a united Colony nearer to the frontier, and thus eliminate Cape Town's control over the east. This was demanded by easterners in the 1830s and 1840s in the interest of border security, but drew from Sir Harry Smith the retort that 'a supreme Government in a wilderness is an embarrassment in time of war', and was no longer taken seriously by 1865, when the telegraph had reached Grahamstown and the frontier was a bare four days from the capital by sea.[3] A third way in which the separatist mood expressed itself was in federalism: not so much in large-scale blueprints like Sir George Grey's for the confederation of all southern Africa (though it would receive considerable encouragement from Carnarvon's proposal of 1875),[4] as in proposals for the subdivision of the Cape Colony into distinct regional administrations. This enjoyed considerable support in official circles: from the Commissioners of Inquiry, for example, and from Governor Sir Philip Wodehouse.[5] But in any assessment of Cape federalism it is necessary to distinguish between proposals for a simple division of the Colony into an eastern and a western province, as put forward by the Commissioners of Inquiry

---

[1] CGH Statutes, 1854, pp. 1–44; Eybers, pp. 45–55 (Constitution Ordinance, 1853).

[2] *The People's Blue Book*, an unofficial compilation of public and private documents on Kaffrarian separation, by S. E. Rowles; D. B. Sole, 'The Separation Movement and the Demand for Resident Government in the Eastern Province, 1828–73', unpublished M.A. thesis, Rhodes University, 1939, Appendix B (Separation Bill of 1861), and Appendix C (Separation Petition of 1872). See also C. 732, pp. 146–9.

[3] e.g. Le Cordeur, pp. 94–95: Godlonton, Paterson, and resident government for the eastern Cape.

[4] See vol. ii.

[5] RCC, xxvii. 360 ff., 376; N. H. Taylor, 'The Separation Movement during the period of Representative Government at the Cape, 1854–1872', unpublished M.A. thesis, University of Cape Town, 1938, Ch. III, quoting Wodehouse to Newcastle, 30 Apr. 1862, in GH 31/9 (Cape Archives).

in the early days of British settlement, by Godlonton in 1857, and by J. C. Chase in 1871,[1] and the alternative proposal of a tripartite federation aimed at giving the midlands an identity of their own, which drew increasing support from about 1860, found clear expression in the report of Barkly's Federal Commission of 1871,[2] and eventually achieved partial realization (though in the context of a unitary constitution) in the Seven Circles Act of 1874.[3]

The hopes of eastern separatists had first been raised by the report of the Commissioners of Inquiry, but were doomed to early disappointment. Andries Stockenström was appointed Commissioner-General of the eastern districts in 1827; but this stormy administrator, who had a seat on the Advisory Council when periodically present in Cape Town, was not in sympathy with the form of government, desired to impose stricter control over the frontier than the settlers in general were prepared to accept, and eventually resigned after a quarrel with Governor Sir Lowry Cole in 1833.[4] The office then lapsed. When Stockenström returned as Lieutenant-Governor in terms of a new Constitution for the Eastern Districts established in 1836, having destroyed his reputation in settler eyes by his evidence before the Aborigines Committee in London,[5] he was placed in the invidious position of having to reverse the frontier settlement of Sir Benjamin D'Urban after the frontier war of 1834–5, while still reporting to D'Urban as his superior.[6] The decline of the lieutenant-governorship was largely bound up in his failure, followed by the undistinguished tenure of his successor, Colonel Hare. Though the appointment of a Frontier Commissioner and Agent General in 1847 indicated that contact with the Xhosa tribes required a diplomatic officer of some standing, the lieutenant-governorship was not adapted to this purpose. After 1853 its administrative responsibilities diminished, while its military responsibilities broadened, extending as far as Natal and St. Helena. This tended to obliterate its regional significance.[7]

Separatism was a force in Colonial politics until after the achievement of responsible government in 1872. One factor which kept it alive was the growth of the wool trade, which brought prosperity and an increased

[1] Le Cordeur, p. 140 (Godlonton); *Grahamstown Journal*, 1 Mar. 1871 (Chase).
[2] *Grahamstown Journal*, 3 July 1871; Sole, ii. 263–5.
[3] Text in Eybers, pp. 64–65. This act created a midland circle as well as three eastern and three western circles, each returning three candidates to the Upper House.
[4] J. D. Pitman, 'The Commissioner-Generalship of Sir A. Stockenström', unpublished M.A. thesis, University of Cape Town, 1939; Sole, i. 23–37; Hutton, *Stockenström*, i. 267–9, 324–32 (appointment and instructions), 426–7, ii. 14–22 (resignation).
[5] Joan M. Urie, 'A Critical Study of the Evidence of Andries Stockenström before the Aborigines Committee in 1835, viewed in the light of his previous Statements and Policies', unpublished M.A. thesis, Rhodes University, 1953.
[6] Eybers, pp. 39–41 (Eastern Districts Government). For the reversal of the D'Urban frontier settlement see Galbraith, *Reluctant Empire*, pp. 112–22.
[7] Fryer, pp. 3–6; Taylor, Ch. II.

population to the east and midlands, and enhanced the commercial importance of Port Elizabeth, creating a demand for railway and harbour works, facilities which were bound to compete with the interests of Table Bay. Secondly, easterners felt the inconvenience of having no supreme court and no deeds office in their vicinity. Thirdly, the law gave generous representation to the east, but covered members' expenses for only fifty days plus travel, with the result that the 'home team'—always the westerners, except in 1864—could reserve contentious votes until the tail end of the session when the visitors had departed. The most determined filibusters, of which there were several, failed against this tactic.[1] Wodehouse's suggestion of alternative sessions in the east and the west was a possible answer to this problem; but the Grahamstown Parliament, convened by Wodehouse in 1864, merely put the problem in reverse. The experiment was not repeated. In any case, it was expensive at an inappropriate time.[2]

The unity of the separatist movement in its early years depended on the ascendancy of Grahamstown, where Godlonton's *Journal* at first held unopposed sway over eastern minds, and whence many an aspirant to political life went out to secure the representation of surrounding districts. In 1859 six of the seven Eastern Province Council seats were held by members who either lived in or had close associations with Grahamstown.[3] The ability of Grahamstown to maintain its ascendancy, however, depended on the good will of Port Elizabeth and the docile acceptance of a subordinate position by Graaff-Reinet and the midlands, and these conditions could be taken less and less for granted as time went on.[4] Economic developments brought disunity, especially after 1861, as Graaff-Reinet and Grahamstown began to compete for the right to control the road and rail links between the coast and the interior. This competition was intensified after 1865, when the incorporation of British Kaffraria in the Cape Colony led to increased rivalry between Port Elizabeth and East London.[5] Dutch farmers in the midlands and the north-east Cape began to work together to resist Grahamstown's domination; Graaff-Reinet found some affinity with the Dutch-speaking Western Province, from which it drew one of its members of Parliament; and midlanders gave considerable backing to Kaffrarian candidates in

---

[1] CGH Constitution Ordinance, ss. 4, 7, 90. The best example of resolute filibustering occurred during the session of 1865, over the question of the representation of Kaffraria.

[2] According to the CGH Blue Books, parliamentary expenses rose from £8,394. 2s. 3d. in 1863 to £14,325. 13s. 2d. in 1864, of which approximately £4,000 were directly associated with the move.

[3] See details in Taylor, Chs. III, IV *passim*. For the influence of Godlonton and the *Journal* see Le Cordeur, pp. 75-78.

[4] Ibid., pp. 79-81.

[5] Ibid., pp. 69-74.

the Council elections of 1868.[1] Kaffrarian settlers, dreaming of expansion into the Transkei under the protective shield of Imperial troops, generally desired to be independent of the Cape; but when doubt arose over the availability of the troops (from 1861), and when London set its face against Transkeian expansion (firmly in 1864), the white Kaffrarians accepted incorporation in the Colony as a *pis aller*. But they were not interested in a separatist solution which would place them under the control of the Eastern Province, and when the Eastern Province Separation League was established in Port Elizabeth in 1872, they replied with a rival Kaffrarian Association to work for continued association with the west.[2]

Separatism failed, in part, because it had sought to live on insubstantial grievances. The allegation that subordination to the Western Province led to injustice in the expenditure of public money was largely beside the point, for although money voted for eastern improvements was sometimes not spent, owing to administrative inefficiency, parliament could not be shown to have neglected genuine eastern needs.[3] The separatists found during the depression of the mid 'sixties that they did not have the resources with which to press for local autonomy, especially when the Imperial Government threatened to withdraw the troops. Wodehouse's settlement of the frontier in 1865 reduced tension on the border and therefore dissatisfaction with the West. Motions in favour of responsible government in 1855 and in 1870-2 split opinion in the East wide open, while the Colony's achievement of responsible government in 1872 effectively destroyed separatism by presenting the Easterners with a *fait accompli*. It was buried by the Seven Circles Act, which broke down the rigid barriers between Eastern and Western constituencies in the Upper House, followed four years later by the accession of the Sprigg ministry to office. The fears of Easterners seemed to be chimerical, if a government could come to power, none of whose members represented a constituency west of Oudtshoorn.[4]

The Cape Colony's experience of representative government coincided almost exactly with two markedly different governorships; that of Sir George Grey (1854-61) and that of Sir Philip Wodehouse (1862-70). Grey's habit of mind was autocratic, but in an age of economic growth he was able to smother discontent without loss of popularity. 'He never

[1] Taylor, Ch. V, quoting *Grahamstown Journal*, 21 Sept., 28 Dec. 1868; *Kaffrarian Watchman*, 12 Aug., 23 Nov., 24 Dec. 1868; *Graaff-Reinet Herald*, 29 Aug. 1868.
[2] Sole, ii. 267-70; Taylor, Ch. VI, quoting *Kaffrarian Watchman*, 8 July, 14 Aug., 11 Sept. 1872.
[3] Fryer defends these conclusions for the period 1825-54 at pp. 4-5; Taylor for the period 1854-72 in Chs. II, III. Sole points out the misrepresentations of the Separation League of 1872 at ii. 272-4.
[4] Eybers, pp. 63-65 (Responsible Government and Seven Circles Acts); R. Kilpin, *The Old Cape House*, p. 170.

openly opposed responsible government', his biographer has written; but he ruled through the Executive Council as 'his own prime minister formulating his own policy, and impressing it upon his councillors', consulting them as and when he thought best, seeking advice outside his Council, drafting his own official speeches, ruling as 'head of all the Departments', and getting away with it because his policies were popular in the Colony and worked in practice.[1] In the absence of a clear-cut party system, policy disputes, or serious financial disagreements, Grey's control of the Executive went unchallenged. During his rule, the legislators tended to assume that a non-responsible executive required something like a separation of powers, for while the constitution prevented Executive councillors from voting in either House, the Legislative Council actually obliged them to engage private members to move and second government motions on their behalf.[2]

During the Wodehouse era there was a notable change of emphasis. Without the margin of prosperity which had so effectively played into the hands of Grey, Wodehouse found himself constantly confronted by a hostile legislature, and was unable to assuage opposition by talking approvingly of the principle of self-government, because he did not believe in it. He told Granville in 1870:

> I have never regarded Responsible Government as applied to a colony, more properly speaking a Dependency, as anything less than an absolute contradiction in terms.... I regard it as my duty, therefore, so long as my connection with this colony lasts, to do what is in me to prevent this change.[3]

This did not make Wodehouse an autocrat, or even a bad Cape patriot. His British patriotism, as he saw it, required him to serve the Cape to the best of his ability, while he strove (as Grey had not) to give his Executive Council a central and responsible role in the formulation of policy.[4] Grey had protested because the Colonial Office ignored his advice in appointing his councillors.[5] Wodehouse believed that it was his duty to act on his councillors' advice. By 1864 Wodehouse's Executive Council had become a well-knit team of uneven quality, meeting regularly, accustomed to handling its own legislative programme, dominating the legislature through its ability to stand outside the interprovincial feud which gave most of the colour to Cape political life. From 1864, however, the atmosphere began to change. It had become necessary to play off one party against another if the policy of the Executive was to find acceptance, and for this kind of tactic the

[1] J. Rutherford, *Sir George Grey*, pp. 295–8.
[2] Mandelbrote, in *CHBE*, viii. 385; Putzel, p. 77.
[3] C. 459 of 1871, p. 15; Kilpin, *Romance of a Colonial Parliament*, pp. 88–89.
[4] M. J. Zeeman, 'The Working of Representative Government at the Cape under Sir P. Wodehouse, 1862–70', unpublished M.A. thesis, University of Cape Town, 1940, Chs. I, II.
[5] Rutherford, pp. 297–9; Zeeman, Ch. II.

constitution of 1853 was entirely unsuited. Even if the officials themselves had had votes in Parliament, they would have found the balancing act difficult. Without votes, it was beyond them.

It was economic crisis that exposed the unworkability of the constitution. Representative government resulted in a sudden rise of twenty per cent. in government expenditure in 1853-4.[1] In 1854-61 expenditure rose steadily from £321,000 to £735,000. Grey and his Executive spent freely, using Imperial funds to govern British Kaffraria, and proceeds from the sale of Crown lands, treated as revenue, to balance expenditure on Colonial public works. Sixteen new magistracies were established in 1859. Large sums were spent on roads, on prisons, on immigration, on the extension of the telegraph, and on hospitals and schools, especially in the closing years of Grey's administration. But budget deficits began in 1859, and continued year after year.[2] To meet the annual charge on the public funds, the Colony depended on indirect taxation, on land sales, and on loans. By far the largest contribution to revenue came from the customs tariff, which normally accounted for about one-third of the total. Land sales fluctuated enormously from year to year: in 1861 they reached one-ninth of the total—an abnormally high figure—and in 1862 fell to a fiftieth. All the other heads of taxation—of which auction, stamp, and transfer duties were the next in importance—contributed relatively low sums. When Grey left the Colony the public debt stood at £565,050, and by 1871 it had risen to £1,160,007. By this time the economy had begun to recover, following the discovery of diamonds and the growth of wool exports; but Colonial finances had been through a very difficult period.

The government and the legislature clashed head on over the question of budgetary policy. Conflict arose from a lack of effective liaison and confidence between the two branches of government, each of which suspected the financial capacity of the other. Parliament normally voted on the budget in August; but as the financial year only ended in December it was unable to appropriate funds for the following year with an adequate knowledge of how the preceding estimates had worked out. The Civil List was reserved, and in hard times this was a source of irritation, leading to demands for the reduction of official salaries, and retaliatory moves by the governor to stop members' allowances. The governor's initial answer to the difficulties was to equalize revenue and expenditure by increased taxation, to separate land sales from ordinary

[1] The following statistical information is derived from the CGH Blue Books.
[2] The existence of a deficit was sometimes concealed in the annual statements of revenue and expenditure by balancing gross revenue (including loans) against expenditure. Towards the end of Wodehouse's administration this practice was discontinued. If *net* revenue, excluding loans, is taken as a basis, there was a deficit every year under Wodehouse until 1870, the largest being £345,000 in 1865.

revenue and place them in a sinking fund for the liquidation of the public debt, and to retrench where possible. The Assembly accepted retrenchment only, and thus obliged the Government in 1862 to raise another loan. In 1863 the Government was able to obtain an increase in transfer duties from 2 per cent. to 4 per cent., and in 1866 to raise the duty on luxuries, to increase the general *ad valorem* duty on non-enumerated imports from 7·5 per cent. to 10 per cent., and to lower that on agricultural implements and construction materials from 7·5 per cent. to 5 per cent. This immediately lifted customs revenue from £285,000 to £330,000 in a year, but it did not stay there. By leasing Crown land on improved terms, the Government increased its revenue from this source from £27,000 to £80,000 between 1862 and 1871. It was also able in 1870, when the crisis was past, to place a small tax on fixed property—the first real attempt at direct taxation, save for Wodehouse's proposal in 1869 of an income tax at 3*d* in the pound; but income tax did not become acceptable to the Colonial legislature until Jameson's Ministry of 1904-8, and until then indirect taxes alone were collected. Wodehouse's individual proposals were turned down year by year, and he encountered as fierce opposition from the wool producers, when a wool tax was debated between 1862 and 1869, as his successors in office would encounter when they tried to place an excise on the liquor interest in 1878.[1] But Wodehouse's successors were better off, for they would enjoy a source of revenue more lucrative than all others put together when the railways came into their own.

Wodehouse met resistance not only to his taxation proposals, but also to his proposals for retrenchment, because he was led in his exasperation to make proposals for the reform of parliament which enabled his opponents to suggest that he was using the financial embarrassment of the Colony to develop his attack on representative institutions.[2] The cost of parliament was small, and did not warrant Wodehouse's attention for financial reasons; but financial difficulties had exposed a constitutional blockage, and Wodehouse was correct in arguing that the Colony had either to move forward to full self-government (which he resisted) or to move back.

'If the colonists will not allow themselves to be governed', Granville wrote to Wodehouse in December 1869, 'it follows that they must adopt the responsibility of governing.'[3] The logic of Granville's observation became

---

[1] See Hofmeyr, *Life*, pp. 147-50.
[2] For Wodehouse's constitutional reform proposals see V. and P., Leg. Co., 1867, pp. 7-8: a single-chamber, 188-member legislature returned from six 3-member constituencies, sitting with three official members; 1869, pp. 91-93: a single-chamber legislature of 15 elective members, plus a president and three official members.
[3] Granville to Wodehouse, 9 Dec. 1869, quoted in P. Lewsen, 'The First Crisis in Responsible Government in the Cape Colony', in *AYB, 1942*, ii. 215.

increasingly clear as Wodehouse's rule advanced, notably during the session of 1869, when a clash between the Governor and his legislature over tax policy ended in the dissolution of the Lower House before supplies for the next year had been voted.[1] There were, however, reasons, from the Assembly's point of view, for not rushing headlong into self-government before the exact nature of the Colony's future responsibilities had been clarified. There was the question of external commitments, in particular the relationship between the Colony and two regions of very recent Imperial expansion—Basutoland (1868) and Griqualand West (1871)—important both in themselves and for future relations with the Orange Free State. There was the question of frontier policy and defence, at a time when Imperial subsidies for British Kaffraria had already been withdrawn, and it seemed as if the withdrawal of Imperial troops which a succession of secretaries of state had insisted on, was about to follow. Eastern separatism, though dying, was not yet dead, and might well become formidable again in the context of renewed federal proposals. Finally, responsible government would require a more sympathetic governor.

The last condition was met when Sir Henry Barkly, who had operated a system of responsible government in Victoria, replaced Wodehouse in December 1870. The actual withdrawal of Imperial troops from the frontier, which began in 1870, became easier to accept when Lord Kimberley undertook to retain an extra regiment at the Cape for some time after responsible government, unless it was needed elsewhere.[2] Basutoland ceased to be a difficulty because the Orange Free State, which had at first objected strongly to Wodehouse's annexation, agreed to sign the Second Convention of Aliwal North in February 1869. A strong desire for territorial expansion grew among the Cape commercial community at the same time. A select committee of the Legislative Council under Godlonton reported in July 1871 that Basutoland offered 'a wide field to profitable commercial enterprise, which it will be sound policy to secure to the Colony', while the Cape Chamber of Commerce frankly stated that it wished to annex the Free State as well, for its inflationary monetary policy had greatly alarmed its creditors.[3] After the Legislative Council had satisfied itself that Basutoland was not 'likely to entail any additional burden at present in the Colony', the Assembly in August carried an Annexation Bill through its second and third readings without any major divisions—helped perhaps by Southey's hint in the Council select committee that Natal might be invited to annex the territory if the Cape were to show reluctance.[4]

[1] Zeeman, Ch. V.
[2] C. 459 of 1871, pp. 66–67 (Kimberley to Barkly, 17 Nov. 1870, quoted in Lewsen, p. 216).
[3] V. and P., Leg. Co., 1871, pp. 85–86; Immelman, pp. 216–19.
[4] V. and P., H. of A., 1871, pp. 508, 518–19. For information concerning Southey's hint I am indebted to Mr. John Benyon.

The Colonial Office hoped that the Cape would be persuaded to take over West Griqualand as well, in return for the grant of responsible government, and it was left to Barkly to persuade it to do so.[1] But the Cape legislature was disinclined to ride roughshod over the claims of the Orange Free State. Therefore in the month in which the Upper House decided to take over Basutoland, the Colonial Secretary moved in the Lower a motion (which Barkly rightly described as 'Delphic'), the purpose of which seems to have been to sound out the opinion of a wary legislature in the hope that it would be won over to annexation by the tactic of gentle persuasion.[2] The House eventually carried this non-committal resolution by 27 votes to 26. No immediate action was possible because the Bloemhof court had not yet sat to test the claims of the South African Republic north of the Vaal.[3] Following the publication of Keate's Award, however, in October Barkly proclaimed sovereignty over Griqualand West in the name of the Crown.[4]

Meanwhile Molteno's campaign for responsible government proceeded. He had carried a motion in favour of the principle by 31 votes to 26 in June. A bill drafted by William Porter, the ex-Attorney-General, had been through all stages in the Assembly by 12 July, but was then thrown out by the Upper House.[5] At last, however, on 13 June 1872, Molteno was successful, after two Legislative councillors who had cast their votes against responsible government in the preceding session had been persuaded to change their minds.[6] But by this time the Griqualand West Annexation Bill had already been withdrawn by the Colonial Secretary. The Colony had decided that responsible government was worth having at a time when, under the stimulus of the diamond discoveries, its finances were beginning to take an upward turn; but it considered itself well free of the administrative and diplomatic headaches which control of the Fields themselves would have involved.[7]

Self-government had arrived after many vicissitudes, and without the éclat which accompanied its arrival in some other parts of the British Empire. It had come before the emergence of stable political parties, before there was any effective rural Afrikaner, let alone Coloured

---

[1] C. W. de Kiewiet, in *CHBE*, viii. 451–6; Agar-Hamilton, *The Road to the North*, pp. 94–95; Lewsen, pp. 215–17.
[2] V. and P., H. of A., 1871, pp. 294–5; A. Wilmot, *Life and Times of Sir R. Southey*, p. 222.
[3] See vol. ii.
[4] De Kiewiet, in *CHBE*, viii. 457.
[5] V. and P., H. of A., 1871, pp. 53, 89, 305; Leg. Co., p. 76.
[6] V. and P., Leg. Co., 1872, p. 68; Kilpin, *Romance of a Colonial Parliament*, pp. 91–96; Eybers, pp. 63–64.
[7] C. 732 of 1872, pp. 50–52: Barkly to Kimberley, 17 June 1872, explaining the withdrawal of the Griqualand West Annexation Bill in terms of an unexpected volte-face by the Cape Parliament.

THE MOVE TOWARDS RESPONSIBLE GOVERNMENT 333

or African, participation in the higher levels of political life, to a community whose political leaders were divided as to its merits. Subsequent developments would show that the governor of the Cape, who had also held the post of High Commissioner beyond the borders of the Colony since 1846, had more power than was desirable for the proper exercise of responsibility by the Colonial government, especially where the Colony's external relations were concerned; but this aroused few objections before the era of Dominion autonomy. Meanwhile the establishment of permanent administrative departments under removable political heads proved to be an effective answer to the deadlocks of the Wodehouse era. The Colony failed to preserve the low franchise qualifications of its 1853 constitution, but that failure belongs to a later phase of its history.

VIII[1]

CO-OPERATION AND CONFLICT: THE ZULU KINGDOM AND NATAL

BETWEEN 1800 and 1870 the situation in both the coastal sector and the plateau of south-eastern Africa, as described in Chapters III and IV, was radically transformed. The change took place in three overlapping phases, as a result of three distinct processes. In the first phase the African system which had existed for several centuries was revolutionized from within. Some of the chiefdoms developed into powerful kingdoms by absorbing other chiefdoms, and large areas were partially depopulated. This process did not have time to work itself out before Afrikaner Voortrekkers began to penetrate into south-eastern Africa from the Cape Colony and to inaugurate the second phase. Voortrekkers then defeated the two most powerful African kingdoms—the Ndebele (1837–8) and the Zulu (1838–40)—and carved out settlements for themselves in the central part of the coastal sector and the central high veld. This process, in turn, did not have time to work itself out before Britain intervened. She annexed Natal, the central part of the coastal sector, in 1843. In the interior Britain vacillated. She annexed all the territory between the Orange and the Vaal in 1848; she renounced responsibility for the Transvaal in 1852 and for the Orange-Vaal area in 1854; and in 1868 she resumed responsibility for Lesotho (Basutoland).

As a result of these events south-eastern Africa became divided into three types of polities: the British Colony of Natal, between the Buffalo-Tukela and the Mzimkhulu, and the Indian Ocean and the Drakensberg;[2] the Afrikaner Republics of the Orange Free State and the South African Republic, on the plateau between the Caledon-Orange and the Limpopo; and, on the peripheries of the British colony and the Afrikaner republics, attenuated African chiefdoms and kingdoms, one of which, 'Basutoland', came under British protection.[3]

[1] For Ch. VIII I owe a great deal to the members of my seminars on the history of south-eastern Africa, held at the University of California, Los Angeles, in the spring of 1964 and the fall of 1965. I am also grateful to Professor Monica Wilson, Mr. Martin Legassick, Dr. T. R. H. Davenport, and Dr. and Mrs. John S. Galbraith, who made many cogent comments on the first draft.

[2] This is the area referred to as Natal in this volume. 'Zululand' was not incorporated in Natal until 1897.

[3] In 1868 'Basutoland' became technically a British Crown Colony; but since white people were not permitted to buy or lease land there, except for the lease of small trading sites, it remained in substance an African kingdom, though under British protection and control.

These processes did not merely create antagonism between African and African, Boer and Briton, black and white. There was also a commingling of peoples and cultures as a result of the dispersion and regrouping of Africans and the intrusion of Voortrekkers and other white settlers, traders, and missionaries. Nguni and Sotho became more interwoven than before. White newcomers transmitted elements of their own cultures to Africans, and in adapting themselves to their new milieu they in turn became conditioned by African cultures.

Starting early in the nineteenth century white people from the Cape Colony organized expeditions beyond the area dealt with in Chapter VI—hunting, and bartering beads, copper bars, blankets, coffee, tea, sugar, brandy, firearms, and ammunition, for ivory, cattle, and cereals. As time went on white traders operated more extensively and more systematically, establishing permanent trading stations and introducing money as a medium of exchange. Missionaries began to penetrate the eastern part of the present-day Republic of South Africa in the second decade of the century. By the time of the Great Trek missionaries from Britain, France, and the United States were settled in many of the African chiefdoms and kingdoms. Although they did not make many enduring converts before 1870, they conducted schools as well as church services, they translated the Bible into Sotho and northern Nguni languages, they sowed seeds of doubt about the efficacy of traditional magic and the validity of traditional value systems, and they encouraged Africans to change their way of life.

Every farm, every trading station, and every mission in south-eastern Africa was a plural society in microcosm. The Voortrekkers arrived with Coloured dependants and they permitted, encouraged, and sometimes coerced Africans to work for them as shepherds, cattleherds, and domestic servants. British settlers and white traders and missionaries also became dependent on African labour.

The community on an Afrikaner farm was an association, formed and maintained mainly for economic purposes, between a dominant, patriarchal white family and client families of Africans and Coloured people, who did most of the manual work in return for the use of a garden plot and some payment in kind, or, more rarely, in cash. The community on a British settler's farm or a trading station was essentially similar. A mission community was different. Most Africans on mission stations were not labourers but peasant farmers, and as their links with traditional society weakened they became, not mere instruments of white enterprise, but individuals with real choices and enlarged opportunities. Interaction spread outwards from both these types of communities into the heart of African society. There was much coming and going, and exchange of goods, services, and techniques.

Wherever they settled the autonomy of white people was tempered by their dependence on African labour; and by 1870 the autonomy of every African community in south-eastern Africa, as well as in the Cape frontier zone, was beginning to recede into the past, as a result of contact with people equipped with a more powerful technology. Cooperation, as well as conflict, marked human relations in south-eastern Africa as in the Cape Colony and the Transkei. Nevertheless, no single pattern emerged in these years before the discovery of diamonds and gold. The experiences of an African varied with the impact upon him of the Shakan revolution and with the intensity and quality of his relationships with African chiefs and with white farmers, traders, and missionaries. The experiences of a white person were almost as varied.

This chapter deals with these processes in the coastal sector; the next with their progress on the plateau.

1. *The Zulu Kingdom*

Our knowledge of the origins of the Zulu kingdom is limited. Apart from castaways from shipwrecks, the first literate people to settle among the northern Nguni did so in 1824, by which time the Zulu kingdom was an established fact and its forerunner, the Mthethwa confederacy, no longer existed. Some of the early traders, notably Henry Francis Fynn (who arrived in Natal in 1824) and Nathaniel Isaacs (1825), wrote accounts of their experiences, and so did some of the early missionaries, notably Allen Gardiner (1835) and Francis Owen (1837).[1] The first person to devote serious attention to collecting the oral traditions of the northern Nguni was A. T. Bryant, a Catholic missionary, who spent many years in Natal from 1883 onwards.[2] He was followed by others, including E. A. Ritter.[3] Northern Nguni traditions, as thus transmitted, give us some understanding of the first steps in the transformation of the Nguni political system—but only a limited understanding. We have very little substantial information on Dingiswayo's Mthethwa confederacy, because it was engulfed by Shaka's Zulu kingdom before 1824, and when an institution has ceased to exist nobody has an interest in preserving its traditions. The original diary of Fynn, who came to know far more about northern Nguni society than any other trader,

[1] Fynn, and extracts from Fynn's writings in John Bird, *The Annals of Natal: 1495 to 1845*, i. 60–71, 73–93, 95–124; Nathaniel Isaacs, *Travels and Adventures in Eastern Africa*, VRS, 1936–7; Gardiner, *Narrative of a Journey to the Zoolu Country in South Africa*; *The Diary of the Rev. Francis Owen, M.A., Missionary with Dingaan in 1837–98: Together with extracts from the writings of the interpreters in Zulu, Messrs. Hulley and Kirkman*, VRS, 1926.

[2] Bryant, *Olden Times, The Zulu People, A History of the Zulu and Neighbouring Tribes*. Of these, the most useful to the historian is the first, and quotations from Bryant are from it, unless otherwise indicated.

[3] Ritter, *Shaka Zulu*.

was buried by Nguni in his brother's grave, and what we have is a later reconstruction, much of it heavily worked over by the author, with the help of others, towards the end of his life.[1] Isaacs was a young man while in South Africa and there is reason to believe that his account has many distortions. Writing for immediate publication,[2] Isaacs stressed the sensational; and as a protégé of James S. King he was deeply involved in the internecine quarrels of the white traders at Port Natal. Though Bryant's voluminous writings constitute most valuable compendia of northern Nguni history, they were compiled two generations and more after the foundation of the kingdoms. Like similar compendia written before the rise of more rigorous methods of investigating the history of pre-literate societies,[3] they do not record the names or the offices of the informants, nor the statements actually made by the informants. They are unsystematic syntheses of oral traditions, travellers' observations, and other published works. Moreover, they have been moulded by Bryant's own mind, which was coloured by the assumptions of his generation and his profession. As for Ritter, though he too was steeped in Nguni traditions, and though he names some of his informants, the book he has published is a highly romanticized biography of Shaka, with scarcely any references to sources, and it is baffling to the historian who is trying to distinguish fact from fiction and to assess degrees of probability. The popular success of Ritter's book has led others to follow in his footsteps, and there has been a spate of popular biographies of nineteenth-century African rulers.[4]

In these circumstances it is not surprising that we do not know precisely why the long-established equilibrium among the small autonomous northern Nguni chiefdoms rather suddenly collapsed. According to the traditions as we have them, the transformation was essentially the work of individuals—Dingiswayo and Shaka. But while the personalities of Dingiswayo and Shaka—and also of Mzilikazi and Moshweshwe —were undoubtedly of great significance, heroic traditions do not explain why heroes should have emerged when they did. The traditions of preliterate hierarchical societies are invariably heroic in character

[1] Fynn, pp. xii–xiii.
[2] Isaacs's book was first published in 1836.
[3] See especially Jan Vansina, *Oral Tradition: A Study in Historical Methodology*; Vansina, Mauny, and Thomas (eds.), *The Historian in Tropical Africa*; and Roland Oliver and John D. Fage (eds.), *JAH*, Cambridge, 1960 ff.
[4] e.g. Peter Becker, *Path of Blood: The Rise and Conquests of Mzilikazi, Founder of the Matabele*; *Rule of Fear: The Life and Times of Dingane, King of the Zulu*; C. T. Binns, *The last Zulu King: The Life and Death of Cetshwayo*. Becker is more reliable than Ritter: Ritter has a very short bibliography and scarcely any footnotes; Becker gives the source of most of his quotations and lists of books with each chapter. Donald R. Morris, *The Washing of the Spears: A History of the Rise of the Zulu Nation under Shaka and its Fall in the Zulu War of 1879*, is imaginative and scholarly, except that it is innocent of footnotes. It is much stronger on the war of 1879 than on the Shaka period.

and reticent on the underlying factors which provided the opportunities for innovators to exploit.

The explanation of the change in Nguni society favoured by most white writers rests on the assumption that the change must have been directly inspired by a white man, or white men. As Bryant puts it, 'the progressive ideas and activities subsequently displayed by Dingiswayo do suggest such extraneous influence; for, as a pure initiation of the Bantu mind and a product of purely Bantu training, they would have been decidedly extraordinary'.[1] This explanation seems to have started with Fynn, who wrote two different accounts of the subject. Common to both of them is the story that while his father Jobe was still chief of the Mthethwa, Dingiswayo had cause to flee from home and become a wanderer. During his travels, the story continues, Dingiswayo met a certain Dr. Cowan, a traveller from the Cape Colony who was trying to get from the high veld to the coast. Dingiswayo became inspired by what Cowan told him about the superior ways of white people, and he acquired Cowan's gun and his horse. In the earlier of the two accounts Fynn says that Dingiswayo met Cowan in 'the year 17–' [sic] and that Dingiswayo became chief of the Mthethwa 'about 1780'.[2] In fact, however, it was in 1808 that Dr. Cowan left the Cape Colony as leader of an ill-starred expedition which perished in the vicinity of the Limpopo river.[3] At some stage Fynn himself seems to have become aware of this, for in his later account he says that Cowan left the Cape in 1806; but even there he makes the assertion that 'Dingiswayo began his reign about 1795',[4] which cannot be reconciled with the role enunciated for Cowan.[5]

Bryant, drawing upon Fynn's earlier version, appreciated that there was a chronological problem. Nevertheless, he endorsed Fynn's basic story and, apparently for no other reason than to make it plausible, he had Dingiswayo assume the Mthethwa chieftainship in 1808.[6] Ritter says the same thing in a brief passage, setting out the Cowan encounter and its effects upon Dingiswayo as a matter of plain fact, without any qualifications or references.[7]

---

[1] Bryant, p. 94.
[2] Bird, i. 62. Bird dates this paper in the year 1839: ibid., p. 60.
[3] I. Schapera (ed.), *Apprenticeship at Kuruman: being the Journals and Letters of Robert and Mary Moffat, 1820–1828*, p. 41, n. 59.
[4] Fynn, pp. 5, 8.
[5] Another document by Fynn relating to the subject is quoted in Andrew Steedman, *Wanderings and Adventures in the Interior of Southern Africa*, ii. 174–5. Evidently Fynn wrote this document in 1834; but it does not specifically relate the Cowan–Dingiswayo encounter to the origins of change among the northern Nguni.
[6] Bryant, pp. 91–95.
[7] Ritter, pp. 21–22. Graham Mackeurtan, *The Cradle Days of Natal (1497–1845)*, pp. 112–14, also follows Fynn.

Theophilus Shepstone, in a paper read in 1875, produced a variant upon the theme of white inspiration. Shepstone's passage is as follows:[1]

It seems that in his travels he [Dingiswayo] had reached the Cape Colony, and must have lived with or entered the service of some colonist. Whether he got his living honestly or not is a question which must now, I fear, for ever remain unsolved. [!!] It was during his stay in the Cape Colony that he acquired the information, or made the observations, which were to effect the great change in his native land and the surrounding countries. . . . He learned the strength of standing armies, the value of discipline and training, as compared with the mobs, called armies, in his own country. He saw that if he could gain possession of his tribe he could gratify his ambition. He had heard of or seen bodies of civilized soldiers. He had ascertained that they were divided into regiments and companies, with regularly appointed officers, and he thought that all soldiers were bachelors. He had no sooner got possession of power than he set to work to organize his tribe in accordance with these ideas.

This story became widely accepted by white people in Natal, and J. Y. Gibson, a Natal official, stated it baldly as a fact in *The Story of the Zulus*, which was published in 1903.[2] It is no more than a wild speculation.

In either version the white-inspiration theory seems to be a white man's concoction, based on an assumption that has vitiated a great deal of writing about African history. Unwilling to envisage a local provenance for significant achievements in Africa, nineteenth-century Europeans attributed the origins of the kingdoms north and west of Lake Victoria to (white) Hamites, and the building of Zimbabwe to (white) Phoenicians, or Arabs, or Jews; and many twentieth-century scholars have doggedly repeated these attributions long after the time when the balance of the evidence was overwhelmingly otherwise.[3] The white-inspiration theory of the origins of the Zulu kingdom is in the same genre. We do not know where Dingiswayo may have wandered or whom he may have met in his youth. What we do know is that long after Dingiswayo had died, Fynn and Shepstone, neither of whom had ever set eyes on him, suggested that he had met white people and that they had had a cataclysmic influence upon him. In detail the suggestions of Fynn and Shepstone are irreconcilable with each other. Fynn's is demonstrably inaccurate; Shepstone's admittedly conjectural.

A third type of explanation has been suggested by Professor Monica Wilson.[4] Trade has been shown to have been the main stimulus to the

---

[1] Bird, i. 163.   [2] J. Y. Gibson, *The Story of the Zulus*, pp. 12–13.
[3] On the Hamitic myth see B. E. Ogot, 'Kingship and statelessness among the Nilotes', in Vansina, Mauny, and Thomas, pp. 284–304; on the Zimbabwe myth see Summers, *Zimbabwe: A Rhodesian Mystery*.
[4] Monica Wilson, *Divine Kings and the 'Breath of Men'*, esp. pp. 23–24, and personal communications.

rise of the Ngonde kingdom north-west of Lake Malawi.[1] Fynn states that Dingiswayo opened up a trade in ivory and cattle with the Portuguese fort at Delagoa Bay and that people from the fort visited Dingane's capital in about 1830.[2] Professor Wilson therefore suggests that Dingiswayo, and later Shaka, extended control over many chiefdoms because they wished to monopolize the trade of northern Nguni country. There are difficulties in accepting this hypothesis. Portuguese power in the Delagoa Bay area was at a low ebb in the late eighteenth and early nineteenth century. The trade passing through Lourenço Marques was small and erratic, and one of the exports was slaves, who did not come from Nguni country.[3] There is no evidence of a significant influx of imported goods from Delagoa Bay into Nguni country in the time of Dingiswayo and Shaka. There was no vestige of an emerging *entrepreneur* class in Nguni society. There is no testimony, apart from Fynn's, that suggests that Dingiswayo's primary motivation was economic. Shaka's was certainly not. Therefore, while trade may have been a subsidiary factor, it does not seem to have been the crucial factor behind political change among the northern Nguni.[4]

A fourth type of explanation has been offered by Professor Max Gluckman. In 1940 he wrote that change among the northern Nguni was sparked off by 'pressure of population'.[5] Recently he has elaborated this hypothesis.[6] He considers that Zulu traditions and the accounts written by castaways indicate that there was a continuous growth of population in Nguni country from at least the sixteenth century onwards, and that by the late eighteenth century, with the Cape Colonial *trekboers* blocking further expansion in a westerly direction, the Nguni population had reached a critical density. Land was no longer available for settlement, either within or beyond the existing chiefdoms. Chiefdoms could no longer split, for a weaker party had nowhere to go. Consequently the Nguni population could no longer be accommodated within the existing political system of small, autonomous, fissiparous chiefdoms. This may well have been the underlying problem which confronted Dingiswayo and Shaka and prompted them to adopt

[1] Godfrey Wilson, *The Constitution of Ngonde*, Rhodes–Livingstone Papers, no. 3, 1939; and Monica Wilson, op. cit.
[2] Fynn, pp. 8, 10, 16, 47–48, 198, 231–2; Bird, i. 63.
[3] Mabel V. Jackson, *European Powers and South-East Africa*; Sidney R. Welch, *Portuguese and Dutch in South Africa, 1641–1806*.
[4] However, research now (1968) being done by Mr. Alan Smith is strengthening the trade hypothesis.
[5] Max Gluckman, 'The Kingdom of the Zulu of South Africa', in Fortes and Evans-Pritchard, p. 25.
[6] Max Gluckman, 'The Rise of a Zulu Empire', *Scientific American*, 202, no. 4, pp. 159–69; also an unpublished manuscript on The Rise of the Zulu Empire, which Professor Gluckman kindly lent me shortly before this chapter went to press.

tougher methods of warfare and to embark on state-making. Such an explanation is far more convincing than the simplistic combinations of heroics and racialism that have usually been offered; and it also seems more probable than the trade theory (though trade may have been a secondary factor). Nevertheless, it has not been conclusively established that population pressure had reached the crucial stage by the time of Dingiswayo. The evidence of demographic trends among the Nguni in the eighteenth century is tenuous and likely to remain so.[1]

The historian is on firmer ground in dealing with the changes wrought in northern Nguni society by Dingiswayo. The main accounts are in substantial agreement on the essentials of the process.[2] After the death of his father, which probably occurred towards the end of the eighteenth century, Dingiswayo ousted his brother from the chieftainship of the Mthethwa, a somewhat typical Nguni unit living in the triangle between the sea and the lower reaches of the Mfolozi and the Mhlatuzi rivers.[3] His crucial innovation was to blend two previously distinct Nguni institutions: the educational and the military (see Chapter III, pp. 124–5). He abolished the circumcision schools and conscripted all the young men of his chiefdom into something like a standing army, organized in regiments of approximately the same age, each regiment wearing a distinctive dress and using shields with hides of a distinctive colour. How far he carried this reorganization is not clear; but it was sufficient to give the Mthethwa a decisive advantage over their neighbours, and step by step Dingiswayo exerted a mastery over most of them. Fynn states that Dingiswayo gave as his reason for his conquests 'that he wished to do away with the incessant quarrels that occurred amongst the tribes, because no supreme head was over them to say who was right or who was wrong'.[4] Sometimes these conquests involved bloody battles, but in such cases Dingiswayo did not annihilate the enemy. He spared women and children, and he often allowed the ruling family to remain in power, provided he could find a member who was loyal. At other times a mere threat or show of force was enough to produce submission. The subject chiefdoms were left

---

[1] In Chs. 1 and 2 of *The Zulu Aftermath: A Nineteenth Century Revolution in Bantu Africa*, which was published after this chapter had been written, J. D. Omer-Cooper sets out the population hypothesis as a fact, but without any fresh supporting evidence.

[2] The basic account is by Fynn, in Bird, i. 62–64. Bryant, pp. 83–118, takes over what Fynn says there and adds data from the oral traditions of various chiefdoms, as well as fanciful embellishments. In Fynn's later account (Fynn, pp. 6–11), which was not available to Bryant, there are additional details, including the dubious statement that the Portuguese sent Dingiswayo a 'company of soldiers' armed with guns to help him in his fighting with the Qwabe.

[3] At the end of Bryant's *Olden Times* there is a map of Zululand and Natal showing 'The Native Clans as located in pre-Shakan Times'.

[4] Bird, i. 64.

intact in many respects; but they supplied men for Dingiswayo's army, which became an integrating factor cutting across the bonds of kinship and local allegiance. Thus the old-style Nguni chiefdom which Dingiswayo took over from his brother expanded into a confederacy of chiefdoms, knit together by the paramountcy of Dingiswayo and the army he controlled. By the time of Dingiswayo's death in about 1818 it extended perhaps from the Mfolozi in the north to the Tukela in the south, and sixty or eighty miles inland from the sea.[1] In the north there had been little expansion, because Zwide, the Ndwandwe chief, had been building up a confederacy along similar lines across the Mfolozi.[2]

One of the many small chiefdoms which acknowledged Dingiswayo as paramount was that of the Zulu, who numbered perhaps two thousand people and who lived between the upper Mhlatuzi and the White Mfolozi, west of the Mthethwa nuclear area. In about 1787 Nandi, a Langeni girl, gave birth to an illegitimate child by Senzangakona, the Zulu chief. The union was regularized when Nandi was taken in by Senzangakona as a junior wife with her baby, Shaka; but mother and child were soon expelled by the chief, and Shaka's childhood was spent among the Langeni (with Nandi's father's people) and the Qwabe (her mother's people). When the boy was about sixteen Nandi took him to Mthethwa relatives, where he worked as a herdboy until, at about 22, he was conscripted into Dingiswayo's growing army. There he acquired a reputation as a brave warrior and a man of original military ideas, and he rose to the command of his regiment.[3]

Chief Senzangakona died in about 1816 and was succeeded by his son, Sigujana. A plot was then hatched at Dingiswayo's place. Ngwadi, a son of Nandi by a later marriage, killed Sigujana, and Shaka then went to the Zulu with an escort provided by Dingiswayo and took over the Zulu chieftainship without opposition.[4]

Shaka at once applied the new Mthethwa military system to the Zulu, with further innovations of his own. He conscripted the men of under forty into three age regiments, each of which wore a distinctive headdress and carried cow-hide shields of a distinctive colour. Each regiment he located at a particular place, under the control of its officers and one or more of Shaka's aged female relatives. He fixed his own headquarters at Bulawayo, the place of the youngest regiment, the Fasimba. Instead of the weapons which were formerly used by fighting men—

[1] The lists of chiefdoms said to have been conquered by Dingiswayo given by Fynn (Bird, i. 64) and Bryant (*Olden Times*, pp. 100–18, esp. p. 103) do not correspond.
[2] We have very little reliable information about the Ndwandwe. See Bryant, *Olden Times*, pp. 158–66, and *History of the Zulu*, pp. 12–15.
[3] Bryant, Chs. 6–9, and Map opposite p. 699; Fynn, in Bird, i. 64–65; Fynn, pp. 12–13; Isaacs, i. 262–5; Ritter, Chs. 1–5.
[4] Bryant, Ch. 13; Fynn, in Bird, i. 65; Fynn, pp. 13–14; Ritter, Ch. 6.

assagais for hurling at the enemy from a distance—he armed each Zulu warrior with a short stabbing spear. This was more effective, because, once he had warded off an enemy's assagais with his shield, a Zulu could close in and cause havoc in hand-to-hand fighting with the spear. Shaka himself had perhaps invented this weapon when he was in Dingiswayo's army; now he had his blacksmiths make one for each member of his own little army.

Shaka made his men relinquish the traditional sandals and go barefoot, for greater speed and mobility. He forbade them to marry, except for the regiment of older men, which formed a reserve. He subjected them to rigorous training and an iron discipline. He taught them new military tactics, including a method of attack by which one regiment fought in the centre, supported by a reserve regiment, and two others formed flanks or horns which advanced and enveloped the enemy. He conscripted young boys as baggage-carriers, and doctors to treat the wounded. He usually tried to catch an enemy by surprise, and he made ingenious use of spies, smoke signals, and stratagems. In place of the limited warfare which was traditional to the Nguni, he aimed at destroying absolutely the capacity of an enemy to resist, by eliminating the ruling family and even, when it seemed expedient, by massacring the women and children as well as the men. Once he had conquered an enemy, he incorporated the survivors into his own system, allotting the men to regiments appropriate for their age. Captured cattle were divided between the regiments according to their colour. Individual warriors had the use of their milk, but the cattle were the property of Shaka.[1]

So long as Dingiswayo survived, Shaka professed to be his loyal subordinate, and he limited his own conquests to the small chiefdoms in his own immediate neighbourhood. In about 1818, however, Dingiswayo became involved in further fighting against his old enemy, Zwide, chief of the Ndwandwe; and Zwide captured Dingiswayo and had him killed. Whether or not, as Fynn avers, Shaka betrayed Dingiswayo to Zwide, he certainly profited from his death. The Mthethwa confederacy soon disintegrated and its members attached themselves to the rising star of Shaka, who killed Dingiswayo's heir and installed a loyal follower as chief of the Mthethwa. Thus Shaka replaced Dingiswayo as the strongest ruler north of the Tukela and absorbed the Mthethwa into his own system.[2]

[1] Bryant, Chs. 13–15; Fynn, pp. 283–6; Isaacs, i. 265–7; Ritter, *passim*. Ritter is strong on the military aspect of Shaka's career and is not in conflict with Bryant, except on the question of footwear, where I have followed Ritter, who gives reasons and references for his opinion on this point, pp. 365–6.
[2] Bryant, pp. 158–67, 202–3; Fynn, in Bird, i. 65; Fynn, pp. 11, 15; Ritter, pp. 113–16. On the circumstances of Dingiswayo's death, Fynn (in Bird, i. 65, and Fynn, p. 15) says that Shaka accompanied Dingiswayo on his Ndwandwe campaign and informed Zwide where

After the death of Dingiswayo Shaka's kingdom expanded rapidly.[1] Besides absorbing the Mthethwa confederacy, Shaka conquered other chiefdoms which had remained independent of Dingiswayo. The decisive conflict was with the Ndwandwe, who were utterly defeated in 1819. Thereafter Shaka's authority extended from the Pongola river in the north to the Tukela in the south, and from the Buffalo to the sea. Within this area all the fit men under about 40 years of age were conscripted into the army; and many of the young women into the parallel organization of women. Ultimately Shaka was able to bring an army of perhaps 40,000 men into the field.[2] Scattered through the kingdom were some fifteen regimental barracks, built to a common plan. The huts of the warriors and the women were tightly packed between two concentric oval stockades, leaving a central arena for military exercises, for dances, and for ceremonies; and the warriors' section was stockaded off from the women's section. Sexual ardour was sublimated in intense military activity and discipline, except on occasions when he permitted the customary form of limited intercourse. Shaka forbade his warriors to marry until they were in their forties, and then he would order a regiment to take wives from designated women's regiments. Shaka acknowledged no children of his own, either because he did not want to risk his authority's being challenged by his sons, or, perhaps, because he was impotent, or because he was a latent homosexual.[3] Each barracks housed two or three thousand warriors and was responsible for several thousand head of cattle.

Shaka himself lived in the women's enclosure of such a barracks, and he changed its location from time to time, with an eye to fresh pasture for the cattle and to the direction of his next military campaign.[4] With him was a small group of councillors, whom he had raised from

Dingiswayo could be found and captured; Bryant (p. 164) says that Shaka failed to carry out Dingiswayo's order to join him on his Ndwandwe campaign; and Ritter (loc. cit.) blandly ignores the possibility of treachery or neglect of duty by Shaka. These differences illustrate the difficulty of obtaining accurate facts for this phase of Shaka's life.

[1] Bryant, *Olden Times*, Chs. 56 and 64, *Zulu People*, Ch. 12; Fynn, in Bird, i. 65-71; Fynn, pp. 15-34; Isaacs, i. 265-86; Ritter, Chs. 12-19.

[2] It is, of course, impossible to be sure about numbers in Shaka's kingdom. Fynn estimated that the Zulu army which passed him on its return from an attack on the Mpondo in 1824 numbered 20,000 (Fynn, p. 62); that the numbers of 'natives in their war attire' at Shaka's kraal on his first visit in 1825 was 80,000, including between 8,000 and 10,000 women (p. 71); and that the 'whole body of men, boys, and women' in the expedition against the Ndwandwe in 1826 numbered 50,000 (p. 123). Elsewhere Fynn says Shaka had 'a body of 50,000 effective followers' (Bird, i. 66).

[3] Shaka told the traders that his refusal to marry or acknowledge children was prompted by political considerations and Bryant agrees (p. 637). Ritter makes Shaka out to be a great lover (pp. 201 ff.). Morris argues that Shaka was impotent (p. 54); Gluckman that he was a latent homosexual (manuscript).

[4] Drawings of Dingane's Mgungundlovu kraal are in Gardiner (opp. p. 28), and in Ritter (opp. p. 209). A plan of the same kraal by James Stuart is in Fynn (opp. p. 326).

different backgrounds and who owed everything to him. He consulted them freely, but it was he, Shaka, who personally made every important decision. He was the senior executive, the ultimate court of appeal, the sole source of laws, the commander-in-chief, and the high priest. He was by far the wealthiest man in the kingdom, owning thousands of cattle and commanding the services of thousands of warriors and hundreds of women. The entire army assembled at the royal barracks annually for the first-fruits ceremony, and before and after major military expeditions, when traditional magic was used for the new purpose of instilling a national morale, transcending traditional particularisms. The traditions of the Zulu royal lineage became the traditions of the nation; the Zulu dialect became the language of the nation; and every inhabitant, whatever his origins, became a Zulu, owing allegiance to Shaka. Fear, too, was an important nation-building factor. Executioners were always at hand to kill people Shaka suspected of disloyalty or cowardice. In these ways an area previously occupied by many autonomous chiefdoms became transformed into a single kingdom; and many tribes became moulded into a single nation.

Within the new institutions, however, the old survived in an attenuated form. Chiefs and headmen, some of them the hereditary incumbents, others Shaka's nominees, administered the territorial divisions and subdivisions of the kingdom. But the threads of authority no longer stopped at the chiefly level, for a chief's tenure was contingent on loyal service and Shaka took steps to prevent chiefs forming combinations against him, by requiring their frequent attendance at court, by playing off chief against chief, and, in the last resort, by replacing or killing a disaffected chief. The homesteads, though deprived of their young men and some of their women, remained the primary units of social and economic life. Children were born and reared in them. Adults returned to them when they were married and demobilized. And their inhabitants owned some of the cattle and produced most of the crops of the nation.

The rise of the Zulu kingdom had repercussions from the Cape Colonial frontier to Lake Tanganyika. Every community throughout approximately a fifth of the African continent was profoundly affected, and many were utterly disrupted.

The inhabitants of Natal, south of the Tukela river, who had been divided among a large number of small chiefdoms,[1] began to be disorganized in the early years of Shaka's reign, when Bhele, Cunu, Hlubi, Ngwane, Zizi, and other refugees came pouring south from Shaka's country. Between 1821 and 1824 Shaka's impis completed the

[1] Bird, i. 124-53, gives details of ninety-four 'tribes' occupying Natal before 1812; and sketch Map No. 1 at the end of Fynn shows the approximate locations of these tribes.

process.[1] By 1824 most of the country between the Tukela and the Mzimkhulu, the Drakensberg and the sea, was devastated. The cattle had been removed, the grain destroyed. Thousands of people had been killed; others had fled further south; and others had been absorbed into the Zulu nation. In Natal organized community life virtually ceased; but San bands survived towards the Drakensberg and a few thousand Nguni maintained some sort of existence in areas sheltered by mountains or bush, living in small groups on roots, game, fish, and even human flesh.[2] Shaka probably had two reasons for initiating and maintaining this devastation. Having founded a military kingdom, he deemed it necessary to provide his army with frequent employment; and being aware that the firearms of the white people in the Cape Colony constituted the most formidable threat to his kingdom, he used a depopulated Natal as a buffer zone between them.

Further south, between the Mzimkhulu and the Mzimvubu, some of the refugees from Natal became amalgamated by Madikane, who founded the Bhaca chiefdom and pressed upon the neighbouring Mpondo chiefdom of Faku. Beyond them large numbers of disorganized refugees sought shelter among the Xhosa chiefdoms. They were known generically as Mfengu ('Fingos' to the white people), meaning 'beggars'.[3]

To the north of Shaka's kingdom the most successful organizer of resistance was Sobhuza, an Nguni chief of the Dlamini clan. Sobhuza's father, Ndungunya, had held off attacks by Zwide and Dingiswayo and begun to amalgamate a number of different communities. Sobhuza, who ruled from about 1815 to about 1836, retreated to defensible positions in the mountains north of the Pongolo river, absorbed Sotho as well as Nguni chiefdoms, created an army on Zulu lines, and laid the foundations of what later became known as the Swazi kingdom— named after Sobhuza's son, Mswazi, who ruled from about 1840 to 1868.[4]

After Shaka defeated the Ndwandwe in 1819 two of Zwide's warriors, with small bands of followers, escaped Shaka's clutches by returning to their homes, and then, in about 1821, by moving northwards. During the next decade one of them, Soshangane, carved out his Gaza kingdom in the lowlands between Delagoa Bay and the lower Zambezi, subjecting the Tsonga inhabitants and destroying the Portuguese settlements at Delagoa Bay, Inhambane, and Sena. The other,

---

[1] Bryant, Chs. 16, 29–33, 39; Omer-Cooper, Ch. 10.
[2] Eyewitness accounts of Natal in 1824 by Fynn, pp. 58–64, 91–98; in 1826 by Isaacs, i. 107–11; in 1835 by Gardiner, pp. 15, 24–25, 311–13.
[3] Bryant, Chs. 38–40; Fynn, pp. 22–24, 98–117; Omer-Cooper, Ch. 11. See Ch. VI above for more information on the Mfengu and the Mpondo.
[4] Bryant, Ch. 35; Kuper, *An African Aristocracy*; Agnes Aidoo, 'Factors in the Founding of the Swazi Kingdom' (unpublished seminar paper, 1965); Omer-Cooper, Ch. 3.

Zwangendaba, settled for a time in the same area, but in 1831 Soshangane drove him westwards, and in 1835 he crossed the Zambezi to establish the Ngoni kingdom along the western side of Lake Malawi (Nyasa) and as far north as Lake Tanganyika, almost two thousand miles from his starting-point. The process was much the same in both cases. Initially the migrant bands consisted of perhaps one hundred warriors each, but they quickly became formidable by receiving fresh refugees from Zulu country and absorbing large numbers of people from the chiefdoms they conquered in their travels. Zwangendaba's followers also threw off splinter groups as they advanced across the Zambezi, and after the death of Zwangendaba in about 1848 there was a disputed succession and the kingdom split.[1]

The Ngwane under Matiwane had formerly lived in the triangle between the upper Pongolo and Buffalo rivers. In about 1818, attacked in quick succession by both Dingiswayo's Mthethwa and Zwide's Ndwandwe, they moved south-west, displacing the Hlubi under Mpangazita, who fled across the Drakensberg. Then in 1822 Shaka drove Matiwane off the land he had taken from the Hlubi, and Matiwane, too, crossed the mountains to the high veld.[2] Meanwhile, Shaka had taken into his service a petty Kumalo chieftain called Mzilikazi, whose father, Mashobane, had been killed by Zwide. In about 1822 Shaka sent Mzilikazi to raid cattle from a Sotho chieftain, but on his return Mzilikazi defied Shaka by retaining some of the cattle he had captured. Next year, threatened by Shaka, Mzilikazi fled with two or three hundred young men to the Sotho country of the eastern Transvaal.[3] The subsequent careers of these three peoples—the Hlubi led by Mpangazita, the Ngwane of Matiwane, and the Ndebele of Mzilikazi—belong to the next chapter.

Before 1824 white people knew very little of these events. The wrecks of Portuguese, Dutch, and British ships had given the south-east African coast a bad name, and mariners generally gave it a wide berth. The nearest approach to a systematic contact had been as far back as 1689, when Simon van der Stel, in command at the Cape, having received favourable reports from survivors of the wrecked *Stavenisse*, sent a galiot to Port Natal to purchase 'that bay with some surrounding land from the king and chief of those parts for some merchandise, consisting of copper arm and neck rings and other articles, upon behalf of the Honourable Company'; but the follow-up was not effective.[4] The early British administrators of the Cape Colony, like their recent Dutch predecessors, were preoccupied with local affairs, while Portuguese

---

[1] Bryant, Chs. 43–44; Omer-Cooper, Chs. 4–5.
[2] Bryant, Chs. 16–17; Omer-Cooper, Ch. 6.
[3] Bryant, Ch. 42; Omer-Cooper, Ch. 9.   [4] Bird, i. 54–56, 59–60.

power in East Africa contracted during the seventeenth and eighteenth centuries and reached its nadir in the early nineteenth century.

In 1822 Captain William Owen, R.N., started a survey of the south-east African coastline for the Admiralty, beginning with the Delagoa Bay area, where he had a brush with Soshangane.[1] As a result of news of Owen's good impressions of the country, of the growth of an English population in the Cape Colony, and of land-shortage among the Afrikaners, a joint stock company was formed in Cape Town to exploit the agricultural and commercial possibilities of Natal. In 1824 Francis Farewell and James King, former British naval officers, and Henry Francis Fynn, a former surgeon's assistant from London, arrived at Port Natal by sea, with a group of Afrikaners, Englishmen, and Coloured servants. The Afrikaners soon departed, and with them went, for the time being, the plan to create an agricultural settlement; but some of the Englishmen and Coloured people remained, and they were joined by others, including Nathaniel Isaacs, a young anglicized Jew from St. Helena. From then onwards there was a small and fluctuating group of British adventurers with headquarters on the Bay of Natal, mainly concerned to collect and export elephant ivory. For a time they were cut off from the outside world by the loss of a ship, stranded on the sand bar at the entrance to the bay. They were tough individualists, ridden with trade rivalries. Fynn made the most effective adaptation to the environment. He became fluent in Zulu; he established good relations with Nguni; he married Nguni women; and he made several protracted journeys to the south as well as the north, laying in caches of ivory and having them carried by African porters to the Bay of Natal for shipment.[2]

Shaka's first reaction to the arrival of these strangers was one of friendly curiosity, and he never ceased to be interested in talking with them. A working relationship soon developed. Shaka liked some of their presents, valued their medical skills (Fynn had had some medical training), and was fascinated by their muskets. He made it known that they were his white people, which meant that wherever they went in his dominions they were safe and were provided with food and shelter. He also put his mark to documents which purported to cede a large part of Natal to them (though no doubt he did not see it in that light);[3]

[1] Fynn, pp. 35–45.
[2] The basic eyewitness accounts are the works by Fynn and Isaacs. In Bird, i. 60–71, 73–101, 103–24, are additional statements by Fynn; ibid., pp. 71–73, 93, 191–5, statements by Farewell; and ibid., pp. 183–5, a statement by King. Percival R. Kirby (ed.), *Andrew Smith and Natal: Documents relating to the early history of that Province*, VRS, 1955, includes some transcriptions made by Smith in the 1830s from Journals of Farewell (pp. 57–67) and Fynn (pp. 67–73).
[3] Bird, i. 193–4, sets out a document purporting to be a grant by Shaka to F. G. Farewell and Company, dated 7 August 1824, 'in consideration of divers goods received', of land

and he allowed them to build up personal followings from among the fragments of the Natal chiefdoms, so that they acquired something like the status of Shaka's chiefs. They in turn knew full well that their lives were in Shaka's hands and that their business success depended on his goodwill, for the tusks of all elephants killed in the Zulu kingdom belonged to Shaka.[1]

In 1828 Shaka tried to make contact with the British Government. James King undertook to lead an embassy, including Chief Sotobe, to King George IV; but the party only got as far as Algoa Bay, where it was roughly handled by Major Josias Cloete, acting on behalf of the Cape Governor.[2]

The first major campaign waged by Shaka after the arrival of the traders was in 1826, when he led his army north against the Ndwandwe, who had revived under Sikhunyana, son of Zwide. Fynn accompanied Shaka on this expedition, which met the Ndwandwe north of the Pongolo river and finally broke their power.[3] On the way back Shaka detached a regiment to deal with a group of Kumalo who, under Beje, had been defying him from a hill in the Ngome forest. The Zulu having failed, Shaka summoned the white people of Port Natal to help him. Isaacs, John Cane, and some Coloured men responded, and Beje submitted early in 1827. It was the traders' muskets that were decisive for, as Beje's people told Isaacs, they 'could not contend with people who spit fire'.[4]

Shaka's next major campaign was in 1828 and to the south. Shaka himself went as far as the Mzimkhulu river, where he remained with a bodyguard near Fynn's trading depot, spending much of his time in the company of Fynn and Farewell. The rest of the Zulu army proceeded in two divisions—one along the coast to deal with the Mpondo and their western neighbours, the other inland to attack the Bhaca and other refugees from Natal. Before they left the Mzimkhulu, Shaka told the officers they were not to become embroiled with white people; and later, persuaded by Fynn or Farewell, he sent messengers ordering them not to attack the frontier chiefs, for fear of drawing retaliation

---

extending thirty-five miles along the coast (including Port Natal) and one hundred miles inland. Mackeurtan, pp. 141–2, cites a document dated February 1828 in which Shaka gives James King 'the free and full possession of my country near the sea-coast and Port Natal . . . together with the free and exclusive trade of all my dominions'. Isaacs, i. 255–6, claims that later in 1828, James King having died, Shaka made him (Isaacs) 'chief of Natal', and granted him a tract of land twenty-five miles by one hundred, including Port Natal.

[1] Felix Okoye, 'Shaka and the British Traders' and 'Dingane and the British Traders' (unpublished seminar papers, 1964).

[2] Bryant, pp. 615, 655–8; Fynn, pp. 141, 154–5; Isaacs, i. 138, 191, 212–27.

[3] Bryant, Ch. 57; Fynn, in Bird, i. 86–90; Fynn, pp. 122–9.

[4] Bryant, Ch. 58; Fynn, pp. 129–31; Isaacs, i. 152–71 (the quotation is from p. 170). Isaacs's account is melodramatic.

from the Cape Colony. In August Colonel Somerset came to the Mthatha river with a force of British regulars, Colonial levies, and African allies, having heard rumours of the Zulu invasion; but by then the Zulu army had withdrawn, and it was Matiwane's Ngwane, who had come down to the Mthatha after devastating the Caledon valley, whom Somerset attacked and routed.[1]

Meanwhile, before his army had had any rest, Shaka ordered it to march northwards against Soshangane—and to do so without its usual baggage-carriers—while he himself remained at his Dukuza barracks (Stanger). The Zulu army skirted Sobhuza's country and the country of the Pedi and then turned towards Soshangane, who was living north-west of Delagoa Bay. Soshangane, who had been given ample warning by a Zulu traitor, drove off the invaders. The Zulu army then retreated in bad order—hungry, fever-ridden, and exhausted. By the time it reached home, Shaka had been assassinated.[2]

From the beginning of his reign Shaka had been a more capricious ruler than the traditional Nguni chief, often ignoring the advice of his councillors and ordering the killing of subjects who displeased him for any reason. His whims were tolerated because of the strength and loyalty of the army and the sheer success of his military adventures, which brought a continuous flow of looted cattle to the kingdom. But, as with other military despots, success gradually went to his head and eventually undermined his sense of reality. By 1824, when the first traders reached him, they observed that he was killing his subjects on the flimsiest pretexts and was giving the impression that he did so, not merely to impress visitors, but because he enjoyed it.[3] He also became isolated from his people. They were obsequious in his presence and he seemed to have no respect for them. His decline reached its final phase after the death of his mother, Nandi, in 1827. Even allowing for exaggeration, the accounts by Fynn and Isaacs show that many thousands of innocent Zulu were then butchered in a wave of mass hysteria, which Shaka encouraged.[4] By 1828, moreover, he seems to have become morbidly concerned about his health. The most urgent order he gave to James King when he left on his embassy was to procure macassar oil, a hair tonic which he understood would rejuvenate him.[5]

There had already been at least one attempt on his life. One night when Fynn was staying at the royal kraal in 1824 Shaka was stabbed while he was taking part in a dance.[6] The would-be assassin was

[1] Bryant, pp. 621–5; Fynn, pp. 143–53; Isaacs, i. 204–5, 227–9.
[2] Bryant, Ch. 63; Fynn, p. 153; Isaacs, i. 229.
[3] Fynn, in Bird, i. 78; Fynn, p. 28.
[4] Bryant, Ch. 60; Fynn, in Bird, i. 91–93; Fynn, pp. 132–6; Isaacs, i. 196–9.
[5] Fynn, pp. 142–3, 155; Isaacs, i. 191–2, 237–8.
[6] Fynn, in Bird, i. 81–84; Fynn, pp. 83–86.

THE ZULU KINGDOM 351

assumed to be Ndwandwe; but his identity was never discovered. Now, in 1828, a plot was hatched by members of his own family. Mkabayi, a full sister of his father, Senzangakona, seems to have been in the centre of the conspiracy. She had long been alienated from Shaka, and she believed that he had killed Nandi. She enlisted the co-operation of Shaka's half-brothers, Dingane and Mhlangana, and his principal servant, Mbopha. The absence of the army on the Shoshangane expedition, and its disaffection at being submitted to excessive strains, gave them their opportunity. Dingane and Mhlangana slipped away from the army and returned home; and they, with Mbopha, slew Shaka outside his cattle-kraal in broad daylight on 24 September 1828.[1]

Soon after the assassination Dingane and Mhlangana organized a force to proceed against Ngwadi—a maternal half-brother whom Shaka had favoured and placed in control of a district, and a potential organizer of retribution on the assassins. Ngwadi and his people were annihilated. Dingane and Mhlangana then fell out among themselves, and by a ruse Dingane had Mhlangana killed. By the time the army returned from the north Dingane was in control of the kingdom. The warriors acclaimed him with some relief, for Shaka would assuredly have killed many of them for their failure to conquer Shoshangane. Dingane then killed Shaka's commander-in-chief and replaced him with an officer whom he trusted; he also placed his own nominees in charge of the districts.[2] What had happened was a rebellion, not a revolution: office-holders had changed, but the kingdom which Shaka had created remained in being.[3]

But Dingane[4] was not Shaka, and the Zulu kingdom began to lose its impetus. No warrior himself, Dingane was unable to exert Shaka's dynamic military leadership. The morale of the army never fully recovered from the strains of the 1828 campaigns; and yet Dingane found it necessary to give the army regular employment, sending it out on annual expeditions against Mzilikazi's Ndebele, Sobhuza's people, Faku's Mpondo, and the Bhaca of Ncaphayi, son of Madikane. Many of these expeditions were failures. Moreover, the Zulu nation itself showed signs of disintegration. The Qwabe under Chief Nqetho, who had been quiescent under Shaka, revolted against Dingane at the beginning of his reign and migrated southwards from their ancestral home in the heart of the Zulu kingdom to the neighbourhood of the upper Mzimvubu, brushing off the Zulu regiments on their way. Others followed the Qwabe precedent and left the Zulu kingdom. As his

[1] Bryant, Ch. 66; Fynn, in Bird, i. 96–97; Fynn, pp. 156–7; Isaacs, i. 258–9.
[2] Bryant, Ch. 67; Fynn, in Bird, i. 97–100; Fynn, pp. 159–64, 221; Gardiner, pp. 44–45.
[3] Max Gluckman, *Order and Rebellion in Tribal Africa*.
[4] Becker, *Dingane*.

prestige declined at home and among the other south-east African states, Dingane, who had started his reign with the declared policy of being a mild ruler, became as tyrannical as Shaka; and he also became desperately anxious to retrieve his military fortunes by obtaining a supply of firearms.[1] The flow of refugees to the south and Dingane's desire for muskets led to increasing involvements between the Zulu kingdom and the white trading community at Port Natal.

Throughout his reign the white presence in Natal became more and more ominous to Dingane. Although James King died in 1828 and in 1829 Francis Farewell was killed by the Qwabe, who regarded him as a spy for their enemy Dingane when they found him travelling through their new country,[2] the number of white traders increased. So, too, did the number of Zulu refugees who attached themselves to the traders. By 1835 there were about thirty white men and 2,500 Africans at Port Natal.[3] Like Shaka, Dingane tried to incorporate the Port Natal community within his political system by treating the traders as subordinate chiefs; but by providing sanctuary for more and more Zulu refugees they seemed to be encouraging the disintegration of the kingdom and to be creating a potentially hostile base.

There were also other signs of white interest in the area. In 1832 the Cape Governor, Sir Lowry Cole, sent Dr. Andrew Smith, of the Army Medical Corps, by the overland route through the Transkei 'to ascertain the real wishes of Dingaan, as well as the nature and capabilities of his country'.[4] In 1834, with Smith's encouragement, 190 merchants and other residents of Cape Town sent a petition asking the British Government to annex 'Port Natal and the depopulated country in its vicinity, which extends about two hundred miles along the coast to the westward ... and inland about one hundred miles'.[5] In the same year a party of thirty Afrikaners from the Uitenhage district, led by members of the Uys family, visited Natal to find out whether it was suitable for a farming settlement.[6] In 1835 Allen Gardiner, a British naval officer turned missionary, visited Dingane and asked permission to give his people religious instruction; and by the end of 1837 there were six American missionaries in Natal and the Zulu kingdom, and Francis Owen had started a mission at Dingane's capital, Mgungundlovu.[7] Though the British Government rejected the petition for annexation,

[1] Bryant, pp. 399–400; Fynn, pp. 164–74, 209–13, 221–9, 265–6; Isaacs, ii. *passim*, especially 21.
[2] Fynn, pp. 167–70; Isaacs, ii. 13–18.
[3] This is the estimate of Gardiner, op. cit., p. 85. [4] Kirby, p. 6.
[5] Ibid., p. 155. [6] Fynn, pp. 230–1.
[7] Gardiner; Owen; D. J. Kotzé (ed.), *Letters of the American Missionaries, 1835–1838*, VRS, 1950. Gardiner and Owen were members of the Church Missionary Society, an Anglican society with headquarters in London; the Americans were under the American Board of Commissioners for Foreign Missions, Boston.

THE ZULU KINGDOM 353

and the Afrikaners returned to the Cape Colony on the outbreak of the frontier war in December 1834, these events were disturbing to Dingane and his councillors; and their effects were intensified by Jacob Msimbiti.

Jacob (as the whites called him) was a Xhosa who had been captured during fighting on the Cape frontier and taken prisoner to Robben Island in Table Bay. From there he had been handed over to Captain Owen, R.N., as an interpreter for his survey work, and Owen passed him on to Francis Farewell. Jacob escaped from Farewell's party at Delagoa Bay in 1823 and walked south to Shaka, who found him useful as an interpreter. Jacob accompanied James King on his embassy to Algoa Bay in 1828, and John Cane on a similar embassy from Dingane in 1830. On both occasions he was handled tactlessly by the Cape officials and on the latter occasion he quarrelled with Cane. As a result of these experiences Jacob became bitterly anti-white, and on his return from the 1830 journey he told Dingane that white people were plotting to take his land and destroy his kingdom.[1] In Fynn's words,[2]

Jacob had reported to the King that as he was going to the Colony he had met a Frontier Kaffir, who told him he wanted to find a home with the Zulus, as there was no living so near the white people; that at first the white people came and took a part of their land, then they encroached and drove them further back, and have repeatedly taken more land as well as cattle. They then built houses among them, for the purpose of subduing them by witchcraft; that at the present time there was an *umlungu*—and a white man's house, or missionary in every tribe . . .; that during his stay at Grahamstown the soldiers frequently asked what sort of a country the Zulus had . . . and had said 'we shall soon be after you'; that he had heard a few white people had intended to come first and get a grant of land as I, Farewell, King and Dambuza [Isaacs] had done; they would then build a fort, when more would come, and demand land, who would also build houses and subdue the Zulus, and keep driving them further back, as they had driven the Frontier tribes.

This report made Dingane and his councillors highly suspicious of white people.

In 1831 Dingane sent a regiment to destroy Cane's property at Port Natal; and though Fynn tried to persuade Dingane that Jacob had been lying and Dingane eventually had Jacob killed, the relations between the Zulu King and the white traders remained strained.[3] There was a further incident in 1833 when a Zulu army, returning in

[1] 'Jacob' is one of the principal characters in the reminiscences of Fynn and Isaacs. See especially Fynn, pp. 179–90 and 196–8, and Isaacs, ii. 204–29; also Bryant, pp. 563–4, who establishes Jacob's real name.
[2] Fynn, p. 196.
[3] Ibid., pp. 188–90, 195–8.

poor condition from an unsuccessful campaign against the Bhaca and the Mpondo, attacked and killed some Coloured hunters and was in turn attacked by the people of Port Natal, black as well as white.[1] The white traders, fearing retaliation, then evacuated Natal; but they were soon back again.

After his arrival at the beginning of 1835 Allen Gardiner tried to bring some order into the situation. He convened a meeting of the white inhabitants, who passed nugatory resolutions to create a municipal government for D'Urban, named in honour of the Cape governor.[2] He also came to an agreement with the Zulu king: Dingane undertook to respect the lives and property of the established community of British traders and their African followers, and Gardiner undertook that future deserters from the Zulu kingdom should be returned to Dingane.[3] If this agreement had been enforced, one of Dingane's major problems would have been solved: Natal would have ceased to promote the disintegration of his nation by providing sanctuary and leadership for disaffected elements. But although Gardiner personally conducted some Zulu deserters to Dingane (who put them to death), some of the traders ignored the agreement. When Dingane heard of this, he forbade his subjects to trade with the whites, held Gardiner responsible for the conduct of the white people in Natal, and debarred all of them except Gardiner and his interpreter from the northern side of the Tukela river.[4] Gardiner then went to England, where he published a *Narrative of a Journey to the Zoolu Country in South Africa*, ending with a plea for British annexation of Port Natal, and gave evidence to the same effect to the Aborigines Committee of the House of Commons.[5] Parliament was not prepared to spend money on Natal; but in the Cape of Good Hope Punishment Act, 1836, it made British subjects in Natal, as elsewhere in Africa south of 25° South latitude, liable to punishment in the Cape courts. Gardiner returned to Natal with an appointment as Justice of the Peace in terms of that Act; but since he had neither funds nor staff, the Natal whites, indignant at the effects of Gardiner's intervention, repudiated his agreement with Dingane and declared themselves independent of British authority.[6] Gardiner then withdrew to his mission station on the Tongati river and ceased to be a factor in politics.[7]

[1] Fynn, pp. 224–9; Gardiner, pp. 289–91.   [2] Gardiner, pp. 187–8, 399–404.
[3] Ibid., pp. 108–42, 398.   [4] Ibid., pp. 145–87, 192–215.   [5] Ibid., pp. 405–8.
[6] The British Government had already done very much the same thing in response to a similar situation in New Zealand. In 1832 it had appointed James Busby as British Resident in the hope that he would protect British commerce and prevent British subjects from committing outrages upon the Maoris, but without providing him with any means to make his authority effective (Vincent Harlow and Frederick Madden, *British Colonial Developments, 1774–1834: Select Documents*, pp. 522–4).
[7] Bird, i. 313–28; Mackeurtan, pp. 192–201.

At the end of 1837 Afrikaner emigrants from the Cape Colony began to pour through the Drakensberg passes into upper Natal.[1] By that time some 4,000 men, women, and children had left their homes in the Colony, hoping to escape from an alien government whose policies they heartily detested and to occupy some Promised Land, where they might make their own arrangements with one another, with their servants, and with the other inhabitants.[2] They took with them perhaps 4,000 Coloured servants, most of whom were of Khoikhoi descent, though some were former slaves who had become apprentices in 1834.[3] They trekked and slept in their covered wagons, which was a style of living to which they had been born and bred as *trekboers*. The hauling capacity of their draft oxen set a limit to the speed of their migration, and the needs of their vast flocks of sheep and herds of cattle for water and pasture made them prefer to travel in small groups and, when sedentary, to spread out over the countryside; but their wagons, their horses, and their muskets, when skilfully co-ordinated, gave them a decisive superiority over all the African communities of south-eastern Africa. The Africans possessed scarcely any of these things, and those they did possess they did not fully understand. For defence, the emigrants could improvise a fortress by forming a *laager* of wagons lashed end to end; for attack, a party of armed horsemen could travel long distances at unexpected speed and take an enemy unawares. By the end of 1837 they had successfully applied both of these techniques against the Ndebele of Mzilikazi.[4]

Initially, the emigrants fanned out on the good pastures between the Rolong town of Thaba Nchu and the Vaal river; but they did not regard that area as their Promised Land, because they wanted access to the sea, preferably at a point remote from British control, where they might obtain regular supplies of sugar, coffee, tea, and other groceries, and especially powder and lead. For the present, they had good stocks of these necessities; most of them had left the Colony with more than 300 pounds of powder apiece.[5]

The emigrants were loosely organized. As in the Cape Colony, their basic social unit was the patriarchal white family with its Coloured dependants. In most cases several families, associated by kin or proximity,

[1] The main collections of documents of the Great Trek are in Bird, op. cit., and Gustav S. Preller (ed.), *Voortrekkermense*. Walker, *Great Trek*, has stood the test of time well; so has C. F. J. Muller, *Die Britse Owerheid en die Groot Trek*.
[2] See above, Ch. VII, pp. 292, 310.
[3] This is a rough estimate of the number of the Voortrekkers' Coloured servants—the 'forgotten people' of the Great Trek. The Cape Government tried to prevent the Voortrekkers taking Coloured people across the border against their will.
[4] See below, Ch. IX, pp. 411–12.
[5] A. J. H. van der Walt, 'Die Groot Trek tot 1838', in A. J. H. van der Walt, *et al.* (eds.), *Geskiedenis van Suid-Afrika*, i. 279.

left the Colony together and remained together while on trek; and in turn groups of families accepted the general leadership of some man of

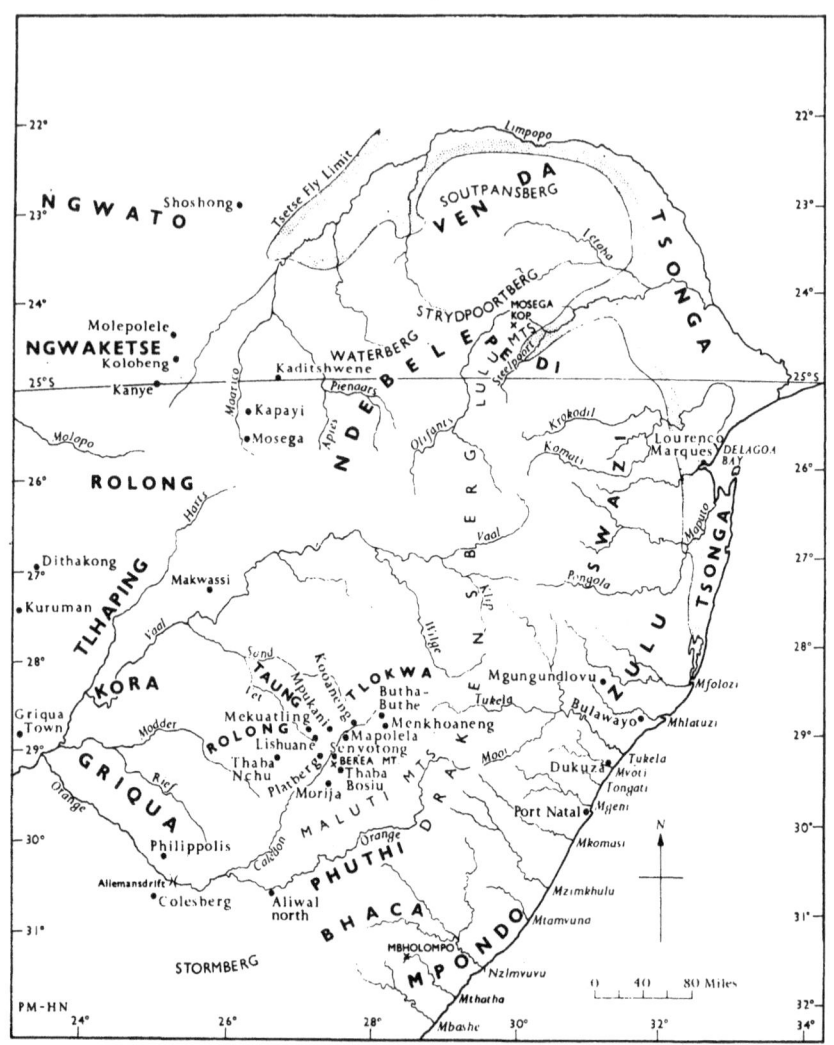

MAP 6. Eastern South Africa c. 1836

striking personality and proven ability. By the end of 1837 there were four considerable leaders among them: Andries Hendrik Potgieter,[1] an experienced commando leader from the Tarka; Gert Maritz,[2] a wagon-maker from Graaff-Reinet; Piet Uys, a young farmer from Uitenhage;

---

[1] Carel Potgieter and N. H. Theunissen, *Kommandant-Generaal Hendrik Potgieter*.
[2] H. B. Thom, *Die Lewe van Gert Maritz*.

and Piet Retief.[1] Retief, the oldest and the most sophisticated, had been born on a wine farm in the western Cape and had lived in Cape Town, Grahamstown, and the Winterberg, where he had won a reputation as a field-commandant. Probably each of the leaders regarded the emigrants as a single *maatschappij* (community) and intended that there should be some over-all unity; but they were individualists and lacked organizational experience beyond the local, subordinate, and primarily military roles to which they had been limited in the Colony. To achieve unity was therefore no easy task, and crises arose as each successive trek party arrived in the Thaba Nchu area.

When the Maritz trek joined the Potgieter trek in 1836, the men of both parties held a general meeting and created a Burgher Council of seven members, with Maritz as President and Judge and Potgieter as Chief Commandant. When Retief arrived in April 1837 another general meeting elected him Governor and Chief Commandant and confirmed Maritz in his offices, but gave Potgieter nothing. In June 1837 a third meeting, at the Vet river, adopted nine Articles of Association, which were to be accepted on oath by all who would join the *maatschappij*. Uys arrived soon afterwards to find that he, like Potgieter, could obtain no office. Thus the embryonic political institutions of the Voortrekkers failed to act as an integrative force, because, in failing to give political offices to the leaders of some of the trek parties, they did not correspond with the realities of Voortrekker organization. The Potgieters and Uyses were at loggerheads with the Retiefs and Maritzes. These jealousies were accentuated by substantial differences.

One dispute concerned religion. No *predikant* accompanied the Voortrekkers, for the Cape Colonial clergy were critical of their emigration; and while Maritz turned to his brother-in-law, Erasmus Smit, who was not an ordained *predikant*, Potgieter attended the services of James Archbell, the Wesleyan missionary at Thaba Nchu.

A more serious dispute concerned the destination of the trek. The Potgieters, who bore the brunt of Mzilikazi's attacks and took the initiative in defeating him, favoured the lands across the Vaal river, and hoped to develop a trade route to the Portuguese fort on Delagoa Bay. Retief and Maritz preferred Natal and its harbour. Uys, too, regarded Natal as the objective, but he considered that he had a right to personal overlordship there, by virtue of his leadership of the *Kommissie* which had visited the area in 1834.

These differences were never fully reconciled; but towards the end of 1837, after Mzilikazi had been driven north, most of the emigrants trekked eastwards towards the Drakensberg passes, with Retief's party in the van.

[1] J. L. M. Franken, *Piet Retief se Lewe in die Kolonie*; Gustav S. Preller, *Piet Retief: Lewensgeskiedenis van die grote Voortrekker*.

Retief knew enough about Natal to realize that if the Voortrekkers were to settle there in peace and security he should treat with the traders, to forestall British intervention, and with Dingane, to prevent a Zulu attack. Therefore, in October 1837 he led a small party by wagon to Port Natal, where he was heartened to find that the bulk of the traders, anxious about their security, would welcome the Voortrekkers in Natal, and that Gardiner lacked the means, if not the will, to oppose their entry. Retief then rode with his fifteen fellows and two of the traders to Mgungundlovu, where, after a display of Zulu warriors and cattle, Dingane assured Retief that he was 'almost inclined' to grant him land in Natal, provided that Retief first demonstrated his goodwill by recovering some cattle which had been stolen from the Zulu by people 'having clothes, horses, and guns'.[1] Retief accepted this condition and sent two Voortrekkers post-haste to reassure the *maatschappij*, while he returned to Port Natal for further discussions with the traders. On receipt of Retief's message the Voortrekkers poured down the Drakensberg passes—Retiefs, Maritzes, and even some Potgieters; and by the end of November, when Retief himself arrived there, the greater part of the emigrants were spread in small groups around the headwaters of the Tukela river and its tributaries.

Retief then led a commando back over the Drakensberg to the country of the Tlokwa, whom he knew to have been responsible for the raid upon the Zulu. He persuaded Sekonyela, the Tlokwa Chief, to meet him at Mpharane (modern Ficksburg) in the garden of James Allison, the Wesleyan missionary. There, by a ruse, Retief placed handcuffs on Sekonyela and said that he would not free him until his people had handed over their cattle, their horses, and their guns. This they did.[2] Retief then returned to the *maatschappij* in Natal and called for volunteers, with whom he rode direct to Mgungundlovu to claim his reward from Dingane—the foundation deed for the Promised Land.

It was difficult for Dingane to find an appropriate response to these events. Hitherto he, like Shaka, had been careful to avoid shedding the blood of white people. He liked the presents the traders brought him, and he respected their fire-arms and what he knew of the power of the British Government which loomed behind them. But by 1837 his relations with the traders had deteriorated, and since Henry Francis Fynn had left Natal in about 1832 there had been none among them in whom he could confide. The missionaries were no substitute. Gardiner, whom Dingane had briefly trusted, had been unable to carry out his

---

[1] Dingane to Retief, 8 Nov. 1837, in Bird, i. 361-2. There is a description of Retief's first visit to Dingane, 4-8 Nov. 1837, in Owen, pp. 58-64.
[2] Eyewitness account of Retief's treatment of Sekonyela by Daniel P. Bezuidenhout, in Bird, i. 369. For Tlokwa versions of the episode see Revd. R. Ellenberger in Owen, pp. 168-70.

commitments. Owen was proving a disappointment. While he was generous with instruction in reading, writing, painting, and religion, these seemed to have no particular relevance to Dingane's immediate problems; and Owen refused to transmit the sources of the white man's power—muskets, powder, lead, and instruction in the use of the few muskets he had obtained from traders.[1] So Dingane had nobody to turn to for informed advice when the Voortrekkers came within his purview, driving the Ndebele across the Limpopo, asking for a grant of land, taking occupation of much of it before he had given permission, and tricking Sekonyela into giving up his most valuable possessions. Gardiner added to Dingane's confusion by writing to remind Dingane that he had already granted *him* the land which the Boers were claiming,[2] and Owen endorsed Gardiner's point.[3] Retief himself exacerbated Dingane's anxieties by trying to intimidate him. 'The great Book of God teaches us', wrote Retief from Port Natal in November, 'that kings who conduct themselves as Umsilikazi does are severely punished, and it is not granted to them to live or reign long; and if you desire to learn at greater length how God deals with bad kings, you may enquire concerning it from the missionaries who are in your country.'[4]

Ndlela, Dingane's commander-in-chief, Dambuza, and other councillors had disapproved of Dingane's decision to allow Owen to settle at Mgungundlovu,[5] and they probably advised him to resist the Voortrekkers. The gathering of the warriors for the first-fruits ceremonies at the end of December generated further pressure for a forceful solution. Owen entered in his diary on 22 December 1837:[6]

> Dingarn sent for me very early to witness a dance. Many hundreds of men in different companies all in their war dresses with shields and spears had assembled to sing and caper, whilst other regiments stood on the neighbouring hills waiting to be called forth. The songs as yesterday, were all in praise of the king. Individuals who had either received some special favour or had lately arrived at the town praised him with loud voices, some of them running to and fro and, all using the greatest vehemence of gesture. One of them said 'Who can fight with thee: no king can fight with thee! They that carry fire cannot fight with thee.'

When Dingane made up his mind to annihilate the Voortrekkers is not certain. If Chief Silwebana is to be believed, Dingane had ordered him to kill Retief and his party when they were travelling from

---
[1] Owen, pp. 64–65, 72–73; Revd. Henry I. Venable to Dr. R. Anderson, 5 Dec. 1837, in Kotzé, p. 219.
[2] Owen, pp. 60, 65. [3] Ibid., pp. 63–64.
[4] Retief to Dingane, 8 Nov. 1837, in Bird, i. 362-4.
[5] Revd. Henry Venable to Dr. R. Anderson, 5 Dec. 1837, in Kotzé, p. 218.
[6] Owen, p. 89.

Mgungundlovu to Port Natal in November, and he refused.[1] It is more likely that the die was not cast until the last moment. When Retief returned to Mgungundlovu in February, he refused to hand over to Dingane the horses and the guns he had taken from the Tlokwa;[2] and Gardiner declined to come to Mgungundlovu, though asked.[3] Dingane then staked his all on eliminating the Voortrekkers, thinking thereby to preserve his kingdom from destruction. Retief and those with him were to be killed at Mgungundlovu; and the rest were to be struck down where they had settled in upper Natal, before they had time to concentrate for defence.[4]

The first part of the plot was carried out as planned. Retief reached Mgungundlovu on 3 February, with seventy-one Voortrekkers and thirty Coloured servants, and the cattle taken from the Tlokwa. They spent most of the next two days watching Zulu displays of war dances and songs performed by the large gathering of warriors whom Dingane had assembled. Some time on 4 February Dingane put his mark to a statement giving 'Retief, and his Countrymen . . . the Place called Port Natal, together with all the land annexed, that is to say from Dogela [Tukela] to the Omsoboebo [Mzimvubu] River westward and from the Sea to the North, as far as the land may be usefull and in my possession.'[5] On the morning of Tuesday, 6 February 1838, Dingane summoned the visitors to the town for a farewell beer drink. Two Zulu regiments encircled them in a war-dance, and when Dingane gave the order they overpowered Retief and his party, their servants, and their English interpreter, dragged them to the execution hill outside the town, and killed them with knobkerries or impaled them. Dingane had sent a message to Owen shortly before the event, and Owen, his wife, his sister, and his young interpreter, William Wood, were helpless witnesses of the massacre from outside Owen's house, which faced the execution hill.[6]

The second part of the Zulu plan was not a complete success, because Dingane had underestimated the number of Voortrekkers in Natal, and perhaps because his impis withdrew prematurely. During the early hours of 16 February they almost annihilated the people in the

[1] Joseph Kirkman (Revd. George Champion's interpreter) in Owen, p. 158; general letter by the American missionaries to Dr. R. Anderson, 2 Apr. 1838, in Kotzé, p. 232.
[2] Owen, p. 105.
[3] R. B. Hulley (Owen's interpreter), ibid., pp. 175–6.
[4] Dingane's own statements of his reasons for wishing to annihilate the Boers: Owen, pp. 112, 116–17, 177; Kotzé, pp. 238–9.
[5] Bird, i. 366.
[6] Eyewitness accounts of events at Mgungundlovu, 3–6 Feb. 1838: Owen, pp. 104–10; William Wood (Owen's interpreter), in Bird, i. 379–82. Accounts by men who reached Mgungundlovu soon after the massacre: Hulley, in Owen, pp. 176–9; American missionaries, in Kotzé, pp. 234–5.

easternmost Voortrekker encampments between the Bushman's and the Blaauwkrans rivers, around what became known as Weenen (Weeping), killing some forty white men, fifty-six white women, 185 white children, and over 200 Coloured servants, and wounding many more. But further west the Voortrekkers rallied and held them off; and the Zulu retired across the Tukela with about 35,000 cattle and sheep, and thereby lost the initiative.[1]

During the next few months the Zulu extinguished one of the white communities in Natal and weakened the other. In March John Cane, with a force of Coloured people and Africans from Port Natal, destroyed several Zulu villages and seized some cattle; but in April, thinking to repeat the success, many of the traders and most of their Coloured and African retainers crossed the Tukela as an undisciplined rabble and were almost annihilated by a Zulu regiment under the command of Mpande, half-brother of Dingane. The Zulu regiment then swept down on Port Natal and razed its buildings to the ground, while the surviving whites took refuge on board the *Comet*, which happened to be in the harbour.[2]

In the same month a Voortrekker expedition fared little better. Weakened by rivalries between their two leaders—Uys and Potgieter—the Voortrekkers were led into an ambush by Ndlela. Most of the Voortrekkers contrived to escape, leaving ten dead, including Piet Uys and his young son, Dirk.[3] The Potgieters then retired to the high veld, followed by accusations of cowardice. Though the Voortrekkers who remained in Natal beat off an attack in August, they were short of food and ridden with illness. Morale was low and their lack of leadership was accentuated by the death of Maritz in September.[4]

The vacuum was filled by Andries Pretorius.[5] Pretorius was an experienced commando leader from the Graaff-Reinet District. In 1837 he had made a reconnaissance of the areas occupied by the emigrants and participated in the fighting against Mzilikazi. He then returned to his home, having decided to organize and lead a trek of his friends and relations to Natal. During April 1838 messengers from Natal urged him to come as soon as possible, and on 20 November he reached Natal, ahead of his trek wagons, with sixty mounted men and a cannon. Appointed Commandant-General, within a few days he was on his

[1] Eyewitness accounts of the Zulu attacks on Voortrekker encampments: Willem J. Pretorius, in Bird, i. 233; Charl Celliers, ibid., pp. 241–3; Daniel P. Bezuidenhout, ibid., pp. 370–3; Anna Steenkamp, ibid., p. 463. See also Jacobus Boshof, ibid., pp. 403–8.
[2] William Wood, in Bird, i. 383–7; Owen, pp. 127–39; Kirkman, ibid., pp. 166–7; Revd. Daniel Lindley in Kotzé, pp. 243–4.
[3] Owen, pp. 134–6; Willem J. Pretorius, in Bird, i. 233–4; Jacobus Boshof, ibid., pp. 408–12.
[4] Jacobus Boshof, ibid., pp. 413–14; Anna Steenkamp, ibid., pp. 464–6.
[5] Gustav S. Preller, *Andries Pretorius*.

way to Zululand with a commando 500 strong and fifty-seven wagons. During the advance he tried to make his men into a disciplined force, exhorting them, establishing a proper chain of command, keeping his officers informed of his tactics, punishing insubordination, posting sentries, sending out scouting parties, and forming strong *laagers* at night. On Sunday 9 December the commando vowed to build a church if it pleased God to grant them a victory; and on the 15th, scouts having reported the presence of the Zulu army in the vicinity, the Voortrekkers *laagered* in a strong defensive position on the banks of the Ncome river. Starting at dawn on the 16th, the Zulu army, some 10,000 strong, spent itself in repeated charges upon the *laager*. Cannon fire combined with musket fire wrought havoc in their ranks, and eventually mounted Voortrekkers issued from the *laager* and routed the exhausted and dispirited Zulu. In the entire engagement no white people were killed, and only three, including Pretorius, were wounded; whereas some 3,000 Zulu died. Blood river, as the Ncome was now called, was a classic example of the devastating superiority of controlled fire, by resolute men from a defensive position, over Africans armed with assagais and spears, however numerous and however brave.[1]

From Blood river Pretorius took his force to Mgungundlovu, which Dingane abandoned. In a leather bag among the corpses on the execution hill the commando discovered Retief's treaty. Soon afterwards a mounted Voortrekker detachment was led into an ambush by the Zulu near the Black Mfolozi; but the Voortrekkers fought their way out, losing only five men and killing about a thousand Zulu, and thereby giving an even more impressive demonstration of fire-power, for the battle was on terrain selected by the Zulu and the Voortrekkers were without wagons. The commando then retired to Natal (January 1839).[2]

After these defeats Dingane sent ambassadors to Natal, promising not to encroach south of the Tukela and undertaking to pay an indemnity in cattle; but the cattle were not sent and the Voortrekkers prepared for another invasion of the Zulu kingdom.

Meanwhile, Dingane sent an impi northwards against the people later known as the Swazi, hoping to restore the morale of the army; but the impi was not successful. The Zulu nation then began to fall apart. Some of the conquered people who had never been fully integrated withdrew their allegiance, and Dingane's half-brother, Mpande, defied

[1] On the campaign against Dingane in Dec. 1838 see the official 'Journal of the Expedition' by J. G. Bantjes, Clerk of the *Volksraad*, in Bird, i. 438–52; official dispatches by Andries Pretorius, 22 Dec. 1838, and 9 Jan. 1839, ibid., pp. 453–8; eyewitness accounts by William J. Pretorius, ibid., pp. 234–6, Charl Celliers, ibid., pp. 243–9, and Daniel P. Bezuidenhout, ibid., pp. 374–5. The Zulu did have a few muskets which Dingane had obtained from traders, but they were not able to use them effectively.
[2] Ibid.

him. Dingane had spared Mpande's life and allowed him to be the regional chief in the Eshowe area because he regarded him as too feeble to be a serious rival. Mpande, who seems to have had a deep-rooted dislike for Dingane, refused to send him effective military assistance for his northern campaign, or to join him at his new capital; and in October 1839, fearing that his life was in danger for his disloyalty, Mpande split the nation, leading 17,000 Zulu across the lower Tukela into Natal, with some 25,000 cattle. The Voortrekkers suspected that this might be a ruse and some of them wished to attack Mpande and seize his cattle; but subtler counsels prevailed. The *Volksraad* interrogated Mpande and sent a commission to his headquarters, as a result of which Mpande became an ally of the Voortrekker Republic and undertook to wage war against Dingane.[1]

In January two forces moved northwards into the Zulu kingdom. Mpande's army, about 10,000 strong, was commanded by Nongalaza. Mpande himself accompanied Pretorius's commando, which consisted of 300 white men and 460 Coloured and African servants. On the way north Pretorius conducted a summary trial of Dambuza and another *induna*, whom Dingane had sent to Natal with presents in a final attempt to ward off the invasion. Mpande declared that they had been largely responsible for the murder of Retief's party and they were both shot. On 30 January Nongalaza inflicted a serious defeat on Dingane north of the Mkuzi river and the Voortrekkers then joined their allies in pursuing and rounding up cattle. Retreating towards the Pongolo, Dingane's army crumbled away and he himself was eventually captured and killed by the proto-Swazi. Pretorius then proclaimed Mpande King of the Zulu, but vassal of the Natal Republic, and returned to Natal with about 36,000 cattle.[2]

Thus the Zulu kingdom which Shaka had created was overwhelmed by circumstances more strange and more formidable than Shaka had ever encountered. But the achievements of Dingiswayo and Shaka were not wholly undone. Mpande ruled from the Buffalo-Tukela to the Pongolo, where there had been a multiplicity of small autonomous chiefdoms before Dingiswayo. His vassalage to Natal lapsed when the republic came to an end in 1843. He pursued a pacific external policy, taking care to avoid giving offence to white people, with their superior technology, and tolerating intrusions into the western part of his kingdom by Afrikaners from the South African Republic. Less energetic than Shaka and Dingane, his internal policy was isolationist and

---

[1] Ibid., pp. 536–44; Becker, Ch. 24; Bryant, pp. 323–5.
[2] On the campaign against Dingane in Jan.–Feb. 1840 see the account by Adolphe Delegorgue in Bird, i. 553–76, and the official Journal by P. H. Zietsman, ibid., pp. 576–99; also Becker, Ch. 25; Bryant, pp. 325–6.

comparatively mild. His reign was consequently a period of recuperation from the strains of the previous decades. The population of the Zulu kingdom increased and so did its wealth in cattle. Most of the conquered peoples became reconciled to permanent membership in the Zulu nation; and those who did not were able to secede from the nation by crossing the Buffalo-Tukela in search of their former homelands in Natal. Mpande's two oldest sons, Cetshwayo and Mbulazi, became rivals for the succession and built up followings of young warriors, and in 1856 the two factions clashed in a tremendous battle near the mouth of the Tukela. Cetshwayo triumphed and thereafter he gradually took over the reins of power from his father. When Mpande died in 1872, Cetshwayo succeeded him without opposition. By that time Zulu cattle-wealth and morale were restored and a new generation of warriors had grown up who had not suffered the devastating effects of fire-arms.[1]

2. *The Voortrekker Republic*

As a result of the Blood river campaign most of the Voortrekkers settled in Natal.[2] They spread out, as their fathers and grandfathers had done in the Cape Colony, establishing claims to farms wherever there were good pastures and perennial water. Those who arrived before December 1839 became entitled by republican law to two farms on the traditional 3,000 morgen scale; later arrivals to one. But in one way and another by 1842 a Voortrekker community of scarcely more than 6,000 men, women, and children claimed almost all the pasture land between the Buffalo-Tukela and the Mzimkhulu, and some of them were already casting covetous eyes beyond those rivers. In the centre of the area they occupied, Pietermaritzburg, named after Piet Retief and Gert Maritz, was laid out as the seat of government. Near what was left of the old trading settlement of Port Natal, a Voortrekker village was founded at Congella; and another at Weenen.

While most of the Voortrekkers were occupied in re-establishing themselves as pastoral farmers, the ambitious and public-spirited were also laying the foundations of a government, adapting and amplifying

---

[1] We need to know more about the Zulu kingdom under Mpande. See Donald R. Morris, pp. 192–9, and C. T. Binns, op. cit.
[2] The principal documents for the history of the Natal Republic are in *SAAR, Natal*, i, ed. J. H. Breytenbach. For the Natal Republic see also J. A. I. Agar-Hamilton, *The Native Policy of the Voortrekkers: An Essay in the History of the Interior of South Africa, 1836–1858*; Bird, op. cit.; [Henry Cloete], *The History of the Great Boer Trek and the Origins of the South African Republics*; A. J. du Plessis, 'Die Republiek Natalia', in *AYB, 1942*, i, Cape Town, 1942; G. W. Eybers, *Select Constitutional Documents Illustrating South African History, 1795–1910*; Muller, op. cit.; Preller, *Voortrekkermense*; Walker, *Great Trek*. As the ground now becomes less controversial and has been covered by a number of historians, less detailed documentation is given in the rest of this chapter.

the improvisations they had made at Thaba Nchu and Vet river to meet their needs as a settled community. In 1838 a committee drew up the framework of a Constitution, with the help of Jacobus Boshof, who was visiting from Graaff-Reinet, where he had been a clerk in the Civil Commissioner's office, and who decided to settle in Natal.[1] The key institution was an elected *Volksraad* of twenty-four men, aged between twenty-five and sixty. The *Volksraad* was not only a legislature; it was also the final court of appeal, and even the executive authority, for there was no other executive. Local government was modelled on the system that had prevailed in the Cape Colony before the British innovations. To each of the three Districts the *Volksraad* appointed a commandant, who was the military officer, and a *landdrost*, the administrative and judicial officer. The *landdrost* and commandant acted in conjunction with *heemraden* and field-cornets, who were unpaid, part-time officials elected by and from the citizen body. Usually there was also a commandant-general in the person of Andries Pretorius; but there was a party in the *Volksraad* which was jealous of Pretorius, which took care that he should not become an independent authority and went so far as to abolish his office for a period.

During 1840 Pretorius went to the high veld to negotiate with Potgieter, as a result of which the Republic was formally enlarged to include the Winburg and Potchefstroom communities, on either side of the Vaal river. These communities were given three representatives in the *Volksraad* at Pietermaritzburg, which became responsible for the entire Republic. There was also a subordinate 'Adjunkt Raad' at Potchefstroom.

Failing to obtain the services of a *predikant* from the Cape Colony, in January 1841 the *Volksraad* pensioned off the unordained Erasmus Smit and appointed as *predikant* an American missionary, Daniel Lindley. A Calvinist from the southern States, Lindley was a sympathetic, though by no means uncritical pastor; and for six years he did his best to serve the entire Voortrekker community, travelling from southern Natal to the Limpopo river, baptizing, confirming, and marrying Voortrekkers and giving them communion.[2]

The Republic of Natal lacked the funds and the personnel to provide more than a sketchy administrative system. The Voortrekkers were running out of the capital they had taken with them from the Cape Colony and had scarcely any means of replenishing it. Revenue, theoretically due in the form of land taxes, customs duties, and trading licences, was meagre. The salaries of the few full-time officials were

[1] Bird, i. 525–31; *SAAR, Natal*, i. 285–8.
[2] Edwin W. Smith, *The Life and Times of Daniel Lindley (1801–80): Missionary to the Zulus, Pastor of the Voortrekkers, Ubebe Omhlope*.

chronically in arrears. There were virtually no police. Moreover, though in moments of stress or for purposes of propaganda leaders spoke of their common blood and common sacrifices, the Voortrekkers were in fact divided by distance and by factional feeling. On the initial cleavage between the different trek parties and leaders, there was now superimposed a new cleavage between those who supported the *Volksraad* and those who supported Pretorius. There were also sharp personal quarrels over land and over the distribution of the booty captured by commandos—especially cattle and 'apprentices'. Consequently, the administrative system of the Voortrekker State was a blueprint rather than a reality. If crime was infrequent, this was due to respect for orderly living rather than to fear of the consequences.

In trying to regulate the transformation of a migrant society into a society settled in a distinct territory, the *Volksraad* had to make far-reaching decisions defining the scope of the community and the status of persons. Who was a member of the community? What strangers were to be admitted to the community and on what conditions? What was the position of strangers who were residents of the territory of the Republic but not Voortrekkers?

In dealing with these problems the members of the *Volksraad* had a clear understanding of the interests and expectations of their constituents. The Voortrekker community was in essence a community of Dutch-speaking people of European descent, born and bred in the Cape Colony, who had quit the Colony to acquire fresh land and labour and to found an independent State.[1] Other people of European origin were to be treated with suspicion, for their loyalties might lie elsewhere; but if they gave proof of their loyalty to the community a few could safely be absorbed, for they were of the same sub-species as themselves. But the Voortrekker *community* was not a complete *society*: it was only the dominant part of a society, distinguished from the subordinate part by prescriptive criteria. The Voortrekkers were dependent on the use of servants of African, or Asian, or mixed descent, and assumed them to be of a different sub-species. They even referred to them in different terms—as *skepsels* (creatures) rather than *mense* (people).[2] These principles had been embodied in the social structure of the Cape Colony ever since the first free burghers left the service of the Dutch East India Company in 1657. They were the principles of the only social order the Voortrekkers had ever known. They were in harmony with the

[1] The Voortrekkers regarded themselves as Dutch-speaking. In fact, their spoken language was already closer to modern Afrikaans than Dutch.

[2] There was, of course, a difficulty in respect of 'Coloured' people—i.e. people who were the product of miscegenation between whites and Khoikhoi, San, Nguni, Sotho, and slaves. Most of them were disowned by their white fathers and relegated to the status of *skepsels*; a few managed to pass into the ranks of the *mense*.

Calvinist religion as they interpreted it. They were implied in the manifesto which Retief wrote for publication before he left the Colony.¹ They were applied during the migration. So engrained were they in the Voortrekker mind that they were unhesitatingly translated into law in the first Voortrekker Republic. That was what custom prescribed, self-interest demanded, and God ordained. That was how it had always been and always must be in South Africa.

Accordingly, the *Volksraad* ruled that Dutch South Africans who joined the Republic from the Cape Colony could easily become citizens and landowners. Other white people—'uitlanders' as they were already called—could become citizens and landowners provided they had lived in the Republic for a year and produced a certificate of good conduct signed by a *landdrost* or field-cornet and two other citizens.² Non-whites had no right to be in the settled parts of the Republic at all, except as servants of white people, and then they were not permitted to own land, firearms, or horses, to participate in the political process, or to be at large without passes signed by white employers.³

The *Volksraad* found that the problem of regulating the relations between the communities was more complicated in practice than in theory, because it was difficult both to provide the requisite number of dark-skinned labourers and to ensure the security of the Voortrekker community. When the Voortrekkers began to settle down as farmers, they needed more servants than the Coloured people they had brought with them from the Cape Colony, and they turned to the African population. At first there were few Africans in the areas the Voortrekkers occupied, so the commandos against Dingane made a point of capturing children as well as cattle for distribution when a campaign was over.⁴ These captives were called 'apprentices', and were meant to become free at the age of twenty-five (twenty-one in the case of girls). However, from the Blood river campaign onwards there was a continual influx of refugees from the Zulu kingdom into Natal, who were returning to the homelands from which they had been absorbed by Shaka two decades earlier; and Africans who had fled south in the time

¹ Eybers, pp. 143–5.   ² Du Plessis, p. 181.   ³ Ibid., pp. 153–61.
⁴ Adolphe Delegorgue, in Bird, i. 564: 'This war that we were waging against the Zulus was looked upon by many of the farmers as simply a hunting expedition; but the chase had much of value in it. More than one regarded it as the starting-point of his fortunes, adding to his share of the results of the commando the cattle which he might acquire, by means well understood and conventionally spoken of as perquisites. And then was it not allowable to bring away three or four young Kafir boys or girls, taken by force from their families, and who by a qualified phrase were called apprentices, in order the better to ward off the idea of slavery? These were destined for household service; but the farmers, as if ashamed to admit their weakness, though they wrangled about the possession of these beings, and bartered them as they would horses or oxen, were constantly repeating: "For my part I would rather not have them; but what would my wife say if I did not bring her some? It is so difficult to obtain servants in Natal."'

of Shaka also came back to Natal. It has been estimated that the African population of the Natal Republic increased from 10,000 in 1838 to 50,000 in 1843.[1] Thus the Voortrekker dilemma shifted from a labour shortage to a threat to security.

The *Volksraad* then decided that concentrations of Africans should be dispersed and not more than five African families should live on one farm. In 1841 the *Volksraad* also resolved that all 'surplus' Africans should be placed between the Mtamvuna and the Mzimvubu rivers at the southern end of the Republic, and instructed Commandant-General Pretorius to send them there, by persuasion if possible, by force if necessary. But this was never done. More and more Africans lived in the Republic without being controlled by the government. *Volksraad* decisions could not be enforced and order could not be maintained, partly because of the inherent weaknesses of the State and partly because its resources were required to deal with a more formidable challenge.[2]

The most serious threat to the survival of the Republic came from Great Britain. British power hung over the Voortrekkers from the moment they left the Cape Colony, because they were British subjects and their actions were liable to continue to affect the Colony. The Voortrekkers themselves had no means of calculating the dimensions of that threat, for they were not aware of the realities of British politics.

In fact, the British response to the Great Trek was confused, half-hearted, and largely ineffective.[3] During the middle years of the nineteenth century, when British naval and industrial power was unchallenged, the primary political objective of the British ruling class, irrespective of party, was financial retrenchment. In the ideal world, the British people would be able to trade freely and profitably everywhere, without the obligation of governing overseas territories. In the world as it was, a British Empire existed, and exerted influences upon the Government. There were colonists of British descent who had links with metropolitan industry and commerce; and there were native inhabitants whose welfare was espoused by missionary societies. When they promoted unremunerative expenditure, these influences were incompatible with the primary political objective of the British ruling class. Hence where possible the cost of defence of a colony was transferred to its inhabitants—a trend which led during the 1850s to responsible government in the Canadian, Australian, and New Zealand colonies. In any case, expansionism had to be checked. There had to be

---

[1] Lieut.-Gov. Scott to Sec. of State Newcastle, 4 Sept. 1862, C.O. 879/2, pp. 8–9, P.R.O.
[2] Agar-Hamilton, Ch. 3; du Plessis, pp. 153–61.
[3] For British policy towards the Voortrekkers see Galbraith, *Reluctant Empire*; Morrell, *British Colonial Policy in the Age of Peel and Russell*; Muller, op. cit.

some compelling commercial or strategic reason to justify an annexation. Evidence was needed, either that the annexation would lead to a significant increase in British trade, which had previously been blocked by the incompetence or the ill will of the inhabitants, or that the territory, left in alien hands, would become a threat to British security.

These fiscal, commercial, strategic, and humanitarian factors provided a framework within which officials thought about imperial questions and set limits to their freedom of action. In particular cases, however, it was often extremely difficult to evaluate each of these factors, and more difficult still to determine the resultant of all the relevant factors, for some might point in one direction and some in another. Consequently, in making a policy decision an office-holder was liable to be affected by an active pressure group or to tilt the balance on the side of his personal ambitions or predilections. This was true of Colonial Office officials and cabinet ministers in London. It was still more true of colonial governors, because distance and slow communications gave them many opportunities to act first and report afterwards.[1]

In the perspective of the British ruling class the Cape Colony was of marginal value in the middle years of the nineteenth century. The Colony had been conquered and held for strategic reasons, but its strategic value was confined to the harbours of the Cape peninsula, which were important links on the trade route to India, the most profitable of all British possessions. For the rest, the Colony was a burden. The cost of civil administration was barely met from local taxation; the military garrison and the frequent frontier wars constituted a huge liability to the British taxpayer. The Cape's trade with Britain was not valuable enough, its British settlers neither numerous nor influential enough, to offset this fundamental defect.

Before the Great Trek, Natal was an even worse prospect. The small population of white traders and their African dependants was clearly unable to pay for an effective administration or to produce a worthwhile volume of trade; and the proximity of the powerful, independent, and potentially hostile Zulu kingdom pointed to large military expenditures. Though Natal, like the Cape, lay athwart the trade route to India, sand bars at the entrance made its only harbour dangerous to small ships and inaccessible to large ones. Consequently London had no hesitation in rejecting the intermittent requests for annexation by Natal traders and Cape merchants, even though endorsed by Governor Sir Benjamin D'Urban in 1835.[2] As for the interior high veld north of

---

[1] Telegraphic communication between London and Cape Town was established in about 1870: *CHBE*, ii, pp. 762–4.
The emigrant ships averaged three months from England to Natal in 1849–51: Alan F. Hattersley, *Portrait of a Colony: The Story of Natal*, p. 31.

[2] Bird, i. 252–73; Kirby, pp. 145 ff.

the Orange river, it was still more remote from British interests before the Great Trek.

These views were not changed by the first reports of the departure of Voortrekkers from the Cape Colony. D'Urban and his successor, Sir George Napier, tried to check the emigration by a mixture of promises and threats, but they did nothing to control the Voortrekkers when they had left. The Cape of Good Hope Punishment Act, 1836, was no more than an empty gesture, because it made no provision for the capture of offenders.

By 1838 the embroilments of the Voortrekkers with the Ndebele and the Zulu evoked stronger pressure from the evangelicals. The Aborigines Protection Society in London petitioned Lord Glenelg, Colonial Secretary, to occupy Port Natal to prevent the Voortrekkers from exterminating Africans. Glenelg, who was sensitive to the evangelical point of view, authorized this; Napier, whose main anxiety was that Voortrekker pressures upon Africans might throw the Cape eastern frontier into turmoil, sent a hundred men to Natal, with orders to try to keep the peace between Voortrekkers and Africans. Two weeks after these first British troops landed at Port Natal, Pretorius's commando defeated the Zulu at Blood river (16 December 1838). Captain Jervis then mediated a peace between Dingane and the Republic, with the Tukela river as the boundary between them, and Napier withdrew the small British force in December 1839, its task seemingly accomplished. But the peace proved to be no more than a truce. By the end of February 1840, with the final defeat of Dingane, the Voortrekkers were supreme in Natal and overlords of Mpande's kingdom, and later that year they wrote to Napier claiming British recognition of the independence they had trekked to obtain.[1]

During the next two years it was touch-and-go whether the Republic would have its way. At one stage Governor Napier was inclined to let it; and so was Lord Stanley, who became Colonial Secretary in September 1841. But two actions by the Republic decided its fate. First, in December 1840 Pretorius led a commando southwards, with African allies, to intimidate the neighbouring tribes into refraining from stealing white men's cattle. On inadequate evidence Pretorius assumed that Ncaphayi, the Bhaca chief, had been responsible for thefts; and he attacked Ncaphayi's people without warning, killing thirty of them and making off with 3,000 cattle and seventeen children for distribution as apprentices.[2] Feeling threatened by this incursion in his vicinity, the

[1] On the first British occupation of Port Natal see Bird, i. 418–37, 458, 492–503, 513–20, 532–6, 547–8, 599, 611–12, 627–30; also Galbraith, pp. 184–8.
[2] On the attack on Ncaphayi see Agar-Hamilton, pp. 139–43; Bird, i. 622–4; *SAAR, Natal*, i. 360–72, 388–90; Walker, *Great Trek*, p. 243.

Mpondo Chief Faku appealed, through his Wesleyan missionary, for protection from the Cape Governor. Napier sent a small detachment to Faku's country early in 1841. Later that year the *Volksraad* passed its rash resolution for the removal of 'surplus' Africans from Natal to the south of the Mtamvuna.[1] When he heard of this, Napier decided to reoccupy Port Natal, and Captain T. C. Smith, with 250 men, marched into the port from Faku's country in May 1842.[2]

The *Volksraad* determined to resist. It was encouraged to do so by the curious conduct of J. A. Smellekamp. A Dutch merchant ship, chartered by the Amsterdam firm of J. A. Klyn & Co., had called at Port Natal to try and open up a trade with the Voortrekkers. Smellekamp, its supercargo, had landed and visited Pietermaritzburg, and without any authority he had led the *Volksraad* to believe that the Dutch Government would take the Republic under its protection.[3] The *Volksraad* therefore tried to mobilize the manpower of the community. The response was slow and inadequate from Natal itself, and the only substantial aid from beyond the mountains was a Transorangia commando led by Jan Mocke. Nevertheless, Pretorius was able to defeat a bungling night attack on his position at Congella, to capture the British ships in harbour, and to besiege the British detachment in its hastily erected fort. Smith was on the verge of being starved out when reinforcements arrived by sea, summoned by Richard King, a member of the trading community, who had made an epic ride from Port Natal to Grahamstown. Colonel Josias Cloete, in command of the relief expedition, then dispersed the Voortrekkers from the port area and demanded the submission of the Republic. Many of the Voortrekkers retreated to the Weenen district or the high veld, but the remaining members of the *Volksraad* invited Cloete to Pietermaritzburg, where, on 15 July 1842, twelve of them submitted to the authority of the Queen in return for a general amnesty (with five exceptions) and general assurances for the future. The Colonel then returned to Cape Town, leaving Smith with 325 men to control the port and its revenues, and holding the *Volksraad* responsible for administration beyond the port, subject to British supremacy and pending the decision of the British Government.[4] That decision was long in coming and longer still in being translated into action.

Lord Stanley's first thought on taking office had been to recall Smith's detachment from Faku's country and leave the Voortrekkers to

[1] *SAAR, Natal*, i. 106–7.
[2] On the background to the second British occupation of Natal see Bird, i. 618–60; Galbraith, pp. 189–92.
[3] Cloete, pp. 144–7; B. J. Liebenberg, 'Nederland en die Voortrekkers in Natal', *Mededelings van die Universiteit van Suid-Afrika*, 51 (1964); *SAAR, Natal*, i.
[4] Bird, i. 700–32, ii. 1–67; du Plessis, pp. 196–200; Walker, *Great Trek*, pp. 272–82.

their own devices, provided they did not attack friendly tribes; but when Stanley heard of the reoccupation of Port Natal he gradually and reluctantly came to the conclusion that Britain should annex Natal. The determining factor was the evidence, from their performance in Natal, that if the Voortrekkers were not controlled they would cause disorder among the African communities and destroy the prospect of stability on the frontiers of the Cape Colony. Stanley hoped that a British Natal would yield a revenue sufficient to pay for its administration, and that by controlling the port of Natal as well as the Cape ports Britain would have the whip hand over all the Voortrekkers. Humanitarian considerations, evoked by Voortrekker disruption of African societies and seizure of apprentices, also entered into his thinking; but they were secondary. Stanley was not moved by the arguments of a recently formed African Land and Emigration Association that Natal had valuable potential for systematic colonization and economic development; nor is there any evidence that he took seriously the rumours that sinister French influences lay behind Smellekamp's activities. As John S. Galbraith says: 'Stanley annexed Natal largely because he was convinced that the independence of the Boers was reconcilable neither with order nor with humanity.'[1]

In announcing this decision to Napier in December 1842 Stanley instructed him to send a special commissioner to Natal. The Commissioner was to tell the Afrikaners that they would be protected in the enjoyment of such lands as they had *bona fide* occupied for the twelve months before the arrival of the Commissioner; to invite them to express their own views about the form of the institutions of local government which were to be established in Natal; and to warn them that Britain would not pay for the expenses of Natal, except those of providing military protection. Stanley added:[2]

It is also necessary that the Commissioner should state most explicitly that, whatever may be the institutions ultimately sanctioned, three conditions are absolutely essential:

1. That there shall not be in the eye of the law any distinction of colour, origin, race, or creed; but that the protection of the law, in letter and in substance, shall be extended impartially to all alike.
2. That no aggression shall be sanctioned upon the natives residing beyond the limits of the colony, under any plea whatever, by any private person or any body of men, unless acting under the immediate authority and orders of the Government.
3. That slavery in any shape or under any modification is absolutely unlawful, as in every other portion of Her Majesty's dominions.

[1] Galbraith, p. 196.
[2] Sec. of State Stanley to Govr. Napier, 13 Dec. 1842, C.O. 49/36, P.R.O.; Bird, ii. 146.

As Commissioner, Napier selected Henry Cloete—lawyer, member of the Cape Legislative Council, and younger brother of Colonel Josias Cloete. He reached Pietermaritzburg in June 1843 to find that the Afrikaners were sharply divided. Some regarded the men who had submitted in July 1842 as traitors to the community, and they had high hopes that, if they held out a little longer, decisive aid would come from Holland. They had heard that Smellekamp had recently returned to South African waters and had been prevented from landing at Port Natal by Major Smith, and they seriously believed that Holland was still a great power and would shortly be taking them under her protection. Cloete was therefore persuaded to postpone the discussions until August. Returning to Pietermaritzburg at that time, Cloete found that Jan Mocke had come back from the high veld with 200 armed men to oppose British authority. While Cloete made himself available to deputations in a private house, the *Volksraad* met in a court-room near by, in the presence of a mob which dominated the proceedings. However, nearly all the recognized leaders of the Natal Voortrekkers were for dealing with the Commissioner. Cloete persuaded them that Dutch support was a myth, parried an indignant deputation of Afrikaner women, and rejected an appeal for an amendment to the condition prohibiting a colour-bar. On 8 August 1843 all but one of the Natal members of the *Volksraad* signed a statement accepting Stanley's terms. Mocke then led his followers back across the Drakensberg, seeking independence on the high veld.[1]

3. *The British Colony*

Britain was very slow in giving effect to these terms. Henry Cloete investigated Afrikaner land claims in accordance with Stanley's instructions. He also treated with Mpande, whom he recognized as the independent ruler of the Zulu kingdom north of the Buffalo-Tukela, except for St. Lucia Bay, which he annexed in case it had potential as a port.[2] He returned to Cape Town in May 1844, leaving Major T. C. Smith in command of Fort Napier, built to control Pietermaritzburg. The final decisions on land claims, the form of government and the southern boundary were not made until 1845, when 371 Afrikaner

---

[1] Henry Cloete himself has left two accounts of these proceedings: one in his contemporary official reports to Cape Town, in Bird, ii. 175–6, 178–81, 186–93, 201–10, 218–19, 221–2, 224–6, 240–6, 249–50, 256–65; the other in a lecture delivered in Pietermaritzburg in 1855, in Cloete, pp. 160–96. The two accounts have substantial differences. The contemporary reports to Cape Town have been preferred, as Cloete was probably speaking from memory in 1855. See also du Plessis, pp. 200–3, and Walker, *Great Trek*, pp. 300–13.

[2] Bird, ii. 290–304.

farms were recognized, subject to payment for survey and a redeemable quitrent, Natal became a detached District of the Cape Colony, and the boundary was fixed at the Mzimkhulu. In December 1845 Martin West assumed duty as Lieutenant-Governor with a handful of other officials. By that time most of the Afrikaners who had waited to see how things would develop had left Natal for the high veld, disappointed with the rejection of their claims to land, the form of government, and the failure of the new régime to control the Africans; and Natal had a population of about 100,000 Africans and 3,000 Afrikaners.[1]

When they reached Natal, West and his colleagues were faced with most of the problems that had baffled the republican *Volksraad*, compounded by the uncertainty and confusion of the years of interregnum.[2] Of the farms which Cloete had recognized, only about a hundred were actually occupied by their owners, for most of the Afrikaners who had not returned to the high veld were assembled in groups, waiting to see what the new régime held for them before they decided whether to stay in Natal or to quit. The Africans were scattered throughout the territory, their social and political cohesion pulverized by the events of the last three decades. Towards the Drakensberg both Afrikaners and Africans were victims of raids by San bands; and towards the Buffalo-Tukela and the Mzimkhulu rivers both Afrikaners and Africans were continually disturbed by fresh waves of immigrants from Mpande's country and Faku's. As with every British colonial administrator in the nineteenth century, West's capacity to deal with his problems was severely restricted by shortage of funds and shortage of personnel.

Cloete had done virtually nothing to place African land-holding on a legal basis, beyond recommending that several areas should be set aside for their use. In March 1846 West appointed a Commission to give effect to this advice. The Commissioners were Theophilus Shepstone, the 'Diplomatic Agent to the Native Tribes', W. Stanger, the surveyor-general, Lieutenant C. J. Gibb, an engineer officer, and two American missionaries—Newton Adams and Daniel Lindley (who returned to missionary work from his Voortrekker congregation at this time). They were to make recommendations for the reservation of land for Africans in the spirit of Stanley's dispatch of December 1842, bearing in mind that 'the public faith' had been pledged to the Africans as well as to the white claimants to land, and they were to take 'especial

---

[1] Bird, ii. 449 ff.; du Plessis, pp. 203–7; Walker, *Great Trek*, pp. 314–43.
[2] For documents on the British Colony of Natal see *SAAR, Natal*, ii–iv, *Records of the Natal Executive Council, 1845–1848, 1849–1852*, and *1853–1856*; ii and iii transcribed and edited by B. A. le Cordeur, iv transcribed by B. A. le Cordeur and edited by V. R. Fourie. The major historian of colonial Natal is Alan F. Hattersley, author of *More Annals of Natal: With Historical Introduction and Notes*; *Portrait*; and *The British Settlement of Natal: A Study in Imperial Migration*.

care that these tracts [of land] are suitable to their wants, and as far as possible to their wishes'.[1]

The Commission defined the sites of four or five 'locations' (i.e. areas to be reserved for Africans) and several 'mission reserves', and it would apparently have defined as many more, with a total area of rather more than two of the twelve-and-a-half million acres of land in Natal, if it had been able to complete its work. In fact, however, it was disbanded in February 1848, before it had dealt with the area south of the Mkomasi river. Nevertheless, it laid the foundations of the land system that has endured in Natal. In 1852 the surveyor-general reported that about a million and a quarter acres had been allotted to Africans;[2] and additions in the 1860s brought the acreage up to about two millions. Most of the locations (as they continued to be called) were immediately south of the Tukela river, but there were also locations south of Durban, west of Pietermaritzburg, and beneath the Drakensberg. The land varied in quality and included a great deal that was rocky and unsuited to cultivation. The best land had already been pre-empted by the Boers.[3]

The Commission also recommended that each of the locations should be supervised by a Resident Agent with assistants, and a police force with white officers and African other ranks. At first African customs should be tolerated, but the people should gradually be brought under the Roman-Dutch law of the colony. There should be schools, including a 'model mechanical school', in each location; and the people should be encouraged to produce goods such as cotton for export.[4]

The recommendations which involved expenditure were never effectively applied, because no one was willing to pay for them, even though the Commission estimated that the recurrent cost of the services would be only about £5,500 a year and that a direct tax on Africans would yield about £10,500 a year. The local government was not willing to appropriate the required sum from its revenue for African development, and the British Government declined to assist. The result was that African education was left to missionaries, whose recources were limited, and African administration was left to the officials on the spot, or rather, to the Official on the spot—Theophilus Shepstone, who was Diplomatic Agent in Natal from 1845 to 1853 and Secretary for Native Affairs from 1853 to 1875.[5]

[1] P.R.O., C.O. 179/1. [2] Smith, p. 266.
[3] Union of South Africa, *The Native Reserves and their Place in the Economy of the Union of South Africa*, U.G. 32/1946, pp. 4–5 and Map at end.
[4] Smith, pp. 254–7.
[5] On Theophilus Shepstone as an African administrator see Edgar H. Brookes, *The History of Native Policy in South Africa from 1830 to the Present Day*, pp. 41–86; Hattersley, *More Annals*, pp. 234–52, *Portrait*, pp. 203–25; J. R. Sullivan, *The Native Policy of Sir Theophilus Shepstone*. There is new material in R. E. Gordon, 'The Shepstone Family in South Africa',

Shepstone's father was an 1820 settler who had become a Wesleyan missionary. Born in Bristol, England, in 1817 and reared on mission stations among the southern Nguni, Shepstone was still a boy when he entered the Cape Colonial Service. He accompanied Sir Benjamin D'Urban as an interpreter in the frontier war of 1835 and Major Charters in the first British occupation of Port Natal in 1838. He then became Resident Agent at Fort Peddie, where he was responsible for keeping the peace between the Xhosa and the Mfengu whom D'Urban had taken under British protection.

A good linguist, Shepstone acquired a reputation for understanding Nguni society and being able to handle Nguni chiefs. In fact, his capacity to perceive the truth about Nguni society was limited by an extremely paternalistic attitude, an unquestioning belief in the superiority of the norms of nineteenth-century Western society, and an ambition which bordered on arrogance. Nevertheless, his energy and self-assurance gained him the confidence of his superiors and for a time he did become a sort of father-figure to many of the African inhabitants of Natal, whose world had disintegrated under the successive blows of the Shakan revolution and the white intrusion.

Shepstone was the driving force in the Locations Commission; and during his first four years in Natal he persuaded most of the African inhabitants, including the latest refugees from Mpande and Faku, to move into the locations. He had to resort to force in only a few cases, and then he avoided bloodshed—as in 1847, when he used white troops and African allies to discipline Fodo, Chief of the Dumesa in southern Natal, who had attacked and plundered Bhaca refugees as they arrived from Faku's country; and in 1849, when he used an African force to move Langalibalele and his Hlubi, refugees from Mpande, from the Klip river area adjoining the Zulu kingdom to the headwaters of the Blaauwkrantz river on the slopes of the Drakensberg.[1]

Shepstone improvised an administrative hierarchy based on the chieftainship. He recognized traditional chiefs and headmen where discernible and created new chiefs and headmen where necessary; he attached every location African to a chief; and he made the chiefs and headmen responsible for law and order, in theory under the Governor, who was proclaimed supreme chief, in practice under himself as a sort of principal *induna*. He sanctioned most elements of traditional Nguni law, including the law of marriage; but he did not codify traditional law, so that there was scope for adapting it to changing conditions. As a start, he made murder a capital offence, and he did not tolerate

unpublished dissertation, University of Natal, 1965. All these accounts are comparatively favourable.

[1] *SAAR, Natal*, ii. 110–20, iii. 98–102, 122–3, 197–202.

accusations of witchcraft. From 1849 onwards he imposed a direct tax of 7s. per hut per annum, payable in cash or in cattle (which he sold to white farmers), and this was soon yielding a revenue of more than £10,000. These improvisations contained many of the ingredients of the policy of indirect rule which Frederick (Lord) Lugard was to apply in northern Nigeria in the first decade of the twentieth century, and which was to become the normal basis of British administration throughout tropical Africa in the second and third decades. In the middle of the nineteenth century such a policy was a new departure in a British colony in Africa. In the short run it was strikingly successful in Natal. Africans seem to have accepted it because, after their experiences in the previous generation, they yearned for security in the land of their fathers. Secretaries of State accepted it because it provided peace in an exposed frontier area at minimal cost.

The Afrikaners were bitterly disappointed. Though West tried to conciliate them, they considered that the government was still slow and niggardly in dealing with their own claims to land and that it was being far too generous to Africans. They also found that the government was not making its presence felt in the only way they wanted—by protecting their farms and their cattle from San and African raiders. Consequently, by the end of 1847 nearly all the Afrikaners had evacuated Natal, except for Andries Pretorius and his followers, and a group under Andries Spies who occupied the Klip river area—a triangle of land between the upper Tukela and the Buffalo. Mpande had already agreed with Cloete that this area should be part of Natal; but in 1847 he ceded it to Spies, who set up a sort of republic. West tried to assert control, but Spies's people baulked at his demand that they should take an oath of allegiance.[1]

When Natal was annexed Andries Pretorius had hoped that his people would be able to retain the substance of power in their own hands, and he had welcomed West with effusive hospitality. By 1847 he was disillusioned. In a final effort to bring his grievances before the British authorities he rode to Grahamstown, where Governor Sir Henry Pottinger, harrassed by the problems of the Frontier War, brusquely refused to see him. Convinced that the British professions of goodwill had been of no avail, Pretorius then returned to Natal and prepared to lead nearly all the remaining Afrikaners to the high veld.[2] In February 1848 they were met by Sir Harry Smith.

A brave soldier, Smith was sadly lacking in judgement and patience. After reaching Cape Town as Governor and High Commissioner on

---
[1] On the Klip River Rebellion see ibid., ii, and Walker, *Great Trek*, pp. 361-3.
[2] Preller, *Pretorius*, pp. 319 ff.

1 December 1847, he wound up the War of the Axe by annexing British Kaffraria, hastened to the high veld to talk with Afrikaner, Griqua, and African leaders, and then made a flying visit to Natal. He met Pretorius and his people at the foot of the Drakensberg and was moved by their plight and their grievances. Scarcely waiting to hear the local officials' side of the story, he issued a proclamation exempting the Afrikaners from the oath of allegiance and he appointed a Land Commission, with instructions to see that every Voortrekker was given a large farm and that 'a distinct line' should be drawn between white and black landholdings.[1] Smith's Commission, which included two Afrikaners but omitted Shepstone and the missionaries, reported that the majority of the Africans in Natal were foreigners with no rights to land, and that the most they should be allowed was a quarter of a million acres, so that nearly all the country would be available for white settlement.[2] In spite of this, the Afrikaner withdrawal from Natal was not arrested.

The Great Emigration from the British Isles took place between 1847 and 1851, as a result of crop failures, the collapse of the railway boom, and commercial distress.[3] An average of over a quarter of a million people left Britain in each of those years. The main flood went to North America and scarcely any would have gone to the distant British colonies in the southern hemisphere without some form of assistance. However, by that time the British Government, influenced by the ideas of Edward Gibbon Wakefield, was accustomed to assisting people to emigrate to the colonies in Australia and New Zealand, financing them with part of the money received from the sale of Crown land in those colonies. The scheme was supervised by a government board—the Colonial Land and Emigration Commissioners. In 1847 the government agreed that purchasers of Crown land could nominate emigrants for free passages. This precedent opened the way to ingenious speculators. One of these was Joseph Byrne, an adventurer who had travelled in Australia and the Cape Colony and claimed to have visited Natal. He set up a 'Natal Emigration and Colonisation Office' in London and approached the government. The government agreed that if he made deposits with the Commissioners at the rate of £10 per emigrant, Byrne would receive the same amount of credit in Crown lands in Natal, where the upset price was fixed at 4s. an acre; he would then be able to select emigrants (subject to the board's approval) and make his own arrangements for their transport to Natal; and he would become entitled to a refund of the £10 deposit when the Natal Government certified that the emigrant had been placed on land in Natal. Byrne then made

[1] *SAAR, Natal,* ii. 362–3. [2] Smith, pp. 261–3.
[3] Hattersley, in the works cited on p. 374 above, deals extensively with British immigration to Natal.

arrangements with shipping companies and advertised for emigrants, offering adults transport and twenty acres of land in Natal at a cost of £10 for a steerage passage (and more for better accommodation). What this amounted to was that for every emigrant taken to Natal the British Government paid nothing, but alienated fifty acres of undeveloped Crown land; for £10 the emigrant was taken to Natal and given twenty acres; and for each refundable deposit of £10 Byrne stood to gain possession of thirty acres of land in Natal—and he would also make an additional gain if the passage money charged by the shipping company, plus his incidental expenses, amounted to less than £10.

Following Byrne's agreement with the government, other promoters made similar agreements, and some people joined the migration at their own expense. The result was that between 1849 and 1851 about 5,000 men, women, and children entered Natal from England and Scotland—two-thirds of them under Byrne's auspices.

The conditions appealed to people who wished to leave Britain but possessed a little capital and had no desire to become part of the distressed flood to North America; especially to those who preferred a British colony to a foreign country for sentimental or cultural reasons, or who were lured by the prospects of a warm temperate climate and cheap African labour. Those who responded came from all parts of England, and some areas of Scotland, both rural and urban. Almost every occupation was represented. There were barristers, blacksmiths, carpenters, doctors, drapers, engineers, merchants, millers, military and naval officers, ostlers, schoolmasters, smallholders, surveyors, solicitors, stage-coach drivers, tenant farmers, tradesmen, and wheelwrights. There were a few agricultural labourers and handloom weavers. There were even an artist, a butler, and a sexton—and a conchologist.[1] Unlike the Irish who flocked to North America at the same time, they carried no deep grievances against the British Government, no sense of alienation from British society; but Alan Hattersley probably goes too far when he says that 'Almost all hoped to stamp the pattern of Victorian respectability on the new land'.[2]

Unforeseen by the emigrants and by Byrne himself, there were many snags in his scheme. Two million acres of the best land in Natal had already been alienated to Afrikaners, under Cloete's arrangements as modified by West and by Smith. Nearly all of them were undeveloped and unoccupied, and many had been bought up by Cape merchants and other speculators, who held them in the hope of a rise in value. Another million and more were being held for Africans. This meant that most of the Crown lands which Byrne's agents were able to acquire had poor soil or inadequate water, and were located at great distances

[1] Hattersley, *Settlement*, Chs. 5–7.   [2] Ibid., p. 120.

from the existing villages and lines of communication. Although twenty acres a head sounded attractive to people accustomed to the productivity of land in nineteenth-century England and Scotland, the productivity of the average Byrne allotment was far below the settlers' expectations. Moreover Byrne was short of capital, and his calculations had hinged on the assumption that he would get quick returns in the form of official rebates and by selling at a good price the lands he acquired from the Crown. Both these assumptions were wildly false. Many settlers did not occupy their allotments; and there was a glut of land on the market as a result of the departure of the Voortrekkers. Consequently Byrne was soon in difficulties and he went bankrupt in 1850; and even though Governor Pine tried to ease things for the settlers by adding twenty-five acres to every twenty-acre allotment, they had hard times before they were firmly established in their new country. Some left Natal as soon as they arrived: one unfortunate family had one look at Natal, re-embarked on the ship that had brought them, and lost their lives when it foundered on its way back to England. Others abandoned farming to settle in Pietermaritzburg or Durban; and those who stayed on the land had years of anxious struggle before they made good—usually after buying up additional land from other settlers, from Byrne's estate, and from other speculators.

After 1851 the British Government stopped further speculative immigration to Natal and the Natal Government was able to help only a few people to migrate from Britain. Consequently the white population increased slowly—to about 8,000 in 1858 and 18,000 in 1870. Only in the extreme north did the few remaining Afrikaners outnumber the British. Elsewhere the settlers of 1849–51 formed a nucleus which absorbed later immigrants. With their British origins and sentiments, they distinguished Natal from all the other territories in South Africa, except the south-eastern part of the Cape Colony.

The development of a modern sector in the Natal economy was a very slow process.[1] Durban remained the only port, and all but the smallest ships had to use the ocean anchorage, which was dangerous with onshore winds, because the sand-bar at the entrance to the harbour was not cleared until the end of the century. Most of the roads were mere wagon tracks; some of the rivers were unfordable in flood; and even the road between Durban and Pietermaritzburg was not much better, though horse-drawn omnibuses made the journey in the 1860s. The only railway in Natal before the 1870s was a short line from Durban Point to Durban Town, opened in 1860. Postal services were provided by African runners.

Farming enterprises were impeded not only by the lack of efficient

[1] Hattersley, *Settlement*, Chs. 9–10.

communications, but also by the settlers' initial ignorance of the potential of the soil and climate, and by diseases of crops and stock. In the subtropical coastal region settlers experimented hopefully with arrowroot, coffee, cotton, indigo, and tobacco, before they identified sugar as the best commercial crop. With the help of a few immigrants who had experience of sugar production in the West Indies and Mauritius, a sugar industry was established with cane from Mauritius and milling machinery from England. By 1870 Natal was producing about 10,000 tons of sugar a year, and there was a tendency for individual holdings to become amalgamated into large estates, owned and operated by companies. In the uplands grassveld region settlers tried their hands with wheat, maize, and potatoes, and with cattle, pigs, and sheep. Gradually wool became the main commercial product in the interior, but it was a long time before disease was eradicated and Natal wool reached the English market in reasonably good and consistent condition.

Over half the white population lived in Pietermaritzburg and Durban, most of them as artisans and small shopkeepers. In Pietermaritzburg, which was far the larger town, a Victorian social tone was set by the officers of the garrison and the senior civil servants. The quarrels which were often associated with isolated colonial communities were intensified in Natal by a remarkable religious controversy.

In 1853 John William Colenso became the first Anglican Bishop of Natal. At the same time Robert Gray, already Bishop of Capetown, was designated under Letters Patent as Metropolitan Archbishop of South Africa. Gray was a staunch High Churchman and so was James Green, Dean of Pietermaritzburg; whereas Colenso, a Fellow of St. John's College, Cambridge, and author of a standard textbook of mathematics, was a Low Churchman with a searching, scientific mind. Soon after he reached Natal, Colenso translated the New Testament and parts of the Old into Zulu, and produced a Zulu dictionary. This work led him far beyond the bounds of contemporary Anglican orthodoxy. As early as 1858 Dean Green was accusing him of heresy. In 1862 Colenso published in England the first of seven volumes on the Pentateuch, which marked an important stage in the growth of Biblical criticism within the Anglican communion. Archbishop Gray convened an ecclesiastical court which tried Colenso *in absentia*, found him guilty of heresy, and sentenced him to deprivation (1863). Colenso appealed to the Judicial Committee of the Privy Council, which upheld his appeal on the grounds that the Letters Patent issued to Gray in 1853 were invalid and Gray had no jurisdiction over Colenso (1864). The legal, theological, and scientific issues in this controversy were understood by few people in Natal; but the local situation was spectacular, with Dean and Bishop competing for physical possession of the cathedral in

Pietermaritzburg; and it became still worse in 1869 when Gray installed William Macrorie as a rival 'Bishop of Maritzburg'.[1]

Among the British settlers were some with a flair for political journalism and it was very largely under their stimulus that an agitation developed for popular participation in the government of Natal. Under the arrangements of 1845 Natal had been a detached District of the Cape Colony, with a Lieutenant-Governor and a small Executive Council of senior officials. In 1847 legislative powers were vested in a Legislative Council, also an official body. Seven years later Pietermaritzburg and Durban became boroughs, with elected municipal councils. In 1856 a Royal Charter made Natal a separate Colony with a representative form of government. The Legislative Council was enlarged to include, besides four officials, twelve members elected by the Colonists who possessed a property qualification; but the Executive Council continued to be responsible to London, the Governor (or Lieutenant-Governor) could withhold his assent to any Bill passed by the Legislative Council or reserve it for Her Majesty's pleasure, and there was a reserved Civil List, with which the Legislative Council could not tamper, covering the salaries of six senior officials and an annual sum of £5,000 set aside for 'Native purposes'. The Governor of the Cape Colony, in his capacity as High Commissioner for South Africa, remained responsible for dealings with independent territories in South Africa. This Charter remained unchanged until 1870.[2]

As in every British colony where a majority of the members of the legislature were responsible to a local electorate and the executive remained responsible to the British government, there was continual constitutional controversy in Natal. Disputes arose on many subjects, above all on 'native policy'. Time after time the legislature tried to gain control over the sum which the Charter reserved for 'Native purposes'. The British government refused to yield, primarily for financial and secondarily for humanitarian reasons, for the franchise was a monopoly of the white colonists, who were protected by a British force paid for by the British taxpayer.[3] As Lord Kimberley, Secretary of State for the Colonies, declared in 1870, '. . . So long as Her Majesty's troops remain in the colony . . ., the Home Government must retain its control over the taxation and. government of the natives . . .; and experience shows that this cannot be done without retaining an effectual control over all policy, whether European or native.'[4]

[1] The Colenso controversy is ably reviewed in Morris, op. cit., pp. 177-82. See also P. Hinchliff, *John William Colenso*.
[2] The Charter of Natal is set out in *SAAR*, *Natal*, iv. 306-16, and much of it in Eybers, pp. 188-97. The background is discussed by Hattersley in *Portrait*, Ch. 4, and *Settlement*, Ch. 11.
[3] For Natal politics under the Charter see the passages in Hattersley's works cited above.
[4] Sec. of State Kimberley to Lieut.-Gov. Keate, 16 March 1870, G. H. 29, Natal Archives.

This controversy generated a great deal of venom. Like other white settler communities in colonies with numerous native inhabitants (such as the 1820 Settlers in the Cape Colony and the later British settlers in Rhodesia and Kenya), many of the Natal settlers very quickly acquired a racialistic attitude to the Colonial situation. The bars to empathy were enormous, for the settlers were ignorant of the history, the language, the social institutions, and the moral norms of the Africans around them; and yet they immediately took Africans into their service, only to become disappointed with their performances as labourers. In the first few years the dominant impressions many settlers had of Africans were a consciousness of their difference, a fear of their numbers, and a disappointment at their instrumental deficiencies. In some cases, too, racialist attitudes were promoted by contacts with Afrikaners, whose own racialism was already deeply engrained.[1]

West's successor, Lieutenant-Governor Benjamin Pine, was himself sympathetic to the settlers' point of view, and in 1852 he appointed a large Commission, consisting of an approximately equal number of Afrikaners and British immigrants, and a few officials, to make recommendations on 'native policy'. The Report of this Commission, dated 1854, was signed by Afrikaners and British immigrants only—not by the officials—and it crystallized the Colonists' views in diametric opposition to the policy which was actually being applied by Shepstone.[2]

The report contained three basic propositions. The first was a stereotype of the African:[3]

When not effectually restrained and directed by the strong arm of power, the true and universal character of the Kafirs, as framed by their education, habits, and associations, is at once superstitious and warlike. Their estimate of the value of human life is very low; plunder and bloodshed are engagements with which their circumstances have rendered them familiar since their childhood; they are crafty and cunning; at once indolent and excitable; averse to labour; but bloodthirsty and cruel when their passions are inflamed. They pretend to no individual opinion of their own, but show the most

---

[1] There is a vast literature on the racial attitudes of white settlers in colonial situations; see especially O. Mannoni, *Prospero and Caliban: The Psychology of Colonization*. But there are no substantial studies of the history of race attitudes among white South Africans, except I. D. MacCrone, *Race Attitudes in South Africa: Historical, Experimental and Psychological Studies*, the historical section of which deals exclusively with the growth of Afrikaner attitudes before 1806.

[2] C.O. 879/1, PRO. The members of the Commission were: John Bird (Acting Surveyor General), Theophilus Shepstone (Diplomatic Agent), and the following Afrikaners and British settlers—J. N. Boshof, R. R. Ryley, Dr. Addison, P. A. R. Otto, Dr. Boast, Henry Milner, Jos. Henderson, G. C. Cato, Frederick Scheepers, S. Maritz, Captain Struben, Theunis Nel, Carl Landman, Evert Potgieter, Ed. Morewood, Dirk Uys, Abram Spies, Caspar Labuscagne, Walter Macfarlane, John Moreland, and Charles Barter. Edmund Tatham was secretary and Henry Francis Fynn was interpreter to the Commission.

[3] Ibid., p. 26.

servile compliance to the rule of a despotic chief, when it is characterized by vigour and efficiency.

Cupidity is another strongly developed feature in the Kafir character; their general habits, like those of other savages, are debased and sensual to the last degree; possessing but a confused, indistinct idea of a future state, and of the existence of a Supreme Being, they cherish a belief in the most degrading system of witchcraft.

The Kafirs recognize no moral delinquency in deceit or falsehood, but are remarkable for a disregard of truthfulness and gratitude.

The second proposition was that the vast majority of the Africans in Natal were 'foreigners',[1] who had no right to occupy land. 'They have been accustomed to settle on unoccupied land when moving from one country to another, and believe they are entitled to dwell there as a matter of course.'[2] The third proposition was that, since 'Natal is a white settlement', the prohibition of racial discrimination in the annexation proclamation had become 'utterly inapplicable'.[3]

The report painted a rosy picture of race relations in the Voortrekker Republic of Natal, where the 'Kafirs' were 'contented and submissive to the authorities' and 'obedient to their employers', because the members of the *Volksraad* had 'a thorough practical acquaintance ... with the true character and habits of the Kafir'.[3] Things had been getting worse ever since the British annexation. The British authorities had begun to go wrong when they had acted on the advice of a Commission which consisted of officials and foreigners, but no settlers. It was 'a fatal error'[4] to set aside so much land for Kafirs. The 'immense locations' 'dried up the source whence an abundant and continuous supply of Kafir labour for wages might have been procured' and allowed Kafirs 'to follow idle, wandering, and pastoral habits'.[5] There was a sad contrast between the 'suicidal illiberality' which gave only five million acres of land to the white people and the 'reckless extravagance' which gave two million acres to the 'Kafirs'.[6] This extravagance encouraged more refugees to come to Natal from Zululand; and it also created a military danger, for the locations included all the natural strongholds of the country. The government should be firm. It should place the Kafirs in smaller locations, allowing three or four acres of land per person, not twenty as at present; the locations should be separated from each other; and they should come directly under magistrates, who should control the Kafirs, prevent them from combining, and distribute their labour fairly throughout the country.

In spite of the manifest bias—and in many places ludicrous naïvety—of this report, Lieutenant-Governor Pine informed the Secretary of

---

[1] C.O. 879/1, PRO., p. 20.   [2] Ibid., p. 30.   [3] Ibid., p. 15.
[4] Ibid., p. 21.   [5] Ibid., p. 19.   [6] Ibid., p. 18.

State that it was 'one of the most able official documents that has proceeded from this district'.[1] Nevertheless, there was no radical change in policy, even after the introduction of representative government in 1856. The press continually criticized 'the present mischievous Kaffir policy', candidates vied with one another in denouncing it at the polls, and Walter Macfarlane formed a group to oppose it in the Legislative Council;[2] but Shepstone remained in office and, except for a period when he quarrelled with Pine, had the approval and the co-operation of governors as well as secretaries of state.

By 1863 Shepstone was able to report that the Natal Africans had accommodated to the subordination of their headmen, *indunas*, and chiefs to white magistrates and senior officials; and that all criminal cases, and civil cases between Africans and whites, were being tried in the magistrates' courts according to the Roman-Dutch law of the Colony, while Roman-Dutch principles were gradually being introduced in civil cases between Africans. For example, Nguni marriage law was being modified by the introduction of the principle that a widow should be able to marry whom she pleased without the permission of her guardian, and even by making the legality of a marriage, when contested, depend upon a clear declaration of consent by the girl. He also noted a widespread use of imported manufactured consumer goods, with cotton and woollen clothes replacing skin karosses, and beads and other imported trinkets replacing traditional ornaments; and remarked that an 1862 proclamation requiring African men to wear trousers in Durban and Pietermaritzburg was being obeyed. The missions were being given small grants-in-aid from the reserved fund for educational purposes, and some mission-trained Africans had become skilled artisans, living in European-style houses on individual land-holdings they had bought. At that time, Shepstone reported, the African population of Natal had reached 210,000 and the average annual number of immigrants from Zululand was 600. Most of the Africans lived in proclaimed locations; but the demarcation of the locations had not been completed, for the Location Commission had been disbanded in 1848, before it had dealt with the area south of the Mkomasi river, where the African inhabitants were still technically squatters on Crown lands. Elsewhere, too, some Africans were squatters on Crown lands, and others were tenants on farms owned by white people, including absentee landlords who collected rent but made no contribution to the development of the Colony.[3]

---

[1] Ibid., p. 54.
[2] Hattersley, *Portrait*, p. 126.
[3] 'Questions proposed by His Excellency the Lieutenant-Governor and Answers by the Secretary for Native Affairs.—October 16, 1863', C.O. 879/2, pp. 20–25, P.R.O.

In 1864 steps were taken to provide greater security for the African land-holdings. Letters Patent were issued vesting in a 'Natal Native Trust', consisting of the members of the Executive Council, the responsibility for holding the location lands in trust for the African population. In the same year a law was passed making it possible for an African who could give proof of ownership of property and ability to read and write to petition the Governor for exemption from 'Native Law'. The Governor could grant or refuse the petition at his discretion. If approved, the African would then become subject to the Roman-Dutch law of the Colony in all respects. This law gave rise to a further law dealing with political rights. Previously all Africans had been excluded from the franchise on the ground that, lacking titles to land, they did not possess the prescribed economic qualifications. In 1865 the Legislative Council passed a law which expressly denied the franchise to the African masses, but permitted an individual, who had been exempted from African law for seven years and had resided in the Colony for twelve years, to apply for the franchise, provided that he produced a certificate of recommendation signed by three white residents and endorsed by a Justice of the Peace. This application, too, could be refused or granted by the governor at his discretion. Thus it became technically possible for an African to pass from the community which was subject to chiefs, and to a modified version of traditional African civil law, into the community which was subject to white magistrates and to Roman-Dutch civil law. In fact, however, the first application for exemption from 'Native Law' was not received until 1876, and no more than a handful of Africans ever acquired the vote in the Colony of Natal.[1]

These exemption and franchise laws were barren because there was a gradual ossification of Shepstone's policy. On the defensive against persistent criticisms from the white community, he could do no more than maintain what he had already accomplished. He could not carry out his original intention to provide the Africans of Natal with opportunities for training and development, because the legislature was not prepared to vote money for such projects; and he himself gradually lost the will to innovate. Even the total reserved fund of £5,000 a year was not always spent on 'Native purposes',[2] and the missionary societies could only touch the fringe of African society with their own resources and their slender subsidies from that fund.

In fact, in spite of their complaints, the interests of the white inhabitants were well served by the Natal Government. They lived in peace,

---

[1] Brookes, pp. 57–60.
[2] In none of the years 1863–7 was the entire £5,000 spent on 'Native purposes' (Govr. Keate to Sec. of State Buckingham, 9 Dec. 1868, G. H. 205, Natal Archives).

though surrounded by overwhelming numbers of people whom they despised.[1] They paid no direct taxes themselves, while Africans paid a hut tax which yielded far more than £5,000 a year, as well as indirect taxes on blankets and other consumer goods, including the trousers they were required by law to possess. African chiefs and *indunas* administered their people as agents of the Government without pay. And Africans performed the manual work for most of the white people at very low wages—on their farms, in their towns and villages, and in their homes.[2]

These conditions caused a gradual shift of African opinion from relief at the defeat of Dingane to dissatisfaction with the new order. Its first overt manifestation was to occur in the Langalibalele affair of 1873; but it did not become widespread until after the guiding hand of Theophilus Shepstone had been removed (1875), the white community had gained control over the executive branch of government (1893), and population growth had caused a serious land shortage and general poverty, when tensions spilled over into rebellion (1906).[3]

Whether, if he had had a more co-operative legislature, Shepstone would have been more successful in the long run, is an open question. Aiming at reforming African society from the top, through the medium of chiefs whom he transformed from responsible rulers of autonomous communities into the instruments of an alien régime, Shepstone's policy was perhaps doomed to failure. The 'Shepstone System' had the fundamental weaknesses of Indirect Rule, wherever it was applied.[4]

There was one group of white settlers whose labour needs were not adequately provided by Africans. These were the coastal planters. Trying to create sugar and cotton industries, they required in their workers interests and skills which were not present in traditional African society, and which were particularly remote from the experience of African men, who left most of the field work to their women folk. The coastal planters were not able to attract sufficient African labourers and they were dissatisfied with those they did attract. So it was they who spearheaded the agitation for the break-up of the locations; and, as the prospects of a change in official policy faded, it was they who proposed that an alternative supply of labour should be provided. They considered various possibilities, including convict labour from Britain, Africans from Portuguese Mozambique, and Chinese; and they eventually turned to India, because there were men among them who had

---
[1] The attitudes of the white community towards the Natal Africans in the 1860s are illustrated in Alan F. Hattersley (ed.), *John Sheddon Dobie: South African Journal, 1862-6*, VRS, 1945.
[2] Hattersley, *Portrait*, pp. 218-21.
[3] L. M. Thompson, *The Unification of South Africa, 1902-1910*, pp. 42-49.
[4] See, e.g. Lucy Mair, *New Nations*, pp. 100-3.

had experience of sugar planting in Mauritius and the British West Indies, where Indian labourers had remedied the shortage created by the emancipation of the negro slaves in 1834–8. Indians, it was realized, had saved sugar industries elsewhere; they might play a crucial role in creating a sugar industry in Natal.[1]

By the 1850s the emigration of labourers from India to tropical and subtropical British and French colonies was being conducted according to regulations laid down by the Indian Government and supervised by Indian officials. Recruiting took place in India under the direction of Emigration Agents appointed by the colonies and approved and supervised by Indian authorities. Emigration was only allowed from Madras, Bombay, and Calcutta. Indentures were for five years and were signed in the presence of a Protector of Emigrants appointed by the Presidency Government. Standards of accommodation and provisions in ships were laid down. At least twenty-five women had to be dispatched with every hundred men. And colonies more distant than Mauritius had to offer the Indians free return passages to India ten years after their arrival.

Under laws passed by the Natal Legislative Council in 1859 and the Indian Government in 1860 this system was extended to Natal. Colonists who wanted to employ indentured Indians were to apply to the Natal Government, which would arrange and pay for the recruitment, transport, and assignment of the Indians. The employers were to repay these costs in instalments. During his five years' indentured service an Indian was to serve the employer to whom he was assigned by the Natal Government, and the employer was to provide him with stipulated wages, food, and accommodation. After the end of five years in Natal the Indian became free to make a private arrangement with an employer, or to branch out on his own as best he could; and after another five years he became entitled to a free return passage to India—but there was nothing to stop him from staying in Natal if he wished, and the governor could at his discretion offer him a grant of Crown land equivalent to the cost of a return passage.

Reporting to the Secretary of State, Lieutenant-Governor John Scott called the scheme 'an experiment' and said that the scale of Indian immigration to Natal would be small.[2] However, the requirement that women should accompany the men and the fact that Indians could remain in Natal if they wished ensured that, once the scheme was started, a permanent Indian population would become established in Natal. This the governor and his advisers failed to foresee.

Between 1860 and 1866 about 6,000 indentured Indians arrived in

[1] On this first phase of Indian immigration into Natal see L. M. Thompson, 'Indian Immigration into Natal, 1860–1872', in *AYB*, 1952, ii.
[2] Govr. Scott to Sec. of State Lytton, 28 June 1859, G. H. 201, Natal Archives.

Natal from Madras and 300 from Calcutta. Some three-quarters of them were men and one-quarter were women. In terms of caste, language, and religion they were heterogeneous, for while the majority were low-caste Hindus there was a sprinkling of Hindus of higher castes, some twelve per cent. were Muslims, and some five per cent. were Christians.

The majority of these immigrants were assigned to sugar planters for their five years' indentured service, and, in spite of serious initial misunderstandings, due to mutual ignorance and to lack of government supervision, the Indians performed the role for which they had been imported. Their labour was a key factor in the development of the Natal sugar industry. Indeed, the white planters soon came to regard Indian labour as indispensable and, with the support of other coastal interests and the co-operation of the executive government, they were able to obtain for Indian immigration financial aid which had not been foreseen in 1859. The government paid more than a third of the total cost of Indian immigration between 1860 and 1870.

As the Indians completed their five years' indentured service, some remained on the coastal sugar estates as labourers; others became semi-skilled workers in a wide range of occupations—especially artisans, cooks, house-servants, tailors, and washermen; others rented or bought land and grew fruit and vegetables for sale in Durban or Pietermaritzburg; others became shopkeepers, catering for Africans or white Colonists; and a few moved to other parts of South Africa.

In 1870 the first Indians who had arrived in Natal became entitled to a free return passage to India. Most of them elected to stay in Natal, but those who did return complained to the Indian authorities that they had been badly treated. By that time Natal planters were wanting to import more Indians, having been unable to do so since 1866 because of economic depression; but the Indian Government prohibited further recruitment for Natal until the complaints had been investigated. A Commission found that there were grounds for some of the complaints: several employers had made arbitrary and excessive deductions from wages and there had been a few cases of brutality.[1] After the Natal Government had undertaken to supervise the treatment of Indians more effectively in the future, the immigration was resumed, with financial aid from the Government, in 1874. As a result of 'an experiment' launched in 1860, a third major community had been established in Natal by 1870; and as a result of the decision to resume Indian immigration, Indians would eventually outnumber the whites in Natal.

In 1870 there were three communities in Natal, distinguished by their history, their social structure, their language, and their knowledge—

[1] Natal Sessional Papers, i, Natal, Archives.

and by their wealth and power in the Colonial situation. The Africans, numbering about a quarter of a million, had experienced two revolutions in the previous fifty years: the Shakan revolution which had temporarily removed them from Natal, and the white revolution which had given them some security on a limited amount of land. The whites, numbering about 18,000, owned most of the land, controlled the legislative branch of government, exerted great influence over the executive branch, and were the only employers of labour. All the whites were comparative newcomers to Natal. The Afrikaner minority had only been there for a generation and the British majority for twenty years. The 6,000 Asians, more recent arrivals still, were beginning to exploit opportunities which, though limited, were greater than those that had been available to them in over-populated India.

Whereas the white and Asian communities were closely interlocked in a white-master Asian-servant relationship, the Africans were not yet, as a community, interlocked with the others, though there was a trend in that direction. Most Africans still had a partial autonomy in the locations; but some were labour tenants or rent payers on white property, others were occasional wage labourers, and all were experiencing the effects of white power and influence, which limited the authority of chiefs, imposed taxes, created new material needs, eroded traditional values, and insinuated new ones.

Natal was still rather sparsely populated and there was elbow-room for all. But the modern sector of the economy was growing very slowly. It lacked a dynamic impulse. The surplus production of the white farmers and their African and Asian workers was meagre; and as peasants in the locations the Africans produced very little for sale to white people or for export.

Britain was doing virtually nothing to promote economic development in the locations, or even in the white areas; nor was she sustaining the non-racial principles set out in the annexation Proclamation. But by keeping ultimate control over the executive government she was still sheltering the African and Asian communities from complete domination by the white community.

IX

CO-OPERATION AND CONFLICT: THE HIGH VELD[1]

1. *The* Difaqane *and its Aftermath, 1822–1836*

DURING the 1820s catastrophe struck many of the inhabitants of the high veld area between the Drakensberg mountains, the Kalahari desert, and the Limpopo river. These disturbances were a result of the rise of the Zulu kingdom, for the primary agents of destruction on the high veld were three bands of refugees from Shaka: Hlubi led by Mpangazita and Ngwane led by Matiwane, who operated in the southern sector between the Vaal river and the Maluti mountains; and Ndebele under Mzilikazi, most of whose operations were to the north of the Vaal river.[2] Several of the Sotho communities who were displaced by the Nguni invaders became secondary agents of destruction—such as Tlokwa in the southern sector and Phuthing, Hlakwana, Fokeng, and Taung in the northern sector.

For several years there was widespread chaos as Sotho peoples competed with Nguni invaders and with one another for diminishing supplies of grain and cattle. Old settlements were abandoned, ancient chiefdoms disappeared; new groups came into being and in turn dissolved; and, as food became scarce, demoralization set in and there was widespread cannibalism. This time of troubles on the high veld is known as the *Difaqane*, a word meaning 'forced migration'.[3]

The impact of the *Difaqane* was uneven. Some communities contrived to preserve a corporate existence: notably the Pedi (p. 134) and Venda (pp. 167–9) chiefdoms in the mountains of the eastern Transvaal, the westernmost Tswana chiefdoms along the fringes of the Kalahari desert, and the Griqua (pp. 68 ff.) on either side of the confluence of the Vaal and the Orange rivers. Moreover, even in the most disturbed areas the process of destruction was followed by a process of regeneration, with the consolidation of the Ndebele kingdom in the central Transvaal and the

---

[1] I am grateful to Professor Monica Wilson and Mr. Martin Legassick who made cogent comments on the draft of this chapter.

[2] The reader is reminded that Nguni spellings are used for Nguni names and Sotho spellings for Sotho names. The Sotho version of Ndebele is Matabele; of Mpangazita, Pakalita; of Mzilikazi, Moselekatse.

[3] I am grateful to Dr. D. P. Kunene for clarifying the meaning of the word *Difaqane*.

rise of the southern Sotho kingdom under Moshweshwe in the Caledon valley.

Our knowledge of these events comes from three types of sources. There are, firstly, the contemporary writings of eyewitnesses. Missionaries founded stations among the Griqua in 1802, the Tlhaping in 1816, the Seleka-Rolong in 1823, the Hurutshe in 1832, the southern Sotho in 1833, the Tlokwa in 1834, and the Ndebele in 1835; and many of their reports and letters have been published.[1] Some of the hunters and traders who travelled in the high veld left accounts of their experiences; and Dr. Andrew Smith, who led a large official expedition from the Cape Colony to the high veld in 1834–6, wrote copious notes.[2] Secondly, some of the African participants subsequently dictated their recollections of the *Difaqane*.[3] Thirdly, the oral traditions of many of the peoples involved in the *Difaqane* were later compiled by white authors, notably D. F. Ellenberger and J. C. Macgregor, who compiled the traditions of the southern Sotho; while a Rolong author, S. M. Molema, included some Sotho traditions in his *The Bantu Past and Present*.[4]

These sources present many difficulties. The contemporary eyewitness accounts have the deficiencies which are to be expected in works by people who were alien to the societies they were describing; and there is

[1] London Missionary Society, *Annual Reports, Quarterly Chronicle of Transactions*; Moffat, *Missionary Labours, Matabele Journals, Apprenticeship*.

Wesleyan Methodist Missionary Society, *Missionary Notices*; Samuel Broadbent, *A Narrative of the First Introduction of Christianity amongst the Barolong Tribes of the Bechuanas, South Africa*. *The Memoirs of the Rev. Thomas Laidman Hodgson: Wesleyan Missionary in South Africa*, ed. Thornley Smith; John Edwards, *Reminiscences of the Early Life and Missionary Labours of the Rev. John Edwards*; G. G. Findlay and W. W. Holdsworth, *The History of the Wesleyan Methodist Missionary Society*, ii.

Société des Missions Évangéliques de Paris, *Journal des Missions Évangéliques*; Thomas Arbousset, *Narrative of an Exploratory Tour to the North-East of the Colony of the Cape of Good Hope*; Casalis, *Basutos*, and *My Life in Basutoland: A Story of Missionary Enterprise in South Africa*.

American Board of Commissioners for Foreign Missions, *The Missionary Herald*; D. J. Kotzé (ed.), *Letters of the American Missionaries, 1835–1838*, VRS, 1950.

[2] *Journals of Andrew Geddes Bain: Trader, Explorer, Soldier, Road Engineer and Geologist*, VRS, 1949; Harris, *The Wild Sports of Southern Africa*; *The Diary of Dr. Andrew Smith, Director of the 'Expedition for Exploring Central Africa', 1834–1836*, VRS, 1939–40. Smith also kept a 'Journal' of the expedition, which is longer and more informative than the *Diary*. The Journal, unpublished, is in the library of the South African Museum, Cape Town (Smith Papers, vols. x and xi).

[3] An Aged Fingo, 'A Story of Native Wars', *CMM*, 2nd Ser. xiv (Jan.–June 1877), 248–52; Moloja, 'The Story of the "Fetcani Horde" by one of themselves', *Cape Quarterly Review*, i. 1882, 267–75; Moshweshwe and Moletsane, in *Basutoland Records*, i. 82–84, 517–18; 'Mziki (A. A. Campbell), *'Mlimo: The Rise and Fall of the Matabele*; N. J. van Warmelo, *History of Matiwane and the Amangwane Tribe as told by Msebenzi to his kinsman Albert Hlongwane*; J. A. Winter, 'The Tradition of Ra'lolo', *Report of the South African Association for the Advancement of Science*, 1912, pp. 87–100.

[4] Ellenberger, *History of the Basuto*; D. R. Hunt, 'An Account of the Bapedi', *BS*, v, 1931, 275–326; Macgregor, *Basuto Traditions*; Molema, *Bantu Past and Present*; Schapera, *Ethnic Composition of Tswana Tribes*; *Praise Poems of Tswana Chiefs*. Bryant, *Olden Times*, contains chapters on the Nguni invaders of the high veld.

the further drawback that before 1833 all these observers lived on or near the extreme western fringe of the high veld area. Moreover, most of the compilations of oral tradition have the defects which have been previously noted in the work of A. T. Bryant (p. 337).[1] For these and other reasons the reconstructions in the established historical works are far from satisfactory.[2] Most of them say far less about the *Difaqane* than is warranted; and virtually all of them have been derived from Theal's versions, which are unreliable and biased.[3]

The origins of the disturbances in the area south of the Vaal river go back to the time of Dingiswayo (p. 341). Matiwane, the Chief of the Ngwane who lived around the sources of the Black Mfolozi, was successively attacked by Dingiswayo and by Zwide. After the second attack Matiwane and his people fled westwards and fell upon the Hlubi— a *tekela*-speaking (p. 76) Nguni people who occupied the country below the highest part of the Drakensberg escarpment. The Ngwane defeated the Hlubi and killed their Chief. The Hlubi then split, some fleeing southwards, others, under Mpangazita, crossing the Drakensberg to the south-eastern high veld. For a while the Ngwane occupied the territory vacated by the Hlubi; but in 1822 they too were displaced, when Shaka invaded upper Natal and drove them across the mountains in the wake of the Hlubi.[4]

The Sotho community which bore the first impact of these invasions was the comparatively large Tlokwa chiefdom which was ruled by MaNthatisi, the widow of the deceased Chief, pending the accession of her young son, Sekonyela.[5] Mpangazita had no compunction in driving the Tlokwa away from their homes and seizing their grain and cattle, because Sekonyela and his circumcision mates had recently murdered Mpangazita's brother-in-law; and when Matiwane appeared in the area he fell with zest upon his old enemy, Mpangazita.[6]

[1] However, Schapera's writings on the Tswana are the work of an expert.

[2] e.g. A. J. H. van der Walt *et al.* (eds.), *Geskiedenis van Suid-Afrika*, i. 281-3; Walker, *History*, pp. 175-6.

[3] Theal, *History of South Africa from 1795 to 1872*, i. Chs. 19-20. William F. Lye, 'Identifying the Mantatee Hordes' (unpublished seminar paper, 1964, to be published in *JAH*), subjects Theal's several accounts, of which the version cited above is the principal, to critical scrutiny. See also J. D. Omer-Cooper, *Zulu Aftermath: A Nineteenth-Century Revolution in Bantu Africa*, which was published after this chapter was written.

[4] The Nguni and Sotho traditions of these events differ. Bryant (p. 139) places a four-year interval between the emigrations of the Hlubi and the Ngwane from Natal, but does not satisfactorily account for the activities of the Hlubi during that period. Moloja (p. 268) says there was a clear interval between the Hlubi and the Ngwane migrations, without setting a time to it. Macgregor (p. 17) says that the Hlubi first attacked the Tlokwa in 1822, and Ellenberger (p. 119) says that both the Hlubi and the Ngwane invaded the high veld in 1822, the latter chasing the former.

[5] On the Tlokwa see Macgregor, pp. 27-35, and Ellenberger, pp. 39-51 and 117 ff., with Genealogy on pp. 352-4.

[6] There are different versions of the death of Mpangazita's brother-in-law, Motshodi, and

This was the beginning of the *Difaqane*. For the next two years three hordes of men, women, and children, led by MaNthatisi, Mpangazita, and Matiwane, devastated the southern high veld, dispersing the inhabitants, colliding with one another, and losing and gaining adherents. MaNthatisi's horde attacked communities as far apart as Butha-Buthe, Kurutlele (near modern Senekal), and the triangle between the Orange and the Caledon; and then returned towards their starting-point. The hordes of Mpangazita and Matiwane did much the same, sweeping westwards towards the Orange-Caledon confluence and doubling back eastwards again.[1]

During 1824 each of the hordes settled on and around a mountain near the Caledon river, selected for defence: MaNthatisi at Kooaneng (near modern Ficksburg); Mpangazita at Mabolela (between Ladybrand and Ficksburg); and Matiwane at Senyotong (near Teyateyaneng). But there was no peace between them. In about March 1825 the struggle between Matiwane and Mpangazita reached finality in a five days' battle on the west bank of the Caledon. Mpangazita was killed and his followers fled or became servants of the Ngwane.[2] However, Matiwane's triumph was short-lived. In 1827 he was attacked successively by a Zulu impi and an Ndebele impi. Matiwane then retreated southwards across the mountains and began to prey upon the southern Nguni, causing Xhosa and Thembu refugees to flee to the Cape Colony. This alarmed the Colonial authorities, who made military probes across the frontier; and in August 1828 Colonel Henry Somerset, with a mixed force of white soldiers and farmers, and Xhosa and Thembu, defeated Matiwane at Mbholompo on the Mthatha River (p. 350). The southern Nguni chiefdoms absorbed the Ngwane survivors—except for Matiwane himself and a few of his loyal retainers, who returned via the Caledon valley to the Zulu kingdom, where Dingane put them to death.[3]

By that time nearly every Sotho community between the Vaal and the Orange rivers had been utterly disrupted. Thousands of the inhabitants had fled—some to the north, where they caused destruction beyond the Vaal (pp. 395 ff.); others to the south-west, where they obtained a footing among the Griqua, or took service with white farmers in the Cape Colony, or joined southern Nguni chiefdoms. In most of the Vaal-Orange area itself the old settlements were abandoned, the stock was

---

different dates are given for the circumcision of Sekonyela (Macgregor, pp. 27-28, Ellenberger, pp. 45-48).

[1] The works by an Aged Fingo, Moloja, and van Warmelo, cited in footnote 3, p. 392 above; Ellenberger, pp. 124-7, 130-42. Recent reconstructions are Marion How, 'An Alibi for Mantatisi', *AS*, xiii, 1954, 65-76, and Lye, op. cit.

[2] An Aged Fingo; Moloja; van Warmelo; Ellenberger, pp. 154-6.

[3] An Aged Fingo; Moloja; van Warmelo; Ellenberger, pp. 176-89.

destroyed, the fields ceased to be cultivated, and in several places the landscape was littered with human bones. Demoralized survivors wandered round singly or in small groups, contriving to live on game or veld plants. Even cannibalism was widespread.[1]

The extent of the collapse of the social and moral order is illustrated by the recollections of a Hlubi survivor of the *Difaqane*. After the Hlubi had been defeated by the Ngwane, the author wandered on his own in the upper Caledon area:[2]

> I was wandering on a path. I saw a man who called to me to stop. He came to me and told me to sit down. He caught hold of my skin mantle. I left it in his hand and ran as fast as I could. He was a cannibal, and wished to kill me. Afterwards I met two children. . . . One was dead. The living one was eating the flesh of the dead one. I passed on. Next I saw a company of people digging plants. I was afraid of them and hid myself. When I was still going I saw a long stone wall, not very high. There were people sitting there cooking. I saw human heads on the ground. I took another way and escaped from these cannibals.
>
> I came to some people of Ngojo [MaNthatisi]. They asked me who I was. I told them. It was night already. They took me to a hut, where I slept. To get warmth I slept in the fire circle, from which the fire had been taken. I found my father with the people of Ngojo. While I was there my father went one day to steal cattle. He returned with two.
>
> From this village we went to another one. We saw on the way some Basutos in a cave under a rock. They asked us to stay with them, but we would not. We were afraid. We saw the skulls of many people beside this rock. . . . I then went to a village. The Amangwana [Ngwane] came there and destroyed the village. I was taken away by them. . . . We became servants. Tshaka sent an army to fight with Matiwana. We were defeated and the Amazulu went back again. . . .

Meanwhile similar disturbances were being caused north of the Vaal river by some of the Sotho who had been ejected from their homes further south, and who formed migrant hordes on the same pattern as those of the Tlokwa, the Hlubi, and the Ngwane. At least four such hordes were active in the north-western high veld: Phuthing, initially under Tshwane, then under Ratsebe; Hlakwana under Nkgaraganye; a branch of the Fokeng, who became known as the Kololo, under Sebetwane; and Taung, who were led by Moletsane after the death of his predecessor in 1824.[3]

At the time the identity of these hordes was falsified by rumour. Robert Moffat, the L.M.S. missionary at Kuruman, wrote of early 1823:

---

[1] On cannibalism in the area see Arbousset, Ch. 7, and Ellenberger, pp. 217-26.
[2] An Aged Fingo, pp. 250-1.
[3] How; notes by I. Schapera in Moffat, *Apprenticeship*, pp. 102-3; Edwin Smith, *Great Lion of Bechuanaland*, pp. 366-79.

For more than a year numerous and strange reports had at intervals reached us, some indeed of such a character as to induce us to treat them as the reveries of a madman. It was said that a mighty woman, of the name of Mantatee, was at the head of an invincible army, numerous as the locusts, marching onward among the interior nations, carrying devastation and ruin wherever she went; that she nourished the army with her own milk, sent out hornets before it, and, in one word, was laying the world desolate.[1]

In spite of Moffat's scepticism, it was widely assumed that the 'Mantatees'—meaning MaNthatisi and her Tlokwa—were responsible for a great deal of damage north of the Vaal river; and historians have repeated the charge.[2] In fact, as has been stated (p. 394), the Tlokwa of MaNthatisi never crossed to the northern side of the Vaal river.[3]

The Tswana chiefdoms, between the Vaal and the Limpopo, the Kalahari and the central Transvaal, bore the brunt of these invasions; and they failed abysmally to co-operate with one another in the face of danger. This was partly because of the settlement patterns of the Tswana. Since most of them lived in concentrated settlements, separated from others by tracts of thinly populated country, they were peculiarly vulnerable to piecemeal attack. Moreover, there were strong traditional rivalries between the Tswana chiefdoms; and several of the most prominent chiefs died or were killed during the early stages of the *Difaqane*.[4]

There are eyewitness accounts of some of the episodes in the *Difaqane* north of the Vaal river. Samuel Broadbent and Thomas Hodgson, Wesleyan missionaries, joined Sefunelo's Seleka-Rolong in January 1823 when, having been dislodged from their homes at Thabeng (near modern Buisfontein) by the Phuthing, the Seleka-Rolong were migrating to Makwassie (near modern Klerksdorp).[5] At the end of May 1823 Robert Moffat, travelling northwards from Kuruman, heard that marauders were in the vicinity and that they intended to attack Kuruman. Moffat returned to Kuruman and explained the situation to a *pitso* (tribal assembly) of the Tlhaping, who resided there. He then proceeded to Griqua Town, where he asked the Cape Government Agent to persuade the Griqua to drive the invaders back. On June 20 George Thompson, an English traveller, went out from Kuruman to

---

[1] Moffat, *Labours*, p. 340. Similarly, Thompson, i. 156–7.

[2] Stow, Ch. 23, 'The Careen of the Mantatee Horde'; Theal, *History*, i. 301–4; van der Walt, *Geskiedenis*, i. 282; Walker, *History*, pp. 175–6.

[3] How (p. 67) and Edwin Smith (*Great Lion*, pp. 370–1) show that by 1912 D. F. Ellenberger himself was convinced that the term 'Mantatees' had been misapplied to the invaders of the Transvaal; Schapera (in Moffat, *Apprenticeship*, p. 102) reached the same conclusion independently; Lye, op. cit., summarizes the history of the error and its correction.

[4] I. Schapera is the author of many monographs on the Tswana, notably those cited in footnote 4, p. 392 above. I am also indebted to Martin Legassick, 'The Ngwato' (unpublished seminar paper, 1965).

[5] Broadbent, Chs. 5–7; Hodgson, op. cit.

investigate, and found that a horde was approaching Dithakong ('Latakoo'), a Tlhaping town fifty miles north-east of Kuruman, and that the inhabitants had evacuated the town. These invaders were probably the Phuthing of Tshwane, who were coming down from the north after attacking the Hurutshe, the Ngwaketse, and the Rolong of Ratlou and Tshidi, and who proceeded to occupy Dithakong. During the next few days another horde, the Hlakwana, also approached Dithakong, suffering grievously from lack of food. On June 26 a Griqua commando, a hundred strong, went into action against the Hlakwana outside Dithakong. As was so often the case, guns and horses offset a tremendous numerical disparity. The Hlakwana, confused by the 'thunder and lightning' of the Griqua horsemen, fled into Dithakong, and the Griqua then drove them and the Phuthing out of town. According to Moffat, the combined strengths of the two hordes was about 40,000; and 500 of the invaders were killed and not a single Griqua. Both Tshwane and Nkgaraganye were among the fallen. As the survivors fled, the Tlhaping, who had taken little part in the previous fighting, fell upon them, killing women and children as well as men, and hacking off the copper rings from their necks, arms, and legs.[1] This engagement did not put an end to the *Difaqane* in the Transvaal area; but, in demonstrating that the marauders could not defeat an armed and mounted force, it caused them to refrain from attacking the Griqua states or the Cape Colony.

After the Battle of Dithakong the Hlakwana horde fled south to the Vaal river, pursued by the Tlhaping. Many Hlakwana were drowned while trying to cross the river, which was in flood, and the horde then disintegrated. The Phuthing fled north-east after the battle and continued to raid the chiefdoms in the western Transvaal. Sebetwane's horde, which was probably in the vicinity of Dithakong at the time and possibly participated in the battle of 26 June, also moved north. It harassed the northern Tswana chiefdoms for several years, until in about 1831 it moved clear out of the area to the north-west. Later the Kololo came to rest in the Zambesi valley, where David Livingstone found them.[2] For a short while after the battle the Taung horde may have acted in concert with the Kololo; but in 1824 the Taung were back near the Vaal river, driving the Seleka-Rolong from Makwassie and sacking the Wesleyan mission station there. However, in August 1824 a combined Griqua and Rolong force engaged the Taung at Phitshani on the Molopo River and the Taung then retreated southwards across the Vaal.[3]

[1] Moffat, *Apprenticeship*, pp. 75–103, *Labours*, Chs. 21–22; Thompson, i, Chs. 8–12, 15–16.
[2] On Sebetwane and the Kololo see Ellenberger, pp. 305–30; Omer-Cooper, Ch. 8; and Edwin Smith, *Great Lion*, pp. 367–410; also Legassick, op. cit.
[3] Broadbent, Chs. 15, 18; Edwards, Chs. 4–6.

The disintegration of the Hlubi and the departure of the Ngwane (p. 394) paved the way for a process of regeneration from the chaos of the *Difaqane* in the area south of the Vaal river. Initially this process was promoted by two chiefdoms: the old Tlokwa chiefdom of MaNthatisi and Sekonyela, centred on Kooaneng; and the new southern Sotho chiefdom of Moshweshwe, centred on Thaba Bosiu.

The Tlokwa survived the *Difaqane* under the able leadership of MaNthatisi. After their migration, they occupied the neighbouring mountains Joalaboholo and Kooaneng, on the northern side of the Caledon river about five miles east of modern Ficksburg. Kooaneng, the principal settlement, was topped by a sheer cliff. The Tlokwa defended the only pass to the summit with a stone wall and a narrow gate, and collected a supply of stones to throw down upon attackers. It was MaNthatisi's policy to attract fresh adherents from the survivors of the shattered Sotho and Nguni communities and to extend her authority as far as possible, and Sekonyela continued that policy when he took over the chieftainship in the early 1830s. By 1834, when Dr. Andrew Smith's expedition travelled through the area, many of the small groups living between the upper Caledon and the Vaal regarded themselves as Tlokwa subjects; and in 1836 Thomas Arbousset, the French missionary, found that the chiefdom extended about thirty miles north of Kooaneng and also some distance to the south, across the Caledon.[1] Both visitors were favourably impressed by MaNthatisi. Arbousset described her as 'a woman of great intelligence' with 'a sweet and agreeable expression' and 'a regular countenance and an elegant figure'.[2] Sekonyela made an unfavourable impression. Arbousset found that he had 'a sullen and unsociable disposition' and that he inspired his own people with 'more of fear than love'.[3] Though Arbousset and Smith were alien witnesses, it does seem likely that it was Sekonyela's mediocrity that caused the leadership of the southern Sotho to slip out of the hands of the Tlokwa into those of a man of humble origin.

Mokhachane, father of Moshweshwe, was no more than a village headman of the Mokoteli lineage—a junior branch of the Monaheng who formed a division of the Kwena. Moshweshwe was born at Menkhoaneng, eight miles south of Butha-Buthe, in about 1786.[4] After his

---

[1] Arbousset, Ch. 5; Andrew Smith, *Diary*, i. 129–31, Papers, x. 174–88.
[2] Arbousset, p. 58; similarly, Andrew Smith, Papers, x. 175–6.
[3] Arbousset, loc. cit.; similarly, Andrew Smith, Papers, x. 174–5.
[4] On the origins of Moshweshwe's Southern Sotho Kingdom, and its history before the arrival of the missionaries in 1833, see Arbousset, Chs. 24–27; Casalis, *Basutos*, Chs. 1–2, 9–17; Ellenberger, *passim*, with Genealogy of Moshweshwe on pp. 378–81; Théophile Jousse, 'Moshesh, roi des Bassoutos', *Le Chrétien Évangélique: revue religieuse de la suisse romande*, pp. 7–17; Macgregor; Mosh[w]esh[we] to the Secretary to the Government, Cape Town, 15 May 1845, *Bas. Rec.* i. 82–87; Nehemiah Mosh[w]esh[we], 'A Little Light from Basutoland', *CMM*, 3rd ser. ii (Jan.–June 1880), 221–33, 280–92; Andrew Smith, *Diary*, i. 105–18, Papers, x.

initiation, he and a circumcision-mate, Makoanyane, like many other young Sotho, indulged in cattle-raiding from neighbouring villages. He also come in contact with Motlumi, a Kwena chief of the senior Monaheng line, who had travelled widely and acquired a reputation as a sage and a man of peace. Motlumi, who died in about 1816, is said to have prophesied that Moshweshwe would become a great chief and advised him to be a tolerant ruler and to oppose the influence of witch-doctors. The *Difaqane* gave Moshweshwe the opportunity to come to the fore. In the general collapse of the southern Sotho chiefdoms he emerged as a man of superior military and political talents. From Butha-Buthe mountain and Menkhoaneng he resisted the first onslaughts of the Hlubi, the Ngwane, and the Tlokwa. In 1824, hard pressed by the Tlokwa, he moved with a small band of followers from Butha-Buthe to Thaba Bosiu, some fifty miles to the south-west. Thaba Bosiu is an inconspicuous mountain among many others in the Little Caledon valley; but it rises some 350 feet on all sides and is topped by a sheer cliff, penetrated by a few narrow passes.[1] Mosweshwe and his father built their villages on the summit—a flat area of about two square miles providing pasture and a fair supply of perennial spring water. Others settled around the base of Thaba Bosiu and on and near neighbouring mountains, using Thaba Bosiu as a refuge in times of danger.

During the next few years Thaba Bosiu withstood a series of attacks. After Matiwane defeated Mpangazita, Moshweshwe tried to find an accommodation with him by paying him tribute; but when Matiwane, nevertheless, appeared threatening, Moshweshwe sent messengers with presents to Shaka. In July 1827, after he had been mauled by the impis of Shaka and Mzilikazi, Matiwane attacked Thaba Bosiu. Moshweshwe defeated him and this was a crucial event in the growth of Moshweshwe's power and reputation. In spite of his humble origins and in spite of the fact that his father Mokhachane was still alive, his fame spread far and wide as the Chief on the Mountain who provided succour in the time of troubles. He encouraged the survivors of the shattered southern Sotho chiefdoms, wherever they had fled, to return and attach themselves to him; and he gave an equally cordial welcome to Nguni. He even gave sanctuary to cannibals without exacting reprisals, providing only that they undertook to mend their ways. Individuals he incorporated directly into villages administered by himself or members of his family; organized groups he allowed to found separate villages and to maintain their own distinctive customs. He enhanced his standing in traditional

---

110–51. Modern historical surveys are in Hugh Ashton, *The Basuto*, London, 1952, Ch. 1; Omer-Cooper, Ch. 7; and G. Tylden, *The Rise of the Basuto*, Ch. 1. R. S. Webb, *Gazetteer for Basutoland*, is invaluable.

[1] G. Tylden, *A History of Thaba Bosiu*.

terms by taking wives from many different chiefly lineages; and he made alliances with more distant chiefs like Moorosi, whose Phuthi lived near the Orange river, below its confluence with the Caledon. Moorosi was particularly useful as an ally in forays which they jointly made into southern Nguni country to build up their wealth in cattle. The result was that by the early 1830s Moshweshwe's people had become known as BaSotho (i.e. *the* Sotho) and Moshweshwe himself was acquiring the prestige of a king.

Sekonyela was jealous of the upstart Sotho whose wealth and power were rivalling those of the Tlokwa; and in 1829, while Moshweshwe and many of his warriors were absent on a cattle raid in Thembu country, he attacked Thaba Bosiu and made off with some of Moshweshwe's wives. Sekonyela was repulsed and made to surrender his booty by the stay-at-homes, including Moshweshwe's senior son, Letsie, and his age-mates, who were in a circumcision lodge at the time. In 1831 a powerful Ndebele impi attacked the mountain, but in a fierce engagement Moshweshwe managed to drive them off and to their surprise he then sent them a present of cattle to speed them on their way. This was another major event in the growth of his prestige. It was also a typical example of Moshweshwe's political technique: he fought enemies when necessary; he conciliated them when possible. As was often to be the case, the technique paid dividends, for Mzilikazi refrained from making further attacks on him.

A different type of threat appeared in 1830. Bands of mounted, gun-carrying 'Bergenaars'—offshoots from the Griqua—and Kora ('Korana') began to raid in the Caledon valley. They caused havoc in many of Moshweshwe's villages and created great anxiety, because the southern Sotho had had no previous experience of horses and firearms. But Moshweshwe was quick to learn. He began to build up stocks of guns and horses—bartering them from Griqua hunters, seizing them from Kora invaders, and encouraging Sotho to bring them to him from farms where they had worked in the Cape Colony. He himself became a good shot and a competent horseman, and the next generation became experts. Furthermore, having heard from a Griqua hunter that missionaries had helped his people to organize themselves into effective states, he sent cattle to Griqua Town to 'buy' a missionary. Kora intercepted the cattle, but a second request reached Griqua Town shortly before three members of the Paris Evangelical Missionary Society—the missionaries Thomas Arbousset and Eugene Casilis and the artisan Constant Gosselin—arrived there from Cape Town and paused to consider where they should found a station. They took the news as a divine sign and hastened to Thaba Bosiu, arriving in June 1833.[1]

[1] Casalis, *Basutos*, pp. 8–14, *Life*, Ch. 8; Ellenberger, pp. 234–6.

Moshweshwe welcomed the missionaries with open arms. Casalis describes their first meeting:

The chief bent upon me a look at once majestic and benevolent. His profile, more aquiline than that of the generality of his subjects, his well-developed forehead, the fulness and regularity of his features, his eyes, a little weary it seemed, but full of intelligence and softness, made a deep impression on me. I felt at once that I had to do with a superior man, trained to think, to command others, and above all himself.[1]

Both Arbousset and Casalis were young, intelligent, perceptive, and freer from cultural prejudices than other South African missionaries of the period; and Moshweshwe for his part was prepared to go a long way to meet their requests, for he was an innovator with an exceptionally rational cast of mind. He placed them at what they called Morija, thirty miles south of Thaba Bosiu in the direction of Kora attacks, and sent his eldest sons, Letsie and Molapo, with their agemates and retainers, to found villages near the mission and be taught by the missionaries. As other French missionaries arrived, he placed them, too, on exposed frontiers, as agents for the expansion of his authority—Bethulie (1833) and Beerseba (1835) in the south-west, and Mekuatling (1837) in the north. He himself regularly attended church services and, although he never learned to read, he eventually acquired a knowledge of the Bible and French Calvinism which astonished visitors. In time he permitted members of his family to be converted, and granted some of his converted wives divorces. He allowed Christian Sotho to be buried by Christian rites. He exposed the chicanery of diviners. He even temporarily forbade traditional initiation rituals. On the other hand he was careful not to split the embryonic nation by straining the allegiance of his more conservative followers too far. As a matter of policy he refrained from being baptized himself, and he made it clear that the missionaries were *his* white men, utterly dependent on his goodwill.[2]

The rivalry between Sekonyela and Moshweshwe for the control of the Caledon valley (including the plains to its north and the Maluti foothills to its south) became complicated by the arrival of newcomers with their own missionaries. In 1823, as we have seen, Wesleyans had begun to work in the neighbourhood of the lower Vaal river, attaching themselves to Sefunelo, Chief of the Seleka branch of the Rolong (a Tswana people), and to various small Coloured bands. Harassed

---

[1] Casalis, *Life*, pp. 176–7. Andrew Smith, too, was impressed by Moshweshwe: 'we were much pleased with his candour and honesty' (Papers, x. 125); 'a man inclined for peace' (ibid., p. 141); 'a man of great observation and very politic in his management of his people' (ibid., p. 147).

[2] Arbousset, Ch. 27; Casalis, *Basutos*, Chs. 3–17, *Life*, Chs. 9 ff.; Jousse, pp. 67–78; *Journal des Missions Evangeliques*, viii ff.

by the wars, food shortage, and droughts, Sefunelo had first tried to establish himself at Makwassie, north of the Vaal river, and then at Platberg-on-Vaal.[1] In 1833 two of the Wesleyans reconnoitred the Caledon valley and obtained permission from Sekonyela and Moshweshwe to bring the Seleka-Rolong and the Coloured communities to settle north of the Caledon and west of Kooaneng, in return for 'Eight Head of Horned Cattle, Thirty Four Sheep, and Five Goats'.[2] Moroka, son and successor of Sefunelo, then moved the Seleka-Rolong to Thaba Nchu and the Coloured groups settled further east—Piet Davids and his Griqua at Lishuane, Carolus Baatje and his 'Bastards' or 'Newlanders' at Platberg-on-Caledon, and Gert Taaibosch and his Kora at Merumetsu. Wesleyans established missions at each of these places, and also at Mpukani (modern Clocholan) among the Tlokwa. Moroka had a substantial following and Thaba Nchu became a Tswana-type concentrated settlement on the plain below the mountain. When Andrew Smith visited it in 1834, he estimated that Thaba Nchu had a population of over 5,000 people. Most of them were Seleka-Rolong, but there were also members of other branches of the Rolong, and some southern Sotho under Moseme. The latter had resided there before the Rolong arrived and recognized Moshweshwe as their superior. Davids, Baatje, and Taaibosch had only a few followers each, but were capable of serious mischief because they possessed guns and horses. Their villages were surrounded by Sotho and Nguni settlements, some of which recognized Moshweshwe, others Sekonyela.[3]

In 1837 Moletsane, a Taung Chief, settled at Mekuatling, between Davids and Taaibosch. Moletsane had started life near modern Winburg and had taken part in the *Difaqane* wars on either side of the Vaal river. He entered the area of Moshweshwe's influence in 1836 and it was Moshweshwe who encouraged him to settle at Mekuatling.[4]

These newcomers created new factors of instability in the Caledon valley. Moroka's and Moletsane's people were inveterate enemies, having clashed repeatedly during the *Difaqane* (p. 397). There was now a natural tendency for Moroka to ally himself with Sekonyela against Moshweshwe and Moletsane, and for the Coloured communities, with their horses and firearms, to add fuel to the flames. These tensions were accentuated by the fact that Moroka, Sekonyela, and the Coloured bands were served by English missionaries and Moshweshwe and Moletsane by French. Each missionary had an interest in inflating the

---

[1] Broadbent, Chs. 5–19; Hodgson, op. cit.

[2] *Bas. Rec.* i. 4; Edwards, Ch. 5.

[3] Arbousset, Chs. 2–4, 22; Casalis, *Life*, pp. 164–71: Edwards, Ch. 6; S. M. Molema, *Chief Moroka*; Andrew Smith, *Diary*, i. 120–7, 147–60, Papers, x. 156–74, 226–43.

[4] Ellenberger, pp. 54–62, 165–9, 173–6; Macgregor, pp. 60–67; Moletsane, in *Bas. Rec.*, i. 517–32.

claims of his own chief. The English missionaries claimed that their chiefs had acquired absolute ownership of extensive lands north of the Caledon by virtue of purchase from Moshweshwe. The French missionaries claimed that Moshweshwe was the ruler of all the territory west of Kooaneng, that Moroka, Davids, Baatje, and Taaibosch were merely his vassals, and that any transfer of cattle, sheep, and goats had been a payment of tribute and not a purchase.[1] These rivalries set the stage for the politics of the Caledon valley area for a generation.

Meanwhile, a regenerative process of a different type was taking place in the Transvaal, following the invasion of the area by Mzilikazi and his Ndebele.[2] Mzilikazi was born in about 1796. His father, Mashobane, was the Chief of a branch of the Kumalo located on a tributary of the Black Mfolozi and a vassal of the Ndwandwe Chief, Zwide. In 1818 Zwide killed Mashobane. Mzilikazi then succeeded to the chieftainship and transferred his allegiance from Zwide to Shaka, who left the little chiefdom intact, apparently intending to use it as an instrument of expansion to the north. In 1822, at Shaka's request, Mzilikazi made a raid on a Sotho chiefdom across the mountains; but on his return he refused to hand over the captured cattle to Shaka, thereby committing an act of rebellion. To escape retribution, Mzilikazi fled northwards with his Kumalo warriors and a few women and children, brushing off Zulu pursuers, seizing cattle, and acquiring fresh adherents as he travelled. In 1823 he settled on the upper Oliphant's river in the eastern Transvaal high veld. During the next few years he conquered the Pedi and other Sotho chiefdoms in that area, and his following continued to grow as he absorbed Sotho survivors as well as more Nguni refugees from Shaka.

The Ndebele and the Pedi traditions of the relations between their two peoples during the 1820s do not agree. According to Pedi tradition, at the time when the Ndebele reached the eastern Transvaal the Pedi were weakened by succession disputes following the death of Chief Thulare; then, in a great battle, the Ndebele defeated the Pedi and killed all the sons of Thulare except Sekwati, who took refuge in the Soutpansberg; later, after Mzilikazi had moved to the Apies river, Sekwati returned to the Steelpoort area, where he re-created the Pedi chiefdom and resisted attacks by the Swazi and the Zulu. What is

[1] e.g. *Bas. Rec.*, i. 57–60, 65–73, 77–79, 82–87, 131–4.
[2] On the Ndebele of Mzilikazi in the Transvaal see: Contemporary eyewitness accounts: James Archbell, in Steedman, ii. 31–34; Harris, Chs. 11–32; Kotzé, pp. 124–42; Moffat, *Journals*, i. 1–138, *Labours*, Chs. 29–31; Jean-Pierre Pellissier, *Journal des Missions Evangeliques*, viii. 5–19; Andrew Smith, *Diary*, ii, Papers, xi. 247 ff. Contemporary second-hand account: Arbousset, Ch. 19. Recollections and traditions subsequently recorded: Bryant, Ch. 42; Ellenberger, Ch. 23. Recent reconstructions: Peter Becker, *Path of Blood*; Edwin Smith, *The Life and Times of Daniel Lindley*, Chs. 3–4; Omer-Cooper, Ch. 9; also William F. Lye, 'The Ndebele Kingdom south of the Limpopo River' (unpublished seminar paper, 1964).

curious is that Ndebele tradition refers to a Pedi victory over the Ndebele, which is not mentioned in Pedi tradition—a reversal of what usually happens, for people recall their victories rather than their defeats.[1]

In about 1825, to put greater distance between himself and Shaka and to escape the effects of a drought in the eastern Transvaal, Mzilikazi moved south-westwards to the Apies river (near modern Pretoria). This fertile area, formerly thickly inhabited by Kwena and other Sotho, had already been devastated. From the Apies river, Mzilikazi extended his power in all directions, sending regiments deep into Shona country across the Limpopo, westwards into Tswana country, southwards to the Caledon valley, and eastwards to the Pedi. But Mzilikazi was still insecure. In 1830, while some of his regiments were beyond the Limpopo, a Zulu army pillaged several of his villages. Soon afterwards Griqua commandos (p. 400) began to raid into his territory, and in retaliation Mzilikazi sent an expedition which destroyed a Coloured band near the Vaal river and returned with captured children, oxen, and wagons. It was still the Zulu whom Mzilikazi feared most, and in July 1832 he moved further westwards, to Mosega on the Marico river (near modern Zeerust), driving away the Tswana inhabitants. Mzilikazi lived in the Mosega area until the arrival of the Voortrekkers.

By that time the Ndebele conquest state had become the dominant power on the entire high veld. Starting with approximately 300 warriors[2] Mzilikazi had successively incorporated Nguni refugees and vanquished Sotho, until he could muster four or five thousand trained and disciplined warriors.[3] Most of these he located in Zulu-type military barracks within a short distance of the capital; but his outposts extended to the Limpopo, the Crocodile, the Vaal, and the Molopo, enclosing an area of about 30,000 square miles; and from time to time, as we have seen, his regiments ranged still further afield.

Mzilikazi was a despotic ruler and his subjects were obsequious in his presence. The dominant element in the Ndebele state was essentially Nguni and the subject element essentially Sotho. Nguni manpower was

[1] For Pedi tradition see Winter and Hunt, op. cit.; also [T. Wangemann], *Maleo en Sekoekoeni*, VRS, 1957, pp. 79 ff. Hunt, p. 284, confuses the issue by saying that Thulare died 'in 1824 on the day of a solar eclipse'. According to Hunt's own account, Thulare must have died before the arrival of Mzilikazi (1823); and in fact there was no significant eclipse in that area in 1824—only an annular eclipse with a centre line passing 400 miles south of Thularestad as shown on Hunt's map. Thulare's death was probably linked with the total eclipse of 14 March 1820, which had a centre line passing 200 miles north of Thularestad (Richard Gray, 'Eclipse Maps', *JAH*, vi, 1965, 260, and Richard Gray, personal communication).
[2] Bryant, p. 423, says 'two or three hundred'; Henry Francis Fynn, in Bird, i. 68, says '300'.
[3] Harris, p. 168, says: 'His standing army of warriors of his own tribe exceeds five thousand men, but numbers of the conquered nations swell his followers to a large amount, and are chiefly employed as guardians of his cattle during the intervals of peace.' See also Kotzé, pp. 129, 168, giving estimates by the American missionaries and others.

divided into three age-groups: the older men, who had been given permission to marry and formed the military reserve; the younger men who were full-time warriors and were forbidden to marry; and the boys, who herded the cattle. Some of the conquered Sotho were permitted to live in their own villages within Mzilikazi's territory; others were used for forced labour, such as the building of military barracks, or were clients of individual Nguni. Thus the Ndebele formed a caste-like society, differentiated by cultural criteria. But the line of division was not absolute. Nguni men took Sotho wives and concubines. One small Sotho group (the Ndiweni), who had joined Mzilikazi during his flight from Shaka, ranked with the dominant element, and later on more Sotho boys were incorporated into the military system.[1] Moreover, the subject peoples tended to absorb Nguni culture (for example, to acquire the Ndebele language), and when Mzilikazi fled north in 1837 he was accompanied by a considerable number of people of Sotho, as well as Nguni, origin.

It is inaccurate to regard Mzilikazi as no more than a bloody tyrant. Once he had rebelled against Shaka, his overriding need was security; and in his search for security, besides causing much destruction, he created a new and viable political community out of diverse ingredients. (Zwangendaba, who fled from Shaka shortly before Mzilikazi, created another new political community further north on strikingly similar lines.)[2] The white people who visited Mzilikazi in the Transvaal were all impressed by the prevalence of law and order in his dominions. Moffat, though a culture-bound Victorian, became curiously intimate with Mzilikazi; and the American missionaries, who settled in his territory in 1836, reported that

> The people, as individuals, are restricted from some crimes which are prevalent among the Bechuana and other tribes, the authority of whose chiefs is comparatively weak. Although this people are accustomed to plundering on a large scale, stealing from a stranger in the community is unheard of. The king's word is law, yet the government is administered with a systematic uniformity, which we infer proceeds from established usages of which we are yet ignorant.[3]

2. *The Great Trek, 1836–54*[4]

In and after 1835 many Afrikaner families disposed of their property in the Cape Colony, bought large supplies of gunpowder, mustered

---

[1] Writing in 1835, Moffat (*Journals*, i. 111) estimated that there were about one hundred Sotho boys in the Nguni system.

[2] J. A. Barnes, *Politics in a Changing Society*; Margaret Read, 'Tradition and Prestige among the Ngoni', *Africa*, 9, 1936, 453–84.

[3] Daniel Lindley and Henry Venable, 18 Aug. 1836, in Kotzé, p. 130.

[4] Besides the sources cited below, see those cited in footnotes on pp. 355–7.

their live-stock, loaded the rest of their movable property in their wagons, and trekked northwards across the Orange river. At the time they referred to themselves as Emigrants. Since the late nineteenth century they have been known as Voortrekkers and their migration as the Great Trek.[1]

Most of the Voortrekkers were derived from the Colonial *trekboer* community of semi-nomadic pastoral farmers (pp. 208–13). It was their *trekboer* mode of life that made it possible for them to become Voortrekkers and determined their manner of migrating and settling in a new terrain. Nevertheless, though several hundred *trekboers* had crossed the Orange before 1835 and others crossed in later years, the Voortrekkers were a new and distinct phenomenon. The *trekboer* movement was a slow and continuous advance of the frontiers of white settlement in South Africa, extending back over four generations to the very beginning of the eighteenth century. It continued to be an unco-ordinated movement of families and small family groups, who had no overwhelming grievances against the Cape Government, regarded themselves as remaining British subjects, and assumed that sooner or later the Government would extend the Cape frontier to incorporate them in their new lands, as had often happened in the past. On the other hand, the Great Trek was an organized migration of several thousand people. By mid 1837 about 5,000 Voortrekkers[2]—men, women, and children—had crossed the Orange river; by 1845, perhaps 14,000.[3] The Great Trek was a sudden, dramatic leap forward, which turned the flank of the southern Nguni chiefdoms, conquered the two most powerful kingdoms in southern Africa, and brought the frontiers of white settlement to the Tukela river and towards the Limpopo. Above all, the Voortrekkers were determined to become 'a free and independent people'[4] in 'a free and independent State'.[5] As Professor C. F. J. Muller says, the Great Trek was 'a rebellion against the British government'.[6] The suppression of the risings of 1795, 1799, and 1815 had shown that disaffected frontiersmen were not capable of staging a successful rebellion *in situ* in the Cape Colony. There remained another mode of rebellion

[1] F. A. van Jaarsveld, 'Die Tydgenootlike Beoordeling van die Groot Trek, 1836–1842', *Communications of the University of South Africa*, C. 36, pp. 5–7.
[2] Van der Walt, *Geskiedenis*, i. 290.
[3] Eric A. Walker, *The Great Trek*, p. 6.
[4] Natal *Volksraad* to Governor Sir George Napier, 4 Sept. 1840: *Annals of Natal*, i. 612.
[5] Natal *Volksraad* to Governor Sir George Napier, 14 Jan. 1841: ibid. 628.
[6] C. F. J. Muller, 'Waarom die Groot Trek geslaag het', *Communications of the University of South Africa*, B. 12, p. 4. On the ideological differences between *trekboers* and Voortrekkers, see also van der Merwe, *Die Noordwaartse Beweging van die Boere voor die Groot Trek*; F. A. van Jaarsveld, *Die Eenheidstrewe van die Republiekeinse Afrikaners*, i: Pioniershartstogte (*1836–1864*), pp. 23–24; and M. C. E. van Schoor, 'Politieke Groeperinge in Transgariep', *AYB*, 1950, ii, Ch. 1.

—escape to a new terrain. The following pages will trace its progress on the high veld from its inception, through its several set-backs, to its partial fulfilment with the acknowledgement by British representatives of the independence of the Voortrekkers north of the Vaal (Sand River Convention, 1852) and between the Vaal and the Orange (Bloemfontein Convention, 1854).

The course of the Great Trek was affected by three main factors: the qualities of the Voortrekkers as individuals and as a community; the environments into which they migrated; and the reactions of the British government and its local representatives.

The product of a frontier situation, every grown male Voortrekker, like every *trekboer*, regarded himself as an independent farmer. To aspire to be anything else was inconceivable.[1] Primarily a pastoral farmer, he would also grow corn and vegetables for his own consumption where possible, and he would take part in occasional hunting expeditions for adventure rather than for profit. Many Voortrekkers were skilled in maintaining their key possessions—wagons and firearms; but all were accustomed to having other services performed for them by people whom they did not regard as members of their own community. In particular, they depended on others to satisfy three basic needs: religion, trade, and labour. Most Voortrekkers were convinced of the necessity of Christian sacraments. In the Cape Colony the Government had always provided Calvinist ministers to conduct *nagmaal* (communion) and the Christian *rites de passage* (baptism, confirmation, marriage, burial); but the synod of the Cape Dutch Reformed Church, composed mainly of Scottish ministers, opposed the emigration on the grounds that it would lead to godlessness and a decline of civilization, and no minister could be persuaded to accompany the Voortrekkers.[2] For the first few years they were therefore dependent on the ministrations of foreign missionaries, such as James Archbell, the Wesleyan missionary at Thaba Nchu, and Daniel Lindley, an American. Secondly, the Voortrekkers required regular supplies of a few commodities they could not themselves produce—tea, coffee, sugar, and other groceries; clothes and clothing materials; and, above all, gunpowder. They could pay for these commodities, not normally in cash, but in sheep and cattle, which constituted their capital accumulation. In the Colony they had been served by *smouse*—travelling traders of British, continental European, or Jewish origin. When they migrated they hoped to become independent of the Colonial commercial network by gaining access to ports beyond the sphere of British control and dealing with Dutch or other non-British traders; but they failed. They had to rely on

[1] Van der Merwe, *Die Trekboer in die Geskiedenis van die Kaapkolonie*, Ch. 4.
[2] Walker, *Trek*, p. 182.

Colonial-based *smouse*, who extended their operations beyond the Orange and the Vaal. Thirdly, the Voortrekkers never had the slightest intention of abandoning the deeply engrained custom of using dark-skinned people as shepherds, cattle-herds, field-workers, and domestic and general servants. They took with them from the Colony as many servants as they could—including former slaves who had become 'apprentices' in 1834. These Coloured dependents were about as numerous as the Voortrekkers themselves. The Voortrekkers recruited more servants from the inhabitants of the areas where they travelled, fought, and settled. The Great Trek was not an act of 'voluntary segregation' as Professor F. A. van Jaarsveld has called it,[1] for true segregation would have produced a self-sufficient Voortrekker society. After removing themselves from the authority of the Colonial Government, the Voortrekkers founded a new society in a new terrain, but it was a society fashioned much as the Colonial society had been before the reforms of the 1820s and 1830s—a loose-knit plural society, in which the Voortrekkers were the dominant minority and their African and Coloured servants were the subject majority.

The Voortrekkers themselves were not united. They left the Colony in a series of trek parties, each of which was organized by a prestigious man and consisted of his kinsfolk, neighbours, and dependents. North of the Orange these trek parties tended to amalgamate for political purposes into larger groups under conspicuous leaders, such as Andries Hendrik Potgieter, Gert Maritz, Piet Retief, Piet Uys, and Andries Pretorius; but different groups settled in widely separated areas, from Natal in the south to the Soutpansberg in the north, and no leader was able to unite all of them into a single political system. This was partly because British power operated differentially in different areas. It was also because of their own intrinsic divisions. Leaders quarrelled and their followers took up their quarrels; and personal disputes became compounded with policy differences. Potgieter believed in personal rule; Maritz and, after him, J. J. Burger preferred that public affairs should be regulated by an elected body. Potgieter believed in ignoring Britain and achieving independence by *fait accompli*; Pretorius deemed it wiser to negotiate with Britain for independence *de jure*. In the course of time the cleavages became intensified as a result of the varied experiences of the different groups. Internal divisions bedevilled the history of the Natal Republic (pp. 364–73); they also bedevilled the history of the Voortrekkers on the high veld.[2]

---

[1] Van Jaarsveld, *Eenheidstrewe*, p. 11.

[2] Van Jaarsveld, *Eenheidstrewe*; van Schoor, op. cit.; also G. D. J. Duvenage, 'Willem Hendrik Jacobsz se rol in die Onafhanklikheid- en Eenheidstrewe van die Voortrekkers op die Hoëveld (1847–1852)', in *AYB*, 1956, i; A. N. Pelzer, *Geskiedenis van die Suid-Afrikaanse*

When the Great Trek began two areas had been reported on, by reconnaissance expeditions which had been made in 1834 and 1835, as fertile and uninhabited; Natal south of the Tukela, and the central high veld on either side of the Vaal river. But the Voortrekkers did not initially understand the realities of the situations in those areas. They did not realize, firstly, that Dingane and Mzilikazi dominated them to safeguard themselves from attacks from the south; and, secondly, that many Africans were alive who regarded them as their homelands. Consequently the first phase of the Great Trek was a military phase; and even when the Zulu and the Ndebele kingdoms had been defeated, the security of Voortrekker settlement in Natal and the central high veld was threatened by influxes of Nguni and Sotho peoples, who were returning to what they regarded as their homes.

In the high veld environment there were other crucial factors. Whereas most of Natal was healthy for man and beast, on the high veld nature set limits to the territory where Voortrekkers could settle and practise their traditional pastoral economy. In the west the high veld merged into the barren Kalahari desert. In the north the Limpopo valley and in the east the low veld were infested with the tsetse fly, which was fatal to cattle, sheep, and horses (p. 132 and map, p. 291), and the malarial anopheles mosquito, which was fatal to human beings who had not acquired immunity by exposure over several generations. That was why the Voortrekkers could not found viable settlements in the north and the east of the modern Transvaal; and that was why they could not open up regular communications with Delagoa Bay, Inhambane, or Sofala, and thereby free themselves from dependence on British-controlled trade routes.[1]

The British Colonial officials could have seriously impeded the Great Trek in its early stages if they had chosen to do so. It was unlawful for British subjects to leave the Cape Colony without permission, to take apprentices with them against their will, or to remove large quantities of gunpowder without licence. Since nearly all the Voortrekkers crossed the Orange river with their wagons by one of six or seven drifts near the later Aliwal North, it would have been a comparatively simple matter to man the drifts and stem the exodus. This was not done. Before they left their Colonial homes the Voortrekkers had no difficulty in buying large quantities of powder—or getting others, such as British settlers, to buy powder on their behalf; they then trekked through the colony to the Orange and crossed the river, with their apprentices and other

Republiek, i; H. B. Thom, *Die Lewe van Gert Maritz*; F. A. F. Wichmann, 'Die Wordingsgeskiedenis van die Zuid-Afrikaansche Republiek, 1838–1860', in *AYB*, 1941, ii.

[1] F. J. Potgieter, 'Die Vestiging van die Blanke in Transvaal, 1837–86' in *AYB*, 1958, ii, gives a good account of the natural impediments to Voortrekker settlement in the Transvaal, with maps.

servants, unmolested.¹ Thereafter they were *de facto* free from British control, notwithstanding the Cape of Good Hope Punishment Act, 1836, which made them liable to punishment for crimes committed south of 25° South. The successful escape of the first Voortrekkers encouraged others to follow. So it was that an emigration that started as a tentative trickle became a flood. By the time Britain had second thoughts it was too late. Through her command of the sea, she was able to annex Natal and gradually to make her authority effective there, but on the high veld it was a different matter. Officials might march troops to or across the Orange river; an impetuous governor might even proclaim the annexation of the territory between the Orange and the Vaal; but no British government was prepared to spend enough money to impose order upon the *trekboers* and Voortrekkers, Griquas and Africans, in that area—let alone to follow the ultimate Voortrekker beyond the last horizon of the seemingly limitless Transvaal. So it became simple realism to let the emigrants have their own way in the interior.²

By 1854 the Voortrekkers had apparently attained their objectives. They had taken possession of more than enough land for their needs, and Britain had recognized them to be free and independent people in free and independent states. The only limitations upon their liberty of action were those imposed by their own shortcomings, their environment, and their continued dependence on the trade routes from the British Colonial ports.

The history of the Voortrekkers in Natal has been reviewed in the previous chapter. Here we are concerned with their activities on the high veld.

The first Voortrekkers were two parties, totalling about 100 white men, women, and children and their servants, led by Louis Trichardt and Janse van Rensburg. They left the Colony in 1835 and joined forces near the Vaal river in April 1836. Swinging to the north-east to avoid the Ndebele, the combined trek went to the Strydpoort area, intending to settle in the hinterland of Delagoa Bay, well beyond the clutches of the British. Trichardt then lingered in the Strydpoort while van Rensburg continued northwards to the Soutpansberg and thence down the Limpopo valley. Weakened by tsetse and anopheles, in August 1836 van Rensburg's party was annihilated by Tsonga in the north-east corner of the modern Transvaal. Two years later Trichardt's party

---

[1] C. F. J. Muller, 'Karel Landman op Trek', *Communications of the University of South Africa*, C. 13, describes Voortrekker Landman's departure from the Colony. Thom, Ch. 8, describes the departure of the Maritz trek.

[2] Galbraith; C. F. J. Muller, *Die Britse Owerheid en die Groot Trek*.

reached Delagoa Bay, where its leader and most of the other adults died of fever. The survivors eventually went by sea to Port Natal, where they joined the main body of Voortrekkers.[1]

Effective Voortrekker settlement on the high veld began with the arrival of the treks led by Potgieter and Sarel Cilliers early in 1836. South of the Vaal river Potgieter found a Taung chief named Makwana and 'bought' from him an undefined area of land for twenty-nine head of cattle. Potgieter then led a small detachment of men to the Soutpansberg, where he met Louis Trichardt and discussed the possibility of settling in that area and opening up trade with Delagoa Bay or Inhambane. Meanwhile the rest of his people spread out over the country on either side of the Vaal.

Scouts had reported the intrusion of Voortrekkers to Mzilikazi. The Ndebele King had always welcomed white visitors who recognized his authority and came to him, after due notice, via Moffat's mission at Kuruman. He had recently been visited thus by Dr. Andrew Smith's expedition, as a result of which he had sent a senior Councillor to Cape Town to put his mark to a treaty of friendship with Governor D'Urban (March 1836). But, harassed by frequent attacks from the south by Zulu impis and Coloured commandos, Mzilikazi was fearful of the new intruders from the same direction, who came without notice, with their women and children, cattle and sheep, and behaved as though they intended to stay. In August 1836 he sent two strong patrols towards the Vaal river. One attacked an elephant-hunting expedition led by Stephanus Erasmus, a Colonial *trekboer*. The other attacked a Voortrekker family called Liebenburg near the modern Parys. Arriving back from the Soutpansberg soon after these events, Potgieter immediately ordered his people to form a laager south of the Vaal, between the Wilge and Renoster rivers, at what became known as Vegkop. On 16 October 1836 the laager was attacked by an Ndebele force of about 5,000 men, who captured nearly all Potgieter's sheep and cattle but were unable to penetrate the laager. In this predicament Potgieter's people were assisted by Chief Moroka of the Rolong (pp. 401–3), who sent oxen to draw their wagons to Thaba Nchu, where he gave them food and asylum. In January 1837, as a result of fresh arrivals from the Colony, including a large party under Gert Maritz, the Voortrekkers felt strong enough to take the offensive against the Ndebele. Potgieter and Maritz led a commando of 107 Afrikaners and forty Coloured men, with sixty Rolong to herd captured cattle. They sacked the Ndebele settlement at Mosega, killing 400 people and making off

[1] B. H. Dicke, 'The Northern Transvaal Voortrekkers', in *AYB*, 1941, i, pp. 67–170; Claude Fuller, *Louis Trichardt's Trek across the Drakensberg, 1837–1838*, VRS, 1932; G. S. Preller (ed.), *Dagboek van Louis Trichardt, 1836–1838*; Walker, *Trek*, pp. 107–13.

with 7,000 cattle, most of which had previously belonged to Potgieter's party. The Ndebele then concentrated further north, around Mzilikazi's headquarters at Kapain. There in November 1837 they were attacked by a commando led by Potgieter and Uys. Beaten in a nine days' battle, Mzilikazi fled northwards across the Limpopo with his Ndebele and some of his Sotho followers.[1] After a period of wandering, they carved out a new 'Matabeleland' at the expense of the Shona inhabitants. Mzilikazi died in 1868 and was succeeded by his son Lobengula, who preserved a precarious independence until he was conquered by the forces of the British South Africa Company in the 1890s.

The Voortrekkers—and especially Potgieter's people—considered that the central high veld was theirs by right of conquest from the Ndebele. But their tenure was not unchallenged. After the ejection of the Ndebele, groups of Sotho who had been displaced by the wars percolated back to their homelands, and Sotho kingdoms and chiefdoms which had been confined to the periphery of the high veld by the Ndebele began to expand. Mobilized and concentrated, the Voortrekkers, with their guns, horses, and wagons, had been more than a match for the most powerful kingdoms in southern Africa; but when they then dispersed in small settlements and resumed their farming occupations, they lacked the means to control the growing African population in their midst, let alone the kingdoms and chiefdoms that surrounded them.

Between 1838 and 1843 Natal was the main focus of Voortrekker settlement (pp. 364–73), but several groups of Voortrekkers remained on the high veld: in 'Trans-Orangia' between the Orange and the Vet rivers; in the Winburg district between the Vet and the Vaal; and north of the Vaal in the Potchefstroom district, where Potgieter and his followers settled when they left Natal after the Battle of Italeni in April 1838 (p. 361). Though Potchefstroom and Winburg became recognized as parts of the Natal Republic, the relationship was never a tight one. Directly Natal became a British colony the high veld representatives left the Pietermaritzburg *Volksraad*; and in April 1844 the Potchefstroom-Winburg *Raad* dissociated itself from Natal's act of submission to the British and adopted thirty-three articles as a sort of constitution.[2] By that time most of the Voortrekkers had left Natal and by 1849 nearly all of them were back on the high veld.

North of the Vaal, Voortrekkers founded a number of separate settlements around nuclear sites, which they selected for the availability and

---

[1] On Voortrekker–Ndebele relations see Carel Potgieter and N. H. Theunissen, *Kommandant-Generaal Hendrik Potgieter*, Chs. 6–9; Edwin W. Smith, *The Life and Times of Daniel Lindley (1801–80)*, Ch. 4; Thom, Ch. 10; Walker, *Trek*, Ch. 4. On Voortrekker–Rolong relations see Molema, *Bantu*, pp. 45–46.

[2] *SAAR, Transvaal*, ed. J. H. Breytenbach and H. S. Pretorius, i. 3–10; Walker, pp. 328–31; Wichmann, Chs. 3–4.

quality of their water, timber, pasture, and soil and used as rallying points in case of attack. The first such settlement was Potchefstroom on the Mooi river, founded in 1838 and moved to its present site in 1842. By 1854 daughter settlements had been founded in several other parts of the south-western Transvaal—around the modern Klerksdorp, Heidelberg, Pretoria, Rustenberg, and Zeerust. The first white settlement in the eastern Transvaal was also founded by Potgieter, as a result of his determination to reduce the risk of British intervention by moving beyond the limit of the Cape of Good Hope Punishment Act and developing a trading connexion through a non-British port. In 1844 he visited Delagoa Bay, where he obtained permission from the Portuguese Governor to settle in the hinterland, and met J. A. Smellekamp, the Dutch supercargo, who assured him that Dutch firms would be willing to supply the Voortrekkers through Delagoa Bay. Potgieter then returned to Potchefstroom and persuaded people to trek to what became Andries-Ohrigstad, in the Steelpoort valley on the western slopes of the Drakensberg. The Ohrigstad settlement was not a success. Anopheles and tsetse took a heavy toll of the settlers and their stock, and made it impossible for them to establish a regular trade route eastwards to the coast; Tsonga, Pedi, and Swazi regarded them as unwelcome intruders; and the whites themselves did not pull together, for one faction recognized Potgieter as their leader, and the other, which included Voortrekkers who had been in Natal, accepted the supremacy of a *Volksraad*. For a time there were two rival governments at Ohrigstad and civil war seemed likely; but in 1848 Potgieter trekked further northwards and founded yet another settlement, at Schoemansdal below the Soutpansberg. Since the northern Transvaal was no healthier for man or beast than the eastern Transvaal and the site of the village of Schoemansdal was singularly ill-selected, the new settlement never became a successful farming community and the death rate in the village was extremely high. Nevertheless, many of the Schoemansdalers enjoyed a period of prosperity as hunters of the elephants which abounded in the area. Some of the ivory was carried down to the east coast by African porters employed by Portuguese traders; most of it was bought by colonial *smouse* and taken by wagon to Grahamstown or Pietermaritzburg, and thence to Port Elizabeth or Durban for shipment to England. The Voortrekkers who remained at Ohrigstad abandoned it in 1849–50 and moved to Lydenburg, in a less fever-ridden area higher up the Steelpoort valley.[1] Meanwhile, dramatic events had been taking place south of the Vaal river.

[1] J. B. de Vaal, 'Die Rol van João Albasini in die Geskiedenis van die Transvaal', in *AYB*, 1953, i; Pelzer, op. cit.; Carel Potgieter and N. H. Theunissen, Chs. 12–19; F. J. Potgieter; *SAAR, Transvaal*, i, Ch. 3; Wichmann, Chs. 4–5.

The area between the Orange and the Vaal was an imbroglio, containing elements of every type of society that existed in southern Africa—hunters, pastoralists, and husbandmen; San, Khoikhoi, Sotho, Afrikaner, and British—and many combinations of different material cultures, physical types, and political systems. By the early 1840s there was a great deal of intermingling among the various peoples in the area, and yet there were no structured relationships among them, except that a few people of San, Khoikhoi, and Sotho descent had become incorporated as servants of Afrikaners. Moreover, each group was divided into rival political communities.

Several bands of San hunters still survived in many different localities throughout the area. In the south-east, on either side of the Caledon river, were the rival Sotho states of Moshweshwe, Moletsane, Sekonyela, and Moroka, each of whom had missionary assistance and was trying to restore order and prosperity, after the turmoil of the *Difaqane*, on the basis of cattle-raising and crop-cultivation (pp. 398–403). In the south-west there were the Griqua and Kora peoples, who were predominantly of Khoikhoi origin, but, through long interaction with white people in the Cape Colony, had become infused with caucasian physical stock and influenced by Afrikaner *trekboer* culture. They were, in varying degrees, hunters and gatherers, pastoralists, hoe-cultivators, and gun-carrying predators. The Griqua had settled around Griqua Town, west of the Harts river, at the beginning of the nineteenth century. In the 1820s they had split into two rival communities. One, under Andries Waterboer, had remained at Griqua Town and became known as the West Griqua. The other had moved to Philippolis, under Adam Kok II, and became known as the East Griqua. Kok died in 1835, and in 1837 his younger son, Adam Kok III, became their leader. Both Griqua communities were assisted by members of the London Missionary Society, who tried to persuade them to become settled farmers with western-type political institutions; but the missionaries were ignored by lawless Griqua elements known as Bergenaars, who preferred a nomadic, marauding life and with their guns and horses were a menace to San and Sotho. Most of the Kora lived much like the Bergenaars; some under Taaibosch and Davids, had attached themselves to Wesleyan missionaries and settled on the northern side of the Caledon river.[1]

Afrikaner *trekboers* had begun to move across the Orange river from the Cape Colony in the 1810s as seasonal visitors. From about 1825 onwards some *trekboers* settled permanently north of the Orange. Most of them were in the Philippolis area, where they lived alongside the East Griqua, from whom they rented land on long leases for trifling considerations. In the 1830s some *trekboers* moved eastwards into the

[1] Marais, *Cape Coloured People*, Ch. 2.

Caledon valley, where they began to mingle with Sotho of Moroka and Moshweshwe. When the Voortrekkers passed through the Philippolis area, on their way to Thaba Nchu from the Orange river drifts, some *trekboers* joined them and became absorbed; but the majority remained aloof, continuing to regard themselves as members of the Colonial society and British subjects. After the annexation of Natal in 1843 *trekboers* remained more numerous than Voortrekkers south of the Modder river and Voortrekkers became far more numerous north of it; but the two communities had become mingled with one another, as well as with Griqua and Sotho. They differed profoundly on the question of allegiance to the Colonial authorities, but they had substantially the same attitude towards their non-white neighbours, and a common interest in ignoring the jurisdiction of Adam Kok and encroaching upon the lands claimed by the southern Sotho chiefs.[1]

During the 1840s Britain was progressively sucked into this scene of anarchy. Dr. John Philip, South African superintendent of the London Missionary Society, which served the Griqua chiefs and had close relations through the French missionaries with Moshweshwe and Moletsane, sought to persuade the British authorities that they had a strategic as well as a humanitarian interest in intervening to protect the East Griqua and the southern Sotho, on account of the location of their territories on the land route between the Cape Colony and Natal. Philip visited Kok and Moshweshwe and found them receptive to the idea that they should enter into a treaty relationship with Britain. In September 1842 Governor Napier issued a proclamation warning Afrikaners that they should not intrude upon Griqua or Sotho lands. In October the Voortrekker Jan Mocke, back in Transorangia from Port Natal, where he had vainly tried to stop the deployment of British troops, threatened to proclaim the land north of the Orange river to be a Voortrekker republic. Hearing of this, Judge William Menzies of the Cape Supreme Court, who happened to be on circuit at Colesberg, proceeded to Alleman's Drift on the Orange river, where he proclaimed the annexation of the territory south of 25° South and threatened Mocke's party with the full rigour of the Colonial law.[2]

Governor Napier disavowed Menzies's unauthorized proclamation, but in 1843 he made treaties with Kok and Moshweshwe. These treaties were based on a precedent of 1834, when Governor D'Urban had made a treaty with the West Griqua chief, Andries Waterboer, giving Waterboer a small annual salary in return for the responsibility

[1] J. J. Oberholster, 'Streekopname van die Suidoos-Vrystaat' (unpublished manuscript); van der Merwe, *Noordwaartse Beweging*, Chs. 7–12; van Schoor, Ch. 1.

[2] Galbraith, pp. 197–203; John F. Midgley, 'The Orange River Sovereignty (1848–1854)', in *AYB*, 1949, ii. 17–23; van Schoor, Ch. 1.

for keeping order in his territory along the northern border of the Colony. Kok and Moshweshwe undertook to maintain order in their territories and assist the Colonial authorities to apprehend criminals and fugitives from the Colony. In return Kok received an annual salary of £100, payable in cash or in arms and ammunition, as he preferred; and Moshweshwe received a similar salary of £75. Kok's treaty said nothing about the territorial limits of his authority; but Moshweshwe's treaty described his territory as consisting of all the land between the Orange and the Caledon rivers, plus a belt 'about 25 to 30 miles north of the Caledon', except in the areas near the source of the Caledon and near its junction with the Orange. These treaties did not bring peace. Moshweshwe's treaty evoked opposition from the Wesleyan missionaries with Moroka and Sekonyela, who denied that Moshweshwe was their overlord. Kok's treaty evoked strong opposition from the Afrikaners of both factions, who were not disposed to accept Kok's jurisdiction over them. There followed several incidents between Afrikaners and Griqua, leading to open fighting in April 1845. Governor Maitland then sent troops to disperse the Afrikaner commando and he himself went to Griqua territory, where he imposed a settlement, designed to preserve for the Griqua a limited sector of land and to allow Afrikaners long-term occupation of the rest of the disputed territory. Transorangia south of a line which ran in part along the lower Riet river was designated 'inalienable'. Afrikaners were to leave that area when their existing leases expired and there were to be no more leases there. The territory north of the line was 'alienable': Afrikaners could continue to lease land in it. A British 'resident' was to be stationed in the northern sector to determine litigation between Afrikaners and Griqua and to receive all payments of rent from Afrikaners, half of which would go towards his own expenses, the other half to Adam Kok. However, since the existing leases in the inalienable sector had a long time to run, Maitland's settlement was not followed by any immediate transfers of population: Afrikaners and Griqua remained intermingled in the inalienable as well as the alienable territory. Moreover the British resident was given no means to impose his authority.[1]

The culmination of the steps towards British involvement in the area is a classic example of the capacity of a nineteenth-century colonial official to commit the British government to responsibilities which it was not prepared to fulfil. Sir Harry Smith, who arrived in Cape Town as Governor and High Commissioner in December 1847, was fully aware that Britain would not spend enough money for the effective administration of new territories in South Africa. Nevertheless, his service as a military officer during the D'Urban régime in South Africa

[1] Galbraith, pp. 203-9; Midgley, pp. 23-34; van Schoor, Ch. 2.

and during a period of British expansion in India, his unquestioning assumption of the superiority of British culture and institutions, his conceit in his own capacity to influence people, and his proneness to oversimplify complex problems, made him a natural expansionist. In two months and two days after his arrival in Cape Town he had extended the frontiers of the Cape Colony to the Orange river in the arid north-west (between Ramah and the Atlantic Ocean), and to the Keiskamma river and the Kraai river basin in the east; and he had annexed two contiguous areas as separate British colonies—British Kaffraria between the Keiskamma and the Kei, and what became known as the Orange River Sovereignty between the Orange and the Vaal. The Colonial Secretary, Earl Grey, accepted these *faits accomplis* with varying degrees of reluctance, on Smith's assurance that they would lead to the pacification of southern Africa and that the costs of the administration of the new colonies would be met from local taxation.[1]

The Orange River Sovereignty might have been a success if it had provided stability, an equitable administration, and a basis for material prosperity; but from the first this hope was jeopardized by lack of funds. The revenue was derived mainly from land taxes and trading licences, imposed on a white farming community which was only just beginning to become established in a new terrain, and it never exceeded £12,000 a year. Since Britain provided no grant-in-aid, this meant that the public service of the entire Sovereignty consisted of no more full-time employees than the Resident (Major Henry Warden), four magistrates in charge of districts, five clerks, eight constables, a Dutch Reformed minister, and four school-masters; and most of them were deficient in training and ability.[2]

The majority of the whites were almost certainly opposed to Smith's proclamation. On his way through the territory to Natal in January 1848 Smith held meetings and received deputations. Most of the white people who participated were *trekboers* ('loyalists') and Smith jumped to the conclusion that the whites were overwhelmingly in favour of annexation. He even seems to have hoped that the Transvaal Voortrekkers, too, would favour British control. Smith then crossed the Drakensberg and on the banks of the Tukela river he met Pretorius and his followers, who had finally abandoned their farms in Natal and were trekking to settle on the high veld. There are conflicting accounts of what then transpired, but it seems probable that, after Smith had

---

[1] C. W. de Kiewiet, *British Colonial Policy and the South African Republics, 1848–1872*, Chs. 2–5; Galbraith, Chs. 10–11; Muller, *Britse Owerheid*, Ch. 5; H. G. W. Smith, *The Autobiography of Sir Harry Smith*, ed. G. C. Moore Smith, Ch. 48; van Jaarsveld, *Eenheidstrewe*, Ch. 3.

[2] Midgley, pp. 188–96, 279–80. On Warden see B. J. Barnard, ''n Lewensbeskrywing van Majoor Henry Douglas Warden', in *AYB*, 1948, i. 307–485.

revealed what was in his mind, he gave Pretorius to understand that he would not annex any high veld territory until Pretorius had had time to sound out Afrikaner opinion and report back to him. Nevertheless Smith annexed the Sovereignty without further ado. An indignant Pretorius then toured the high veld settlements from Winburg to the Soutpansberg, stirring up opposition. He also put out feelers to Moshweshwe, Mpande, and the Portuguese Governor at Delagoa Bay. The African rulers, the Portuguese Governor, and the Afrikaner loyalists would have nothing to do with him; and not many Voortrekkers were prepared to risk their lives in an armed rising under Pretorius's leadership. By remaining under British rule in Natal for four years Pretorius had forfeited the confidence of many high veld republicans, and Potgieter and his people had no wish to compromise their own position in the Transvaal by challenging British authority further south. Nevertheless, some Winburg republicans invited Pretorius to come to the Sovereignty, which he did in July; and his force grew to about 1,200 men as he swept through the country and drove the British officials across the Orange river. But when Smith appeared from the Cape Colony with 800 regulars, many of Pretorius's men melted away; on 29 August 1848 Smith defeated Pretorius at Boomplaats, and Pretorius fled across the Vaal. Smith then declared the property of rebels forfeit, set up a commission to sell the confiscated land and exact fines, and returned to the Cape, leaving a detachment of 250 men behind him in a fort at Bloemfontein.[1]

It was not long before Warden began to become involved in disastrous quarrels with Africans. In September 1848 Smith interviewed the Sotho, Griqua, and Kora chiefs and told them that, though they had become British subjects, the Government would not interfere in their internal affairs or restrict their landholdings. Nevertheless, Smith instructed Warden to establish boundaries between the different communities in the Caledon river area on the basis of occupation, and explicitly told him that he was to act on the principle that, wherever white and non-white landholdings overlapped, no white farmer should be disturbed.[2] In addition, Warden himself favoured the lesser chiefs where their claims conflicted with those of Moshweshwe, because he was influenced by the Wesleyan missionaries and also because he thought it sound policy to create counterpoises to the strongest Sotho ruler. The result was that the 'Warden Line', which was promulgated in December 1849, greatly reduced the area which Governor Napier, in

[1] Duvenage, Ch. 2; Midgley, Chs. 2–4; van Jaarsveld, *Eenheidstrewe*, Ch. 3; van Schoor, Chs. 4–9; Wichmann, Ch. 6.
[2] Richard Southey (Sir Harry Smith's secretary) to Henry Warden, 12 Apr. 1849: Orange River Sovereignty, S.C. 3/1, Orange Free State Archives.

1843, had accepted as coming under Moshweshwe's control. A triangle of land seventy miles long between the Orange and the lower Caledon was recognized as falling within the white area; and nearly all the land north of the Caledon was recognized as belonging either to whites or to one of the lesser Sotho or Kora chiefs. The Warden Line was a serious setback for Moshweshwe. It deprived him of authority over a great deal of arable land which he had had reason to regard as part of Lesotho. Also, in giving independent recognition to the lesser chiefs, it arrested the process of state-building on which he had been engaged since the *Difaqane* wars. Under duress, Moshweshwe gave his formal consent to the Line; but his brothers and sons strongly disapproved of this, and they proceeded to ignore the Line, with Moshweshwe's tacit support. Consequently Warden found that it was one thing to draw a Line on a map; another to force everyone into his prescribed area. The promulgation of the Line was followed by contests for occupation of land and by a wave of cattle-rustling. In general, Moshweshwe's people acted in concert with Moletsane's Taung against Afrikaners, Moroka's Rolong, Sekonyela's Tlokwa, and Kora and Griqua bands led by Taaibosch and Davids. Losing patience, Warden eventually abandoned all pretence of impartiality and, mustering a composite force of whites, Africans, and Coloured people, he attacked Moletsane's villages on Viervoet mountain; but Moshweshwe's Sotho came to the aid of their allies and inflicted a crushing defeat on Warden (30 June 1851). Viervoet was followed by a collapse of authority throughout the Winburg district. Afrikaners refused to turn out for burgher service; and some of them tried to come to terms with Moshweshwe and Moletsane, or to obtain help from their kinsfolk across the Vaal river.[1]

Warden had been particularly foolish in coming to blows with Moshweshwe at that time, because since December 1850 nearly all the British troops in South Africa had been heavily engaged in warfare on the eastern frontier of the Cape Colony. The outbreak and course of this long war, as well as the breakdown of law and order in much of the Orange River Sovereignty, caused the British Government to lose confidence in Smith and his expansionist policies. In the middle of 1851 Earl Grey appointed two officers with South African experience— William S. Hogge and C. Mostyn Owen—as assistants to the High Commissioner, with general, but undefined, responsibilities in the British territories beyond the Cape Colony; and since Smith was committed to directing the campaign on the eastern frontier, he sent the assistant commissioners to the Sovereignty soon after they reached South Africa and gave them virtually a free hand there. By the time they reached Bloemfontein, Warden had been humbled at Viervoet

[1] Midgley, Chs. 6, 7, 9; *Bas. Rec.* i; Tylden, *Basuto*, pp. 35-48; van Schoor, Chs. 10-13.

and the territory was full of rumours of Sotho invasion and Afrikaner intrigue. Pretorius had written to Warden, saying that he had been asked by Moshweshwe and some of the Afrikaner inhabitants to intervene in the Sovereignty, and that he had been appointed head of a Transvaal delegation to make a treaty with the British Government. Hogge and Owen jumped at this opportunity of removing the danger of Transvaal intervention in the Sovereignty by giving the Transvaalers a formal recognition of their independence.[1]

In presenting himself as the leader of a delegation which could speak with authority for the Transvaal Voortrekkers, Pretorius had shown great skill. Their dispersal in widely separated settlements, the tensions at Ohrigstad between Potgieter and the *Volksraad* party, and the personal rivalry between Potgieter and Pretorius had in fact made unity unattainable. In 1849 a meeting at Derdepoort, attended by Pretorius (who had settled near the modern Pretoria) and by members of the Ohrigstad *Volksraad* party, but not by Potgieter, decided to establish a united government for all Transvaalers, under a representative *Volksraad*. But although the *Volksraad* met at different places three times a year, the only way to get a quorum was by co-opting members of the local community, so that each session was dominated by the population of the region where it met. There was no head of State and, after January 1851, there were four men with the title Commandant-general, one for each of four regions: Andries Pretorius for Magaliesberg and Mooi River, A. H. Potgieter for the Soutpansberg, W. F. Joubert for Lydenburg, and J. A. Enslin for Marico. When the Winburg republicans and Moshweshwe got in touch with him in 1851, Pretorius convened a meeting of the *Krygsraad* (war council) and of the general public at Magaliesberg, in his own region, and the meeting authorized him to try to come to an understanding with Britain. A similar meeting held at Rustenburg in December appointed a delegation of fifteen members, headed by Pretorius, and specified its powers; and these decisions were confirmed by a meeting of the *Volksraad* (which included locally co-opted members) held at Potchefstroom on 10 January 1852. Thus Pretorius and his fellow delegates were able to meet Commissioners Hogge and Owen with some sort of authority to act in the name of all Transvaal Afrikaners, even though Potgieter had stood aloof from all the proceedings.[2]

The negotiations at the Sand river proceeded without a hitch and on the second day, 17 January 1852, Hogge and Owen signed an agreement with Pretorius and his fellow delegates. The Commissioners guaranteed to the Transvaal Afrikaners 'the right to manage their own

[1] De Kiewiet, Chs. 4–5; Galbraith, pp. 242–58.
[2] *SAAR, Transvaal*, i–ii; Wichmann, Chs. 6–7.

affairs and to govern themselves according to their own laws, without any interference on the part of the British government'. More than that; they also disclaimed 'all alliances . . . with . . . the coloured nations to the north of the Vaal River', and they committed the British Government to a partisan control of the arms trade in South Africa: 'It is agreed that no objection shall be made by any British authority against the emigrant Boers purchasing their supplies of ammunition in any of the British Colonies and Possessions of South Africa, it being mutually understood that all trade in ammunition with the native tribes is prohibited both by the British Government and the emigrant farmers on both sides of the Vaal River.' In return, the Transvaalers undertook that 'this system of non-interference [should be] binding upon both parties' and that slavery would not be permitted or practised in the Transvaal.[1]

By the time of the Sand River Convention Earl Grey and Prime Minister Lord Russell had reached the conclusion that Smith should be recalled and the Orange River Sovereignty should be disannexed. Hogge and Owen also favoured disannexation, but proposed first to see whether conditions in the Sovereignty would become stable following the removal of the threat of Transvaal intervention. In fact the situation in the Sovereignty did not improve. Relations between the different communities continued to be chaotic; but legal considerations and changes of office-holders in England and South Africa caused delays before action was taken. The Derby Ministry, with Sir John Pakington as Colonial Secretary, succeeded the Russell Ministry in February 1852, and was in turn followed by the Aberdeen Ministry in December that year; while in March Sir George Cathcart replaced Smith as High Commissioner and Henry Green replaced Warden as Resident. Cathcart's first task as Governor was to terminate the war on the eastern frontier. By the time that was done he had reached the conclusion that the Sovereignty should be abandoned; but the information he had received from Bloemfontein persuaded him that the prestige of British arms should first be restored by teaching Moshweshwe a lesson, and he assumed that this would be a simple matter. Accordingly, in December 1852 Cathcart led a force of 2,000 infantry and 500 cavalry to Platberg-on-Caledon, where he interviewed Moshweshwe and ordered him to hand over 10,000 head of cattle and 1,000 horses within three days. Moshweshwe did hand over 3,500 head of cattle in the allotted period, but his request for more time to collect the remainder was then rejected, and on 20 December Cathcart's force crossed the Caledon in

---

[1] Text of the Sand River Convention, in G. W. Eybers, *Select Constitutional Documents Illustrating South African History*, pp. 358–9; commentaries in de Kiewiet, pp. 63–65, Galbraith, pp. 256–60, and Wichmann, pp. 110–17.

three columns, two of which proceeded to round up cattle on Berea mountain, where they received a serious check from Sotho horsemen and infantry. That night, on Thaba Bosiu, Moshweshwe dictated a letter to Cathcart, who had made his camp near the foot of the mountain:[1]

> Your Excellency,—This day you have fought against my people, and taken much cattle. As the object for which you have come is to have a compensation for the Boers, I beg you will be satisfied with what you have taken. I entreat peace from you,—you have shown your power,—you have chastised,—let it be enough I pray you; and let me no longer be considered an enemy to the Queen. I will try all I can to keep my people in order for the future.

The next day Cathcart withdrew with his force.[2]

Back in the Cape Colony Cathcart advised the new Colonial Secretary, the Duke of Newcastle, that the Sovereignty could not be maintained without a permanent garrison of 2,000 men. This clinched the fate of the Sovereignty. Newcastle appointed Sir George Clerk as Special Commissioner to prepare the inhabitants for abandonment. When Moshweshwe learned that the British were going to withdraw, he prepared for the struggle which he foresaw with his Afrikaner neighbours by delivering the *coup de grâce* to Sekonyela's Tlokwa and their Kora and Griqua allies, who had been a thorn in his flesh so long as they had been encouraged by the Sovereignty Government. He drove them from their strongholds and dispersed them, with the result that virtually all the southern Sotho who remained in the Caledon river area came directly or indirectly under his control, with the exception of Moroka's Rolong at Thaba Nchu. Clerk devoted most of his time and energy to the white inhabitants of the Sovereignty. He was placed in the anomalous position of having to cold-shoulder the loyalists, composed of British traders and Afrikaners of *trekboer* origin, and to encourage the republicans to produce leaders who were willing to treat with him and assume the responsibility for taking over the government of the country. He had the white inhabitants elect delegates, whom he dismissed when they insisted that conditions should be fulfilled before abandonment; and by means which are not clear he constituted another group of 'representatives', with whom he signed what became known as the Bloemfontein Convention on 23 February 1854.[3]

---

[1] *Bas. Rec.* i. 627.

[2] *Bas. Rec.* i; de Kiewiet, pp. 65–69; Galbraith, pp. 260–7; Midgley, Chs. 12–14; Tylden, *Basuto*, pp. 48–63.

[3] *Bas. Rec.* ii. 51–100; W. W. Collins, *Free Statia: Reminiscences of a Lifetime in the Orange Free State*, Chs. 3–4; de Kiewiet, Ch. 6; Galbraith, pp. 267–73; Midgley, Chs. 15–18; J. M. Orpen, *Reminiscences of Life in South Africa from 1846 to the Present Day*, Chs. 36–41; SAAR, *Orange Free State*, i, ed. W. B. van der Vyver and J. H. Breytenbach, pp. 3–15; Tylden, pp. 63–65; van Schoor, Chs. 16–17.

The Bloemfontein Convention released the inhabitants of 'the Orange River Territory' from their allegiance to the Crown and transferred the government to the representatives who signed the document. It declared that the British Government had no alliances with 'any native Chiefs or tribes' north of the Orange River, except Adam Kok, and that 'Her Majesty's Government has no wish or intention to enter hereafter into any treaties which may be injurious or prejudicial to the interests of the Orange River Government'. It also said that the treaty with Kok would be amended 'to remove all restrictions preventing Griquas from selling their lands', and that the new Government would be able to buy ammunition in British territories and would not permit slavery or the slave trade.[1]

This Convention was in many ways a remarkable document. A feature besides the irregularities of its origin was that it said nothing about the boundaries of the new State. All the parties understood that the new State would not include the territories of Moshweshwe and his ally, Moletsane; but while Clerk and the other signatories regarded the Warden Line as forming the boundary between them, Moshweshwe assumed that the situation reverted to what it had been before the annexation—that is to say, to the Napier Line of 1843. In his last few days north of the Orange river Clerk completed his business by browbeating Kok into accepting the abrogation of his treaty. Since the East Griqua had depended on the British presence for the preservation of their land holdings, this decision hastened the disintegration of the East Griqua community in Transorangia.[2] As for Moshweshwe, he visited Bloemfontein to try to persuade Clerk to settle the boundary question before he left, but Clerk evaded the issue, merely suggesting that land disputes between Afrikaners and Sotho should be settled by arbitration.[3] Thus Clerk carried out his instructions to eliminate British commitments beyond the Orange river; but in so doing he treated all parties most shabbily, paving the way for the collapse of the East Griqua community and for a collision between the whites and the southern Sotho.

The British policy of trying to control the Voortrekkers, which had started with the Cape of Good Hope Punishment Act and culminated with the annexation of the Orange River Sovereignty, had failed. It had failed because laws enacted by the Parliament at Westminster and annexations proclaimed by a peripatetic high commissioner could not be translated into a systematic power structure without a financial

---

[1] Text of the Bloemfontein Convention in Eybers, pp. 282-5.
[2] De Kiewiet, pp. 82-83; Midgley, pp. 563-7; Orpen, pp. 193-5.
[3] *Bas. Rec.* ii. 99-105, iii. 93-96; de Kiewiet, p. 82; Midgley, p. 571; Orpen, pp. 181-8; Tylden, *Basuto*, p. 67.

commitment which no British government was willing to make. In the process of failure the pendulum had swung right over, from a treaty system which was designed to protect Africans and other non-white people from disruption by turbulent British subjects, to a convention system which amounted to a British alliance with independent white communities, who were assured the right to acquire ammunition supplies, against their non-white neighbours, who were denied that right.

By 1854 both A. H. Potgieter and Andries Pretorius had died. Between them they, more than any other individuals, had secured the primary political objective of the Voortrekkers—Potgieter by his steadfast refusal to have any dealings with the British, Pretorius by his skill in seizing the opportunities which were created by the collapse of British policy in the Sovereignty. The Voortrekkers had become 'free and independent', but they were poor, scattered, disunited, politically inexperienced, and virtually surrounded by Africans.

3. Afrikaner Republics and African States, 1854–70

After the British withdrawal, Afrikaners and Africans were left jostling one another in innumerable sectors in the area between the Orange and the Limpopo. With the advantage of interior lines, the Afrikaners had the better opportunity for concerted action. Nevertheless, the great distances between their main pockets of settlement, their persistent internal antagonisms, and intermittent British diplomatic interference made it extremely difficult for the independent Afrikaners to co-operate with one another. Those in the former Orange River Sovereignty held together, but it was not until 1860 that all the Transvaalers accepted a Constitution, and they had scarcely done so when they fell apart again in civil warfare (1860–4); while all efforts to combine the Orange Free State and the South African Republic came to nothing.

These divisions within independent Afrikanerdom helped the Africans to preserve the integrity of their own states. The Pedi chiefdom in the eastern Transvaal and several of the Tswana chiefdoms in the west held their own against Afrikaner expansion. The Venda chiefdoms in the north, assisted by the tsetse fly and the anopheles mosquito, actually reversed the flow of Afrikaner settlement (1867). In the south, Moshweshwe's southern Sotho kingdom defeated the Orange Free State in a brief war in 1858 and was only conquered in 1865–8 in a long and mutually exhausting conflict.

It was not merely a confrontation of two societies along a series of shifting boundaries. Each society changed its own character by absorbing aliens. The Afrikaner republics incorporated considerable numbers of Africans as unfree labourers, and the African chiefdoms admitted Colonial hunters and traders and European missionaries. The Afrikaner republics were greatly assisted by the arms clauses of the Conventions. While Afrikaners could openly acquire arms and ammunition from the British Colonies, Africans could only obtain them clandestinely. Both sides were well aware of the importance of arms and ammunition. African rulers did everything possible to accumulate them and the Afrikaner governments tried their best to prevent it. The one president who ignored the embargo, Josias Hoffman of the Orange Free State, was forcibly dismissed (1855). Missionaries such as David Livingstone, who were believed to trade arms to Africans, were ejected or their property was looted. Actions like these estranged many of the missionaries and gave rise to a series of sweeping charges that the republics were enslaving and ill-treating Africans.

For several years the British Government remained unmoved by these complaints, and in the late 1850s it rejected a plea by High Commissioner Sir George Grey for the reannexation of the Orange Free State as part of a British South African federation; but by 1866 the officials in the Colonial Office were regretting the non-intervention policy embodied in the Conventions, and in 1868 Britain annexed Basutoland in response to repeated requests from Moshweshwe for protection from the victorious Orange Free State.

Until gold and diamonds were discovered, the white population of the Afrikaner republics remained meagre and thinly spread. It probably numbered no more than 45,000 in 1870, at a time when the Cape Colony had nearly 200,000 white inhabitants.[1] Moreover, lacking local markets and separated from the Colonial towns by great distances, the republican Afrikaners remained essentially *trekboers*, occupying vast areas of land without improving it, living on their herds and flocks, and producing very little for exchange. Though large tracts passed into the hands of absentee speculators, land was still available for young Afrikaners in the Transvaal until after 1870, so that there was no necessity for them to modify the extensive farming methods of their ancestors. Some of the less successful attached themselves to relatives; but that had always happened, and there were still no great differences in living

---

[1] According to census returns, the Cape Colony had a white population of 181,582 in 1865 and 236,783 in 1875 (C. G. W. Schumann, *Structural Changes and Business Cycles in South Africa, 1806–1936*, p. 38). From an incomplete census it has been estimated that the Transvaal white population was about 30,000 in 1873 (F. J. Potgieter, 'Die Vestiging van die Blanke in Transvaal (1837–1886)', in *AYB*, 1958, ii. 107). J. W. Silver estimated that the Orange Free State had a white population of 13,000 several years before 1875, but some other estimates are considerably higher (Schoeman, pp. 38–39).

standards between landowner and *bijwoner*. They lived in the same sorts of houses, wore the same sorts of clothes, and ate the same sorts of food.[1]

Such trade as there was was conducted by foreigners, mainly of British or Jewish origin, who worked in association with Colonial firms. The travelling *smous* gradually gave way to the village shopkeeper, who allowed extensive credit to most of his customers and expected to be paid once a year, usually from the wool clip or in cattle. Paper money was issued by the governments of both the republics, but it depreciated in value. Other services, too, were performed by non-Afrikaners. Both republics employed *predikants*, teachers, and government secretaries from Europe. The only newspapers in the republics—the Bloemfontein *Friend* (1850) and the *Transvaal Argus* (Potchefstroom, 1867)—were owned and operated by English-speaking people. The republican Afrikaners themselves remained an undifferentiated community of pastoral farmers, with scarcely any distinctions of wealth, occupation, or class.

The absence of a money economy placed serious limitations on the governments of the republics. Chronically short of funds, they could employ only a minute number of full-time officials, whose salaries were often in arrears. Local administration depended on the services of unpaid or poorly paid, part-time officials, drawn from the farming community. It was not possible to make roads or build bridges, and the construction of a railway through the fever-ridden low veld to the east coast, which would have been the only way of breaking out of the British Colonial trading network, was beyond the bounds of practicability. Nor was it possible to provide more than the sketchiest public services. There was a salaried *predikant* as well as a *landdrost* in each district, but education remained largely a matter of transmitting a smattering of the three Rs in the family from generation to generation, supplemented, perhaps, by an occasional visit from a travelling teacher.[2]

In all these respects there were differences between conditions in the south and the north. The Orange Free State took over the administrative apparatus of the Sovereignty, such as it was, and came within the range of the expanding market economy of the Cape Colony and Natal. The quality of stock was improved, some wool was produced for export, banks were founded in the 1860s, there were elementary schools of sorts in some of the villages and a high school at Bloemfontein. Most of

---

[1] On economic conditions in the Republics see Arndt, pp. 70–121, 302–59; S. P. du T. Viljoen, 'Die Boerestate tot 1870', in *Geskiedenis van Suid-Afrika*, ii. 212–39.

[2] On education in the Republics, see J. de W. Keyter, 'Die Opvoedingsideaal en Opvoedingstrewe van die Afrikaner', in C. M. van den Heever and P. de V. Pienaar, *Kultuurgeskiedenis van die Afrikaner*, ii. 293–361; E. G. Malherbe, *Education in South Africa, 1652–1922*; G. S. Nienaber, 'Die Afrikaanse Kultuurstryd tot 1870', in *Geskiedenis van Suid-Afrika*, ii. 611–33.

the Transvaal remained a pure frontier area. The country was quite devoid of schools and banks, and the primitive quality of its public service is shown by the fact that as late as 1867 a *Volksraad* commission found that in the preceding year the Treasurer of the South African Republic had kept no books and the only documents he had were hopelessly confused.

The career of Marthinus Wessels Pretorius, son and political heir of Andries Pretorius, was the central thread in white politics on the high veld throughout this period. His objective was that of his father. The achievements of the Voortrekkers were to be consummated by the fusion of all the white people north of the Orange river into a single republic, which was to be made absolutely independent of Britain in all respects.[1]

The economic factors which have been mentioned above were prodigious obstacles to the realization of this objective. There were also psychological obstacles. The freedom the republican Afrikaner believed in and was prepared to fight for was first and foremost the freedom of the family to do as it willed in its own domain; secondly, the freedom of the regional group to regulate its own communal affairs in its own way; and only thirdly and tenuously did it encompass the interests of a larger community—let alone the entire community of independent Afrikaners. African chiefs exploited these weaknesses; and British high commissioners could at any time exert pressure by manipulating the British elements among the white population, or by threatening to cut off the supply of arms and ammunition to the republics. Moreover, M. W. Pretorius's own talents were not commensurate with his ambitions. Too often he took short cuts which had the opposite effects to those he desired.

By the mid 1850s there were three groups of Afrikaners north of the Vaal river: Pretorius's own people, who lived in the Potchefstroom area in the south-west and called their state the South African Republic; the Soutpansbergers in the north who were followers of Stephanus Schoeman, the political heir of A. H. Potgieter; and the Lydenburgers in the east, who had previously formed the anti-Potgieter party at Ohrigstad. There was, nevertheless, one common institution—a *Volksraad*, which met at various places, was normally attended merely by the representatives of the region where it happened to be sitting, and was liable to be overawed by the general public of that region.

In 1853, as a step towards ecclesiastical autonomy, Pretorius encouraged the Potchefstroom congregation to break away from the Cape Colonial Synod of the Dutch Reformed Church (*Nederduitse Gereformeerde Kerk*) and found what became the independent *Nederduits Hervormde Kerk*, served by *predikants* from the Netherlands; but this action

[1] Van Jaarsveld, *Eenheidstrewe*.

precipitated an ecclesiastical schism, for the Lydenburgers, refusing to follow the Potchefstroom lead, remained associated with the Cape Synod. A further split took place in 1859, in Pretorius's own south-western District at Rustenburg, where the *Gereformeerde Kerk van Suid-Afrika* (the 'Dopper' Church) was founded by Fundamentalists who objected to the singing of hymns in church.[1]

In spite of these setbacks, Pretorius proceeded with the work of political amalgamation. At a *Volksraad* meeting held at Pienaar's river in the south-western region in September 1855 a drafting committee was appointed, consisting of Jacobus Stuart, a Hollander, Paul Kruger, a young Afrikaner of great strength of character who was making a reputation as a commando leader, and seven others. The committee, acting largely on the advice of Stuart, prepared a long constitutional document, which was considered by the *Volksraad* and such members of the general public as were present at a meeting at Potchefstroom in November 1855. The draft was accepted with the proviso that every burgher was to be able to lodge his criticisms of it within twelve months. In addition, Pretorius was 'provisionally' elected President.

The south-western Transvaalers were generally content with this Constitution, which became operative in their region. Not so the Soutpansbergers and Lydenburgers. Although Schoeman had taken part in the Potchefstroom meeting he repudiated its decisions and carried his people with him; while the Lydenburgers, who had boycotted the Potchefstroom meeting, acted completely independently from the other Transvaalers.

Between December 1856 and January 1857 a committee met at Potchefstroom and made amendments to the Constitution. At the *Volksraad* meeting that followed, the amended document was treated as the law of the land and Pretorius took the oath as provisional President of the Republic. But Schoeman incited his people to oppose Pretorius and the two regions drifted into a state of warfare. In January 1858 fifty supporters of Schoeman assembled under arms at Rustenburg, where it had been arranged that a 'court' would decide upon the questions at issue. Fighting was narrowly averted and a reconciliation took place. A committee of representatives of both parties met and, taking the existing Constitution of the south-western Transvaal as a basis, made several amendments to meet the wishes of the Soutpansbergers. The revised document was then considered by a specially convened *Volksraad*, which accepted it unanimously on 16 February 1858, and administered the prescribed oaths to Pretorius as President and Schoeman as Commandant-general. When Lydenburg joined the South African

[1] On the Dutch Reformed Churches in the Republics, see the chapters by G. B. A. Gerdener, S. P. Engelbrecht, and S. du Toit in *Kultuurgeskiedenis van die Afrikaner*, ii. 188–292.

Republic in 1860, all the Transvaal Voortrekker communities were united.[1]

Meanwhile, the Orange Free State had come into being south of the Vaal river. The committee which signed the Bloemfontein Convention elected from its members a provisional Government under the presidency of Josias P. Hoffman, a farmer who had played a prominent part in the events leading to the Convention. The provisional Government arranged for the election of a *Volksraad*, which served both as a legislature and as a constituent assembly. One of its members, J. G. Groenendaal, a Hollander who had been a schoolmaster in the Sovereignty administration, submitted a draft Constitution, which he had derived in part from the Constitution of the United States of America, of which he happened to have a copy. Other proposals emanated from J. M. Orpen, an Irish immigrant who had been a land surveyor in the Sovereignty, and Adolph Coqui, a trader of Portuguese origin. The *Volksraad* discussed Groenendaal's draft section by section, when the other members, nearly all of whom were Afrikaners, injected their own ideas. On 10 April 1854 the *Volksraad* promulgated a Constitution,[2] which was subsequently amplified by ordinary laws and proclamations.[3]

The resultant constitutional system of the Orange Free State was an amalgam of the Cape Colonial system of local administration, the legislative system which had existed in the Republic of Natalia, and several ingredients taken over from the United States Constitution, with, perhaps, some infusions from the Netherlands and France. The Orange Free State was a unitary republic, divided into Districts and Wards. Dutch was the sole official language. All white people who had lived in the republic for at least six months were citizens, and the franchise was open to male citizens who had registered for military service. The legislature was a uni-cameral *Volksraad*, whose members were elected in single-member constituencies. Executive power was in the hands of a President, directly elected for five years, and an Executive Council, consisting of some officials and some *Volksraad* nominees.

[1] On the making of the South African Republic see J. S. du Plessis, 'Die Ontstaan en Ontwikkeling van die amp van die Staatspresident in die Zuid-Afrikaansche Republiek', in *AYB*, 1955, i, Chs. 3–5; *SAAR, Transvaal*, iii; L. M. Thompson, 'Constitutionalism in the South African Republics', in *Butterworths South African Law Review*, 1954, pp. 50–72; Wichmann; A. Wypkema, *De invloed van Nederland op ontstaan en ontwikkeling van de staatsinstellingen der Z. A. Republiek tot 1881.*

[2] On the making of the Orange Free State Constitution see J. H. Malan, *Die Opkoms van 'n Republiek*; Orpen, pp. 198–207; *SAAR, O.F.S.*, i. 31–47; G. D. Scholtz, *Die Konstitutie en Staatsinstellings van die Oranje Vrijstaat, 1854–1902*, Amsterdam, 1937, Ch. 1. The text of the Constitution as promulgated in 1854 is in *SAAR, O.F.S.*, i. 194–201, and Scholtz, pp. 186–92.

[3] Notably, laws and proclamations making Dutch the official language (*SAAR, O.F.S.*, i. 303), giving instructions to field-cornets (ibid. i. 304–6), concerning the military system (ibid. i. 312–15, ii. 438–42), concerning presidential elections (ibid. ii. 265–70), and concerning the courts and the legal system (ibid. ii. 272–93, 427–8, 433–4, 455–81).

The President appointed a *landdrost* of each district, subject to *Volksraad* approval. The field-cornet of each Ward and the field-commandant of each District were the elected, unpaid officers of the citizen commandos, and in time of war they elected a Commandant-general. Since the field-cornets were the only office-holders at the ward level, they also had police, administrative, and quasi-judicial duties. The *landdrosts* presided over District courts, assisted in some cases by appointed *heemraden*; and jurisdiction in major cases was vested in a circuit court of three *landdrosts*, with appeal to the Executive Council. The courts applied Roman-Dutch Law, with English rules of procedure as introduced into the Cape Colony by the British, including the jury system in criminal cases. Though the *Volksraad* possessed 'the highest legislative authority', the Constitution debarred it from making laws prohibiting peaceful assembly and petition, asserted that there should be equality before the law without respect of persons, and guaranteed the right of property. It also guaranteed personal freedom and freedom of the press, subject to law. Any amendment of the Constitution required the support of three-quarters of the members of the *Volksraad* in three successive annual sessions. The Constitution was a great advance on previous Voortrekker experiments, such as that in Natal, which had lacked an adequate executive authority. It remained in force, with comparatively few amendments, until the fall of the republic in 1900.[1]

The Transvaal Constitution was quite a different matter. Jacobus Stuart, who was mainly responsible for its drafting, was evidently neither so wise nor so well informed as Groenendaal. While the Orange Free State document, with sixty-two crisp articles, was systematically organized and limited in content to items of constitutional importance, the Transvaal document, with 232 articles, was ambiguous and unsystematic, and included much that was trivial. The institutions it created were similar to those in the Free State. The principal exception was that in the Transvaal the Commandant-general was a directly elected official with a seat on the Executive Council, and the office was filled in peace as well as in war. The Transvaal Constitution did not clearly define the conditions for citizenship, but the central question was settled obliquely in the well-known Article 9: 'The people are not prepared to allow any equality of the non-white with the white inhabi-

---

[1] Commentaries on the Orange Free State Constitution in Scholtz; Thompson; and A. J. H. van der Walt, 'Die Ontwikkeling van Boere-Bestuursinstellinge', in *Geskiedenis van Suid Afrika*, ii. 70–98. The Constitution was amended in 1866, 1879, 1891, 1894, and 1898 (Scholtz, pp. 7–17). Eybers, pp. 288–96, gives the text of the Constitution as amended in 1866, with an English translation. The 1866 amendment changed the amending article: the consent of three-quarters of the members of the *Volksraad* was thereafter required to be given in two successive annual sessions, instead of three as formerly. On all occasions the amending procedure laid down in the Constitution was complied with.

tants, either in Church or State.' The *Volksraad* was declared to be 'the supreme authority and the legislative power of the country' (Article 29), but elsewhere limitations were imposed on the powers of a bare *Volksraad* majority. For example, 'Any matter discussed shall be decided by three-fourths of the votes recorded' (Article 42), while several articles implied that sovereignty remained with the white people ['het volk'], from whom all office-holders exercised a delegated authority. In practice the Transvaal Constitution was not taken very seriously until long after 1870. Legislation was often enacted without a three-quarters majority vote and there was nobody to challenge its validity. In a frontier state there were no lawyers, and political authority depended on physical power rather than constitutional formulas.[1]

The Orange Free State made a shaky start. The provisional Government was confirmed in office in May 1854, when Hoffman was elected President under the Constitution. Hoffman tried to conciliate the white inhabitants who regretted the withdrawal of British control, appointing several of them to administrative offices. He was also conciliatory towards Moshweshwe, whom he already knew and respected. In March 1854 the provisional Government entertained Moshweshwe at a public dinner in Bloemfontein, where the Sotho King made a cordial speech and Hoffman thanked 'our old friend Moshesh'. Hoffman then sent J. M. Orpen to Thaba Bosiu to pave the way for an amicable solution of the boundary problem. On parting, Hoffman promised to grant Moshweshwe's request for a small keg of gunpowder and later he sent it to him. This was too much for many of the Free State burghers. When the *Volksraad* met in February 1855, some members accused Hoffman of treason for giving gunpowder to Moshweshwe and, failing to get the three-quarters majority constitutionally necessary for impeachment, they seized the Bloemfontein fort and trained its guns on the presidential house; whereupon Hoffman resigned.[2] Hoffman's successor was Jacobus N. Boshof, who had been Secretary to the Natal Republic and had continued to live in Natal after the British annexation. He, too, looked to the Cape Colony rather than the anarchic Transvaal for assistance.

In February 1857 Pretorius made a clumsy bid for power in the Orange Free State, negotiating with Moshweshwe and visiting Bloemfontein to inform the *Volksraad* that he had inherited from his father a personal right to authority over all the land between the Orange and the Vaal. When the Bloemfontein *Volksraad* rejected his claim, he

[1] The text of the S. A. R. Constitution as adopted in February 1858 is in Eybers, pp. 362–410 (with English translation), and *SAAR, Transvaal*, iii. 496–525. Commentaries are in du Plessis, Ch. 5; Thompson, op. cit.; van der Walt, *Geskiedenis*, ii. 70–98; E. F. W. Gey van Pittius, *Staatsopvattings van die Voortrekkers en die Boere*; Wypkema, op. cit.

[2] *Bas. Rec.* ii; Orpen, Chs. 41–43, 46–51, 57, 61–62; *SAAR, O.F.S.*, i; van Jaarsveld, *Eenheidstrewe*, Ch. 5; Wichmann, Ch. 13.

returned to the Transvaal, leaving behind him a fiery Proclamation denying the legality of the Orange Free State Government. Boshof then made an alliance with Pretorius's Transvaal rival, S. Schoeman, and called up a commando and led it northwards towards the Vaal. Pretorius, in turn, mobilized a commando and came southwards. The two forces confronted one another in the northern Free State, near the Renoster river; but bloodshed was avoided and the leaders signed an agreement recognizing the autonomy of both states (1 June 1857).[1]

High Commissioner Sir George Grey had mediated between the Orange Free State and the southern Sotho at Boshof's request in October 1855, when both parties agreed to accept the Warden Line as their boundary; but the situation remained turbulent and some of the Sotho refused to withdraw within the Line. In March 1858 Boshof declared war. Commandos invaded Lesotho from the north and the south and converged on Thaba Bosiu. There they faltered, while armed and mounted Sotho bands raided Afrikaner farms in their rear. Burgher morale then collapsed and the commandos disbanded, leaving Moshweshwe the victor. Again Grey was invited to mediate. At Aliwal North he patched up an agreement between representatives of the governments of the Orange Free State and the Sotho kingdom, confirming the Warden Line as the boundary in the north and transferring some territory between the Orange and the Caledon to the Sotho (29 September 1858).[2]

In face of these disasters Boshof had tried to get help from the Cape Colony. When that was not forthcoming, he reluctantly turned to Pretorius, who made it clear that the price of his assistance would be the incorporation of the Orange Free State in the South African Republic.[3]

Grey watched every step in this drama with apprehension. Even before the war of 1858 he had reached the conclusion that the Conventions had been a mistake. He reasoned that the division of the white South African communities into separate polities had destroyed their capacity to deal wisely and effectively with the Africans who faced them on innumerable frontiers; and he suspected (probably falsely) that Moshweshwe had been involved in the cattle-killing by the Xhosa on the eastern frontier (p. 259). He was alarmed by the prospect that the Voortrekker communities might unite into a single independent state, fearing that such a state might ultimately become powerful

---

[1] Eileen M. Attree, 'The Closer Union Movements between the Orange Free State, South African Republic and Cape Colony (1838–1863)', in *AYB*, 1949, i, Ch. 3; Collins, Ch. 7; *SAAR, O.F.S.*, ii; van Jaarsveld, *Eenheidstrewe*, Ch. 6; Wichmann, Ch. 13.

[2] *Bas. Rec.* ii; Collins, Ch. 8; J. J. G. Grobbelaar, 'Die Vrystaatse Republiek en die Basoetoe-Vraagstuk', in *AYB*, 1939, ii; Tylden, *Basuto*, Ch. 5; Jean van der Poel, 'Basutoland as a Factor in South African Politics (1852–1870)', in *AYB*, 1941, i, Ch. 1.

[3] Ibid.

enough to threaten the British Colonies, and that its increased pressures on Africans would cause more disturbances on the Colonial frontiers. Grey therefore took it on himself to inform the governments of the republics that, if they united, Britain would consider that the Conventions had ceased to operate, and would assume a free hand in treaty-making and in the arms and ammunition trade north of the Orange river. This threat was effective. In the Transvaal it strengthened the hands of the isolationists. In the Orange Free State it caused many white people to believe that their only salvation lay in some form of reunion with the Cape Colony. This suited Grey admirably. His prescription for South Africa was a federation under the British Crown of all the white states and colonies, including the Orange Free State and, ultimately, the Transvaal. He therefore encouraged the Orange Free State *Volksraad* to adopt a resolution in favour of a closer relationship with the Cape Colony, and he placed the resolution before the Parliament in Cape Town with his blessing.[1]

Grey had counted on being able to persuade the British Government of the wisdom of his prescription; but he failed. All the colonial secretaries who held office during Grey's high commissionership were agreed in maintaining the Convention policy of non-intervention beyond the Orange river, for the same reason that the policy had originally been applied: they were not prepared to face the cost of adding to British territorial responsibilities in South Africa. Indeed, Grey's encouragement of the Bloemfontein *Volksraad* and the Cape Town Parliament to work towards a federation was in direct defiance of orders from London; and he was therefore recalled in June 1859.[2]

With the collapse of Grey's federation scheme, Boshof and the loyalists were discredited in the Orange Free State and opinion veered towards the alternative method of strengthening the state—unification with the South African Republic. Disillusioned, Boshof resigned and Pretorius was elected as his successor. Pretorius intended to use the Free State presidency as an instrument for integrating the two republics; but before he had achieved anything, Transvaal opinion turned against him, for isolationists feared lest the dual presidency should evoke British intervention and imperil the independence of the Transvaal. The Pretoria *Volksraad* told him that he was to choose between the two presidencies (September 1860). Pretorius then resigned from the Transvaal, but instead of confining his attention to the affairs of the Free State he encouraged his Transvaal supporters, who now included his former rival, Stephanus Schoeman, to rebel. A mass meeting at Potchefstroom repudiated the authority of the Transvaal *Volksraad*, declared that Pretorius was still President and Schoeman was his deputy, and

[1] De Kiewiet, Chs. 7–8.   [2] Ibid., Ch. 8.

appointed a committee of five to give effect to these decisions. The *Volksraad* set up a special court to try this revolutionary committee, but Potchefstroom ignored the court's verdict and rival governments claimed

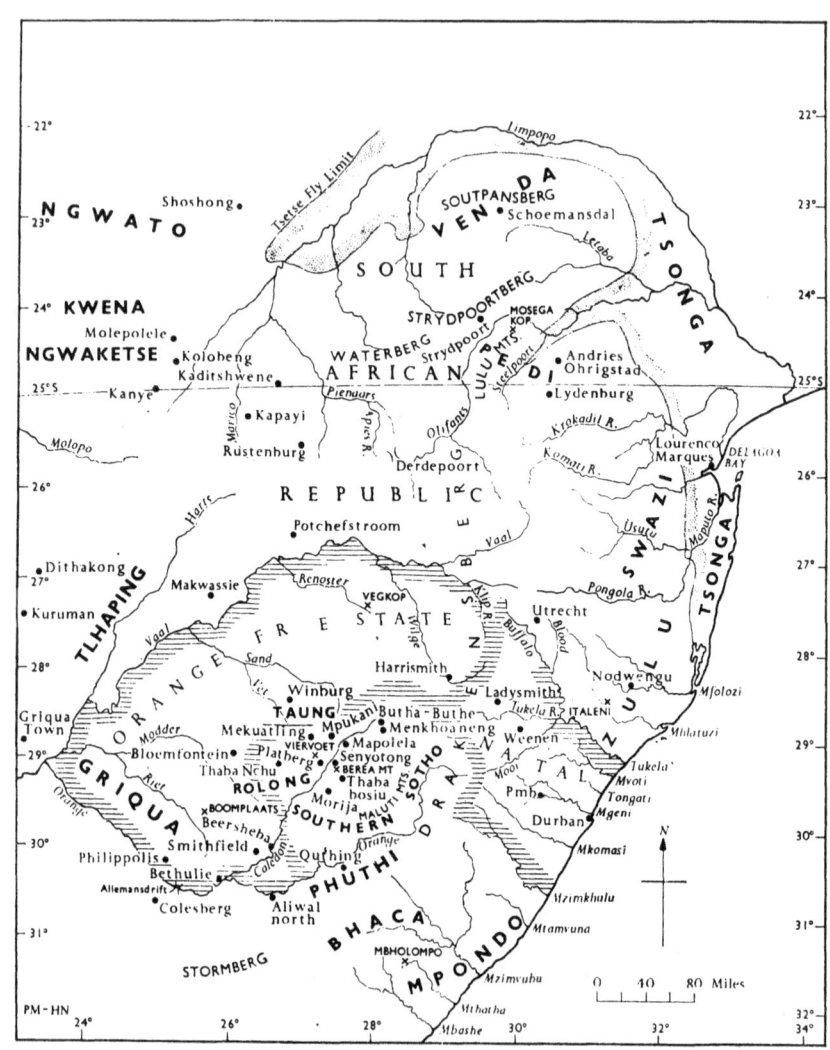

MAP 7. Eastern South Africa *c.* 1860

the allegiance of Transvaalers: the constitutional Government, with W. C. J. van Rensburg as President and Paul Kruger as Commandant-general, and the revolutionary Government, whose real leader was the absentee Pretorius, acting through Schoeman and J. W. Viljoen. The constitutional Government was strong among the Doppers and in

Lydenburg, which had never overcome its suspicion of leaders who acted independently; the revolutionary Government, in Marico and Waterberg; but in many parts of the republic neighbour was at odds with neighbour, and brother with brother. After four years of anarchy peace was restored in 1864. By that time Pretorius had tired of the Orange Free State and reached the conclusion that it was not possible to unite the two republics. He resigned from the Bloemfontein office and was re-elected President of the Transvaal.[1]

The period of contention about the Voortrekker state system was over. Unification was dead; and the two republics proceeded to develop along somewhat different lines—the South African Republic under President Pretorius (1864–71), in isolation; the Orange Free State, under President Jan Hendrik Brand (1864–88), son of the Speaker of the Cape House of Assembly, as a bridge between the colonial south and the republican north.

The growth of Afrikaner settlement, following upon the *Difaqane* wars, presented the African inhabitants of the high veld with their second massive challenge in a generation. A few Africans quickly became clients of Afrikaner families and were thus incorporated in the white-controlled society in the subordinate status of labour-tenants. The majority attached themselves to one of the many African chiefs who were striving to re-establish the institutions of autonomous, corporate life. The success of such a chief depended on the size of his following and his geographical location. In the central high veld, where the disruption wrought by the *Difaqane* had been most severe, many chiefdoms had scarcely begun to re-form when they were surrounded by white settlers and became their vassals. At the other extreme, a few chiefdoms, which had escaped the full brunt of the previous turmoil and which occupied particularly strong defensive positions, absorbed large numbers of new followers after the departure of the Ndebele. Some of these remained effectively autonomous until the last quarter of the nineteenth century. They included, in the west, the Kwena under Chief Sechele in the Kolobeng area, the Ngwaketse under Chief Gaseitsiwe in the Kanye area, and the Ngwato under Chiefs Sekgoma and Macheng in the Shoshong area; in the north, the Venda chiefdoms in the Soutpansberg; and in the east, in the Lulu mountains west of the white settlements of Ohrigstad and Lydenburg, the Pedi chiefdom of Sekwati and Sekhukhune.

The laws of the South African Republic concerning African subjects were derived from those of the Natal Republic. Africans were not

[1] Theal, *History of South Africa from 1795 to 1872*, iv, Chs. 81–83; van Jaarsveld, *Eenheidstrewe*, Ch. 8.

permitted to possess firearms, ammunition, or horses, nor could they be at large without a pass signed by an employer or an official. A white farmer was entitled to have four African families on his farm and to use their services. Those Africans who were not labour tenants on farms were allotted 'locations', where they were administered by chiefs or headmen recognized by the Government. It was Government policy to have a location in each ward of each District, so that the African population would be divided into small groups and a labour supply would be close to all farming settlements. Generally, the farmers edged the Africans out of the more fertile and better watered land. The Government required each location chief to pay taxes in cattle and to provide manpower on demand. Men thus conscripted would be allotted to the farmers to work for not longer than a year at a time, at a wage of one heifer for a year's work; or they might be used as auxiliaries in military campaigns against the enemies of the Republic.

The administration of these laws was vested in the military officers—the Commandant of each District and, especially, the field-cornet of each ward. It was the field-cornet's duty to see that the peace was preserved and that each white farmer had a supply of African labour. It was he who told the Africans where they could live; it was he who requisitioned the chiefs for labour and distributed the men between the farmers; and it was he who registered the contracts of service, without which no labour engagement was legally valid. The African servant had the right to complain of ill-treatment to the *landdrost*; but 'frivolous' complaints were punished.

In practice, the Government of the South African Republic lacked the means to enforce these laws systematically. Before 1877 locations were neither surveyed nor clearly delimited and African land tenure was on sufferance. Conditions varied greatly with time and place. If the Africans were quiescent and the whites were stable, the Africans had security of life and limb and the opportunity to produce their own food in return for the obligation to perform intermittent compulsory labour for the white farmers. If the Africans resisted the impositions or the whites were disorderly, there was anarchy. The latter was sometimes the case in the early stages of the white settlement of an area, while the whites were still engaged in subjecting the Africans to their will, and again during the civil war. It was almost always the case in the Soutpansberg district, where the white community lacked internal discipline and its officials were themselves guilty of the most flagrant abuses.[1]

---

[1] On the condition of Africans in the South African Republic see J. A. I. Agar-Hamilton, *The Native Policy of the Voortrekkers*, Chs. 5–10; W. Kistner, 'The Anti-slavery Agitation against the Transvaal Republic, 1852–1868', in *AYB*, 1952, ii, Ch. 3; F. A. van Jaarsveld, 'Die Veldkornet en sy Aandeel in die opbou van die Suid-Afrikaanse Republiek tot 1870', in *AYB*, 1950, ii, Chs. 3, 5.

AFRIKANER REPUBLICS AND AFRICAN STATES 437

An institution that attracted special attention was that known as 'apprenticeship'. It was derived from the apprenticeship system that had been applied to Khoikhoi and San children in the Cape Colony between 1812 and 1828 and to the former slaves between 1834 and 1838, and the system which operated in the Natal Republic and, with some modifications, in the Colony of Natal. Under the laws of the South African Republic, African children who had been captured in warfare could be 'apprenticed' to farmers by the military officers; and, by extension, so could African children who were voluntarily handed over by their parents for some consideration. The law drew a distinction between apprenticeship, as sanctioned, and slavery, which was prohibited. An apprentice could not be sold by one master to another, nor could he be held after the age of twenty-five (twenty-one in the case of girls), nor, if his parents were known, could he be held without their consent. Nevertheless, the institution often enabled farmers, with or without the knowledge and participation of their field-cornets, to indulge in military expeditions for the purpose of obtaining children; and it also enabled farmers to put pressures on African parents to part with their children, in return for food and immunity from attack.[1]

Some of the missionaries who worked in the chiefdoms adjacent to the Republic, and some of the traders who travelled through the Republic, were shocked by what they saw and heard. They criticised the treatment of Africans by the farmers in communications to the Government of the Republic, to the press in the Cape Colony and Natal, and to their friends and the headquarters of their societies in England and Europe. In some cases, too, they defied the republican laws against the sale of fire-arms and ammunition to Africans. These actions intensified the endemic distrust of the Voortrekker community for foreigners in general, and British missionaries and traders in particular. In response, the Government of the South African Republic harassed traders whom it suspected of selling arms and ammunition to Africans, and it forbade members of the London Missionary Society to settle in the Republic. On the other hand, it encouraged German Lutheran missionaries, who were content to work within the framework of the existing social order, without questioning it.[2]

The areas where the African inhabitants were effectively subjected to republican law shaded off into areas where they were virtually autonomous. Initially the Voortrekker leaders had tried to acquire titles to specific portions of land by negotiations with African chiefs, and they

[1] Agar-Hamilton, Ch. 9 and Appendix 3; Kistner, Chs. 5–6; van Jaarsveld, pp. 284–5.
[2] Agar-Hamilton, Chs. 6–10; [Baines], *Journal of Residence in Africa, 1842–1853*, VRS, 1964; Livingstone, *Missionary Travels and Researches in South Africa*; [Livingstone], *Missionary Correspondence, 1841–1856*; *Private Journals*; *Family Letters, 1841–1856*.

and their successors continued to make treaties with chiefs when it seemed expedient; but when they had defeated the Ndebele they saw themselves as having acquired by conquest the succession to Mzilikazi's entire Transvaal empire, which they construed in the largest terms as embracing everything between the Vaal and the Limpopo and between the Kalahari desert and the Drakensberg escarpment. They claimed to have liberated all the African inhabitants from Ndebele oppression and to be justified in treating them as vassals. The African chiefs saw things differently. Some, like those of the Ngwato and the Venda, had never been effectively ruled by Mzilikazi; others, such as the Pedi chiefs, had been temporarily subjected; but in either case they strove to achieve and maintain autonomy after the Ndebele had been driven out, especially when they became aware of the obligations which the republican authorities demanded of vassals. British traders and missionaries encouraged them to adopt this attitude, and by providing them with arms and ammunition increased their capacity to resist republican demands. From time to time the chiefs tried to co-operate with one another for this purpose. Messengers were constantly on the move with the latest news between chiefdom and chiefdom. But, located as they were around the periphery of the white settlements, and divided as they were by traditional feuds and personal rivalries, each chief had to depend very largely on his own resources; so that the republican authorities were generally able to deal with them piecemeal. Moreover, the Republic could often exploit the fissiparous nature of Sotho and Venda chiefdoms by giving sanctuary to the rival of an incumbent chief. In this way several traditional chiefdoms were split into two parts—one autonomous, the other under republican control.

By the time of the Sand River Convention some of the Tswana peoples,[1] including most of the Hurutshe, the Ratlou-Rolong, and the Kgafela-Kgatla, had been subjected by the Transvaal farmers. Others, notably the Tlhaping around the Harts river in the south and the Ngwato under Chief Sekgoma in the Shoshong hills in the north, were beyond the range of regular contact with Transvaalers, though some of the Tlhaping came into conflict with both republics in 1858. In between the Tlhaping and the Ngwato several Tswana communities contrived to hold their own against the Afrikaner farmers of the Marico district—notably the Kwena under Chief Sechele around Dimawe and the Ngwaketse under Chief Gaseitsiwe around Kanye. Immediately after

---

[1] On the Tswana in this period see J. A. I. Agar-Hamilton, *The Road to the North*; James Chapman, *Travels in the Interior of South Africa*; J. Mackenzie, *Ten Years North of the Orange River*; *The Matabele Journals of Robert Moffat, 1829–1860*; S. M. Molema, *The Bantu Past and Present*; I. Schapera, 'A Short History of the BaNgwaketse', *AS*, i, 1942, 1–26, and *The Ethnic Composition of Tswana Tribes*; A. Sillery, *The Bechuanaland Protectorate*; Smith, *Great Lion*; and the works by David Livingstone cited in the previous footnote.

signing the Sand River Convention the Transvaalers determined to subject these chiefdoms, because traders, hunters, and missionaries were supplying them with firearms and using their territories as a route to the north. Commandant P. E. Scholtz summoned all the chiefs of the area to a meeting at the place of a subject chief, Mosielele of the Mmanaana-Kgatla, and told them that they were subject to taxation and labour service. Soon afterwards Mosielele fled for protection to Sechele, who had refrained from attending the chiefs' meeting. At the end of August 1852 Scholtz led a commando to Dimawe but Sechele refused to hand over Mosielele. The commando then attacked the towns of the Kwena and the Ngwaketse, destroyed their crops, captured over 200 women and children, and sacked the residence of Sechele's missionary, David Livingstone, who was known to be highly critical of the Afrikaners and was suspected of supplying the Kwena with firearms, but was himself absent in the Cape Colony at that time. On its return journey the commando also attacked the vassal Chief Montshiwa of the Tshidi-Rolong, who had ignored an order to supply men to serve with the commando. R. Edwards and W. Inglis of the London Missionary Society, who had been working with vassal chiefs, criticized the conduct of the commando and were promptly expelled from the Transvaal; and thereafter no members of the London Missionary Society were allowed to settle in the area under Afrikaner control.

Sechele's Kwena and Gaseitsiwe's Ngwaketse survived these attacks. Strengthened by the accession of Mosielele's Kgatla-Mmanaana and other refugees from the South African Republic, they continued to preserve a tenuous autonomy between the white farms and the Kalahari desert, and to provide a route by which hunters, traders, and missionaries could penetrate to the north without coming under the surveillance of the republican authorities. Further north, the Ngwato also remained independent, though they had to deal with attacks by their Ndebele neighbours and were weakened by internal divisions, which resulted in the chieftainship's alternating between Sekgoma and Macheng. In the south the Tlhaping, too, were autonomous, though they never regained their pre-*Difaqane* strength and unity.

The Pedi kingdom was the principal African state in the eastern Transvaal. During the 1820s, when the area was devastated successively by the impis of Mzilikazi, Soshangane, and Sobhuza, Sekwati, a junior son of the deceased chief Thulare, had fled northwards to the Soutpansberg. Returning to his homeland in about 1829, Sekwati established himself in defensible mountain positions west of the Steelpoort river, first at Phiring and later at Mosego Kop in the Lulu mountains, from which he beat off attacks by Sobhuza, came to terms with Mpande, and rallied the remnants of the northern Sotho chiefdoms, in much the same way as Moshweshwe was rallying the southern Sotho. Sekwati held his own in the face of the intrusion of Voortrekkers to Ohrigstad and Lydenburg, and in 1852 he narrowly survived a sustained attack by a large commando led by A. H. Potgieter. Five years later he and delegates of the Lydenburg republic agreed to recognize the Steelpoort river as the boundary between the republic to the east and the Pedi kingdom to the west;[1] and in 1861 he admitted two Lutheran missionaries of the Berlin Mission Society. Sekwati died in the same year. His successor, Sekhukhune, continued the policy of building up the kingdom by welcoming and absorbing refugees. He, too, had reformist tendencies, but when the missionaries began to make converts he came to the conclusion that they were undermining his authority and intriguing with Afrikaners. He told the missionary Alexander Merensky: 'I am no longer king in the country; you have taken my people away from me . . .; you are spies of the Boers.'[2] By 1866 he had expelled the missionaries and proscribed Christianity. Sekhukhune also built up a supply of arms and ammunition against the day when, as he foresaw, Afrikaner commandos would again invade his kingdom.[3]

By 1848, when A. H. Potgieter founded the Schoemansdal settlement, there had been a partial recovery from the devastations wrought in the northern Transvaal by Shaka, Mzilikazi, Soshangane, and Sobhuza. The most powerful organized communities were the Venda chiefdoms, which had survived the *Difaqane* in their fastnesses in the Soutpansberg and absorbed survivors from other chiefdoms. Further south-west, in the mountains on either side of what became known as the Nyl river, Sotho chiefs such as Makapane organized other survivors; while in the east, between the Venda and the Pedi, there was a continual influx of Tsonga (whom the Afrikaners called Magwamba or 'knobnoses'), who had been displaced by Soshangane.

The first serious attempt to challenge white settlement in the northern Transvaal was made by Makapane, who massacred a hunting expedition in 1854. In retaliation, an Afrikaner commando blockaded many of Makapane's people in a cavern and killed about 3,000 of them.[4]

If the Venda had been united, they might have preserved themselves intact; but the Venda chiefdoms, like the Xhosa and the Tswana, were

---

[1] Theal, *History of South Africa from 1873 to 1884*, i. 258, says that Sekwati 'acknowledged himself a vassal of the republic', but his statement is not borne out by D. R. Hunt, 'An Account of the Bapedi', *BS*, v, 1931, 290–1, who cites the agreement between Sekwati and the Lydenburg Republic.

[2] [Theodor Wangemann], *Maléo en Sekoekoeni*, VRS, 1957, p. 106.

[3] Hunt, op. cit., pp. 275–306; Theal, *History of South Africa from 1795 to 1872*, ii. 505, iii. 386–9, *History of South Africa from 1873–1884*, i. 256–9; T. S. van Rooyen, 'Die Sendeling Alexander Merensky in die Geskiedenis van die Suid-Afrikaanse Republiek (1859–1882)', in *AYB*, 1954, ii, Chs. 4–5; Wangemann, op. cit.

[4] Theal, *History of South Africa from 1795 to 1872*, iii. 415–19.

AFRIKANER REPUBLICS AND AFRICAN STATES 441

prone to fission after the death of a chief. The Venda were already divided by the time of the *Difaqane* and there were further secessions from the principal chiefdom on the death of Ramavhoya in about 1836, and on the death of his successor, Ravele (Ramabulana), in 1864; and after both events the disappointed claimant to the chieftainship sought white assistance. Furthermore, individual Venda took service with white farmers and hunters. The situation in the Soutpansberg was complicated by two others factors. First, the whites in the area were particularly disorderly. They included adventurers of British, Portuguese, and Russian, as well as Afrikaner origin, who made their living from elephant hunting, and since horses and cattle could not survive the tsetse, they used Africans as porters and in many cases provided Africans with firearms to hunt for them. Secondly, Tsonga politics impinged on the area, especially after the death of Soshangane in about 1858, when his successors tried to control the Tsonga refugees in the Soutpansberg district.[1]

In 1859 S. Schoeman appointed João Albasini superintendent of the African tribes east of the village of Schoemansdal. This was an unwise choice. Albasini was a Portuguese trader engaged in exporting slaves from the Soutpansberg area through Delagoa Bay and, though his wife was an Afrikaner, he had no deep loyalty to the Afrikaner community. He antagonized the leading Venda and Tsonga chiefs by giving sanctuary to their rivals and, with a following of some two thousand Africans, he raised a tribute for the Government and booty for himself by making unprovoked attacks on Venda villages. The local commandant and field-cornets did much the same. In retaliation, the Venda raided white farms and caused the white community to go into laagers.[2]

When the civil war was over, the republican government tried to restore order, but it was not able to bring sufficient force to bear, for the burghers of the southern districts had no stomach for Soutpansberg adventures and the Republic was so short of funds that it could not supply the commandos with enough ammunition. The climax came in 1867. Paul Kruger, commandant-general of the Republic, arrived at Schoemansdal with 400 men. Finding that his force was insufficient to master the Venda in their mountain strongholds, he asked Pretorius for more men and more ammunition, but these were not provided. At the same time, the high court of three *landdrosts*, sitting in Schoemansdal, tried Albasini, Commandant S. Venter, and Field-Cornet J. H. du Plessis for the illegal seizure of African cattle, and when it had sentenced du Plessis to a fine, a white mob stormed the court and released

[1] Theal, iv. 473–91; van Warmelo, *Contributions*, and *Copper Miners*.
[2] J. B. de Vaal, 'Die Rol van João Albasini in die Geskiedenis van die Transvaal', in *AYB*, 1953, i.

the prisoner. Kruger then withdrew from Schoemansdal and the white inhabitants followed him, while Chief Makhado's Venda destroyed the village. The collapse spread to the Nyl river, where Makapane and other Sotho chiefs rose in rebellion. Almost the entire Soutpansberg district, from the Limpopo to the Oliphants river, was abandoned by whites, and some of those who remained paid tribute to Africans for immunity from attack. Nevertheless, lacking a man of the calibre of Moshweshwe among them, the Africans were unable to consolidate their advantage. Venda remained divided against Venda, Sotho against Sotho, and the Soutpansberg area was again ravaged by Mzila, successor of Shoshangane, and Mswazi, successor of Sobhuza.[1]

Unlike the South African Republic, the Orange Free State did not assume the responsibility for controlling non-white communities. The farmers employed Coloured or African labourers, some of whom were labour tenants, while others came to the farms from their own territories and worked for limited periods.

It was not long before most of the Coloured communities lost their land. Warden's client communities in the Caledon valley were all swept away by Moshweshwe after the Berea battle. Several small groups who lived along the left bank of the Vaal river disintegrated in 1858, when they were dispersed by Orange Free State commandos, after they had plundered farmers' cattle while the Republic had been at war with Moshweshwe.[2] Adam Kok's Griqua fared somewhat better. Realizing that if they stayed where they were there could be only one end to the process by which they were selling their land to white farmers, in 1861 Adam Kok sold out his rights north of the Orange river to the Free State Government and led his people on a trek through lower Lesotho and across the Drakensberg, to found Kokstad and a new East Griqualand, where they held together until white farmers began to intrude there, too, in the 1870s.[3] That left the Orange Free State with indeterminate western frontiers with the Tlhaping and the various West Griqua communities, which was a matter of no great consequence before diamonds were discovered there (vol. ii).

After 1854 the Rolong of Moroka at Thaba Nchu were all that was left of Warden's grand alliance in the Caledon valley against Moshweshwe. The Free State Government treated Moroka as a friendly and independent chief and received his help in its wars with Moshweshwe; but the chiefdom showed signs of schism after 1865, when,

---

[1] de Vaal, Chs. 12–15; F. J. Potgieter, op. cit., pp. 74–76 and Map opposite p. 107; Theal, iv. 480–91.   [2] Theal, iii. 455, 483.
[3] S. J. Halford, *The Griquas of Griqualand*, Chs. 17 ff.; Marais, *Cape Coloured People*, pp. 56–73; Theal, iv. 194–7; W. Dower, *The Early Annals of Kokstad and Griqualand East*.

with Moroka ageing, the newly arrived Church of England missionary favoured Samuel Moroka as heir, while the Wesleyans associated with the senior son, Tshipinare.[1]

Moshweshwe's southern Sotho kingdom was the core of African resistance to white expansion in south-eastern Africa throughout the 1850s and most of the 1860s. To the task of maintaining the strength and integrity of his kingdom Moshweshwe brought a remarkably clear-sighted appraisal of the realities of the situation. He continued to gain fresh adherents. Most of the Tlokwa joined him after he had finally routed Sekonyela in 1853 (p. 422); the Kholokwe joined when a Free State commando drove them out of Witsie's Hoek in 1856;[2] and there was a continuous influx of refugees from the Transvaal communities which were engulfed by the farmers. He also tightened his authority over his kingdom, by placing his brothers and senior sons in charge of Districts, while leaving some latitude to the leaders of the original groups of followers at the village level. Moorosi's Phuthi and Moletsane's Taung he treated differently. They were allies with considerable autonomy; but both of them accepted Moshweshwe's leadership in the conduct of their relations with white people, because it paid them to do so. Notwithstanding the arms clauses of the Conventions, Moshweshwe continued to modernize his military system. Horses were bred locally as well as pilfered from farmers; and there were always traders to sell him guns and deserters from the British army to repair the guns and make powder and shot from local ingredients; so that in the war of 1858 (p. 432) Moshweshwe disposed of about 10,000 mounted men, most of them armed with muskets, some with rifles. Having experienced the failure of white authorities to stand by their engagements (notably, the Napier Line of 1843), Moshweshwe had become a master of *Realpolitik*. He turned a blind eye to his young men's cattle-rustling expeditions, and reacted to each approach from the Free State Government in the light of the power situation of the moment—complaining, justifying, explaining, admitting, or promising, and sometimes actually disgorging a few cattle, but always encouraging his people to hold firmly to the land they occupied and the horses and firearms they possessed. Though skilfully exploiting the divisions between Boer and Boer, and between Boer and Briton, he was careful to leave a good impression with British officials, as with Cathcart, for he was aware that in the last resort the British might be serviceable allies. Ever since he had turned to Shaka for protection against Matiwane, he had known the art of offsetting a neighbour's capacity to damage him by calling in a more distant

---

[1] Theal, iii. 481, iv. 192, 282-3; I. S. J. Venter, 'Die Sendingstasie Thaba Nchu, 1833-1900', *Communications of the University of South Africa*, C. 18.
[2] Theal, iii. 348-50, 450-1, 461-2.

Power. He saw that in an emergency Britain was capable of disposing better-disciplined and better-armed forces than the Afrikaners, as at Boomplaats, but that, unlike the Afrikaner republics, Britain did not covet his land. He also saw that British policy was subject to sudden shifts which he could not predict or control; while the terms of the Conventions and the events on the eastern frontier of the Cape Colony demonstrated that white people generally acted in concert against black people throughout the sub-continent. Moshweshwe therefore tried to build up a defensive African alliance. For this purpose the central position of Lesotho in south-eastern Africa was admirably suited. His envoys were continuously on the move, from the Soutpansberg to the Kei river, and envoys of distant chiefs were often at Thaba Bosiu. Nevertheless, since nearly every African chiefdom was threatened by its own neighbouring white frontiersman, it was not possible to devise an effective system of mutual aid; and the extent to which other chiefs acted upon Moshweshwe's advice is not known.[1]

By the mid 1860s the relative strengths of the Orange Free State and the southern Sotho kingdom had changed. With increasing age Moshweshwe (born c. 1786) was losing control over his senior sons, and they were intriguing and indulging in uncoordinated raids on farmers' property with the object of building up their own followings and their own prestige in preparation for a struggle for the succession. Moreover, the white population of the Orange Free State had grown in numbers, and with the election of J. H. Brand in 1864 the Republic at last had an able President. Thus the Free State developed an unprecedented capacity to act firmly at the very time when the southern Sotho were losing their cohesion.

War broke out in 1865. Though the Sotho gained some early successes and staved off several assaults on Thaba Bosiu, the commandos then resorted to destroying crops and capturing cattle, and playing off chief against chief. Moshweshwe's second son, Molapo, whose district covered the northern part of Lesotho, made a separate peace; and Moshweshwe himself came to terms. According to the Treaty of Thaba Bosiu (April 1866), the Free State acquired the greater part of Lesotho, and Moshweshwe was left with a narrow strip of arable lowlands and a somewhat larger mountainous area. But Moshweshwe had no intention of vacating the ceded territory and further fighting broke out in 1867. The commandos systematically cleared some of the mountain strongholds and seemed on the verge of achieving a complete victory over a demoralized and famished enemy, when, dramatically, Sir Philip Wodehouse, High

---

[1] *Bas. Rec.* ii and iii; J. J. G. Grobbelaar, 'Die Vrystaatse Republiek en die Basoetoevraagstuk', in *AYB*, 1939, ii; *Journal des Missions Evangeliques*; Tylden, *The Rise of the Basuto*; Jean van der Poel, 'Basutoland as a Factor in South African Politics (1858–1870)', in *AYB*, 1941, i.

Commissioner, cut off the Free State's ammunition supply and proclaimed that 'the tribe of the Basutos shall be . . . British subjects; and the territory of the said tribe shall be . . . British Territory' (12 March 1868).[1]

When Wodehouse arrived in South Africa in 1861, he had received from Moshweshwe a request that he and his people should be received forthwith as British subjects; and when the war broke out in 1865 Moshweshwe reiterated this request, considering that the best hope for his kingdom lay in British protection. Wodehouse sympathized with the southern Sotho and believed that they would suffer grievously if Britain did not intervene. Like Sir George Grey before him, he also believed that the Convention policy of non-interference north of the Orange river had been an error, leading to divisions, conflicts, and general poverty, contrary to the interests of Great Britain and all the South African communities. As the dominant Power in South Africa, Britain should resume her responsibilities and, as a first step, take Moshweshwe's people under protection.

The initial response of the officials in the Colonial Office to the outbreak of the war was to insist on complete neutrality on the part of the British Colonies. Nevertheless, by that time their confidence in the policy of non-intervention had been eroded. There was dismay at the persistent reports that slavery existed in the Transvaal, and African chiefdoms were continually harassed by commandos; this sentiment was intensified when news arrived of the severe terms of the Treaty of Thaba Bosiu and of the expulsion by the Orange Free State Government of the French Protestant missionaries from the conquered territory. There was also anxiety lest, if the Free State were not checked, it might gain control of a route to the sea at Port St. Johns and thereby drive a wedge between Natal and the Cape Colony, and open up the republics to alien European influences. There were, too, dispatches from the Lieutenant-Governor of Natal showing that Moshweshwe would be happy for his country to be incorporated in Natal. The crucial decision was taken in December 1867, when the British Cabinet decided to instruct Wodehouse that Moshweshwe's prayer might be granted, provided that Basutoland was annexed by Natal rather than directly by Britain, and that this was done at the request of the Natal legislature and with the consent of the Orange Free State.

Wodehouse modified this mandate to suit his own convictions. He knew that the Free State would resent any British intervention, and he suspected that if Moshweshwe's country was incorporated in Natal, Shepstone and the white community of the Colony would abuse their powers. That was why he cut off the Free States ammunition supply

[1] Jean van der Poel, op. cit.; also Theal, iv, Chs. 73–75.

from the Cape ports, annexed Basutoland as a Crown Colony, and sent up a detachment of the Cape Frontier Mounted Police to give effect to the annexation. In the ensuing year Wodehouse played a game of bluff with the Free State, Natal, and the British Government, knowing full well that Britain would not spare a single soldier in the event of conflict. He had his way. The annexation stood and at Aliwal North he negotiated with President Brand a boundary between the Orange Free State and the Colony of Basutoland which ran along the Caledon river from its source to Jammerdrif, and thence south-eastwards to the Drakensberg (12 February 1869). This was a considerable improvement for Moshweshwe on the Treaty of Thaba Bosiu, though its provisions compared unfavourably with those of the Convention of 1859, for he lost all his land north of the Caledon and some land between the Caledon and the Orange.[1]

In March 1870, the month in which the Convention of Aliwal North was ratified by Brand and Wodehouse, Moshweshwe died on Thaba Bosiu. He had experienced all the crucial changes which had taken place on the South African high veld—from the comparative stability of traditional societies in his youth, through the anarchy of the *Difaqane*, to the intrusion of French missionaries, Afrikaner farmers, and British officials. More skilfully than any other African confronted with similar problems, he had managed to create a kingdom out of chaos and to steer that kingdom through manifold dangers to what was probably the best destiny that was open to it in the changed world of the late nineteenth century.

In sanctioning the annexation of Basutoland, the British Cabinet resumed responsibilities in an area which, as far as it knew, was still a wilderness, devoid of exploitable wealth. But in the same month of December 1867, when the Cabinet came to that decision, Carl Mauch was in Pretoria reporting that he had found rich and extensive goldfields on the Tati river in Ngwato country, and a stone, which children had been found playing with in the Hopetown district of the Cape Colony, was on exhibition in Cape Town, having been identified as a diamond. These discoveries, coinciding with the British decision to return to the high veld, paved the way for a new era in South African history.

[1] C. W. de Kiewiet, *British Colonial Policy and the South African Republics, 1848–1872*, Chs. 9–14, is a detailed and masterly account of the change in British policy leading to the annexation of Basutoland.

INDEX

NB. Page numbers before 40 refer to OHSA, vol. i.

Abambo people, settlement in Natal, 86, the Mpondo *and*, 93 n. 3. *See also* Mbo.
Aborigines Committee of House of Commons, Andries Stockenström *and*, 325, Allen Gardiner *and*, 354; *and* Khoikhoi population figures (1837), 68.
Aborigines Protection Society, 370.
Acheulian culture, 2, 14 f., 17, sites, 15-16; pre-Chelles/Acheul stone culture, 13.
Adams, Newton, American missionary, *and* African lands in Natal, 374.
African Land and Emigration Association, 372.
Africaner, leader of lawless raiders, 70.
Africans: meaning of term, xi; *and* agriculture and sheep, 263; *and* schools, 261, 270; *and* firearms, 425, 435, 437, 439, 441; *and* franchise, 386.
British policy towards, 371-5, 382-7, 390, 421, 423-4.
in Natal, 374-8, 382-7, 390, at Port Natal, 352; locations, 375 f., 384-7, 390; *and* Sir Harry Smith's Land Commission, 378; funds for 'Native purposes', 386 and n. 2; characteristics according to Natal report of 1854, 383-4.
and 'Difaqane', 392 and n. 3; divisions among, 440-2.
and Voortrekkers, 366-8.
in Orange Free State and Transvaal, *see under* Afrikaners.
See also under Labour; Land; Population; South African Republic; Veld; *and under* separate headings of various peoples.
Afrikaner Bond, topics at congresses of, 310.
Afrikaners; xi and n. 1, 197, 231, 244, 270 ff., 274; characteristics, 425-7, racialism, 383 and n. 1, treatment of Coloured people, 245, resistance to anglicization, 283, 285.
in Natal, 348, 352 f., 355, 377, 380; *and* land, 372-5, 378 f.; *see also* Natal Republic *under* Natal.
in Orange Free State and Transvaal, relations with Africans, 424, 430-1, 433, 435, 442-5; *and* arms and ammunition, 425, 427.
See also under Boers; Dutch; Great Trek; Trekboers; Voortrekkers.

Agriculture, 31, 72, 80, 85, 103, 248, 263, 296; methods, 110 f., 142, 154, 161, 173, 177, 425, carried on by women, 83, 111, 240, 387.
Crops, 109-10, 142, 192 ff., 197 f., 201, 248, 253, 381, *see also* sugar; tobacco; wheat; wine. Over-production problem, 198-9, 209.
White settlers *and*, 184, 192, 194-8, 209, 244, 282, 296; Christian missionaries *and*, 239, 263.
See also Farmers; Farms.
Albany District, rock paintings, 29.
British settlers in, 244, 278-9 and n. 2, 280 f.; 292, 302, 315, 383; *and* representative institutions, 319; Albany Levy disbanded, 280.
Albasini, João, 441.
Alberti, L., with reference to travellers, 115; to buck, 254.
Alexandersfontein, Griqualand West, archaic tools in, 19.
Aliwal North, agreement between Orange Free State and southern Sotho at, 432; Voortrekkers *and*, 409; First Convention of (1859), 446, Second Convention of (1870), 331, *and* Basutoland, 446.
Alleman's Drift, 415.
Allison, James, Wesleyan missionary, 358.
Amber, trade in, 177.
American, ships at Cape, 274; missionaries, 352 and n. 7, 365, 374, 392 n. 1, 407, with reference to Mzilikazi, 405.
Ancestors, cult and veneration of, 53, 62, 126-7, 171 n. 2, 178, 182, 270; Sotho *and*, 161; Xhosa *and*, 256-7.
Angola, hunters in, 47.
Animals, 5, 50, 54, 82, 96, 109 f., 128, 162, 179, 254; domestic animals, 22-3, 29, 31 47, 55-57, 72; wild animals venerated, 162, 170, exterminated, 225, witches *and*, 269; animal sacrifices, 161-2, 173.
Buck, 254; dogs, 104, 107, 155, for hunting, 48, 82, 110, 117; elands, 52, 54, 71; elephants, 150 and n. 1, 179, 234-5, 238, 254, 349, 411, 413, 441, *see also* Ivory; fowls, 109, 177; goats, 55, 71, 104, 107, 142, 109, 177; horses, 69, 71, 109, 235, 237 f., 242, 251, 259, 397, 400, 443, exported to India, 294, forbidden to Africans, 435; pigs, 109, 381.
See also Cattle; Sheep.

I i

INDEX

Anthropologists, vii, x.
Anti-Convict Association, 321.
Apies river area, Mzilikazi *and*, 98, 404.
Arbousset, T., with reference to stone building, 140; to metallurgy, 144; to Pedi trade, 151; to trade routes, 152; to Sotho and fish, 167; to MaNthatisi and Sekonyela, 398; mission to Thaba Bosiu, 400-1.
Archaeology, vi, viii, xi f.
 Artefacts, *see* Glass; Hand-axes; Tools and Weapons.
 Cultures, 1 and n. 1; *see also* Acheulian; Early Stone Age; First Intermediate; Iron Age; Late Stone Age; Middle Stone Age; Second Intermediate: Smithfield; Wilton.
 Sites, 1 and n. 3, 17-18, 22-23, 25 (map), 32, 37. *See also* Bambandyanalo; Buispoort; Cave of Hearths; Elandsfontein; Florisbad; Hopefield; Hyrax Hill; Kanjera; Khami; Klipplaatdrif; Klipriviersberg; Kromdraai; Lydenburg; Leopard's Kopje; Mabveni; Makapan; Makapansgat; Mapungubwe; Matjes River; Melkbosch; Melville' Koppies; Mwulu's Cave; Oakhurst shelter; Olduvai Gorge; Olieboompoort; Peers Cave; Pietersburg; Rustenburg-Zeemst; Sterkfontein; Steynsrus; Swartklip; Swartkrans; Taung; Tuinplaats; Uitkomst; Vereeniging; Zimbabwe; *and under* Acheulian; Orange Free State; Rhodesia; Transvaal; Zambia.
Archbell, James, Wesleyan missionary, 357, 407.
Architecture, *see* Building.
Arms trade, *see under* Firearms.
Arnot, David, land speculator, 293.
Ashton, E. H., with reference to Sotho settlements, 154.
Asians, xi, 274, 298 n. 2, 366.
Asiatic Possessions, Council for, 288.
Assembly, freedom of, 314-15, 317, 430.
Atherstone, W. G., scientist, 281 n. 2.
Australia, primitive tools in, 18; Macarthur's merinos in, 290.
Australopithecus africanus, 1 ff., 5 f., described, 8-14.
Australopithecus robustus, 5, described, 8-14.
Ayliff, Revd. J., missionary, 281 n. 6.

Baatje, Carolus, 402 f.
Babanango hill, Malandela *and*, 90.
Backhouse, J., with reference to Thaba Nchu, 153; to school at Swellendam, 261; to schools in the Tyhume, 262.
Bain, A. C., with reference to Bechuana stone town, 140.
Bains, Thomas, *and* hunting painting, 49; *and* 'Namaqua Hottentot on Riding ox and his Bushman', 63.
Bamaliti stone town, 140.
Bambandyanalo, Northern Transvaal, archaeological site, 32-35, 146 f., 168, 175.
Bambe, chief near Lourenço Marques, 86-87; 'a great thief', 81.
Bamboesberg, refugees in the, 240.
Banks, 295-6, 426.
Bantu, xi, 1, 33, 338; Bantu speakers, ix, 21, 29 f., 32, 37 ff., 41, 56, 59, 72 f., 105, 146, 233; area occupied by, 31, 39; ancestor veneration, 53, 62; *and* cattle, 104, 166; *and* Pygmie clients, 64 n. 1.
Barber, Mary E., scientist, 281 n. 2.
Barkly, Sir Henry, Governer of the Cape, *and* Federal Commission of 1871, 325; *and* responsible government, 331-2.
Barkly West, rock paintings, 29.
Barnard, Lady Anne, 275.
Barolong kings, power of, 140, 153; dance in honour of iron, 145. *See* Rolong.
Barotseland, Sotho in, 131 n. 3.
Barrow, J., with reference to San dancing, 54; to riding ox, 108; to Xhosa and beer, 110; to Nguni villages, 111; to Nguni social structure, 124; to expedition of 1801, 137; to articles of trade between Xhosa and settlers, 238; to trade and boundaries, 240, 289; to Ngqika, 246; to Khoikhoi and Coloured in Graaf Reinet district, 247; to game, 254; to punishments, 273; to Dutch settlers, 275.
'Bastards', 68-70, 226 f., 248, 402.
Basutoland, rock paintings, 30; Cape Colony *and*, 331; Britain *and*, 334 and n. 3, annexed (1868), 425, 445-6. *See also* Lesotho.
Batavia, 186, 188, 217 f., 298, hospital at, 189; *and* rice, 192 f.; *and* Cape wheat, 206; Governor-General in council at, 214; Statutes and High Court of Justice, 214, 297, 299 and n. 1, 300, Council of Justice, 220.
Batavian Republic, *and* the Cape, 273, 275, 277, 313 f., 318, economic policy, 288-9, 291, 294 f. and n. 1, 301, 303; *and* office of Independent Fiscal, 299-300. Department of Indian Affairs, 183.
Bathurst, Henry, third Earl, 315, *and* Albany settlement of 1820, 279 n. 2, 280; *and* Somerset's Proclamation regarding slaves, 306 f.
Beads, 34, 54 ff., 106, 238, found at Zimbabwe, 163, 175; trade in, 61, 65, 106, 149-53, 235, 238, 242.
Beaufort West, Scots clergy at, 285.

INDEX

Bechuanaland, Sotho in, 131 n. 3, 134, stone town, 140. *See also* Botswana.
Bedford, South Africa, school at, 261.
Beje, Kumalo leader, 349.
Belgians, in British-German Legion, 283.
Bennie, Revd. John, missionary, 239, with reference to stone buildings, 140.
Berea battle, 442.
Berg Damara, *see* Negro hunters.
'Bergenaars', attack Moshweshwe's kingdom, 400; in Orange-Vaal area, 414.
Bessie, daughter of Mpondo chief and survivor from shipwreck, 92 f., 233.
Bethelsdorp, mission station, 239 f., 246 f.
Beutler, Ensign, *and* inquiry relating to trade, 234, 240, 246.
Bezuidenhout, Frederik, 310.
Bhaca, the, chiefdom, 120, 346, clans, 117, military organization, 124; *and* cattle racing, 108; attacked by the Zulu, 349, 351, 354, by the Dumesa, 376. *See also* Madikane; Ncaphayi.
Bhele, the, 97, 101, 120, 249, 345.
Birwa, the, 163, chiefdom, 134.
'Black Circuit' court, 225.
Blair, Collector of Customs, libelled, 315.
Bleek, Dorothea, with reference to Naron and Nama languages, 43; to children among Naron, 53; to San religion, 54.
Bleek, W. H. I., with reference to languages, 44, 73.
Blesius, Fiscal, 297 n. 1.
Bloemfontein, fort at, 418, 431; school at, 263, 426; Convention of 1854, 407, 422–3, 425, 429, 432 f., 443 ff.
Bloemhof court, 332.
Blood river, Zulu defeat at, 362, 364, 367, 370.
Board of Trade and Plantations, *and* representative government in Cape Colony, 323.
Boers, 195, characteristics, 281; predominance in Cape white population, 232. *See also* Great Trek; *Trekboers*; Voortrekkers.
Boers, William Cornelius, Fiscal, 297 n. 1, 298 and n. 2; *and* burgher petition of 1779, 219–20.
Bomvana, the, population, 255.
Bond, C., with reference to past climate, 6.
Boomplaats, battle at (1848), 418, 444.
Borcherds, P. B., with reference to Europeanized Khoikhoi, 70; to expedition of 1801, 137; stone ruins at Dithakong, 139; to Tlhaping and metal, 143; to Xhosa, 236; to schools, 276.
Boshof, Jacobus, *and* constitution of Natal Republic, 365; President of Orange Free State, 431–3.

'Bosjemans', 57.
Botswana, x; hunters in, 44, 47, 72; clientship in, 63, 180; Sotho in, 145, 153, 155. *See also* Bechuanaland.
Bourke, Sir Richard, Lieutenant-Governor of eastern Cape, 304, 307, *and* petition for representative assembly (1827), 319.
Bowker family, 281 n. 7.
Boxer, C. R., with reference to the advantages of the Cape, 188; to white settler community at the Cape, 231.
Boyce, with reference to Mpondo villages, 111; to language, 248.
Brain, C. K., with reference to past climate, 6.
Brand, Christoffel, 322.
Brand, Jan Hendrik, President of Orange Free State, 435, 444, 446.
Brandberg, rock paintings, 29.
Breutz, P.-L., with reference to dating of arrival of Kwena and Hurutshe, 134; to stone buildings, 139 and n. 2, 140; to Transvaal metal workers, 146.
Brijckje, the, *see* Tlhaping, the.
Brink, eighteenth-century journal of, 135.
British, *and* emancipation of slaves, 301, 307–8.
British conquests of the Cape, *see under* Cape, the.
British Foreign Legion and British-German Legion, 282 f. and n. 1.
British government at the Cape, *see under* Cape Colony.
British Imperial Government:
  Colonial policy, 368–70, 382, 415–17, 419–21, 423–4, 433, 445 f.
  and Natal, 352, 354 and n. 6, 368–9, 371–3, 378–80, 382, 390.
  and Orange River Sovereignty, 417, 421–4.
  and Orange-Vaal area, 415–17, 419.
  and Transvaal independence, 420–1.
  and arms trade, 421, 423; funds, 329, 331, 382; slavery, 306–9, 372, 421, 423; tension between Africans and Afrikaners, 425.
  See also Colonial Office; Crown; *and under* Voortrekkers.
British Isles, emigration of 1847–51 from, 378–80; Colonial Land and Emigration Commissioners, 378.
British settlers, characteristics, 280–1, 334–5; nineteenth-century immigrants, 274, 283; on eastern Cape frontier, 252–3; in south-east Cape, 380; in western Cape, 281 n. 3; relations with Afrikaners, 244, 281, 321–3, with Shaka, 349.
See also under Albany, *and under* Natal.
See also Missionaries.

INDEX

British South Africa Company, *and* Matabeleland, 412.
British troops, 327, 331, 415, 419, deserters, 443.
Broadbent, Samuel, Wesleyan missionary, with reference to the *Difaqane*, 396.
Broken Hill skull, Zambia, 9.
Brownlee, Charles, missionary, 239, with reference to the Gona, 61; to Xhosa cattle-killing, 257 n. 1, 258 f.; to sheep, 263; to Christian converts, 265.
Brownlee, Mrs. Charles, 257 n. 1.
Brownlee, John, missionary, 239, with reference to the Xhosa and the Gona, 102; to the Xhosa and cultivation and hunting, 110; to areas occupied by the Khoikhoi and the Xhosa, 236.
Bryant, A. T., Catholic missionary, writings of, 337; with reference to dialect spoken around Durban, 85; to location of Nguni, 87; to length of reigns and generations, 89 and n. 4; to movements of Zulu, 90; to the Dlamini, 90; to the Nguni, 100, 117, 129–30, 336, 338, 393; to racial intermixture, 105; to Dingiswayo, 338, 341 n. 2; to Shaka, 343 nn. 1 and 2, 344 n. 3.
Buchanan, Revd. John, with reference to power of chiefs, 264.
Building, in stone, 31–32, 34–39, 112, 139–42, 174, 181. Huts, of reed mats, 80, of mud and wood, 139; Nguni and Khoikhoi huts, 104–5, 112; San huts, 112. *See also* cattle byres *under* Cattle.
Building at the Cape, 230, 281, 287, at Cape Town, 275, 288.
Buispoort, Transvaal, culture, 33–36, 38, 135.
Bulawayo, 98, 342.
Burchell, W. J., with reference to Dithakong huts, 139; to grain trade, 142; to metallurgy, 143; to Dutch settlers, 274.
Burger, J. J., 408.
Burghers, grievances and petitions, 218–22 and n. 10, 227–8, 287–8, 298–9 and n. 1, 310 f., *see also* 'Kaapse Patriotte', *and under* Trade.
 Legal position, 223–4, 299, members of High Court of Justice, 220, of administrative Councils, 222–3, 227; *and* Council of Justice, 312, *and* Council of Policy, 311; ignorance of Romano-Dutch law, 297.
Burgher Senate, Cape Town, 223, 227–8, 312 f., 319, abolished 318.
 and British military government, 313; Fiscal W. C. Boers, 298; military service, 226–7; Ngqika, 245; slaves, 307.
Burials, 10, 33, 37, 46, 171 and n. 2, 175, of heads of homesteads, 127, of Nguni chiefs, 90–95, 127; 'beast burial', 33.

Burnett, Mr. Bishop, 280 n. 1.
Burton, R. F., with reference to Ngoni raiders, 99 f.
Bush, increase in, 254 and n. 6.
Bush-boskop stock, ix, 20, 22, 105, 146 f.
Bushmen, ix, *see also* San, The. 'Bushmanoid' skull, 10.
Buxton, Sir Thomas Fowell, *and* slaves, 306, 308.
Buytendag, Carl, banishment of, 222, Fiscal Boers *and*, 297 n. 1, 298.
Byrne, Joseph, *and* 'Natal Emigration and Colonization Office', 378–80.

'Caffers', meaning of term, 298 n. 2.
Caledon, Earl of, *and* Dutch schools, 284; Proclamations regulating labour, 303 and n. 5, 304 and n. 1.
Caledon, school at, 284, Scots clergy *and*, 285.
Caledon river, battle between the Ngwane and the Hlubi at, 394.
Caledon valley, settlements in, 402–3, 414–14, 442, boundaries of African and white settlements, 418–19.
 See also Kingdom in Caledon valley *under* Moshweshwe.
Calvinism, *see* Dutch Reformed Church.
Campbell, John, missionary, with reference to art, 46; to displacement of Khoikhoi by Dutch settlers, 68–69; to Kora hordes, 69; to 'Bastards', 70; to buildings in Hurutshe capital, 139 n. 2; to the Thamaga and trade in grain, 142; to Hurutshe and tobacco, 142; to metallurgy, 143–4; to gold and silver ornaments, 146; to leather work, 147; to regent of Kaditshwene and trade, 149–50, 152; to beads and money, 152–3; to Sotho settlements and chiefs, 153, 158; to Makoon, San chief, 165; to languages, 165.
Cane, John, 349, 353, 361.
Cannibalism, 391, 395, 399.
Canning, George, *and* slavery, 306.
Cape, the:
 Rock paintings in, 23, 29 f.
 Cape Station established, 187–90, defects and advantages, 190–2. *See also* Table Bay. Characteristics, 185, 188, 190–1, of eighteenth-century society, 228–32; problems in late eighteenth century, 183–4, 198–9.
 British conquests of the Cape, 273, 275, 277, 288 f., 312; military government (1795–1803), 313.
 Changes in political control (1795–1815), 273, 275, 287–9.
 Dutch government: Council of Justice,

INDEX

215 f., 219 f., 223, 225, 228, 297 ff. and n. 1, 312 f. Council of Policy, 215–23, 225–8, 297, 299 n. 1, 311, 313, 318. Governor, 216–19, 222, 228, 297; Vice-Governor, 217, 219 f. Captain, 217. Independent Fiscal, 217, 219–20, 222, 297 and n. 1, 299–300, 314.
Abuses and weaknesses of Executive, 221–2, 297, unchecked by judiciary, 221–2, increase in bureaucracy, 217, interference with interaction between whites and non-whites, 238, 240; corruption and weakness of officials, 214 f., 217–19. Opposition by burghers, 213–14, 218, 220–2 and n. 10, *see also* Burghers.
Local government, 223–6, 312 f.
See also Batavian Republic; Dutch East India Company; *and under* Commissioners of Inquiry; Education; Finance; Frontiers; Law and Justice; Population.
Cape Chamber of Commerce, 294, 331.
Cape Colony:
British government:
Governor, 307, 314, 317 f., 320, 323, 333, 382, *see also* High Commissioner for South Africa; Ordinances.
Advisory Council, 304, 307, 317 f. 320, 325.
Executive Council, 318, 320, 323, 328.
Legislative Council, 320–3, 328, 331.
Fiscal, 318; Secretary, 318.
Local government, 318–19, elective municipal boards, 319, 322 f.
Constitution of 1853, 285, 323–4, 329, 333. Parliament, Upper House, 323, 328, Lower House, 328, 331, Parliament *and* budget, 329; *and* English language, 283, 285. Acts relating to African labour, 309, 311.
See also Representative government; Responsible government.
British government, problems in 1806, 277–8; economic policy, 288–90, 294 f., *and* burghers' trade grievances, 288; *and* expeditions, 135; policy regarding settlers and the Xhosa, 241–4; *and* 'border ruffians', 245; *and* annexation of Basutoland and Griqualand West, 331–2 and n. 7; *and* Great Trek, 355 n. 3, 370–1, *see also under* Voortrekkers.
See also Law and Justice; Ordinances.
Cape of Good Hope Punishment Act (1836), 354, 370, 410, 413, 423.
Cape of Good Hope Trade Society, 294.
Cape Town, 190, 201, 211, 213, 232; Bishop of, 258, *see also* Gray, Robert; Burgher Council, 223, 227–8; Court of Petty Cases, 220, 223; Matrimonial Council, 222–3; Orphan Chamber, 222–3, 226; Philanthropic Society, 308.
Banking, 296; market for meat etc., 235, 237, 288; Commercial Exchange, 294; Commercial Hall, 319, diamond exhibited in, 446; shops, 294.
Architecture, 281; church founded, 230, Groote Kerk, 286; hospital, 191, 197; schools, 276; George's Coffee House, Berg Street, 294.
Population, 196; slaves at, 205; rule of law, 298; political supremacy challenged, 324; petition (1834) for annexation of Port Natal, 352; Xhosa visit, 240.
'Cargo Cults', 260.
Carnarvon, Henry Herbert, fourth Earl of, *and* federalism, 324.
Casalis, Eugene, 267; mission to Thaba Bosiu, 400–1; with reference to settlement of Sotho, 134.
Cathcart, Sir George, High Commissioner for South Africa, 421–2, 443.
Cattle:
Rock paintings of, 23, 29 f.; breeds, Afrikander, 108 and n. 1, 109, 166, Gona and Xhosa, 103, long-horned Sanga, 142, Zulu, 107; numbers, 107; stock-breeding, 71–72, *see also* Stock farming.
Used for racing, riding, and transport, 56, 58, 100, 108, 142–3, 154, in war, 56, 58.
Barter and trade, 64–65, 81, 83, 121, 143 f., 147, 149 152, 189, 194, 197 f., 208, 212, 234 f., 237 f., 240, 251, 340, 407. Captured and handed over in war, 362, 367 and n. 4, 411, 421, 441.
Stealing and raids, 64 f., 70, 72, 234, 237, 240, 242, 244, 266 and n. 6, 268, 280, 281 n. 4, 370, 399 f., 419, 442 f.
Kaffirs *and*, 80, 82 f.; Khoikhoi *and*, 55–58, 107–8 and n. 1, 253; Ngoni *and*, 108, 173; Nguni *and*, 96, 101 f., 104, 107, 110, 120–1, 127, 130, 142; Shaka *and*, 343, 345; Sotho *and*, 142–3, 153 ff., 162 and n. 3; Tswana *and*, 132, 142; Xhosa 'Cattle-killing', 129, 256–60, 264, 432.
Cattle byres, 110–13, 127, 148.
See also under Clientship; rinderpest *under* Diseases; Tsetse.
Cave of Hearths, Transvaal, 1, 8 f., 18.
Central Africa, peoples of, 111, 130; slavery in, 121.
Cetshwayo, Zulu chief, *and* riding ox, 108 n. 6; his great place, 111 n. 5; succeeds Mpande, 364.
Chalmers, William, missionary, 239.

INDEX

Chase, J. C., *and* regional division of the Cape, 325.
Chiefdoms, evolution of, viii; fragmentation of, 250–4, 440–1; indirect rule through chiefs, 376–7, 385, 387. *See also under* separate peoples.
Children, apprenticed, 248, 304 f., 367, 370, 437; captured by commandos, 71, 208 and n. 4, 367 and n. 4, 370, 437; disposal of unwanted, 53, 60.
China, early trade with, 148.
Chinese labour, 66, 193, 387.
Christianity and Christians, 66, 69, 73, 216, 238; *and* the apocalypse, 260; converts, 265–6; Indian, 389; slaves, 300 f., 305 f.; among southern Sotho, 401; Voortrekkers *and*, 407; white settlers *and*, 244, 270; Xhosa reaction to, 256–60, 268.
See also 'Dopper' Church; Dutch Reformed Church; Lutherans; Missionaries; Roman Catholics.
Cilliers, Sarel, 411.
Cira, Mpondomise chief, son of a San woman, 106.
Circuit Commissions of 1812 and 1813, 304 and n. 3.
Civil liberties, *see* Assembly, freedom of; Press, freedom of the; Rule of Law *under* Law and Justice.
Clark, J. D., with reference to wooden artefacts, 17.
Clerk, Sir George, Special Commissioner for disannexation of Orange River Sovereignty, 422 f.
Clientship, 155, 180, 405, between hunters and herders, 63–64, 164–5, between settlers and hunters, 71; between Africans and Coloured, 335, between Afrikanders and Africans, 435; among Nguni, 120–1, among Sotho, 153, among Tswana, 155–6; dependent on cattle, 164–5, 179.
Climate, 101, past, 6–7; at the Cape, 190–1, 211 f.; *and* settlements, 171–2; drought, 238, 270. *See also* Rainfall.
Cloete, Henry, special Commissioner to Natal, 373 and n. 1, 374, 377, 379.
Cloete, Josias, 349, 371.
Cloth, 173 f., 177.
Clothing and ornaments, 49, 55, 103, 110, 113, 147–8, 385, 387, of Kaffirs, 80, 82–83, of Sotho, 131; Kaross, 147–8, 385; missionaries *and*, 239–40, 265 f.
See also Cloth.
'Cochoquas', 68.
Coen's regulations for Indian Empire, 218.
Cole, Sir Galbraith Lowry, Governor of the Cape, 325; *and* agitators, 317; *and* the Zulu, 352.
Colenso, John William, bishop of Natal, 271, controversy concerning, 381–2.
Colesberg, banking at, 296.
Collett family, 281 n. 7.
Collins, Colonel, with reference to size of bands of hunters, 49; to Khoikhoi movements, 57; to commandos and children, 71; to Nguni cattle, 107; to Nguni order and security, 122, 124; to ritual regarding milk, 127; to Khoikhoi and Kaffirs, 247; to Xhosa population, 255.
Colonial Office, policy of, 369, 425, 445; *and* amelioration of slavery, 308; appointment of councillors, 328; Commission of Inquiry of 1823, 317; freedom of the Press, 315; German immigrants, 282; Griqualand West, 332. *See also under* Glenelg.
Coloured people, xi, 165 f., 184, 249, 270, 335, graziers, 250; *and* frontier defence, 280, 322; *and* intermarriage, 245–6; *and* free labour, 293; *and* schools, 261, 284; *and* Xhosa land, 252; ill-treatment by 'border ruffians', 245.
Removal of disabilities, 303–5, 309, 322, white opposition to, 310, 322.
represented on local and municipal councils in Cape Colony, 319.
In Caledon valley, 401–2, 404; in Kat valley, 244–5, 248; in Natal, 348, 366 n. 1, 367; in Orange Free State, 442; *and* Great Trek, 355 n. 3, 360 f.
See also dependents *under* Voortrekkers, *and under* Labour.
Commandos, origin and composition of, 226–7; rock painting of, 106; *and* stock raiding, 242; expeditions against hunters, 50, 71, 208, 212 f., 226–7, against Xhosa, 237, 268.
Transvaal and Orange Free State commandos, 432, 439–42, 444 f.; Voortrekker, 411–12, 416; *and* Great Trek, 358, 362; Griqua commandos, 404; Khoikhoi and Coloured people in, 246–7, 411.
See also under Children.
Commissioners of Inquiry, *and* Cape government, 214–15, 217, 314 n. 2, 317–19; *and* office of Independent Fiscal, 297 n. 1; *and* freedom of the press, 315; *and* regional division of the Cape, 324 f.
Congella, Natal, 364, 371.
Congo, clientship in, 64 n. 1.
Constitutions:
See under Cape Colony, British government; *under* Eastern Cape; Republic

INDEX

and British Colony *under* Natal; *under* Orange Free State; *under* Transvaal. *See also* Federalism.
Convention of 1815, *and* status of Cape Colony, 314.
Cooke, C. K., with reference to archaic fauna, 3.
Cooke, H. B. S., with reference to rainfall, 7, 16. *See also* Wells, L. H. and Cooke, H. B. S.
Copper, 38, 56, 81, 114, 150-1, 168, 177, 180 f., 238, 294, 296, Sotho *and*, 143 f., 146 f. Musina mines, 173-4, 180.
Coqui, Adolph, *and* Orange Free State Constitution, 429.
Corranas, the, 43, 165. *See* Kora.
Cotton, 173, 375, 381, 387.
Cowan, Dr., traveller, *and* Dingiswayo, 338 and n. 5.
Cradock, Governor, Proclamation of 1813, 292; *and* education, 283; *and* slaves, 305 f.; *and* tenure of farms, 291 and n. 5.
Cradock, Scots clergy at, 285.
Craig, Major-General, *and* abolition of torture, 297.
Crime, increase in, 305.
Crown, reserve powers of, 318. *See also* Crown lands *under* Land.
Cungwa, Xhosa chief, 238, 240.
Cunu, The, 345.
Customs tariff, 329 f.

Dale, Langham, Superintendent-General of Education, 284.
D'Almeida, *and* skirmish with Khoikhoi (1510), 187.
Dama, *see* Negro people.
Dambuza, Dingane's councillor, 359, 363.
Dancing, 54, 128 f., 145, 162, 266; Kaffir, 81; Zulu war dances, 359 f. *See also under* Khoikhoi; San; Xhosa.
Dange, the, 250.
Daniell, Samuel, *and* expedition of 1801, 135; *and* homesteads in Dithakong, 139; *and* metal ornaments and tools, 143; *and* ostrich feather parasols, 147.
Danish ships at Cape, 274.
Dapper, O., seventeenth-century journal of, 45; with reference to Khoikhoi camps, 58.
Darling, Sir Charles Henry, Lieutenant-Governor of the Cape, 323.
Dart, R. A., with reference to tool-making, 11-14.
Das, Claas, interpreter for Dutch, 66.
Davids, Piet, *and* the Griqua, 402 f., 414, 419.
Debe Nek, 235.
De Buys, Coenraad, 240.

De Chavonnes, Captain D. P., Governor at the Cape, 215 f., *and* schools, 276, *and* white immigration, 200.
De Jong, C., with reference to social conditions of Cape settlers, 232; to lack of education, 276.
De Kiewiet, C. W., *A History of South Africa: Social and Economic*, vii.
Delegorgue, Adulphe, with reference to cattle and children captured by commandos, 367 n. 4.
Delagoa Bay, 78, 148, 150-1, 340, 346, 348, 357, 410 f., 413, 441.
De Mist, J. A. M., Commissioner-General, 275; memorandum (1802) on the Cape, 183; *Kerkenordre* of 1804, 275 and n. 7; *and* Cape law, 299 n. 1; *and* finance, 313; press, 314; schools, 276, 283, 313; trade, 288 f.
Denyssen, Fiscal, with reference to status of slaves, 300; to political meetings, 315.
Derdepoort, Transvaal Voortrekker meeting at, 420.
De Salis, R. A., *and* private business, 294.
De Suffren, Admiral, 275, 287.
De Villiers, Chief Justice J. H., with reference to English language, 283.
Diamonds, 1, 252, 293, 329, 332, discovery of, 425, 442, 446.
Diaz, Bartholomew, 78, 80, 187.
Dicke, B. H., with reference to trade routes, 151, to Venda marriage rites, 171.
Difaqane, the, meaning, 391; 391-9, 402, 414, 419, 435, 440 f., 446; sources of information for, 392-3, 396.
Dimawe district, the Kwena in, 438 f.
Dingane, Shaka's half-brother, murders Shaka and succeeds him, 351-3; murders Matiwane, 394; his kraal, 344 n. 4; *and* Swazi, 362; *and* Voortrekkers, 358-63, 367, 370, 387, 409; *and* white traders, 353 f., 358; *and* trade, 251, 340; *and* capture of cattle, 108.
Dingiswayo, Nguni chief, 87, 115, 119, 121, 129, 251, 336 f., 363; military changes, 124, 160, 339, 341-2; innovations, 341-4; wars, 341, 343, 346 f., 393; *and* Shaka, 342-3 and n. 2; *and* Dr. Cowan, 338; *and* trade, 340.
'Diplomatic Agent to the Native Tribes', *see* Shepstone, Theophilus.
Diviners, 263, 269 f.
Diseases and epidemics: causes of, 269 f.; dysentery, 101, 178; malaria, 101, 132, 178, 409 f., 413, 424; rinderpest, 132; scurvy, 188-9; smallpox (1713, 1735, 1767), 68, 184, 204, 210; tuberculosis, 293. Remedies, 106; vaccination, 150. *See also* Tsetse areas.

INDEX

Dithakong, 135, 139, 141 f., 145, 152, 154, 166, 179 f.; battle of, 397; population (1801), 153.

Dlamini people, in Swaziland, 90, 93, 97, 164, 346; chiefs and burial sites, 90. *See also under* Mpondo, the; Ndungunya.

Donkin, Sir Rufane, acting Governor at the Cape, 279–80.

'Dopper' Church, 428, 434.

Dordrecht, rock paintings, 29.

Douglas, Commissioner, 215, 227.

Drakensberg, the, 38, 44, 97 f., 102; rock paintings, 23, 29, 50; nineteenth-century paintings, 72; occupants in eighteenth century, 90.

Drakenstein, Huguenots at, 196; difficulties, 201; subordinate to Stellenbosch, 223; church founded at, 230; rule of law, 298.

Drury, Robert, with reference to slave trade, 121.

Dugmore, Revd. H. H., 281 n. 6; with reference to Nguni chiefs' retinue, 119.

Dumesa, the, in southern Natal, 376.

Du Plessis, Field-Cornet J. H., 441–2.

D'Urban, Sir Benjamin, Governor of Cape, 354, 376, 416; annexation of Xhosa land, 243; settlement of the Mfengu, 274; Legislative Council, 320; *and* frontier settlement, 325; *and* annexation of Natal, 369; *and* Voortrekkers, 370; *and* Mzilikazi, 411; treaty (1834) with Waterboer, 415.

Durban, 83–84, 251, 354, 380 f., 413; pottery, 35; banking, 296; Indians in, 389. *See also* Port Natal.

Dutch, early settlers at the Cape, 57, 103, 107, 135, 187–9, 193–202; immigrants in eighteenth century, 231, 274; *and* aboriginal inhabitants, 40, 44, 65–69, *and* African languages, 66; struggle with San and Xhosa, 183–4; political standing, 213–14; *and* British government at Cape, 278; *and* slaves, 307. *See also* Afrikaners; Boers; Burghers. Trekboers; Voortrekkers; White settlers.

Dutch East India Company, government of the Cape, *see under* Cape, the, *and* Seventeen, Chamber of the.

Origin, composition, and powers, 183–6; *and* Cape station, 189–203, 205, 231; *and* the Remonstrance of 1649, 188, 190; *and* immigration, 196–201.

Economic privileges, 287; finances, 287–8, 295; trade, 201–3; *and* frontier, 245; *and* defence, 226; religious policy, 275, 286, *and* Dutch Reformed Church, 229; *and* burghers, 220, 222. Opposition to, 311–12.

Dutch Eastern Empire, 185 ff., 206, 213, 218, 231, political structure, 214. *See also* Batavia.

Dutch Reformed Church, 220, 229–31, 270, 275 ff., 285–6 and n. 2, 314, 366–7, *and* Voortrekkers, 407. *Kruiskerk* movement, 277. Cape Colonial Synod, 427–8. *See also* 'Dopper' Church.

Dzata, Venda capital, 174.

Early Stone Age, 1 n. 1, 10–17.

East Africa, Acheulian cultures in, 14 f.; influence on Stone Age cultures, 20, 28; hypothetical migration from, 23; pottery, 23–24.

East India Company (English), 187, 288 f., 294.

East Indies, deportations to, 298 n. 3.

East London, 282, 294, 326.

Eastern Cape, 320, 1836 Constitution for, 325; Lieutenant-Governorship, decline of, 325; Eastern Province Council, 326–7, Separation League, 327. *See also* Separation movement, *and under* Frontier.

Edict of Nantes, revocation of, *and* immigration at Cape, 196.

Education:

schools, 239, 248, 261–3, 272, 283–5, 335, 375, village schools, 239, 248, schools and libraries established by British settlers, 244, 281, 315, Bible and Schools Commission, 283–4; seminaries for teacher training, 239.

Education at Cape in eighteenth century, 230, 276; in Afrikaner republics, 426–7; Natal Africans *and*, 385; Ngoni *and*, 99; slaves *and*, 308 and n. 3.

Education Commission of 1863, 276, 283.

Education Act of 1865, 284–5.

Edwards, 'a certain', *and* libelling of Blair and Lord Charles Somerset, 315.

Edwards, Dr. Isobel, with reference to slavery, 308.

Edwards, R., missionary, *and* Afrikaners, 439.

Elandsfontein, near Hopefield, fossil remains at, 8.

Ellenberger, D. F., and Macgregor, J. C., with reference to dating of Sotho migrations, 134; to stone buildings, 139 f.; to lasting ties between boys circumcized at same time, 160; *and* traditions of the *Difaqane*, 392.

Emboas, the, on Natal coast, 86–87.

English, interlopers, 187; landing at False Bay (1795), 190, 238; *and* Afrikaners, 270 f.; predominance in urban areas, 272; settlers, 279 n. 2, 284. *See also* British, *and under* Albany.

INDEX

Enslin, J. A., 420.
Erasmus, Stephanus, *trekboer* leader of elephant-hunters, 411.
Europe, wooden spears in, 16; hunter-gatherer communities in, 27.
Europeans, advance of, 57; adventurers in Soutpansberg district, 441; traders and teachers in Afrikaner republics, 426. *See also* White settlers.
Eva, niece of Herry, married to Pieter van Meerhoff, 66.
Ewer, R. F., with reference to archaic fauna, 3, 5.
Expedition of 1801, to the Sotho, 135, 137.
Eyasi, Tanzania, fossilized skull from, 9.

Fairbairn, John, 315 f., 322 f.
Fairs and markets, *see under* Trade.
Faku, Mpondo chief, 89, 93, 255 f., 259, 346, 351, 371. *See also* Mpondo, the.
False Bay, archaeological evidence at, 15; English landing at (1795), 190. *See also under* Shipwrecks.
Famine, 242, 254 f., caused by Xhosa 'cattle-killing', 258.
Farewell, Francis, *and* Natal, 348 and n. 3; *and* Shaka, 349; *and* Jacob Msimbiti, 353; killed by the Qwabe, 352.
Farmers, ix, 47, 55, 57, 194, 196, 198, 270, patriarchal character, 232; Afrikaner farmers, 426, 436; peasant farmers, 335; protest (of 1705-6), 199; *and* dependent clients, 63; *and* slaves, 121, 232; forbidden to employ Xhosa, 238. *See also* Agriculture; Boers; Stockfarming.
Farms: individual tenure of, 263-4; loan farms, 287 f., 291-2; perpetual quitrent tenure, 291 and n. 5, 292 n. 1. Afrikaner and British farms, community of, 335.
Farms of Voortrekkers in Natal, 364, 374, 377 f.
Fauna, archaic, 3, 5.
Faure, Abraham, 315.
Fauresmith culture, 3, 6, 15, 17 f.
Federalism, 324-5, 331, 425, 433.
Feirrera, 'border ruffian', 245.
Finance:
lack of capital at the Cape, 202. Revenue and taxation, 192, 203-4, 207, 216, 329 and n. 2, 330; assessment for, 225; income tax, 330; taxation of Africans, 436, of grazing land, 210-12; local taxes, 223, 225.
Dutch East India Company *and*, 287. Organization of, 295-6, 313-14.
Government Expenditure under Constitution of 1853, 329 and n. 2, 330; Civil List, 329.

Finance in Afrikaner republics, 426-7; in Natal Republic, 365-6; in Natal Colony, 375, 377, 386-7; in Orange River Sovereignty, 417.
See also Banks; Crown lands *under* Land; Money; Independent Fiscal *under* Dutch government *under* Cape, the.
'Fingos', *see* Mfengu.
Firearms and gunpowder, changes caused by, 63 f., 132, 165, 346; Khoikhoi *and*, 69, 181; forbidden to Africans, 435, 437, 443. Trade in, 238, 242, 251 f., 259, 352, 359, 405, 407, 409, 421, 423-5, 427, 433, 439. Superiority over African weapons, 252, 349, 362, 397, 400, 402.
First Intermediate culture, 1 n. 1, 3.
Fitzgerald, J. P., *and* hospital at King William's Town, 263, 270.
Fleck, minister of Dutch Reformed Church, 276.
Florisbad, Orange Free State, archaic deposits at, 7 f., 10, 18 f.
Fodo, chief of the Dumesa, 376.
Fokeng, the, 133 f., 144, 154, 165, 391, 395, *and* iron, 180. Fokeng chief married to San woman, 106 and n. 5, 165.
Food: of herders, 55, 60; of hunters, 47-49, 52, 54, 60; of Kaffirs, 79, 81 f.; of Nguni, 110-11; of Sotho, 142; at the Cape, 192 ff., 288; *see also under* Xhosa. Food supply, 63 f., 107. Game, 235, 254.
Honey, 48, 55, 193.
Fish, 48, 50, 55, 82, 96-97, 167, 177; *see also under* Taboos.
Meat, 55, 82, 235.
Milk, 55, 60, 80, 82 f., 110, 127, 142, 162, 235, 242.
See also crops *under* Agriculture.
Foreigners, incorporated in Nguni clans, 120 f.
Forests, reduced, 110; on frontier, 249.
Fort Beaufort, banking, 296.
Fort Brown, *see* Hermanus Kraal.
Fort Napier, 373.
Fort Peddie, 376.
Fort Willshire, fair at, 241 f., 251, 279 f.; frontier post, 248.
Fossils, 2 f., 5 f., 8-10, 21.
Franchise, 273, 319, 322-4, 333; in Natal, 382, 386; in Orange Free State, 429.
Frankfort, Orange Free State, building and pottery, 38; hut settlements, 35 f.
Frazer, D., with reference to education of the Ngoni, 99 n. 10.
Frederiksburg, military colony at, 279 f.
French immigrants at the Cape, 231, 283, *see also* Huguenots; missionaries, 392 n. 1, 400-2, 415, 445, Paris Evangelical Missionary Society, 400.

INDEX

French Revolution, influence in South Africa, 312.
Frontier: in eighteenth century, 211–13; boundary shifts, 252, 268, 273, 417, advanced by Great Trek, 406; administrative districts, 212 f.
Policy regarding, 241, 243–4, 260, 278, 280, 327, 331, 377, Sir Harry Smith *and*, 417.
Struggle for land on, 235–7, 240–1, 243, 249–52, 268, *see also under* Wars.
Defence, 278 ff.; disaffection, 406; 'border ruffians', 245; stock raids, 242, 281 and n. 4, 292; Cape Frontier Mounted Police, 446; Frontier Commissioner and Agent General, 325.
Coloured people *and*, 249; *trekboers* and, 292.
Eastern Cape frontier, 233–46 *passim*, 370, 372, 419, 421, 444.
Frykenius, Commisioner-General, 218, 274, 287, 297 n. 1, 299.
Furs, 147, 177.
Fynn, Henry Francis, diary, with reference to northern Nguni, 336–40; to Dingane, 353, 358; to Dingiswayo, 115, 338, 341 and n. 2, 343 and n. 2; to Shaka's Zulu army, 344 n. 2; *and* Natal, 348, 383 n. 2; *and* Shaka, 349 f.

Galbraith, John S., with reference to British annexation of Natal, 372.
Galton, Francis, with reference to hunting in the Kalahari, 48–49.
Gama, Vasco da, 78, 150, with reference to copper trade, 177; Arab pilot of, 168.
Gardiner, Allen, missionary, 352 n. 7; information from, 336; *Narrative of a Journey to the Zoolu Country in South Africa*, 354; with reference to Nguni cattle byres, 112; *and* mission to Zulu, 352; *and* relations between Natal and Dingane, 354; *and* Voortrekkers, 358–60.
Gasa kingdom, *see under* Shoshangane.
Gaseitsiwe, chief of the Ngwaketse, 435, 438 f.
Gcaleka, the, campaign against, 242; war with the Mfengu, 249; senior chief, 250 and n. 1; population, 255.
Genadendal village, 247.
Genootskap van Regte Afrikaners, 285.
Geology: eras, Holocene, 6, 8, Pleistocene, 2, 6–9, 12 f., Pliocene, 2, Quaternary, 2, 7, Tertiary, 6.
George, school at, 284.
Germans, at the Cape, 186, 194, 231, 274; frontier settlements, 244, 252–3, 281–2 and n. 2; British-German Legion, 282 f. and n. 1.

See also Lutherans.
Gezani, Daniel, 261.
Gibb, Lieutenant C. J., and African lands in Natal, 374.
Gibson, J. Y., *The Story of the Zulus*, 339.
Girls, schools *and*, 262, 276.
Glass, artefact from, 27.
Glen Grey District, sheep in, 263.
Glen Lyndon, settlers and Coloured people in, 270.
Glenelg, Charles Grant, Baron, Colonial Secretary, reverses D'Urban's annexation of Xhosa land, 243; *and* protection of Africans against Voortrekkers, 370.
Gluckman, Professor Max, with reference to pressure of population among northern Nguni, 340; to Shaka, 344 n. 3.
Godeffroy, Hamburg firm of, *and* German immigrants, 282.
Goderich, Frederick John Robinson, Viscount, *and* freedom of the press, 316 and n. 9.
Godlonton, Robert, *Journal*, 326; with reference to population of Kaffraria, 255; *and* Basutoland, 331; *and* Legislative Council, 322; *and* regional division of the Cape, 325.
Gold, 146 f., 168 and n. 3, 173, 177, 193, discovery of, 425, 446.
Goldswain, Jeremiah, journal, 281 n. 1.
Gona, the, 57, 61, 68, 70, 102–3 and n. 7, 107, 246, 248.
Gonnema, the, of Saldanha Bay, war with Dutch, 65.
Goodwin, A. J. H., with reference to van Riebeeck's diary and cattle, 23.
Gordon, Colonel R. J., *and* colony of Europeanized Khoikhoi, 69–70; *and* Spanish merinos, 290.
'Gorinhaiquas', the, 68.
Gosselin, Constant, mission to Thaba Bosiu, 400.
Govan, William, founder of Lovedale school, 263.
Gqunukwebe, the, 103, 236, 250.
Graaff-Reinet, 279 n. 2, administrative district, 213, 223, 227 f.; banking at, 296; Chamber of Commerce, 294; church at, 230, 270; Khoikhoi and Coloured in, 247, 303; revolt at, 185, 227, 240, 312 and n. 5; school, 284; *and* Grahamstown, 326.
Grahamstown, architecture, 281; banking, 296; battle of, 247; Bishop of, 258; British settlers *and*, 244, 279; exports from, 242; fair at, 241; Parliament at, 326; school, 261; separatist movement in, 322, 326; Xhosa attack, 256.

INDEX 457

Granville, second Earl, Colonial Secretary, 328, *and* responsible government, 330.

Gray, Robert, Bishop of Cape Town, 263, Metropolitan Archbishop of South Africa, 381–2.

Grazing, 40–41 and n. 7, 49, 56–57, 84, 108; extension in eighteenth century, 211–12; decrease, 254; disputes regarding, 65, 106–7, 240; grants and licences, 210–12; white settlers *and*, 184, 194, 208–12, 235, 244, 250, 253, 269, 291. *See also* sheep-walks *under* Sheep.

'Great-place' of chiefs, 111 n. 5, 264–5.

Great Trek, the, 245, 292 and n. 7, 293, 310, 355–63, 368, 370, 405–24; rebellion against British government, 406. *See also* Voortrekkers.

Green, Henry, Resident in Orange River Sovereignty, 421.

Green, James, Dean of Pietermaritzburg, 381.

Greig, George, 315 ff.

Grevenbroek, seventeenth-century journal of, 45; with reference to Dutch authority in the Cape, 67.

'Grigriqua' hordes, 67, 70.

Grey, Sir George, governor of Cape Colony, biographical information and policy, 260–4, 268, 296, 327–9, 432–3, 445; *and* chiefs, 264; *and* education, 261 f.; *and* farming, 263; *and* federalism, 324, 425, 433; *and* Orange Free State and southern Sotho, 432; with reference to population and settlement of Kaffraria, 255, 282.

Grey, Sir Henry George Grey, third Earl, Colonial Secretary, *and* annexation of Kaffraria and Orange River Sovereignty, 417, 419, 421; *and* convicts, 331; *and* representative government, 321, 323.

Griqua, the, 68 and n. 6, 70 f., 84, 102 n. 4, 293, 394, 396–7, 400, 402, 410, 414–16, 419, 422, 442; British *and*, 418, 423; commandos, 404; mission stations among, 392; East Griqualand founded, 442; Griqualand West, Cape Colony *and*, 331 f. and n. 7. *See also* Kok, Adam; Waterboer, Andries.

Groenendaal, J. G., *and* Orange Free State Constitution, 429 f.

Gumban 'B' stone-bowl culture, 24.

'Gunjeman', 65, 79, 103.

Gwali, son of Xhosa chief, Tshiwo, 236.

Gwali, the, 250.

G/wi, the, 43 f., 48 ff., 52 ff.

Hahn, Theophilus, with reference to Namaquas, 43; to Nama religion and customs, 45 f., 61 f.; to Khoikhoi trade, 61.

Hammond-Tooke, W. D., with reference to Nguni political units, 119 n. 4.

Hancock, Sir Keith, with reference to security and trade, 240.

Hand-axes, 1 ff., 5 f., 8 f., 13–16, 18.

Hangklip, archaeological evidence at Cape, 15; Thembu defeated near, 249.

Hare, Colonel, Lieutenant-Governor of Eastern Cape, 325.

Harris, Cornwallis, with reference to stone building, 140.

Hattersley, Alan, with reference to British emigrants to Natal, 379.

Healdtown, school at, 261.

Heidelberg, Transvaal, Voortrekker settlement at, 413.

Heikum, the, 45.

Hemp, smoking of, 142.

Herders, ix, 10, 22, 28 f., 80, 159, hunters become, 71–72; *and* settlers, 65; *and* traders, 64–65. *See also* Khoikhoi, *and under* Clientship.

Herero, The, 70.

Hermanus Kraal, 235.

Herry, van Riebeeck's interpreter, 55, 66.

Herschel District, rock paintings, 29.

Hessequas, the, independent villages of, 67; *and* Dutch authority, 67; *and* European employers, 66; *and* herds, 65.

Heupenaer, *and* ivory trade with the Thembu, 234, 246.

Heyns, Commissioner, 215.

High Commissioner for South Africa, 333, 382; *and* Afrikaner republics, 427.

Hintsa, Xhosa chief over sub-chiefs, 118, 152, 245, 250 and n. 1, 251, 255, *and* wives, 269.

Hintsati, Khoikhoi chief, 236.

Historiography of Africa, v—viii, x.

Hlakwana, the, 391, 395, 397. *See also* Khgaraganye.

Hlubi, the, 97, 101, 115, 345, 347, 376; chiefdom, 90, 249, genealogies of chiefs, 90–91; *and the Difaqane*, 391, 399; defeated, 393 and n. 4, 395, 398. *See also under* Marriage; *and also* Langalibalele; Mpangazita; Poto.

Hodgson, Thomas, Wesleyan missionary, with reference to the *Difaqane*, 396.

Hoernlé, Winifred, with reference to Khoikhoi clans, 58–59; to rituals, 62.

Hoffman, Josias, President of the Orange Free State, 425, 429, 431.

Hogge, William S., assistant to Sir Harry Smith, 419–21.

Hoja, the, 139, 142.

Hominids, 8 f., 11 f.

Homo erectus, 8 f., 12.

Homo habilis, 12 f.
Homo sapiens, 8, 10, 21.
Hop, Hendrik, with reference to the Sotho, 135.
Hopefield, archaeological site, 3, 6, 8 f., 12.
Hopetown District, Cape Colony, diamond *and*, 446.
Horton, Sir Robert John Wilmot, *and* representative government at the Cape, 319.
Hospital and Orphan Chamber at the Cape, 217.
Hottentots, ix, *see also* Khoikhoi.
Howieson's Poort culture, 20 f.
Huguenots, settled at Cape, 196–7, 213, 274, 281 f.; immigration stopped, 198.
Huising, Henning, leader of free farmers, 199.
Hume, *and* ivory trade, 148.
Hunters, ix, 10, 22, 28, 43–44, 47, 154, 159, 165, 425, 439, distribution, 105, 181; independent, 63–64; of the Kalahari, 41; hunted by Khoikhoi and settlers, transformed into herders, 70–72.
See also Naron; San; *and under* Clientship.
Hunting, land for, 235, 240, 254; methods, 48–49; Xhosa *and*, 110.
See also game *under* Food.
Hurutshe, the, 133–4, 139 and n. 2, 140, 148, 153, 158, 179, 181, 397, 438; *and* metals, 143 ff.; *and* tobacco, 142.
Hyrax Hill, Kenya, pottery, 23–24.

India, 187, trade route to, 369. Statutes of, *see* Statutes *under* Batavia.
Indian labourers in Natal, 387–90.
Indian Mutiny, 282.
Indonesia, settlers from, 172, 193 n. 9, slaves from, 205.
Inglis, R., missionary, *and* Afrikaners, 439.
Insurance companies, 295.
Intermingling of peoples, 120 f., 233–4, 236.
See also Intermarriages *under* Marriage.
'Inhaca', *see* Nyaka.
Irish settlers, 279 n. 2, 282.
Iron, 33, 35, 49, 79, 81, 102, 106, 114, 135, 151 f., 180; Sotho *and*, 143 ff., 147.
See also under Taboos.
Iron Age, xii, 1 n. 1, 24, 31–39; immigrants, 30, 37; villages, 30 ff., 34 ff., 141.
Isaacs, Nathaniel, early trader, 336 f., 348 and n. 3, 349 f., 353.
Italeni, Battle of (1838), 361, 412.
Italians, 283.
Ivory, trade in, 69 f., 78, 106, 110, 121, 148, 150, 177, 179 f., 193, 234 f., 238, 240, 242, 251, 340, 348, 413; carving, 147 f.

Jabavu family, 100.
Jameson, L. S., ministry of 1904–8, 330.
Janssens, Governor, 238, 240, 245 f., 275 f.
Java, 186 f.; ricefields destroyed, 206.
Jele, the, 99 f. and n. 2.
Jervis, Captain, *and* peace between Dingane and Natal Republic, 370.
Jews, 276 and n. 1, 283 n. 1, 294, traders, 407, 426.
Jobe, chief of the Mthethwa, father of Dingiswayo, 338.
Johannesburg, Chamber of Commerce, 294.
Joubert, W. F., 420.
Judicial Committee of the Privy Council, *and* Colenso controversy, 381.
Junod, Revd. H. A., *The Life of a South African Tribe*, with reference to the Tsonga, 176.
Juridical customs, among hunters, 51, 60–61; among Nguni, 121–3; among Tswana, 158; among Sotho, Tsonga, and Venda, 182; among Lobedu, 158.
Jury, trial by, instituted, 302.

Kaapse Patriotte, 183, 214, 220, 222, 228, 287, 298–300.
Kaditshwene, Tswana town, 139, 141, 143, 146 f., 152 ff., 158, 179 f.; paintings in chief's hut in, 46; statement on trade by regent of, 149–50; *and* vaccination, 150.
Kaffirs, 57, 264; described, 80, 383–4; Portuguese *and*, 78–80; 'Kaffir Employment Act,' 310.
See also Africans, *and under* Wars.
Kaffraria, 255, 329, 331; settlement of, 281–2; separation policy *and*, 324; incorporated in Cape Colony, 326–7, annexed, 378, 417; Kaffrarian Association, 327.
Kalahari, hunting in the, 48–49.
Kalambo Falls, Zambia, wooden artefacts at, 16.
Kalomo village, 32.
Kamer van Commercie established, 294.
Kanjera, fossilized skulls at, 9.
Kano, trading town, 181.
Kanye area, the Ngwaketse in, 435, 438.
Kapain, Voortrekkers defeat Mzilikazi at, 412.
Karanga, the, 163.
Karroo, 7, 19, 103, 107, 290.
Kat River Settlement, 248, 305, Rebellion (1851), 322.
Kay, S., with reference to Kaditshwene, 154.
Kazembe, Lunda chief, 180–1.
Keate's Award, 332.
Keurboomstrand, *see* Matjes River.
Kgalagadi, the, 133 f., 142, 155.
Kgatla, the, settlement near Mabotsa, 144,

INDEX

146; chiefdom of, 134, 158. Kgafela-Kgatla, the, 438. Mmanaana-Kgatla, the, 439.
Kgwakgwe, population (1824), 153.
Khama, Ngwato chief, 155–6.
Khami ruins, Rhodesia, 36.
Khawuta, minor Xhosa chief, homestead of, 111.
Khgaraganye (or Nkgaraganye), leader of the Hlakwana, 395, 397.
Khoikhoi, the, 10, 20 ff., 24, 28, 43–47, 78, 84, 165 f., 181, 204, 231; areas of occupation, 40–41, 56–58, 93, 236, 248, 414; traditions regarding migrations from the East, 45–46.
Social organization, 58–62, clans and hordes, 58–61, disintegration of landless hordes, 67–70; kinship, 58–62; camps, 55 f., 58–59; groups, 65 n. 5; population in 1652, 68; leadership, 59–62; judgements, 60; marriage, 59–60.
Gods and heroes, 62; rituals, 55 f., 59–62, 64, 105; dancing, 62; and Christianity, 69 f., 73, 239.
Economy, 55–58, trade, 61, 64–65, 147 f.; and hemp, 142.
Under Dutch Company, 66–67; Europeanized, 69–70, 73; learn Dutch language, 66; interpreters, 234, 239, 246; and white settlers, 40, 65–66, 184, 189, 192, 194, 208 f., 215–16, 224–5, 234, 246–7, 312 and n. 5.
Emancipated, 272, 292, conditions of life, 293; and land, 293 and n. 4; legal position, 300 f.; rebellion of 1799, 303; regulation and protection, 303 n. 5, 304 n. 1; work passes, 241.
See also Cattle; Quama; and under D'Almeida; Hintsati; Hunters; Nguni; Sotho; Wars; Xhosa.
Kholokwe, the, 443.
Khwane, councillor of Tshiwo, 102–3.
Kimberley, John Wodehouse, first Earl of, Colonial Secretary, 331, 382.
Kimberley, 252.
King, James S., 337, 352 f., and Natal, 348 and n. 3; and Shaka, 349 f.
King, Richard, Natal trader, 371.
King William's Town, population of district, 255; Christian converts at, 265; Grey hospital in, 258, 263, 270; bank at, 296.
Kingdoms formed by amalgamation of African chiefdoms, viii, 334.
Kinship, 52 f., 58–59, 62, 96, 158, 182, 267. See also under Khoikhoi; Nguni; Sotho; Tsonga.
Kirby, P. R., with reference to building in stone, 36, 174.
Kirsten, J. F., economic grievances of, 287.
Klerksdorp, rock paintings, 29. Voortrekker settlement at, 413.
Klip river area, 376 f.
Klipplaatdrif, archaeological site at, 14.
Klipriviersberg, Iron Age village, 34.
Klyn, J. A. & Co., Amsterdam firm, and trade with Natal Republic, 371.
Knight's case, 301.
Koeberg farmers, and resistance to amelioration of slavery, 308.
Kok, Adam, II, 414.·
Kok, Adam, III, 414 f.; treaty (1843) with Governor Napier, 415–16, 423; trek through Lesotho, 442.
Kok, Cornelis, 442.
Kolb, P., with reference to hunting areas, 50; to fighting bulls, 56; to Khoikhoi camps, 58, judgements, 60, rituals, 61; to hunter and herder clientship, 63; to cattle stealing, 64; to employment of labour, 66; to disintegration of the Khoikhoi, 67; to the Nama, 68.
Kolobeng area, the Kwena in, 435.
Kololo, the, defeat Ngoni raiders, 99; and malaria, 101; and canoes, 150; migrant horde, 395; in Zambesi valley, 397.
See also Linyanti; Sebetwane; Sekelutu.
Koni, the, 98.
Kooaneng, Tlokwa capital, 398.
Kora, the, 61, 68 and n. 5, 69 ff., 152, 166, 400 ff., 414, 419, 422, raids, 165 f.; and Sotho, 166; British and, 418.
Koyi, William, and the Ngoni, 99.
Krige, Eileen, with reference to hired labour, 149.
Kromdraai, Transvaal, cave deposits at, 2, 6.
Kropf, Revd. A., author of Xhosa dictionary, and report on cattle-killing, 257 n. 1.
Kumalo, the, 347, 349, 403.
!Kung, hunters, 44, 49–53, 60, 71.
Kruger, Paul, and constitution of South African Republic, 428; Commandant-general of Transvaal, 434, 441.
Kuper, H., with reference to the Dlamini, 90.
Kuruman, 396–7, 411.
Kwena, the, 132, 134, 140, 148, 154; and veneration of crocodiles, 162; and fish taboo, 167; Monaheng division of, 398 f.; in Kolobeng area, 435; and Afrikaners, 438 f. See also Motlumi; Sechele; Sekano.
Kyungu, the, 251.

Labour, 66, 269; based on contract, 293, 436; domèstic, 66, 205, 241, 262, 367

INDEX

Labour, (cont.):
n. 4; farm servants, 71, 149, 241, 256, 258, 293; industrial, 73; migrant, 258, see also under Tswana; white, 195, 201, 204-5, 301, compared with slave, 200, 204; convict, 321, 387.
Khoikhoi and Coloured servants, 246-7, 249, 355, 414, 442; Xhosa herdsmen and labourers, 238, 296, 310.
at the Cape, 192-4, 196, 200, 204; in Natal, 383 f., 387; in Orange Free State and Transvaal, 425, 442; South African Republic and, 435-7, 439; Voortrekkers and, 408, 414; white settlers dependent on African labour, 335-6, 366-7 and n. 4.
Christian missionaries and, 239-40; emancipation of slaves and, 272, 292 and n. 7; freed servants, 193 and n. 7, 194, craftsmen, 293.
Apprenticeship, 280, 309, 355, 366, 408, 437, see also under Children. Regulation of labour, 303-6, 309, 311; work passes, see Passes, and under Khoikhoi.
See also Chinese; Clientship; Indians; Slavery; Truck wages.
Lala, The, 110-11, 114.
Land: competition for, 249-56, 292-3; shortage, 348, 387; grants, 278-80, 282; Crown land, 320, 329-30, 378-80, 385, 388.
African locations in South African Republic, 435 f.; Africans in Natal, 374-5, 379, 384 ff.
Afrikaners in Natal and, 372-5, 378 f., in Orange Free State and Transvaal, 425, in South African Republic, 437-8.
British emigrants in Natal and, 378-80, 384.
Xhosa and, 268-9.
See also under Farms; Frontier; Grazing; Hunting.
Langalibalele, Hlubi chief, 376, 387.
Langeni, the, 342.
Language and physical type, ix.
Languages, 43-44, 50, 64, 66, 72-74, 76, 85, 93, 101 f., 115 f., 129-30, 165 f., 239; changes in, 95-96 and n. 1. Interpreters, 55, 66, 285, 353 f., 360, 376, 383 n. 2, see also under Khoikhoi.
Afrikaans, 66, 70, 184, 231, 248, 285, 366 n. 1.
Bantu, 21, 32, 43, 73 n. 3, 104, 109, 169, see also Bantu speakers under Bantu.
Chinese, 64, 274.
Click, 39 ff., 47, 73, 82 f., 102, 104, 165.
Dutch, 66, 104, 196, 207, 231, 246, 248, 272, 274, 278, 284-5, 305, 366 and n. 1.

English, 66, 272, 274, 280-6, 315, 317, made the official language, 283 and n. 4, 285.
French, 196, 213, 276.
German, 282.
Gona dialect, 246, 248.
G/wi, 43.
Hadza, 47.
Herero, 43, 133.
Italian, 276.
Javanese, 274.
Kaffir, 80-81.
Khoikhoi, 10, 20, 29, 40-41 and n. 6, 43, 45, 47, 53, 66, 69 f., 73, 103 f., 109, 133, 166, 181, 248.
Kora, 166.
!Kung, 44.
Lala dialect, 76, 90.
Latin, 276.
Malay, 274.
Nama, ix, 29, 43, 45, 133.
Naron, 43.
Ndebele, 405.
Ngonde dialect, 169.
Nguni, 38, 56, 75 and n. 2, 76, 95, 98, 101, 104 f., 109, 116, 129, 166, 335.
Nyakyusa, 169.
Pedi, 131.
San, 10, 20, 29, 41 and n. 6, 43 f., 47, 66, 73, 105 and n. 5, 248.
Sandawe, 47.
Sarwa, 133 and n. 5.
Shona, 104 n. 4, 167 and n. 6, 169, 173.
Sotho, 55, 76, 97 f., 104 and n. 2, 131, 133, 165 f., 335.
Swahili, 173.
taal, 184, 231.
tekela dialect, 85, 90, 93, 97, 393.
Tsonga, 76, 104, 176.
Tswana, 131.
Venda, 104 and n. 4, 133, 164, 167 ff.
Xhosa, 75 and n. 3, 81 f., 93, 103 f., 239, 246, 248, 272.
Zulu, 75 f., 85, 98 f., 101, 104, 108, 345, 348, 381.
Late Stone Age, 1 n. 1, 2, 20, 21-31, 33; cultures, see Smithfield; Wilton.
Law and Justice:
at the Cape, 214-17, 219-22, abuses and shortcomings, 221-2, 297, 298-9 and n. 1.
High Court of Justice created (1783), 220; appeal courts, 300 and n. 3; circuit courts, 314; local courts, 223-5, 297, and slaves and Khoikhoi, 224-5; enforcement, 273; Cape placaaten, 297, 299 f., 314.

INDEX

English legal system introduced, 302 and nn. 2 and 6, anglicized courts, 285.
Charter of Justice (1827), 302, 318 n. 1; Chief Justice, 318. Rule of law defended, 298–300. Legal system *and* emancipation of slaves, 309. *See also* Jury, trial by. *See also* Cape of Good Hope Punishment Act; Council of Justice *under* Dutch government *under* Cape, the; Roman-Dutch law; Torture.
in British colony of Natal, 375 f., 385, exemption from 'Native Law', 386.
in Orange Free State, 429 n. 3, 430.
League of Nations, report of 1928 with reference to Khoikhoi and San, 45.
Leather and leather-working, 147–8.
Legends, 86–87.
Leiden, Holland, university, 277.
Lemba, the, *and* gold, 147; *and* the Venda, 172–3, 175.
Leopard's Kopje culture, Rhodesia, 34 f., 39.
Lesotho, x, formation of, 131; San in, 165; Sotho in, 131 n. 3, 145, 155, 419, 444; size of villages in, 154; *and* Xhosa cattle-killing, 259; invaded by Orange Free State commando, 432.
See also Basutoland.
Lestrade, G. P., with reference to Venda language, 169; to Venda settlement, 175.
Le Sueur, cellarer, dispute with Independent Fiscal, 297 n. 1.
Lete, the, *and* iron, 144 and n. 8.
See also Mokgosi.
Letsie, Moshweshwe's senior son, 400 f.
Le Vaillant, F., painting of fighting ox, 56; of Gona people, 103; portraits of 'Tamboeki', 106.
Libombo, Tsonga chief, 176.
Lichtenstein, M. K. H., with reference to Kora chiefs, 61; to Europeanized Khoikhoi, 69–70; to Nguni social structure, 124; to riding oxen, 143; to Xhosa, 114 f., 123, 236, 243, 253, 269.
Liberty of the subject, 272–3, 430.
Libraries, South Africa Public Library, 315.
See also under Education.
Liebenburg, Voortrekker family, 411.
Liesbeeck river, 192, 194.
Limpopo river, as trade route, 150–1, 177.
Lindley, Daniel, American missionary, *predikant* to Natal Republic, 365; *and* African lands in Natal, 374; *and* Mzilikazi, 405 and n. 3; *and* Voortrekkers, 407.
Linyanti, Kololo capital, population (1853), 180.
Liquor, ravages of, 293; excise on, 330; beer, 110, sacrificial beer, 127; brandy, 65, 193, 238. *See also* Wine.

Lishuane, the Griqua at, 402.
Literature and learning, 281.
Literary and Scientific Society (1824), 316.
Livingstone, David, with reference to malaria, 101; to stone walls, 141; to the Makololo and oxen, 143; to metallurgy, 144, 146; to trade in skins, 148; to ivory, 148; to absence of slavery among Sotho, 148; to chiefdoms, 156; to first fruits ritual, 158; to fish taboos, 167; to chiefs and trade, 179; to arms trade, 425, 439. Attacked by Afrikaners, 439.
Lloyd, Lucy, with reference to language, 44.
Lobedu, the, 137, 149, 163; chiefdom, 134, 155; *and* stone walls, 141; legal customs, 158; marriage, 159, 163 n. 1; *and* veneration of wild pigs, 162; rituals, 164; *and* Tsonga, 164; *and* Venda, 168.
Lobengula, son and successor of Mzilikazi, 412.
'Lobola', *see under* Marriage.
Lourenço Marques, 78 f., 81 f., 177, 235, 251, 340; chiefdoms north of, 119.
See also Bambe.
Lovedale, school and training seminary at, 99, 239, 261–3, 270.
Lugard, Frederick, Lord, *and* indirect rule, 377.
Lunda, Kazembe's capital, 180–1.
Lungu clan, descended from survivor of shipwreck, 233.
Luspance, Kaffir chief, 80 f., 83, 95.
Lutherans, 229, 275, 283; missionaries in South African Republic, 437; *and* the Pedi, 440.
Luzac, Elie, *and* 'The Power and the Liberties of a Citizen Association', 311 n. 2.
Lydenburg, Transvaal, archaeological evidence, 39; Voortrekker settlement at, 413, 420, 427, 440; *and* S. A. Republican Constitution, 428; *and* Dutch Reformed Church, 428; *and* Transvaal political struggles, 435.
Lynx, chief in the Bamboesberg, 49.

Mabveni, in Chibi Reserve, Iron Age village settlement, 32.
Macfarlane, Walter, 385.
Macgregor, J. C., *see* Ellenberger, D. F.
Macheng, chief of the Ngwato, 435, 439.
Maclean, Colonel, *and* Xhosa and Thembu population, 255.
Macrorie, William, 'Bishop of Maritzburg', 382.
Madikane, Bhaca chief, 346.
Madura, chief of hunting band, 49.

Magaliesberg, 132 f., Sotho settlements, 141; Voortrekkers in, 420.
Magamma, Xhosa chief, 84.
Magistrates, 243, 264; English system of, 302, 305, 307, 385; Resident Magistrates and Civil Commissioners, 318 f.; new magistracies, 329.
Magosian culture, 20.
Magossche, the, 122.
Magwamba 'knobnoses', *see* Tsonga.
Maitland, Sir Peregrine, Governor of the Cape, *and* the Griqua, 416.
Makanda (or Makana), a diviner, Xhosa war leader, 256, 265, 268, 278.
Makapan valley, 6, Limeworks cave, 11.
Makapane, Sotho chief, 440, 442.
Makapansgat, Transvaal, cave deposits, 2, 11 ff.
Makhado, Venda chief, 442.
Makoanyane, Moshweshwe's circumcision mate, 399.
Makololo, the, and oxen, 143. *See* Kololo.
Makoon, San chief, 165.
Malandela, founding ancestor of Zulu chiefs, 89 n. 4, 90 f., widow of, 117.
Malawi, 99; the Ngoni in, 100 f.; pottery, 169; ivory trade *and* slaves, 235, schools, 262.
Malays, at the Cape, 321; religious freedom under British, 275.
Mambo, Lobedu descent from a, 163.
Mansfield, Earl of, judgement on slavery, 301.
Mantatees, refugee labourers, 241, 280, 393 n. 3, rumours of, 396 and n. 3.
MaNthatisi, chieftainess of the Tlokwa, 393–6, 398.
Mapungubwe, Northern Transvaal, archaeological site, xii, 32–35, 37 ff., 146 ff., 168, 175.
Maqoma, Xhosa chief, 247 f.
Marais, report (1761–2) on the Sotho, 135.
Marais, J. S., *Cape Coloured People*, 45; with reference to exploitation of Khoikhoi, 69; to extermination of hunters, 71; to emancipation of slaves, 310; to republican movement, 312.
Mardykers, 193 and n. 9.
Marico district, Voortrekkers in, 420, 438; revolutionary government in, 435.
Maritz, Gert, 356–8, 361, 364, 408, 411.
Marriage:
among Hlubi, 159; Khoikhoi, 59–60; !Kung and G/wi, 50–53; Swazi, 97, 159; Tsonga, 96, 178; Venda, 171, 175; Xhosa, 83, 97, 267, 269, 271; Zulu, 97. *See also under* Lobedu; Nguni; Sotho; Tswana.

Intermarriages, 66, 101 f., 105 f., 117, 120, 165 f., 245–6, 248, 271, 281, 286, 348, 405.
Levirate, 59; 'lobola', 266; polygyny, 83, 111, 119, 125, 266, 269, 271, 400.
Marshall, Mrs., with reference to !Kung hunters, 50 f., 53, 60.
Maseu, 154.
Mashobane, father of Mzilikazi, 403.
Mason, R. J., with reference to Stone Age culture, 14; to pottery, 36; to stone buildings, 139; to Sotho settlements, 141.
Masweu, population of (1820), 153.
Matabele, the, *see* Ndebele, the.
Matabeleland, 76 n. 4, 412.
Matiwane, Ngwane chief, 350, 391, 394; *and* total war, 243; attacked by Shaka, 347, 399, by Dingiswayo and Zwide, 393; attacks Moshweshwe, 399, 443; defeated by Cape forces and allies, 394.
Matjes River archaeological site, 24–27.
Mauch, Carl, *and* gold, 446.
Maun, Tswana capital, 155.
Mauritius, sugar planting in, 388.
Maynier, H. C. D., *Landrost* of Graaf-Reinet, *and* cattle raids, 237; *and* regulation of labour conditions, 303; *and* republican movement, 312.
Mazelspoort, archaic tools in, 19.
Mbalu, the, 250.
Mbholompo, battle (1828) at, 394.
Mbo, the, 84.
Mbopha, Shaka's servant, 351.
Mbulazi, son of Mpande, 364.
Mekuatling, the Taung at, 402.
Melkbosch, archaeological site, 6.
Melville Koppies, Transvaal, archaeological site, 35; iron workings at, 135, 145.
Mentzel, O. F., with reference to Cape hospital, 191; to illiteracy and primitive life at the Cape, 230.
Menzies, William, Judge of the Cape Supreme Court, *and* annexation of Orange-Vaal area, 415.
Merensky, Alexander, German missionary, *and* the Pedi, 440.
Merumetsu, the Kora at, 402.
Metallurgy, 21, 31, 33, 38 f., 56, 63, 114, 135, 143–7, 180, f. *See also* copper; iron; tin. Trade in metal, *see under* Trade.
Mfengu, the, 346, frontier settlements of, 244, 249, 252, 263; population, 255, 274; allied with white settlers, 249, 252, 258 f., 265; *and* Christianity, 265; under British protection, 376. *See also under* Xhosa.
Mgungundlovu, Dingane's capital, 352, 358 ff., 362; Voortrekkers massacred at, 360.

Mhlakaza, seer and councillor of Sarili, 256-7, 259.
Mhlangana, Shaka's half-brother, 351.
Middle Stone Age, 1 n. 1, 2 f., 5 f., 8 ff., 15, 17-21.
Military service, 213, 226-7, 293, and Africans in S. A. Republic, 436. *See also* Commandos.
Militia at the Cape, 194, 198 f., 280.
Millennium, the, Xhosa cattle-killing *and*, 257-8, 260.
Mining, 39, 56, 143, 146 f., 173-4, 180.
Missionaries, 241, 246 f., 265-71, 281 and n. 6, 335 f., 368, 400-1. London Missionary Society, 238 f., 245, 271, 293, 304, 352 n. 7, 382 n. 1, 395, 414 f., 437, 439, 442-3; Methodists, 239, 245; Scots, 239, 245, 261, 271; Wesleyan, 248, 271, 357 f., 371, 376, 392 n. 1, 396, 401-2, 407, 414, 416, 418, 443.
Reports of, 392 and n. 1; rivalry between English and French, 402-3; changes advocated by, 266-9; used by white governments and African chiefs, 267, 425, 438-9.
Mission stations, 239 f., 258, 264 ff., 335, 385, 392, 397, 401 f.
Reserves, 264-6, 293, 375, *and* the Ngoni, 99 and n. 10; the Xhosa, 238-9, 243, 265. In Orange-Vaal area, 414 f., *and* S. A. Republic, 437 ff.; *and* Voortrekkers, 407.
and arms trade, 425, 439; drought, 270; intermarriage, 245; schools, 261-3, 284; slaves, 301.
See also under Americans; French; Lutherans; Natal; Zulu.
Mkabayi, sister of Senzangakona, 351.
Mlanjeni, witch-finder, 256 f., 259, 265.
Mocke, Jan, 371, 373, 415.
Moedwil, ruins at, 140.
Moffat, Robert, missionary, 267, with reference to linguistic variety, 43-44, 50; to Tswana and clients, 63, to absence of slavery among, 149; to Mzilikazi, 98, 100, 405, 411; to Ndebele huts, 112; to stone buildings, 139-40; to riding on oxen, 143; to Hurutshe and copper, 144; to Sarwa, 149; to river transport, 150; to Kgwakgwe, 153; to clientship and the poor, 153-4; to rumours of MaNthatisi and the Tlokwa, 395-6; to attack on Kuruman, 396; to battle of Dithakong, 397.
Mogale, ancestor of the Kwena, 132.
Mohammedans, 231, 389; slaves, emancipation of, 305 and nn. 3 and 8.
Mokgosi, Lete chief, 144.
Mokhachane, father of Moshweshwe, 398 f.

Molapo, son of Moshweshwe, 401, 444.
Molema, S. M., Rolong author, *The Bantu Past and Present*, 392.
Moleta, Ngwaketse chief, 140.
Moletsane, chief of the Taung, 395, 402, 414 f., 419, 423, 443.
Molita, *and* metal trade, 179.
Molteno, Sir John Charles, *and* responsible government, 332.
Money and monetary system, 295-6; in Afrikaner republics, 426; white traders *and*, 335; paper money, 287-8, 295; rix-dollars, 210 n. 4, 295 and n. 1.
Monomotapa, 163, 168, 180 f.
Montagu, John, Colonial Secretary at Cape, 294, 318, 323.
Montshiwa, Tshidi-Rolong chief, 439.
Moodie, Benjamin, *and* Scottish settlers, 278.
Moorosi, Phuthi chief, 400, 443.
Moroka, son of Sefunelo, Seleka-Rolong chief, 402 f., 411, 414 ff., 419, 422, 442.
Moroka, Samuel, 443.
Morolong, founding ancestor of the Rolong, 135, 145.
Morris, D. R., with reference to Shaka, 344 n. 4.
Mosega, Ndebele settlement at, 411.
Moseme, *and* southern Sotho, 402.
Moshweshwe, Sotho chief, 131, 134, 152, 251, 256, 259, 337, 440; biographical information and achievements, 398-403, 442-4; kingdom in Caledon valley, 392, 398-403, 414 ff., 422 ff., 443, 446; treaty with Governor Napier, 415-16; war with Orange Free State, 432, 442; war of 1858, 443.
and rival African chiefdoms, 422, 443-4; British, 443-5, British annexation of Basutoland, 425; Sir George Cathcart, 421-2, 443; Hoffman, 431; missionaries, 400-2, 415; Pretorius, 418, 420; Shaka, 443; Governor Warden, 418-19; Xhosa cattle-killing, 418.
Mosielele, chief of Kgatla-Mmanaana, 439.
Mossel Bay, 56, archaic tools at, 19.
Mothibi, Tlhaping chief, mother of, 165-6.
Motlumi, Kwena chief, 399.
Motshodi, murdered brother-in-law of Mpangazita, 393 and n. 6.
Mount Coke, school at, 261.
Mozambique, possible cultural influence, 39; African labour from, 387; European traders *and*, 187; Ngoni and Tshangane *and*, 101.
Mpande, Dingane's half-brother, 361-3; king of the Zulu, 363-4, 370, 373 f., 376 f.; *and* Pretorius, 418; *and* Sekwati, 439; *and* Voortrekkers, 363.

Mpangazita, Hlubi chief, 347, 391, 393 f., 399.
Mpondo, the, 84, 93 and n. 3, 95, 105, 120, 250, 346, population, 255; villages, 111; chiefdom, 120, genealogy and burial places of chiefs, 91–93; military organization, 124; attacked by Zulu, 344, 349, 351, 354; refugee immigrants in Natal, 374, 376.
and circumcision, 125; cultivation, 110 f.; Dlamini, 93; metals, 114; *and* Mpondomise, 93; San, 106; Swazi, 93. *See also* Faku; Xwabiso.
Mpondomise, the, 84, 86 f., 95, 120; chiefdom, 120, genealogies and graves of chiefs, 87, 93; *and* circumcision, 125. *See also* Cira; *and under* Mpondo; San.
Msi or Musi, founding hero of southern Ndebele, 98.
Msimbiti, Jacob or Jacot, 353 and n. 1.
Mswazi, Swazi chief, 346, 442.
Mthethwa, the, 87, 176, 336, 338, 341–4, 347. *See also* Jobe.
Muller, Professor C. F. J., with reference to Great Trek, 406.
Mumbos, the, problem of identity of, 86–87.
Murray, Revd. Andrew, of Graaf-Reinet, 286 n. 1.
Murray, Sir George, Colonial Secretary, with reference to liberties for all in South Africa, 304; to slavery, 320.
Musina, *see under* Copper.
Mwulu's Cave, archaeological site, 18.
Myburgh, A. C., with reference to Sotho stone huts, 140.
Myths, 53–54; and visions, 257; regarding white influence on early African kingdoms, 338–9 and n. 3.
Mzila, Tsonga chief, 442.
Mzilikazi, Zulu headman and Ndebele chief, 150, 337, 351, biographical information and achievements, 98 ff., 403–5, 412, violence and tyranny of, 124; his army, 101, 404 and n. 3, 439; on high veld, 391, 440; *and* Matiwane, 399; *and* Moshweshwe, 400; *and* A. Smith, 140; *and* Voortrekkers, 355, 357, 361, 409, 411–12, 438. *See also under* D'Urban; Shaka.

Nama, the, 29, 47, 55, 57, 59, 61, 63 f., 70, 135; population, 68; religion and rituals, 45, 61; *and* metallurgy, 21, 56, 146; and Sotho, 166.
Namaqualand, 212, 246, 294.
Namaquas, the, 43, 57. *See* Nama.
Names, spelling of, x.
Nandi, junior wife of Zulu chief, Senzangakoma, mother of Shaka, 342, 350 f.

Napier, Sir George Thomas, Governor of the Cape, *and* abolition of office of political commissioner, 286; *and* Moshweshwe's kingdom, 418–19, 423; *and* Voortrekkers in Natal, 370 ff.; *and* protection of Griqua and Sotho against Voortrekkers, 415.
Napier Line, 423, 443.
Naron, the, hunters, 43, children, 53, myths, 54.
Natal:
rock paintings, 30; pottery, 32–33, 35 f.; inhabitants, 87, tribes, 345 n. 1, Sotho in, 132; *see also* Abambo people; Emboas; Vambe kingdom. Portuguese *and*, 78 f.; trade, 251.
Chiefdoms, 118–19, 249; unrest in, 259; annexed by Britain (1843), 334 and n. 2, separate colony (1856), 324. British in, 348–50, 378–81, 387–90.
Devastation and depopulation by Shaka, 345–6, *and* refugees from Zulu kingdom, 345 f., 349, 385.
Missionaries *and*, 352, 374 f., 378, mixed schools, 261.
Voortrekkers *and*, 355, 357, 360–73, 412. Natal Republic, 363–73, 384, 408 f., 412, 429 ff., 435, 437.
Submits to British, 371, terms of annexation, 372, rebellion of 1906, 387.
British Colony, 373–90, 410, royal charter, 382, administration, 382, 385–7, 390, 437, native policy; 382–7 and n. 1, Commission of 1854, 383–5, members listed, 383 n. 2.
Land system, 374–5, Sir Harry Smith's Land Commission, 378.
and Basutoland, 331, 445.
See also Indian labourers; *and under* British Imperial Government; Population.
Ncaphayi, Bhaca chief, 351, 370.
Ncome river, *see* Blood river.
Ndebele, the, 347, 351; population, 76 n. 4; migrations and raids, 98, 101; relations with Shona and Sotho, 101; language, 101 f.; cattle, 108; huts, 112; *and* total war, 243.
Defeated by Voortrekkers, 334, 355, 359, 370, 409 411–12, 438; in central Transvaal, 391, 403–5, 435; mission stations among, 392.
and Moshweshwe, 400; the Ngwato, 439. *See also* Msi; Mzilikazi.
Ndlambe, Xhosa chief, 238, 240, 242, 250 ff., 255.
Ndlela, Dingane's commander-in-chief, 359, 361.

INDEX

Ndungunya, Nguni chief of Dlamini clan, attacked by Zwide and Dingiswayo, 346.
Ndwandwe, the 342 and n. 2, 343 and n. 2, 344, 346 f., 349, 351. *See also* Sikhunyana; Zwide.
Neanderthal man, 9.
Nederburgh, Commissioner-General, 218, 274, 287, 299.
Negro people, 156, hunters, 43, 45; clients to Nama herders, 63; immigrants from East Africa, 231; *and* metallurgy, 63, copper smelting, 56, 146.
Negroid population, ix, 10, 23, 29, 103, 105, 147, among Sotho, 133.
Netherlands, characteristics in eighteenth century, 231-3.
Netherlands East India Company, *see* Dutch East India Company.
Netherlands States-General, *and* VOC's charter, 185-6; *and* Cape government and laws, 214, 299; burghers' appeal to, 299 f.
Newlands, garden at, 197.
Newspapers and periodicals, growth of, 317 and n. 2. Bloemfontein *Friend*, 426; *Cape Town Gazette and African Advertiser*, 314; Godlonton's *Journal*, 326; *Journal* and *Tijdschrift*, 315 f., *New Organ*, 316; *S.A. Commercial Advertiser*, 315 ff.; *Transvaal Argus*, 426.
Newcastle, Henry Clinton fifth Duke of, Colonial Secretary, *and* Orange River Sovereignty, 422.
New Zealand, British Imperial Government *and*, 354 n. 6.
Ngonde, kingdom, language, rituals, 169-70, 175, 251, 340; *see also* Nyakyusa-Ngonde.
Ngoni, the, 98-102, 168, 172-3, 175, kingdom established, 347; *and* education, 262; total war, 124. *See also* Nqaba; Zwangendaba.
Ngqika, Xhosa chief, 250-1, rule of, 122-3; *and* Barrow, 246; *and* Cape government, 240, 245, 279; De Buys *and* his mother, 240; *and* missionary, 238; riding ox, 108; *and* travellers, 115; *and* rebellious burghers, 245.
Ngqika, the, population, 255.
Nguni, Cape, pottery, 38.
Nguni, the: 38-39, 55, 58, 182. Distribution and area of occupation, 76 f., 86, 90, 100-2, 107, 129-30, 164, 253, 402; in Mizilikazi's Ndebele kingdom, 404-5; peculiarities, 95-98, 101, 128-9; no slave trade, 121, 130, 340; problems relating to, 129-30. Chiefs, genealogies of, 85, 90; powers of, 56. Chiefdoms, 116-19 and n. 4, 120, 122, 125 f., 250, 252 f., 337, 340 ff. and n. 1. Kingdoms, 121-2, 124, 155, 237; political system, transformation of, 336-41; law, 120-3.
Economy, 107-16, methods of cultivation, 110, crops, 109-10, grain storage, 113; hunting, 110; villages, dwellings, settlements, 111-13, 154-5, 159; pottery and clothing, 113; metals, 114; trade, 114-15, 340 f., ivory trade, 110; weapons, 113-14; raids, 164; warfare, 124-5, 343.
Social structure, 116-30, kinship, 96, 116-18, 121, 126-7 162, lineages, 116-17, 120, 126-7, 162, clans, 116-18, 120, 127, royal clan, 120, 127, homesteads, 116; age-groups, 405. Marriage laws and customs, 96, 115, 117-20, 125-7, 159, 163, 376, 385.
Rituals, 62, 96, 109 f., 118, 125-9, 160, 162; language and poetry, 56; *and* Christian missionaries, 239.
Relations with Khoikhoi and San, 102-7, with Sotho and Tsonga, 95-98, 335; incorporated in Cape Colony, 274; *and* Voortrekkers, 409.
Population pressure, 340-1; survivors from Shaka's wars, 346; on high veld, 391, 393 and n. 4, 394, 398 f.; *and* refugees and survivors from shipwrecks, 233-4; *and* Fynn, 348; *and* Shepstone, 376.
See also Cattle; Dingiswayo; Foreigners; *and under* Clientship; Torture; Taboos; Witchcraft.
Ngwadi, killer of Sigujana, 342, 351.
Ngwaketse, the, 143, 397, 439, chiefdom, 134, 140, 153, 179, 435, 438. *See also* Gaseitsiwe; Moleta.
Ngwane, the, 345, 347, 350, 391, 393 and n. 4, 394 f., 398 f. *See also* Matiwane.
Ngwato, the, chiefdom, 134, 155, 435, 438 f.; *and* gold, 446; *and* ivory, 148.
See also Khama; Macheng; Sekgoma; Tsikidi.
Nkudzi Bay, Lake Nyasa, cemetery at, 37.
Nolthenius, Commissioner, *and* legal status of Khoikhoi, 224-5.
Nongalaza, Zulu commander, 363.
Nongqanse, *and* Xhosa 'cattle-killing', 256-60.
Nonkosi, *and* prophecies regarding Xhosa 'cattle-killing', 259.
North Africa, archaeological evidence in, 8, 12, 16.
Nqaba or Nxaba, leader of Ngoni raiders, 99, 101.
Nqetho, Qwabe chief, 351.
Ntinde, the, 246, 250.

Ntsikana, Christian convert, 265.
Ntsuanatsatsi, hill of origin of Lesotho ruling lineage, 133 f., 145.
Ntungwa, the, 98.
Nyaka, Tsonga chief, 78.
Nyakyusa-Ngonde of Tanzania and Malawi, 164, 169-71, 173.
Nyanja cemetery, 37.
Nyiha, the, *and* iron smelting, 146.
Oakhurst shelter, near George, archaeological site, 26 f.
Oba, Xhosa chief, 267.
Ohrigstad, Voortrekker settlement, 413, 420, 427, 440.
Olduvai Gorge, Tanzania, archaeological site at, 2 f., 8 f., 12-15.
Olieboompoort, archaeological site at, 3.
Opperman, Veldkommandant, 227.
Opzoomer, scholar of Utrecht, 277.
Orange Free State, 331 f., 334; Late Stone Age evidence in, 27, archaeological sites, 32, 35 f., 39. Independence of, 424-6, Constitution, 429 and n. 3, 430 and n. 1, administration and progress, 426, 429, 444; frontiers; 442, 446. And Africans, 442-5; Cape Colony, 433, 435; missionaries, 445; S. A. Republic, 433; southern Sotho, 431 f., 442-6. *See also under* Volksraad.
Orange River Sovereignty, 417-24.
Orange-Vaal area, relinquished by Britain, 334; destruction and cannibalism in, 394-5; Voortrekkers in, 407-10, 414-16; occupants of, 414-15; British annexation proclaimed and disavowed, 415. *See also* Orange River Sovereignty.
Ordinances of Cape Governor-in-Council, 318. Constitution Ordinance of 1853, 324; Slave Ordinance of 1826, 319. Ordinance of 1828, 247, 304 and n. 5, 305, 309 f.; of 1841, 309; of 1843, 286, 319. Other references, 304, 307, 310.
Orpen, J. M., with reference to gods of the San, 53; *and* Orange Free State Constitution, 429; *and* boundary with southern Sotho, 431.
Ostrich egg shells, 48 f., 54; feathers, 193, 291; feather sunshades, 55, 147.
Owen, Francis, missionary, 336, 352 and n. 7, 359 f.
Owen, C. Mostyn, assistant to Sir Harry Smith, 419-21.
Owen, Captain William, *and* survey of south-east African coast, 348, 353.

Paarl, Dutch settlement at, 196; schools, 276, 285.
Pakington, Sir John, Colonial Secretary, 421.
Palgrave, W. C., with reference to Khoikhoi hordes, 58.
Parker, William, 280 n. 1.
Passes and passports, 303 ff., 311, 367, 436.
Paravicini, W. B., with reference to Xhosa area, 236.
Pastoral farming, *see* Grazing; Stockfarming; 'Trekboers'.
Pedi, the, 124, 131, 137, 151, 172; cattle, 142; chiefdom, 134; crops, 142; iron, 144; in Eastern Transvaal, 391, 403-4 and n. 1, 424, 435, 439-40; *and* Tsonga, 176; *and* Voortrekkers, 413, 438. *See also* Sekhukhuni; Sekwati; Thulare.
Peers Cave, south-west Cape, archaeological site at, 3.
Phalaborwa, 38, 181, iron working at, 135, 144 f., 177; chiefdom, 134; people, 163.
Philip, Dr. John, missionary, 247; *Researches in South Africa*, 304; *and* Caledon's Proclamation of 1809, 303 n. 5; *and* Ordinance 50, 305; *and* Griqua and southern Sotho, 415.
Philippolis, 414 f.
Phitshane, on the Molopo river, population (1824), 153; battle at, 397.
Phuthi, the, 400, 443. *See also* Moorosi.
Phuthing, the, 391, 395 ff. *See also* Ratsebe; Tshwane.
Pienaar's river, South African *Volksraad* meeting at, 428.
Pietermaritzburg, capital of Natal, 364 f., 371, 373, 380 f., 412; bank at, 296; cathedral, 381-2; chamber of commerce, 294; Indians in, 389.
Pietersburg, archaic tools at, 19, stone building, 36.
Pigot, Major, *and* sheep farming, 290.
Pine, Sir Benjamin, Governor of Natal, 380, 383-5.
Pithecanthrope, 8 f.
Pitje, Godfrey, with reference to initiation among the Sotho, 160.
Platberg-on-Calendon, 402, 421.
Platberg-on-Vaal, 402.
Plettenberg, Governor, *and* Xhosa, 236 f.; *and* boundary of white settlement, 237.
Plural society, growth of a, 335.
Poles, 283.
Police, headmen as, 264.
Political Commissioner, 286, 314.
Political units, formation of, 74, 182.
Pondoland, 78, 253, circumcision in, 125.
Population, limitation of, 53, 60; pressure as agent of change, 340-1.

INDEX   467

Population estimates:
Cape, early estimates, 254–6; census of 1805, 68; of 1960, 76 n. 4. 'Bushmen', 72–73, herders, 55, 58 and n. 3, 60, 67–69, 74; hunters, 49 f., 60, 71, 73 f.; Khoikhoi and Coloured, 273; Ndebele, 76 n. 4; Nguni, 76 and n. 4, 168; slaves, 204 ff., 273; Sotho, 131 and n. 3, 153 f., 168; Swazi, 76 n. 4; Tsonga, 176; Venda, 146, 168; white settlers, 196, 201 and n. 3, 206, 272–4, 425 and n. 1; Xhosa, 76 n. 4, 107, 253–6, 258, 274; Zulu, 76 n. 4.
Natal, Africans, 368, 374, 385, 390; Afrikaners, 374, 390; British, 380, 390; immigrants from Zululand, 385; Indians, 388–90.
Orange Free State, 425 and n. 1.
Transvaal, 425 and n. 1.
Port Elizabeth, *and* ascendancy of Grahamstown, 326; banking, 296; export trade, 294, 326, 413; school at, 263.
Port Natal, 364, 370–3, 376, 411; attempts to annex, 352, 354; ceded to Voortrekkers by Dingane, 360, 362; destroyed by Zulu, 361; white traders at, 337, 347 f., 352–4, 358.
Porter, William, Attorney-General at the Cape, *and* representative institutions, 323; *and* responsible government, 332.
Portuguese, early contacts with South Africa, 78–86, 187–8; shipwrecked, 56, 108, *see also* Ships; trade, 55, 61, 152, 185, 340; decline in East Africa, 347–8; settlements destroyed by Shoshangane, 346; *and* Pretorius, 418; *and* Voortrekkers, 413.
Potchefstroom, 365, Voortrekkers in district of, 412 f., 427 f., meetings at, 420, 428, 433–4; ecclesiastical independence, 427–8.
Potgieter, Andries Hendrik, 151, 356–8, 361, 365, 408, 411–13, 418, 420, 424, 427, *and* the Pedi, 440.
Poto, Mpondo chief, 90.
Pottinger, Sir Henry, Governor of the Cape, 321, 377.
Pottery, 23–24, 27, 31–39, 56, 113, 135, 148.
Press, freedom of the, 281, 314 and n. 5, 315–16 and n. 9, 317, 430.
Pretoria, Chamber of Commerce, 294; Voortrekker settlement at, 413.
Pretorius, Andries, biographical information, 361–2, 408, 424, 427; *and* battle of Blood river, 362, 370; *and* invasion of Zulu kingdom, 363; *and* Natal Republic, 365 f., 368, 370 f.; *and* Natal Colony, 377–8; *and* British annexation of Orange River Sovereignty, 417–18, 420; *and* Transvaal Voortrekkers, 420.

Pretorius, Marthinus Wessels, policy of, 427–8, 433; President of S. A. Republic, 428, 433 ff., 441, *and* Orange Free State, 431–3, 435.
Pringle, Thomas, with reference to language, 248; *and* freedom of the press, 315 f.
Pringle family, 281 n. 7.
Prinslo, Willem, 234, 237, 250.
Printing press, missionaries *and*, 239; for Dutch Company, 299.
Punga (Phunga), problem of identity of, 87.
Punishments, 273, 297, 305–8, 311.
See also Cape of Good Hope Punishment Act.
Pygmies, 51, 64 n. 1, 156.

Qwabe, the, 341 n. 2, 342, 351 f. *See also* Nqetho.
Quæna, Khoikhoi chief, 57.
Queenstown, rock paintings, 29, nineteenth-century paintings, 72, 105; caves as headquarters of hunting bands, 50.

Radiocarbon dating, 1, 3, 15, 18, 25, 32, 34, 39.
Rainfall, 7, 16, 41 and n. 7, 235, 270, ritual relating to, 62. Rainmakers, 106, 143, 161.
Ramavhoya, Venda chief, 441.
Rarabe, Xhosa chief, 106.
Rason, R. W., Secretary at Cape, 318.
Ratsebe, leader of the Phuthing, 395.
Read, —, missionary, 245.
Refugees, 107, 240 f., 248 f., 252, 280, 345, 352, 354, 367, 374, 376, 384, 391, 394, 403, 439, 441, 443. *See also* Difaqane.
Ravele, Venda chief, 441.
Reitz, F. W., 322.
Religion and rituals, 44–45, 47, 51–56, 59–62, 104–6, 109 f., 120, 134, 177, 180, 182, 256–60, 270, 384, 401. Circumcision, 52, 80, 85, 97, 103, 112, 119, 125, 129, 159–60, 172, 178, 393 and n. 6, 398–9, lodge, 400, schools, songs of, 167, 341.
See also Ancestors; Christianity; Mohammedans; *and under* Ngonde; Nguni; Sotho; Tsonga; Venda; Zulu.
Religious toleration, 231, 272, 275–7, 286, conflict with Calvinism, 277.
Representative government, 296, 309, 319–24, 327–30, 382. *See also* Franchise.
Republican movement, 312–13.
Resident Agents, 375 f., 416 f., 421.
Responsible government, 297, 323, 327–8, 330–3, 368.
Retief, Piet, 357–60, 362 ff., 408, Manifesto, 310, 367.

Rhodesia, archaeological sites in, 3 and n. 5, 32, 36, rock paintings, 23, 29, stone building, 36; languages in, 101 f., 167 f.; pottery, 32, 37 f.; sheep and cattle, 30–31; Ndebele in, 76 n. 4, 102; Shona in, 163; Sotho in southern, 131 n. 3. Rhodesioids, 9. *See also* Leopard's Kopje.
Ritter, E. A., with reference to Nguni traditions, 336 ff.; to Shaka, 343 nn. 1 and 2, 344 n. 3.
Rixdollar, *see under* Money.
Robben Island, Table Bay, prison on, 256, 353.
Robinson, J. T., with reference to *Telanthropus*, 9; to transition from tool-using to tool-making, 11.
Robinson, K. R., with reference to Leopard's Kopje culture, 34; to pottery, 37.
Rock art, 22 f., 29–30, 44 ff., 72, 74, 105–6, herders riding, 56, sacred paintings in hunters' caves, 50.
Rolong, the, 133 ff., 143, 158, 162, 166, 179, 181, 397, 402, 442. Ratlou-Rolong, 438; Tshidi-Rolong, 439.
See also Molema, S. M.; Montshiwa; Morolong; Seleka-Rolong; Tau.
Roman Catholics, 275, 283 and n. 1.
Roman-Dutch law, 220 f., 297, 302, *and* status of slaves, 300 f.; in Natal, 375, 385 f.; in Orange Free State, 430.
Rondebosch, garden at, 197.
Roodezand, church founded at, 230.
Roos, eighteenth-century report by, 135.
Ross, John, missionary, 239; with reference to Zizi refugee, 249.
Royal African Corps, 279.
Rozwi, the, 163 f.
Russell, Lord John, *and* colonial policy, 421.
Russians, Xhosa rumours concerning, 256–7.
Rustenburg, Transvaal, archaeological site, 35; Voortrekker settlement at, 413, meeting at, 420, 428; 'Dopper' Church founded at, 428.
Ruyter, Coloured grazier, 250.

St. Helena, 187 f., 325, trade, 295.
St. Lucia Bay, annexed by Britain, 373.
St. Marks, school at, 261.
St. Matthews, school at, 261.
'Saldanhars', the, 55, 58, 64, 68, chiefs, 61.
Salem, 243, school at, 261.
San, the, 10, 20 ff., 28, 43–48, 70, 231, 253, 346; area of occupation and hunting, 41, 50, 107, 165, 236 f., in Orange-Vaal area, 414; turned into herders and 'tamed', 71–73; cattle raids, 237, 374, 377.
Social structure, 49–54, camps, 51–52, 54; huts, 112; kinship system, 59; leadership, 50–51; marriage, 50–53; judgements, 51, 60 f.
Religion and rites, 45, 52–54, 106; dancing, 52 ff., 112; paintings, 54 f., 237.
and clientship, 63–64; smoking of wild hemp, 142; Sotho, 165 ff.; white settlers, 183 f., 209, 212–13, 215–16, 226–7, 312, resistance to extermination by settlers, 71, 184, 212; total war, 242. *See also* Makoon.
Sand River Convention (1852), 407, 420–1, 425, 432 f., 438, 443 ff.
Sandile, Xhosa chief, 242, 258.
Sarili, Xhosa chief, 89, 250 n. 1, 251, 255–9, 267.
Sarwa, the, 73, 133, 147 ff., 155–6, 165 f.
Schapera, Isaac, *The Khoisan Peoples of South Africa*, 45; *The Early Cape Hottentots*, 45; with reference to early metallurgy, 21; to Sotho settlement, 134; to stone building, 140; to Tswana, 137, 156, 393 n. 1.
Schimmelpenninck, Dutch Pensionary, 289.
Schoeman, Stephanus, *and* Africans, 441; *and* Afrikaners of Soutpansberg area, 427; *and* Boshof, 432; *and* Constitution of S. A. Republic, 428; *and* M. W. Pretorius, 432 ff.
Schoemansdal, Voortrekker settlement at, 413, 440 ff.
Schofield, J. F., with reference to pottery, 35, 37.
Scholten, Leiden scholar, 277.
Scholtz, Commandant P. E., *and* African chiefs, 439.
'School people', 265, 271. *See* Education.
Schryver, with reference to Khoikhoi and San in 1689, 236.
Schultz, A. H., with reference to cave deposits, 12.
Scots settlers, 247, 278, 279 n. 2, 280, clergy, 285–6 and n. 2, 407. *See also under* Missionaries.
Scott, John, Lieutenant-Governor of Natal, 388.
Sea, changes in level of, 6 ff., 15, 19.
Second Intermediate culture, 1 n. 1, 20 f.
Sebetwane, Kololo chief, 132, 395, 397.
Sechele, Kwena chief, 435, 438 f.
Secunde, see Vice-Governor *under* Dutch government *under* Cape, the.
Sejunelo, chief of the Seleka-Rolong, 396, 401–2.
Sekano, Kwena chief, 140.
Sekelutu, Kololo chief, 179.
Sekgoma, Ngwato chief, 435, 439.
Sekhukhuni, Pedi chief, 435, 440.

INDEX 469

Sekonyela, Tlokwa chief, 358 f., 393 and n. 6, 398, 400, 414, 419, rivalry with Moshweshwe, 401-2, 416, 422, 443.
Sekwati, Pedi chief, 403, 435, 439-40.
Seleka-Rolong, the, mission stations among, 392; forced migration, 396 f., in Caledon valley, 402.
See also Moroka; Sefunelo.
Selouskraal, ruins at, 140.
Senthumule, Venda chief, 169.
Senzangakona, Zulu chief, 342.
Separation movement of east and west Cape, 320, 324-7, 331. See also Bourke, Sir Richard.
Serowe, and trade, 179.
Serrurier, Dutch Reformed clergyman, 276.
Seven Circles Act (1874), 325, 327.
Seventeen, Chamber of the, in Holland, 65, 185 f., 190, 193, 196, 311-12 and n. 2; powers of, 214-17, 219 f., and High Court of Justice, 220; and emigration to Cape, 198; and free farming, 197; and Law at the Cape, 299.
Shaka, Zulu chief, 76, 87, 90, 98 f., 111 f., 129, 251, 336 f., 363; biographical information, career, and wars, 342-3 and n. 2, 344 and n. 2, 345-51, 393, 440, violence and tyranny of, 124, 345, 350; extent of kingdom, 344; military reforms, 342-4; refugees from wars of, 107, 367-8; and death of Dingiswayo, 343 n. 2; and Moshweshwe, 399, 443; and Mzilikazi, 347, 403 ff.; and Natal traders, 348 and n. 3, 349; and trade, 340. See also under Cattle.
Sheep, rock paintings of, 23, 29 f.; fat-tailed, 55, 57, 290, Ormuz breed, 81, 107; words for, 104; used in ritual, 56, 61-62, 142, 161; stolen and traded, 64 f., 234, 237, 242; wool farming, 244, 290, 381; Voortrekkers and, 407; Xhosa and, 263. Sheepwalks, 290. See also Stock-farming; Wool.
Shepstone, Theophilus, 376, 445, Commissioner for African Lands in Natal, Diplomatic Agent to Native Tribes, Secretary for Native Affairs, 374-6, 378, 383 and n. 2, 385-7; with reference to Dingiswayo, 115, 339; to Nguni occupation, 112.
Shiloh mission, 239.
Ships, statistics relating to, 192, 206, visiting Cape, 274-5, 294, time of voyages, 369 n. 1, Dutch East India Company ships, 215.
Centaurus, 83-84; Comet, 361; Grosvenor, 85, 233 n. 6; Haarlem, 65, 188; Neptune, 321; Nossa Senhora de Belem, 82-83; Santo Alberto, 79-80, 83 ff., 95, 115; São Bento, 78-79, 84, 90, 111, 114; São João, 78; São João Baptista, 81-82, 85; Santo Thome, 79; Stavenisse, 83-84, 93, 102, 106, 109, 113, 121, 123, 128, 236, 347.
Shipwrecks, wreck of 1647, 83, 108; off False Bay, 190-1; on south east African coast, 347. Survivors of, ix, 120, 336, 340, 347, absorbed by Africans, 233. See also Ships, names.
Shona, the, 99, 101, 147, 155, 168-9, 171 and n. 10, 181, 412; and cattle, 142, 173; Lobedu, 164; mining, 146, 163; Sotho, 63; stone building, 163; Tsonga, 176. See also under Venda, the.
Shoshangane, overlord of the Tsonga, 100 f., 176, 441; his Gasa kingdom, 346; drives off Zulu, 350 f.; devastation in Transvaal, 440; and Zwangendaba, 347; and Pedi, 439; and British naval survey, 348.
Shoshong area, the Ngwato in, 435.
Sibasa, Paramount chief of the Venda, stone village for, 36, 174.
Sigujana, Zulu chief, 342.
Sikhunyana, chief of the Ndwandwe, 349.
Silberbauer, G. B., with reference to language of the G/wi, 43; to size of bands, 49; to initiation rites, 53; to dancing, 54.
Silwebana, Chief, and Voortrekkers, 359.
Simons, Commissioner J., and Cape militia, 199; criticism of the administration, 215, 217-18, 221.
Slagters Nek Rebellion, 304 n. 3, 310.
Slavery and Slaves, and clientship, 64; at the Cape, 184, 194, 196 f., 200-1, 204-5, 207-8, 232, regulations regarding, 207-8, legal status, 224-5; value of, 292 n. 7; escaped slaves, 234, 240, 242; immigrant slaves, 231; children of slaves, 248, 308.
Liberated slaves, 193 and n. 9, 215, 355, 437; individual manumission, 305 and n. 7, 306.
Absence among Sotho, 148-9; rejected by Nguni, 121, 130; in Transvaal, 445.
Emancipation, 272, 280, 292 and n. 7, 293, 296, 301-2, 305-9; resisted, 302, 306 ff.; status, 300-1; Slave Registry, 306; Protector of the Slaves, 308.
Slave Trade, 121, 149, 178, 340, 441, abolished, 274, 301, 305.
Smellekamp, J. A., and Natal Republic, 371 ff.; and Voortrekkers, 413.
Smit, Erasmus, and Voortrekkers, 357, 365.
Smith, Dr. Andrew, with reference to stone buildings of the Kwena, 140; to annexation of Port Natal, 352; to Moshweshwe, 401 n. 2, to population of Thaba Nchu, 402. Expedition (1834-6) to high veld, 392 and n. 2, 398, 411.

INDEX

Smith, Sir Harry, Governor of the Cape and High Commissioner, 260, 323, 416–17, 421, characteristics, 417; defeats Pretorius at Boomplaats, 418. *And* Africans in Natal, 378; annexation of British Kaffraria and Orange River Sovereignty, 417–19, 421; convicts, 321; freedom of speech, 317; land allotment in Natal, 379; Legislative Council, 322. Pretorius, 377–8; separation of east and west Cape, 324; Xhosa chiefs, 243, 245. With reference to African marriages, 266; to accusations of witchcraft, 269.
Smith, Captain T. C., in Port Natal, 371, 373.
Smithfield culture of Late Stone Age, 24–28.
Smuggling, 288.
Sobhuza, Swazi chief, 90, 346, 350 f., 439 f.
Soga, J. H., with reference to Theal's speculation regarding Mumbos, 87; to Hlubi, 90; to Gona, 102; to Xhosa cattle-racing, 108; to Nguni chiefdoms, 119 n. 4; to Nguni migrations, 129.
Solomon, Saul, *and* 'Voluntary Principle' in ecclesiastical affairs, 286.
Somerset's case, 301.
Somerset, Lord Charles, autocratic rule of, 314–15, 317; *and* advisory Council, 317; Dutch Church, 285; language, 283 n. 3; law reform, 315; political meetings, 315; press, 316; schools, 284; slaves, 306 ff.; trade, 289; Zuurveld, 278–80.
Somerset, Colonel Henry, 279, 350, defeats Matiwane at Mbholompo, 394.
Somerset East, 236, 280, encounter between Xhosa and white settlers near, 234, 236.
Somerville, *and* expedition of 1801, 135.
Sonquas, the, 63.
Sotho, the, 38–39, 51, 55, 57 f., 70 f., 87, 95, 97 f.; painting, 46; pottery, 38, 135, 163. Physical types, 133; distribution and settlements, 131 and n. 3, 132–5, 137–9, 141, 145, 153–5, 159, 165, 181, 414, huts, 49–50, 111–13.
Chiefdoms, 134, 153, 155–8, 438 f., genealogy of royal line, 136; powers of chiefs, 61, 155, 161, limited, 158; kingdom, 250.
Economy, 142–53, 162, craftsmanship, 143, 147–8, 163, leather-work and carving, 147–8; metallurgy, 143–7, 163, 181, iron, 135; stone building, 139–41, 163; *and* fish. *See also under* Cattle; Food. Trade, 61, 142–3, 146–53, 181.
Social structure, 153–63, age-groups, 159–61, military organization, 160; lineages, 155, 159, identified with wild animals, 162; kinship, 96, 155, 162; marriage, 96, 101, 159 f., 162.
Rituals, 62, 125, 142, 158–62; circumcision, 52–53, 159–60, 165.
On high veld, 391, 440; *and* Voortrekkers, 409, 412, rebellion against South African Republic, 442.
Questions relating to, 180–2; *and* Khoikhoi, 166–7.
See also Kazembe; Makapane; Sebetwane; *and under* Kora; Nama; Ndebele; Nguni; Population; San; Shona; Tsonga; Venda.
Southern Sotho: Moshweshwe's kingdom in Caledon valley, 392, 398–401, 418, 423, 443; attacked on high veld, 393 and n. 4, and disrupted, 394–5, 398 f. *and* British, 418, 423; Mzilikazi, 403–5; Orange Free State, 424 f., 432; Voortrekker, 415, 423.
Mission stations among, 392; in Thaba Nchu, 402.
See also Moseme; Moshweshwe.
Sotobe, Chief, *and* attempted embassy to King George IV, 349.
South African Republic, 334, 424, 427, 435; in Potchefstroom area, 427. Constitution of 1858, 428–9; local administration: Commandant, 436, 439, 441, fieldcornets, 436 f., 441. Laws relating to African subjects, 435–7; *and* African chiefdoms, 437–42; *and* Orange Free State, 432 f. *See also* Transvaal.
Southey, Sir Richard, secretary to Cape Government, 318, *and* annexation of Basutoland, 331 f.
South West Africa, rock paintings, 23; hunters in, 44, 47, 72; clientship in, 63; Sotho in, 131 n. 3.
Soutpansberg district, 410 f., 420, 439, 441–2, abuses in, 436; *and* South African Republic, 427 f; the Venda in, 435, 440.
Sparrmann, Andrew, Swedish botanist, with reference to grazing, 57, 253; to horses, 69; to Xhosa attack on white traders, 234; to ivory trade, 235; to wild animals and domestication, 254; to punishments, 273.
Spices, trade in, 185 ff., 288.
Stayt, H. A., with reference to the Venda, 169, 174 f.
Spies, Andries, 377.
Sprigg, Sir John Gordon, Cape Ministry of, 327.
Stanford, W., 243, with reference to marriage between Thembu and San, 106; to Xhosa cattle-killing, 259.
Stanger, W., *and* African lands in Natal, 374.

INDEX

Stanley, Edward, fourteenth Earl of Derby, Colonial Secretary, *and* representative institutions, 320 f.; *and* Natal Republic, 370-3, *and* British annexation of Natal, 372-4.
Steedman, A., with reference to Mpondo population, 255 and n. 4.
Stellenbosch, 234, 236 f., Dutch settlement at, 196, 201, church at, 230, schools, 276, 284, theological seminary, 261, 270, 277. Administrative district, 212, 215, 220, 223, 228, judicial powers, 224-5, rule of law, 298. Resistance to limitations on slave-owners, 307. *And* commandos, 226-7, 246.
Sterkfontein, Transvaal, cave deposits at, 2, 5, 11-14.
Stewart, James, missionary, 239, with reference to Lovedale school, 261; to a university, 263; to aims of missionaries, 267.
Steynsrus, Orange Free State, stone hut settlement, 35 f., pottery, 38.
Stillbay, archaic tools at, 19.
Stockenström, Landdrost Andries, murdered by Xhosa, 237-8; *and* treaties with Xhosa, 243; regulations of labour conditions and passes, 303-5; experiments in sheep, 290; with reference to Kaffirs and Khoikhoi, 247.
Stockenström, the younger, *and* Xhosa chiefs, 245; *and* regulation of labour, 303; *and* Legislative Council, 322; *and* constitutional reforms, 323. Commissioner-General of the eastern districts of the Cape and Lieutenant-Governor, 325.
Stock-farming, 184, 192 ff., 197, 201, 208-12, 272, 280.
Stow, G. W., *and* rock art, 44 f., 105-6; with reference to honey, 48; to bands of hunters, 49-51; to San dancing, 54.
Strandlopers, the, 48, 72.
Stuart, Jacobus, 428, 430.
Sudan, the, 102, *see also under* Transkei.
Sugar, Natal *and*, 381, 387-9.
Sutu, mother of Xhosa chief Sandile, 258.
Suurveld or Zuurveld, the, 46, 236 f., 254, 278-9.
Swartklip, fossils at, 6.
Swartkrans, Transvaal, cave deposits at, 2, 5 f., 8 f., 12 f.
Swazi, the, 99, 126, 403, population, 76 n. 4, 154, dwellings, 113, 154; circumcision, 125; slave raids, 121; kingdom, 250, 346; law, 97; *and* Dingane, 362 f.; *and* Voortrekkers, 413. *See also under* Marriage; Mpondo; Mswazi; Sobhuza.
Swaziland, 76 and n. 4, 93; Sotho in, 164. *See also* Dlamini.

Swellendam, administrative district, 212, 220, 223, 228, judicial powers, 224 f.; settlement difficulties, 201; labour conditions, 303; revolt at, 185, 227, 312; school, 261.

Table Bay, as refreshment station, 184 f., 187, 191-2, 238; fortifications, 190; gardens, 197; trade and exports, 294, 326. *See also* Cape Station *under* Cape, the.
Table Valley, population, 196.
Taaibosch, Gert, 402 f, 414, 419.
Taboos, breaches of, 161; drum, 171 f.; fish by the Kwena, 167, by the Nguni, 96 and n. 6, 97, 167, by some Sotho, 167; by the Venda, 173; iron smelting, 146; women, 127, 146.
Tanganyika, 85.
Tanzania, click languages in, 47; Ngoni in, 100 f.; Nyakyusa in, 119, 146; Nyiha in, 146.
Tas, Adam, 199, 287.
Tau, Rolong chief, 166.
Taung, northern Cape, cave deposits at, 2, 5; population (1824 and 1836), 153.
Taung, the, 142, 391, 395, 397, 402, 443. *See also* Moletsane.
Taverns, 194 ff., 207.
Tawana, chiefdom of, 134.
Tea, trade in, 288 f., 294.
Telanthropus, 9.
Tembe, the, 176.
Ten Rhyne, seventeenth-century journal of, 45; with reference to stock of the Hessequas, 65.
Thaba Bosiu, 154, Moshweshwe's capital, 398 ff., 422, 431 f., 444, 446; French missionairies at, 400, 445 f. *See also under* Treaties.
Thaba Nchu, population, 153, 402; mission at, 407; Seleka-Rolong at, 402, 411, 422, 442; Voortrekkers *and*, 357, 365.
Thamaga, the, 142.
Theal, G. M., with reference to population figures of Khoikhoi, 68; to shipwrecked Portuguese, 78-80; to Mumbos, 86-87; to *Difaqane*, 393 and n. 3.
Thembu, the, 84, 87, 95, 114 f., 120, 236, 249 f., 264, 394, 400, population, 255; chiefdom, 119-20, genealogies and burial places of chiefs, 87, 94-95; military organization, 124; trade, 234; *and* circumcision, 125; *and* limited war, 243; *and* San, 106; *and* Xhosa 'cattle-killing', 259.
Thom, George, 285.
Thomas, E. M., with reference to dancing and miming, 54.

Thompson, George, with reference to the Xhosa, 236, 255 f.; to labourers, 241; to the Tlhaping, 396-7; to trade, 289 f.
Thompson, William, missionary, 239.
Thulare, Pedi chief, 403, 404 n. 1, 439.
Thunberg, C. P., with reference to Xhosa and Khoikhoi, 103, 234, 236; to language, 246.
Tin, 150-1, 168, Sotho *and*, 143 f.
Tiyo Soga, minister of Free Church of Scotland, 245, 250 n. 1, 265 ff.; with reference to Xhosa 'cattle-killing', 257 n. 1, 259.
Tlhaping, the, 55, 133, 139, 153 f., 166, 180, 439; *and* fish, 167; metallurgy and mining, 143, 145; riding, 143, 166; trade, 149; mission stations among, 392; attacked during *Difaqane*, 396-7; *and* Afrikaner republics, 438, 442. *See also* Mothibi.
Tlokwa, the, chiefdom, 134, 393 and n. 4, 398, settlements, 154; migrant hordes on high veld, 391, 393 and n. 4, 395-6, 399; regeneration of, 398; mission stations among, 392, 402; *and* Moshweshwe, 443; *and* Voortrekkers, 358, 360. *See also* Kooaneng; MaNthatisi; Sekonyela.
Tobacco, 49, 65, 106, 109 f., 142, 148 f., 235, 238.
Tobias, P. V., with reference to human evolution, 9; to physical anthropology of Khoikhoi, 45, 47.
Tobias, P. V. and von Koenigswald, G. H. R., with reference to human evolution, 8.
Togu, Xhosa chief, 84, 89, 93, 95, 120; sons and grandson, 102.
Toka, the, 173.
Tolo, the, 97, 100 n. 2, 101.
Tonga, the, areas occupied by, 176.
Tools and Weapons: bone, 11, 14, 46, 48, horn, 11, ivory, 46, metal, 56, 114, 143-5, stone, 2, 8 f., 11-22, wooden, 16 f., 19.
Assegais, 79, 82 f., 110, 113 f., 259, 342; bows and arrows, 48 f., 51, 107, 113, 177; cleavers, 14, 16; digging-stick, 48, 114; hoes, 177; javelins, 236; Zulu spears, 343.
Tool-making, 11-14, 16-21; tool-using, 11 f. Trade, 149, 152.
See also Firearms, *and under* Nguni; Venda.
Torture, among Nguni, 123, 128; in judicial cases at the Cape, 220, 222 f., 297.
Tot Nut Van 't Algemeen, 276, 285, 290.
Totems, 145, 156.
Towns, origin and growth of, 180-1.
Trade, 64-66, 81, 114-15, 242, 272; in grain, 142, 149; meat, 287; metals, 146, 150-2, 177, 179, 235, 238, 242; pelts, 69 f., 147-9, 155, 179 f., 193; timber, 288. *See also* Amber; Beads; Cattle; Ivory; Firearms; Spices; Tea; Wheat; Wine; Wool.
Fairs and markets, 152, 241 f., 251, 279 f., limited markets, 198-201; contraband trade, 202 and n. 3, 206.
Trade routes, 149-53, 177, 187-8, 282, 357, 369, 409 f., 413. Dutch *and* Eastern trade, 185 f., 288.
Exports from the Cape, 193, 202, 206-7, 281 n. 3, 288-91, 294; expansion and depression, 287-8, 296-7. Burghers' grievances regarding trade, 287-8.
Settlers at the Cape *and* trade, 185, 235.
Trade between Nguni and San, 106; between settlers and Xhosa, 238, 240, 279; linked with large settlements and chiefdoms, 179-81, 250-1.
Chambers of Commerce, 294; private business, 294; retail trade, 294.
Afrikaner Republics *and* trade, 426; trade *and* political change, 339-41.
See also economic policy *under* Batavian Republic *and under* British government *under* Cape Colony; Finance; Sotho; Transport; Voortrekkers.
Traders, in relation to herders, 64-65; white traders, information from, 336, quarrels among, 337. Trading stations established, 335. Africans *and* traders, 425; Afrikaner Republics *and*, 426, 437 ff. *See also under* Port Natal.
Tradition, viii, 336 ff., 392 f. and n. 4.
Transkei, 84-85 and n. 2; links with Sudan, 130; stone buildings in, 141; clans descended from survivors of shipwrecks, 120; Kaffrarian settlers *and*, 327; Nguni in, 38, 85; Sotho in, 132; Thembu and Xhosa in, 87; Wellington movement in, 259.
Transorangia, boer settlements in, 292, Griquas in, 423; commando *and* Natal Republic, 371; Voortrekkers *and*, 412, 415-17.
Transport and Communications: African porters, 149, 151, 413, 441; animal, 149-50 (*see also under* Cattle); facilities for, 235; wagons, 70, 202, 235; water, 150. In Afrikaner Republics, 426; at the Cape, 202-3; in Natal, 380. Railways, 330, 380; Roads, 294, road boards, 319, 322 f.; Postal services, 380; Telegraph, 294, 324, 369 n. 1. *See also* Trade routes *under* Trade.
Transvaal: archaeological sites, 32-36, 39; climate and natural features, 409, 413; gold mining, 146; language, 101 f.; raided by Zulu, Ndebele, and Ngoni, 98-99; Sotho and Venda in, 141, 145.

INDEX 473

Destruction and disturbances by hordes, 391-8, 400, 440. Mzilikazi *and*, 403-5.
Voortrekkers *and*, 412-20, 422-4; relinquished by Britain and independence recognized, 334, 420-1; frontier characteristics, 426-7; Constitution, 424, 428, 430-1; *and* Orange Free State, 433; political struggles, 433-5.
See also South African Republic; *Volksraad.*
Treaties: Amiens (1802), 273; Cobden (1860), 290; Thaba Bosiu, 444 ff.; between D'Urban and Waterboer (1834), 415; between Napier and Kok and Moshweshwe (1843), 415.
'Trekboers', 212-13, 223, 228, 291 f., 340, 355, 406 f., 410, 414-15, 417, 423, 425. *See also* Great Trek.
Trevor-Roper, Professor H., with reference to the content of history, viii.
Trichardt, Louis, Voortrekker leader, 410 f.
Trinidad Order-in-Council *and* Ordinance 19 regarding slaves, 306-7 and n. 1.
Truck wages, 293.
Truter, *and* expedition of 1801, 135.
Truter, Fiscal J. A., *and* tenure of farms, 291 and n. 5, 292 n. 1.
Truter, P. J., *and* schools, 284.
Tsatsu, Jan, Xhosa interpreter, 239, 246.
Tsetse areas, 101 f., 132, 138, 149, 153, 155, 164, 173, 177, 409 f., 413, 424, 441.
Tshangane, the, raids and migrations, 101 f.
Tshiwo, Xhosa chief, 57, 102-3, 236.
Tshwane, Phuthing leader, 395, 397.
Tsikidi, Ngwato Regent, 155-6.
Tsipinare, Moroka's senior son, 443.
Tsonga, the 95-98, 100, 149, 164, 346, 441; areas of occupation, 176-7, 182, 440; culture, 176; raided by Swazi, 121; kings and chiefs, 79, 176, 178, lineages, 176. Economy: crops, 177; fishing, 177; trade, 177 f., 181, slave trade, 178. Social structure: settlements, 177-8, 180; kinship, 96, 177-8; *see also* Marriage. Rituals, fowls *and*, 109, 177 f.
And Sotho, 177; *and* Voortrekkers, 410, 413.
See also Libombo; Shoshangane; Tembe; Tshangane; *and under* Mzila; Nguni: Nyaka; Pedi; Shona; Venda.
Tswana, the, areas and settlements, 131 f., 139, 145, 154 f., 180, 391, 396; chiefs and chiefdoms, 155 f., 175, 440, lineage, 159; military organization, 124; *and* law and justice, 158; marriage, 159, 162-3, 165; *and* clients, 63, 148-9, 155-6, 165; migrant labourers, 141; *and* copper, 114. Information relating to, 137 and n. 6.

And Afrikaners, 424, 438; the *Difaqane*, 396 f.; Khoikhoi, 165; Sarwa, 165.
See also Kaditshwene; Maun; *and under* Cattle.
Tuinplaats, Transvaal, human fossils at, 10.
Tukela valley, Natal, pottery, 35.
Tulbagh, Ryk, governorship of, 217 f.
Tulbagh, school at, 284; local government, 313.
Turnbull, C. M., with reference to clientship between negroes and pygmies, 156.
Twa, Nguni for 'San', q.v.
Tyhume valley, mission station in, 239, 243, schools, 262.

Ugie, mixed school at, 261.
Uitenhage, Afrikaners of, 352; banking, 296; local government, 313; school, 261, 284.
Uitkomst, Transvaal, culture, 33-39, 135.
Uitlanders, 367.
Ullbricht, missionary, 245.
Umhala, Xhosa chief, 259.
Utrecht, Holland, university, 277.
Uys, Dirk, 361.
Uys, Jacobus, 245.
Uys, Piet, Voortrekker, 292 n. 5, 356-7, 361, 408, 412.
Uys family, *and* Natal, 352.

Vaal River, deposits in valley of, 1 f., 6, 14 f.; Nguni and Sotho *and*, 87; Voortrekkers north of, 407. *See also* Orange-Vaal area.
Vagrancy, 303 ff.
Valkenier, Commissioner, 215.
Vambe kingdom, in Natal, 86-87.
Van den Brouck, Commissioner, 195.
Van der Capellen, Joan Derk, leader of *Patriot* party in Netherlands, 312.
Van der Graaf, governor of the Cape, 287.
Van der Kemp, J. T., missionary, 238-40, 245 f., 267, 270; rock portrait of, 105; with reference to area of occupation of San and Xhosa, 107; to Xhosa moderation in drink, 110; to chief Ngqika, 122-3, 238; to escape from torture, 123-4; to Nguni social structure, 124; to population, 254-5.
Van der Merwe, Professor P. J., with reference to slave children, 208; to tenure of farms, 291.
Van der Stel, Frans, 198 f.
Van der Stel, Simon, 198 f., 294; governorship of, 217; colonization policy of, 198; *and* Port Natal, 347; *and* stock barter, 209; with reference to hunter and herder clientship, 63; to authority of Dutch Company over Cape Africans, 67.

474 INDEX

Van der Stel, Willem Adrian, 198 f., 297 n. 1; administrative abuses of, 213, 217, 221-2; impeached, 234; *and* stock barter, 208 n. 8.
Van der Walt, Johannes, *and* employment of hunters as farm servants, 71.
Van Gennep, A., with reference to rituals, 61.
Van Goens, Commissioner Rykloff, 194, 215, 221.
Van Hogendorp, G. C., 289, *and* settlement of Tzitzikama coast, 288.
Van Jaarsveld, Professor F. A., with reference to Great Trek, 408.
Van Jaarsveld, Adrian, *and* campaign against Xhosa (1781), 237.
Van Lijnden, Fiscal Baron, 297 n. 1.
Van Meerhoff, Pieter, explorer and surgeon, 66.
Van Pallandt, Baron A., 289, 314.
Van Plettenberg, tour (1778), 212; *and* Carel Buytendag, 298; petitions against, 299 n. 1.
Van Polanen, R. G., 294.
Van Reenen, Jacob, with reference to Mpondo woman, Bessie, 92 f., 233.
Van Reenen, J. G., *and* employment of hunters as farm servants, 71.
Van Rensburg, Janse, Voortrekker leader, 410.
Van Rensburg, W. C. J., President of Transvaal, 434.
Van Rheede tot Drakensteyn, Commissioner-General H. A., 214-16, 219.
Van Riebeeck, Jan, 44, diary, with reference to cattle, 23; to Khoikhoi language, 41; to camps of herders, 55; to hunters' fear of herders, 64; to war between Dutch and Cape herders, 65; to employment and numbers of Khoikhoi, 66-68; *and* the Cape Station, 187, 189-93, 195, 198; *and* cattle trade, 64; *and* slavery, 204.
Van Riet Lowe, C., *and* Vaal deposits, 2; *and* stone culture, 13.
Van Ryneveld, Fiscal W. S., *and* his office, 297 n. 1; *and* interests of Dutch Company, 311; *and* meat and wool trade, 288.
Van Warmelo, N. J., with reference to trade routes, 151.
Vedder, H., with reference to area occupied by Khoikhoi, 41; to boundaries of hunting areas, 50; to Portuguese trade, 55-56.
Veld, the high, characteristics, 409; explorers, hunters, and traders on, 392 and n. 2; refugees and warfare on, 391, 393-9; African chiefdoms *and* autonomy, 435.
See also Grazing; Voortrekkers.

Venable, Henry, American missionary, *and* Mzilikazi, 405 and n. 3.
Venda, the. 98, 164, 168, areas of occupation, 167-9, 171; cemetery and pottery, 37, 169, 174-5; population and settlement, 141, 6, 168, 174 f., 180; building, 141, 174; chiefdoms, 169 f., 172-5, 438, 440-1.
Economy, 173-5; grain storage, 103, 174; *and* copper, 168, 173, 181; *and* mining, 146; tools and weapons, 172-3.
Social structure, 175; myths and rituals, 169-74.
In eastern Transvaal, 391, 435.
And Afrikaners, 424, 438, 441 f.; Nyakyusa-Ngonde, 169-71, 174; Shona, 169, 171, 174; Sotho, 172, 175; Tsonga, 173, 177.
See also Makhado; Ramavhoya; Ravele; Senthumule; Sibasa; *and under* Lobedu.
Venter, Commandant S., 441.
Verburgh, Commissioner, 196, 221.
Vereeniging, archaeological evidence at, 14.
Viervoet mountain, battle at, 419.
Viljoen, J. W., *and* Transvaal political struggle, 434.
Villages, 49-50, 79-82, 84. *See also under* Iron Age; Nguni; Sotho; Zulu.
Volksraad, of Natal Republic, 365-8, 371, 373 f., 412; of Orange Free State, 429-30, 431, 433; of Transvaal, 412, 420, 427 f., 431, 433 f.
VOC, *see* Dutch East India Company.
Von Koenigswald, G. H. R., *see* Tobias, P. V., and von Koenigswald, G. H. R.
Voortrekkers, 98, 151, 168, 292 and n. 7, 293, 310, 334, 355-63, 405-15; characteristics, 407-8; numbers, 406; dependants of, 335, 355, 360 f., 366-7, 407-8; disputes among, 357, 361, 366, 373, 408, 413, 420; trade, 413, commodities required, 407-8; *and* food supply, 142, *And* British Government, 368, 371-3, 409-10, 423; Griqua, 416; Orange-Vaal area, 415-17; Pretorius, 418, 420.
Voortrekker Republic, *see* Natal Republic *under* Natal.
See also Great Trek; *and under* Transvaal; Zulu.

Wagenaar, successor to Van Riebeeck at the Cape, 195.
Wakefield, Edward Gibbon, 378.
Walker, E. A., with reference to Theal's speculation regarding Mumbos, 87; to Xhosa cattle-killing, 259; to Voortrekkers, 292.

INDEX

Walton, J., with reference to Sotho homesteads, 141, 174.

Warden, Major Henry, British Resident in Orange River Sovereignty, 417, 420 f.; defeated at Viervoet, 419; *and* Africans, 418–19, 442.

'Warden Line', the, 418–19, 423, 432.

Warner, J. C. with reference to civilizing of Kaffir tribes, 264, 267.

Wars:
Anglo-Dutch, 190, 196, 206, 275; between settlers and Khoikhoi (1658–60), 65, 194; (1673–7), 65, 196; between settlers and San, 212; between Mfengu and Gcaleka (1878), 249; Java, 206; 'Kaffir', 213, 247; War of the Axe, 378; wars of 1822–38, 139; Crimean war, 282, influence on Xhosa, 256.

Frontier Wars, 183–5, 226–7, 234, 237–8, 240, 242, 247, 249, 252, 278, 292, 322 f., 325, 353, 376 f., 419, 421.

Xhosa Wars, 240–4, 248, 252, 256, 260, 265, 268.

Animals used in war, 56; total war, 238, 242 f., 343, 397; war-doctor, 256.

See also 'Difaqane'; *and under* Moshweshwe; Shaka; Zulu.

Waterberg, revolutionary government in, 435.

Waterboer, Andries, Griqua chief, 72, 414, 442, treaty (1834) with D'Urban, 415.

Watermeyer Commission, *and* English language in schools, 284.

Weaving, 173, 175.

Webb, W. J., 243.

Weenen, village, 364, Voortrekkers massacred at, 361.

Wells, L. H., with reference to human fossils, 10; and Cooke, H. B. S., with reference to fossil remains at Makapan, 5–6.

Welsh settlers, 279 n. 2.

Wessels, Jan, with reference to hunters' caves, 51.

West, Martin, Lieutenant-Governor of Natal, 374, 377, 379.

West Indies, slavery in the, 307 ff., Jamaica slave rebellion of 1831, 309; sugar planting, 388.

Westphal, Professor E. O. J., with reference to Naron and G/wi languages, 43; to click languages, 47.

Wheat, 198, 201, 205 ff., 244, 287 f., production statistics, 206 and nn. 1 and 2.

White settlers, xi, characteristics in eighteenth century, 213, 232, limitations, 230–1, communal character, 228–9, 231; areas of occupation, 237, 252–3; population density, 256.

In relation to herders, 65–69, marriages and concubinage with Khoikhoi, 66; exterminate hunters, 70–71; *and* African languages, 66.

and black Africans, 233–43, 268–71, 335; growing gulf between white and non-white, 232, 268–71.

See also Afrikaners; British; Dutch; English; Germans; French; Irish; Portuguese; Scots; Welsh; *and under* Agriculture; Caledon valley; Khoikhoi; Labour; San; Xhosa.

Wicht, J. H., 322.

Wikar, H. J., eighteenth-century Swede, with reference to Portuguese trade, 55–56; to Tlhaping trade, 149; to copper, 56; to smelting, 146; to leather, 147; to hunters and herders, 63 f.; to Sotho, 135; to mixture of Tswana and Khoikhoi, 165.

Williams, Joseph, missionary, 239, 246, 248, 268.

Willowmore district, rock paintings, 29.

Wilson, Professor Monica, with reference to the Nguni, 38, to trade as agent of political change, 339–40.

Wilton culture of Late Stone Age, 24, 26–28.

Winburg district, Voortrekkers in, 412, 418.

Wine, 80, 193, 197, 202, 205, 207, 287, 290, 294 f.

Witchcraft, 102, 123, 127–8, 158, 171, 240, 266, 269–70, 353, 377, 384, 399; purification from, 256–60.

Witsie's Hoek, 443.

Wodehouse, Sir Philip, Governor of Cape and High Commissioner, 285, 297, 327–31, 333; *and* regional divisions, 324; *and* Grahamstown Parliament, 326; *and* frontier settlement, 327; *and* reform of Parliament, 330 and n. 2; *and* annexation of Basutoland, 444–6; opposition to responsible government, 328, 331.

Women, *and* pottery, 113, 148; employment of, 241, 262, 269; spared in war, 243; Shaka's military organization of, 344 and n. 2.

See also Marriage; Girls; *and under* Agriculture; Taboos.

Wood, William, Francis Owen's interpreter, 360 and n. 6.

Wool, merino, 288, 290, 296; trade, 325–6; exports, 294, 329, value of, 290–1; taxation of, 330; in Natal, 381; in Orange Free State, 426.

Wreede, G. F., *and* first Khoikhoi vocabulary, 66.

Xhosa, the, viii, 70 f., 84, 86 f., 95, 97 f., 120, 152, 394; described, 82–83.

Xhosa, the (*cont.*):
Area occupied, 107, 236, 243; huts and villages, 112-13.
Chiefs and chiefdoms, 117 ff., 234, 241, 243-4, 250-1, 263-4, 440, genealogies of chiefs, 87-89, burial places, 93, 253; homesteads and 'great place,' 264-5; government officials *and* chiefs, 245; treaties, 243; rule of headmen, 244, 264.
Military organization, 124; limited warfare, 242-3, 271, *see also under* Wars; weapons, 113-14, 236, 252.
Economy: cattle, 107 ff., raids, 237, 242; crops, 109 and n. 3, 110; food, 235, 254, beer, 110; hunting, 110, 235; *and* metals, 114, 145; sheep, 263; employment of women and girls, 262, work passes, 241, absence of slavery, 121; clothing, 113. *See also under* Labour; Trade.
Circumcision, 125; dancing, 236; hospitality, 121 f., 128; poetry and oratory, 128; respect for law, 121-3, 128; Christian converts *and* pagans, 265-7.
and white settlers, 184, 212-13, 227, 237-46, 249, 252, 256, 267 f., 271, 281 f., 292, 312 n. 5, 325, encounter of 1702, 234, 236 f.
Dispossession, 252-3, 255; cattle-killing of 1857, 129, 256-60, 264, 432; become Cape Colonials, 274; treated as 'native foreigners', 310-11.
and Khoikhoi, 102-5, 166, 236, 248, 250; Mfengu, 249, 252, 271, 376; refugees from Shaka's wars, 346; San, 106.
See also Cungwa; Gwali; Hintsa; Khawuta; Magamma; Makanda; Maqoma; Ndlambe; Ngqika; Oba; Rarabe; Sandile; Sarili; Sutu; Togu; Tsatsu; Tshiwo; Umhala; *and under* Marriage; Population.

Xwabiso, Mpondo chief, 233.

Yonge, Sir George, Governor of Cape, 314.

Zambia, archaeological evidence in, 3, 9, 15 f., 32, pottery, 37.
Zeerust, archaeological sites, 35; Voortrekker settlement at, 413.
Zimbabwe culture, 147, 175, 339, *see also under* Beads.
Zizi, the, 97, 101, 114, 120, 152, 249, 345, trade with Sotho, 164; *and* smelting, 145, 180.
Zonnebloem, school at, 261, chiefs' sons at, 263.
Zulu, the:
population, 76 n. 4; migrations and raids, 98, 165; villages and dwellings, 112-13, homesteads, 345. Chiefs, 345, genealogy of, 89, 91, burial sites, 90.
Cattle, 107-8, 343; clothing, 113, 343; metals, 114.
Circumcision, 125; customs, 106, 345; *and* missionaries, 352, 359.
Warfare: military organization, 129 f., 342-4 and n. 2; barracks, 111; weapons, 114, 343, 362 n. 1; total war, 243, 343. *See also* Shaka; *and under* Dancing.
Kingdom, 250, 336, 342, 344-5, decline, 351, 354, 362-3, deserters from, 354; defeated by Shoshangane, 350; recuperation under Mpande, 363-4.
and Voortrekkers, 334, 358-63, 370, 409; vassal of Natal, 363, 370; refugee immigrants in Natal, 374, 376, *and* Natal traders, 352; raids in Transvaal, 403 f.
See also Cetshwayo; Dingane; Malandela; Mpande; Mzilikazi; Nongalaza; Senzangakoma; Sigujana; Sotobe; *and under* Marriage.
Zululand, incorporated in Natal, 334 n. 2.
Zwangendaba, *and* the Ngoni, 99 ff., 347, 405.
Zwartland, 212, church founded at, 230.
Zwide, chief of the Ndwandwe, 342 f. and n. 2, 346 f., 393, 403.

For Product Safety Concerns and Information please contact our EU
representative GPSR@taylorandfrancis.com
Taylor & Francis Verlag GmbH, Kaufingerstraße 24, 80331 München, Germany

www.ingramcontent.com/pod-product-compliance
Lightning Source LLC
Chambersburg PA
CBHW071136300426
44113CB00009B/993